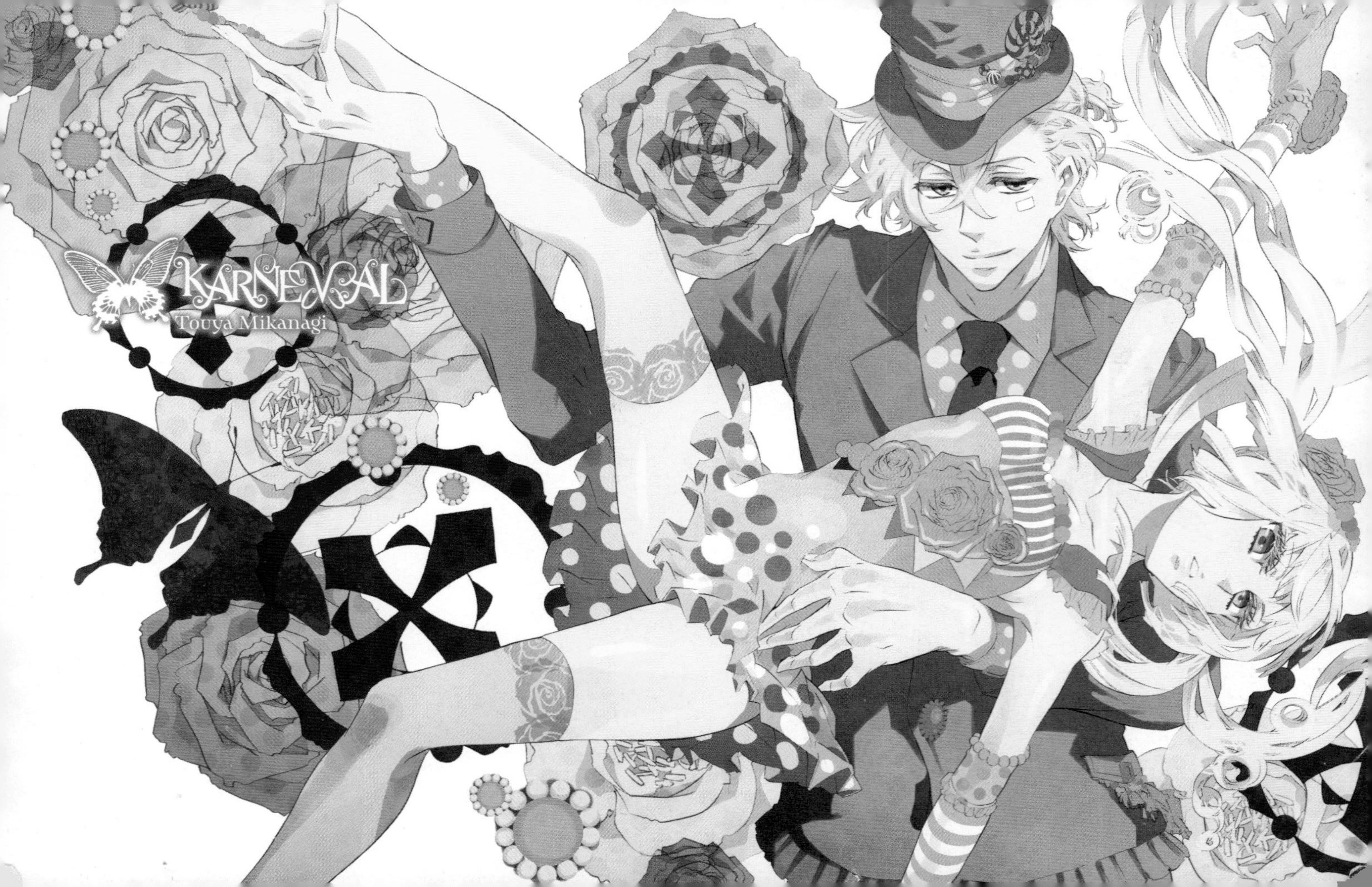
KARNEVAL
Touya Mikanagi

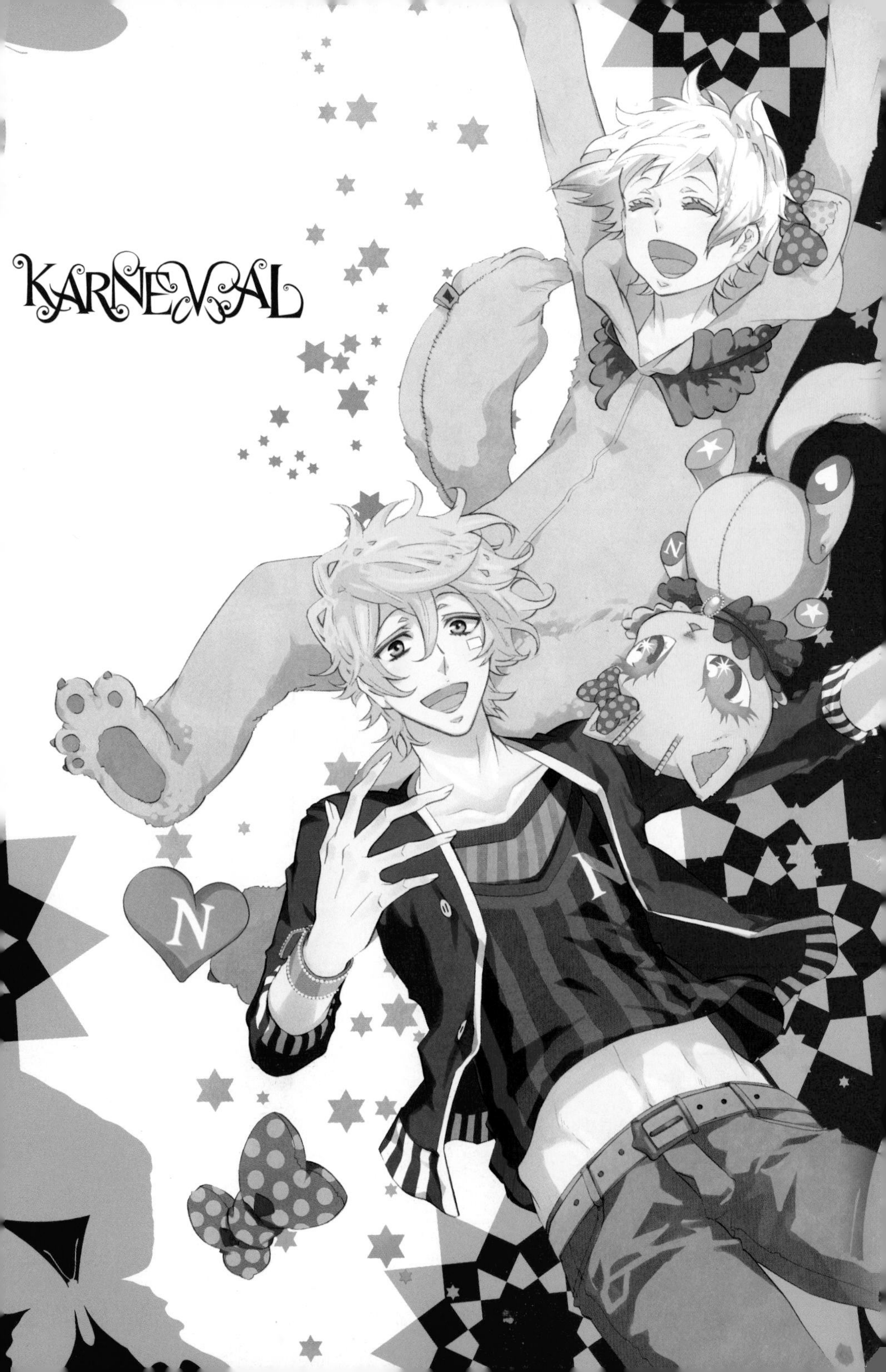
KARNEVAL
N
N
N

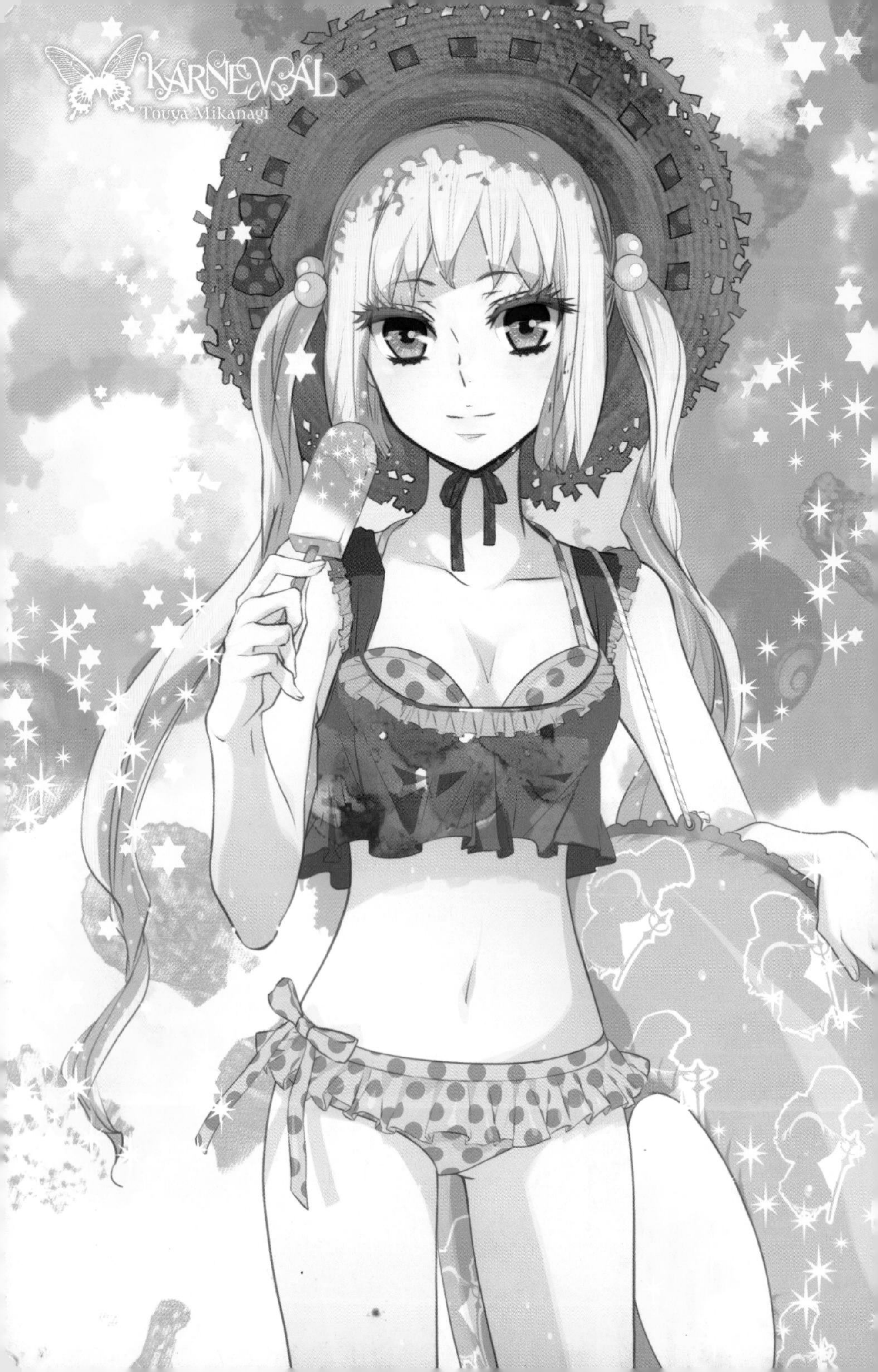
KARNEVAL
Touya Mikanagi

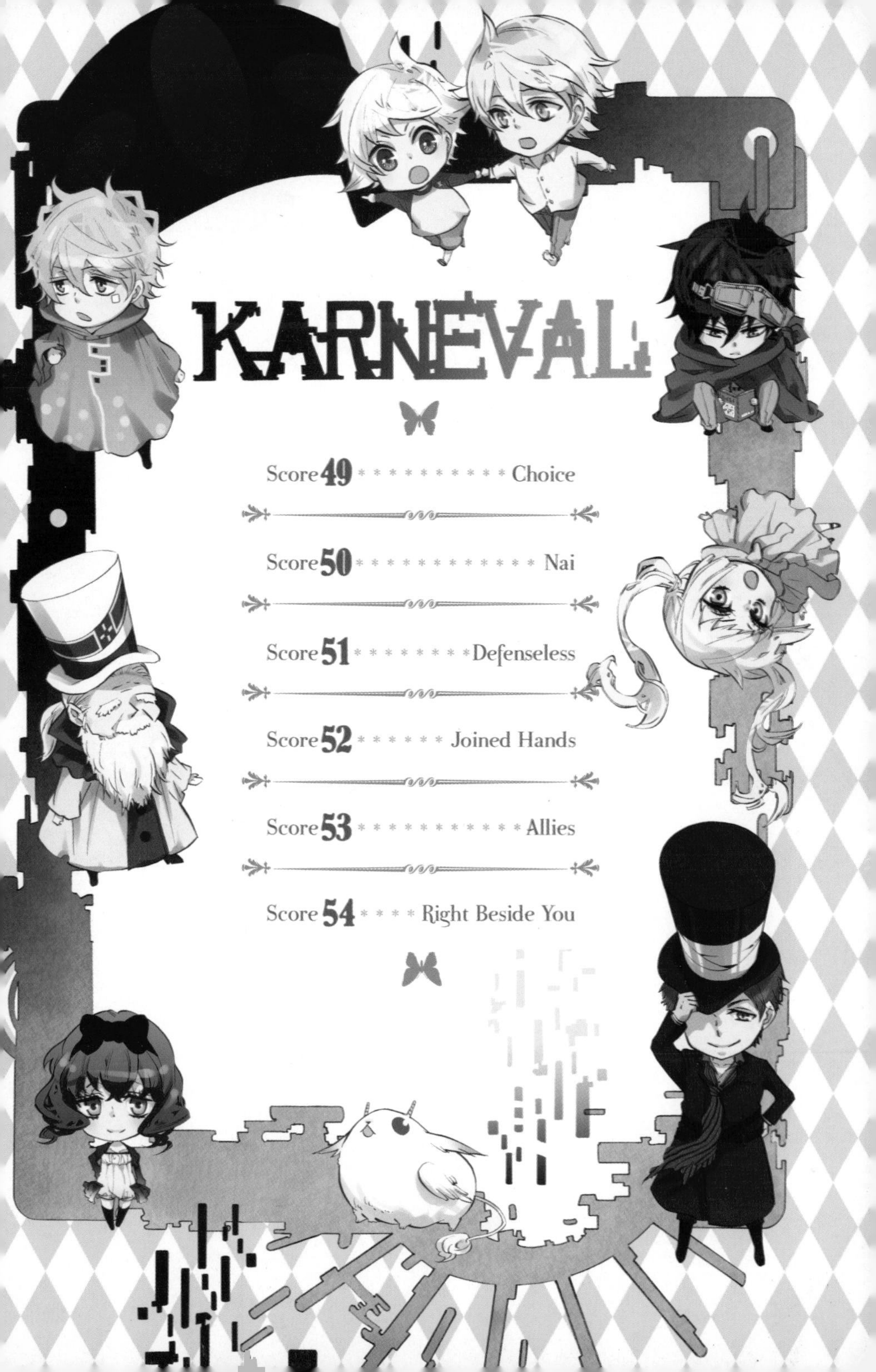

KARNEVAL

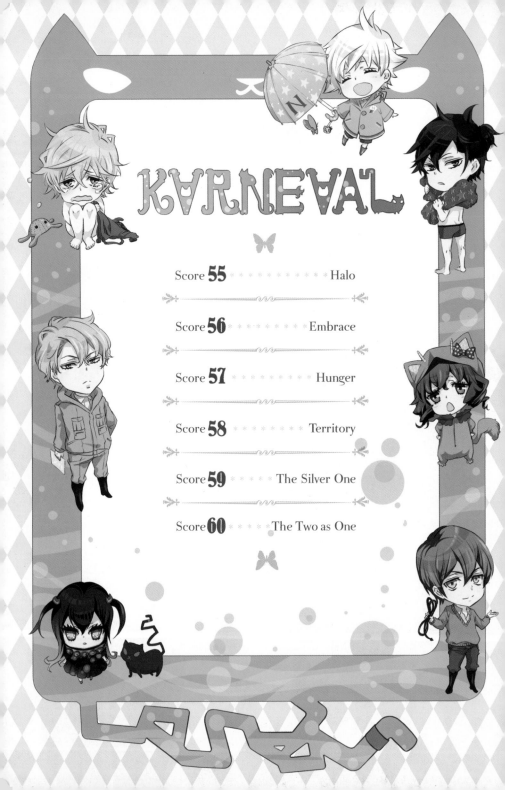

KARNEVAL

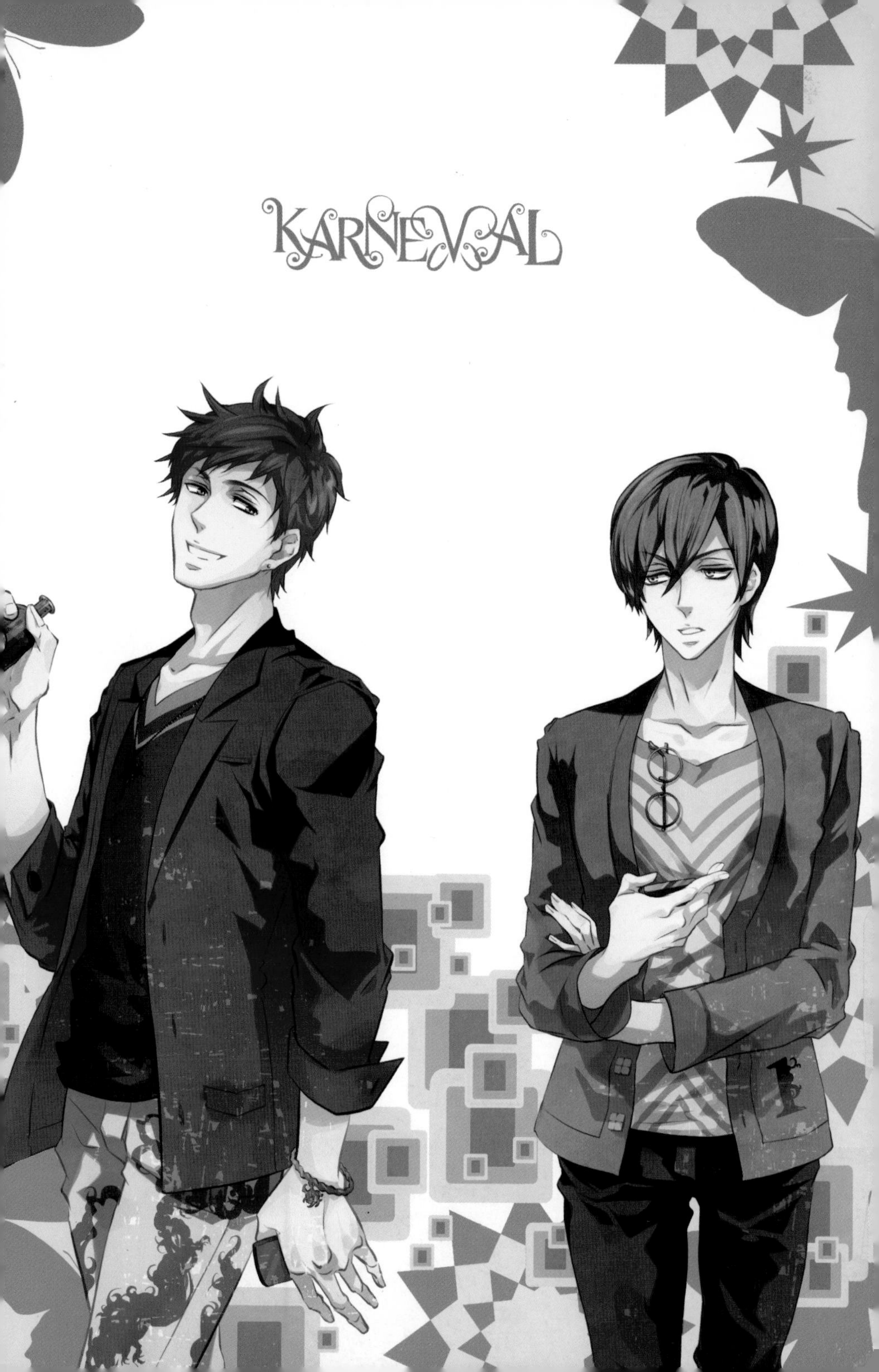
KARNEVAL

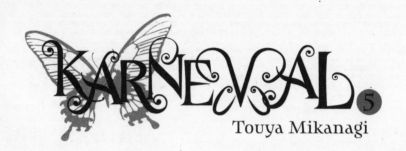

KARNEVAL 5

Touya Mikanagi

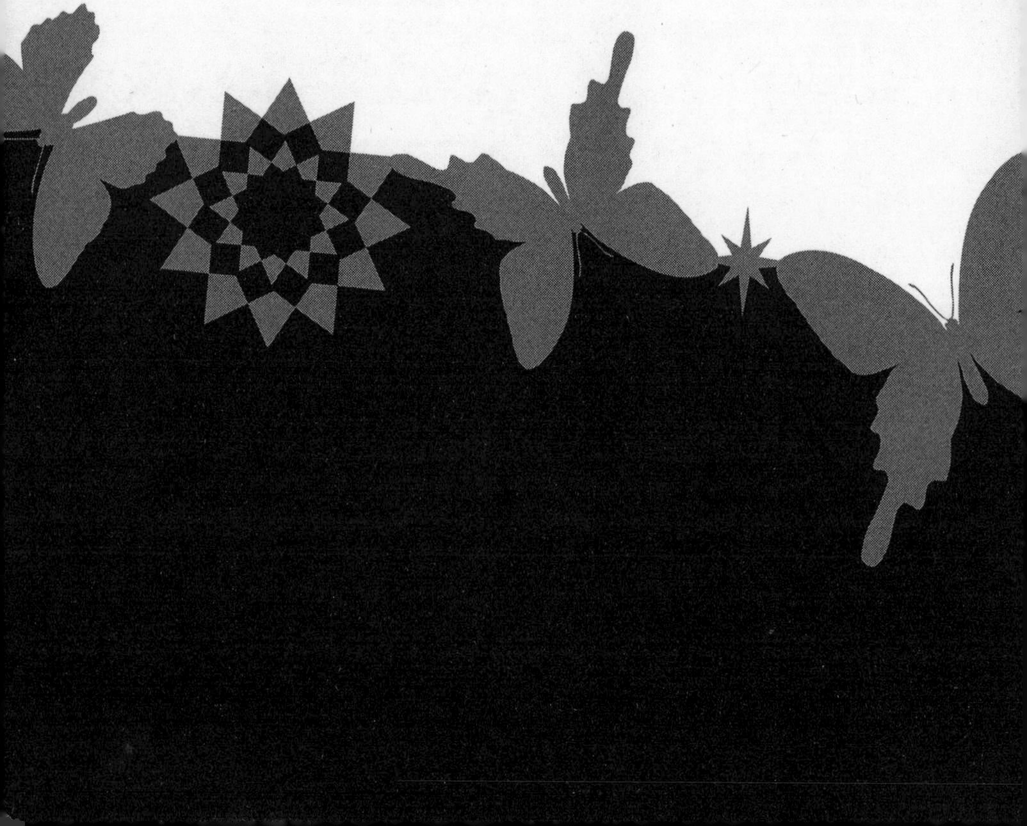

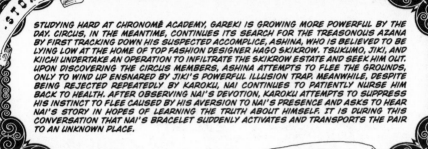

STORY

STUDYING HARD AT CHRONOMÉ ACADEMY, GAREKI IS GROWING MORE POWERFUL BY THE DAY. CIRCUS, IN THE MEANTIME, CONTINUES ITS SEARCH FOR THE TREASONOUS AZANA BY FIRST TRACKING DOWN HIS SUSPECTED ACCOMPLICE, ASHINA, WHO IS BELIEVED TO BE LYING LOW AT THE HOME OF TOP FASHION DESIGNER HAGO SKIKROW. TSUKUMO, JIKI, AND KIICHI UNDERTAKE AN OPERATION TO INFILTRATE THE SKIKROW ESTATE AND SEEK HIM OUT. UPON DISCOVERING THE CIRCUS MEMBERS, ASHINA ATTEMPTS TO FLEE THE GROUNDS, ONLY TO WIND UP ENSNARED BY JIKI'S POWERFUL ILLUSION TRAP. MEANWHILE, DESPITE BEING REJECTED REPEATEDLY BY KAROKU, NAI CONTINUES TO PATIENTLY NURSE HIM BACK TO HEALTH. AFTER OBSERVING NAI'S DEVOTION, KAROKU ATTEMPTS TO SUPPRESS HIS INSTINCT TO FLEE CAUSED BY HIS AVERSION TO NAI'S PRESENCE AND ASKS TO HEAR NAI'S STORY IN HOPES OF LEARNING THE TRUTH ABOUT HIMSELF. IT IS DURING THIS CONVERSATION THAT NAI'S BRACELET SUDDENLY ACTIVATES AND TRANSPORTS THE PAIR TO AN UNKNOWN PLACE.

CHARACTERS OF KARNEVAL

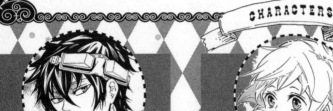

GAREKI

HE MET NAI INSIDE AN EERIE MANSION THAT HE HAD INTENDED TO BURGLARIZE. CURRENTLY ENROLLED IN THE CIRCUS PROGRAM AT THE GOVERNMENT TRAINING SCHOOL CHRONOMÉ ACADEMY.

NAI

A BOY WHO POSSESSES EXTRAORDINARY HEARING AND HAS A SOMEWHAT LIMITED UNDERSTANDING OF HOW THE WORLD WORKS. HE IS CURRENTLY LIVING ABOARD CIRCUS'S 2ND SHIP ALONGSIDE KAROKU.

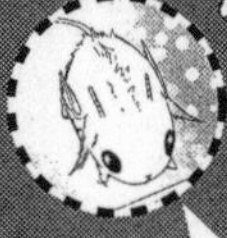

NIJI

THE ANIMAL FROM WHICH NAI WAS CREATED. THEY EXIST ONLY IN THE RAINBOW FOREST, A HIGHLY UNUSUAL ECOSYSTEM THAT ALLOWED THE NIJI TO EVOLVE AS THEY DID.

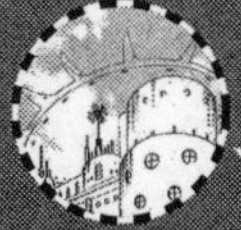

CHRONOMÉ

A VOCATIONAL SCHOOL FOR THOSE HOPING TO WORK FOR THE GOVERNMENT. ITS FOUR PROGRAMS OF STUDY ARE CIRCUS, ENGINEERING, MEDICAL & BIOLOGICAL SCIENCES, AND MANAGEMENT & INTELLIGENCE.

TAKING CARE OF

NATIONAL SUPREME DEFENSE FORCE "CIRCUS" 2ND SHIP

HIRATO

CAPTAIN OF CIRCUS'S 2ND SHIP. NAI (AND GAREKI), WHO BROUGHT HIM A BRACELET BELONGING TO CIRCUS, ARE CURRENTLY UNDER HIS PROTECTION.

GUARDING ON SHIP

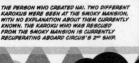

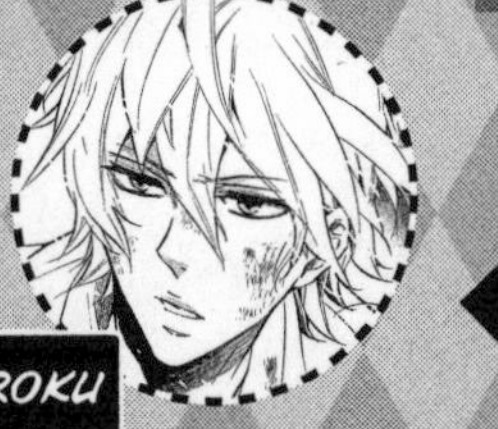

KAROKU

THE PERSON WHO CREATED NAI. TWO DIFFERENT KAROKUS WERE SEEN AT THE SMOKY MANSION, WITH NO EXPLANATION ABOUT THEM CURRENTLY KNOWN. THE KAROKU WHO WAS RESCUED FROM THE SMOKY MANSION IS CURRENTLY RECUPERATING ABOARD CIRCUS'S 2ND SHIP.

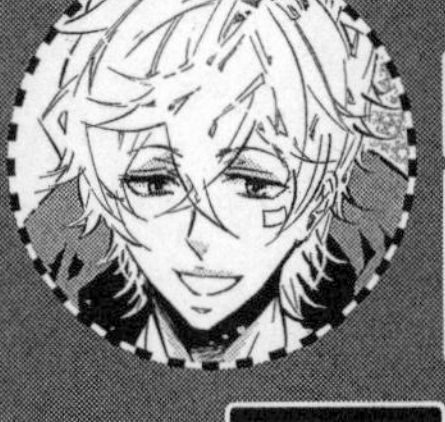

YOGI

CIRCUS'S 2ND SHIP COMBAT SPECIALIST. HE HAS A CHEERFUL, FRIENDLY PERSONALITY. WHEN THE PATCH HE WEARS ON HIS FACE RUNS OUT OF POTENCY, HIS PERSONALITY CHANGES.

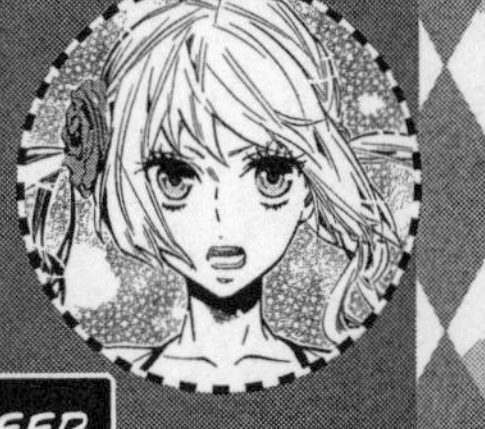

TSUKUMO

CIRCUS'S 2ND SHIP COMBAT SPECIALIST. A BEAUTIFUL GIRL WITH A COOL, SERIOUS PERSONALITY. RECENTLY, SHE SEEMS TO HAVE TAKEN UP SEWING STUFFED TOYS AS A PASTIME.

SHEEP

A CIRCUS DEFENSE SYSTEM. DESPITE THEIR CUTE APPEARANCE, THE SHEEP HAVE SOME VERY POWERFUL CAPABILITIES.

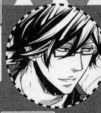

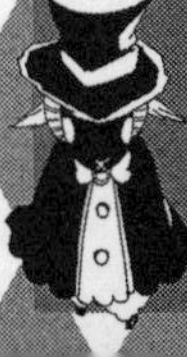

Q: WHAT IS CIRCUS?

A: THE EQUIVALENT OF THE REAL-WORLD POLICE. THEY CONDUCT THEIR LARGE-SCALE "OPERATIONS" WITHOUT FOREWARNING TO ENSURE THEIR TARGETS WILL NOT ESCAPE ARREST, UTILIZING COORDINATED, POWERFUL ATTACKS!! AFTER AN OPERATION, CIRCUS PERFORMS A "SHOW" FOR THE PEOPLE OF THE CITY AS AN APOLOGY FOR THE FEAR AND INCONVENIENCE THEIR WORK MAY HAVE CAUSED. IN SHORT, "CIRCUS" IS A CHEERFUL (?) AGENCY THAT CARRIES OUT THEIR MISSION DAY AND NIGHT TO APPREHEND EVIL AND PROTECT THE PEACE OF THE LAND.

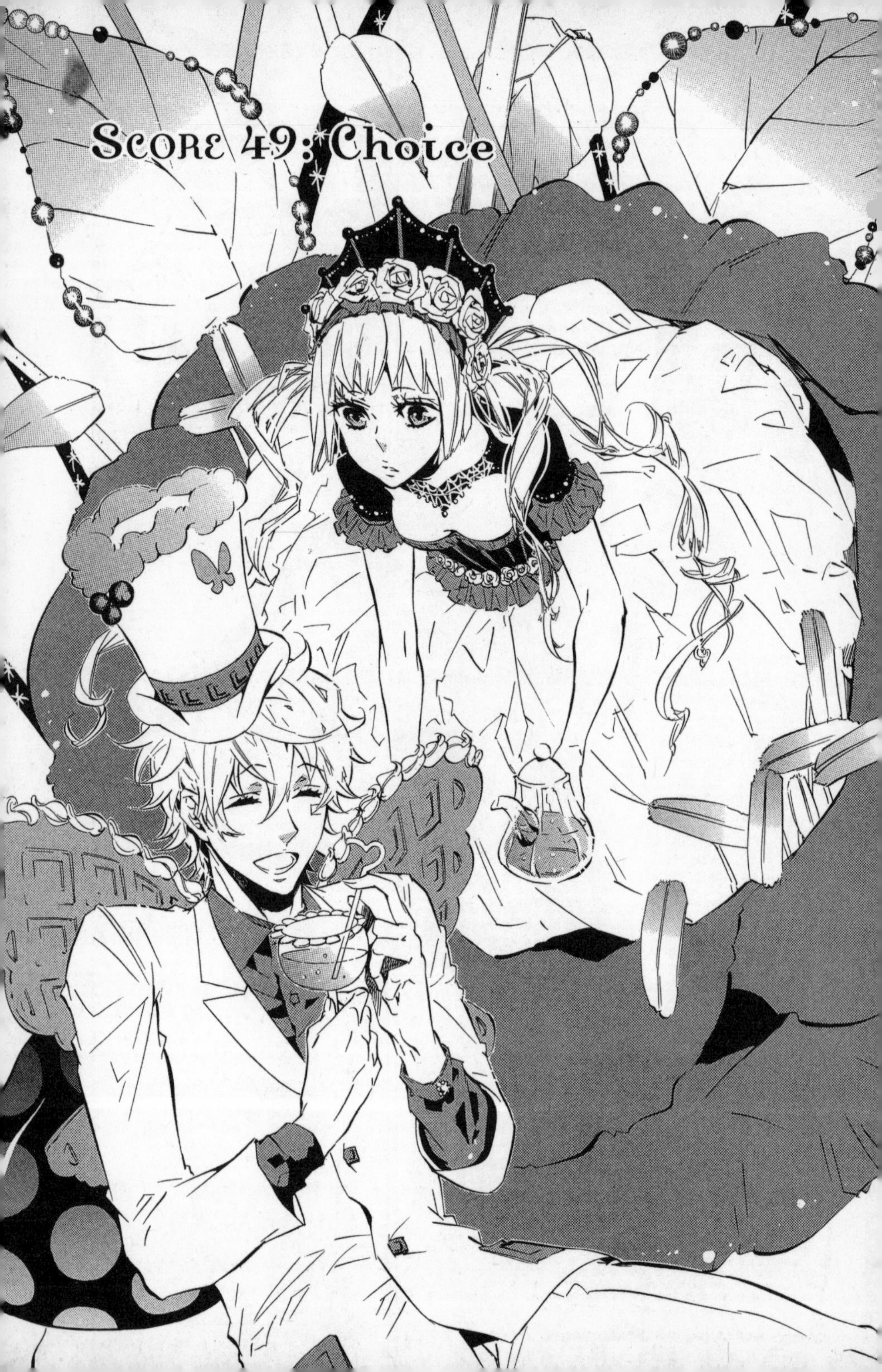
Score 49: Choice

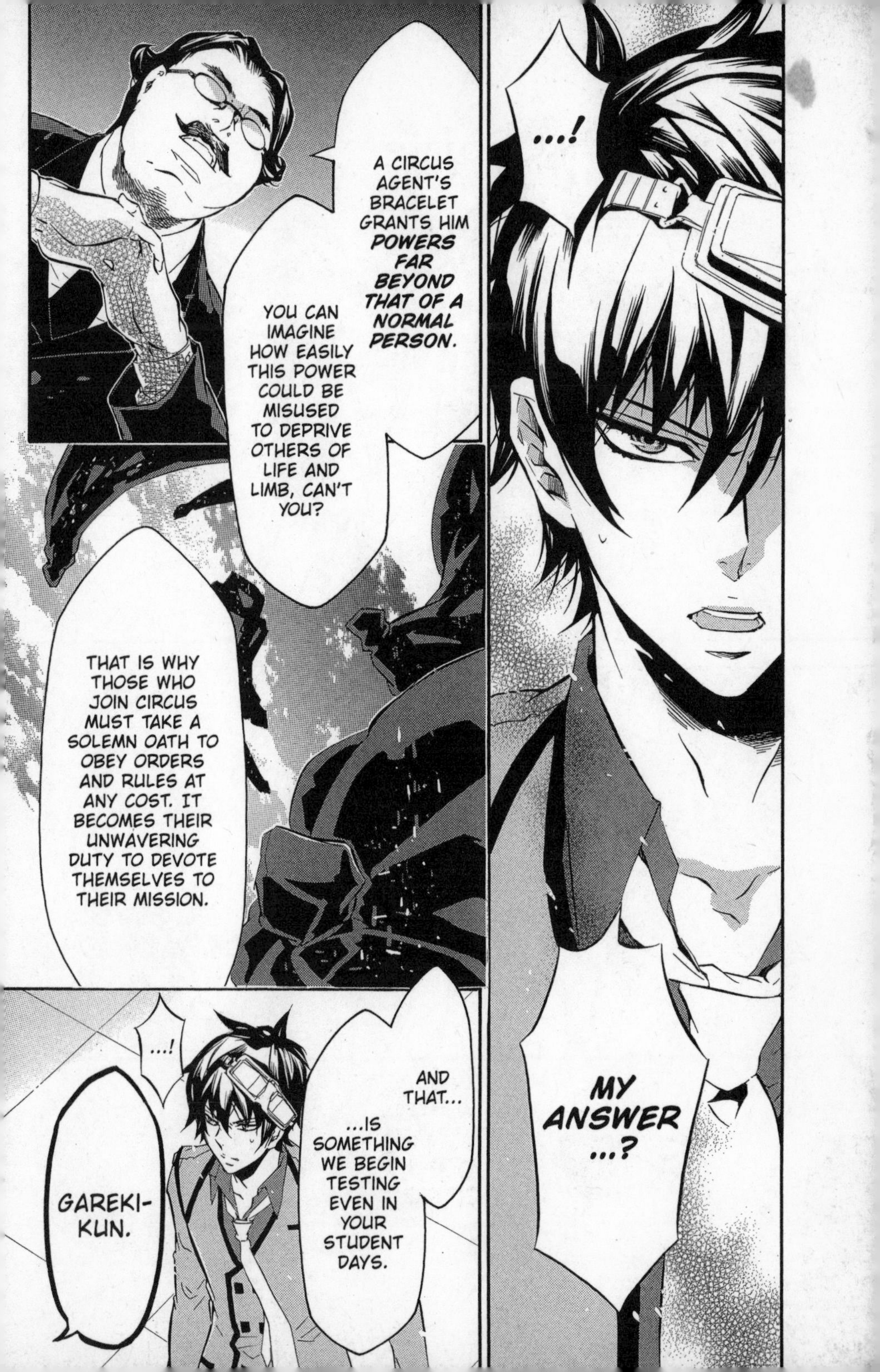
...!
MY ANSWER ...?
A CIRCUS AGENT'S BRACELET GRANTS HIM POWERS FAR BEYOND THAT OF A NORMAL PERSON.
YOU CAN IMAGINE HOW EASILY THIS POWER COULD BE MISUSED TO DEPRIVE OTHERS OF LIFE AND LIMB, CAN'T YOU?
THAT IS WHY THOSE WHO JOIN CIRCUS MUST TAKE A SOLEMN OATH TO OBEY ORDERS AND RULES AT ANY COST. IT BECOMES THEIR UNWAVERING DUTY TO DEVOTE THEMSELVES TO THEIR MISSION.
AND THAT...
...IS SOMETHING WE BEGIN TESTING EVEN IN YOUR STUDENT DAYS.
...!
GAREKI-KUN.

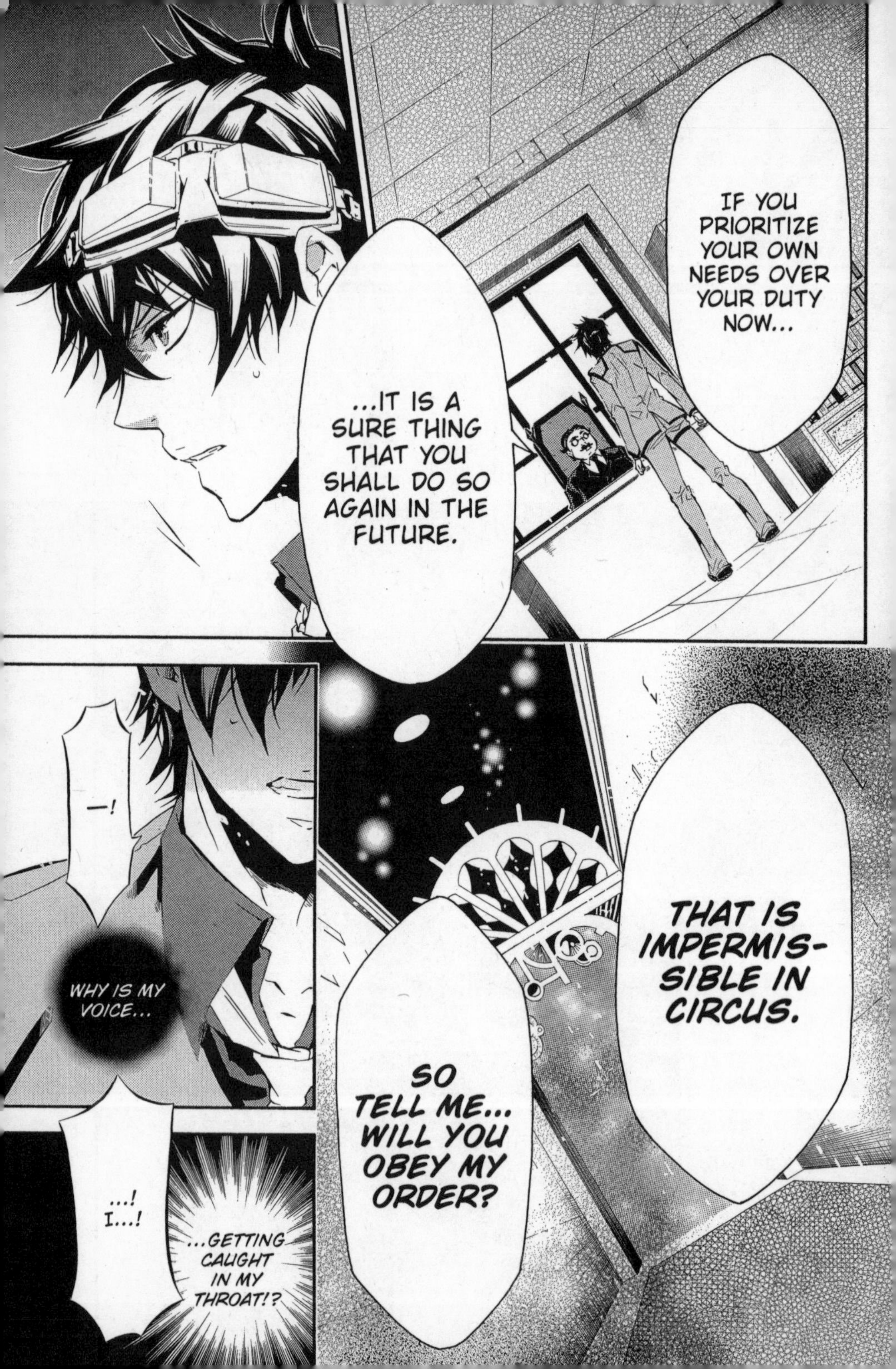
IF YOU PRIORITIZE YOUR OWN NEEDS OVER YOUR DUTY NOW...
...IT IS A SURE THING THAT YOU SHALL DO SO AGAIN IN THE FUTURE.
THAT IS IMPERMIS-SIBLE IN CIRCUS.
SO TELL ME... WILL YOU OBEY MY ORDER?
—!
WHY IS MY VOICE...
...! I...!
...GETTING CAUGHT IN MY THROAT!?

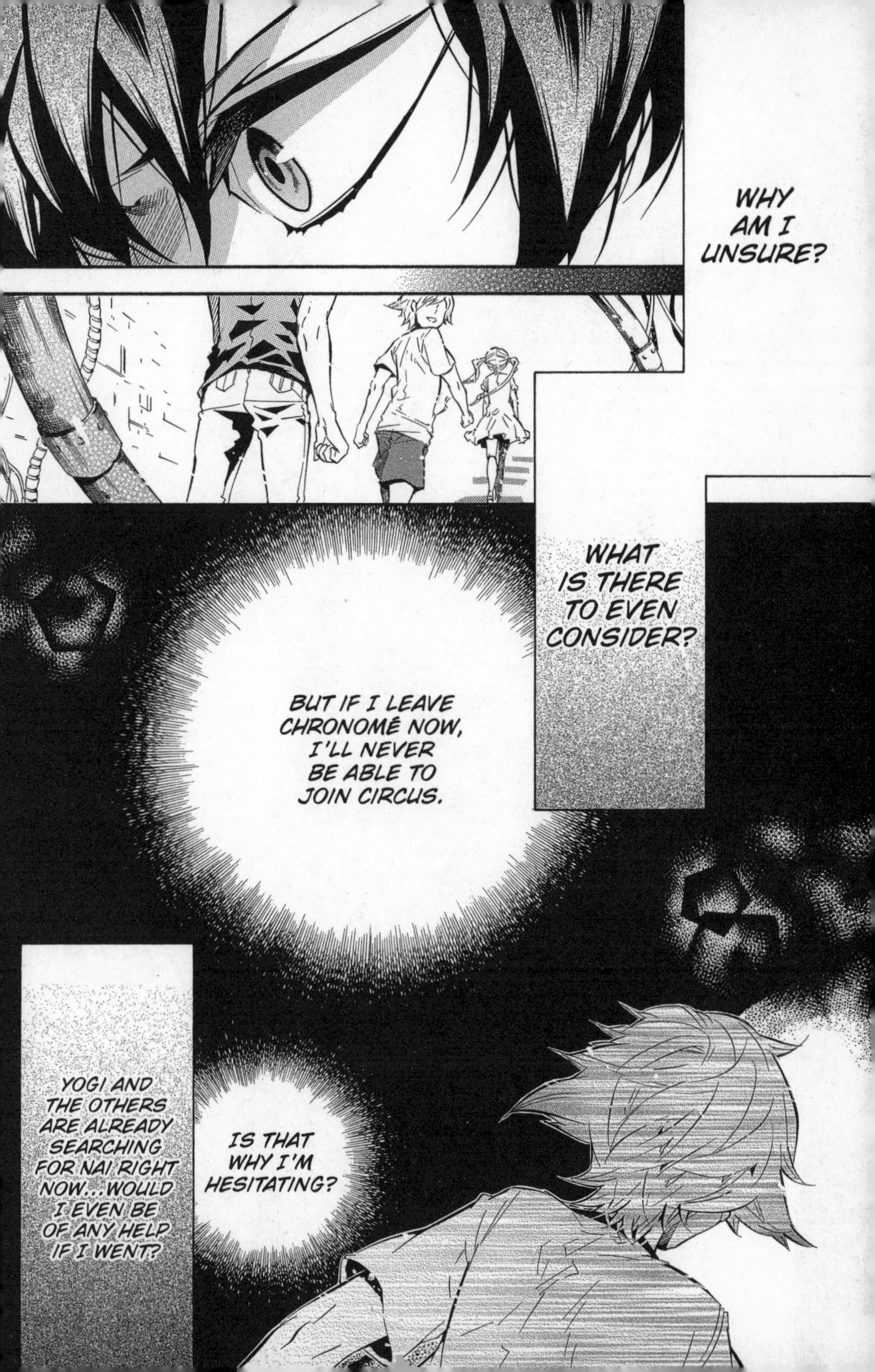
WHY AM I UNSURE?
WHAT IS THERE TO EVEN CONSIDER?
BUT IF I LEAVE CHRONOMÉ NOW, I'LL NEVER BE ABLE TO JOIN CIRCUS.
YOGI AND THE OTHERS ARE ALREADY SEARCHING FOR NAI RIGHT NOW...WOULD I EVEN BE OF ANY HELP IF I WENT?
IS THAT WHY I'M HESITATING?

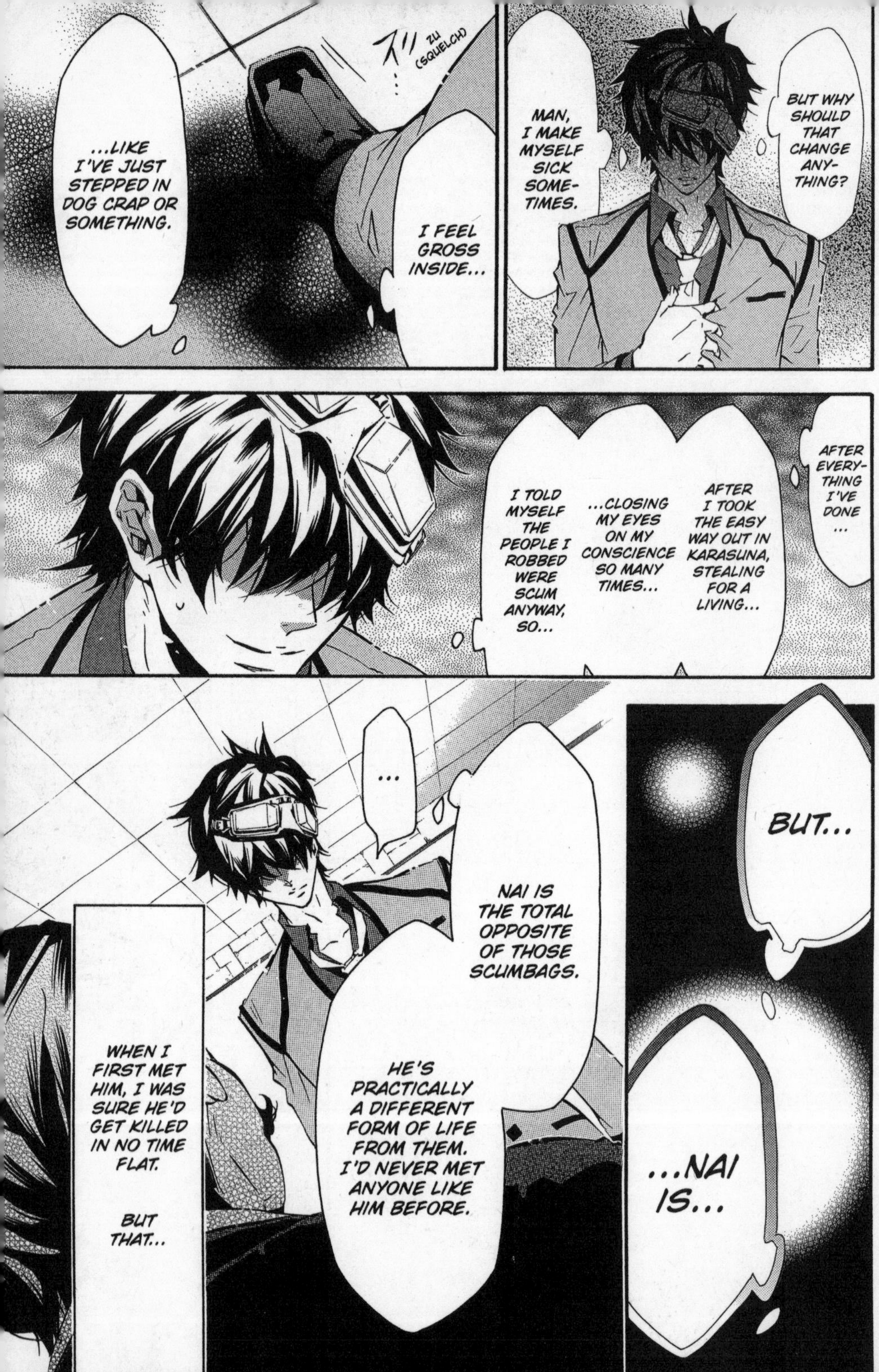
BUT WHY SHOULD THAT CHANGE ANY-THING?
MAN, I MAKE MYSELF SICK SOME-TIMES.
ズリ ZU (SQUELCH)
I FEEL GROSS INSIDE...
...LIKE I'VE JUST STEPPED IN DOG CRAP OR SOMETHING.
AFTER EVERY-THING I'VE DONE...
AFTER I TOOK THE EASY WAY OUT IN KARASUNA, STEALING FOR A LIVING...
...CLOSING MY EYES ON MY CONSCIENCE SO MANY TIMES...
I TOLD MYSELF THE PEOPLE I ROBBED WERE SCUM ANYWAY, SO...
BUT...
...NAI IS...
...
NAI IS THE TOTAL OPPOSITE OF THOSE SCUMBAGS.
HE'S PRACTICALLY A DIFFERENT FORM OF LIFE FROM THEM. I'D NEVER MET ANYONE LIKE HIM BEFORE.
WHEN I FIRST MET HIM, I WAS SURE HE'D GET KILLED IN NO TIME FLAT.
BUT THAT...

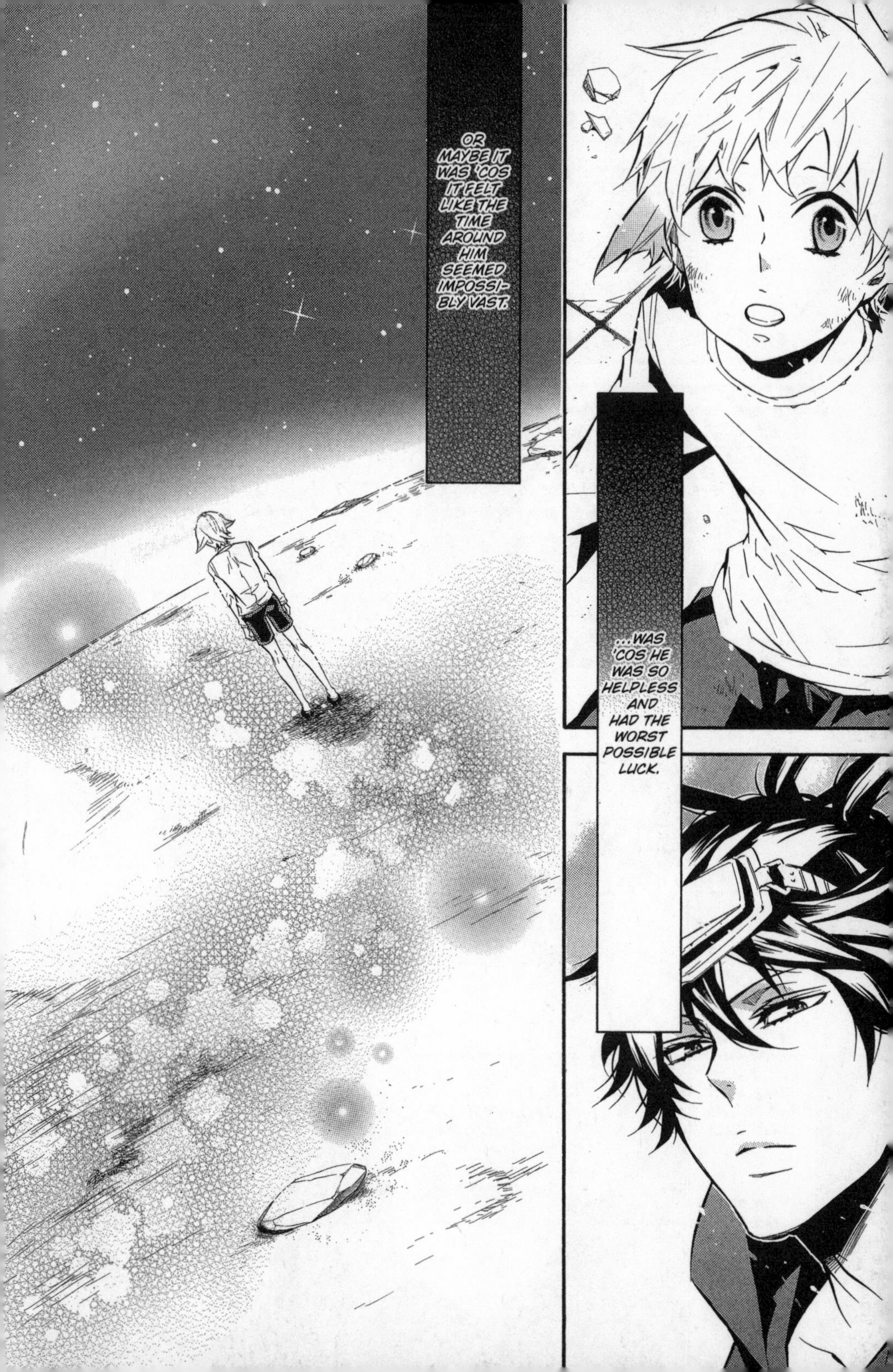
OR MAYBE IT WAS 'COS IT FELT LIKE THE TIME AROUND HIM SEEMED IMPOSSIBLY VAST.
...WAS 'COS HE WAS SO HELPLESS AND HAD THE WORST POSSIBLE LUCK.

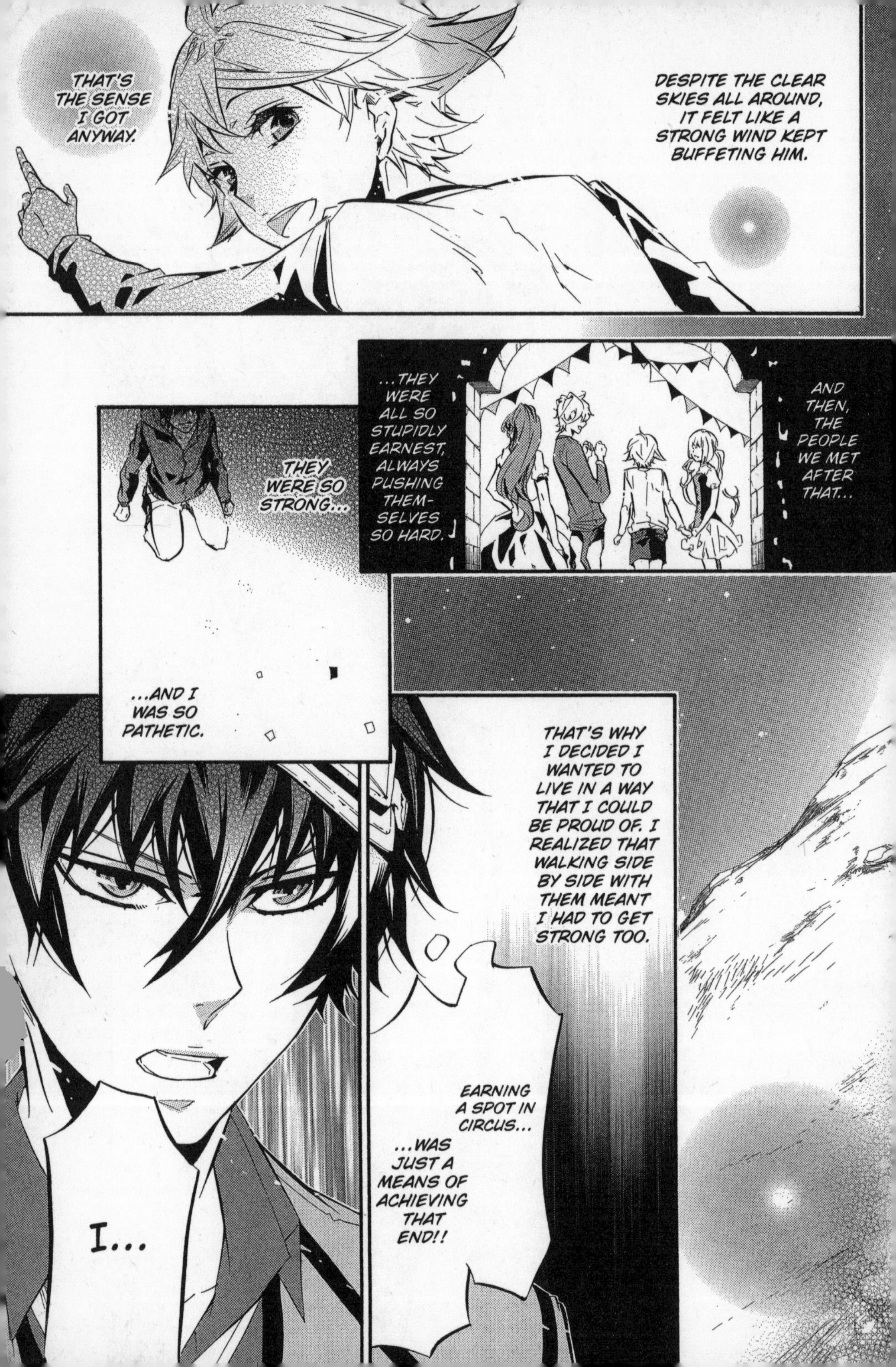
DESPITE THE CLEAR SKIES ALL AROUND, IT FELT LIKE A STRONG WIND KEPT BUFFETING HIM.
THAT'S THE SENSE I GOT ANYWAY.
AND THEN, THE PEOPLE WE MET AFTER THAT...
...THEY WERE ALL SO STUPIDLY EARNEST, ALWAYS PUSHING THEM-SELVES SO HARD.
THEY WERE SO STRONG...
...AND I WAS SO PATHETIC.
THAT'S WHY I DECIDED I WANTED TO LIVE IN A WAY THAT I COULD BE PROUD OF. I REALIZED THAT WALKING SIDE BY SIDE WITH THEM MEANT I HAD TO GET STRONG TOO.
EARNING A SPOT IN CIRCUS...
...WAS JUST A MEANS OF ACHIEVING THAT END!!
I...

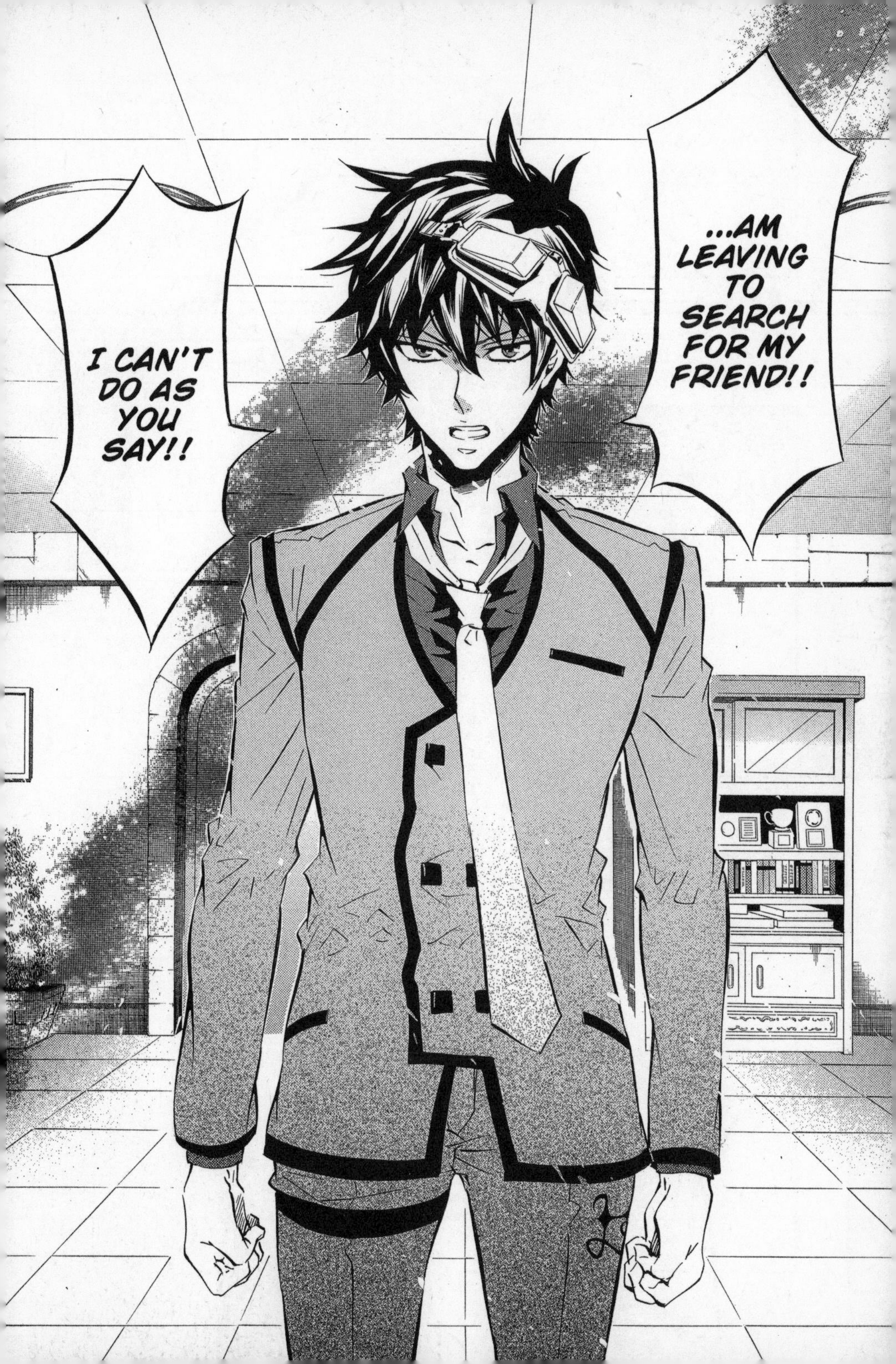
...AM LEAVING TO SEARCH FOR MY FRIEND!!
I CAN'T DO AS YOU SAY!!

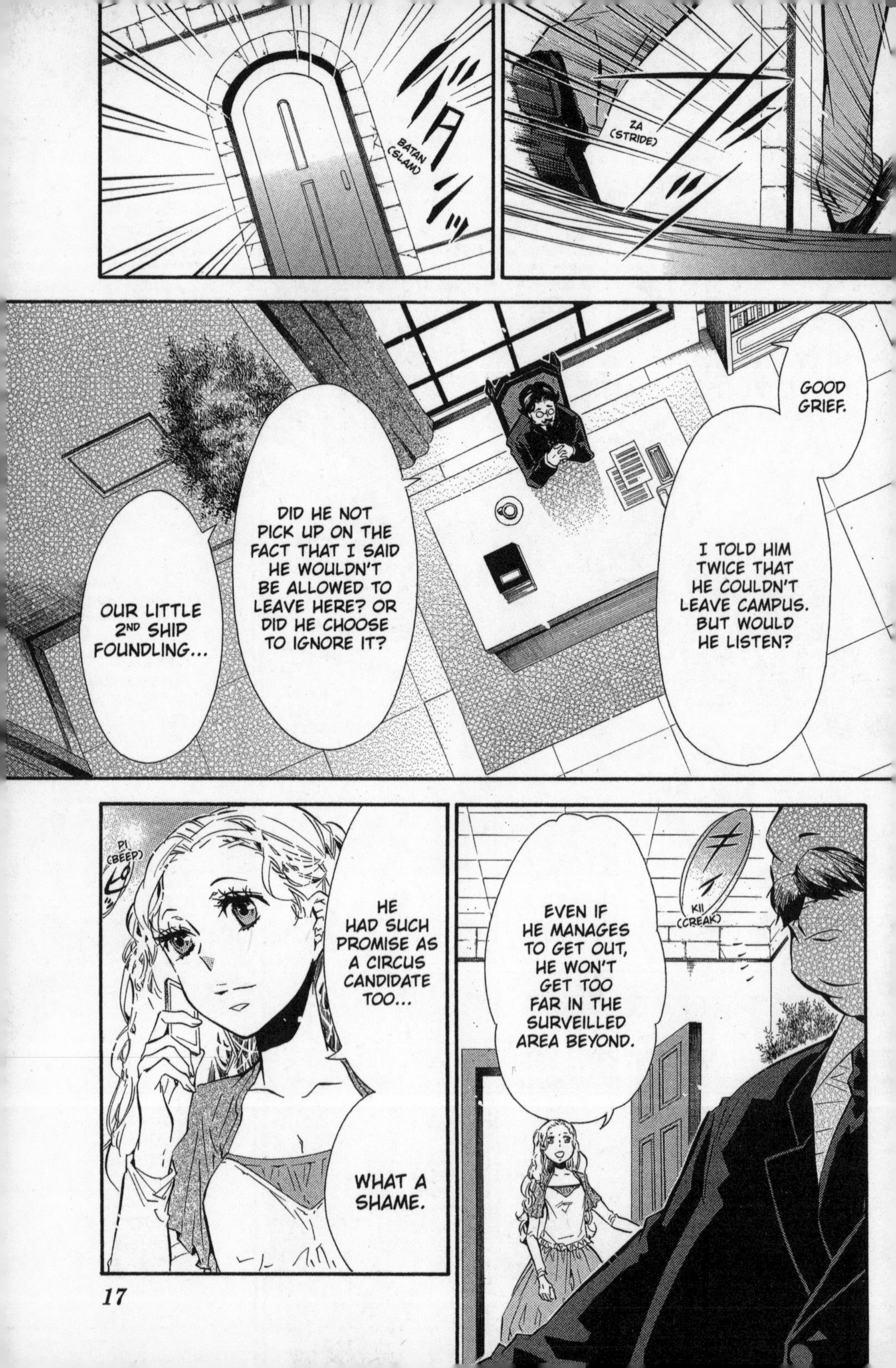
ZA (STRIDE)
BATAN (SLAM)
GOOD GRIEF.
I TOLD HIM TWICE THAT HE COULDN'T LEAVE CAMPUS. BUT WOULD HE LISTEN?
DID HE NOT PICK UP ON THE FACT THAT I SAID HE WOULDN'T BE ALLOWED TO LEAVE HERE? OR DID HE CHOOSE TO IGNORE IT?
OUR LITTLE 2ND SHIP FOUNDLING...
KII (CREAK)
EVEN IF HE MANAGES TO GET OUT, HE WON'T GET TOO FAR IN THE SURVEILLED AREA BEYOND.
PI (BEEP)
HE HAD SUCH PROMISE AS A CIRCUS CANDIDATE TOO...
WHAT A SHAME.

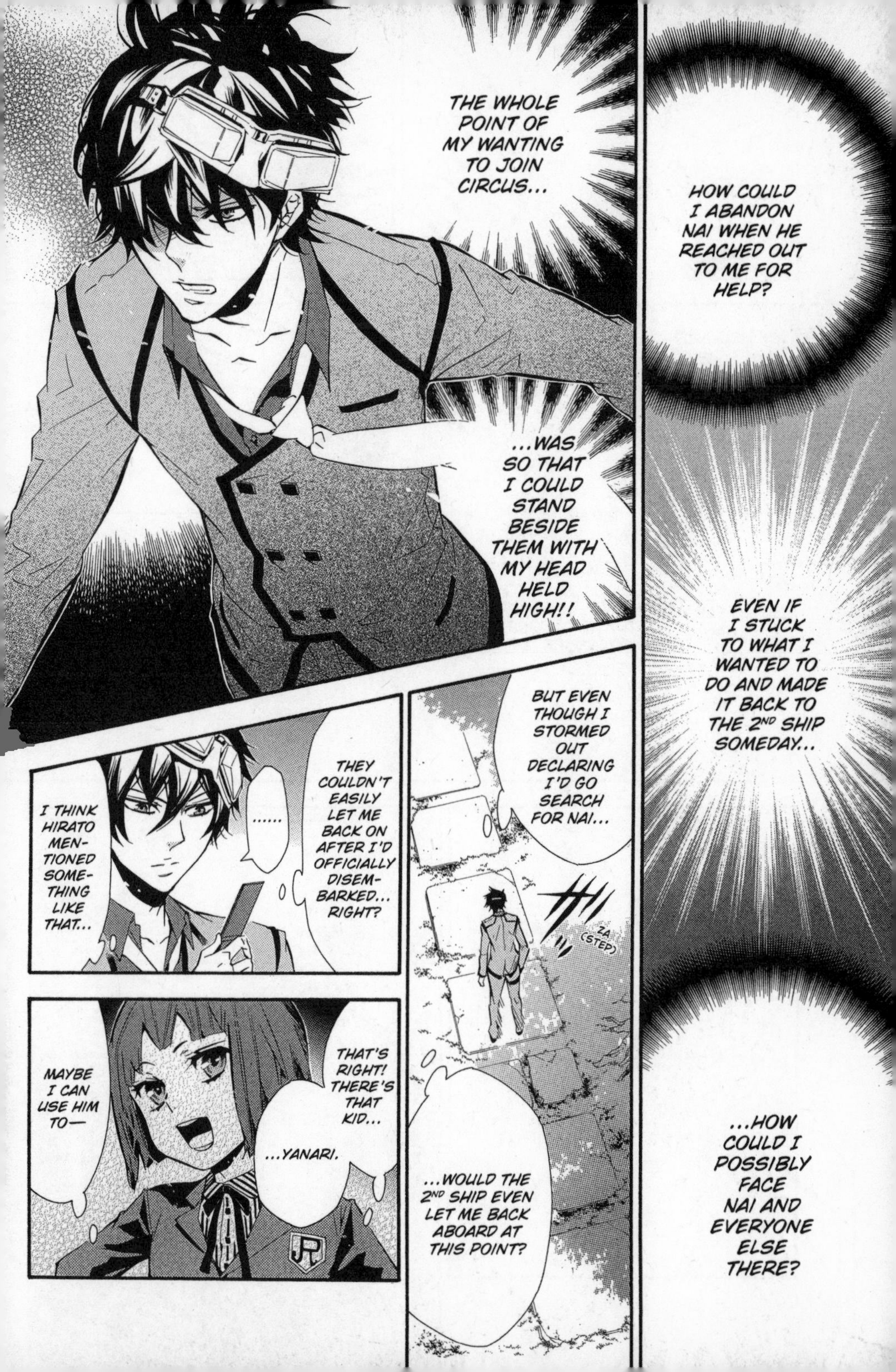
HOW COULD I ABANDON NAI WHEN HE REACHED OUT TO ME FOR HELP?
EVEN IF I STUCK TO WHAT I WANTED TO DO AND MADE IT BACK TO THE 2ND SHIP SOMEDAY...
...HOW COULD I POSSIBLY FACE NAI AND EVERYONE ELSE THERE?
THE WHOLE POINT OF MY WANTING TO JOIN CIRCUS...
...WAS SO THAT I COULD STAND BESIDE THEM WITH MY HEAD HELD HIGH!!
BUT EVEN THOUGH I STORMED OUT DECLARING I'D GO SEARCH FOR NAI...
ZA (STEP)
...WOULD THE 2ND SHIP EVEN LET ME BACK ABOARD AT THIS POINT?
THEY COULDN'T EASILY LET ME BACK ON AFTER I'D OFFICIALLY DISEMBARKED... RIGHT?
......
I THINK HIRATO MENTIONED SOMETHING LIKE THAT...
THAT'S RIGHT! THERE'S THAT KID...
...YANARI.
MAYBE I CAN USE HIM TO—

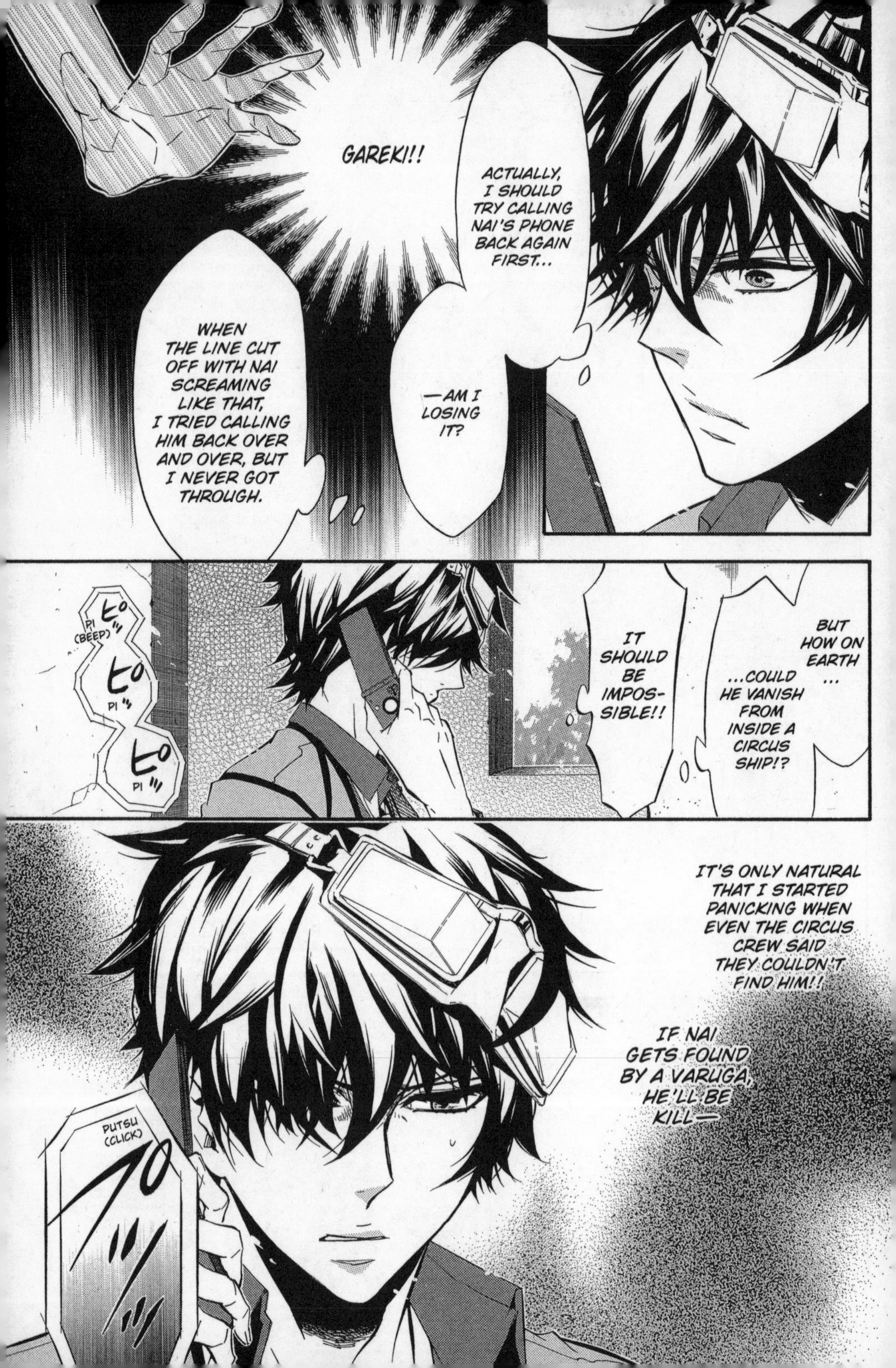
ACTUALLY, I SHOULD TRY CALLING NAI'S PHONE BACK AGAIN FIRST...
GAREKI!!
—AM I LOSING IT?
WHEN THE LINE CUT OFF WITH NAI SCREAMING LIKE THAT, I TRIED CALLING HIM BACK OVER AND OVER, BUT I NEVER GOT THROUGH.
BUT HOW ON EARTH...
...COULD HE VANISH FROM INSIDE A CIRCUS SHIP!?
IT SHOULD BE IMPOSSIBLE!!
PI (BEEP)
PI
PI
IT'S ONLY NATURAL THAT I STARTED PANICKING WHEN EVEN THE CIRCUS CREW SAID THEY COULDN'T FIND HIM!!
IF NAI GETS FOUND BY A VARUGA, HE'LL BE KILL—
PUTSU (CLICK)

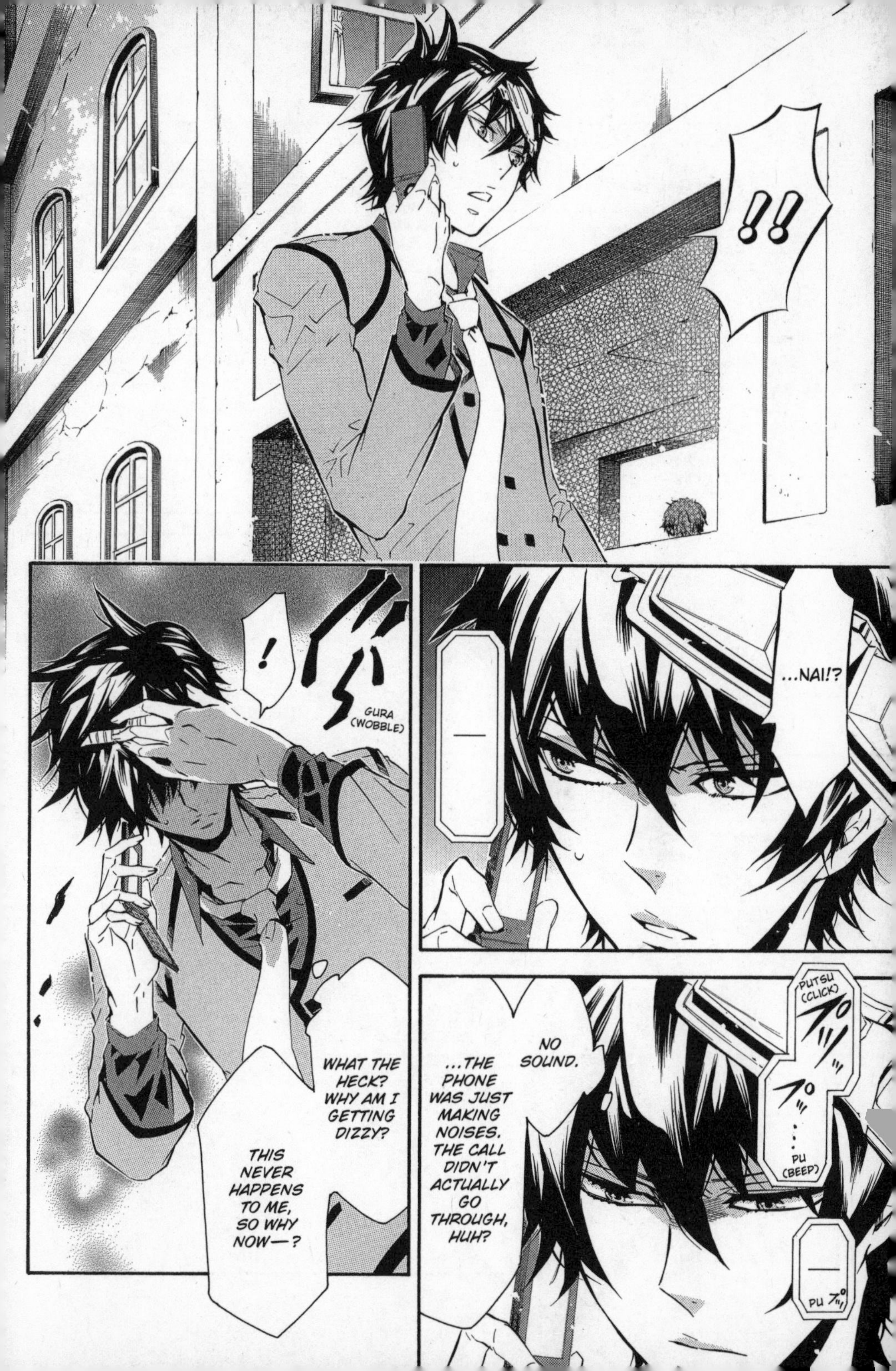
!!
...NAI!?
—
PUTSU (CLICK)
PU (BEEP)
NO SOUND.
...THE PHONE WAS JUST MAKING NOISES. THE CALL DIDN'T ACTUALLY GO THROUGH, HUH?
—
PU
!
GURA (WOBBLE)
WHAT THE HECK? WHY AM I GETTING DIZZY?
THIS NEVER HAPPENS TO ME, SO WHY NOW—?

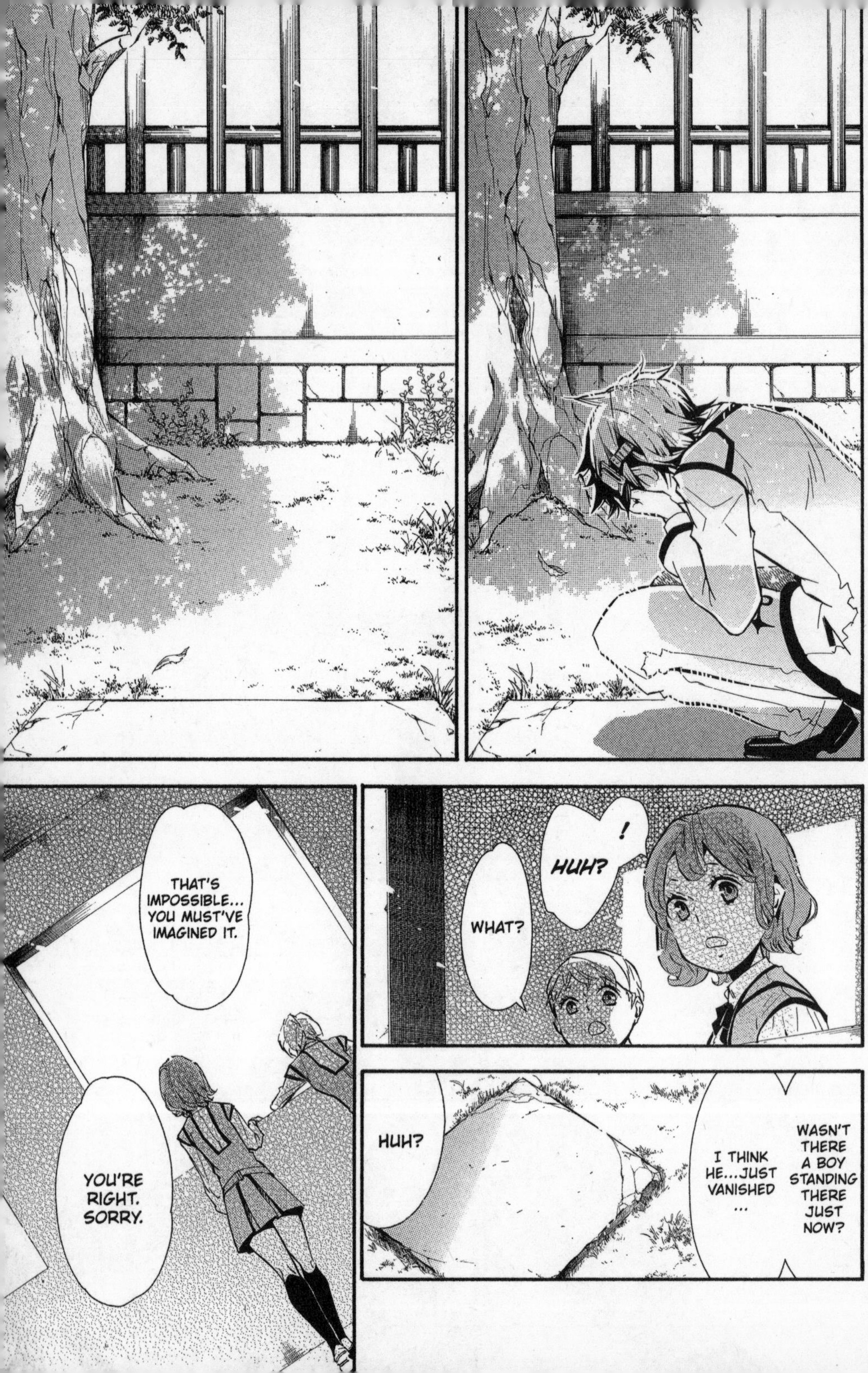
HUH? !
WHAT?
WASN'T THERE A BOY STANDING THERE JUST NOW?
I THINK HE...JUST VANISHED...
HUH?
THAT'S IMPOSSIBLE... YOU MUST'VE IMAGINED IT.
YOU'RE RIGHT. SORRY.

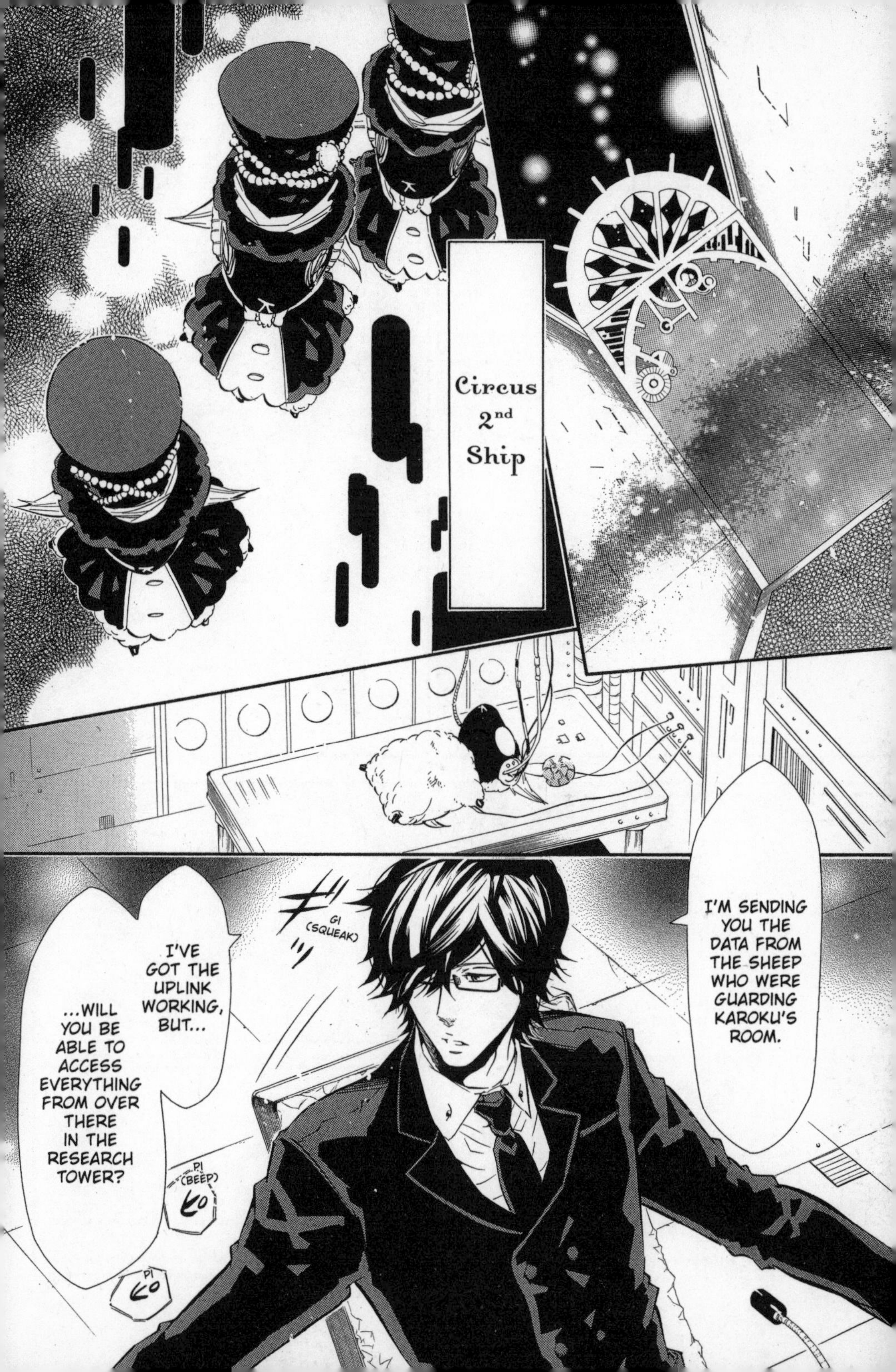
Circus 2nd Ship
I'M SENDING YOU THE DATA FROM THE SHEEP WHO WERE GUARDING KAROKU'S ROOM.
GI (SQUEAK)
I'VE GOT THE UPLINK WORKING, BUT...
...WILL YOU BE ABLE TO ACCESS EVERYTHING FROM OVER THERE IN THE RESEARCH TOWER?
PI (BEEP)
PI

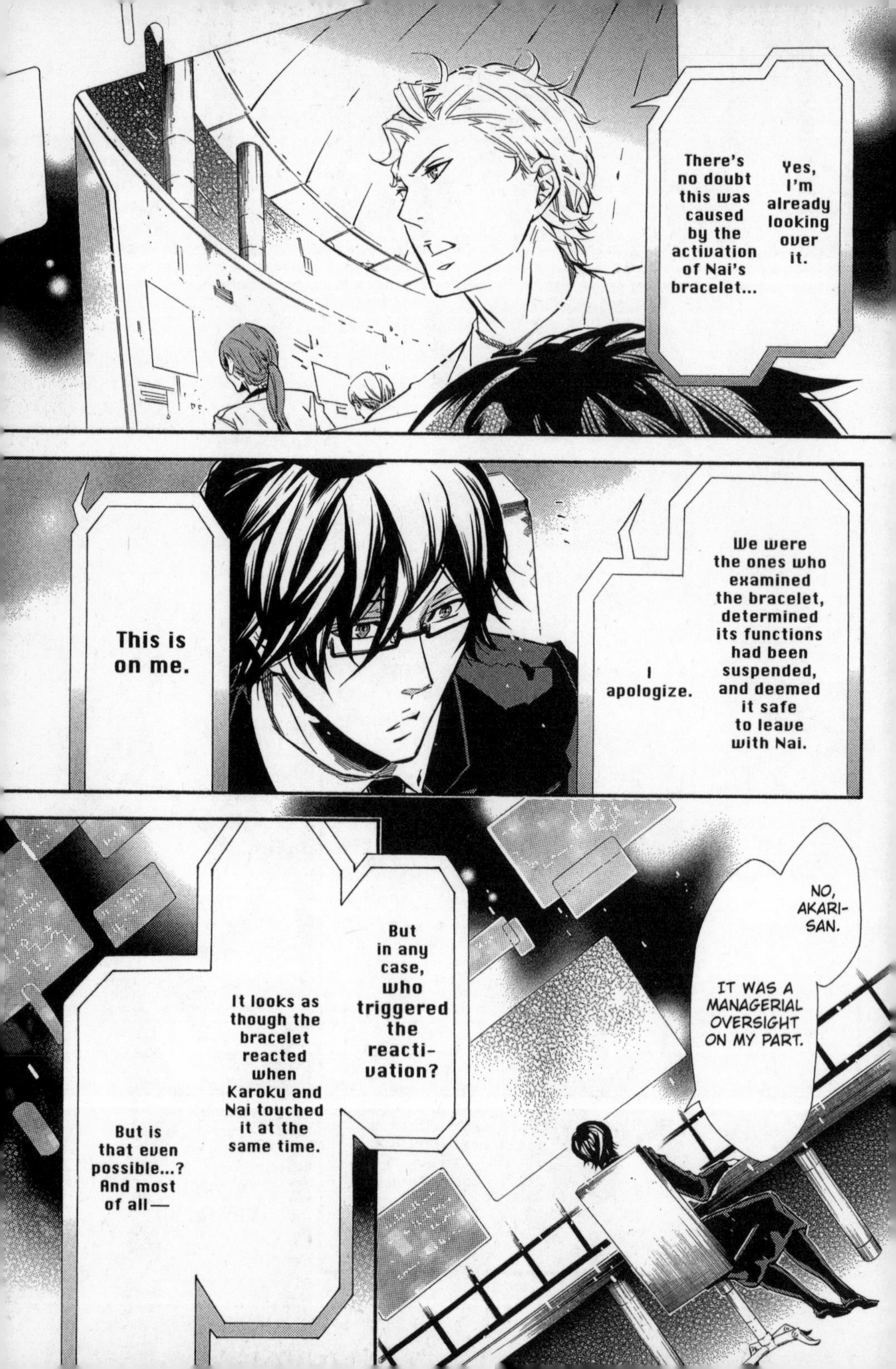
Yes, I'm already looking over it.
There's no doubt this was caused by the activation of Nai's bracelet...
We were the ones who examined the bracelet, determined its functions had been suspended, and deemed it safe to leave with Nai.
I apologize.
This is on me.
NO, AKARI-SAN.
IT WAS A MANAGERIAL OVERSIGHT ON MY PART.
But in any case, who triggered the reacti-vation?
It looks as though the bracelet reacted when Karoku and Nai touched it at the same time.
But is that even possible...? And most of all—

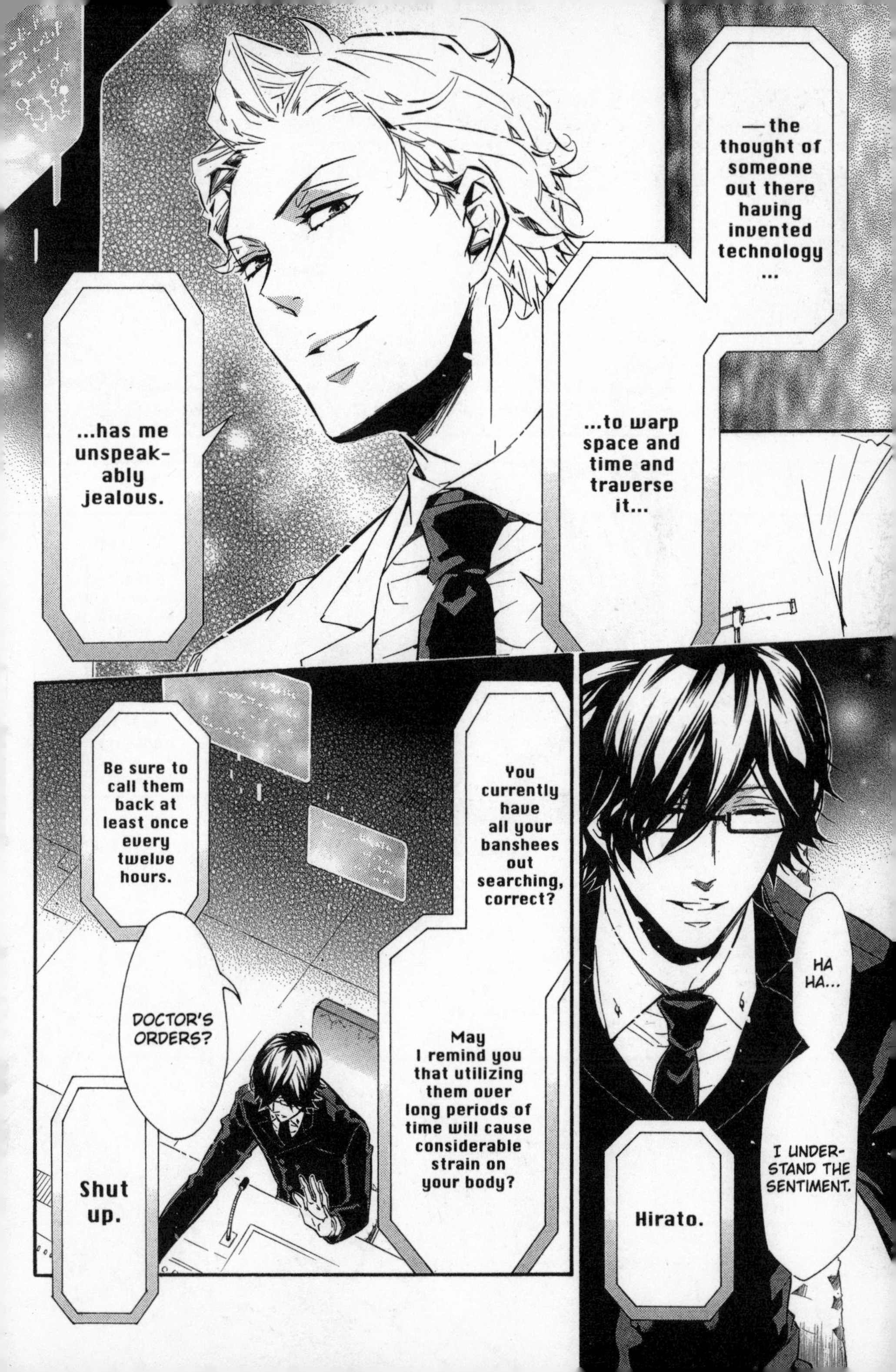
—the thought of someone out there having invented technology...
...to warp space and time and traverse it...
...has me unspeak-ably jealous.
HA HA...
I UNDER-STAND THE SENTIMENT.
Hirato.
You currently have all your banshees out searching, correct?
Be sure to call them back at least once every twelve hours.
DOCTOR'S ORDERS?
May I remind you that utilizing them over long periods of time will cause considerable strain on your body?
Shut up.

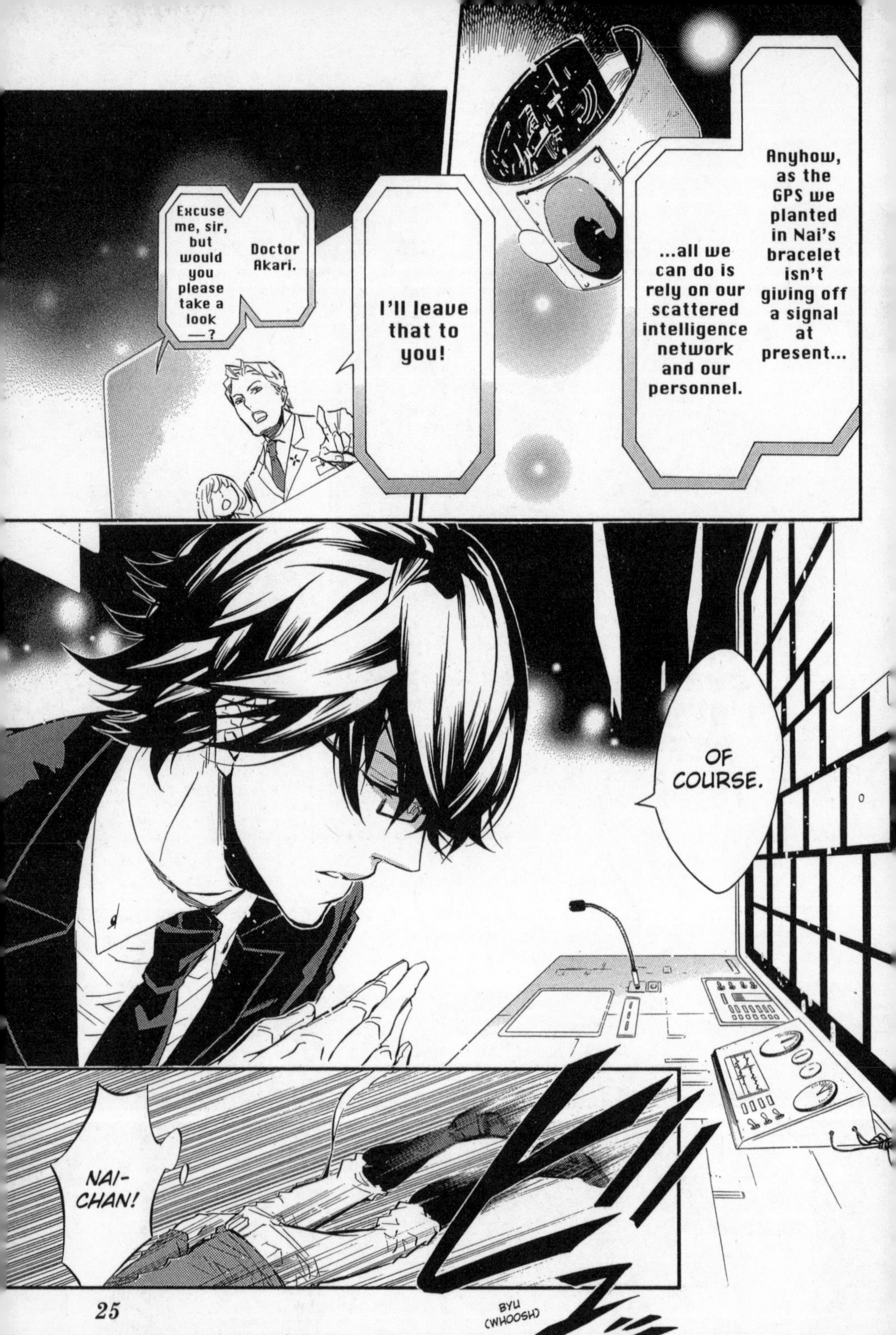
Anyhow, as the GPS we planted in Nai's bracelet isn't giving off a signal at present...
...all we can do is rely on our scattered intelligence network and our personnel.
I'll leave that to you!
Doctor Akari.
Excuse me, sir, but would you please take a look—?
OF COURSE.
NAI-CHAN!
BYU (WHOOSH)

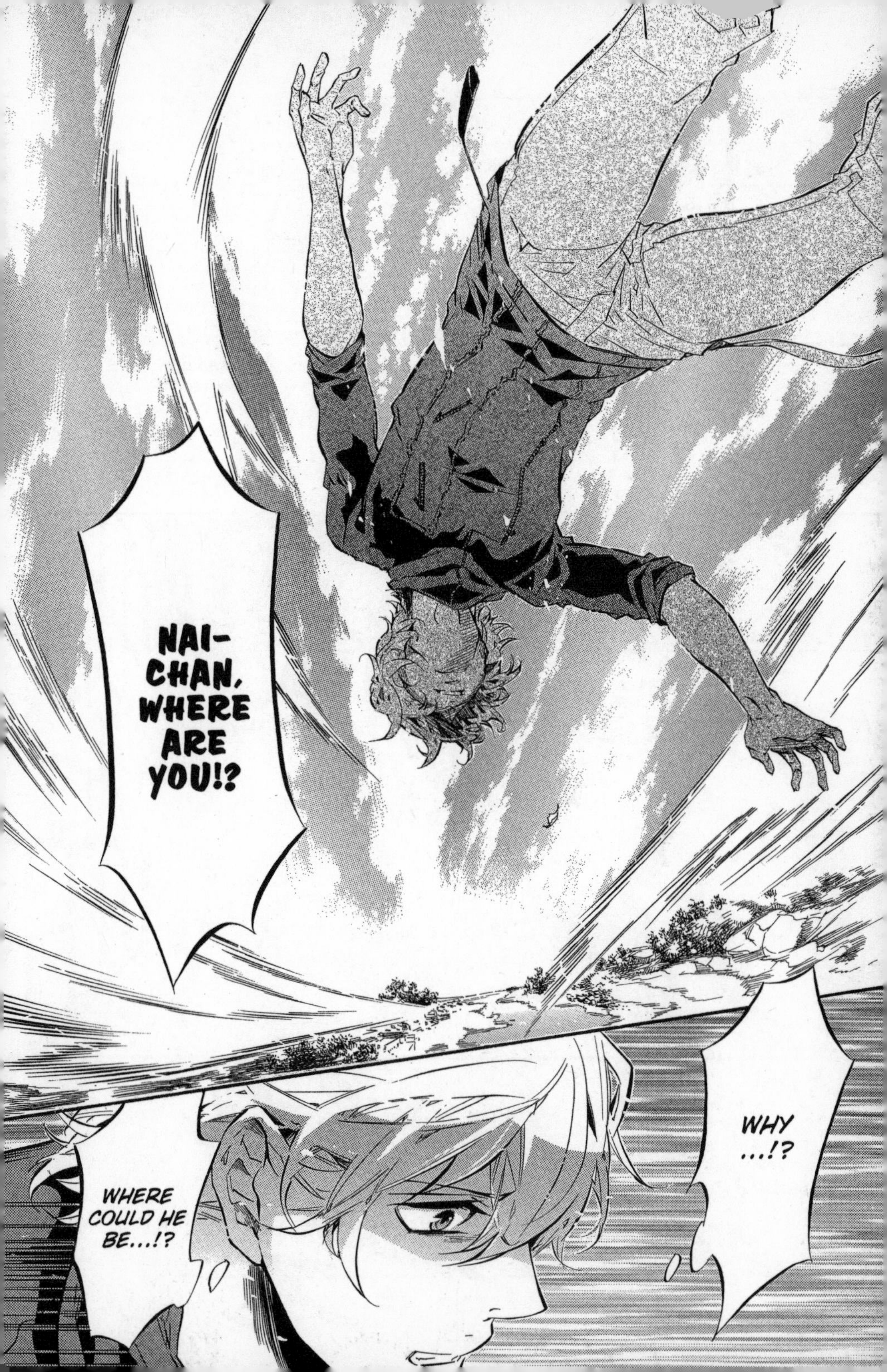
NAI-CHAN, WHERE ARE YOU!?
WHY ...!?
WHERE COULD HE BE...!?

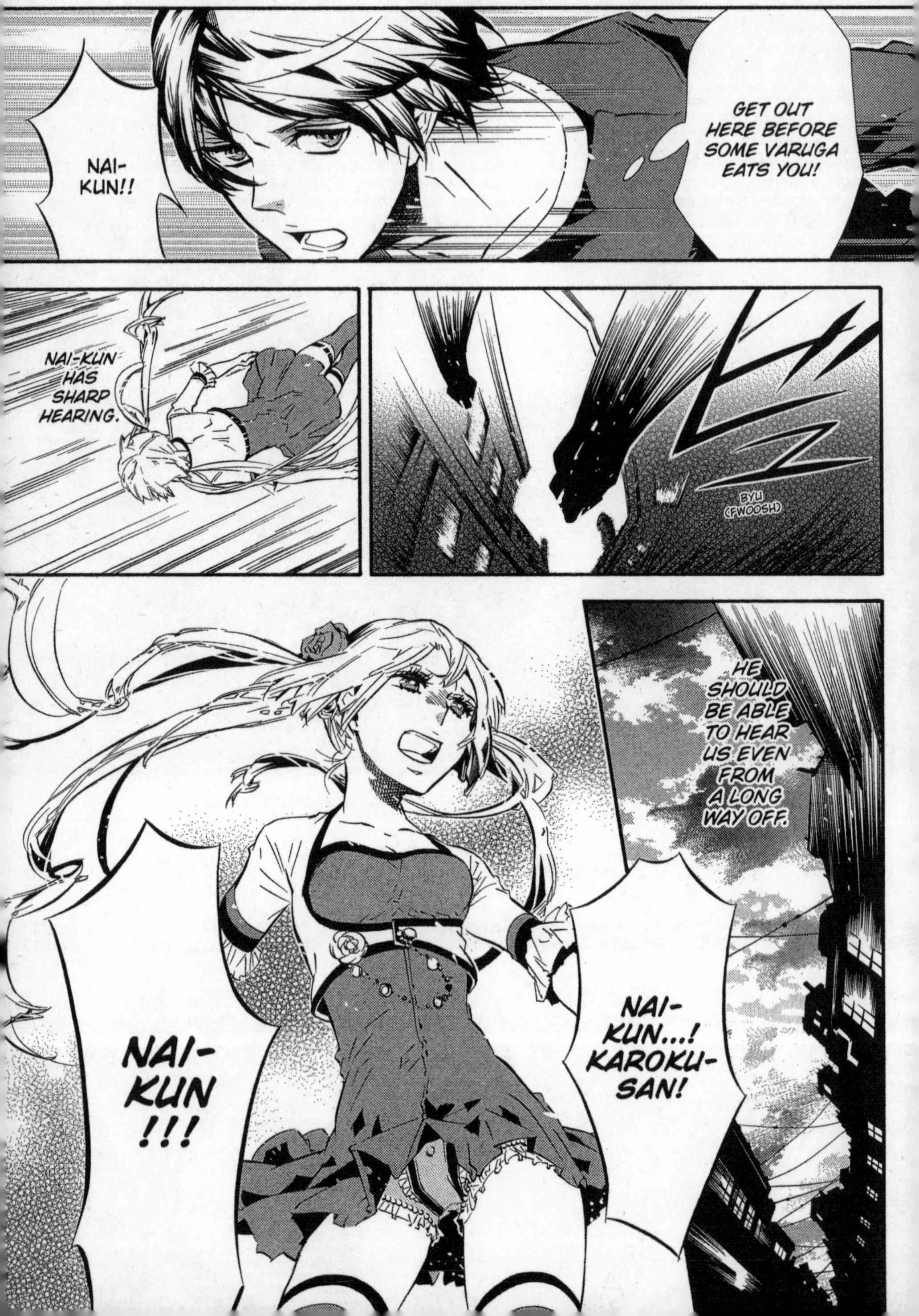
GET OUT HERE BEFORE SOME VARUGA EATS YOU!
NAI-KUN!!
BYU (FWOOSH)
NAI-KUN HAS SHARP HEARING.
HE SHOULD BE ABLE TO HEAR US EVEN FROM A LONG WAY OFF.
NAI-KUN...! KAROKU-SAN!
NAI-KUN!!!

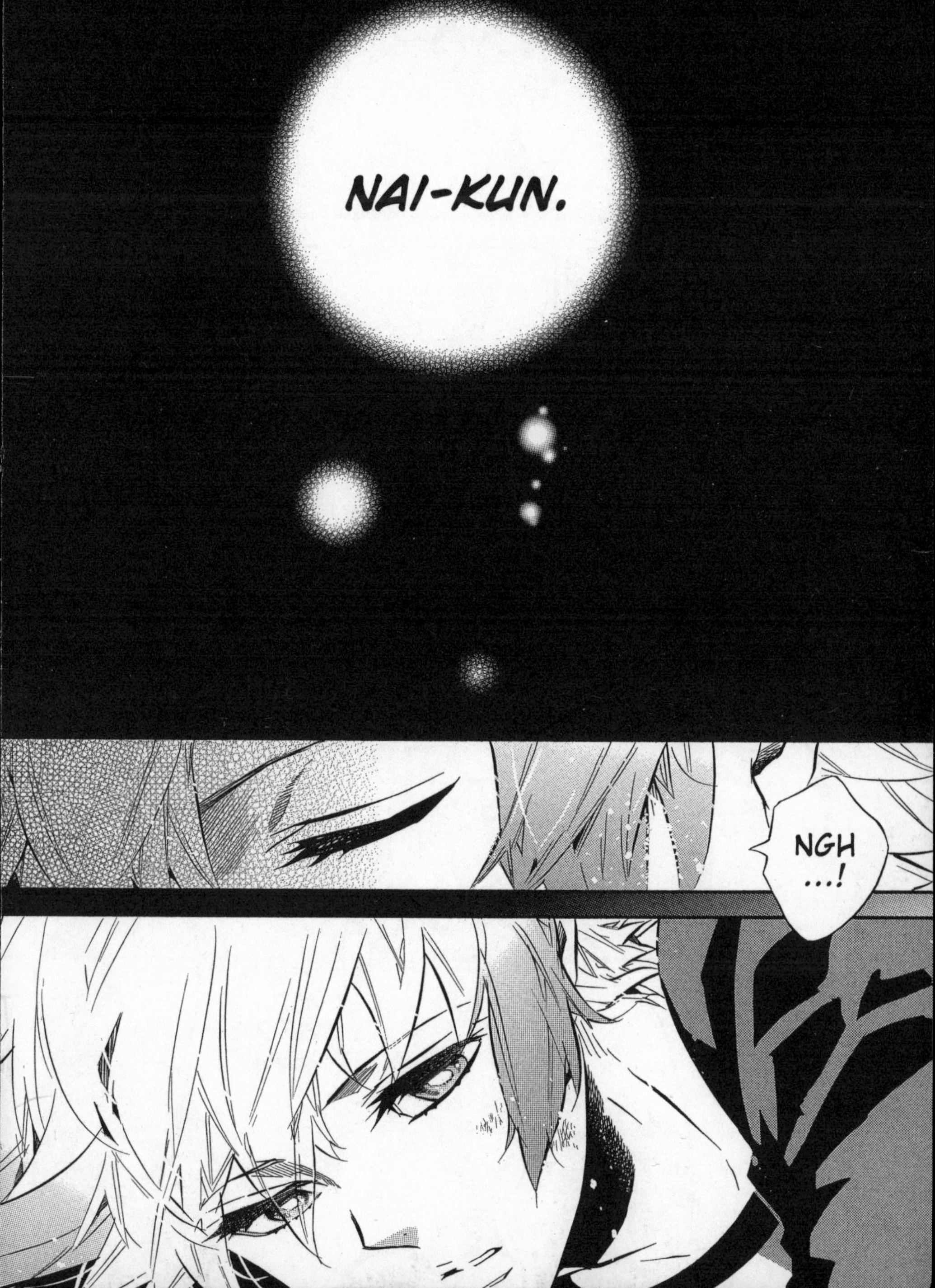
NAI-KUN.
NGH ...!

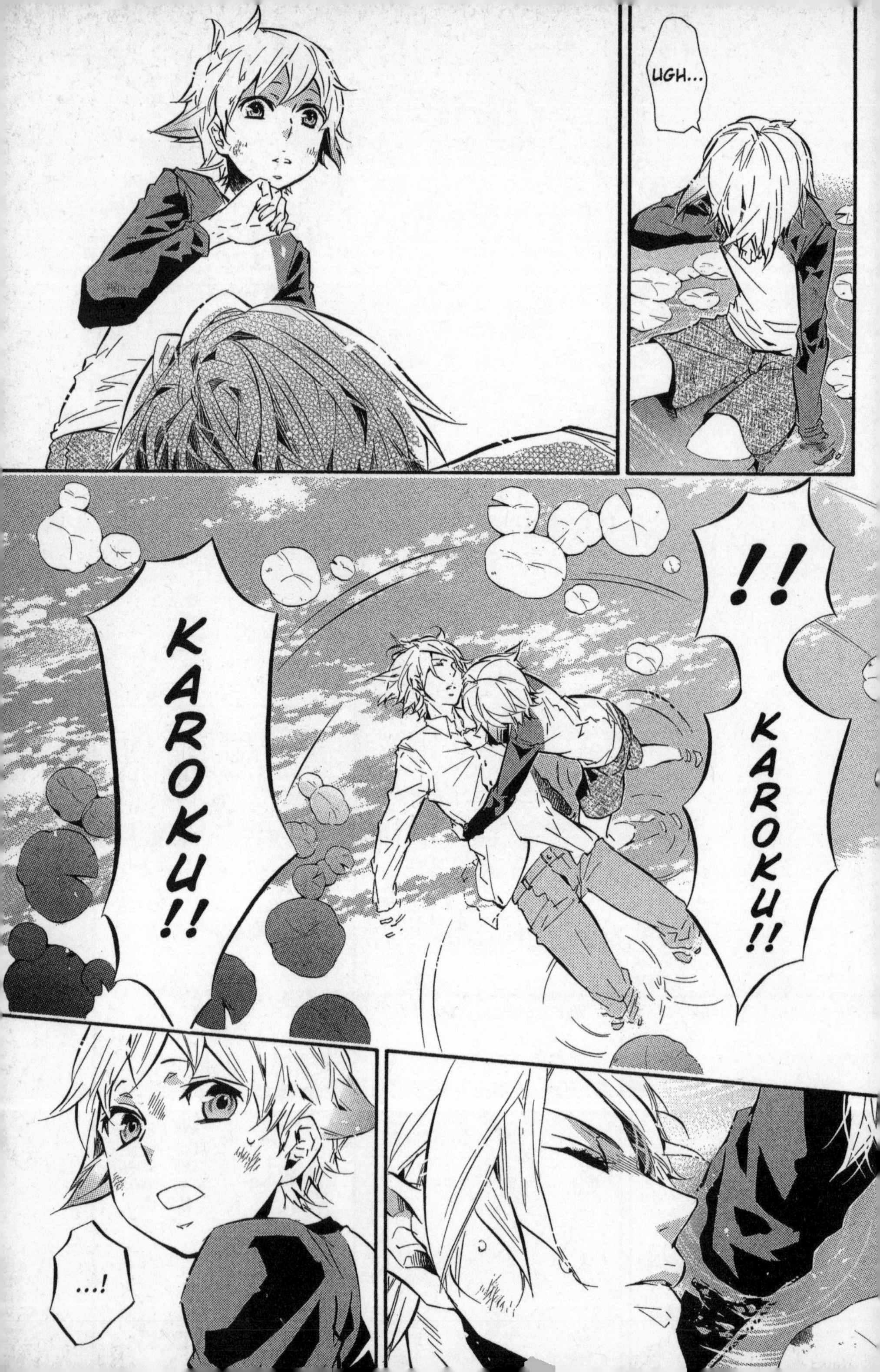
UGH...
!!
KAROKU!!
KAROKU!!
...!

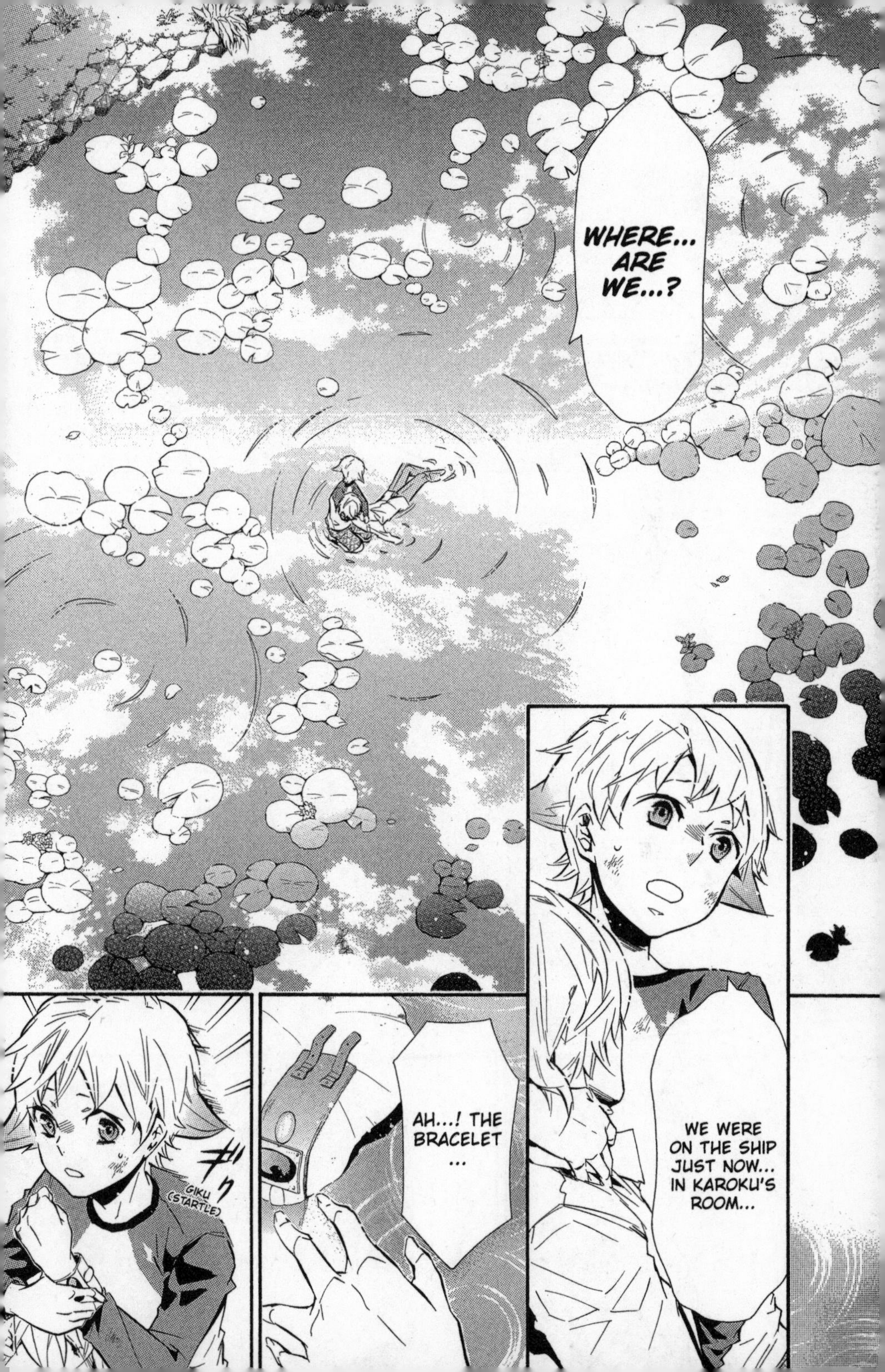
WHERE... ARE WE...?
WE WERE ON THE SHIP JUST NOW... IN KAROKU'S ROOM...
AH...! THE BRACELET ...
GIKU (STARTLE)

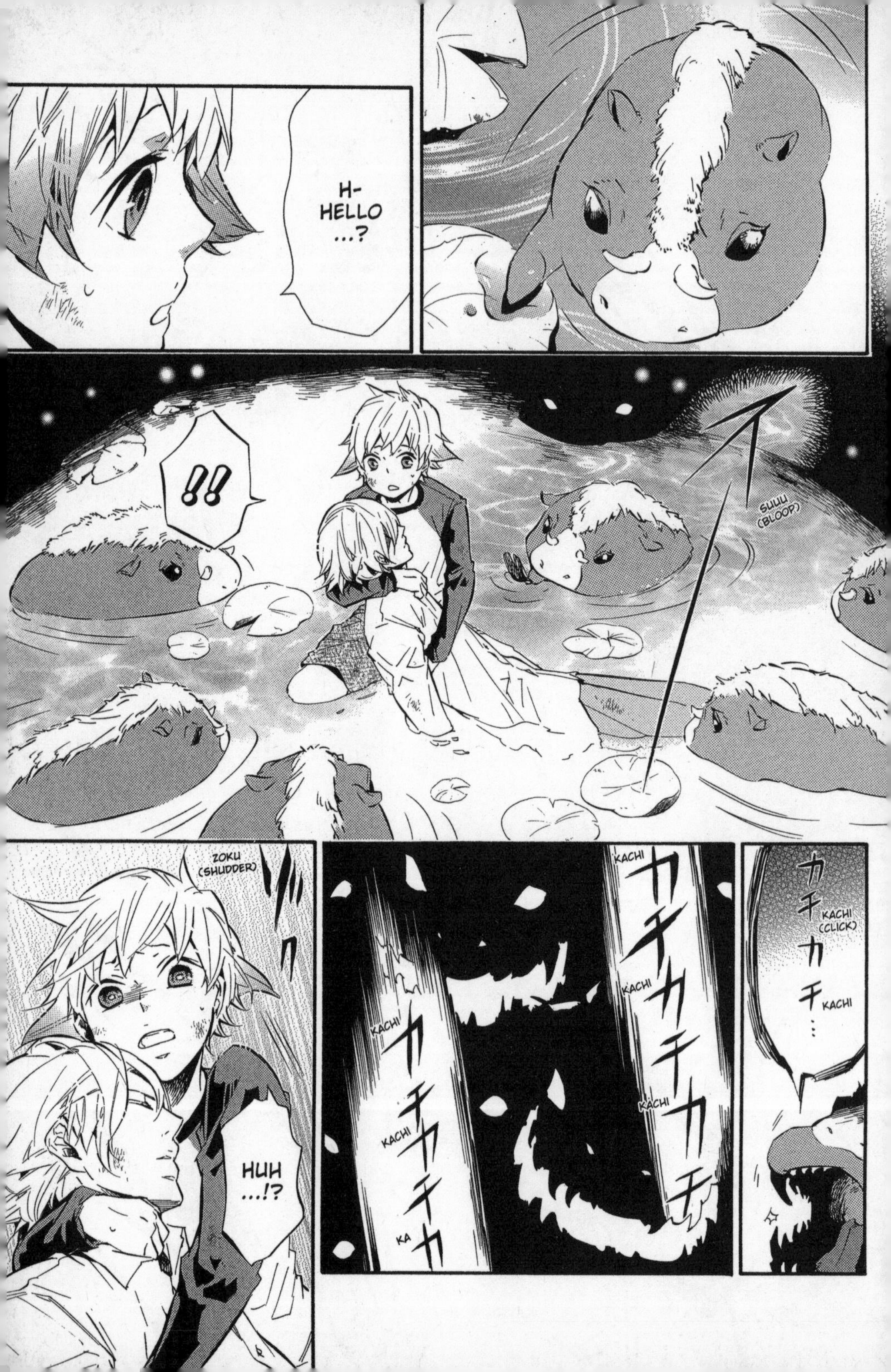

H-
HELLO
...?
SUUU
(BLOOP)
!!
カチカチ…
KACHI
(CLICK)
KACHI
カチカチ
KACHI
KACHI
カチカチカ
KACHI
KACHI
KA
ゾク
ZOKU
(SHUDDER)
HUH
...!?

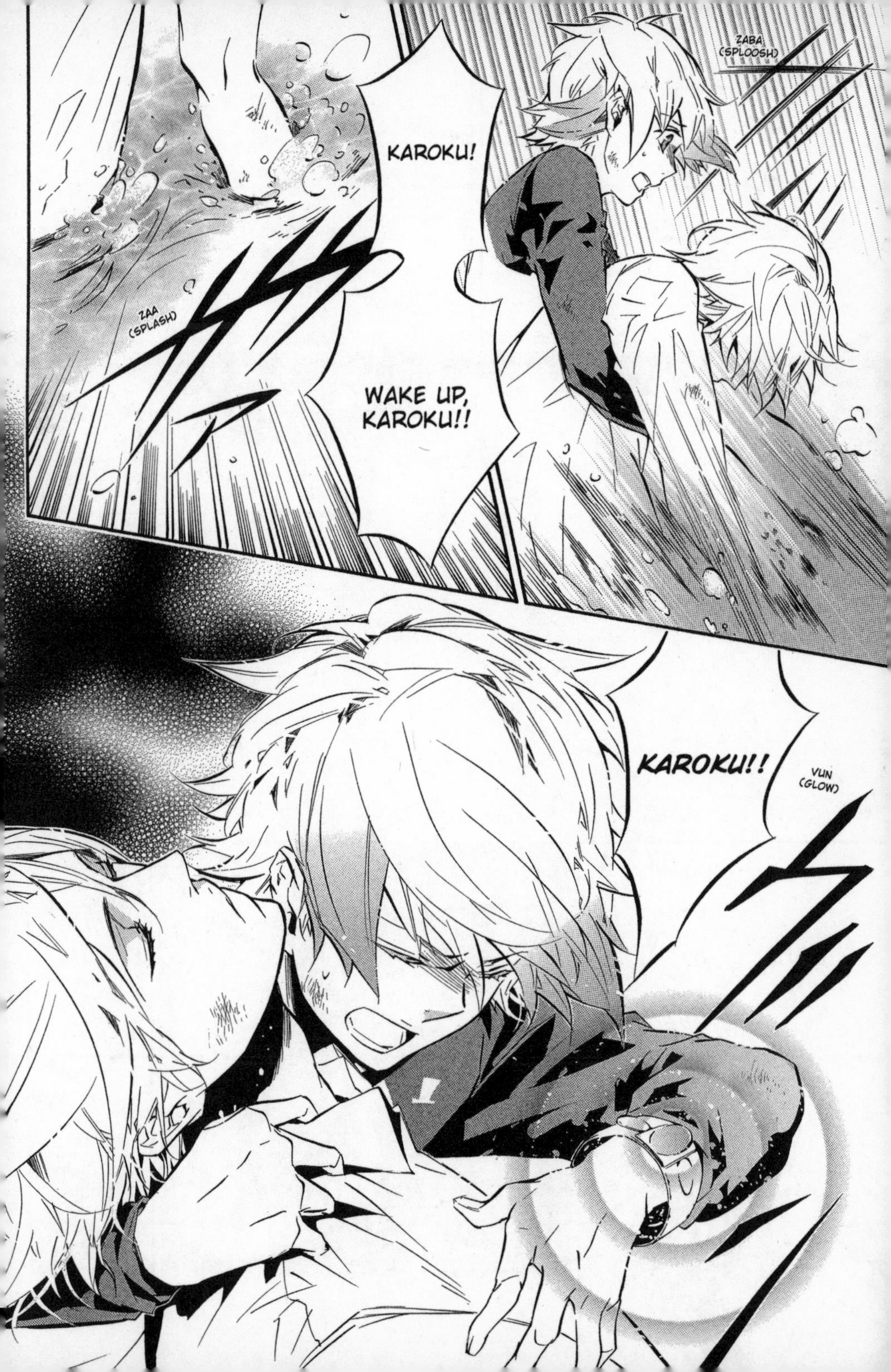
ZABA
(SPLOOSH)
KAROKU!
WAKE UP,
KAROKU!!
ZAA
(SPLASH)
KAROKU!!
VUN
(GLOW)

KARNEVAL

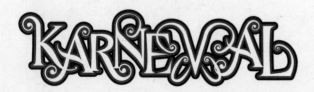

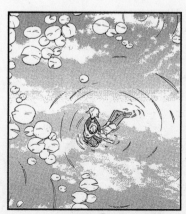

KARNEVAL

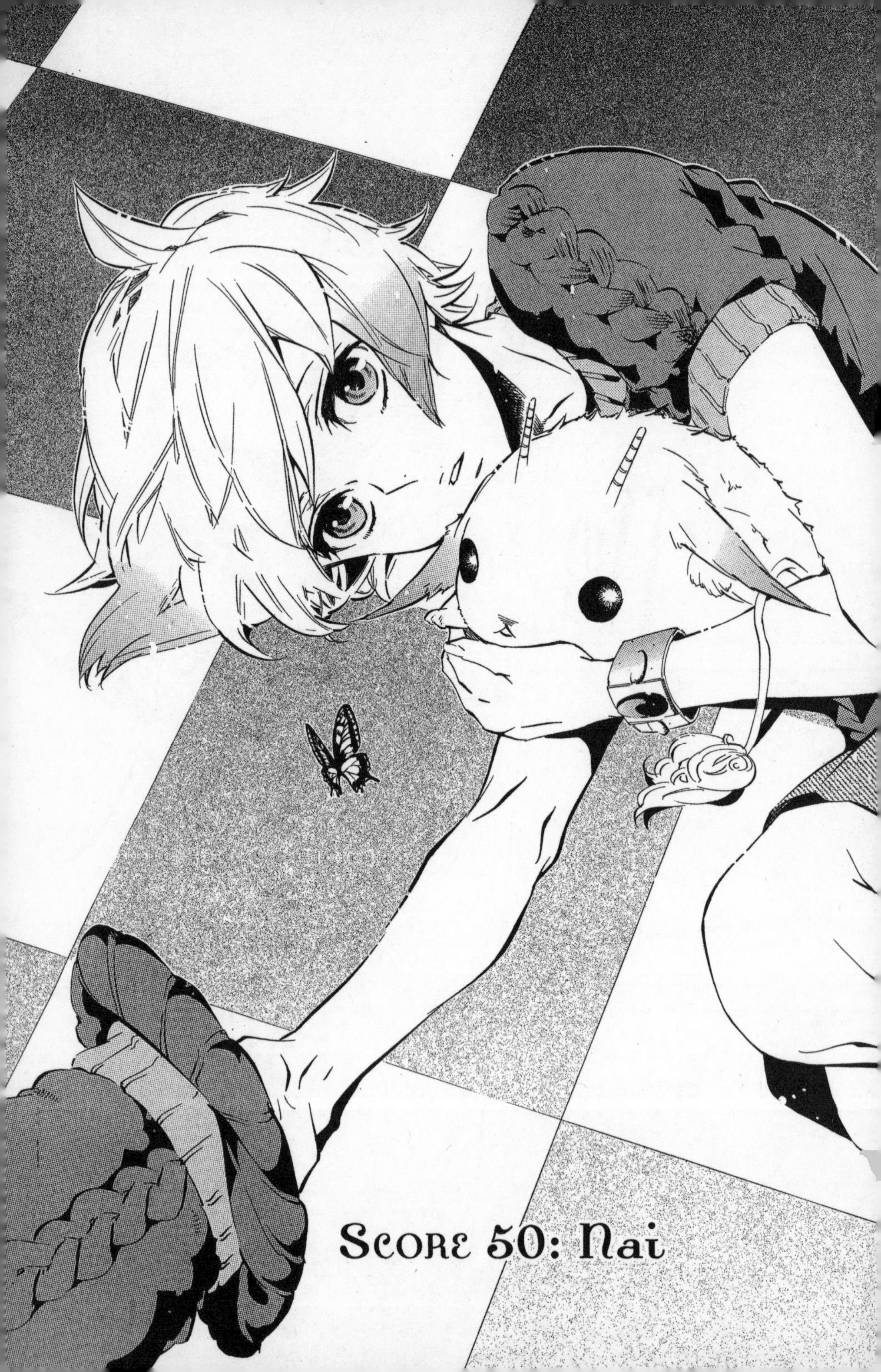
Score 50: Nai

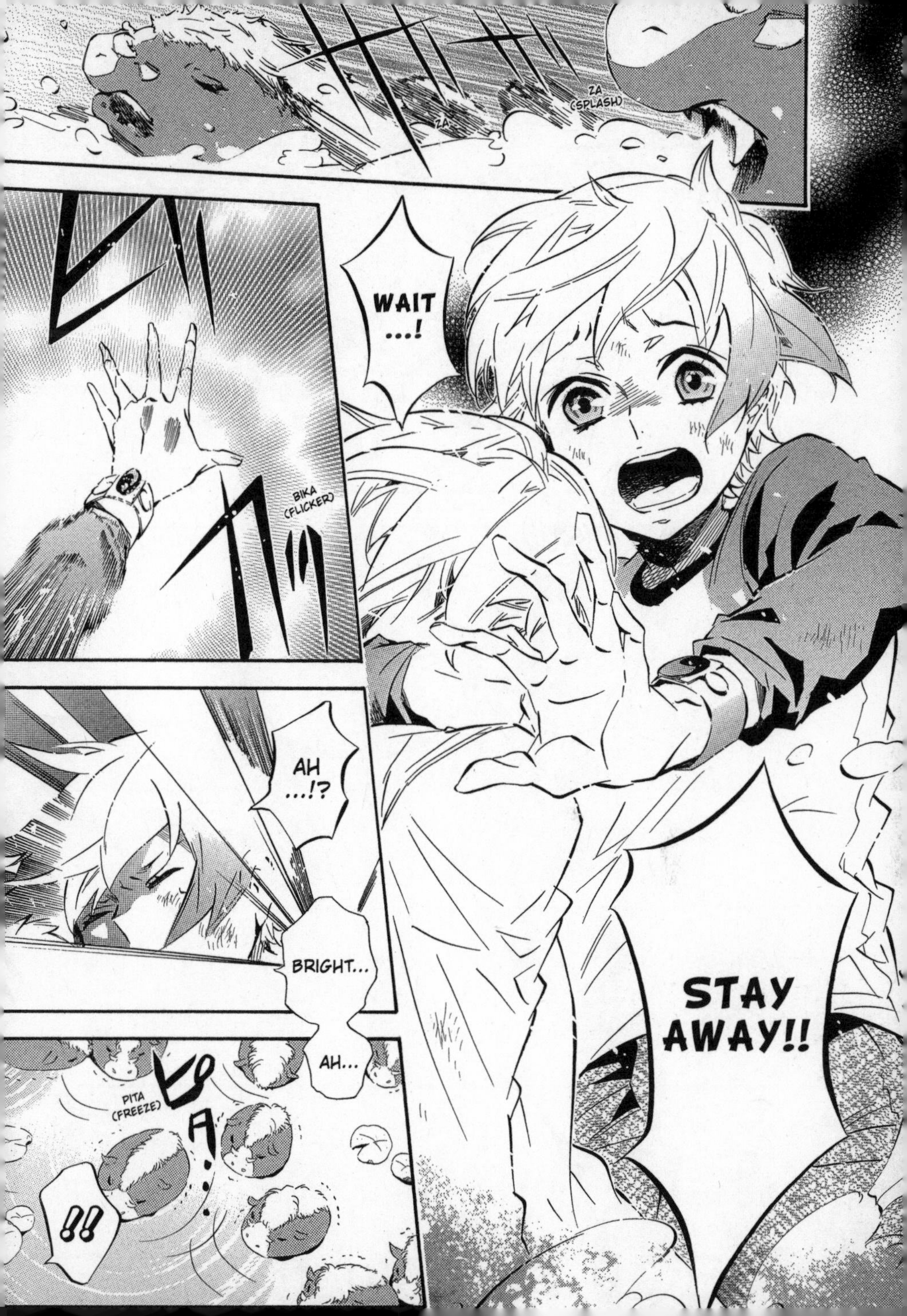
ZA
(SPLASH)
ZA
WAIT
...!
STAY
AWAY!!
BIKA
(FLICKER)
AH
...!?
BRIGHT...
AH...
PITA
(FREEZE)
!!

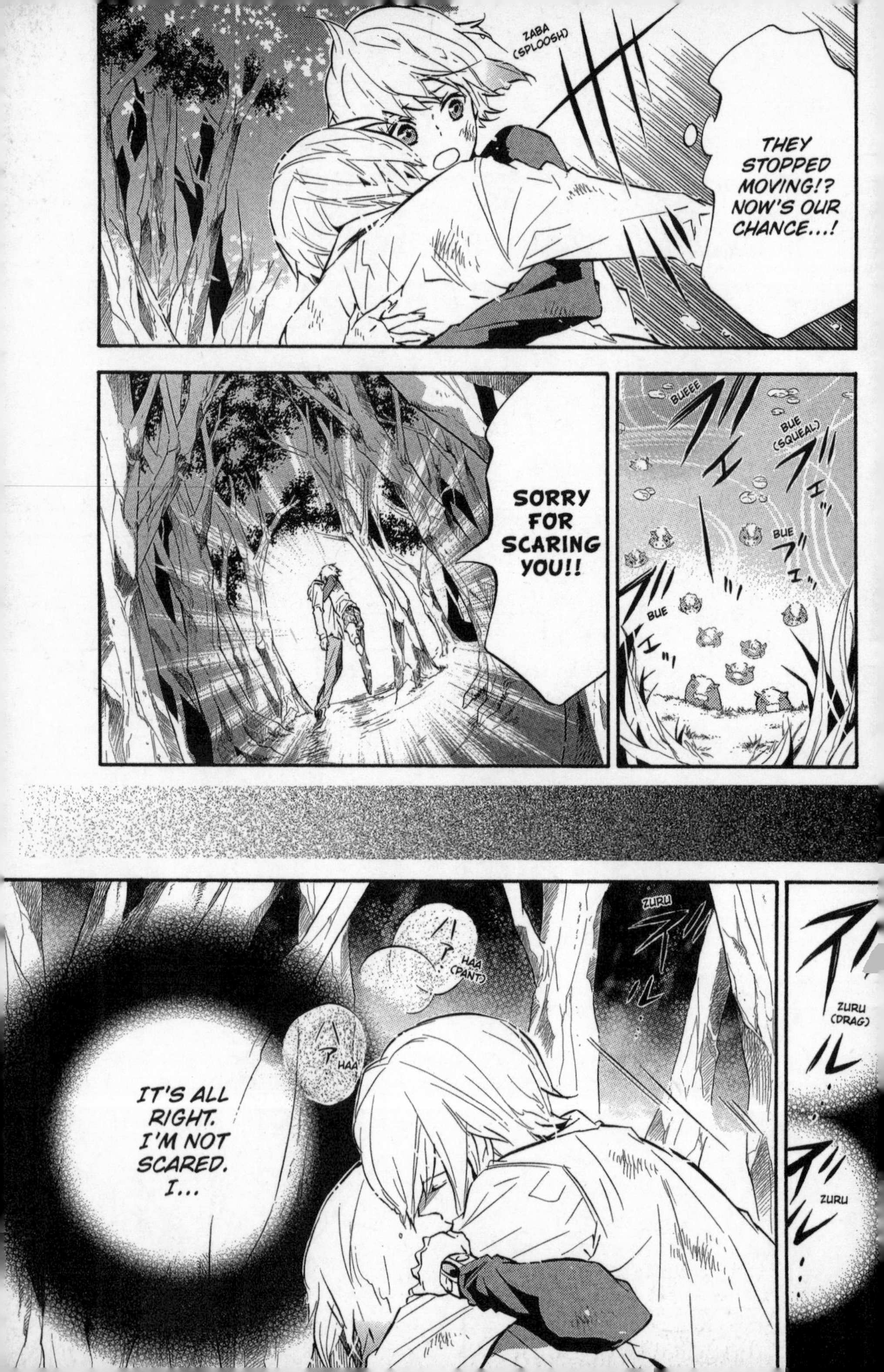
ZABA
(SPLOOSH)
THEY STOPPED MOVING!? NOW'S OUR CHANCE...!
BUEEE
BUE
(SQUEAL)
BUE
BUE
SORRY FOR SCARING YOU!!
ZURU
(DRAG)
ZURU
ZURU
HAA
(PANT)
HAA
IT'S ALL RIGHT. I'M NOT SCARED. I...

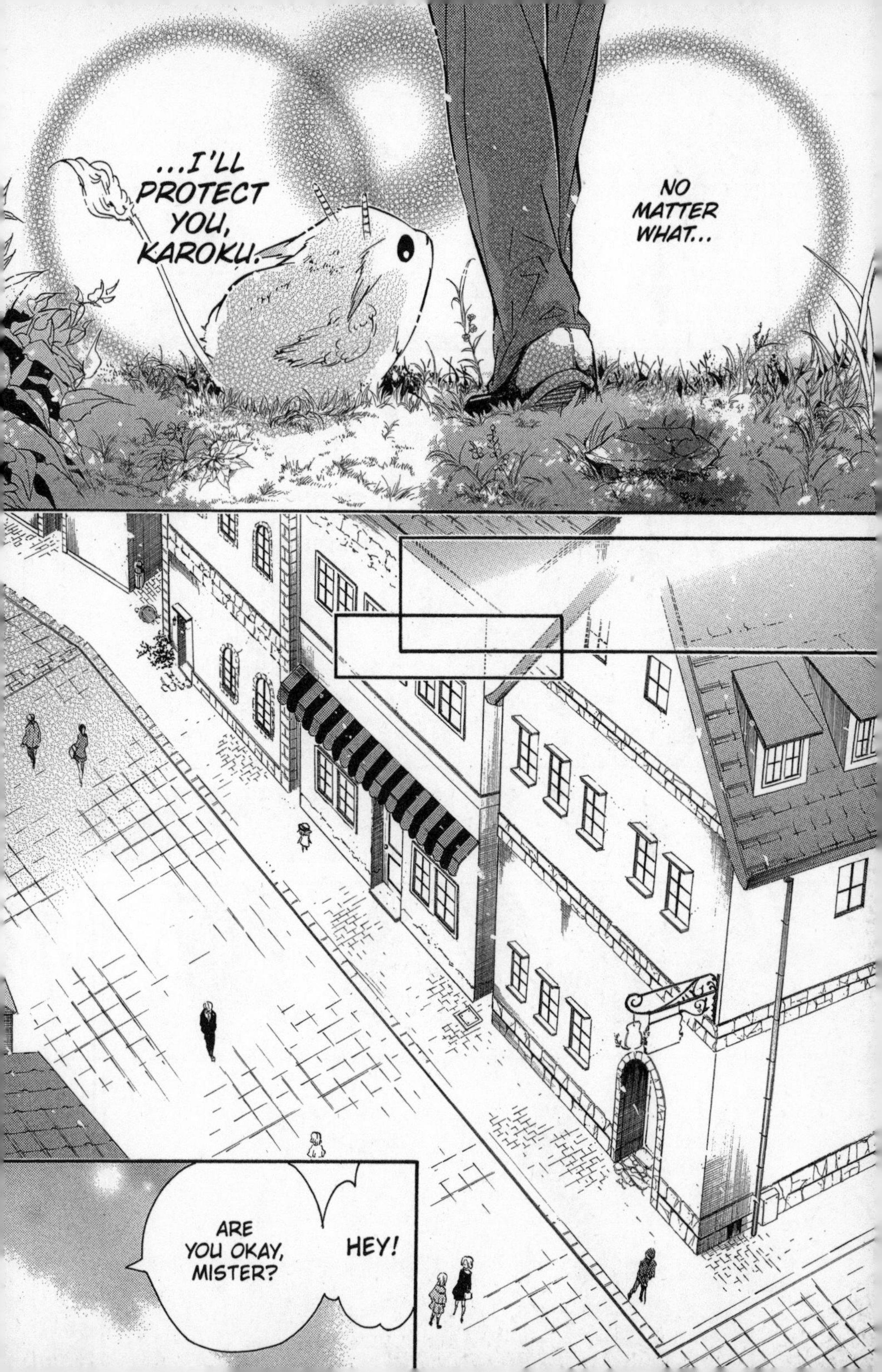
NO MATTER WHAT...
...I'LL PROTECT YOU, KAROKU.
HEY!
ARE YOU OKAY, MISTER?

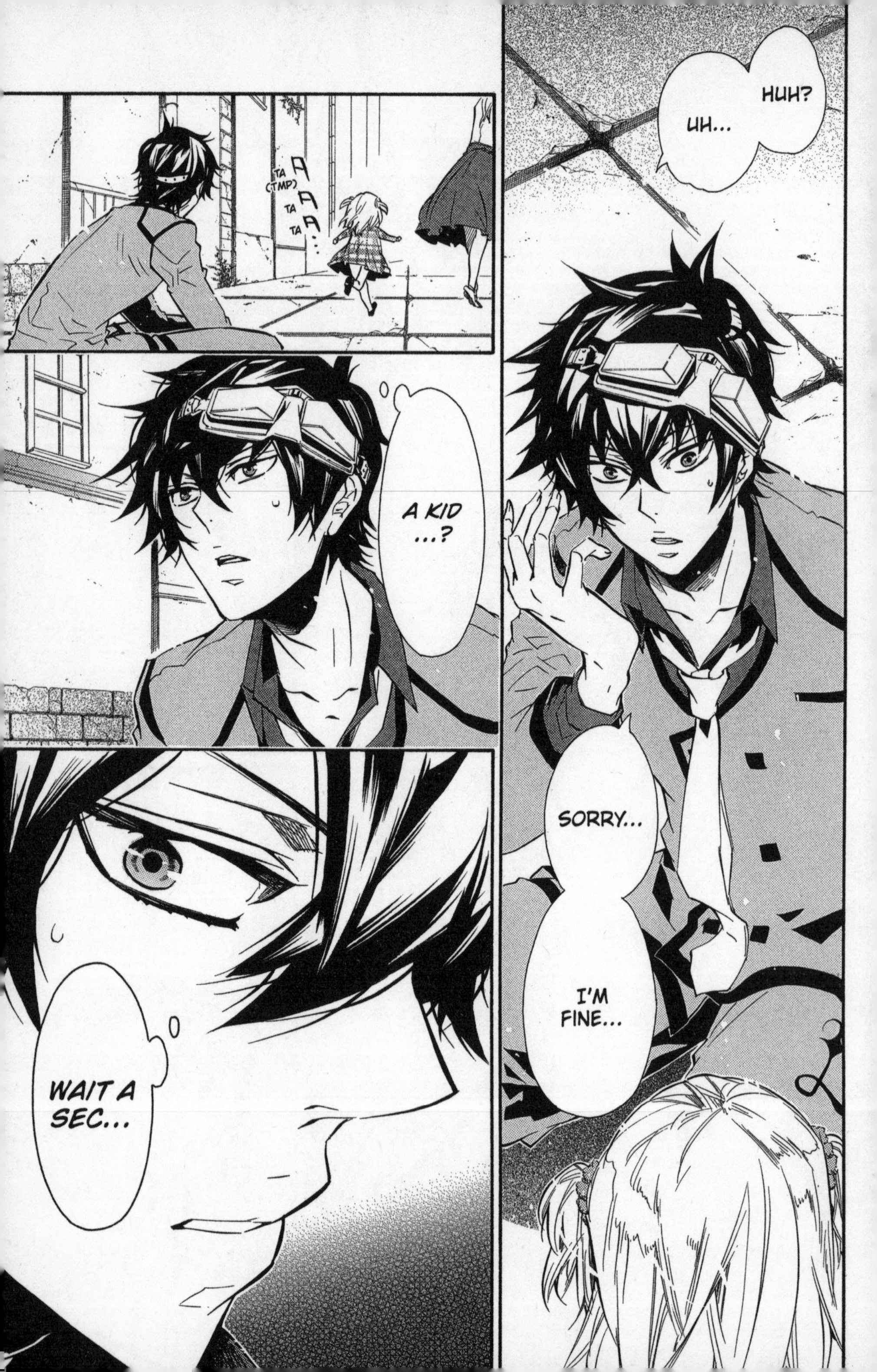
HUH?
UH...
SORRY...
I'M FINE...
TA (TMP) TA TA
A KID ...?
WAIT A SEC...

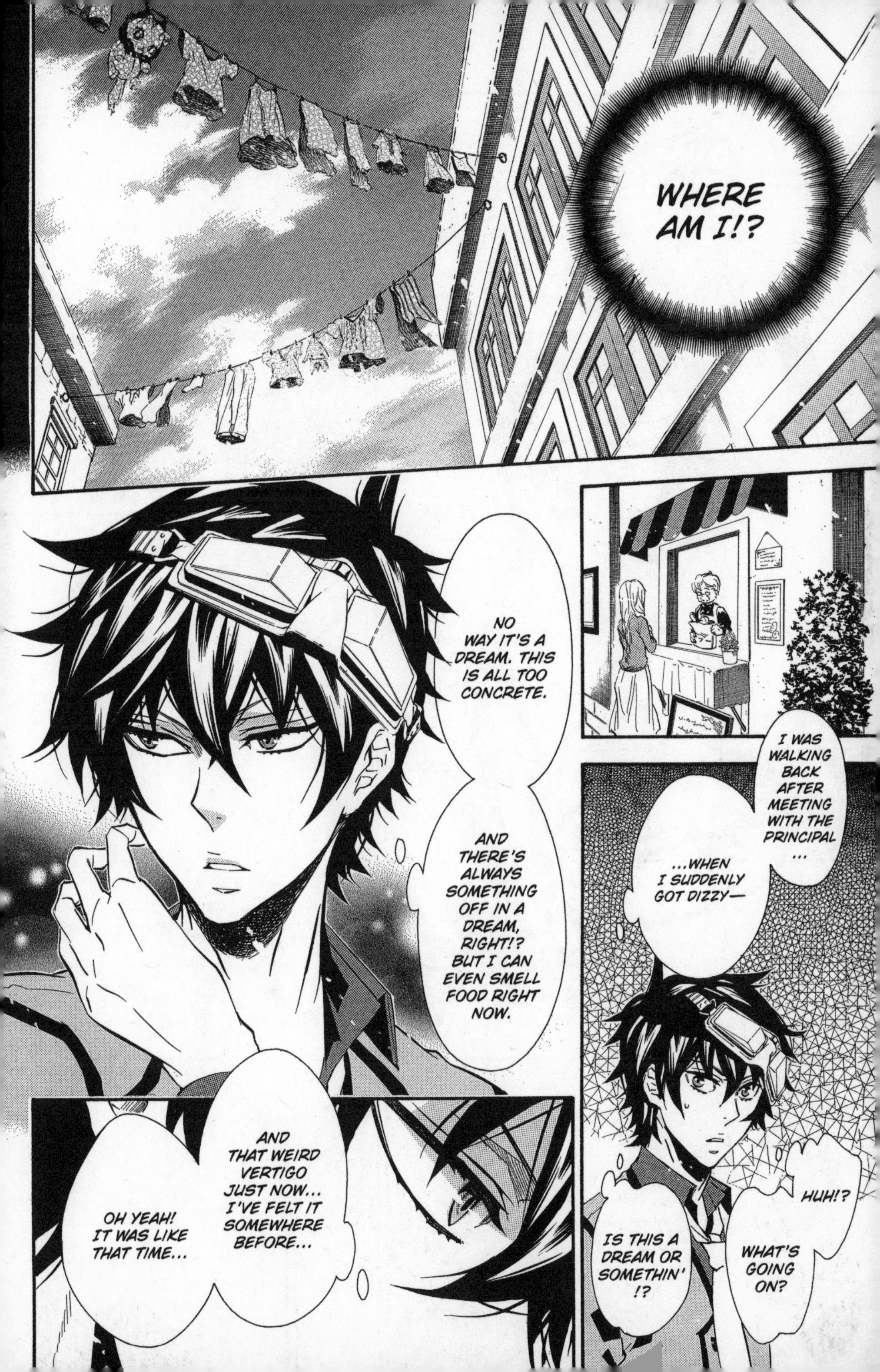
WHERE AM I!?
I WAS WALKING BACK AFTER MEETING WITH THE PRINCIPAL...
...WHEN I SUDDENLY GOT DIZZY—
HUH!?
WHAT'S GOING ON?
IS THIS A DREAM OR SOMETHIN'!?
NO WAY IT'S A DREAM. THIS IS ALL TOO CONCRETE.
AND THERE'S ALWAYS SOMETHING OFF IN A DREAM, RIGHT!? BUT I CAN EVEN SMELL FOOD RIGHT NOW.
AND THAT WEIRD VERTIGO JUST NOW... I'VE FELT IT SOMEWHERE BEFORE...
OH YEAH! IT WAS LIKE THAT TIME...

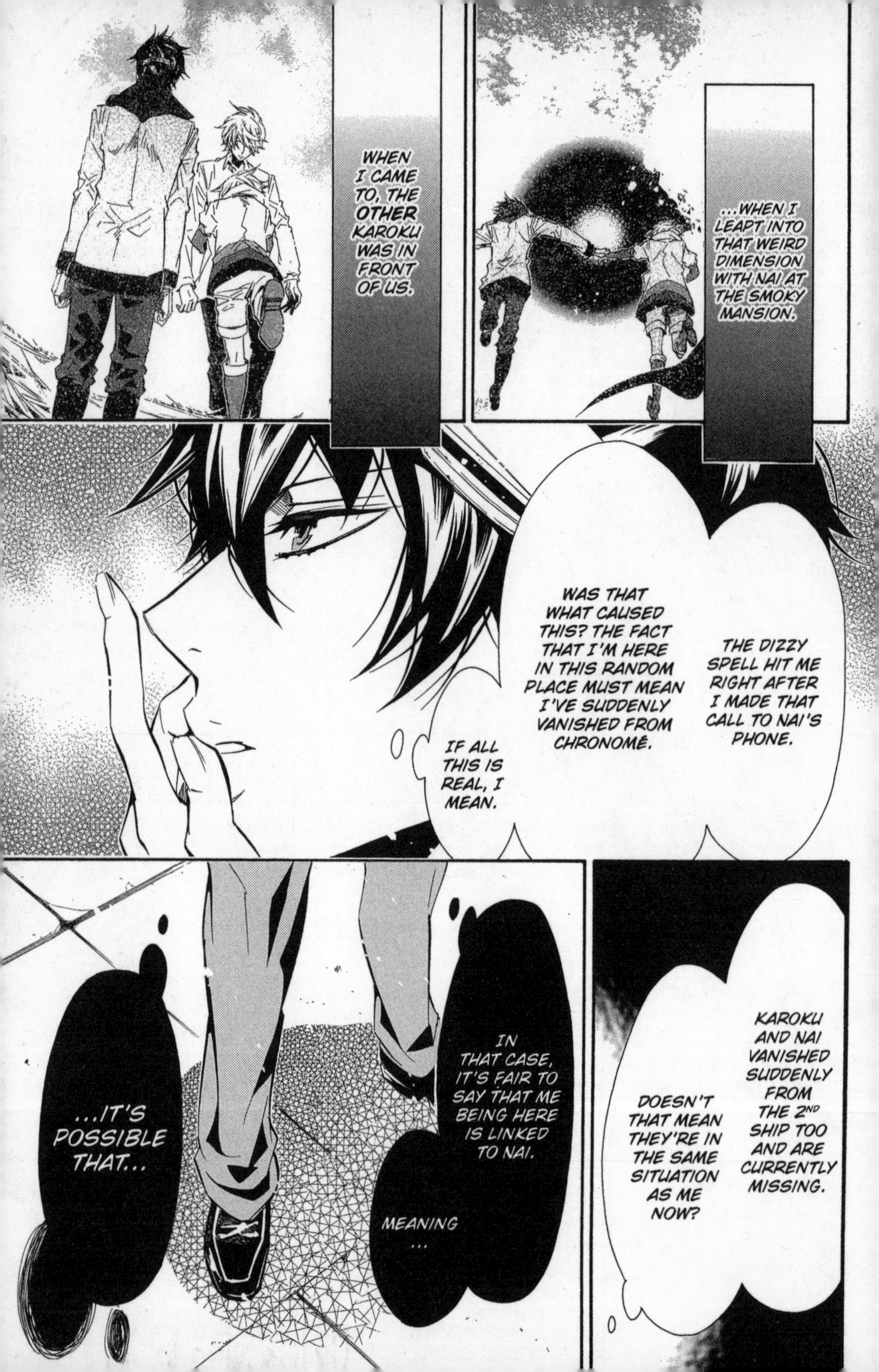
...WHEN I LEAPT INTO THAT WEIRD DIMENSION WITH NAI AT THE SMOKY MANSION.
WHEN I CAME TO, THE **OTHER** KAROKU WAS IN FRONT OF US.
THE DIZZY SPELL HIT ME RIGHT AFTER I MADE THAT CALL TO NAI'S PHONE.
WAS THAT WHAT CAUSED THIS? THE FACT THAT I'M HERE IN THIS RANDOM PLACE MUST MEAN I'VE SUDDENLY VANISHED FROM CHRONOMÉ.
IF ALL THIS IS REAL, I MEAN.
KAROKU AND NAI VANISHED SUDDENLY FROM THE 2ND SHIP TOO AND ARE CURRENTLY MISSING.
DOESN'T THAT MEAN THEY'RE IN THE SAME SITUATION AS ME NOW?
IN THAT CASE, IT'S FAIR TO SAY THAT ME BEING HERE IS LINKED TO NAI.
MEANING...
...IT'S POSSIBLE THAT...

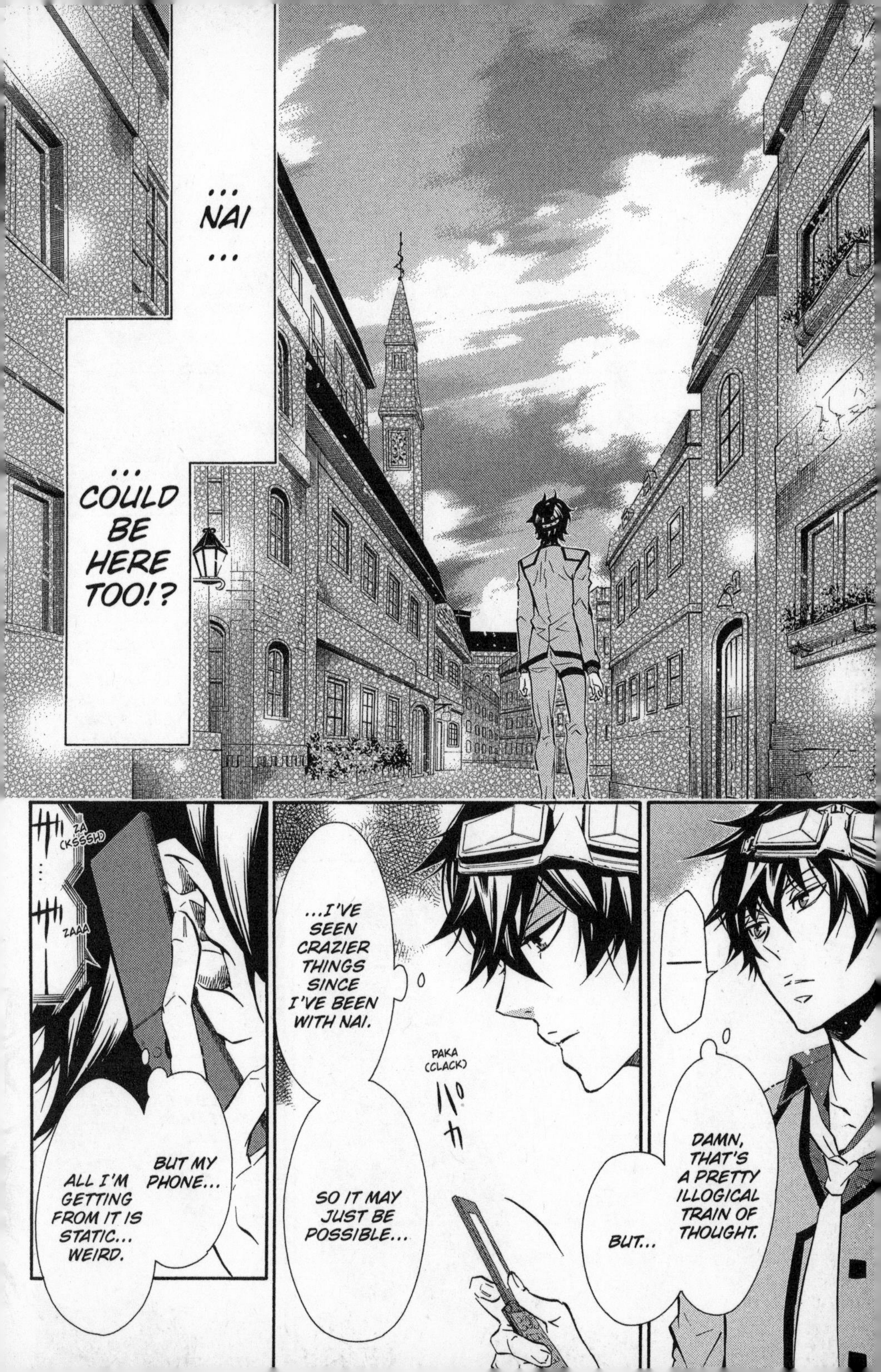
...NAI...
...COULD BE HERE TOO!?
—
DAMN, THAT'S A PRETTY ILLOGICAL TRAIN OF THOUGHT.
BUT...
...I'VE SEEN CRAZIER THINGS SINCE I'VE BEEN WITH NAI.
PAKA (CLACK)
SO IT MAY JUST BE POSSIBLE...
ZA (KSSSH)
ZAAA
BUT MY PHONE...
ALL I'M GETTING FROM IT IS STATIC... WEIRD.

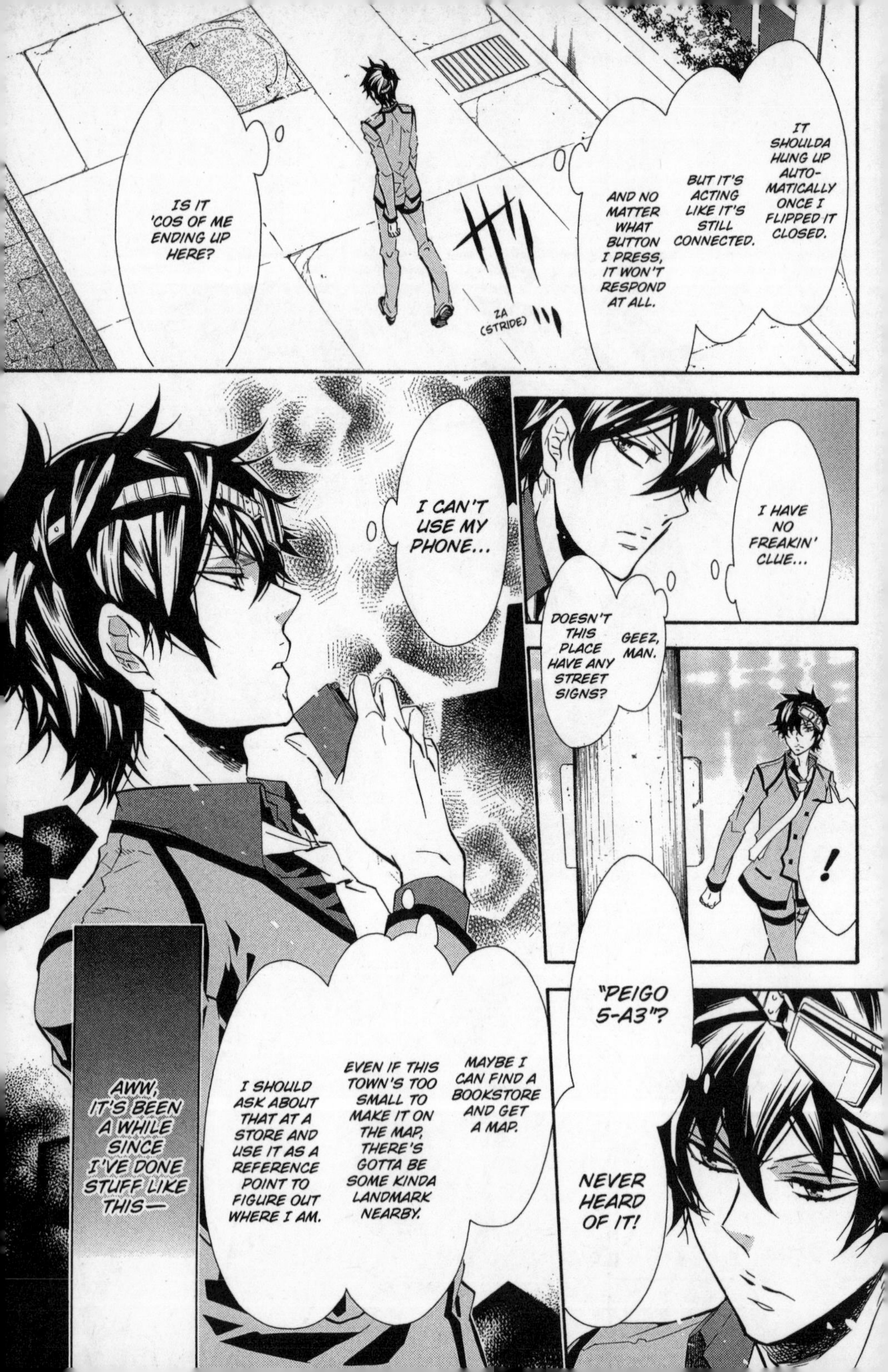

IT SHOULDA HUNG UP AUTO-MATICALLY ONCE I FLIPPED IT CLOSED.
BUT IT'S ACTING LIKE IT'S STILL CONNECTED.
AND NO MATTER WHAT BUTTON I PRESS, IT WON'T RESPOND AT ALL.
ZA (STRIDE)
IS IT 'COS OF ME ENDING UP HERE?
I HAVE NO FREAKIN' CLUE...
GEEZ, MAN.
DOESN'T THIS PLACE HAVE ANY STREET SIGNS?
!
"PEIGO 5-A3"?
NEVER HEARD OF IT!
I CAN'T USE MY PHONE...
MAYBE I CAN FIND A BOOKSTORE AND GET A MAP.
EVEN IF THIS TOWN'S TOO SMALL TO MAKE IT ON THE MAP, THERE'S GOTTA BE SOME KINDA LANDMARK NEARBY.
I SHOULD ASK ABOUT THAT AT A STORE AND USE IT AS A REFERENCE POINT TO FIGURE OUT WHERE I AM.
AWW, IT'S BEEN A WHILE SINCE I'VE DONE STUFF LIKE THIS—

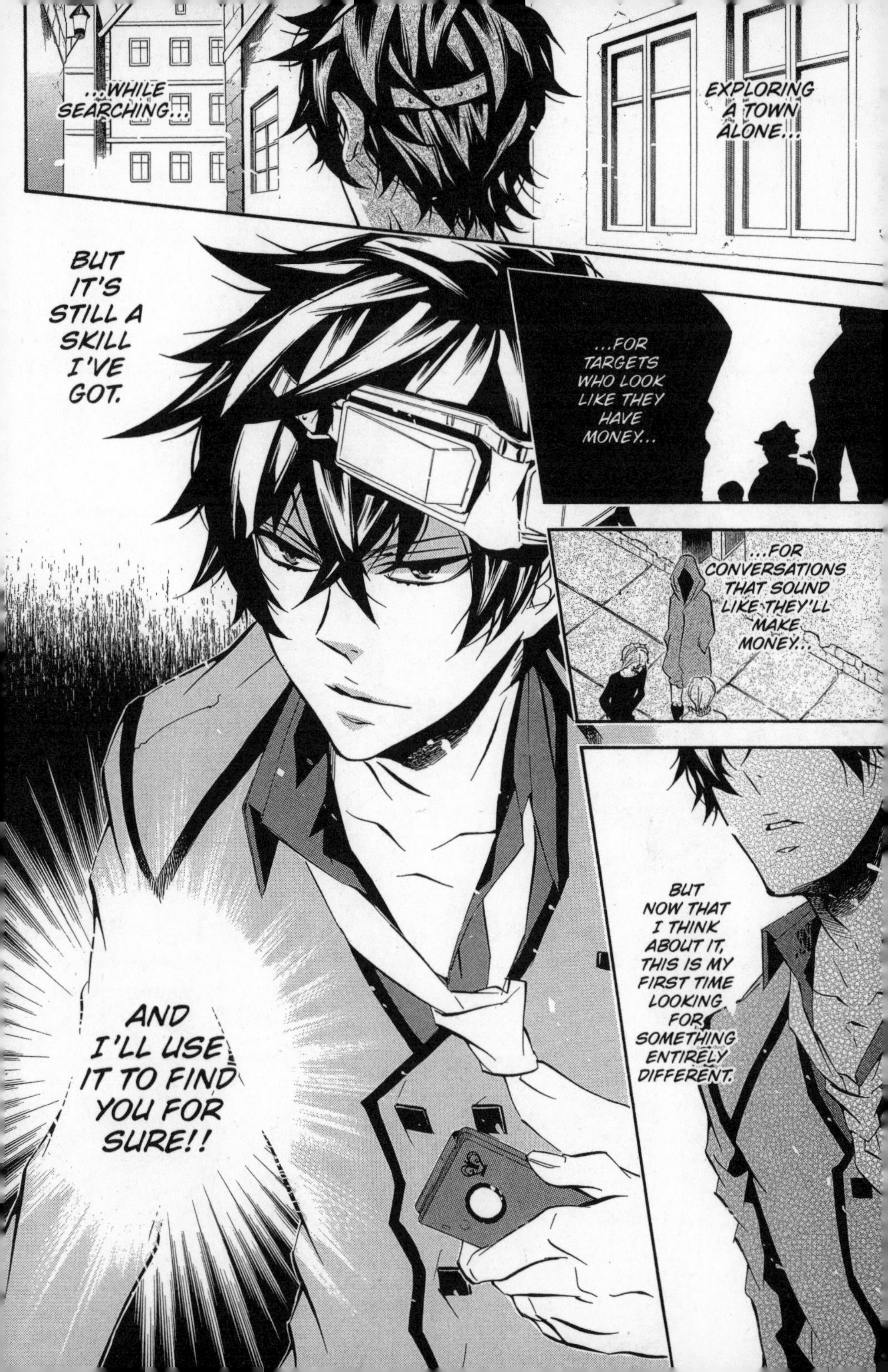
EXPLORING A TOWN ALONE...
...WHILE SEARCHING...
...FOR TARGETS WHO LOOK LIKE THEY HAVE MONEY...
...FOR CONVERSATIONS THAT SOUND LIKE THEY'LL MAKE MONEY...
BUT NOW THAT I THINK ABOUT IT, THIS IS MY FIRST TIME LOOKING FOR SOMETHING ENTIRELY DIFFERENT.
BUT IT'S STILL A SKILL I'VE GOT.
AND I'LL USE IT TO FIND YOU FOR SURE!!

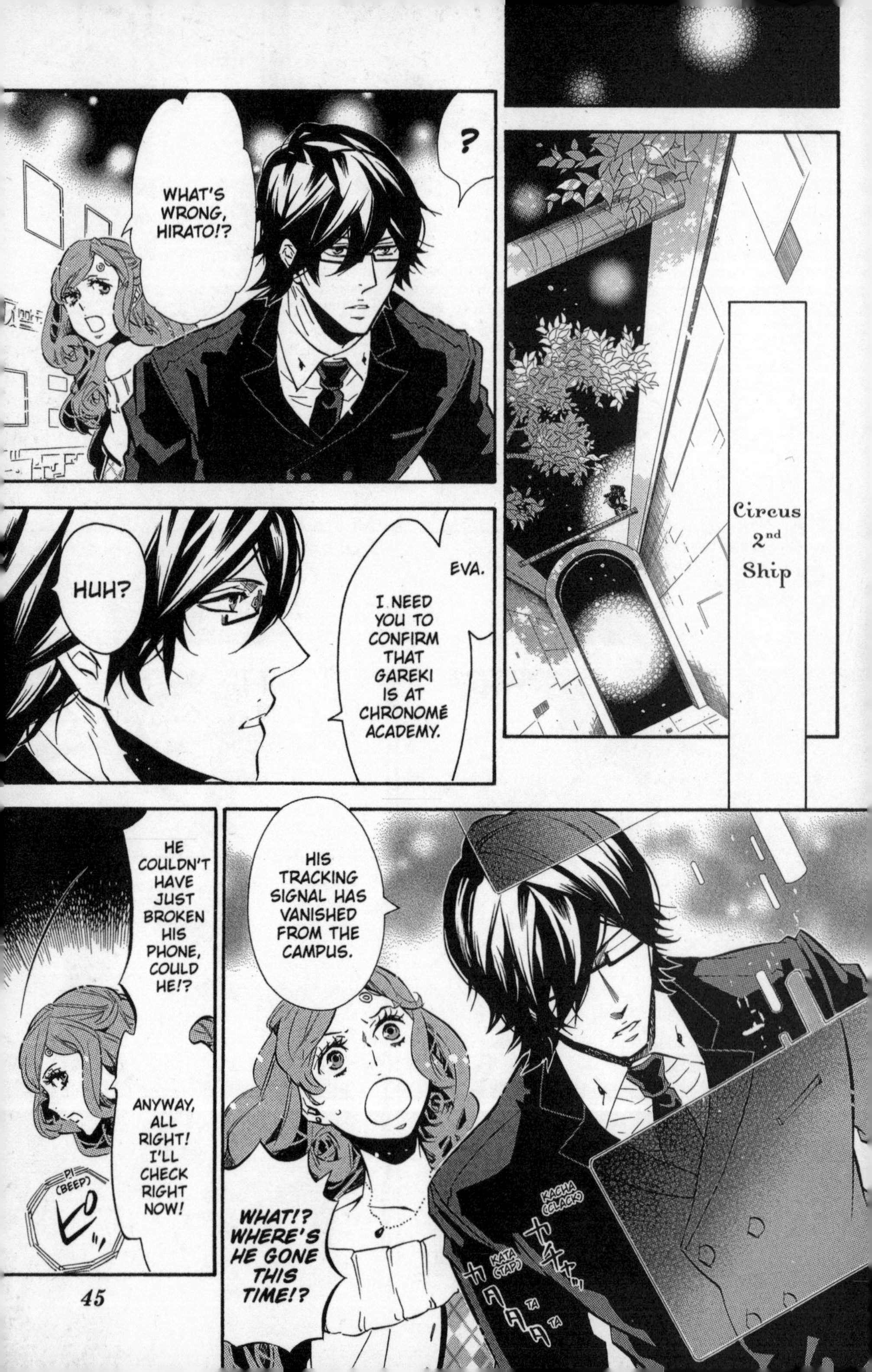
Circus 2nd Ship
?
WHAT'S WRONG, HIRATO!?
EVA.
I NEED YOU TO CONFIRM THAT GAREKI IS AT CHRONOMÉ ACADEMY.
HUH?
HIS TRACKING SIGNAL HAS VANISHED FROM THE CAMPUS.
KACHA (CLACK)
KATA (TAP)
TA TA
WHAT!? WHERE'S HE GONE THIS TIME!?
HE COULDN'T HAVE JUST BROKEN HIS PHONE, COULD HE!?
ANYWAY, ALL RIGHT! I'LL CHECK RIGHT NOW!
PI (BEEP)

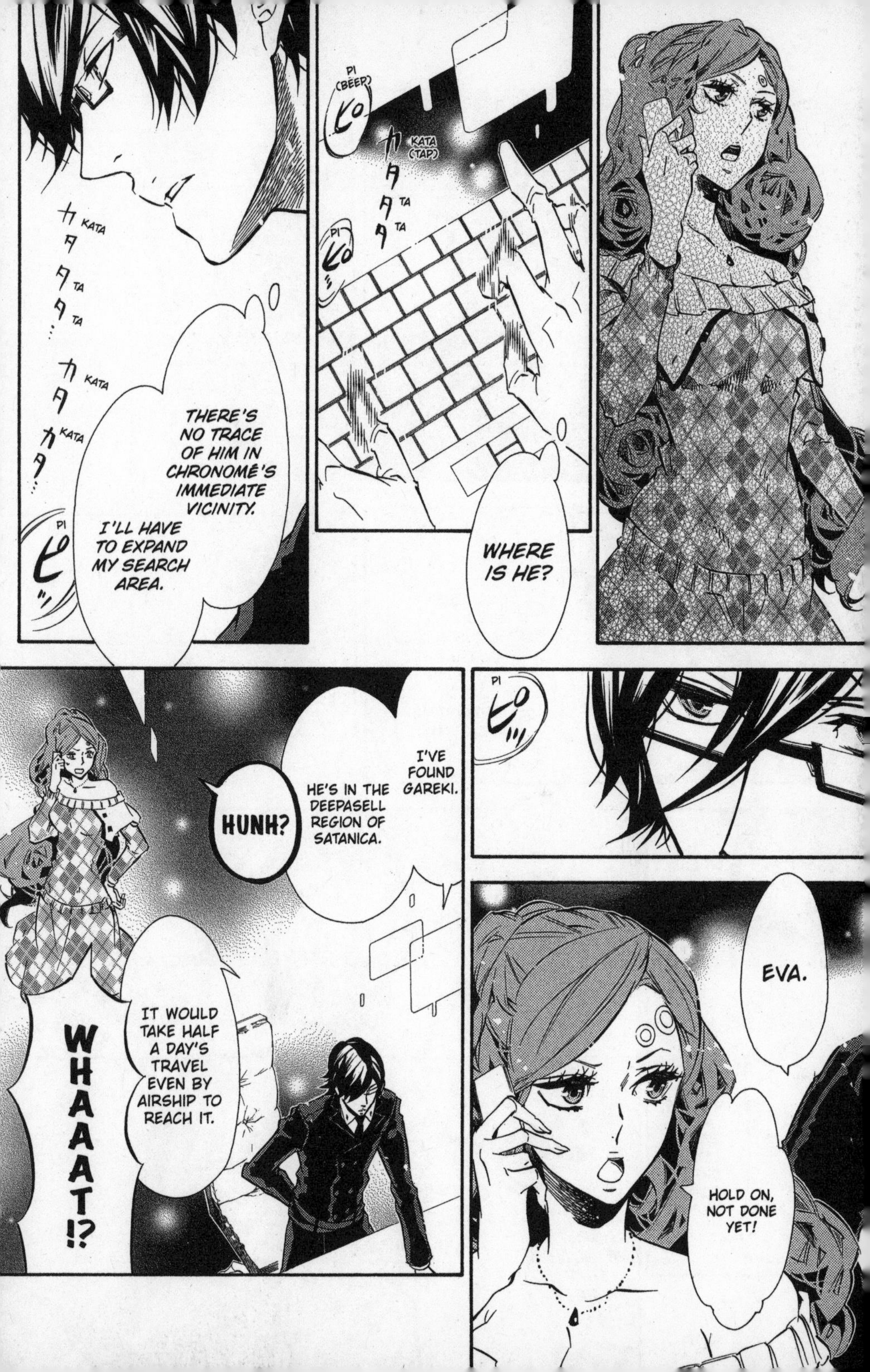
WHERE IS HE?
PI (BEEP)
KATA (TAP)
TA
TA
PI
KATA
TA
TA
KATA
KATA
PI
THERE'S NO TRACE OF HIM IN CHRONOMÉ'S IMMEDIATE VICINITY.
I'LL HAVE TO EXPAND MY SEARCH AREA.
PI
I'VE FOUND GAREKI.
HE'S IN THE DEEPASELL REGION OF SATANICA.
HUNH?
IT WOULD TAKE HALF A DAY'S TRAVEL EVEN BY AIRSHIP TO REACH IT.
WHAAAAT!?
EVA.
HOLD ON, NOT DONE YET!

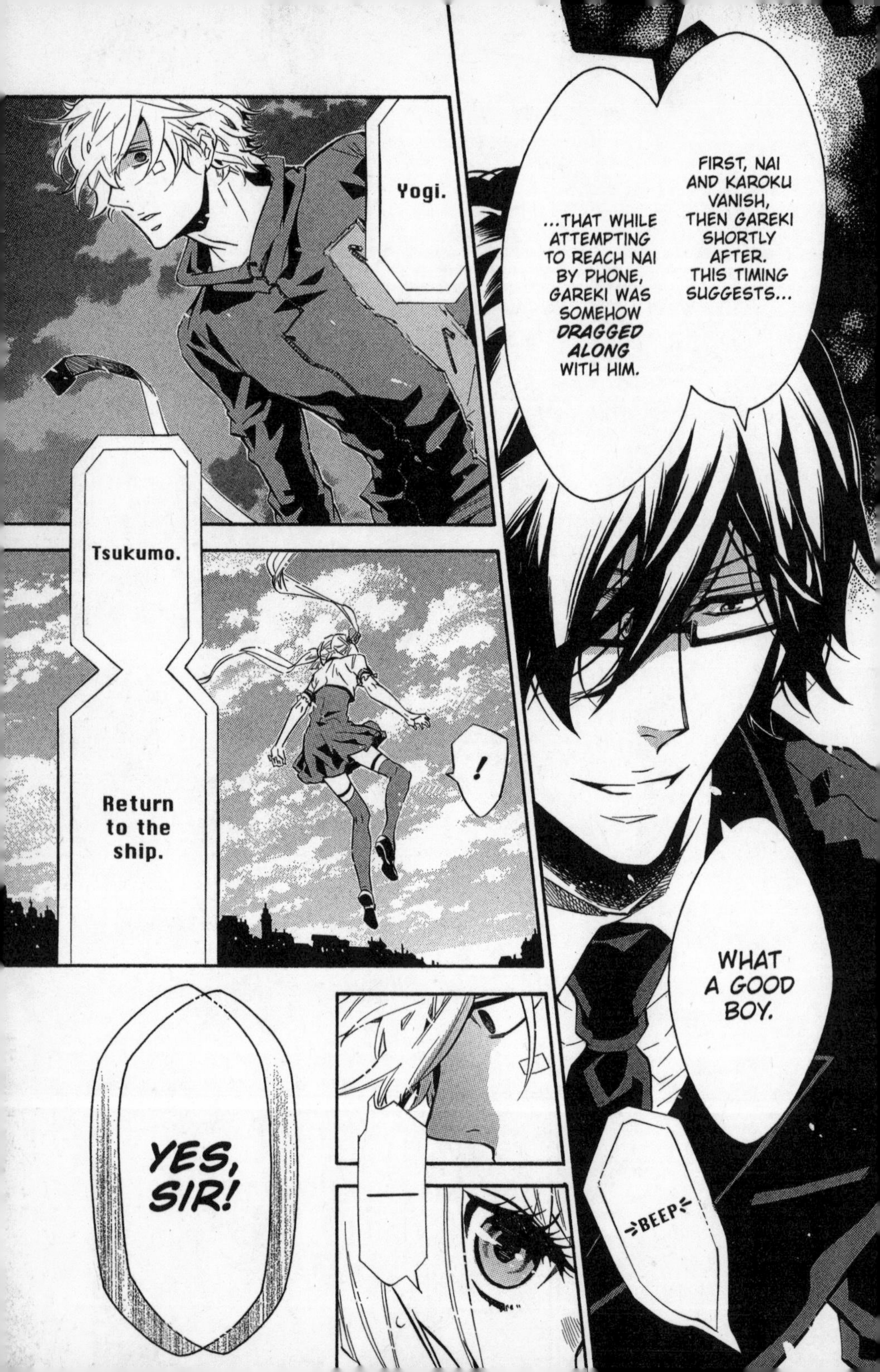
FIRST, NAI AND KAROKU VANISH, THEN GAREKI SHORTLY AFTER. THIS TIMING SUGGESTS...
...THAT WHILE ATTEMPTING TO REACH NAI BY PHONE, GAREKI WAS SOMEHOW *DRAGGED ALONG* WITH HIM.
WHAT A GOOD BOY.
BEEP
Yogi.
Tsukumo.
!
Return to the ship.
—
YES, SIR!

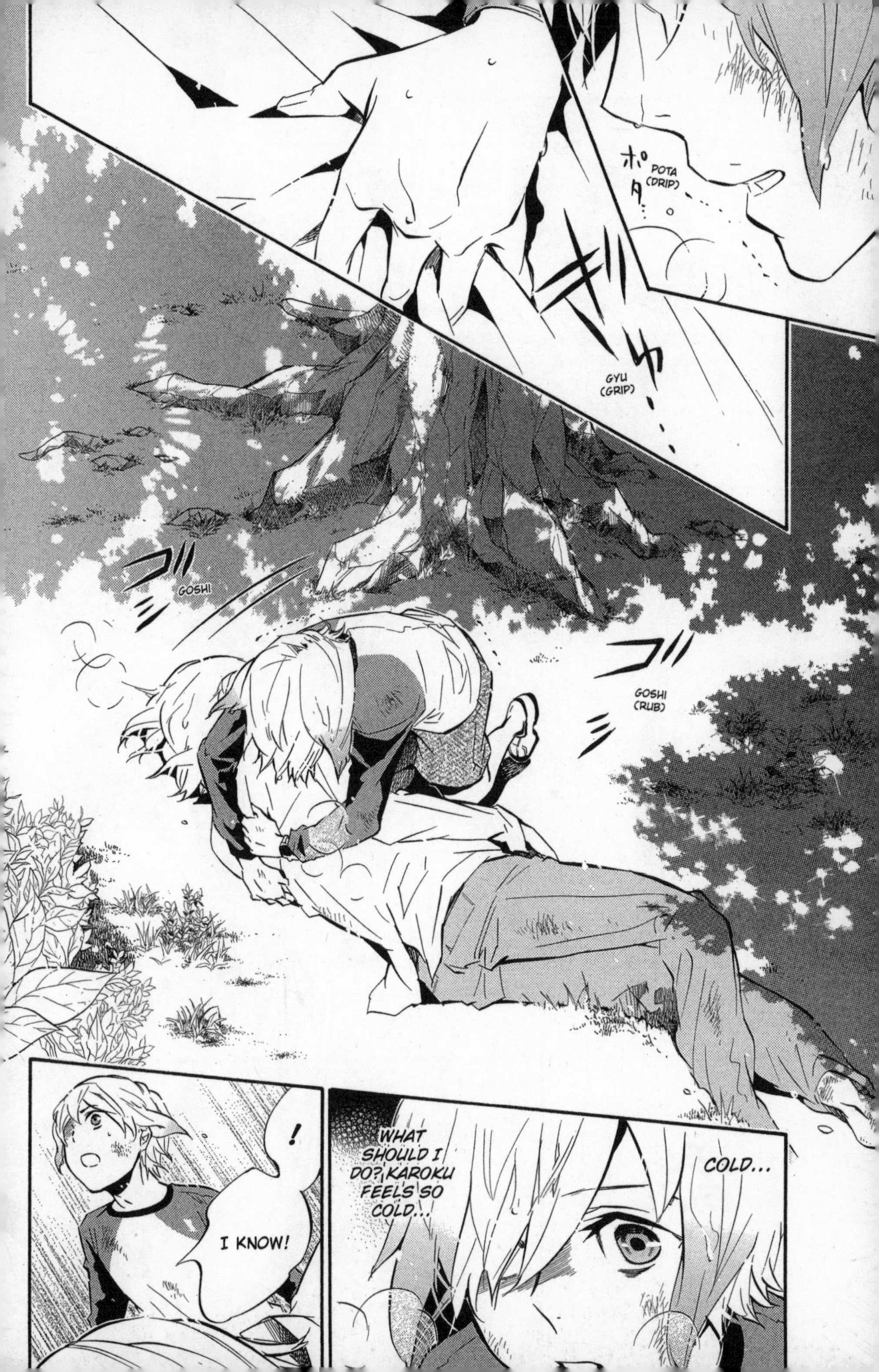
ポタ
POTA (DRIP)
GYU (GRIP)
GOSHI (RUB)
GOSHI
COLD...
WHAT SHOULD I DO? KAROKU FEELS SO COLD...
!
I KNOW!

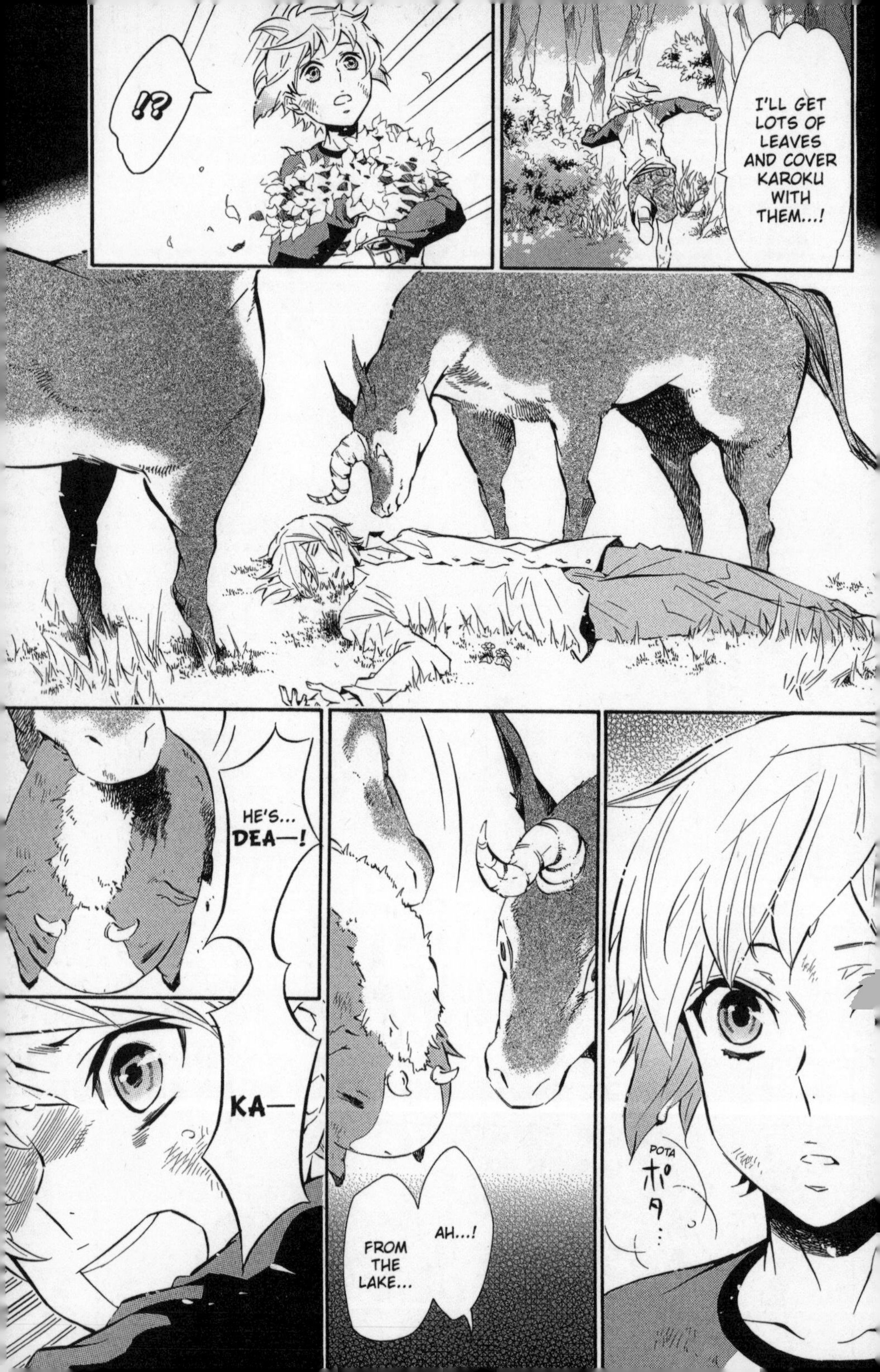

I'LL GET LOTS OF LEAVES AND COVER KAROKU WITH THEM...!
!?
POTA
ポタ...
AH...!
FROM THE LAKE...
HE'S... DEA—!
KA—

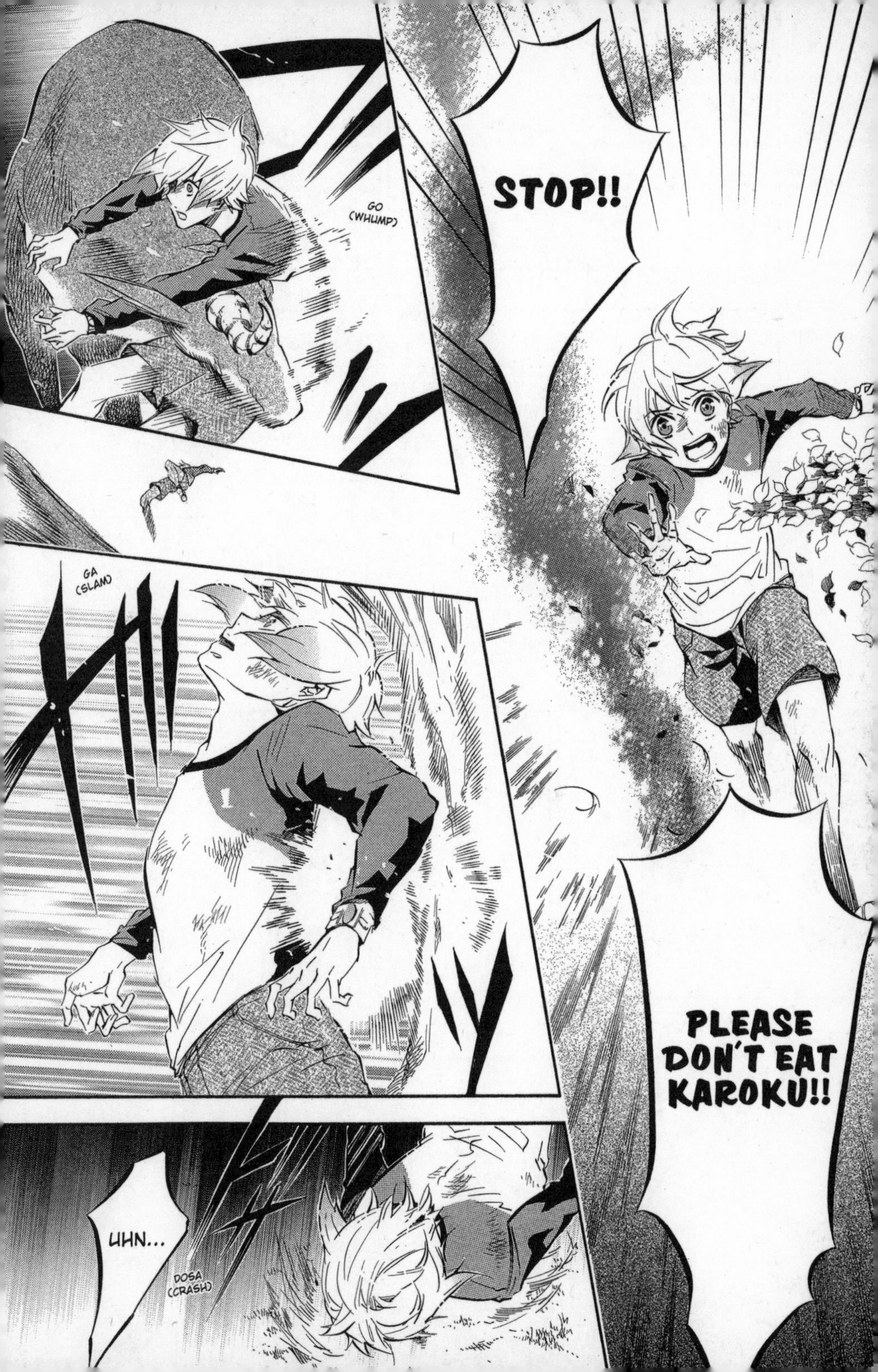
STOP!!
PLEASE DON'T EAT KAROKU!!
GO (WHUMP)
GA (SLAM)
UHN...
DOSA (CRASH)

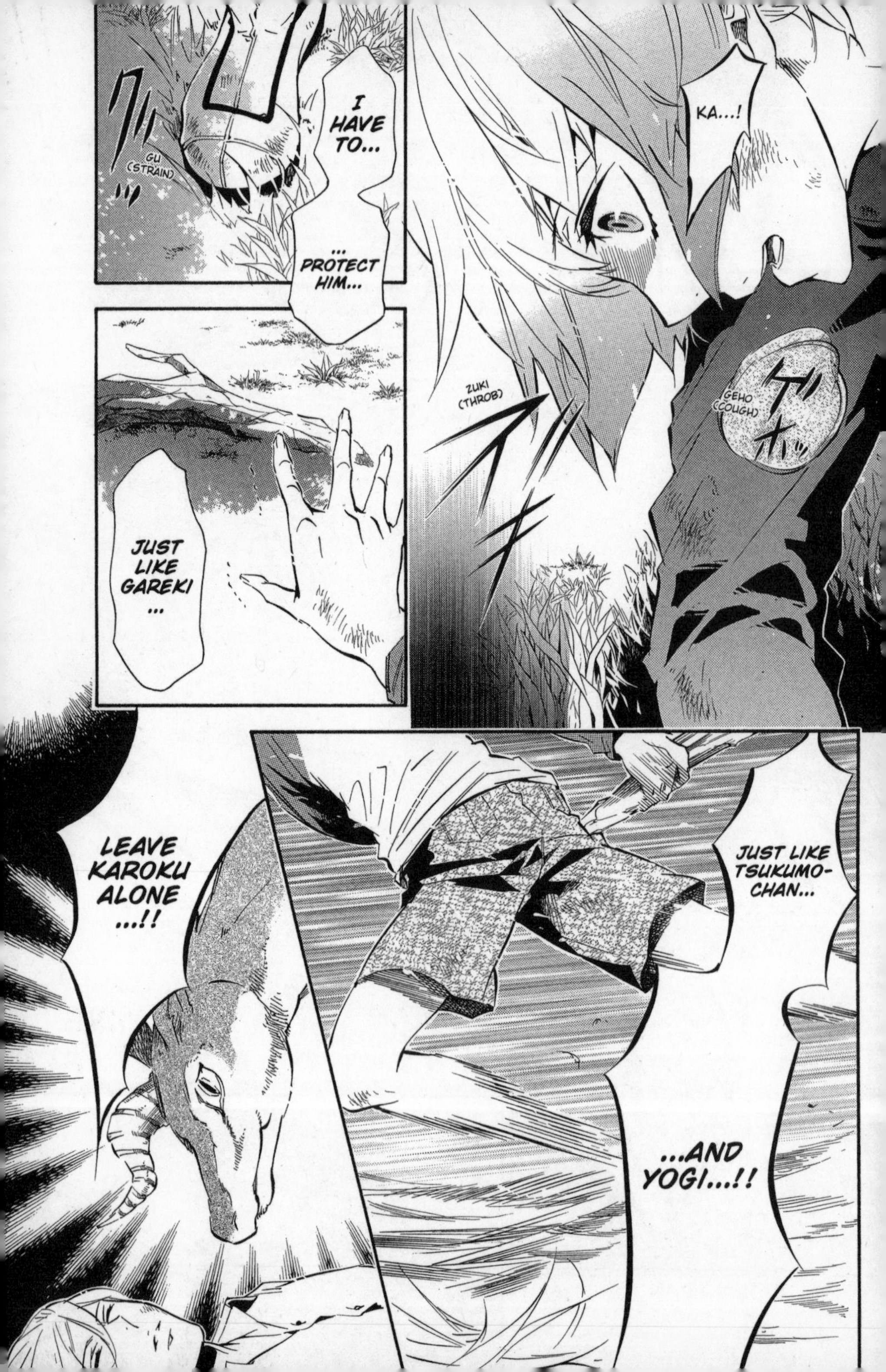
KA...!
GEHO (COUGH)
ZUKI (THROB)
I HAVE TO...
GU (STRAIN)
... PROTECT HIM...
JUST LIKE GAREKI ...
JUST LIKE TSUKUMO-CHAN...
...AND YOGI...!!
LEAVE KAROKU ALONE ...!!

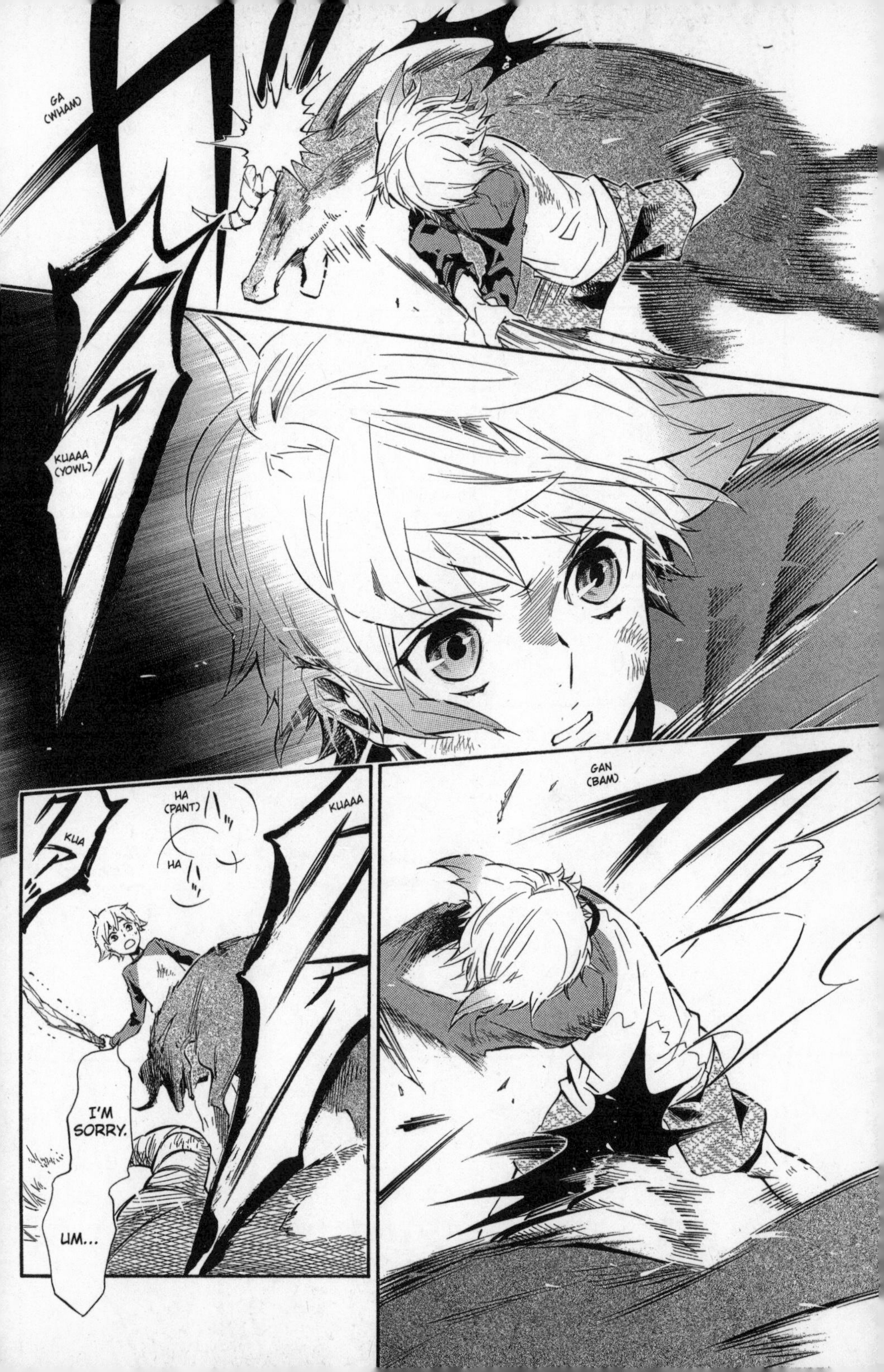
GA (WHAM)
KUAAA (YOWL)
GAN (BAM)
KUAAA
HA (PANT)
HA
KUA
I'M SORRY.
UM...

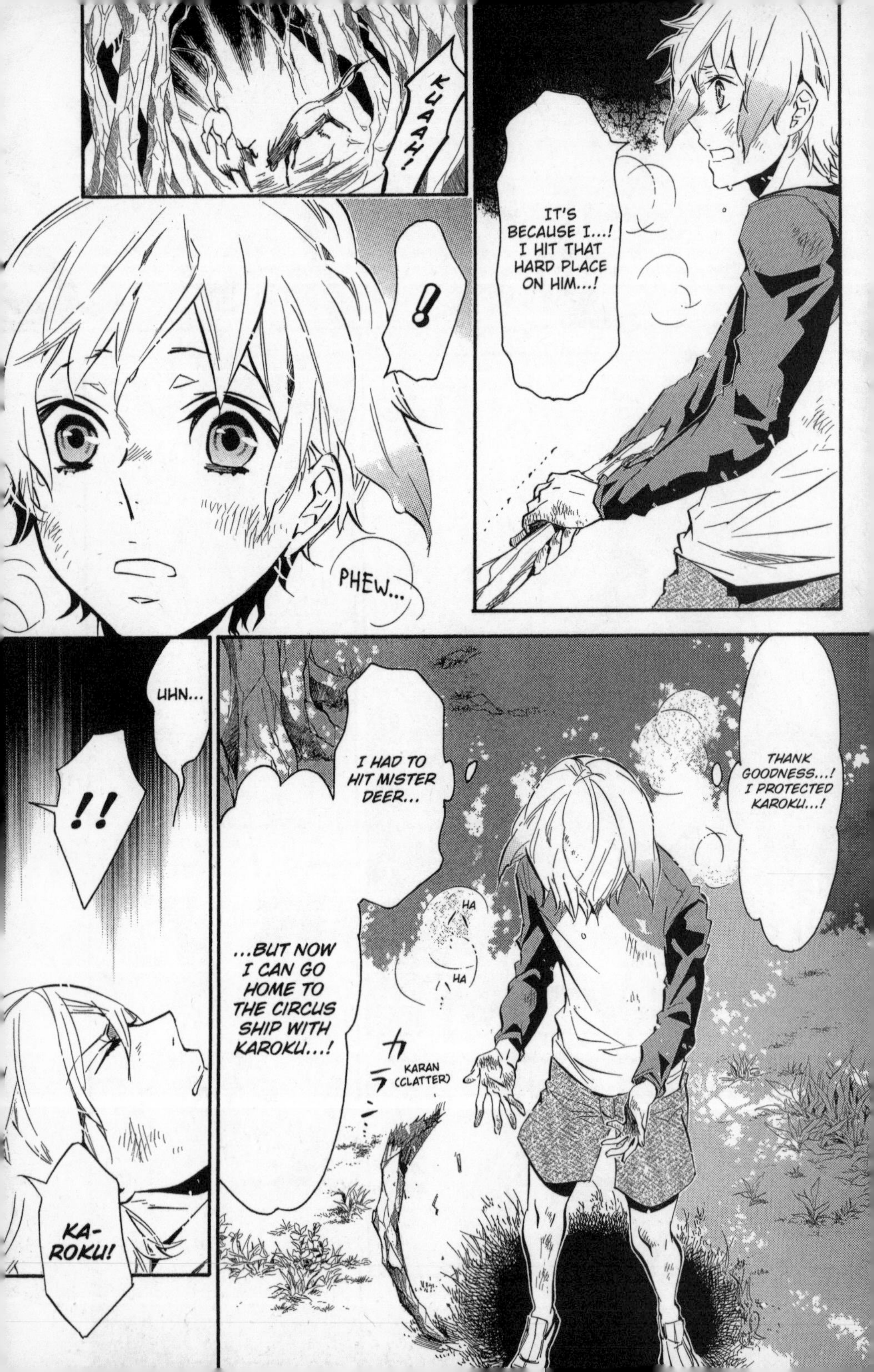
IT'S BECAUSE I...! I HIT THAT HARD PLACE ON HIM...!
KUAAAH!
!
PHEW...
THANK GOODNESS...! I PROTECTED KAROKU...!
I HAD TO HIT MISTER DEER...
HA
HA
...BUT NOW I CAN GO HOME TO THE CIRCUS SHIP WITH KAROKU...!
KARAN (CLATTER)
UHN...
!!
KA-ROKU!

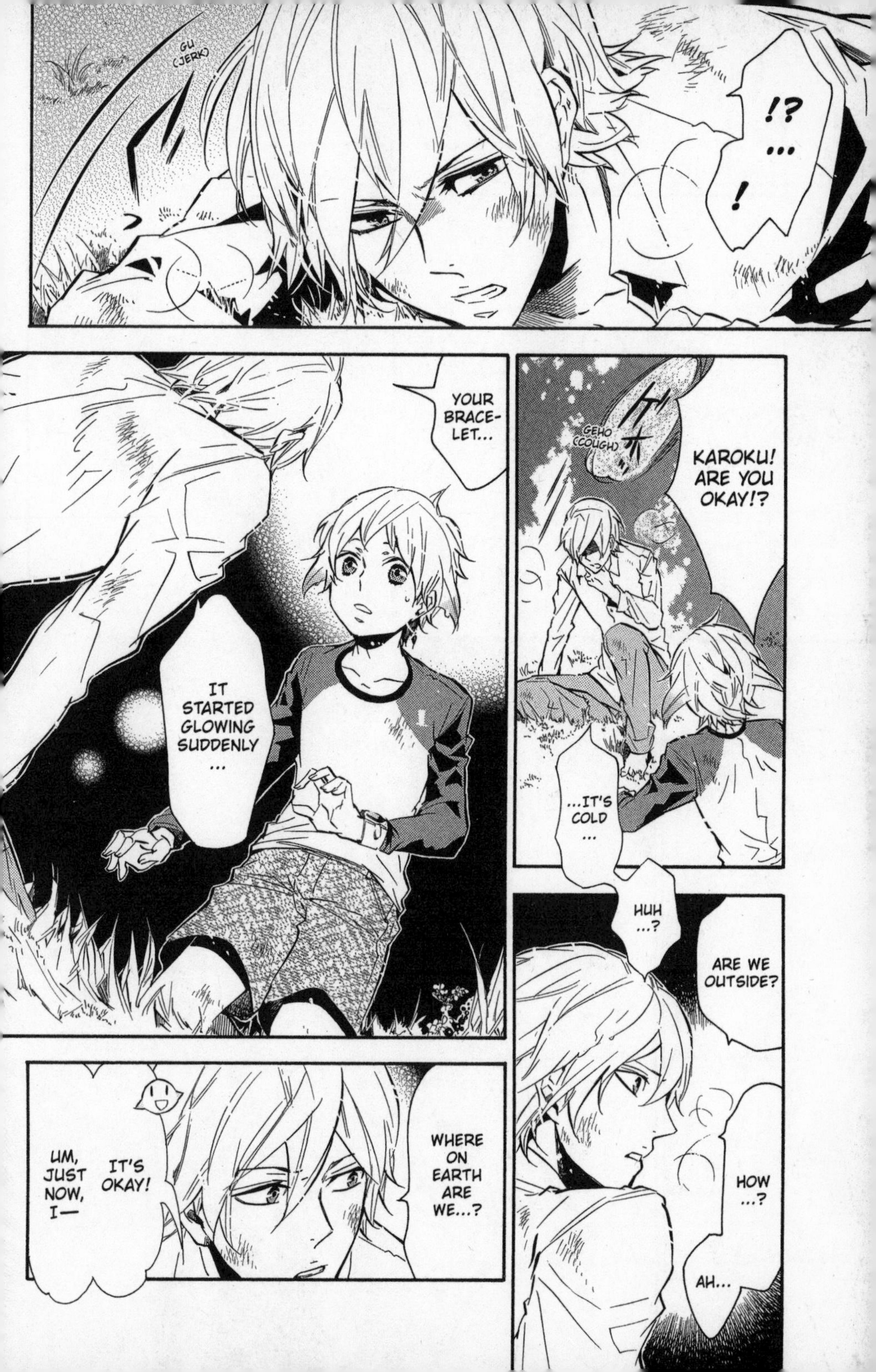
!? ... !
GU (JERK)
KAROKU! ARE YOU OKAY!?
GEHO (COUGH)
...IT'S COLD ...
YOUR BRACELET...
IT STARTED GLOWING SUDDENLY ...
HUH ...?
ARE WE OUTSIDE?
HOW ...?
AH...
WHERE ON EARTH ARE WE...?
IT'S OKAY!
UM, JUST NOW, I—

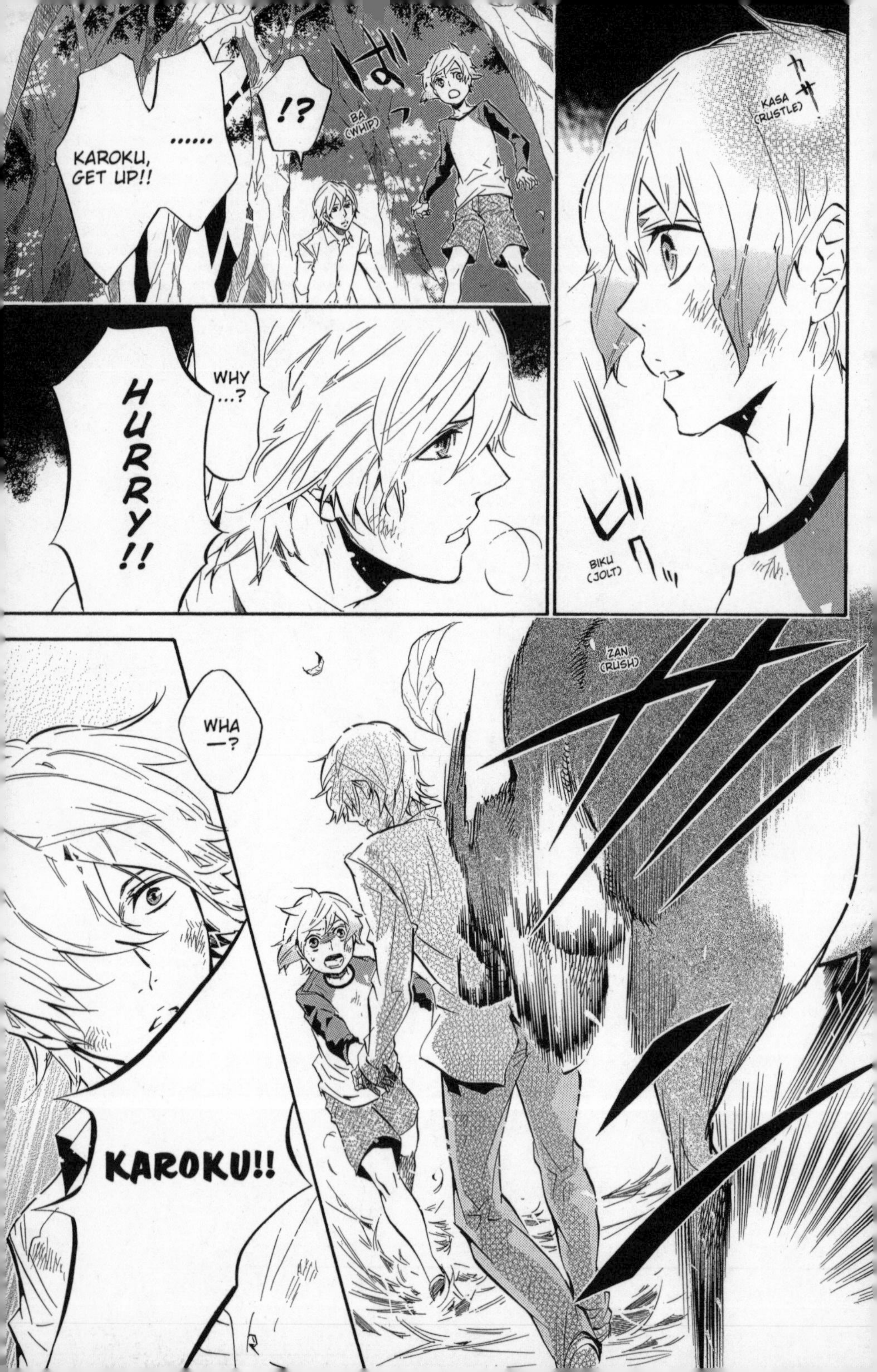
KASA (RUSTLE)
BIKU (JOLT)
BA (WHIP)
!?
......
KAROKU, GET UP!!
WHY ...?
HURRY!!
ZAN (RUSH)
WHA—?
KAROKU!!

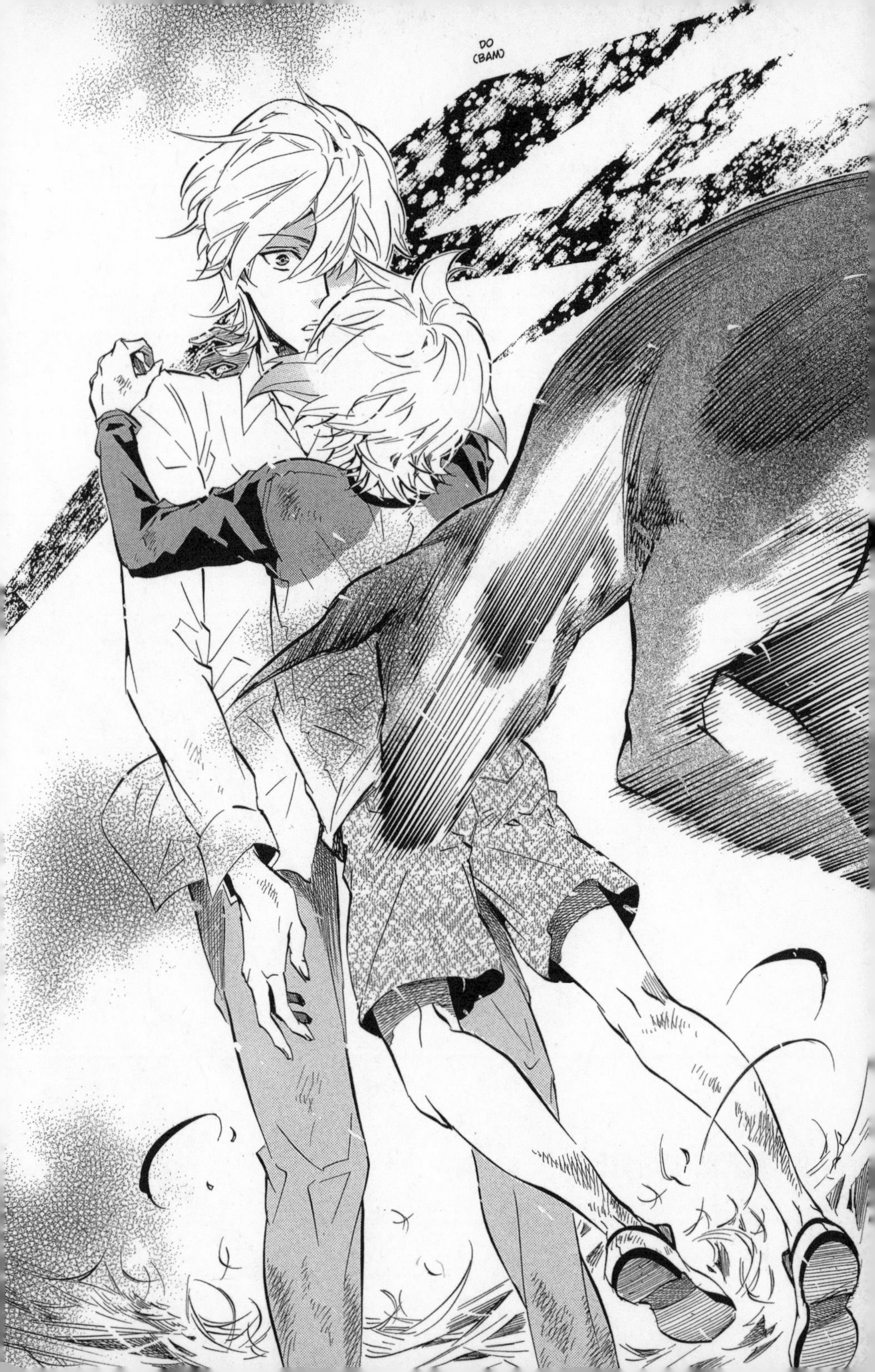
DO
(BAM)

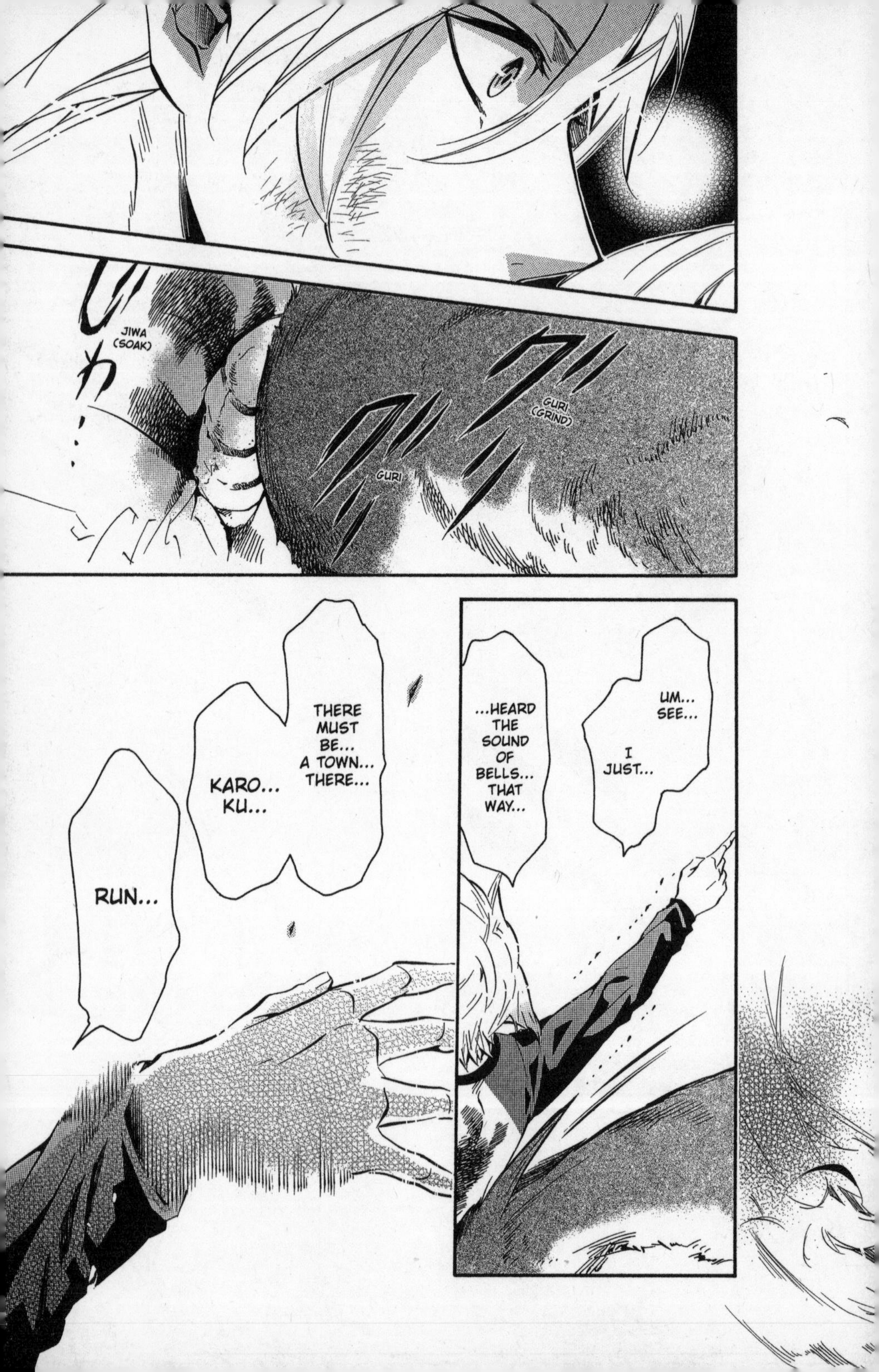
GURI (GRIND)
GURI
JIWA (SOAK)
UM... SEE...
I JUST...
...HEARD THE SOUND OF BELLS... THAT WAY...
THERE MUST BE... A TOWN... THERE...
KARO... KU...
RUN...

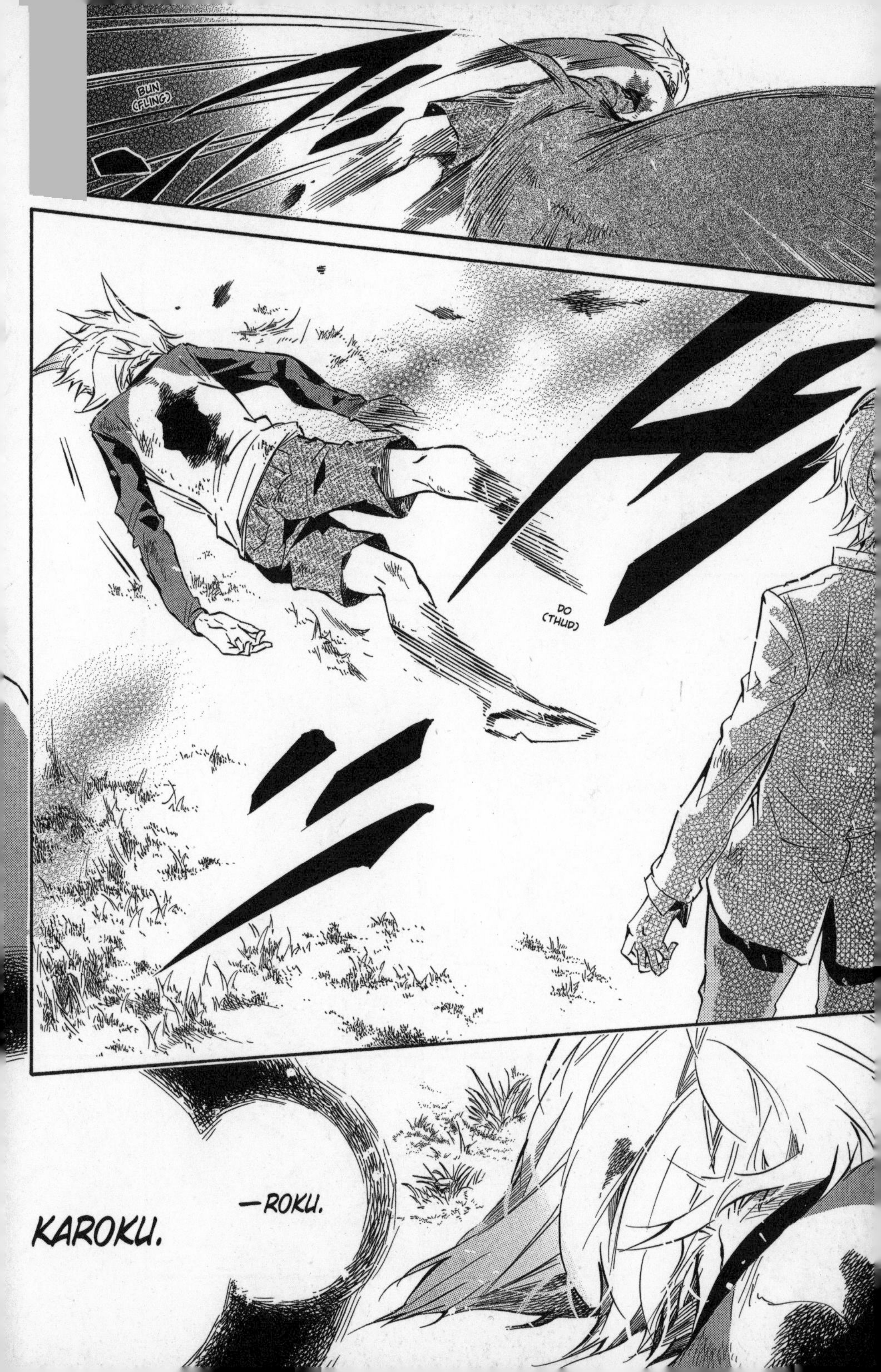
BUN (FLING)
DO (THUD)
—ROKU.
KAROKU.

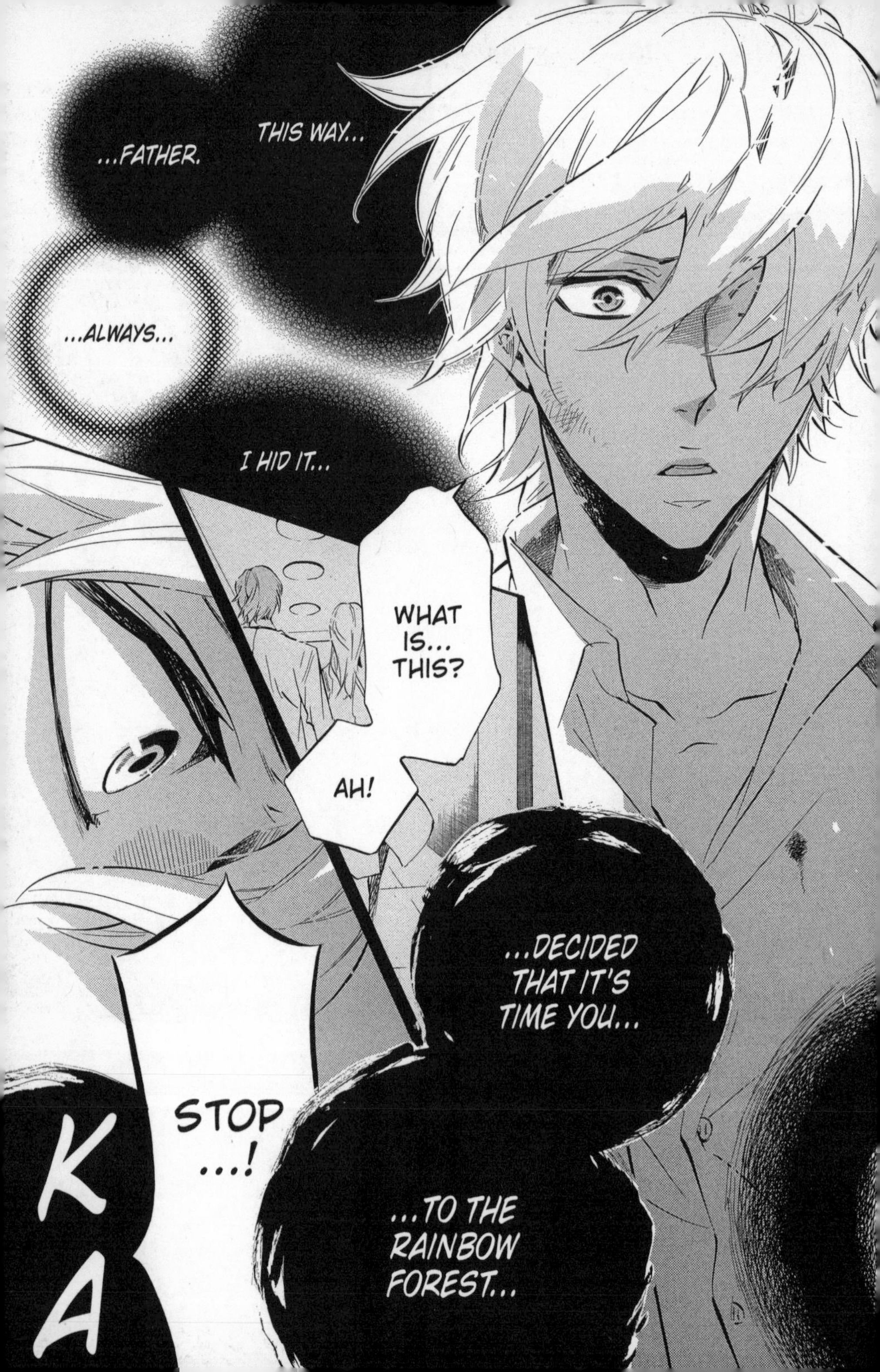
THIS WAY...
...FATHER.
...ALWAYS...
I HID IT...
WHAT IS... THIS?
AH!
...DECIDED THAT IT'S TIME YOU...
STOP ...!
...TO THE RAINBOW FOREST...
KA

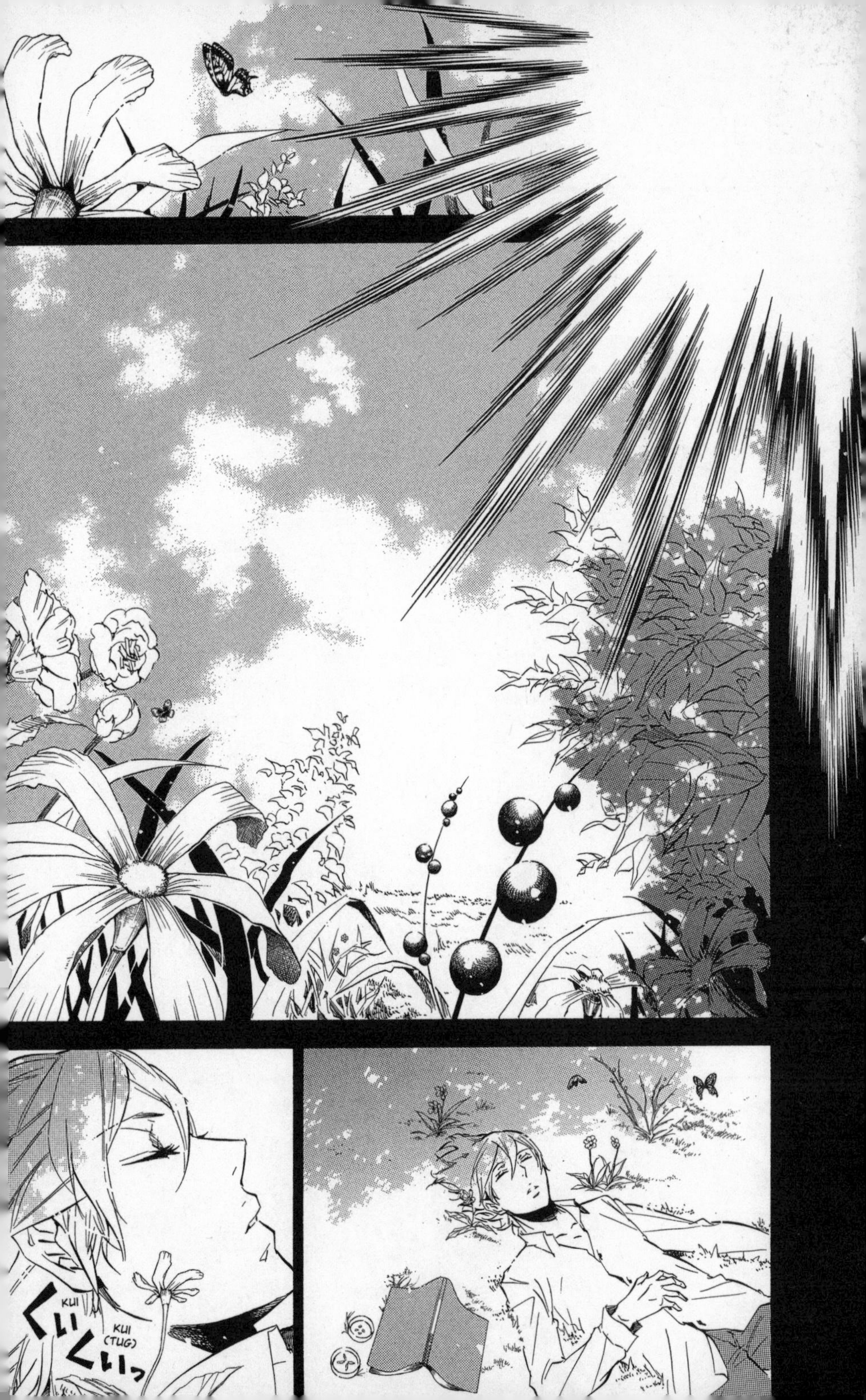
くい
KUI
くいっ
KUI
(TUG)

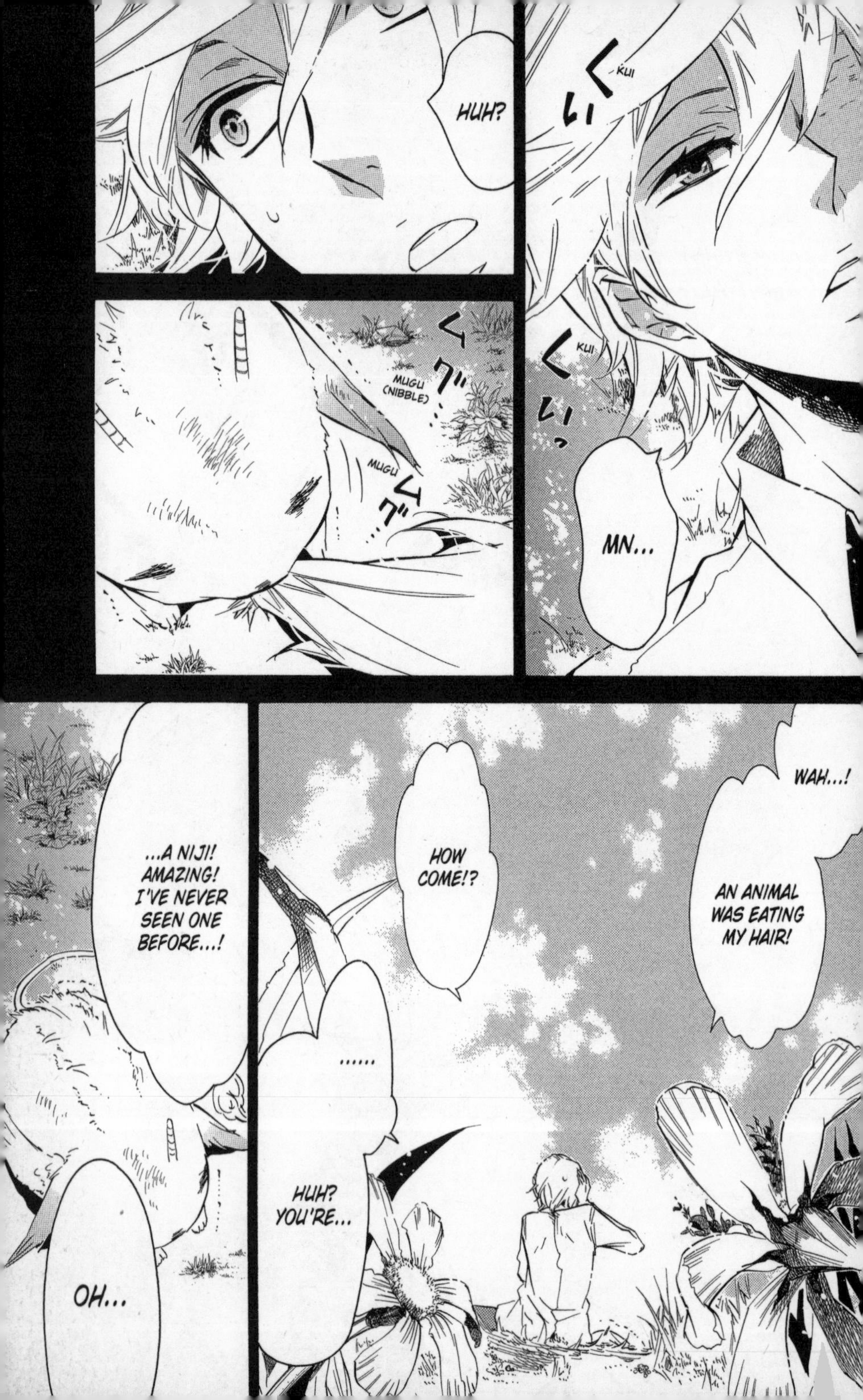
KUI
KUI
MN...
HUH?
MUGU (NIBBLE)
MUGU
WAH...!
AN ANIMAL WAS EATING MY HAIR!
HOW COME!?
......
HUH? YOU'RE...
...A NIJI! AMAZING! I'VE NEVER SEEN ONE BEFORE...!
OH...

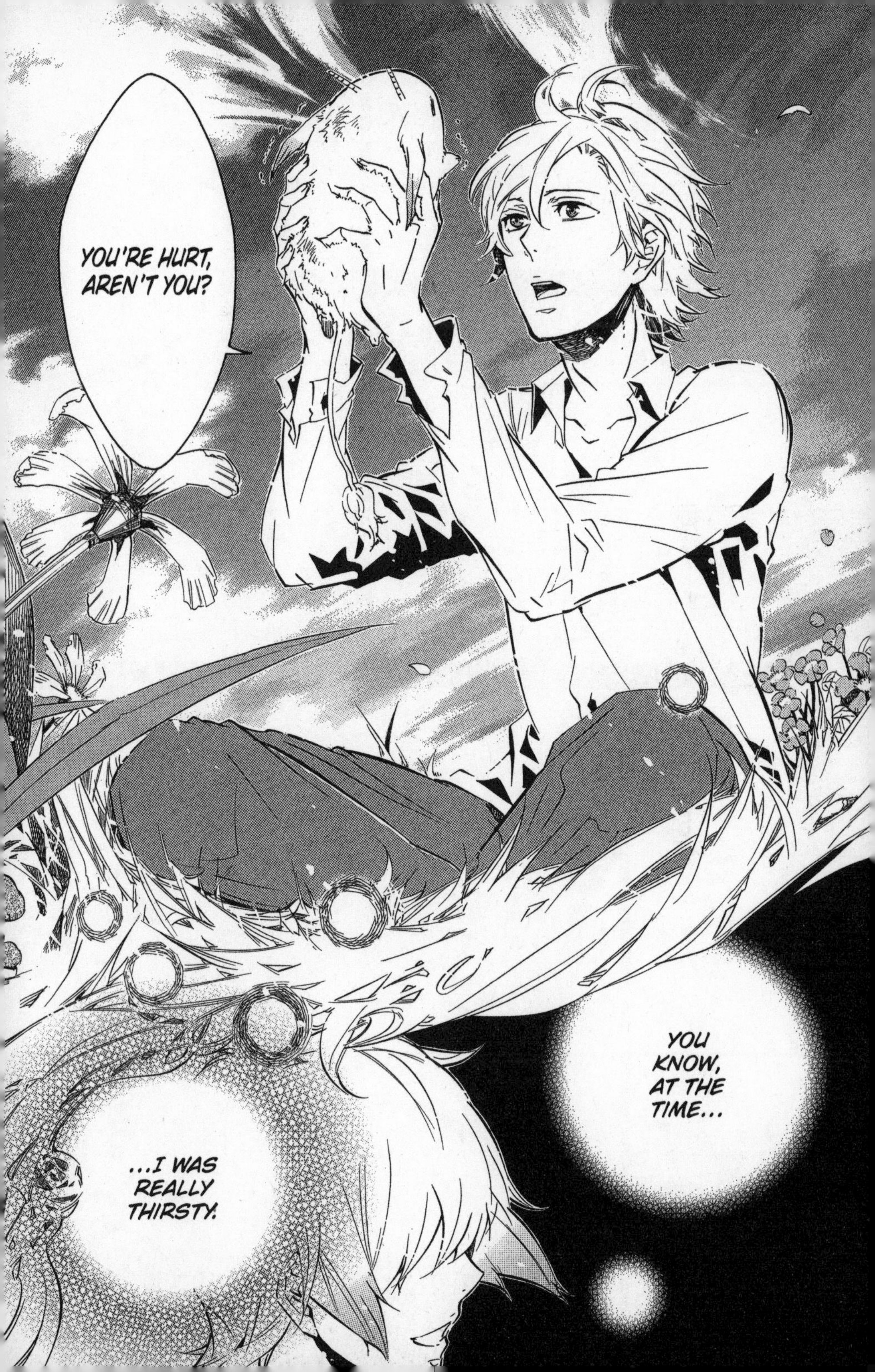
YOU'RE HURT, AREN'T YOU?
YOU KNOW, AT THE TIME...
...I WAS REALLY THIRSTY.

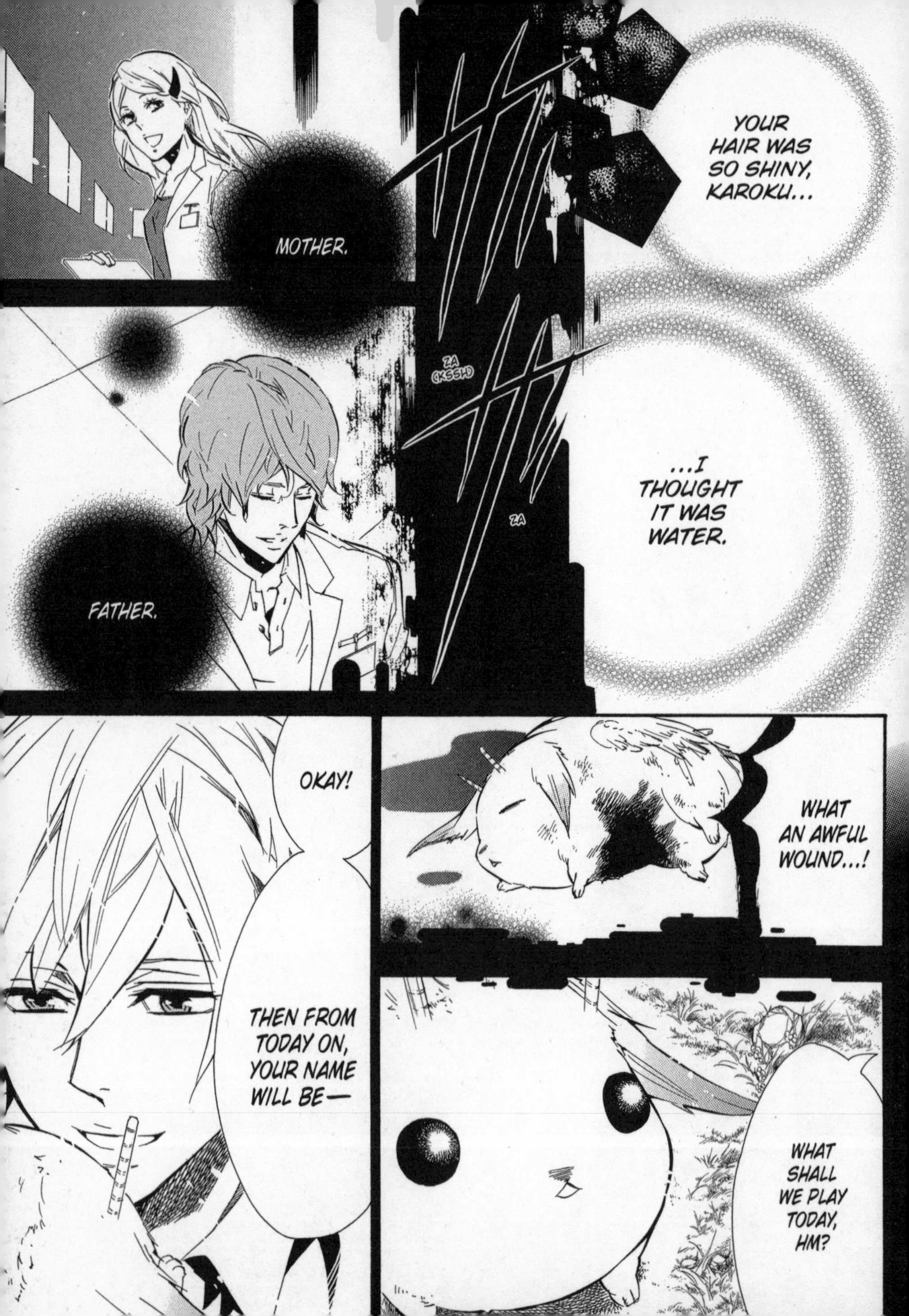
YOUR HAIR WAS SO SHINY, KAROKU...
ZA (KSSH)
...I THOUGHT IT WAS WATER.
ZA
MOTHER.
FATHER.
WHAT AN AWFUL WOUND...!
WHAT SHALL WE PLAY TODAY, HM?
OKAY!
THEN FROM TODAY ON, YOUR NAME WILL BE—

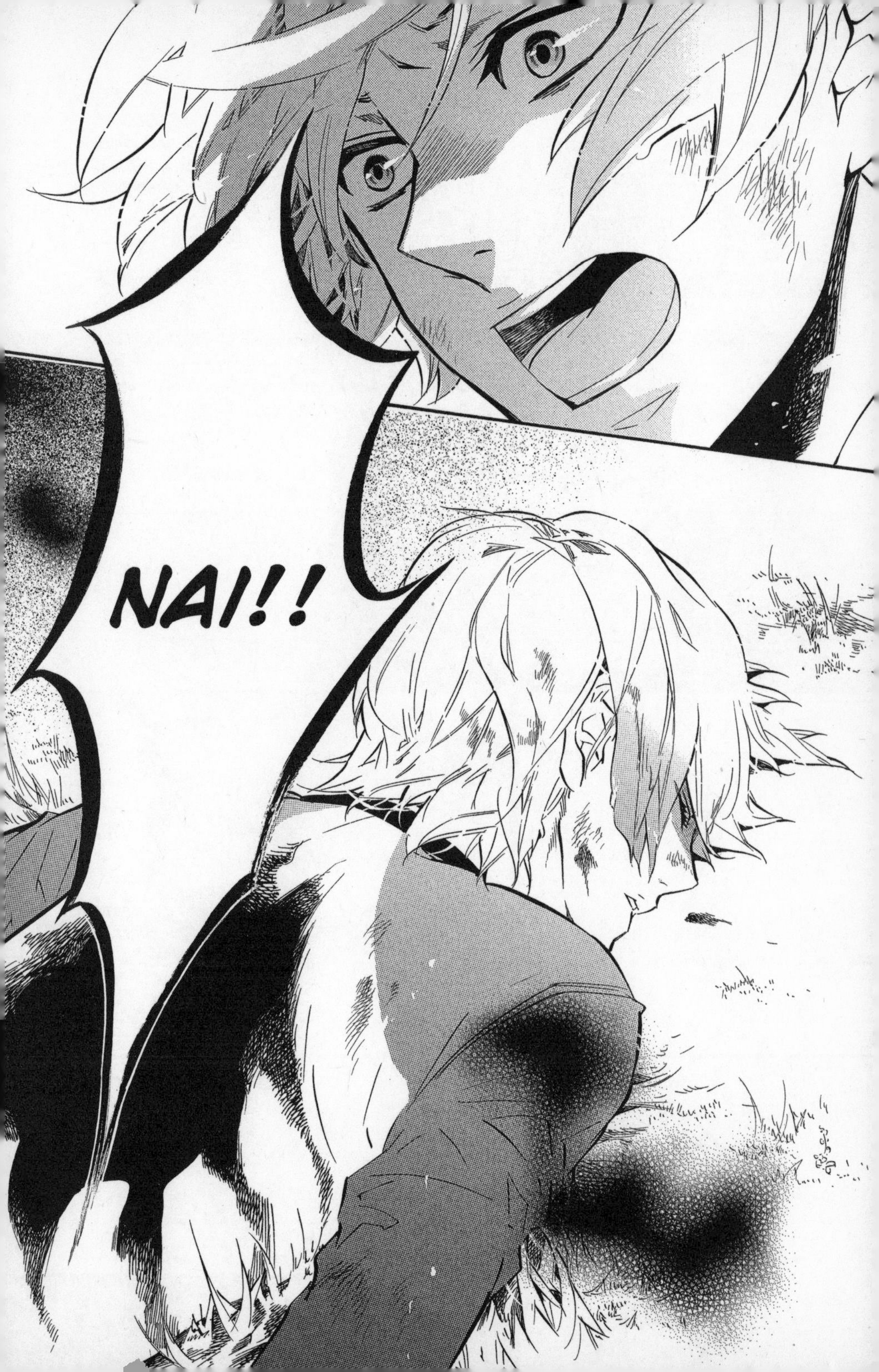
NAI!!

KARNEVAL

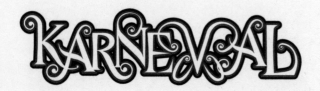

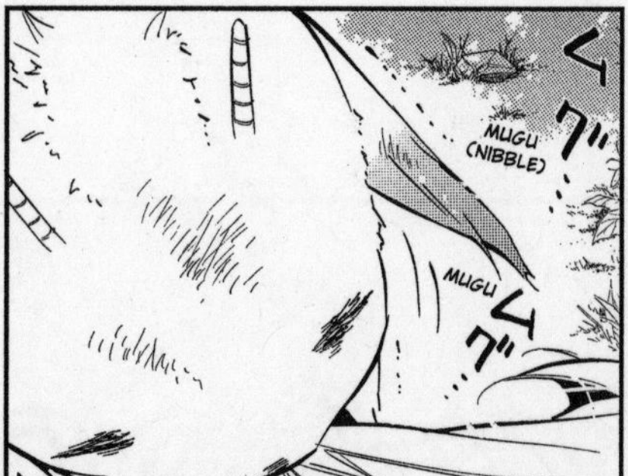
ムグ
MUGU (NIBBLE)
ムグ
MUGU

KARNEVAL

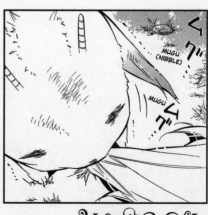

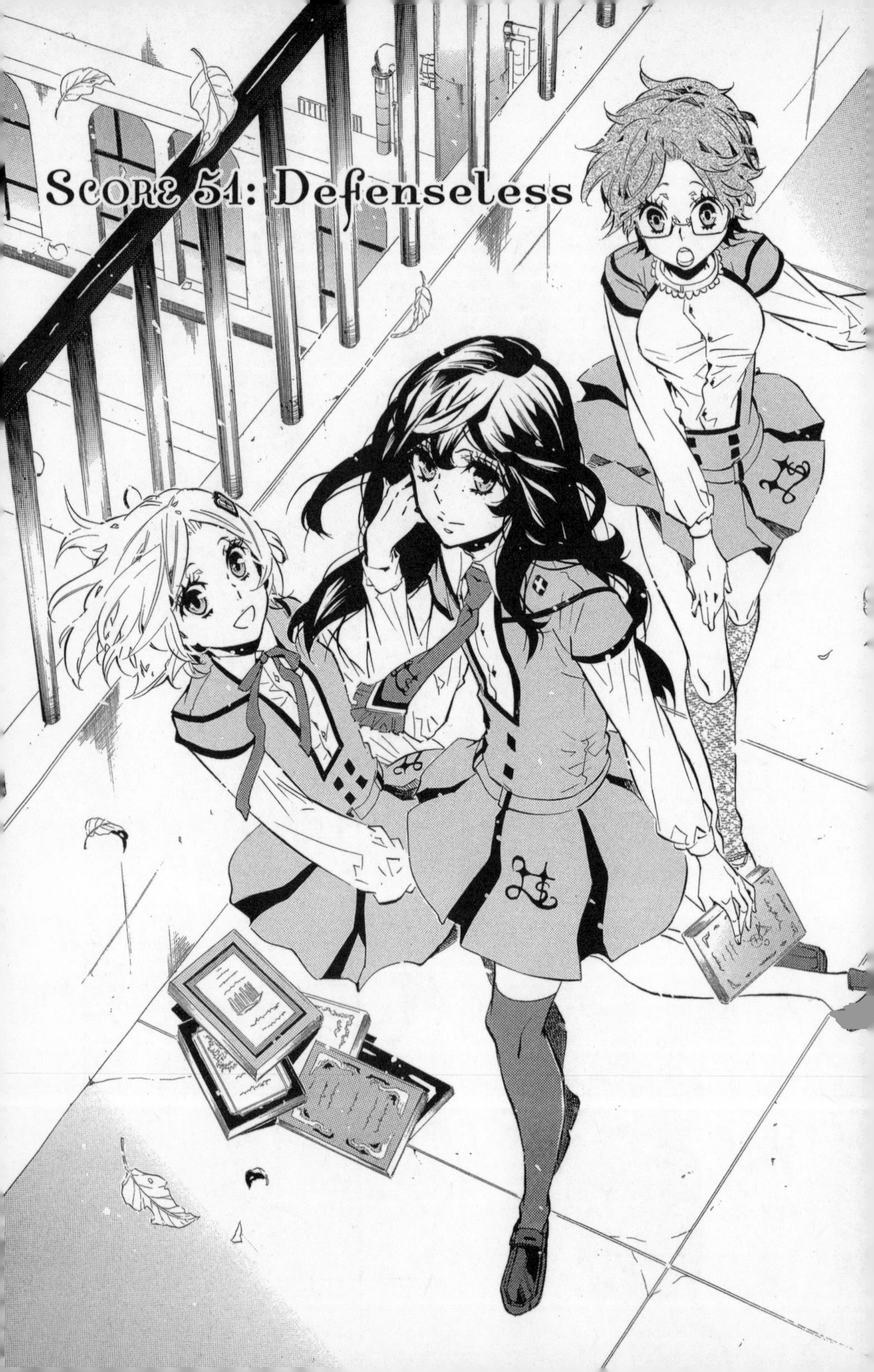
Score 51: Defenseless

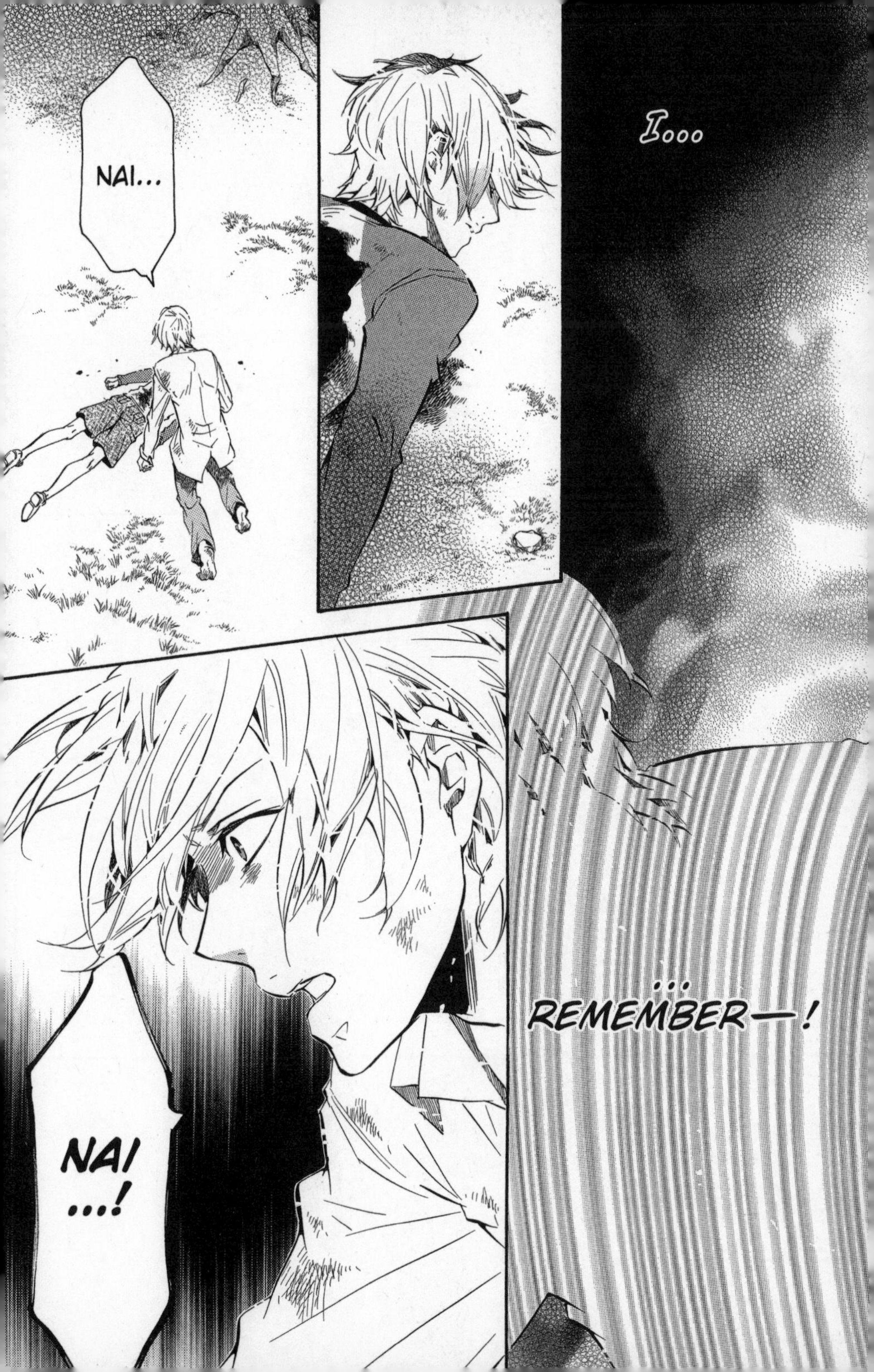
I...
NAI...
...REMEMBER—!
NAI...!

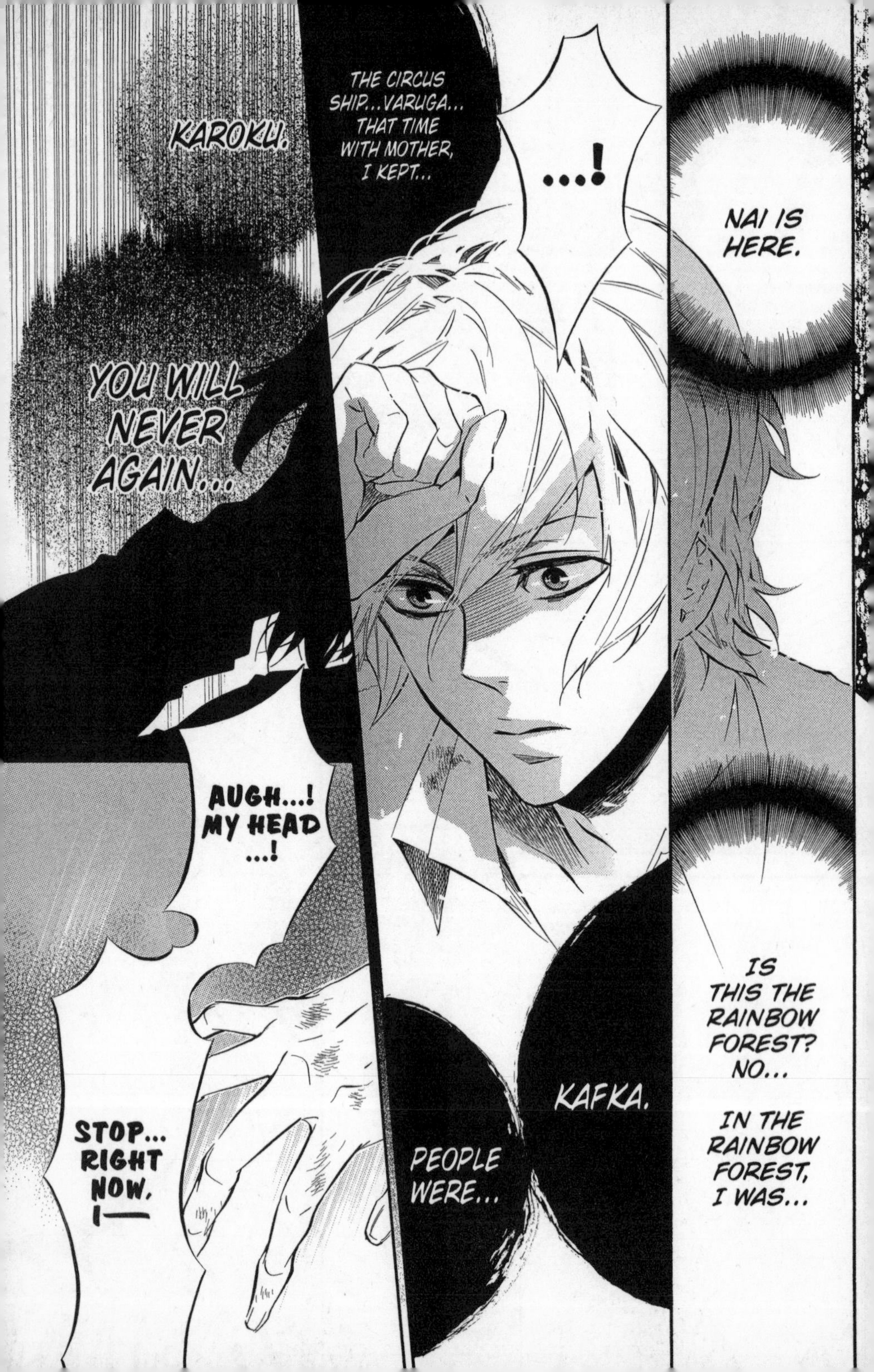
NAI IS HERE.
IS THIS THE RAINBOW FOREST? NO...
IN THE RAINBOW FOREST, I WAS...
...!
THE CIRCUS SHIP...VARUGA... THAT TIME WITH MOTHER, I KEPT...
KAFKA.
PEOPLE WERE...
KAROKU.
YOU WILL NEVER AGAIN...
AUGH...! MY HEAD ...!
STOP... RIGHT NOW. I—

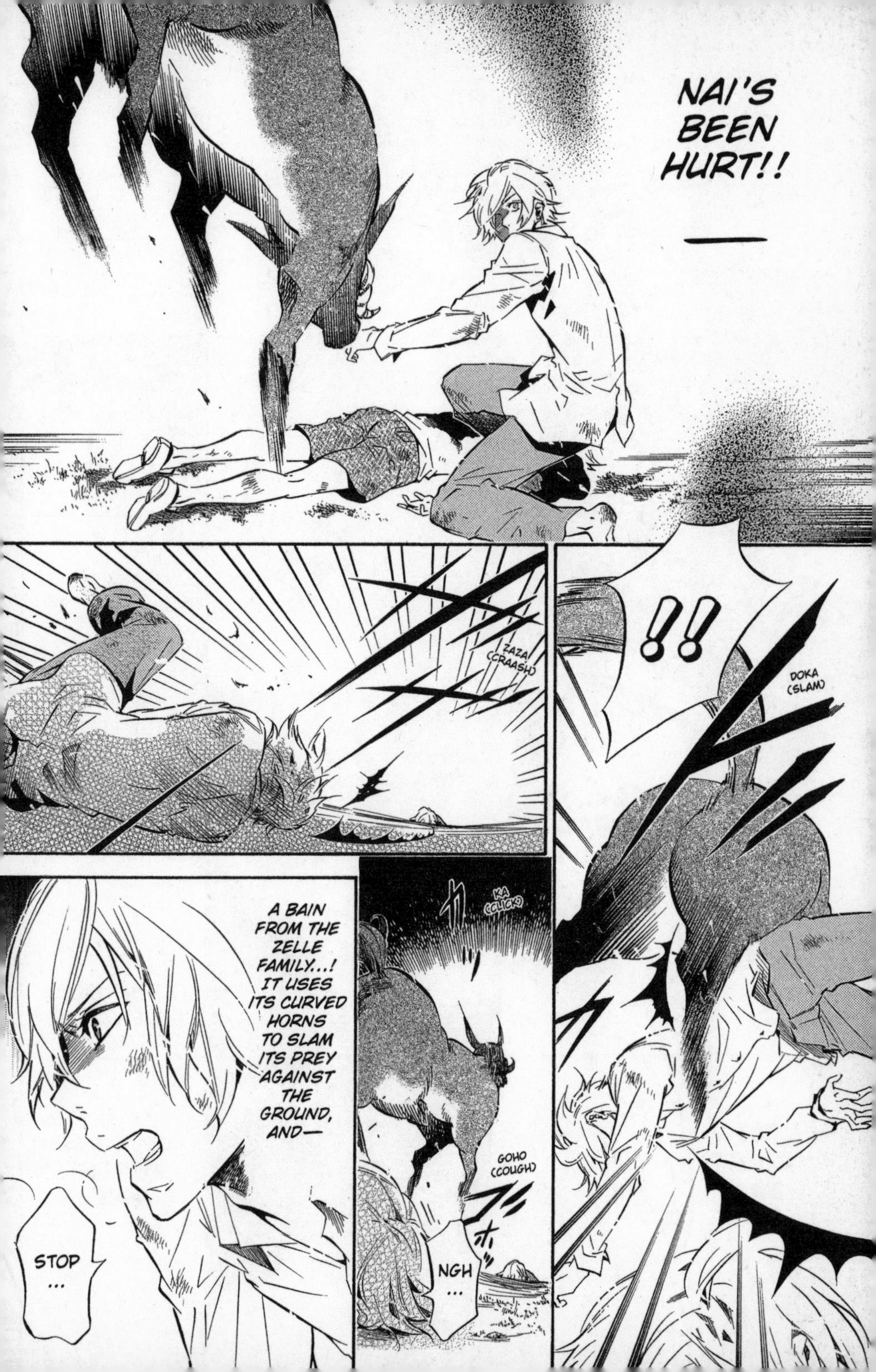
NAI'S BEEN HURT!!
—
!!
DOKA (SLAM)
ZAZA (CRAASH)
KA (CLICK)
GOHO (COUGH)
NGH ...
A BAIN FROM THE ZELLE FAMILY...! IT USES ITS CURVED HORNS TO SLAM ITS PREY AGAINST THE GROUND, AND—
STOP ...

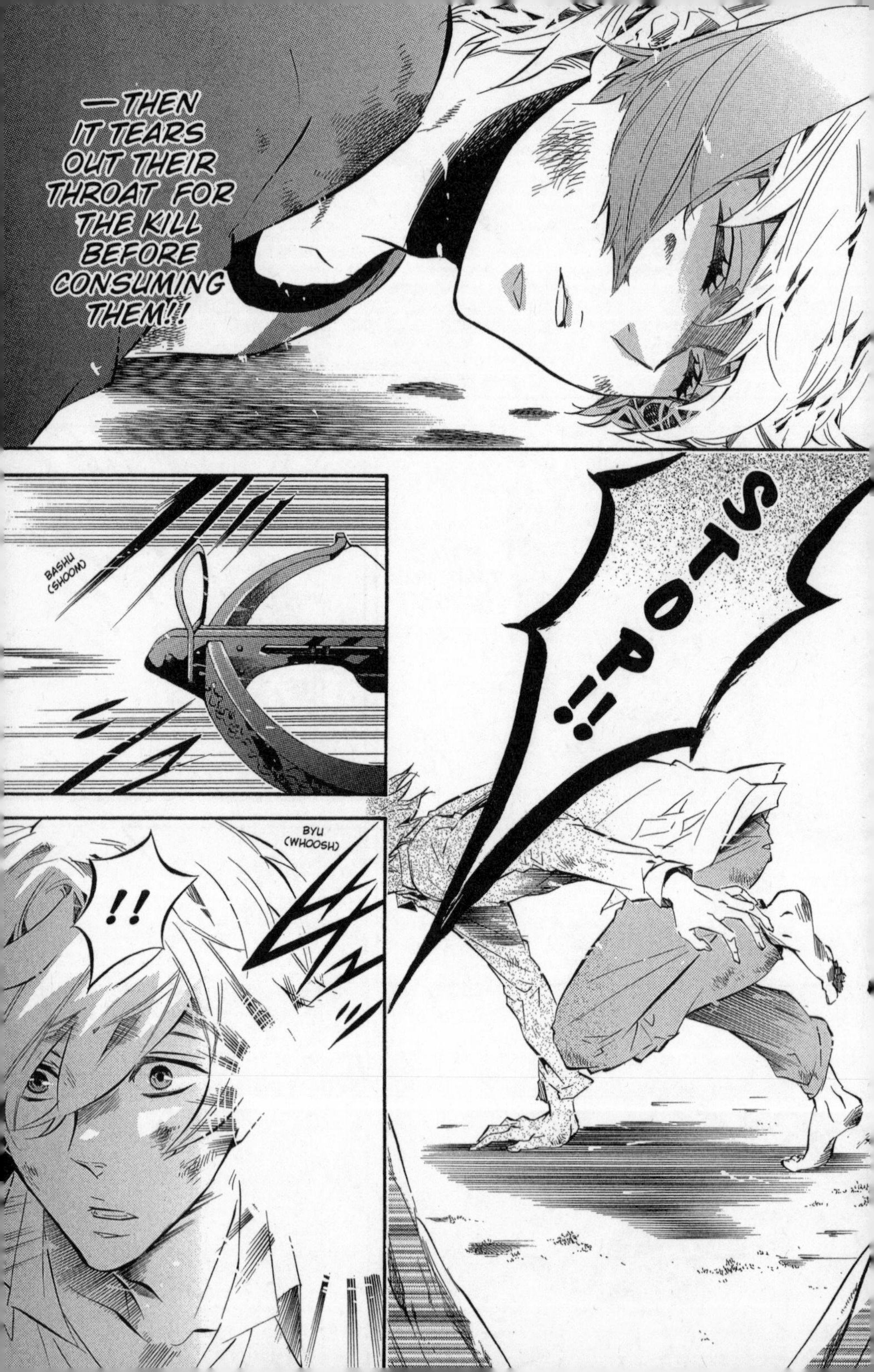
—THEN IT TEARS OUT THEIR THROAT FOR THE KILL BEFORE CONSUMING THEM!!
STOP!!!
BASHU (SHOOM)
BYU (WHOOSH)
!!

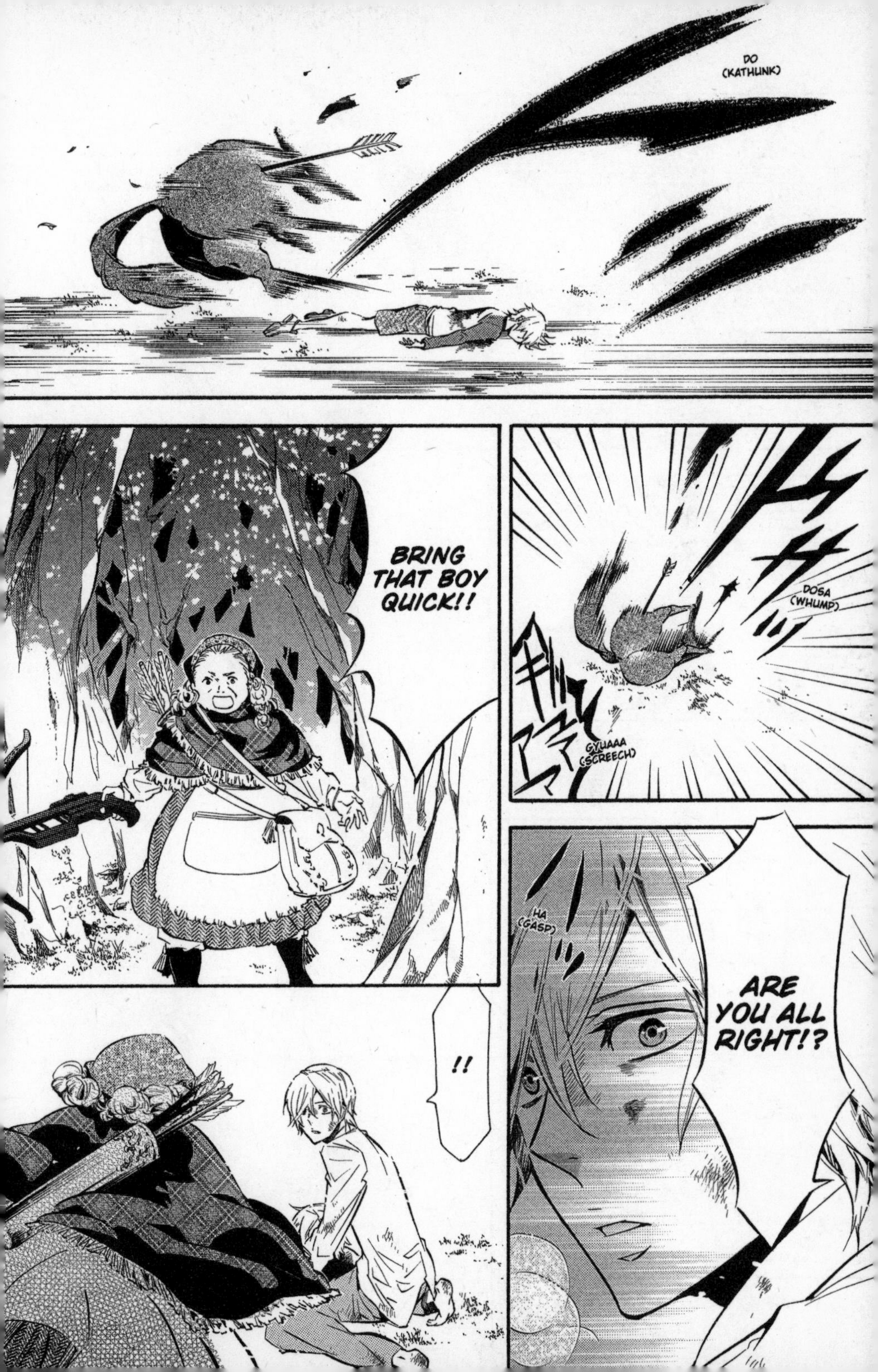
DO
(KATHUNK)
DOSA
(WHUMP)
GYUAAA
(SCREECH)
BRING THAT BOY QUICK!!
HA
(GASP)
ARE YOU ALL RIGHT!?
!!

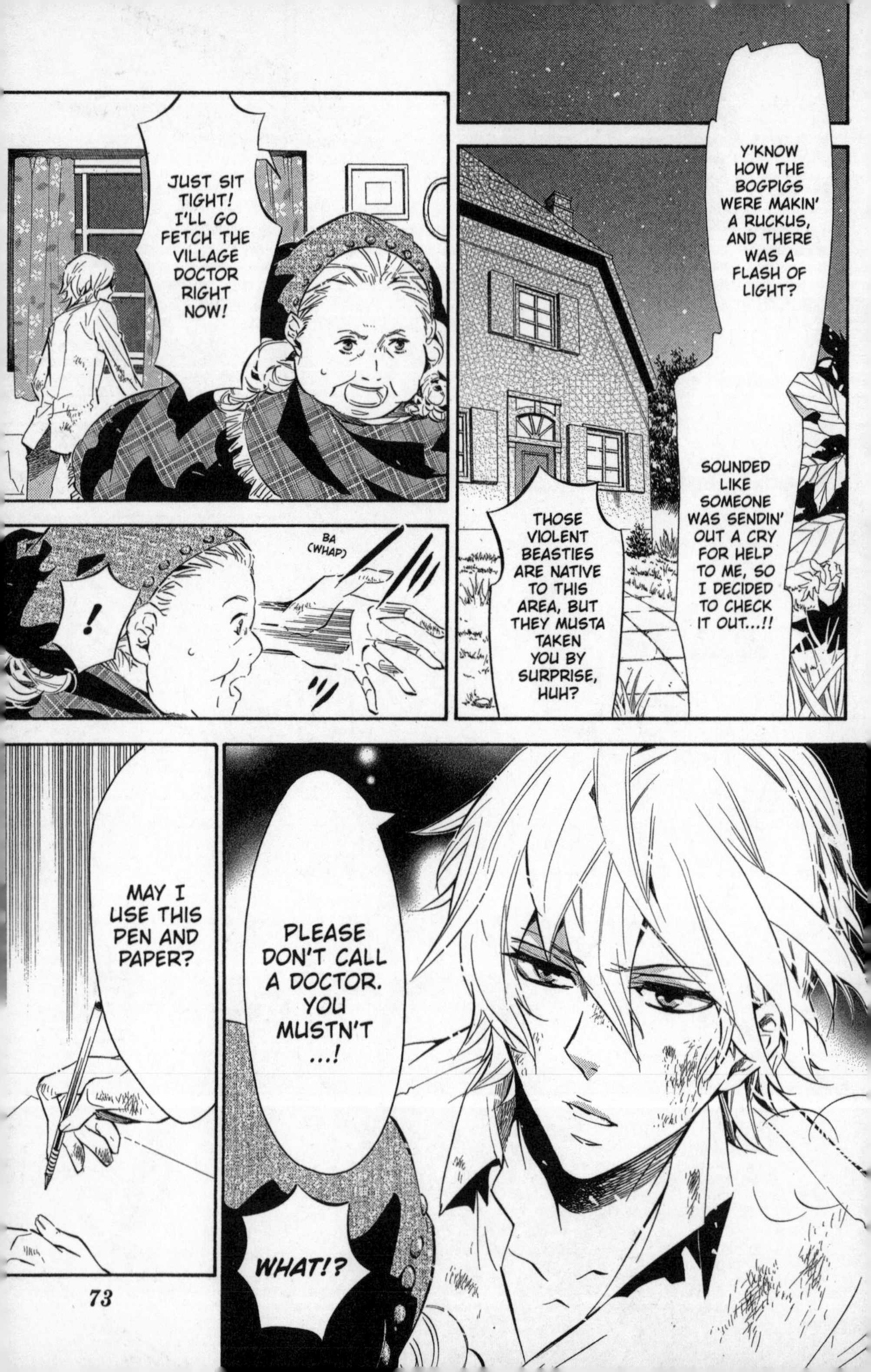

Y'KNOW HOW THE BOGPIGS WERE MAKIN' A RUCKUS, AND THERE WAS A FLASH OF LIGHT?
SOUNDED LIKE SOMEONE WAS SENDIN' OUT A CRY FOR HELP TO ME, SO I DECIDED TO CHECK IT OUT...!!
THOSE VIOLENT BEASTIES ARE NATIVE TO THIS AREA, BUT THEY MUSTA TAKEN YOU BY SURPRISE, HUH?
JUST SIT TIGHT! I'LL GO FETCH THE VILLAGE DOCTOR RIGHT NOW!
BA (WHAP)
!
PLEASE DON'T CALL A DOCTOR. YOU MUSTN'T ...!
WHAT!?
MAY I USE THIS PEN AND PAPER?

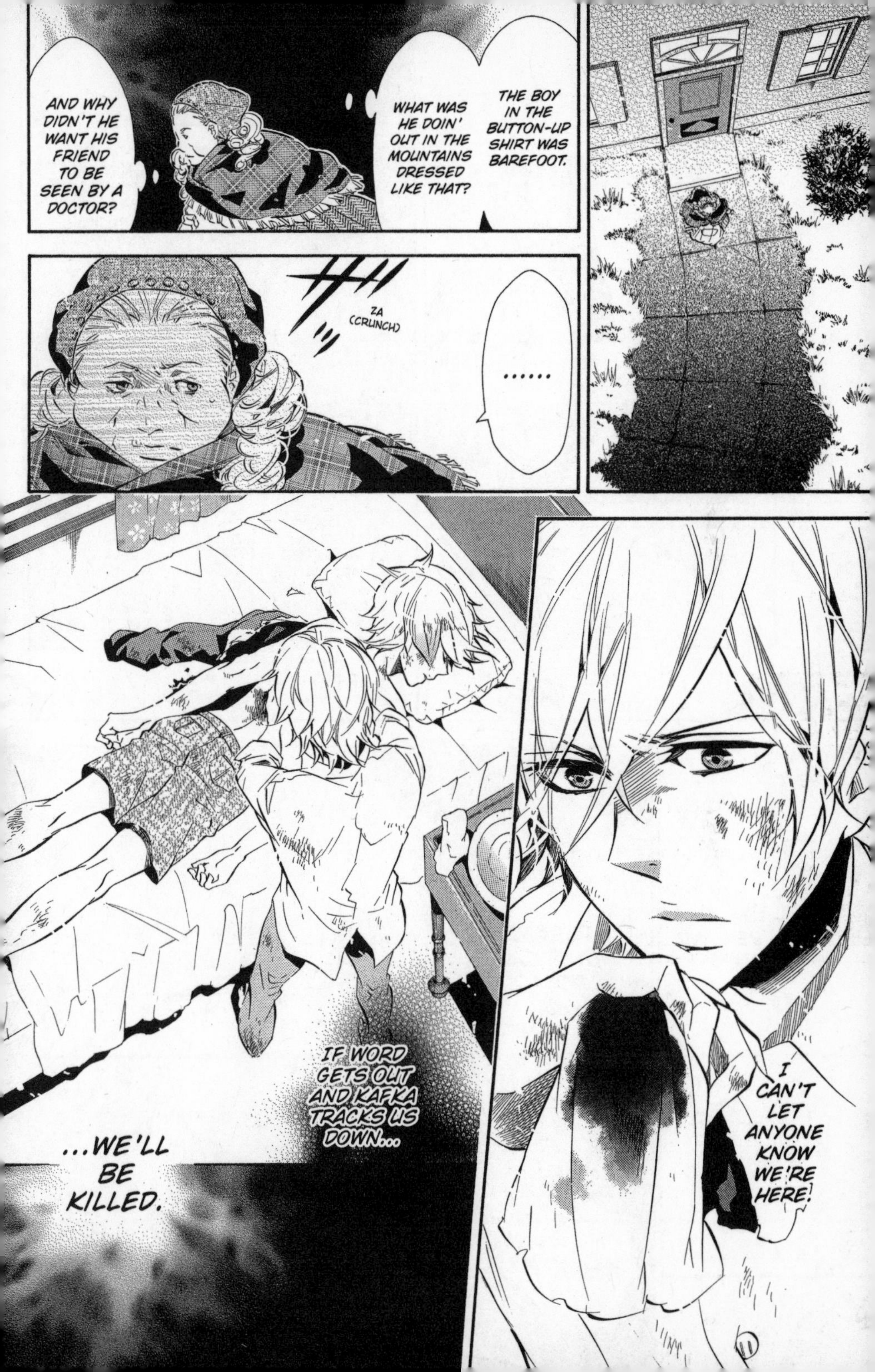
THE BOY IN THE BUTTON-UP SHIRT WAS BAREFOOT.
WHAT WAS HE DOIN' OUT IN THE MOUNTAINS DRESSED LIKE THAT?
AND WHY DIDN'T HE WANT HIS FRIEND TO BE SEEN BY A DOCTOR?
......
ZA (CRUNCH)
I CAN'T LET ANYONE KNOW WE'RE HERE.
IF WORD GETS OUT AND KAFKA TRACKS US DOWN...
...WE'LL BE KILLED.

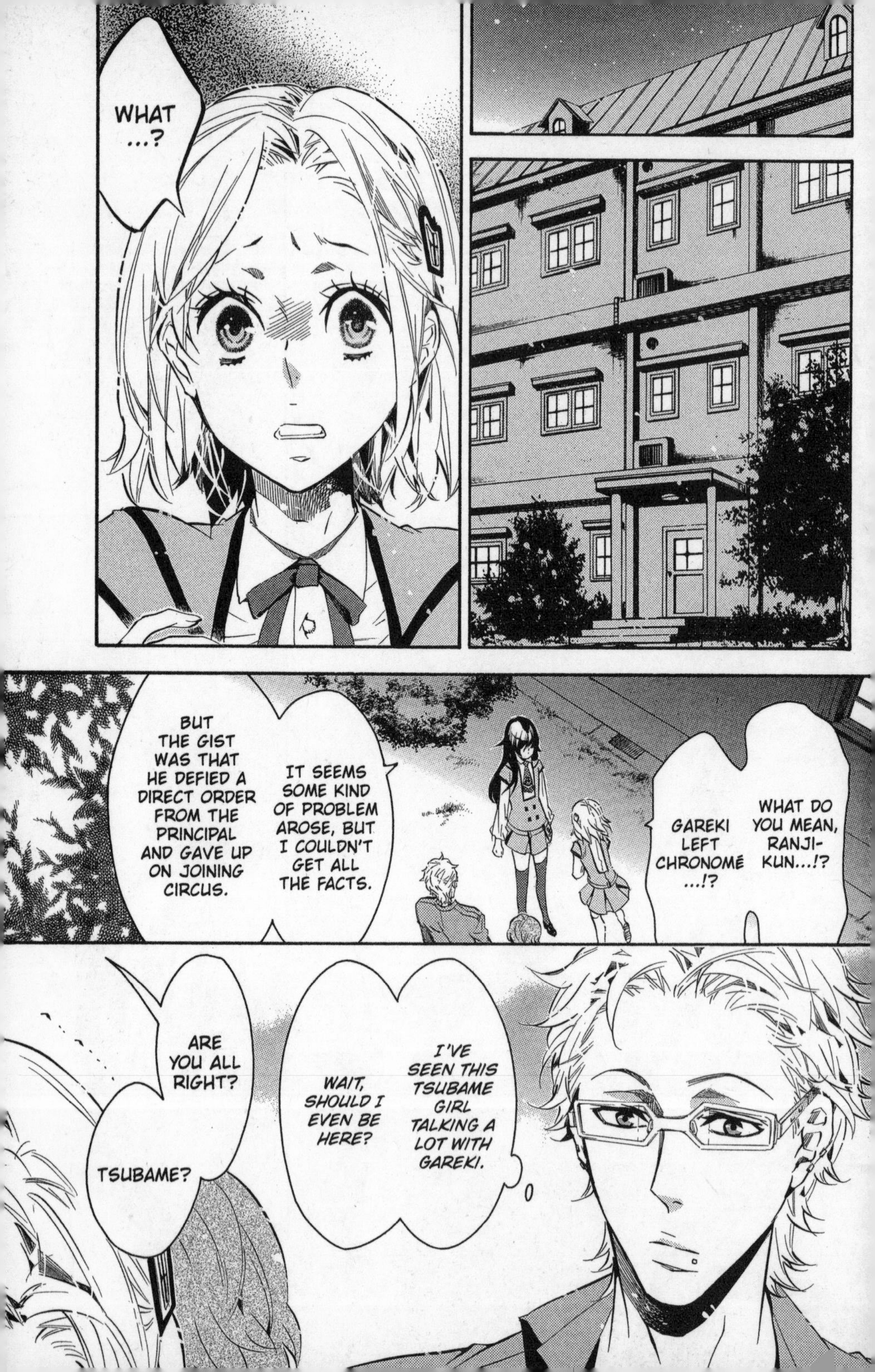
WHAT ...?
WHAT DO YOU MEAN, RANJI-KUN...!?
GAREKI LEFT CHRONOMÉ ...!?
IT SEEMS SOME KIND OF PROBLEM AROSE, BUT I COULDN'T GET ALL THE FACTS.
BUT THE GIST WAS THAT HE DEFIED A DIRECT ORDER FROM THE PRINCIPAL AND GAVE UP ON JOINING CIRCUS.
I'VE SEEN THIS TSUBAME GIRL TALKING A LOT WITH GAREKI.
WAIT, SHOULD I EVEN BE HERE?
ARE YOU ALL RIGHT?
TSUBAME?
...

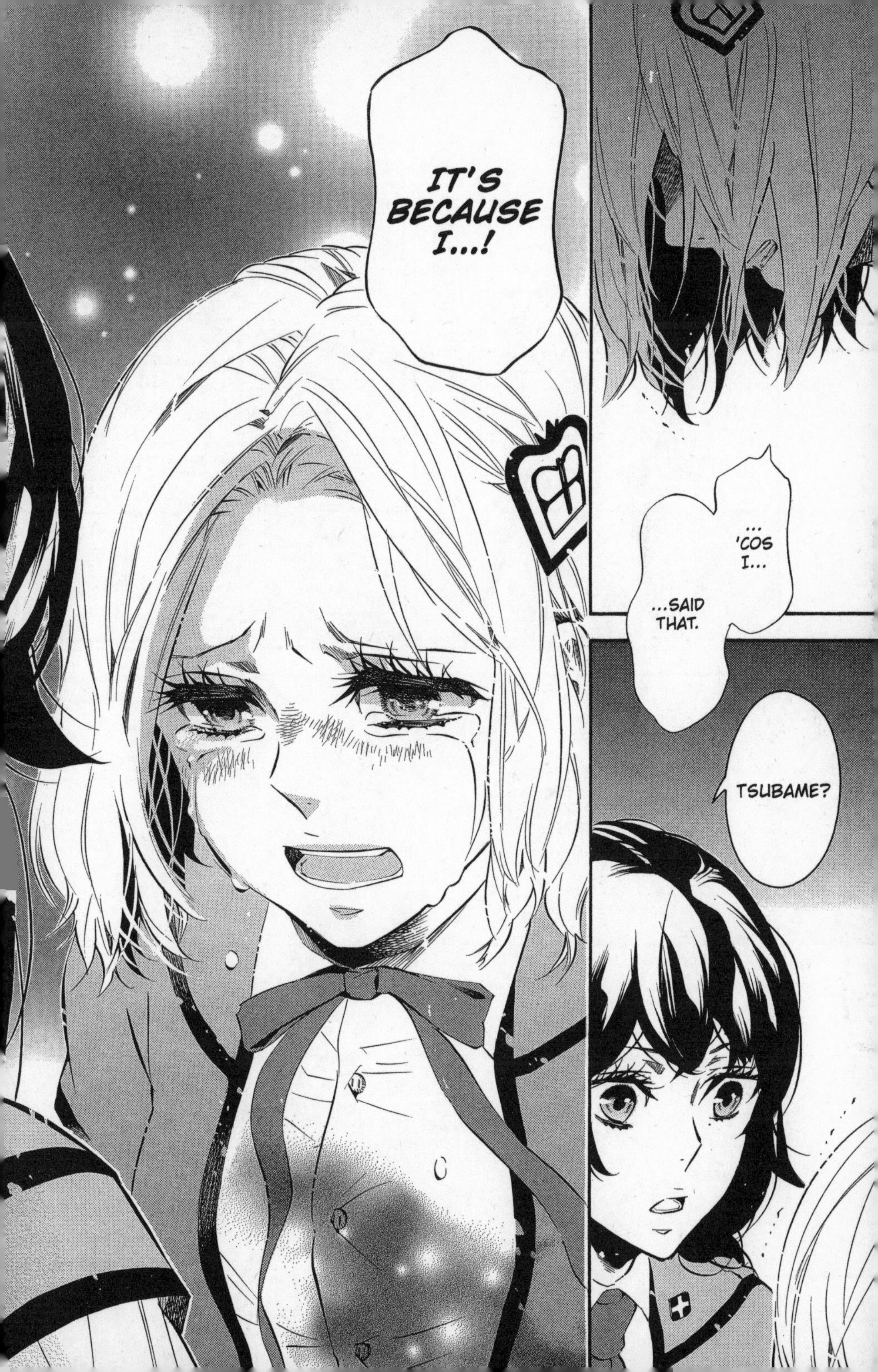
...'COS I... ...SAID THAT.
TSUBAME?
IT'S BECAUSE I...!

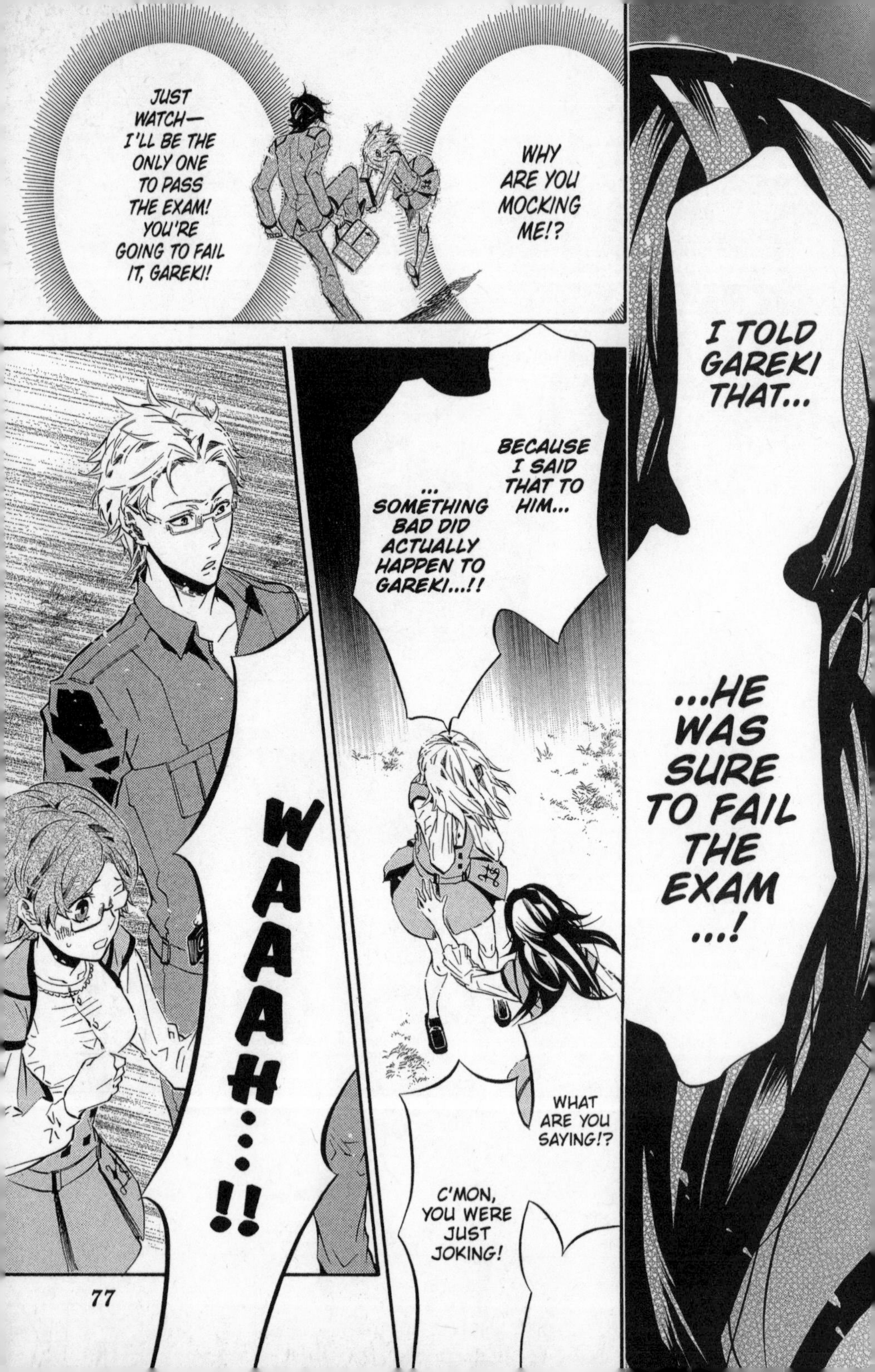
I TOLD GAREKI THAT...
...HE WAS SURE TO FAIL THE EXAM ...!
WHY ARE YOU MOCKING ME!?
JUST WATCH— I'LL BE THE ONLY ONE TO PASS THE EXAM! YOU'RE GOING TO FAIL IT, GAREKI!
BECAUSE I SAID THAT TO HIM...
... SOMETHING BAD DID ACTUALLY HAPPEN TO GAREKI...!!
WHAT ARE YOU SAYING!?
C'MON, YOU WERE JUST JOKING!
WAAAAH...!!

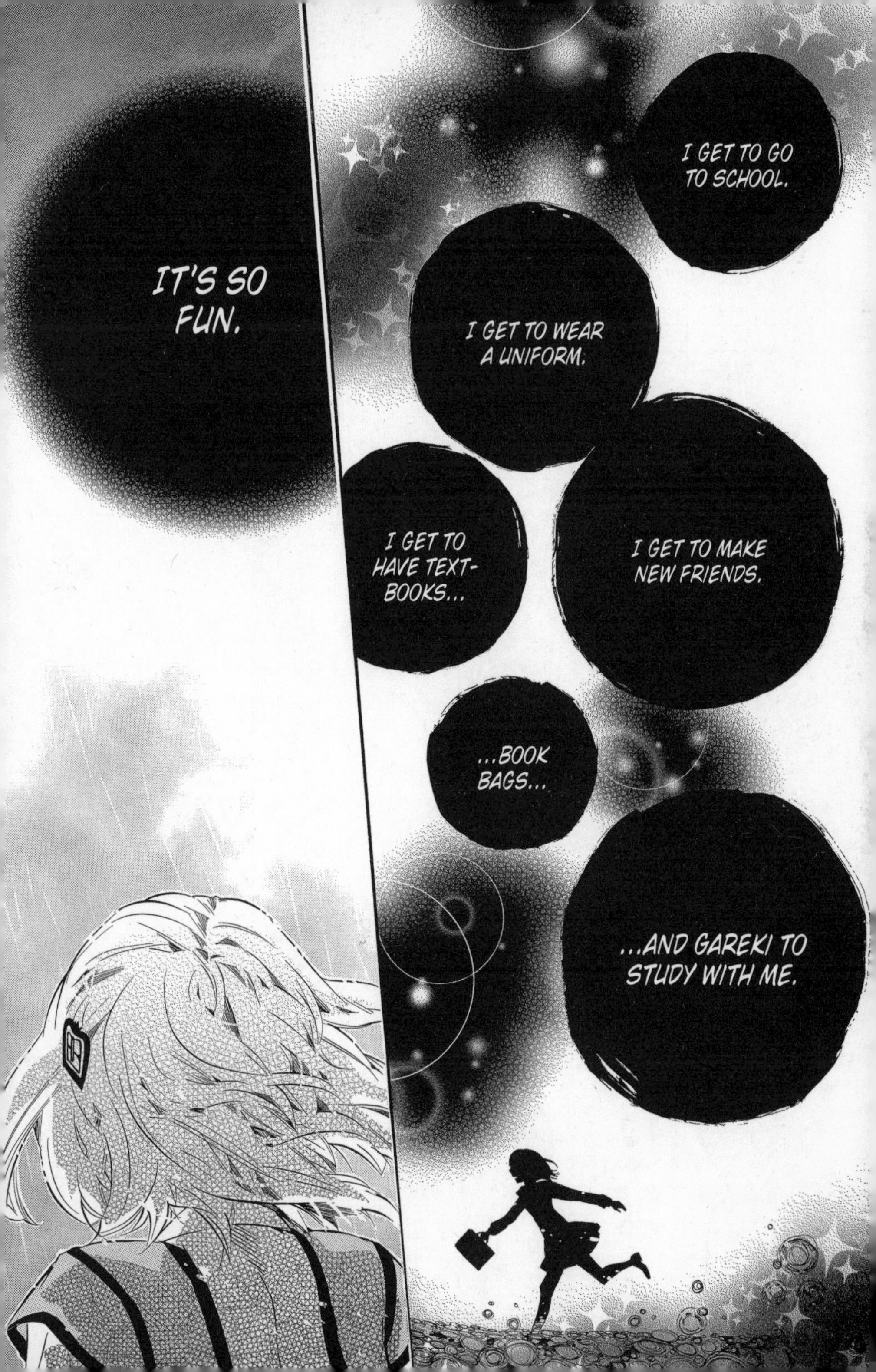
I GET TO GO TO SCHOOL.
I GET TO WEAR A UNIFORM.
I GET TO MAKE NEW FRIENDS.
I GET TO HAVE TEXT-BOOKS...
...BOOK BAGS...
...AND GAREKI TO STUDY WITH ME.
IT'S SO FUN.

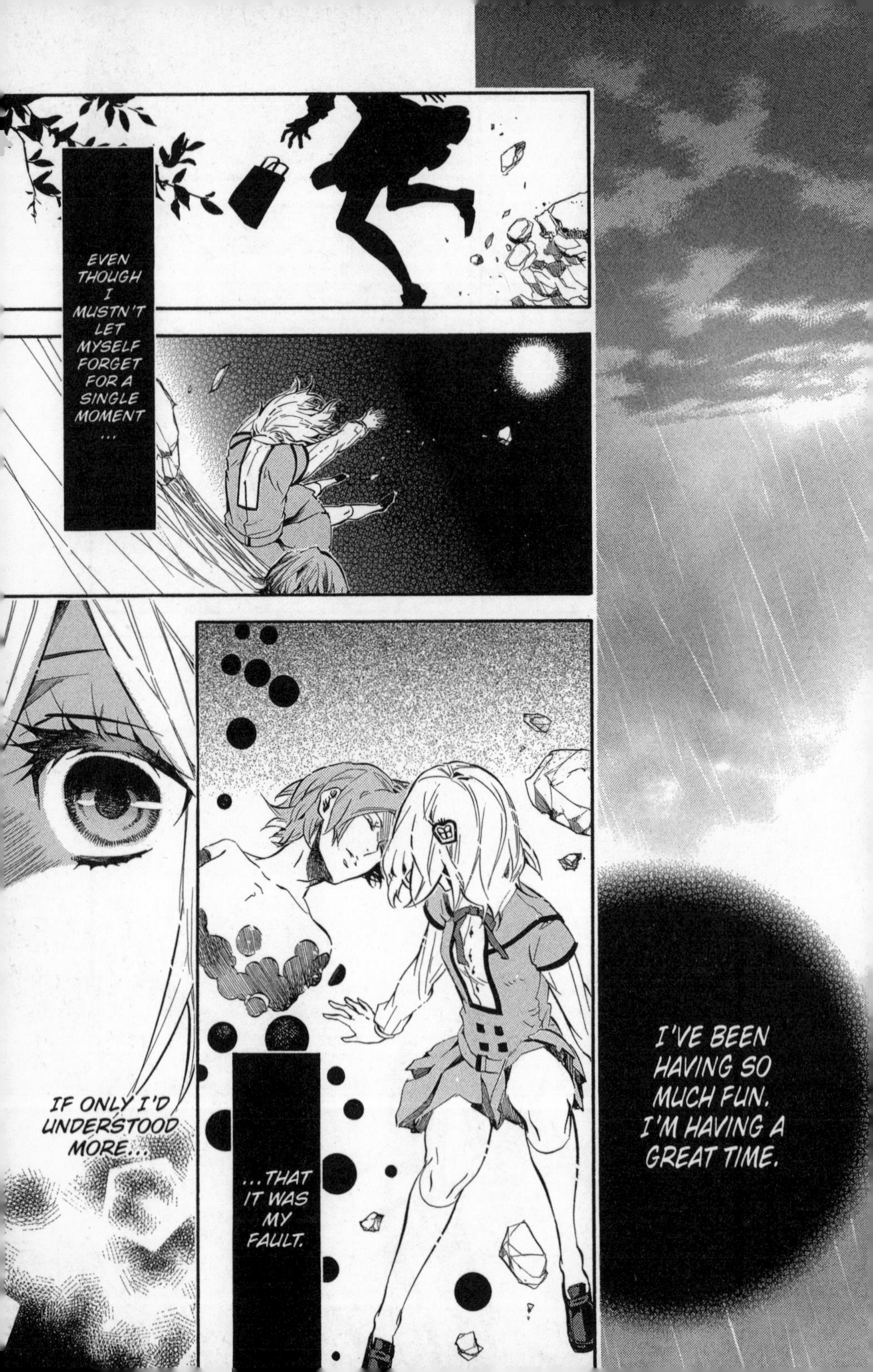
I'VE BEEN HAVING SO MUCH FUN. I'M HAVING A GREAT TIME.
EVEN THOUGH I MUSTN'T LET MYSELF FORGET FOR A SINGLE MOMENT...
...THAT IT WAS MY FAULT.
IF ONLY I'D UNDERSTOOD MORE...

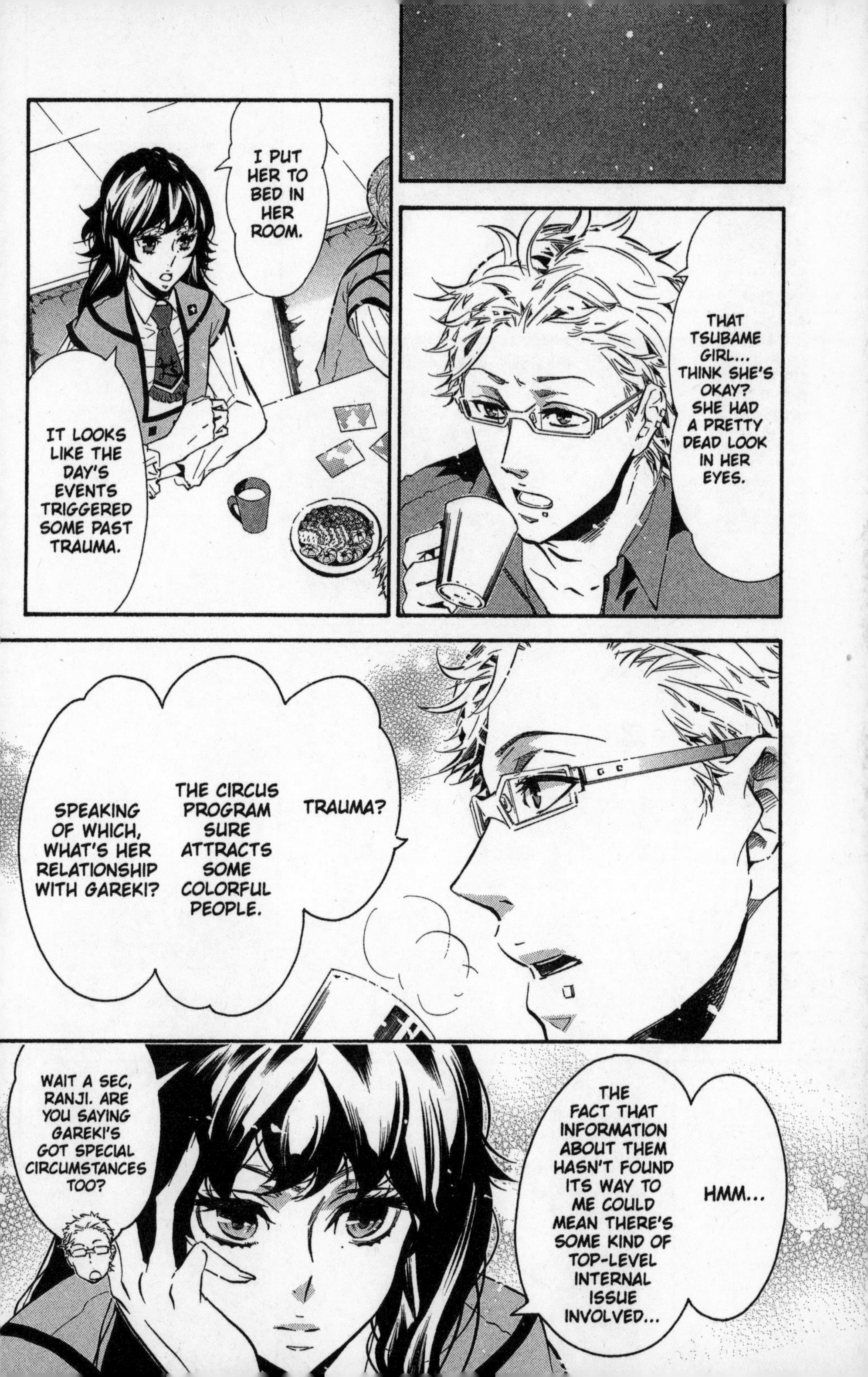
THAT TSUBAME GIRL... THINK SHE'S OKAY? SHE HAD A PRETTY DEAD LOOK IN HER EYES.
I PUT HER TO BED IN HER ROOM.
IT LOOKS LIKE THE DAY'S EVENTS TRIGGERED SOME PAST TRAUMA.
TRAUMA?
THE CIRCUS PROGRAM SURE ATTRACTS SOME COLORFUL PEOPLE.
SPEAKING OF WHICH, WHAT'S HER RELATIONSHIP WITH GAREKI?
HMM...
THE FACT THAT INFORMATION ABOUT THEM HASN'T FOUND ITS WAY TO ME COULD MEAN THERE'S SOME KIND OF TOP-LEVEL INTERNAL ISSUE INVOLVED...
WAIT A SEC, RANJI. ARE YOU SAYING GAREKI'S GOT SPECIAL CIRCUMSTANCES TOO?

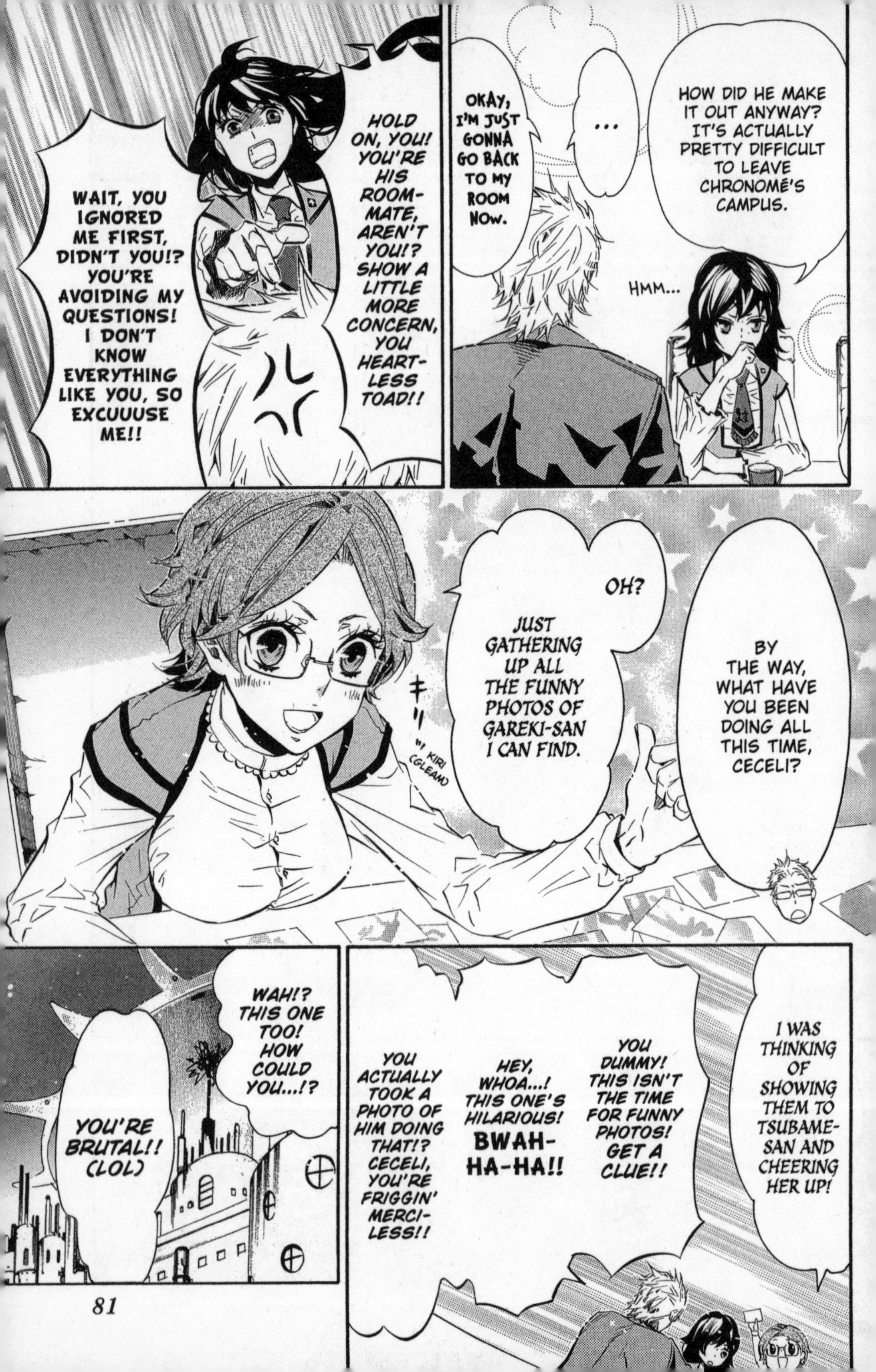
HOW DID HE MAKE IT OUT ANYWAY? IT'S ACTUALLY PRETTY DIFFICULT TO LEAVE CHRONOMÉ'S CAMPUS.
HMM...
...
OKAY, I'M JUST GONNA GO BACK TO MY ROOM NOW.
HOLD ON, YOU! YOU'RE HIS ROOM-MATE, AREN'T YOU!? SHOW A LITTLE MORE CONCERN, YOU HEART-LESS TOAD!!
WAIT, YOU IGNORED ME FIRST, DIDN'T YOU!? YOU'RE AVOIDING MY QUESTIONS! I DON'T KNOW EVERYTHING LIKE YOU, SO EXCUUUSE ME!!
BY THE WAY, WHAT HAVE YOU BEEN DOING ALL THIS TIME, CECELI?
OH?
JUST GATHERING UP ALL THE FUNNY PHOTOS OF GAREKI-SAN I CAN FIND.
キリ
KIRI (GLEAM)
I WAS THINKING OF SHOWING THEM TO TSUBAME-SAN AND CHEERING HER UP!
YOU DUMMY! THIS ISN'T THE TIME FOR FUNNY PHOTOS! GET A CLUE!!
HEY, WHOA...! THIS ONE'S HILARIOUS! BWAH-HA-HA!!
YOU ACTUALLY TOOK A PHOTO OF HIM DOING THAT!? CECELI, YOU'RE FRIGGIN' MERCI-LESS!!
WAH!? THIS ONE TOO! HOW COULD YOU...!?
YOU'RE BRUTAL!! (LOL)

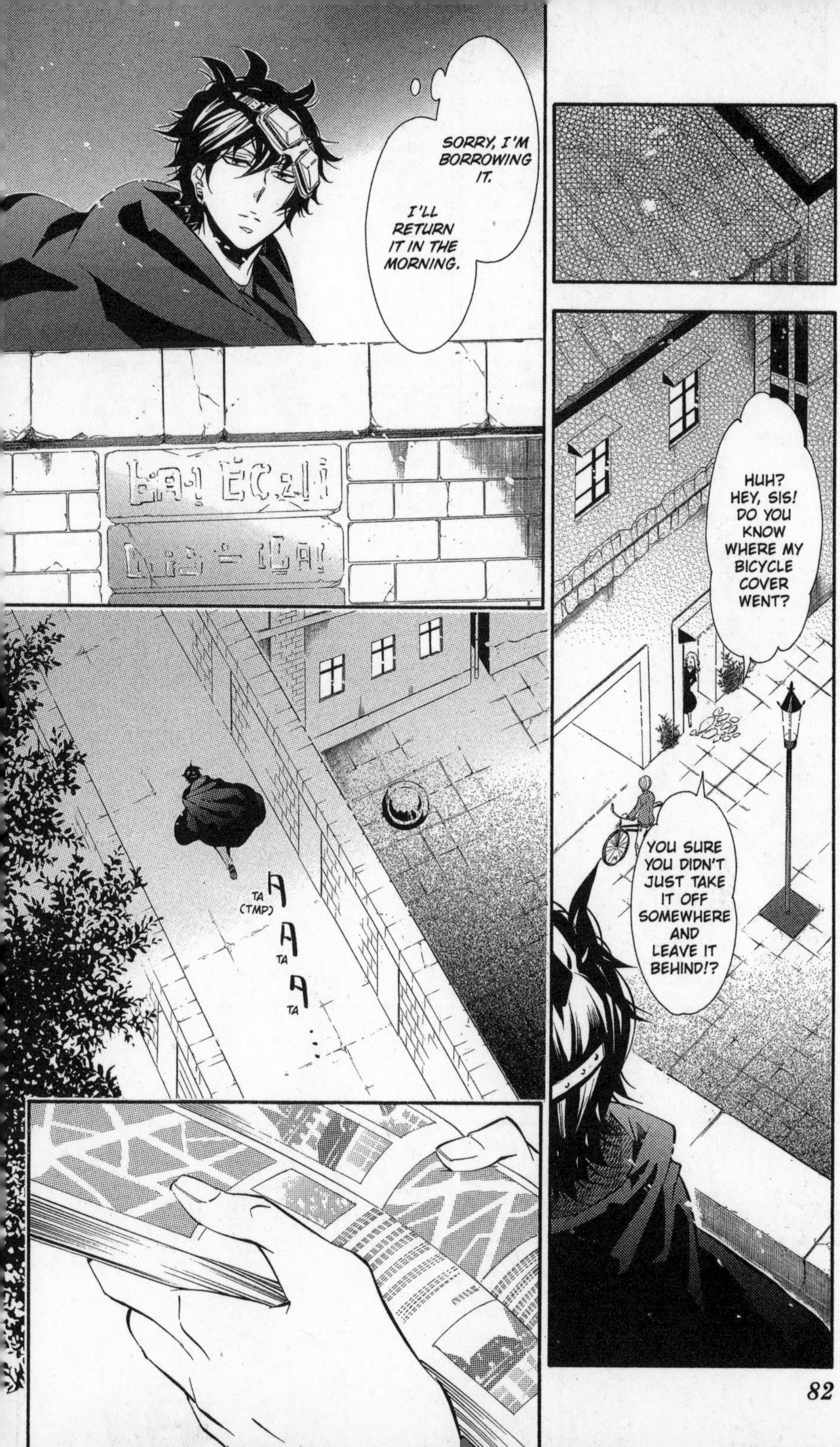
HUH? HEY, SIS! DO YOU KNOW WHERE MY BICYCLE COVER WENT?
YOU SURE YOU DIDN'T JUST TAKE IT OFF SOMEWHERE AND LEAVE IT BEHIND!?
SORRY, I'M BORROWING IT.
I'LL RETURN IT IN THE MORNING.
TA (TMP)
TA
TA

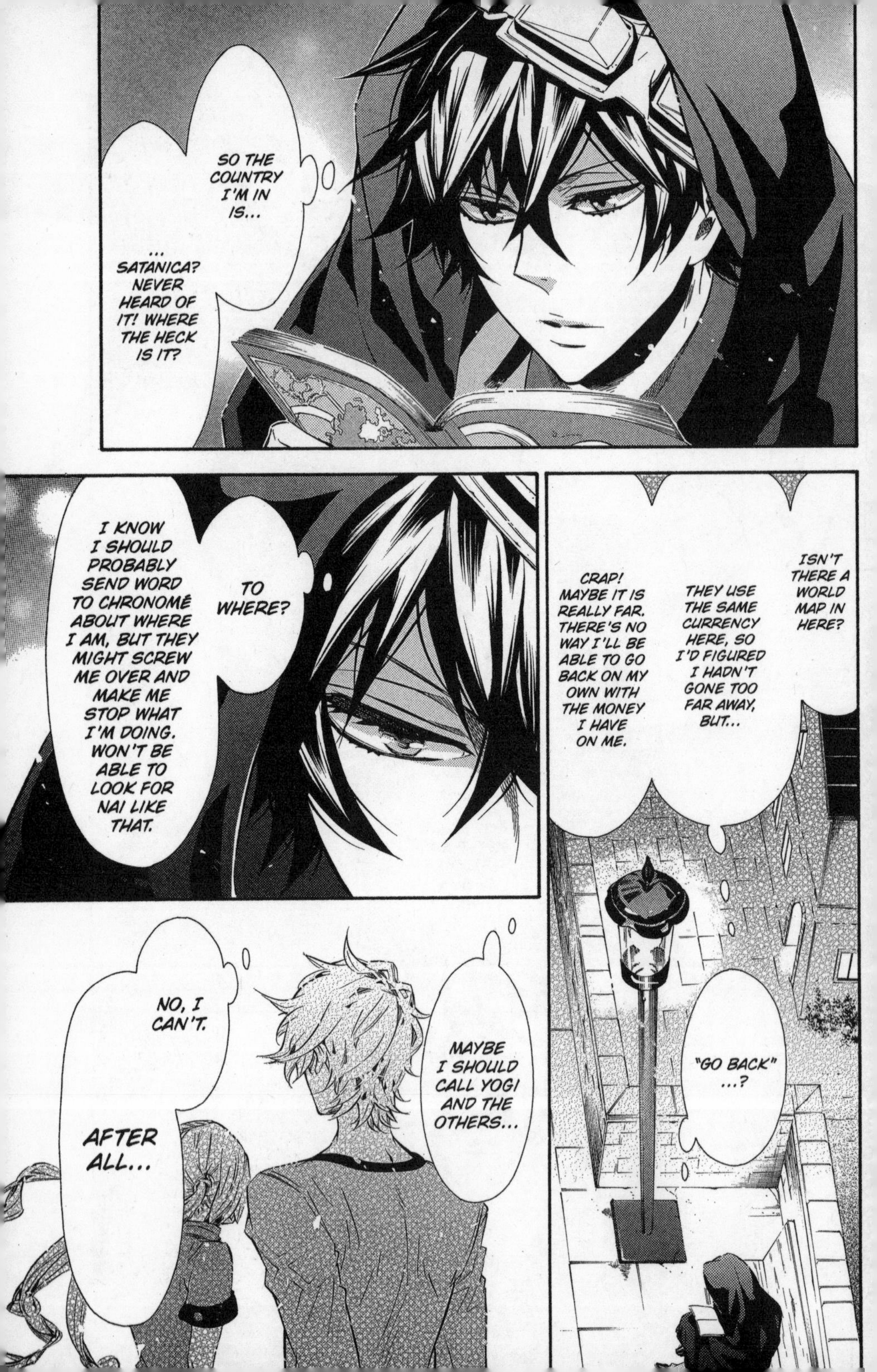
SO THE COUNTRY I'M IN IS...
...SATANICA? NEVER HEARD OF IT! WHERE THE HECK IS IT?
ISN'T THERE A WORLD MAP IN HERE?
THEY USE THE SAME CURRENCY HERE, SO I'D FIGURED I HADN'T GONE TOO FAR AWAY, BUT...
CRAP! MAYBE IT IS REALLY FAR. THERE'S NO WAY I'LL BE ABLE TO GO BACK ON MY OWN WITH THE MONEY I HAVE ON ME.
"GO BACK" ...?
TO WHERE?
I KNOW I SHOULD PROBABLY SEND WORD TO CHRONOMÉ ABOUT WHERE I AM, BUT THEY MIGHT SCREW ME OVER AND MAKE ME STOP WHAT I'M DOING. WON'T BE ABLE TO LOOK FOR NAI LIKE THAT.
MAYBE I SHOULD CALL YOGI AND THE OTHERS...
NO, I CAN'T.
AFTER ALL...

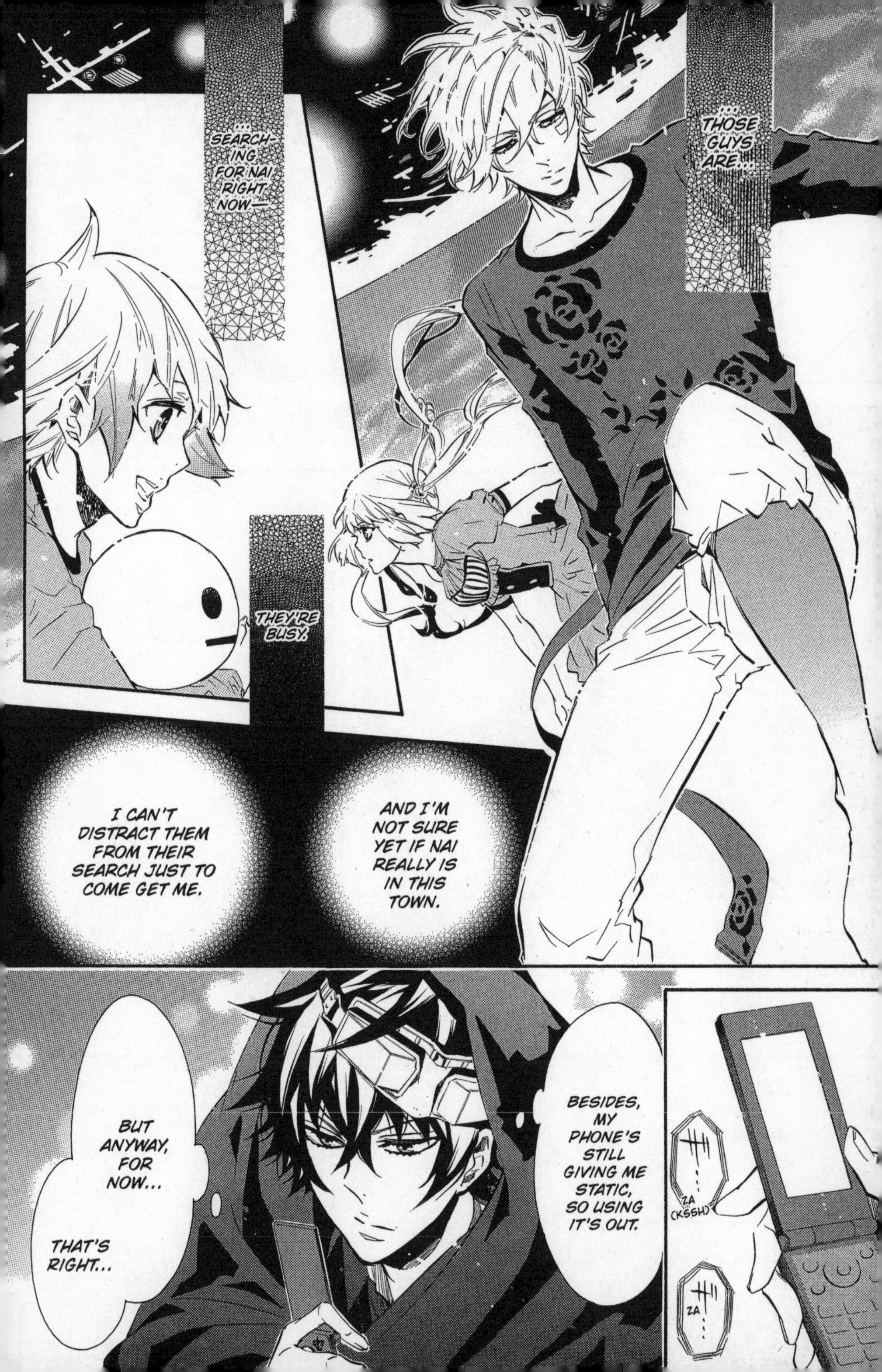
...THOSE GUYS ARE...
...SEARCHING FOR NAI RIGHT NOW—
THEY'RE BUSY.
I CAN'T DISTRACT THEM FROM THEIR SEARCH JUST TO COME GET ME.
AND I'M NOT SURE YET IF NAI REALLY IS IN THIS TOWN.
ZA (KSSH)
ZA
BESIDES, MY PHONE'S STILL GIVING ME STATIC, SO USING IT'S OUT.
BUT ANYWAY, FOR NOW...
THAT'S RIGHT...

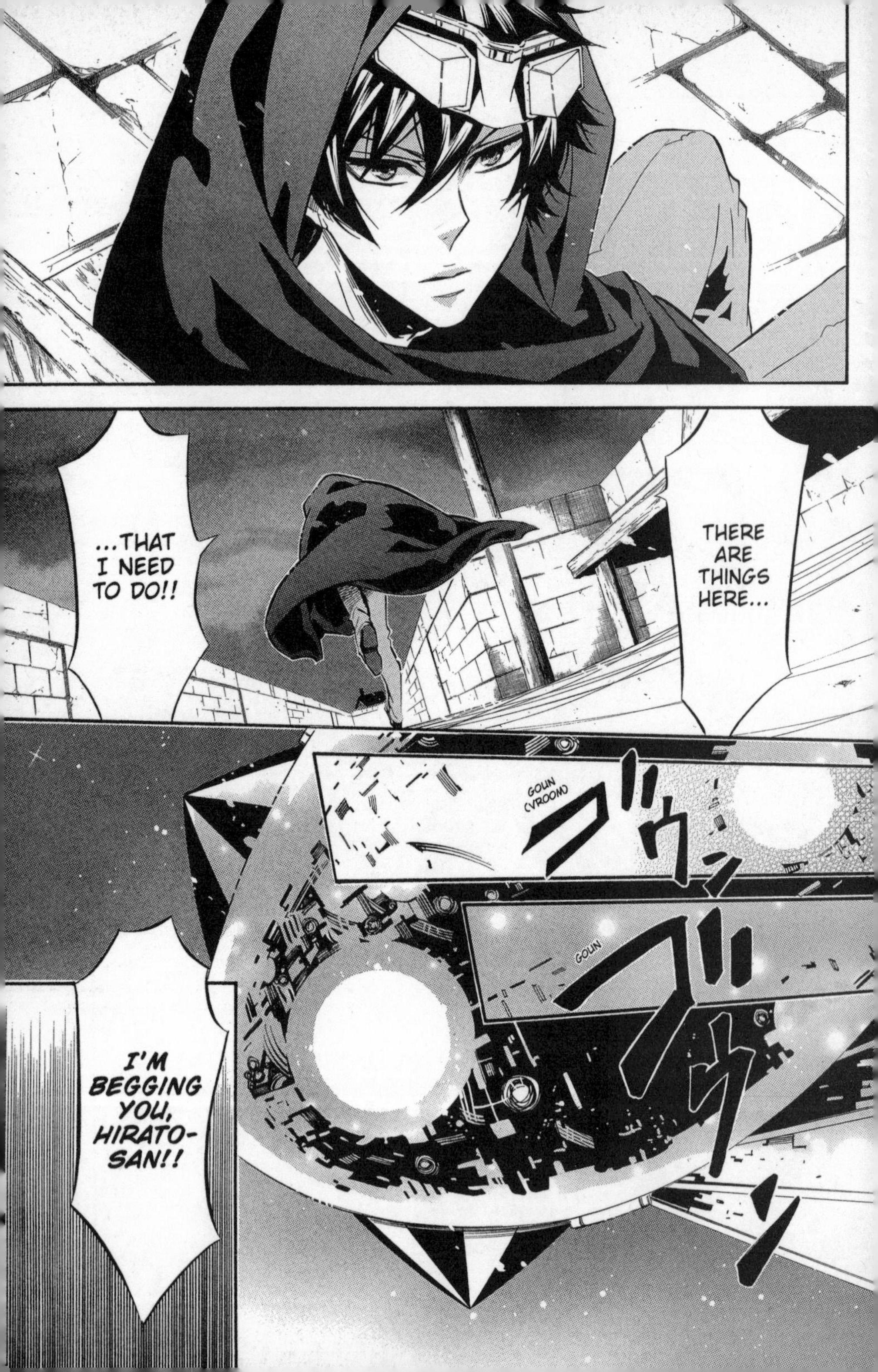
THERE ARE THINGS HERE...
...THAT I NEED TO DO!!
ゴウン
GOUN (VROOM)
ゴウン
GOUN
I'M BEGGING YOU, HIRATO-SAN!!

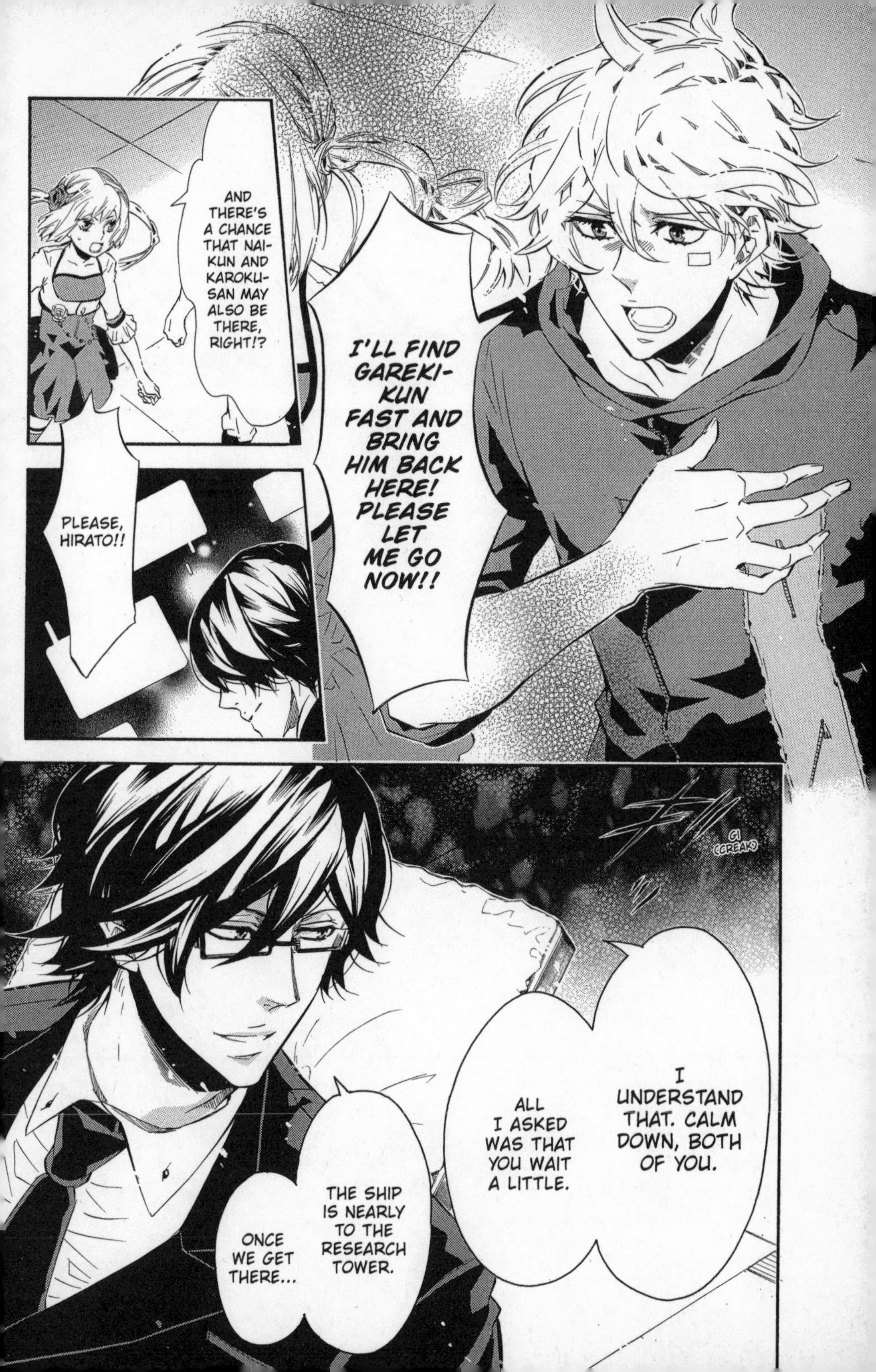
I'LL FIND GAREKI-KUN FAST AND BRING HIM BACK HERE! PLEASE LET ME GO NOW!!
AND THERE'S A CHANCE THAT NAI-KUN AND KAROKU-SAN MAY ALSO BE THERE, RIGHT!?
PLEASE, HIRATO!!
GI (CREAK)
I UNDERSTAND THAT. CALM DOWN, BOTH OF YOU.
ALL I ASKED WAS THAT YOU WAIT A LITTLE.
THE SHIP IS NEARLY TO THE RESEARCH TOWER.
ONCE WE GET THERE...

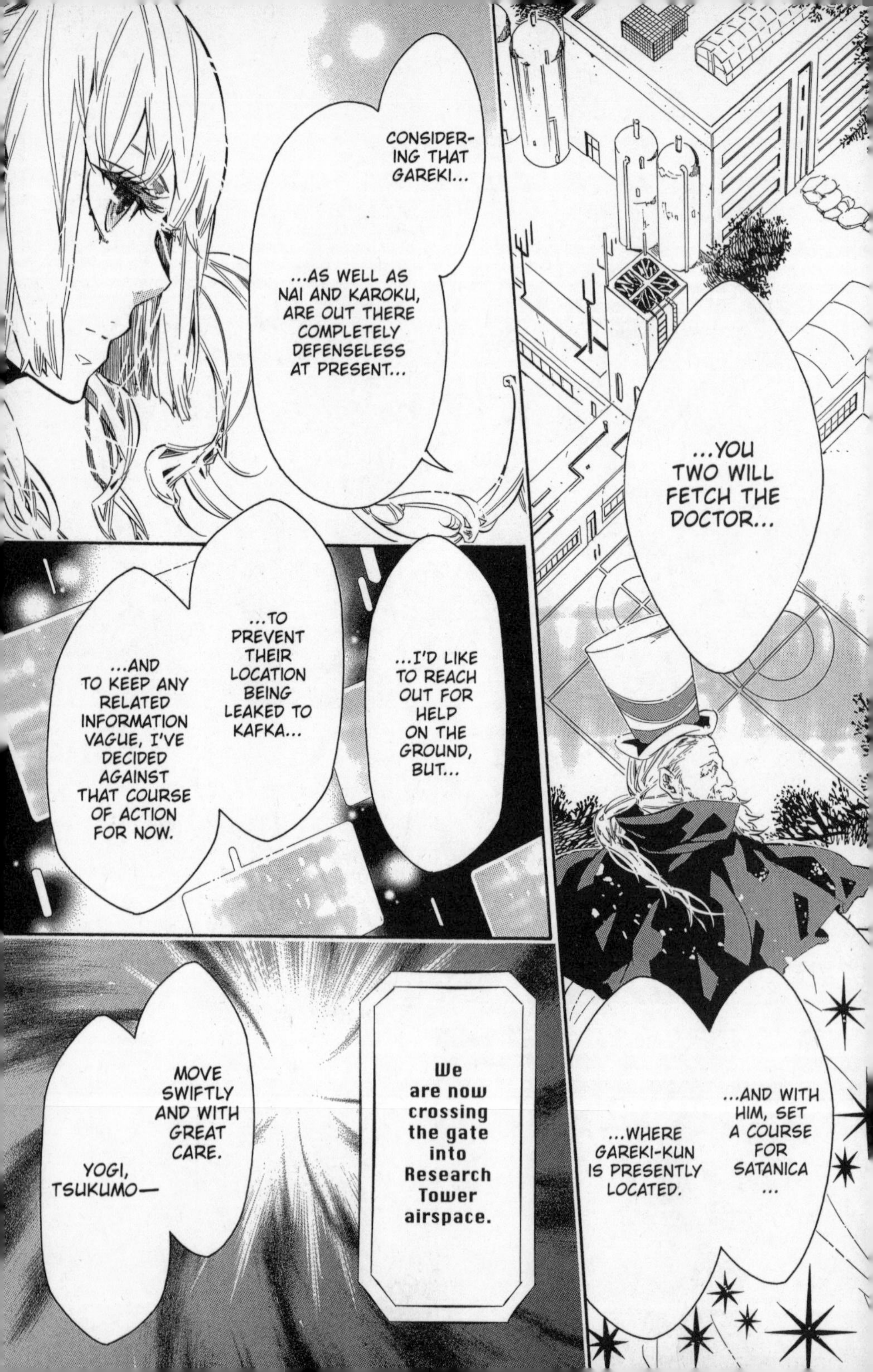
...YOU TWO WILL FETCH THE DOCTOR...
...AND WITH HIM, SET A COURSE FOR SATANICA ...
...WHERE GAREKI-KUN IS PRESENTLY LOCATED.
CONSIDER-ING THAT GAREKI...
...AS WELL AS NAI AND KAROKU, ARE OUT THERE COMPLETELY DEFENSELESS AT PRESENT...
...I'D LIKE TO REACH OUT FOR HELP ON THE GROUND, BUT...
...TO PREVENT THEIR LOCATION BEING LEAKED TO KAFKA...
...AND TO KEEP ANY RELATED INFORMATION VAGUE, I'VE DECIDED AGAINST THAT COURSE OF ACTION FOR NOW.
We are now crossing the gate into Research Tower airspace.
MOVE SWIFTLY AND WITH GREAT CARE.
YOGI, TSUKUMO—

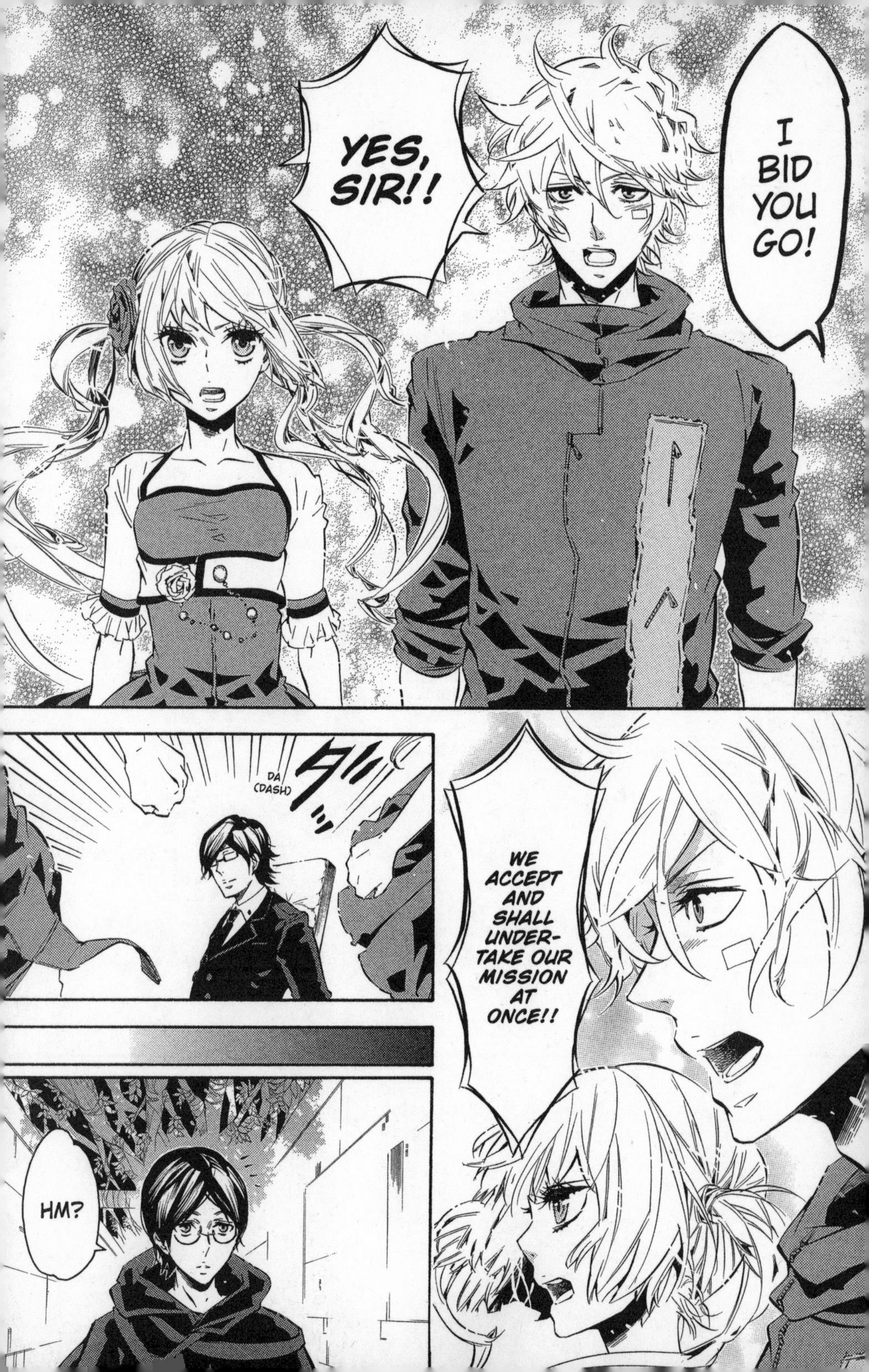
I BID YOU GO!
YES, SIR!!
WE ACCEPT AND SHALL UNDER-TAKE OUR MISSION AT ONCE!!
DA (DASH)
HM?

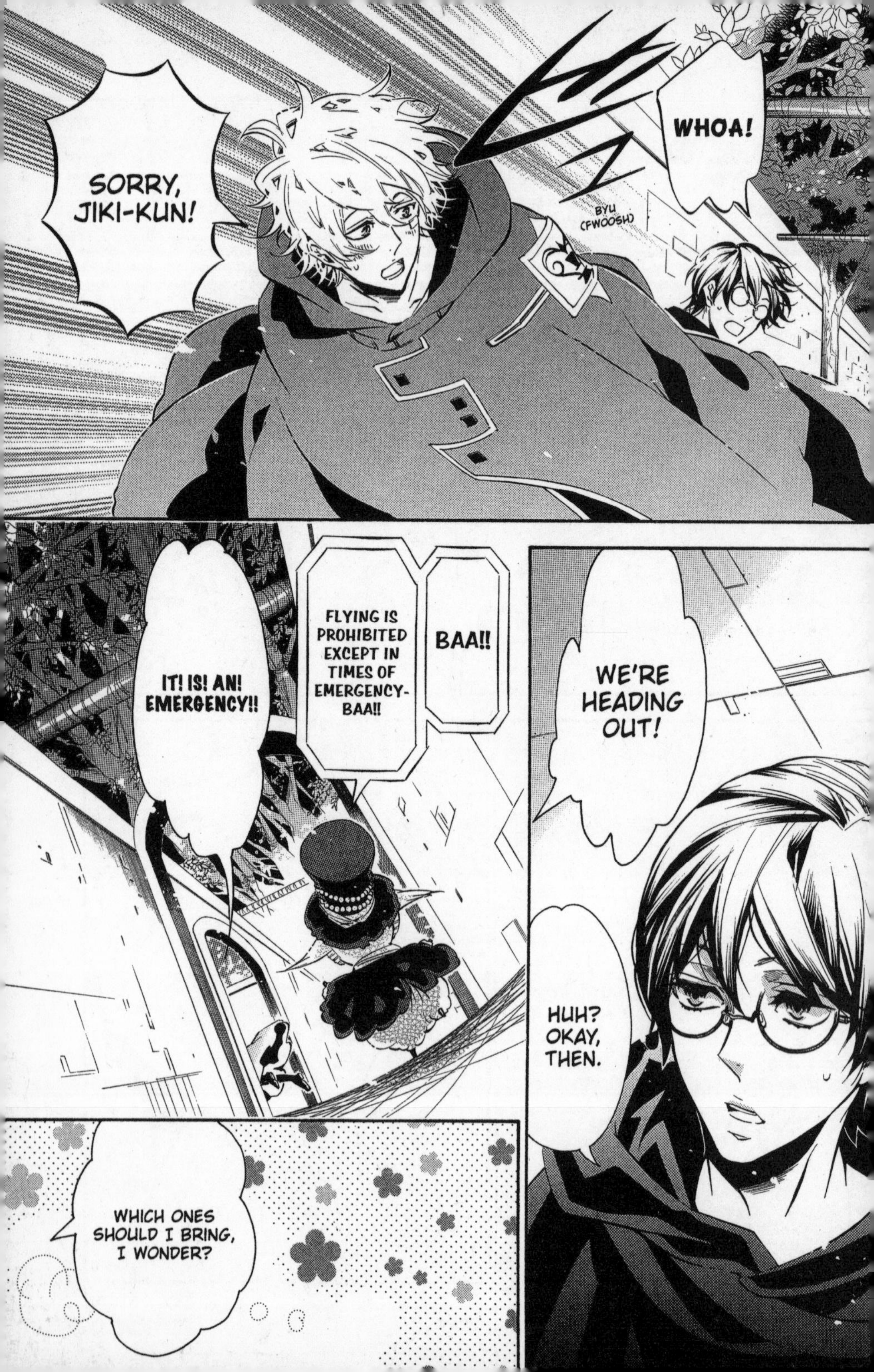
WHOA!
BYU (FWOOSH)
SORRY, JIKI-KUN!
WE'RE HEADING OUT!
HUH? OKAY, THEN.
BAA!!
FLYING IS PROHIBITED EXCEPT IN TIMES OF EMERGENCY-BAA!!
IT! IS! AN! EMERGENCY!!
WHICH ONES SHOULD I BRING, I WONDER?

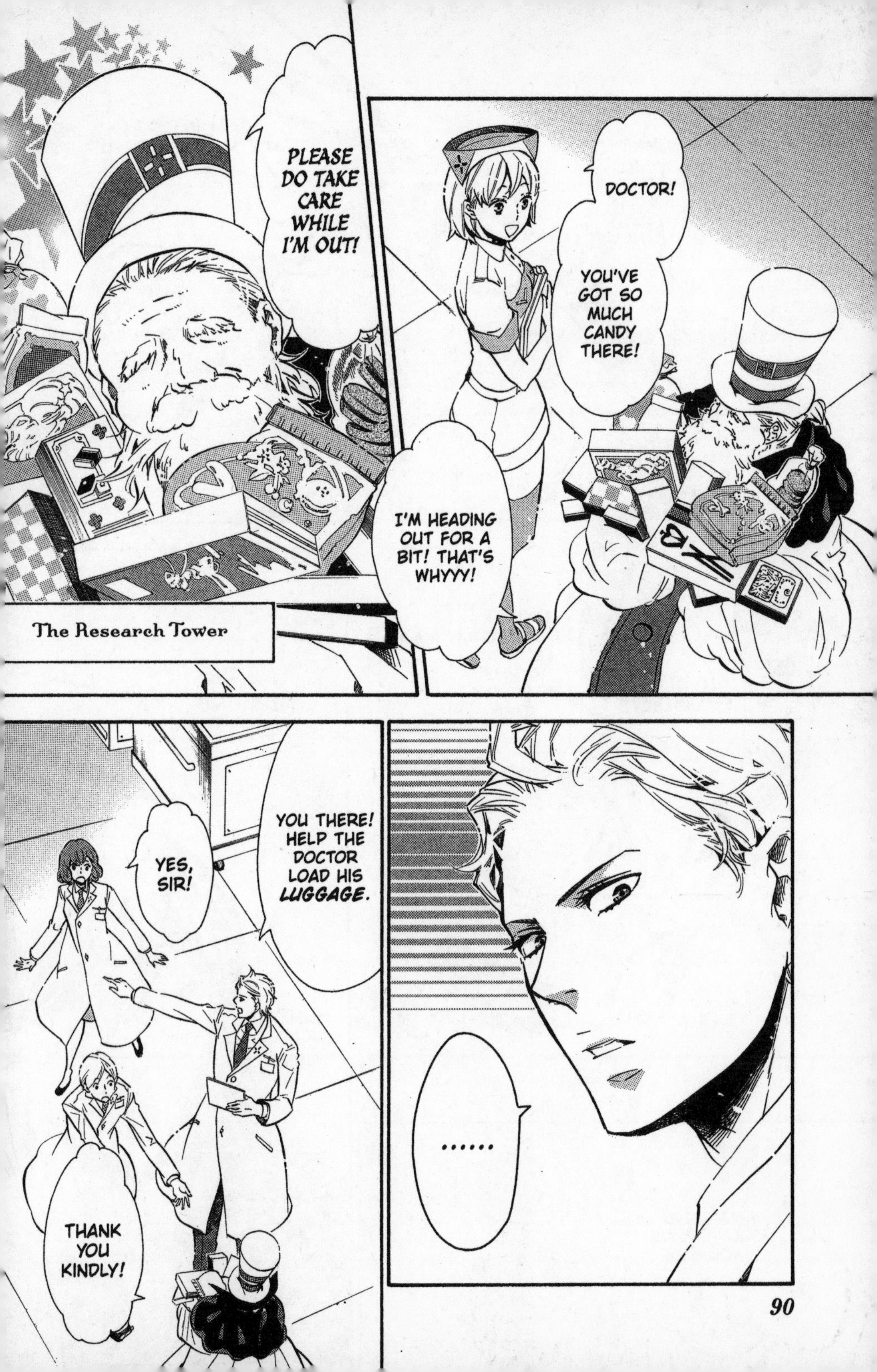
DOCTOR!
YOU'VE GOT SO MUCH CANDY THERE!
I'M HEADING OUT FOR A BIT! THAT'S WHYYY!
PLEASE DO TAKE CARE WHILE I'M OUT!
The Research Tower
......
YOU THERE! HELP THE DOCTOR LOAD HIS LUGGAGE.
YES, SIR!
THANK YOU KINDLY!

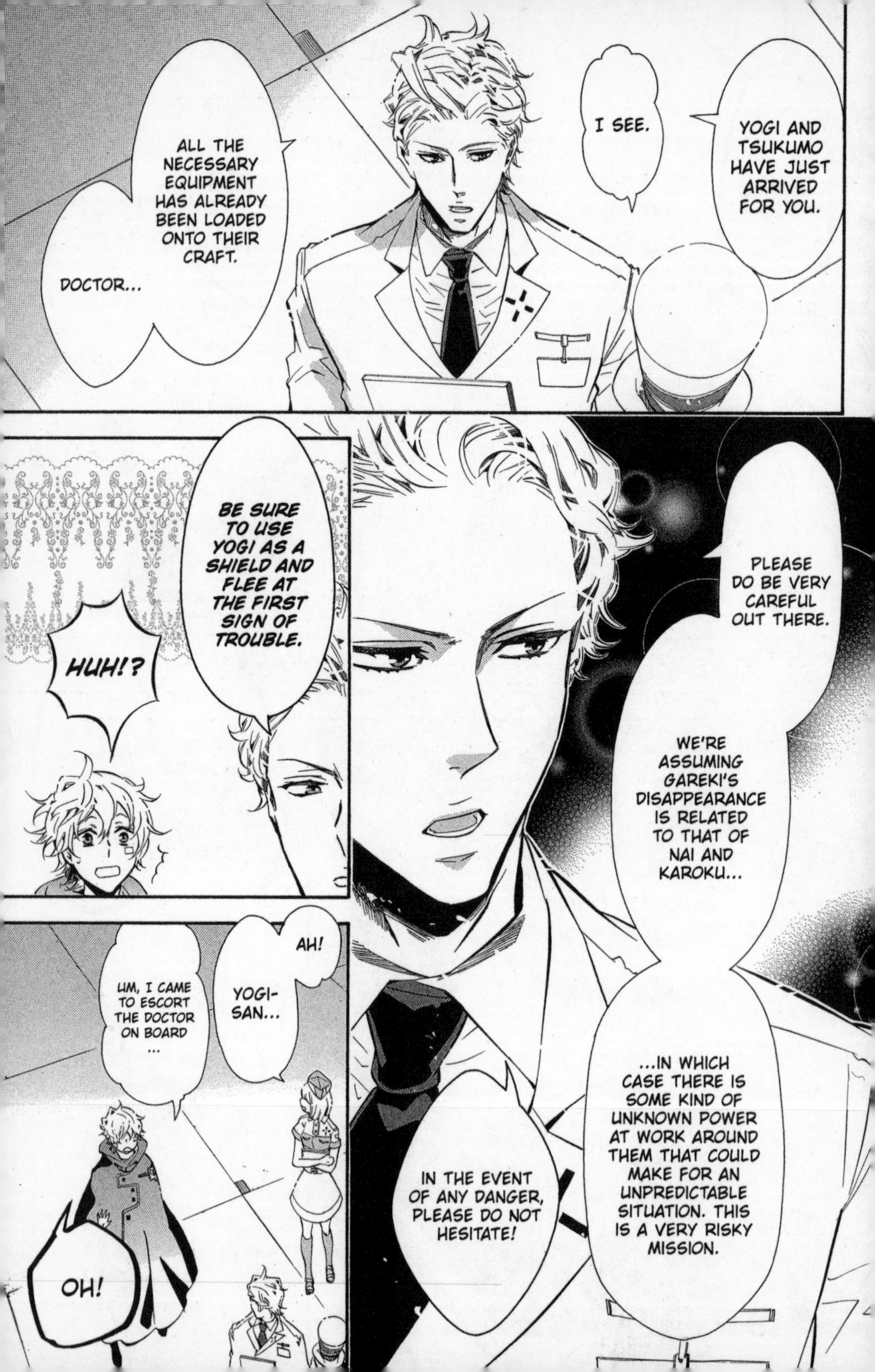
YOGI AND TSUKUMO HAVE JUST ARRIVED FOR YOU.
I SEE.
ALL THE NECESSARY EQUIPMENT HAS ALREADY BEEN LOADED ONTO THEIR CRAFT.
DOCTOR...
PLEASE DO BE VERY CAREFUL OUT THERE.
WE'RE ASSUMING GAREKI'S DISAPPEARANCE IS RELATED TO THAT OF NAI AND KAROKU...
...IN WHICH CASE THERE IS SOME KIND OF UNKNOWN POWER AT WORK AROUND THEM THAT COULD MAKE FOR AN UNPREDICTABLE SITUATION. THIS IS A VERY RISKY MISSION.
IN THE EVENT OF ANY DANGER, PLEASE DO NOT HESITATE!
BE SURE TO USE YOGI AS A SHIELD AND FLEE AT THE FIRST SIGN OF TROUBLE.
HUH!?
AH!
YOGI-SAN...
UM, I CAME TO ESCORT THE DOCTOR ON BOARD ...
OH!

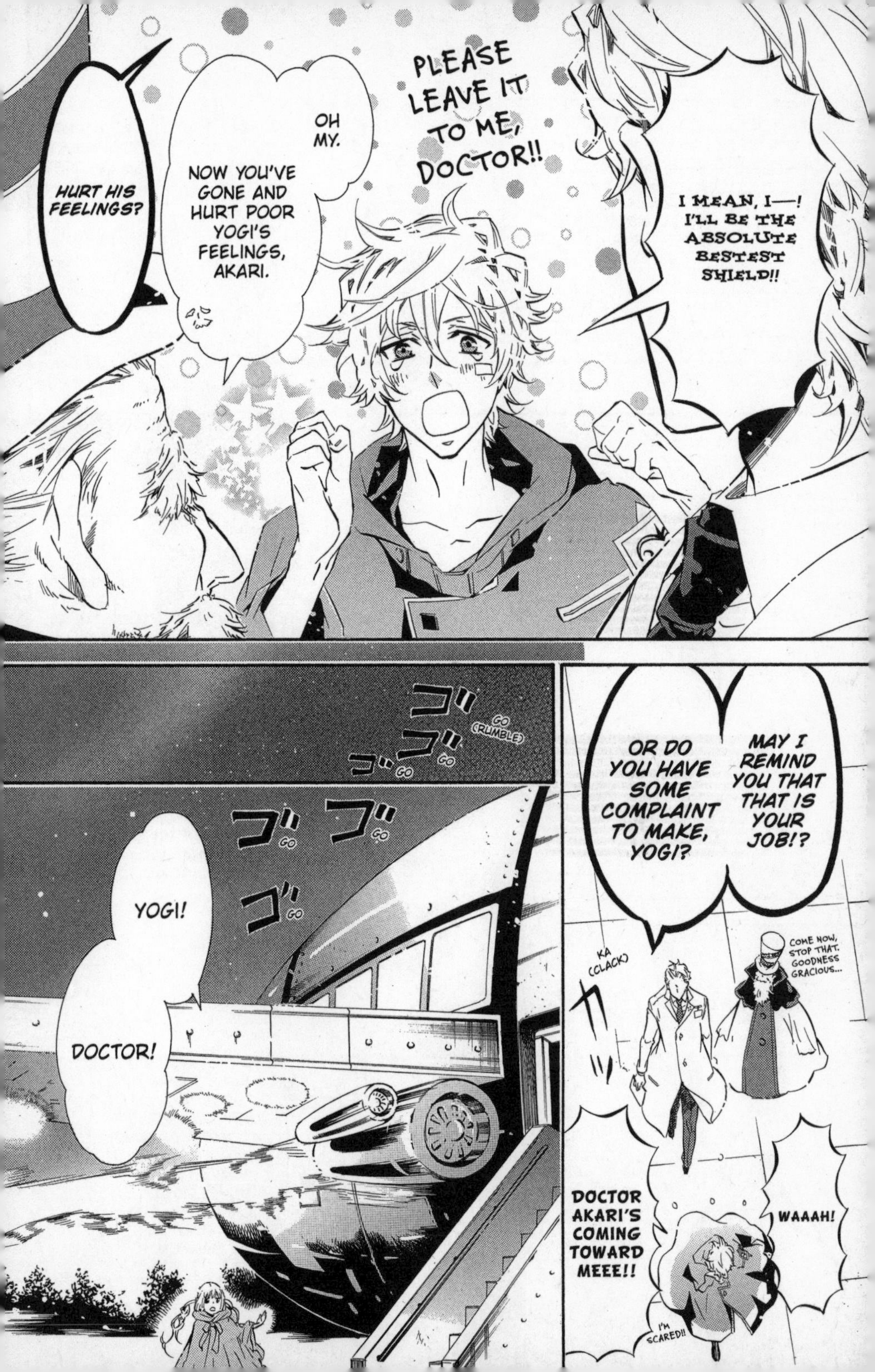
I MEAN, I—! I'LL BE THE ABSOLUTE BESTEST SHIELD!!
PLEASE LEAVE IT TO ME, DOCTOR!!
OH MY.
NOW YOU'VE GONE AND HURT POOR YOGI'S FEELINGS, AKARI.
HURT HIS FEELINGS?
MAY I REMIND YOU THAT THAT IS YOUR JOB!?
OR DO YOU HAVE SOME COMPLAINT TO MAKE, YOGI?
COME NOW, STOP THAT. GOODNESS GRACIOUS...
KA (CLACK)
WAAAH!
DOCTOR AKARI'S COMING TOWARD MEEE!!
I'M SCARED!!
GO (RUMBLE)
GO
GO
GO
GO
GO
YOGI!
DOCTOR!

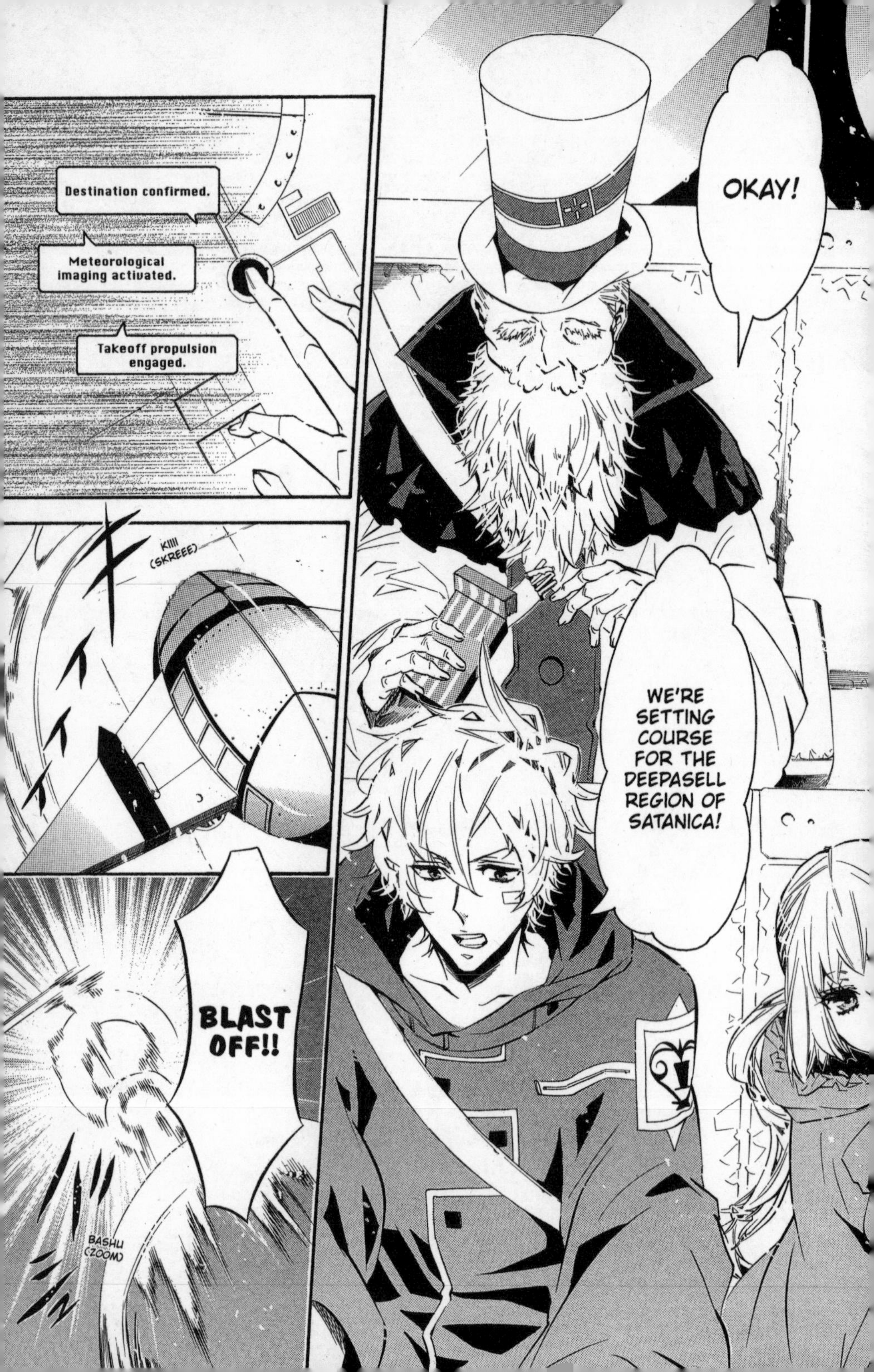
OKAY!
WE'RE SETTING COURSE FOR THE DEEPASELL REGION OF SATANICA!
Destination confirmed.
Meteorological imaging activated.
Takeoff propulsion engaged.
KIIII (SKREEE)
BLAST OFF!!
BASHU (ZOOM)

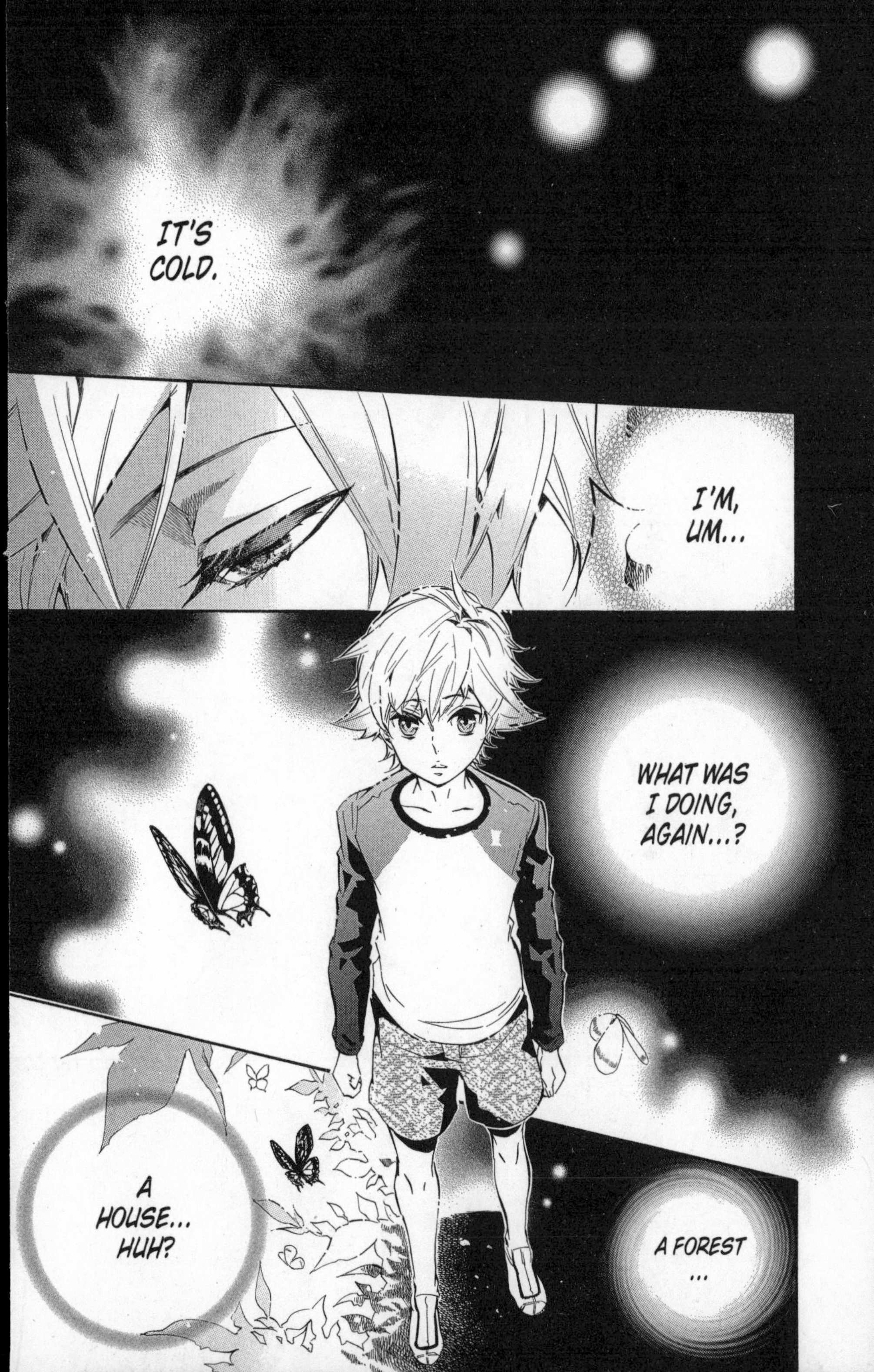
IT'S COLD.
I'M, UM...
WHAT WAS I DOING, AGAIN...?
A FOREST ...
A HOUSE... HUH?

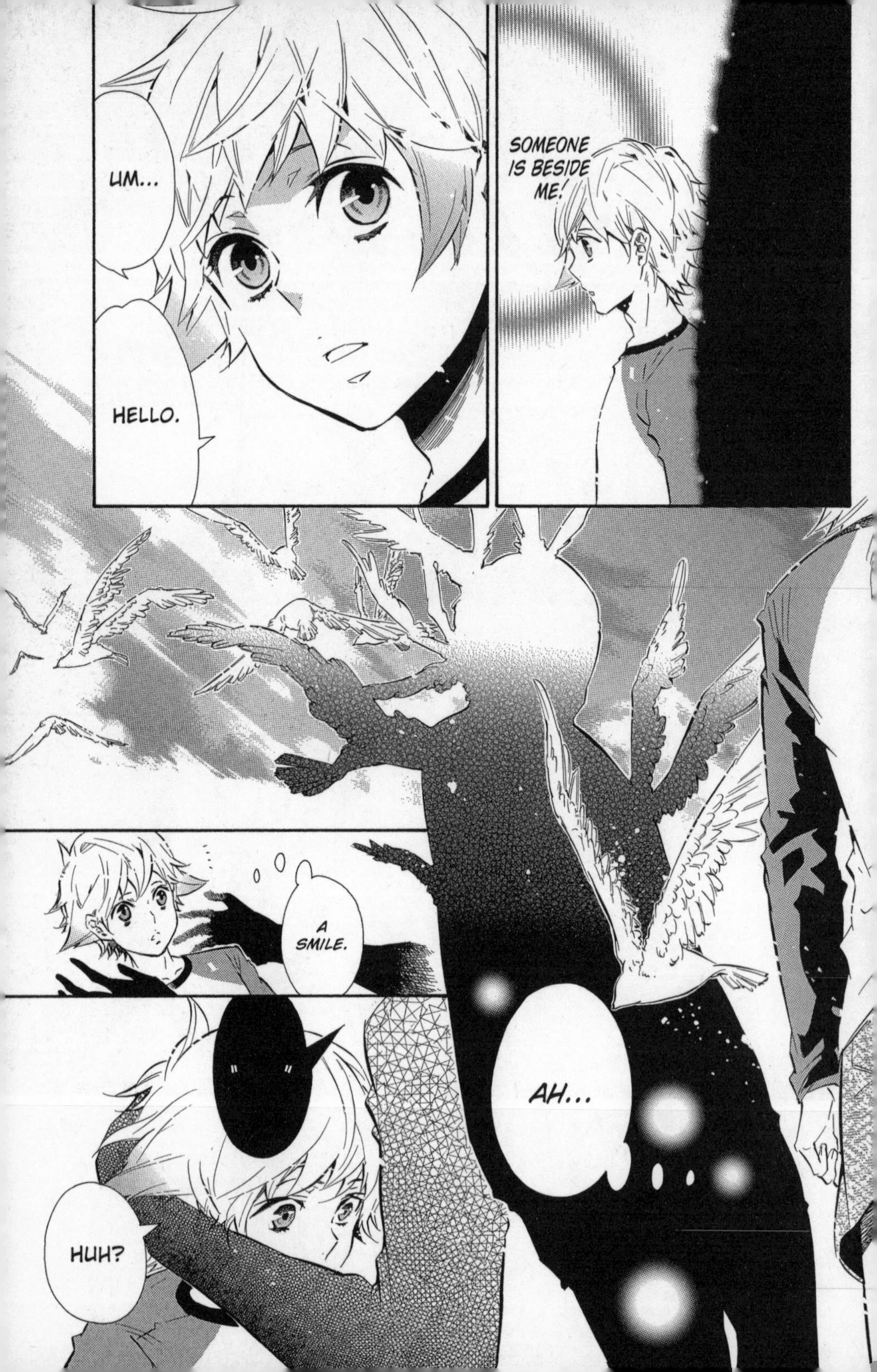
SOMEONE IS BESIDE ME!
UM...
HELLO.
AH...
A SMILE.
HUH?

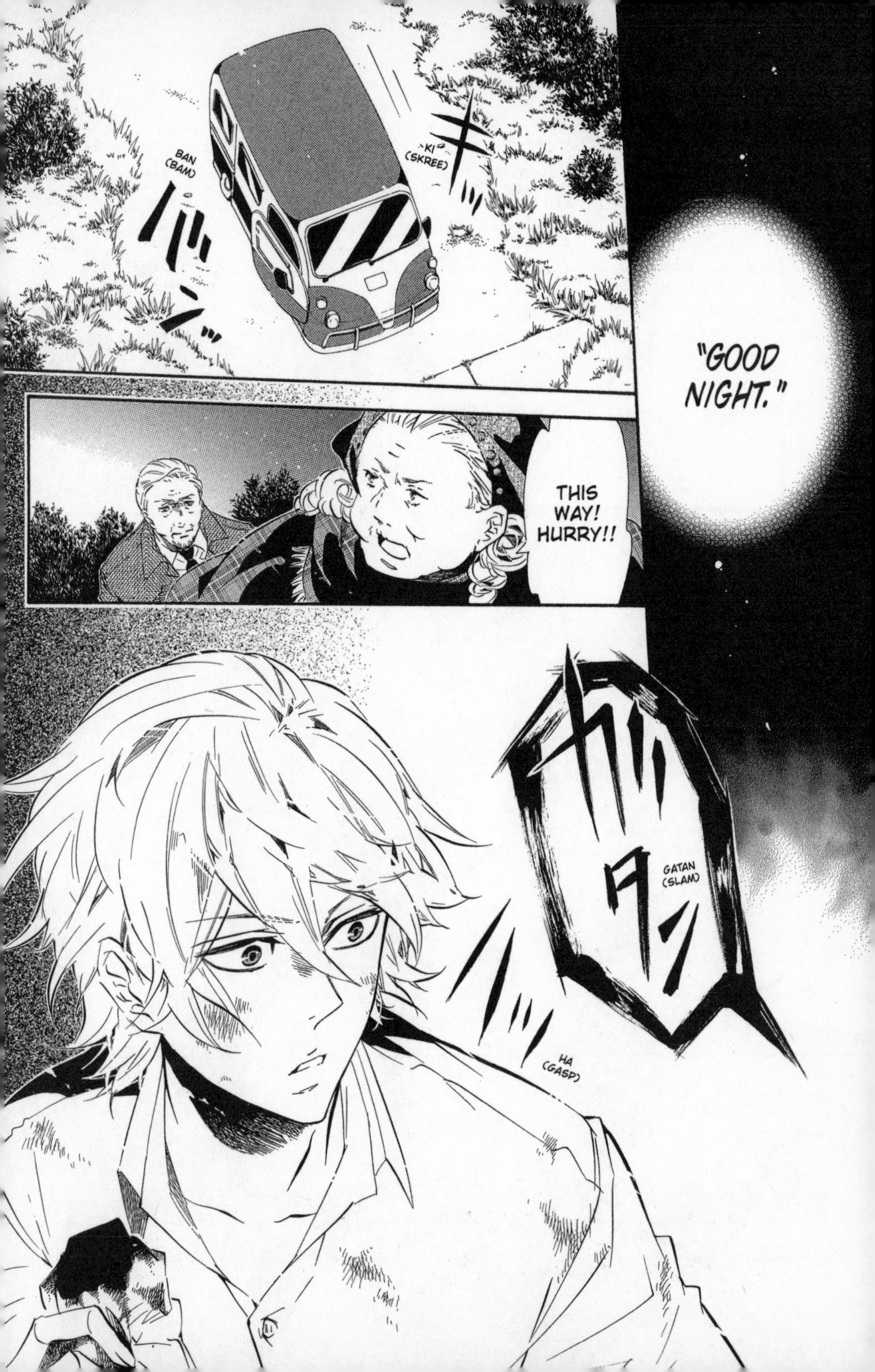
"GOOD NIGHT."
KI (SKREE)
BAN (BAM)
THIS WAY! HURRY!!
GATAN (SLAM)
HA (GASP)

KARNEVAL

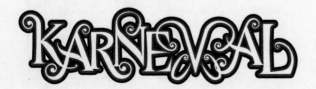

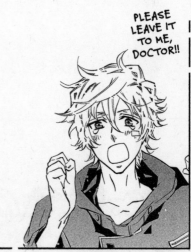

PLEASE
LEAVE IT
TO ME,
DOCTOR!!

KARNEVAL

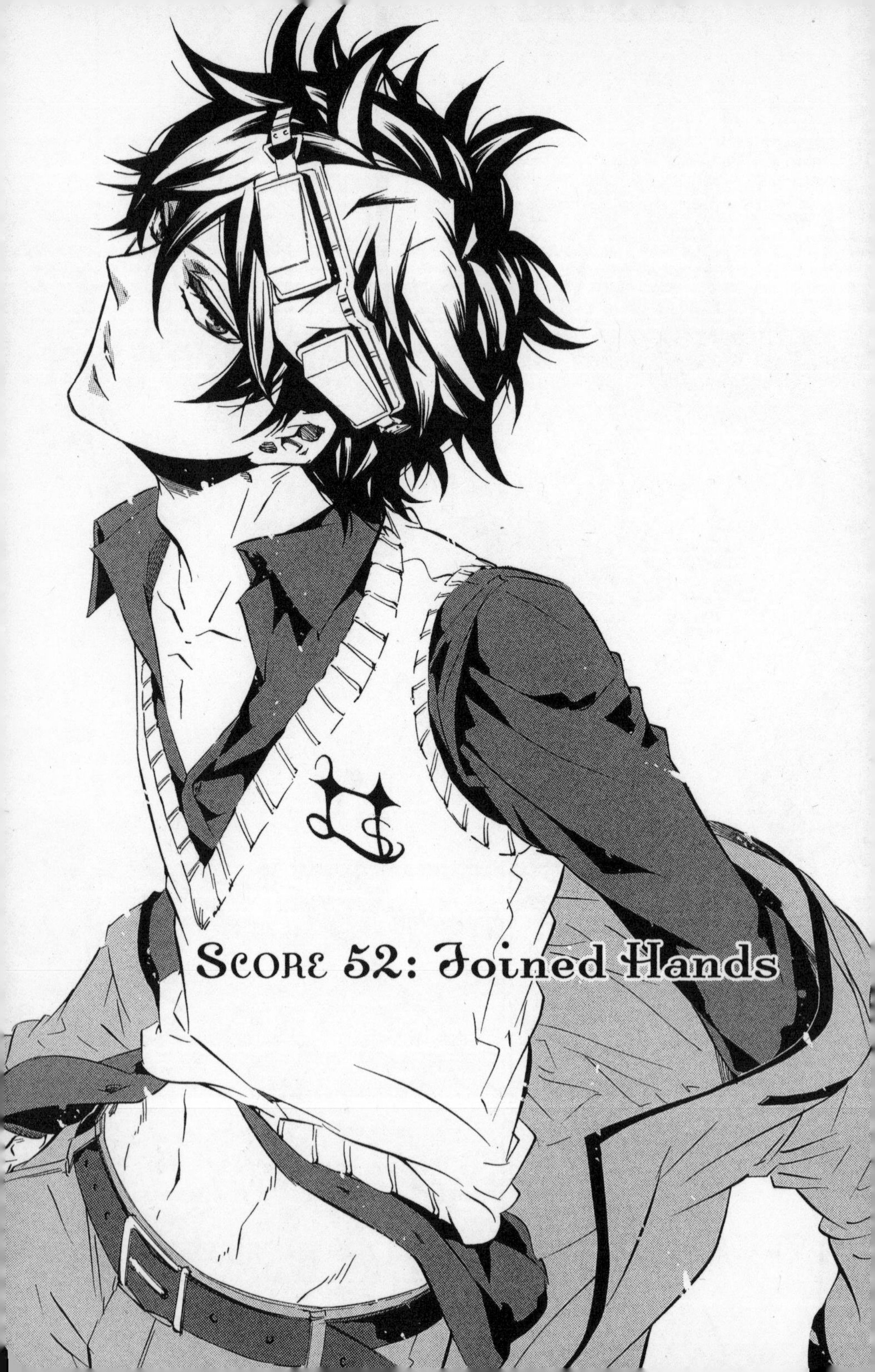
Score 52: Joined Hands

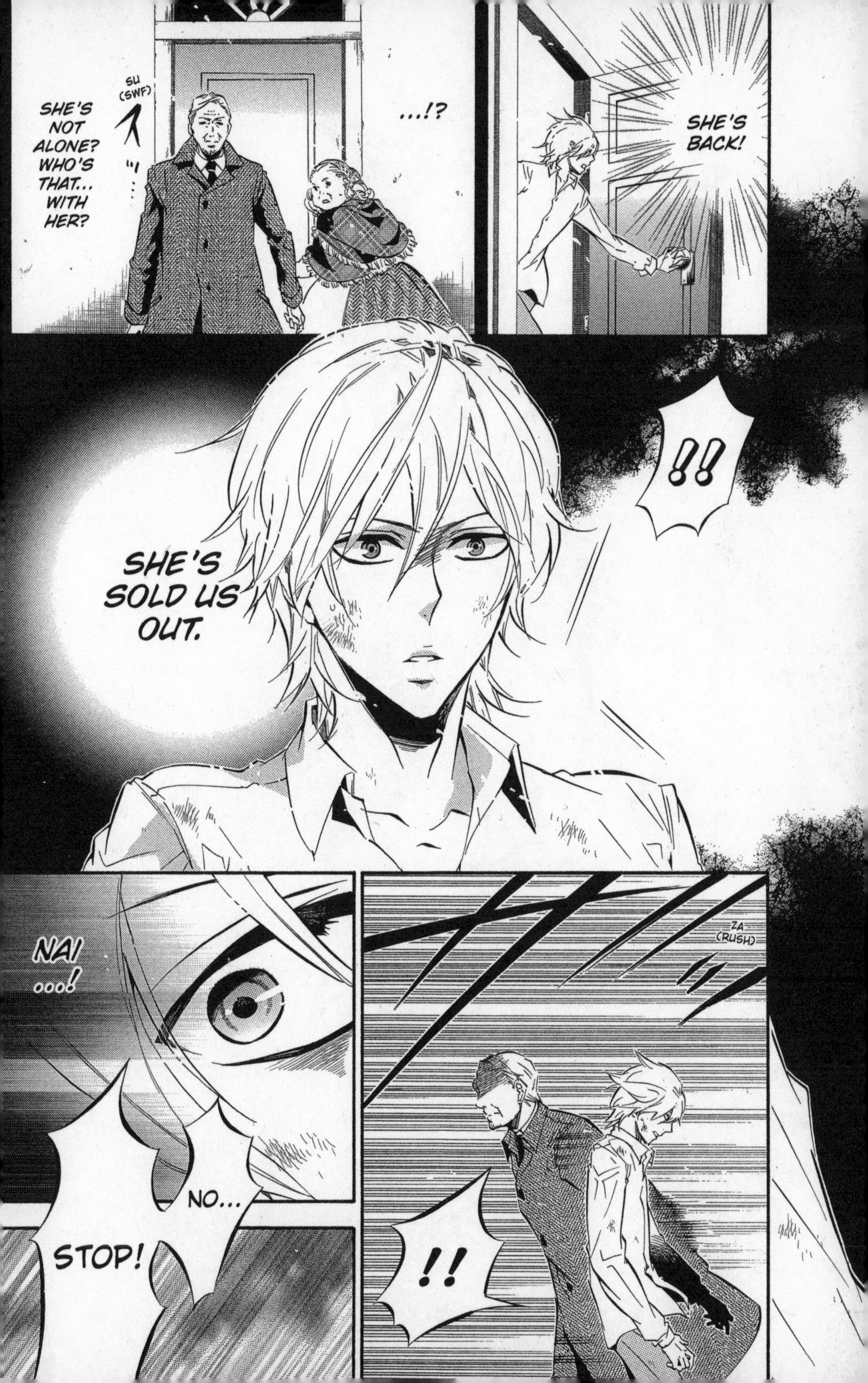
SHE'S BACK!
...!?
SU (SWF)
SHE'S NOT ALONE? WHO'S THAT... WITH HER?
!!
SHE'S SOLD US OUT.
ZA (RUSH)
!!
NAI ooo!
NO...
STOP!

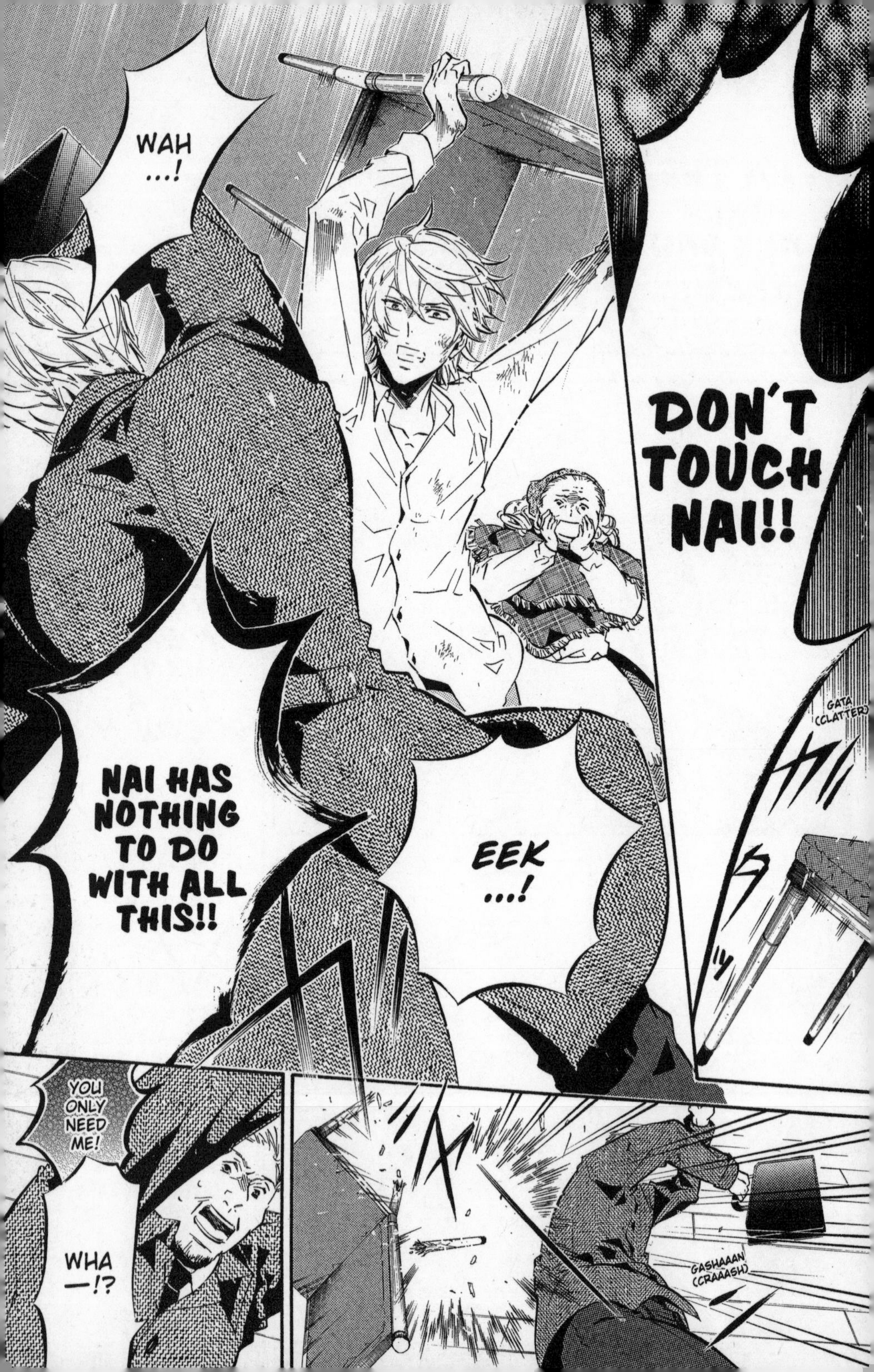
DON'T TOUCH NAI!!
GATA (CLATTER)
WAH ...!
NAI HAS NOTHING TO DO WITH ALL THIS!!
EEK ...!
GASHAAAN (CRAAASH)
YOU ONLY NEED ME!
WHA—!?

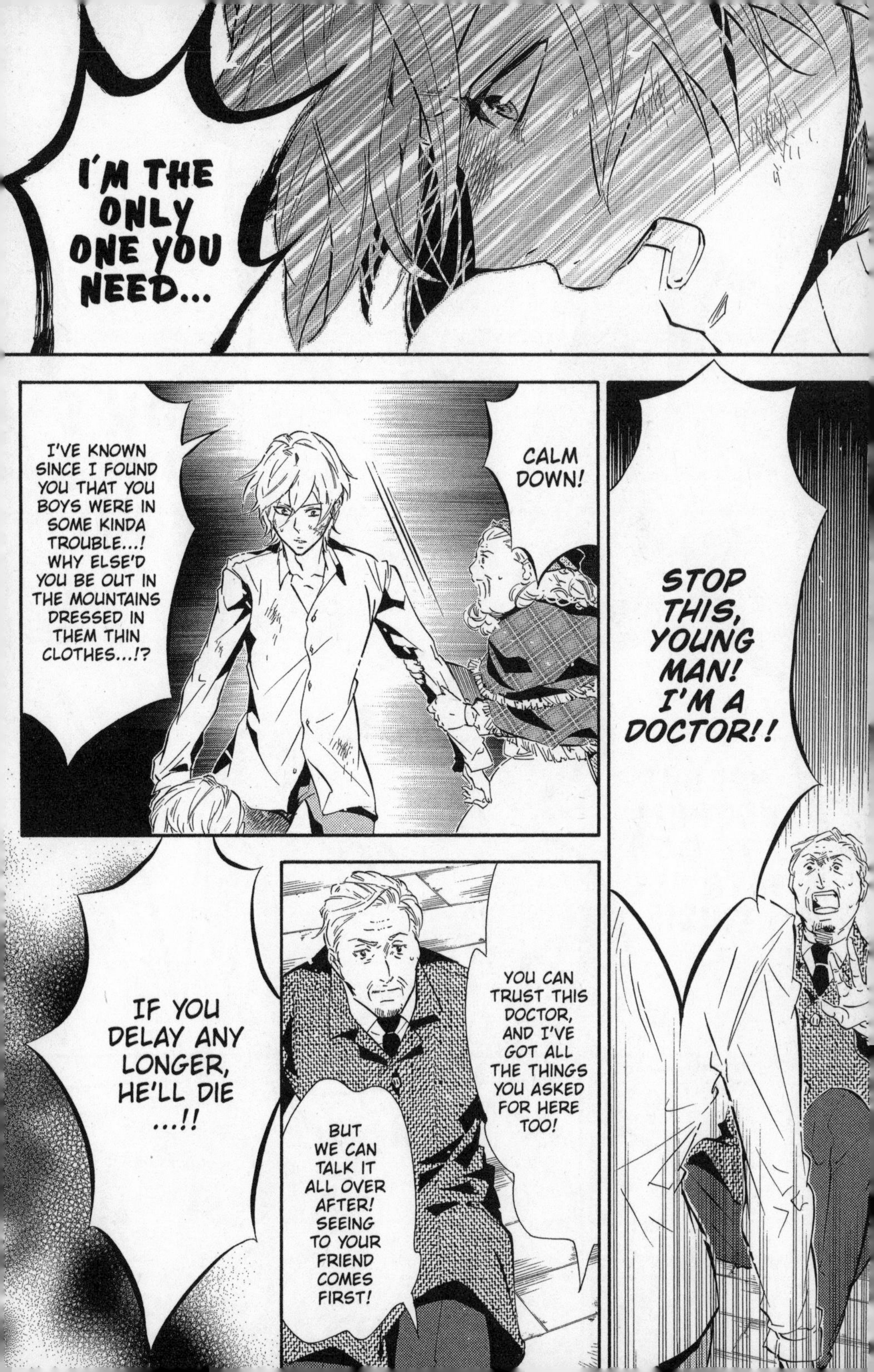
I'M THE ONLY ONE YOU NEED...
STOP THIS, YOUNG MAN! I'M A DOCTOR!!
CALM DOWN!
I'VE KNOWN SINCE I FOUND YOU THAT YOU BOYS WERE IN SOME KINDA TROUBLE...! WHY ELSE'D YOU BE OUT IN THE MOUNTAINS DRESSED IN THEM THIN CLOTHES...!?
YOU CAN TRUST THIS DOCTOR, AND I'VE GOT ALL THE THINGS YOU ASKED FOR HERE TOO!
BUT WE CAN TALK IT ALL OVER AFTER! SEEING TO YOUR FRIEND COMES FIRST!
IF YOU DELAY ANY LONGER, HE'LL DIE ...!!

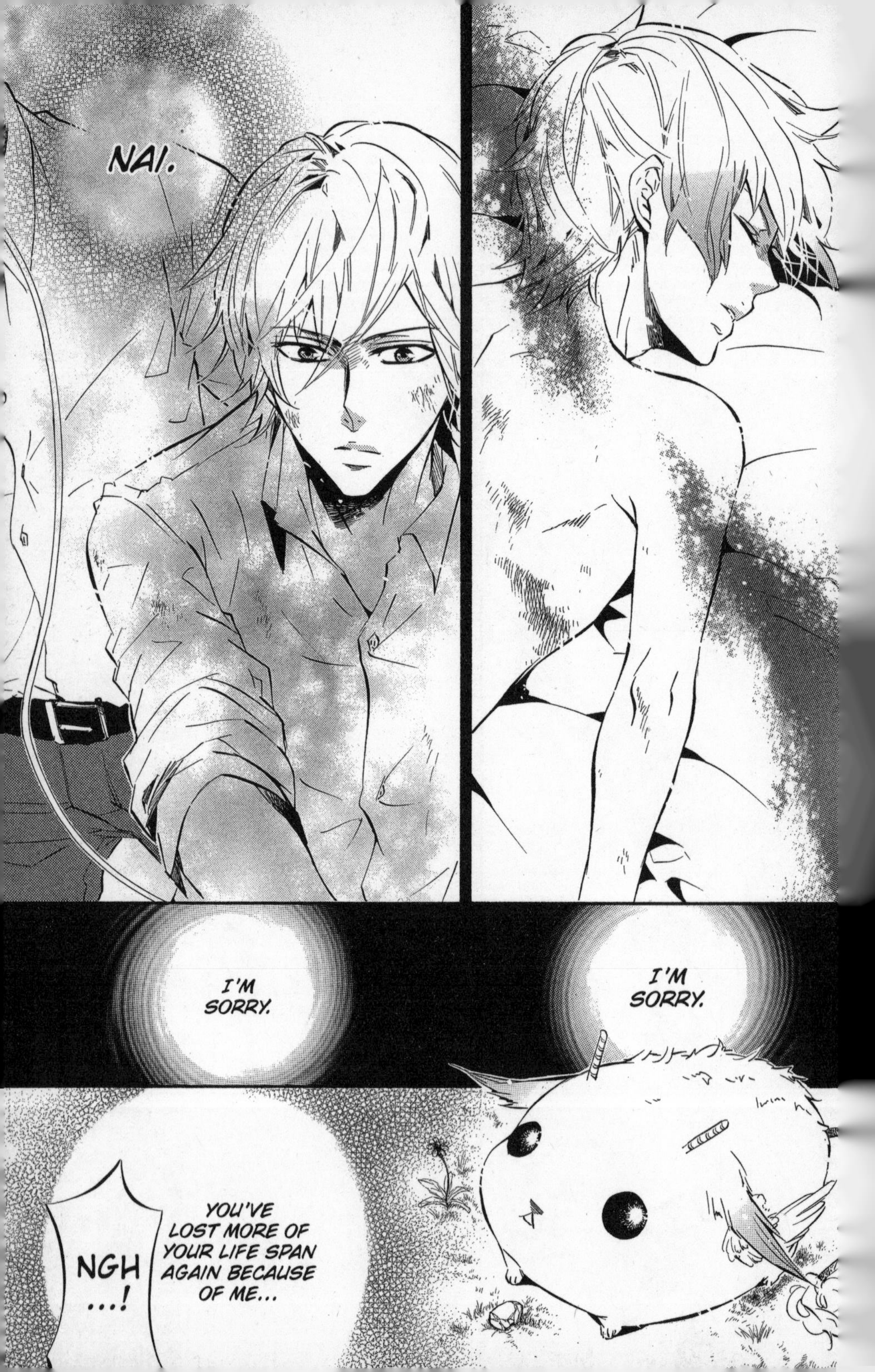
NAI.
I'M SORRY.
I'M SORRY.
YOU'VE LOST MORE OF YOUR LIFE SPAN AGAIN BECAUSE OF ME...
NGH ...!

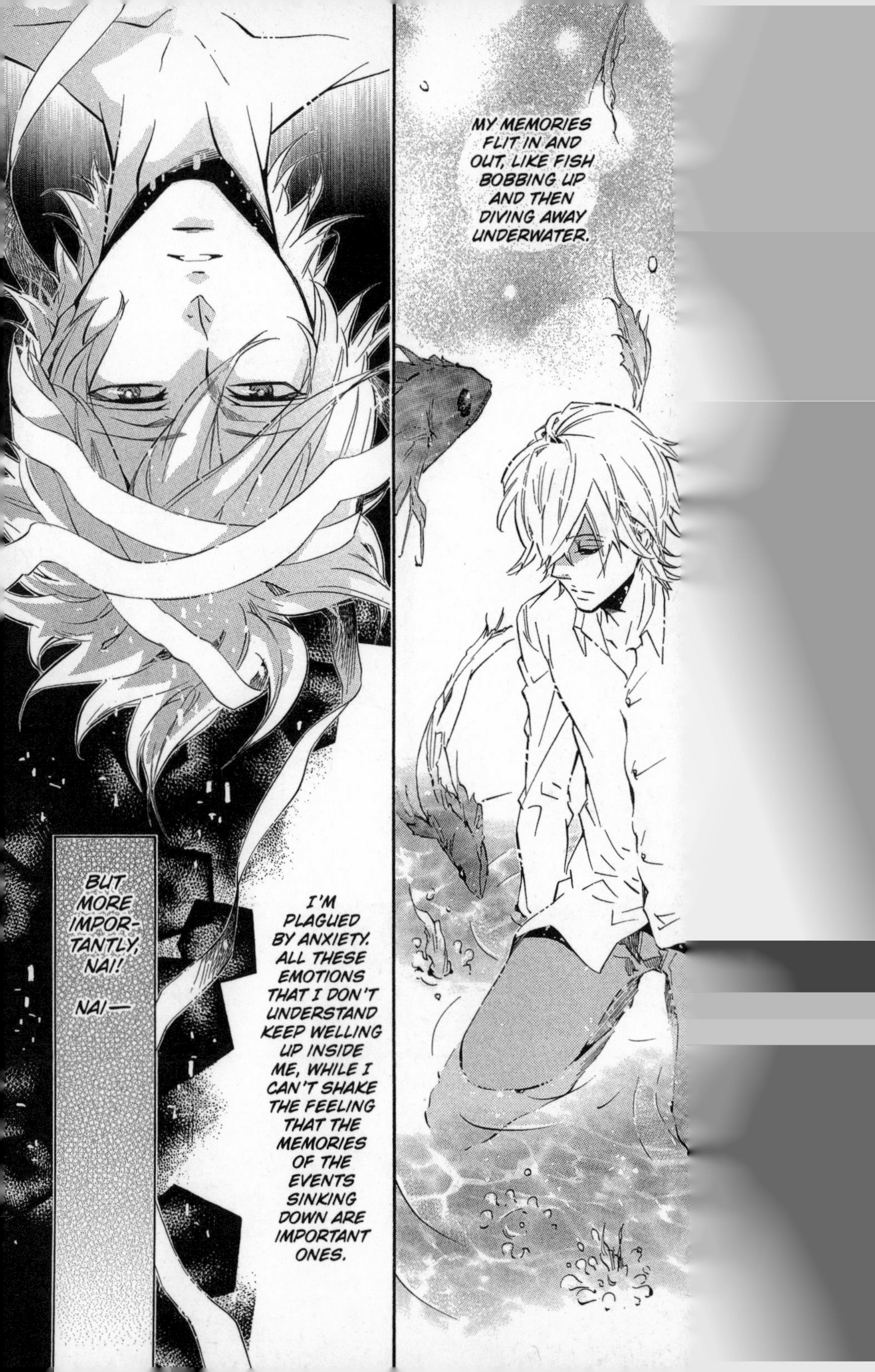
MY MEMORIES FLIT IN AND OUT, LIKE FISH BOBBING UP AND THEN DIVING AWAY UNDERWATER.
I'M PLAGUED BY ANXIETY. ALL THESE EMOTIONS THAT I DON'T UNDERSTAND KEEP WELLING UP INSIDE ME, WHILE I CAN'T SHAKE THE FEELING THAT THE MEMORIES OF THE EVENTS SINKING DOWN ARE IMPORTANT ONES.
BUT MORE IMPORTANTLY, NAI!
NAI—

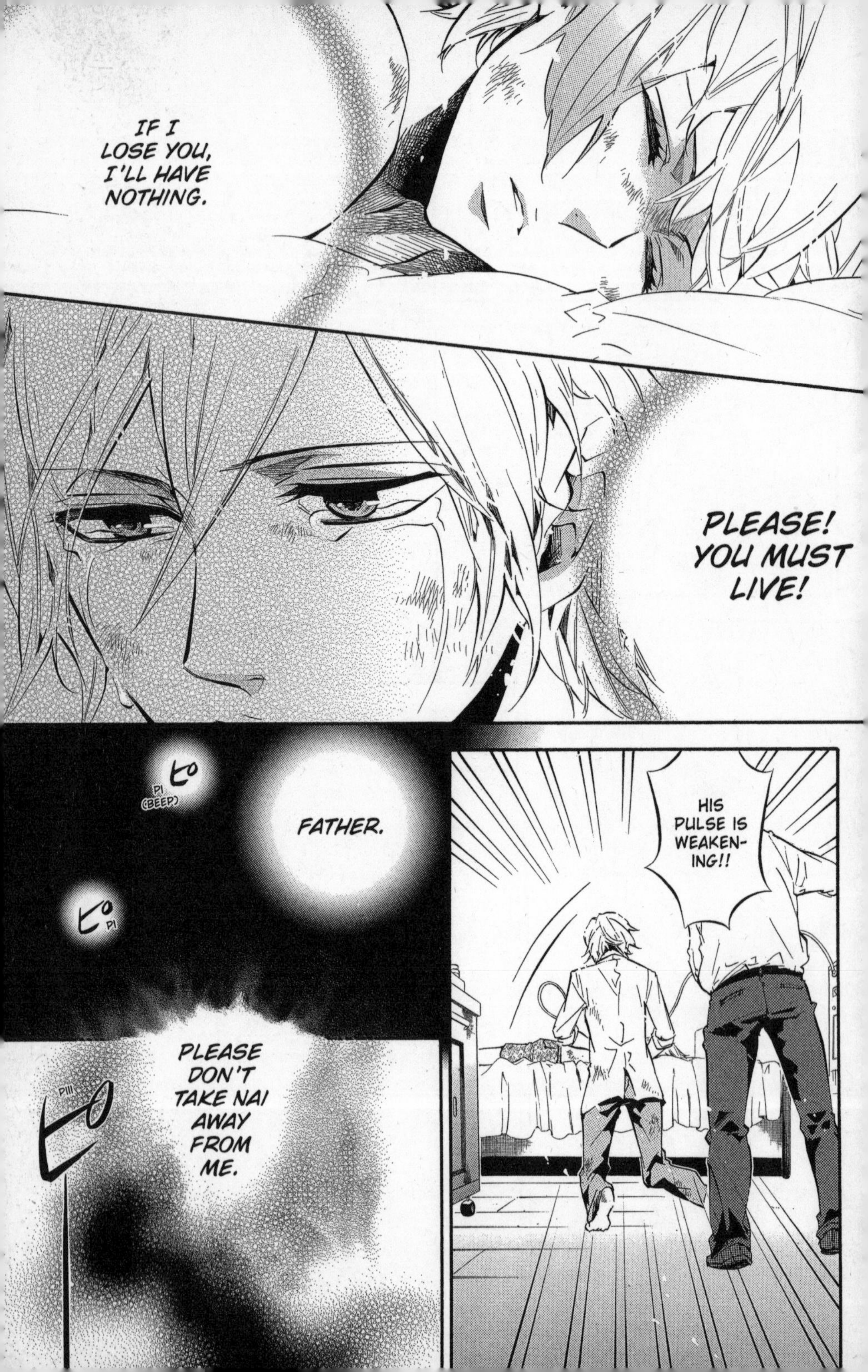
IF I LOSE YOU, I'LL HAVE NOTHING.
PLEASE! YOU MUST LIVE!
HIS PULSE IS WEAKEN-ING!!
ピ PI (BEEP)
FATHER.
ピ PI
PLEASE DON'T TAKE NAI AWAY FROM ME.
ピー PIII

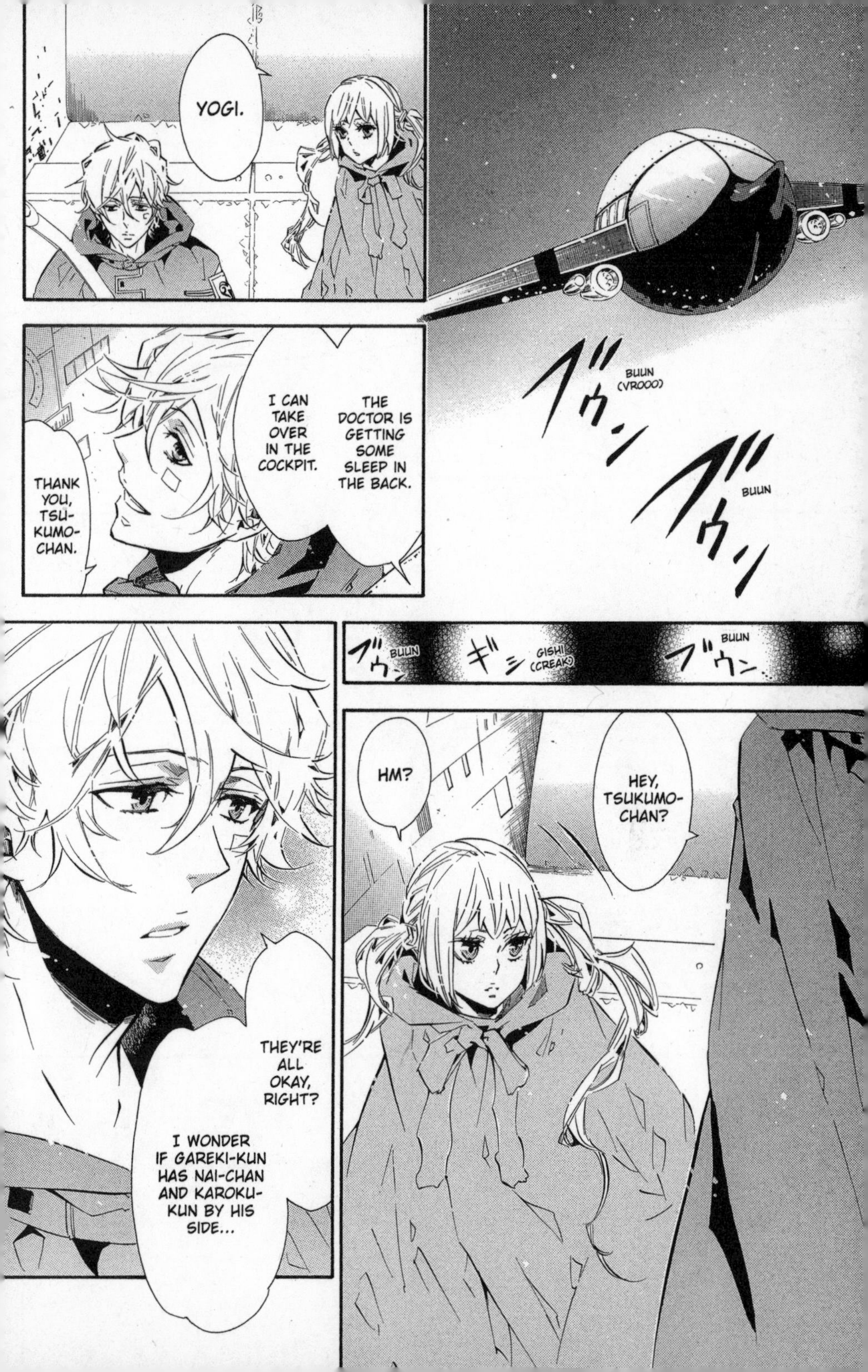
BUUN (VROOO)
BUUN
YOGI.
THE DOCTOR IS GETTING SOME SLEEP IN THE BACK.
I CAN TAKE OVER IN THE COCKPIT.
THANK YOU, TSU-KUMO-CHAN.
BUUN
GISHI (CREAK)
BUUN
HEY, TSUKUMO-CHAN?
HM?
THEY'RE ALL OKAY, RIGHT?
I WONDER IF GAREKI-KUN HAS NAI-CHAN AND KAROKU-KUN BY HIS SIDE...

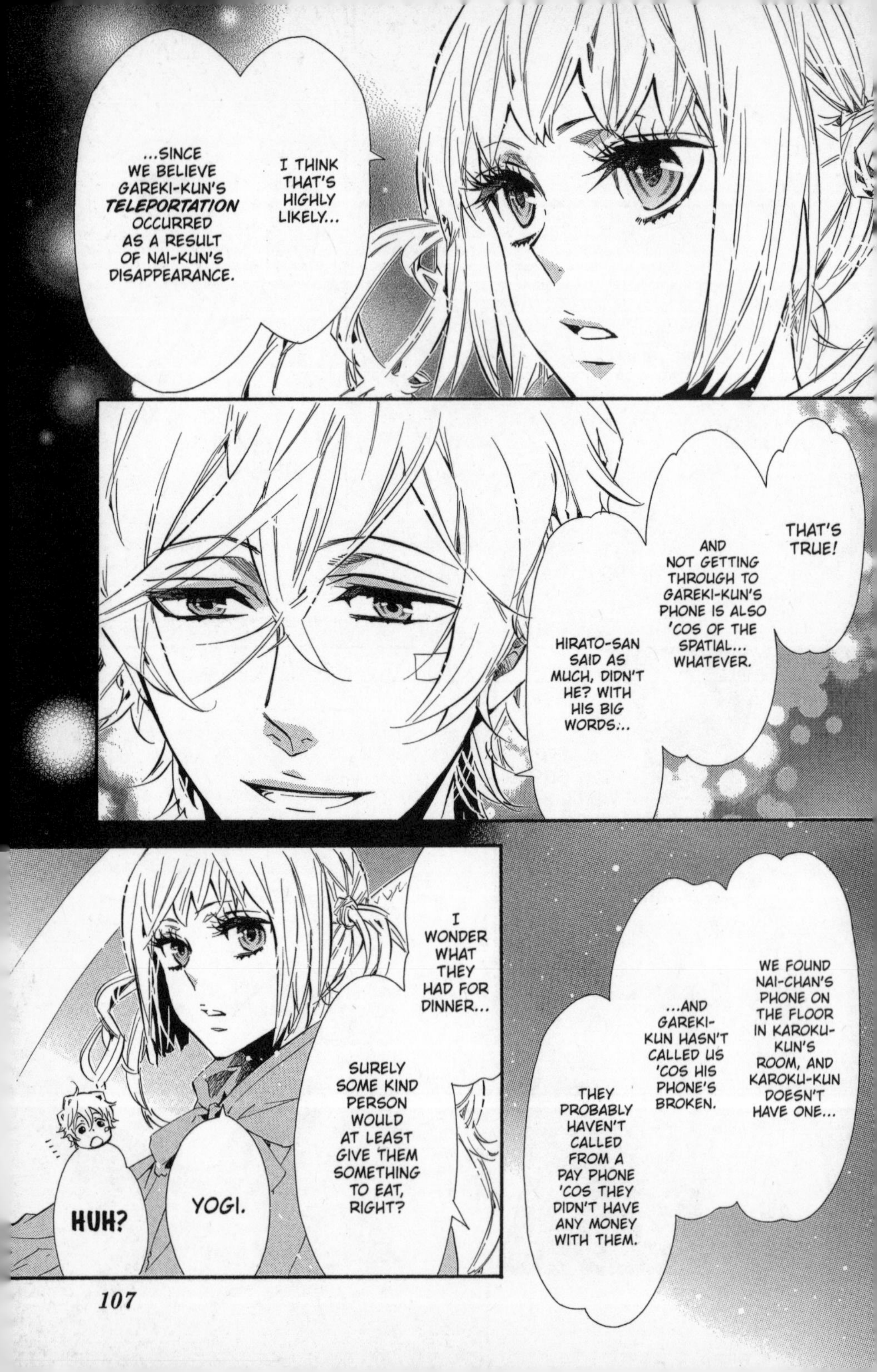
I THINK THAT'S HIGHLY LIKELY...
...SINCE WE BELIEVE GAREKI-KUN'S ***TELEPORTATION*** OCCURRED AS A RESULT OF NAI-KUN'S DISAPPEARANCE.
THAT'S TRUE!
AND NOT GETTING THROUGH TO GAREKI-KUN'S PHONE IS ALSO 'COS OF THE SPATIAL... WHATEVER.
HIRATO-SAN SAID AS MUCH, DIDN'T HE? WITH HIS BIG WORDS...
WE FOUND NAI-CHAN'S PHONE ON THE FLOOR IN KAROKU-KUN'S ROOM, AND KAROKU-KUN DOESN'T HAVE ONE...
...AND GAREKI-KUN HASN'T CALLED US 'COS HIS PHONE'S BROKEN.
THEY PROBABLY HAVEN'T CALLED FROM A PAY PHONE 'COS THEY DIDN'T HAVE ANY MONEY WITH THEM.
I WONDER WHAT THEY HAD FOR DINNER...
SURELY SOME KIND PERSON WOULD AT LEAST GIVE THEM SOMETHING TO EAT, RIGHT?
YOGI.
HUH?

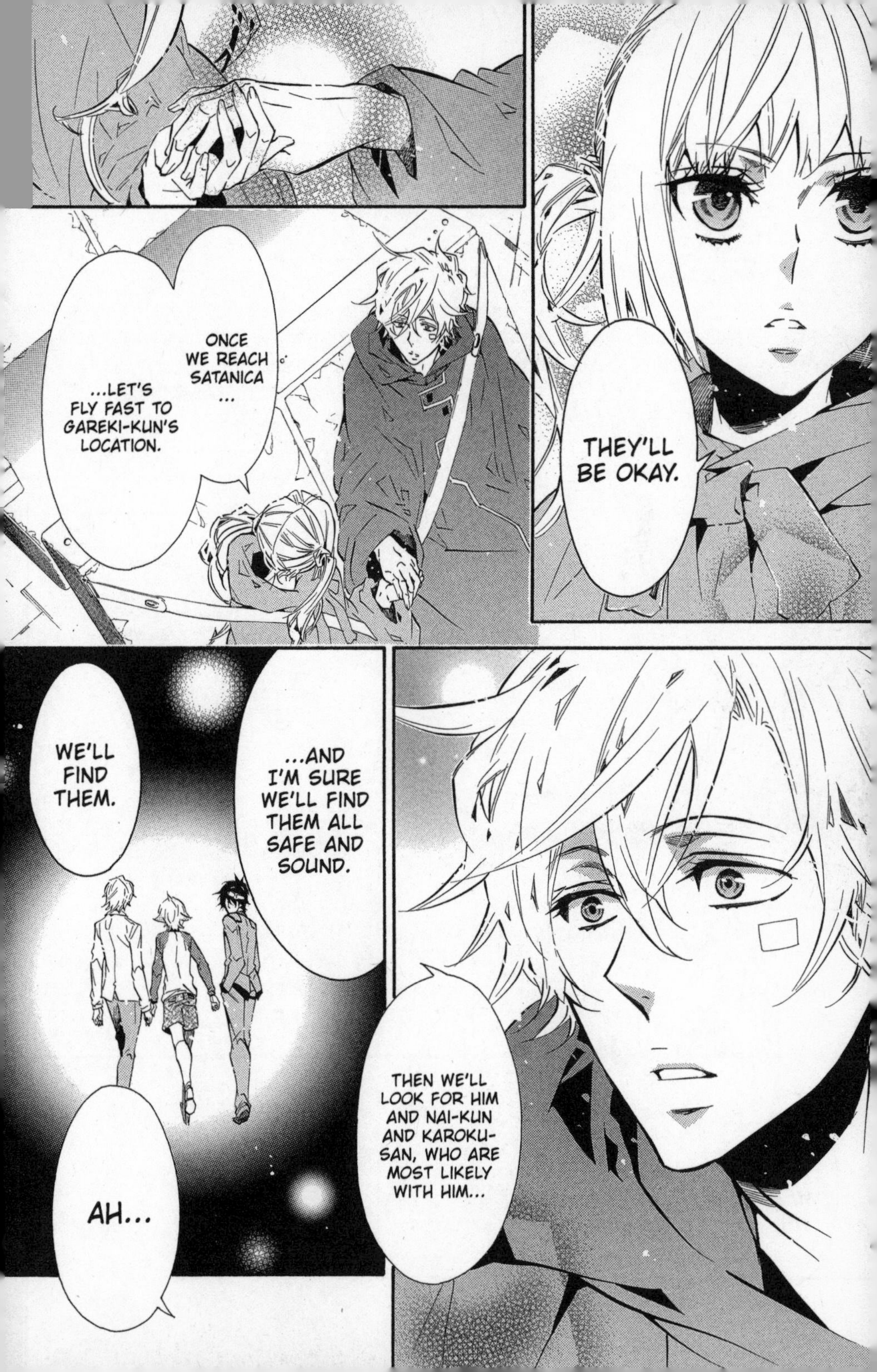
THEY'LL BE OKAY.
ONCE WE REACH SATANICA ...
...LET'S FLY FAST TO GAREKI-KUN'S LOCATION.
THEN WE'LL LOOK FOR HIM AND NAI-KUN AND KAROKU-SAN, WHO ARE MOST LIKELY WITH HIM...
...AND I'M SURE WE'LL FIND THEM ALL SAFE AND SOUND.
WE'LL FIND THEM.
AH...

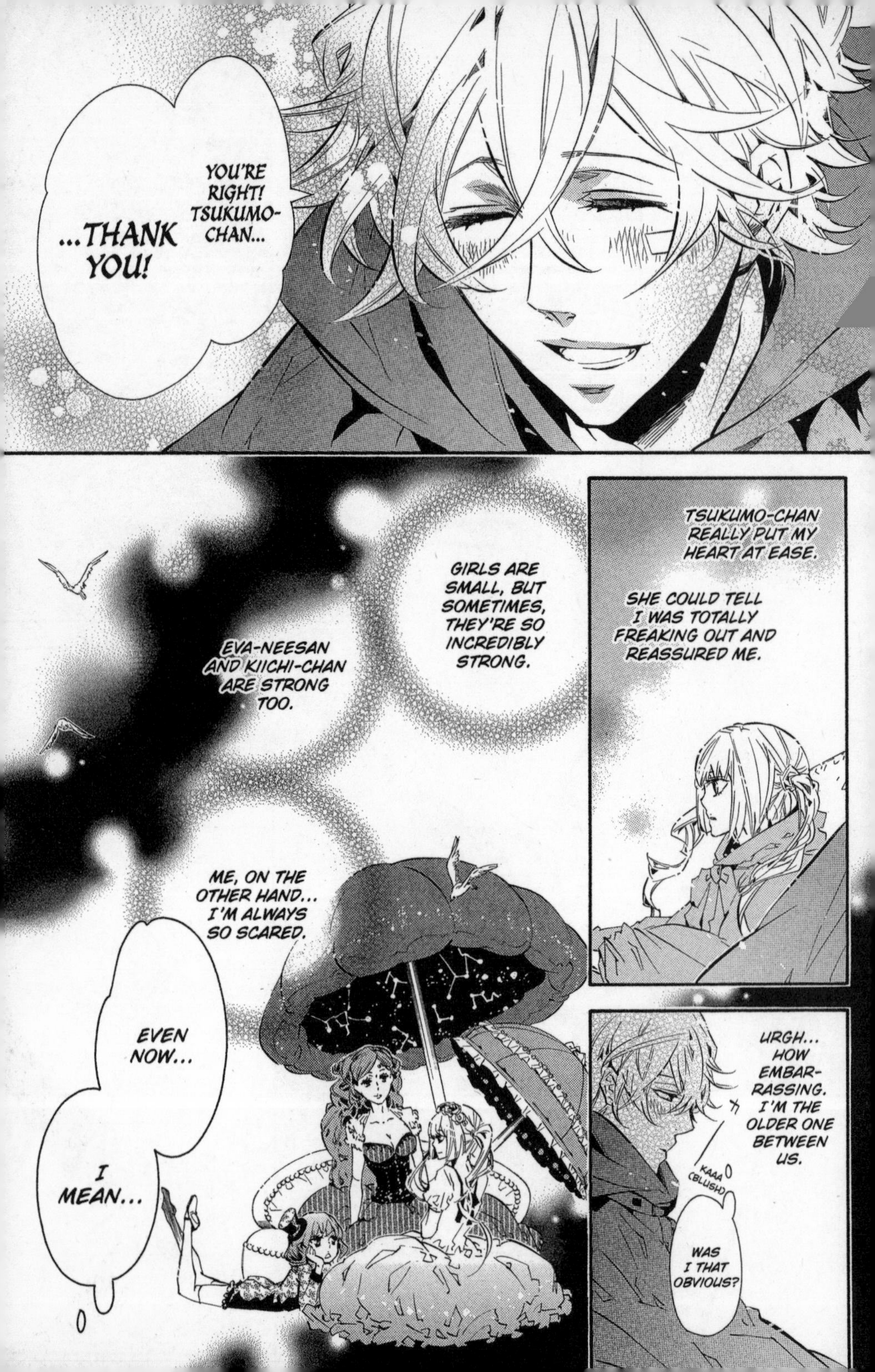
YOU'RE RIGHT! TSUKUMO-CHAN...
...THANK YOU!
TSUKUMO-CHAN REALLY PUT MY HEART AT EASE.
SHE COULD TELL I WAS TOTALLY FREAKING OUT AND REASSURED ME.
URGH... HOW EMBARRASSING. I'M THE OLDER ONE BETWEEN US.
KAAA (BLUSH)
WAS I THAT OBVIOUS?
GIRLS ARE SMALL, BUT SOMETIMES, THEY'RE SO INCREDIBLY STRONG.
EVA-NEESAN AND KIICHI-CHAN ARE STRONG TOO.
ME, ON THE OTHER HAND... I'M ALWAYS SO SCARED.
EVEN NOW...
I MEAN...

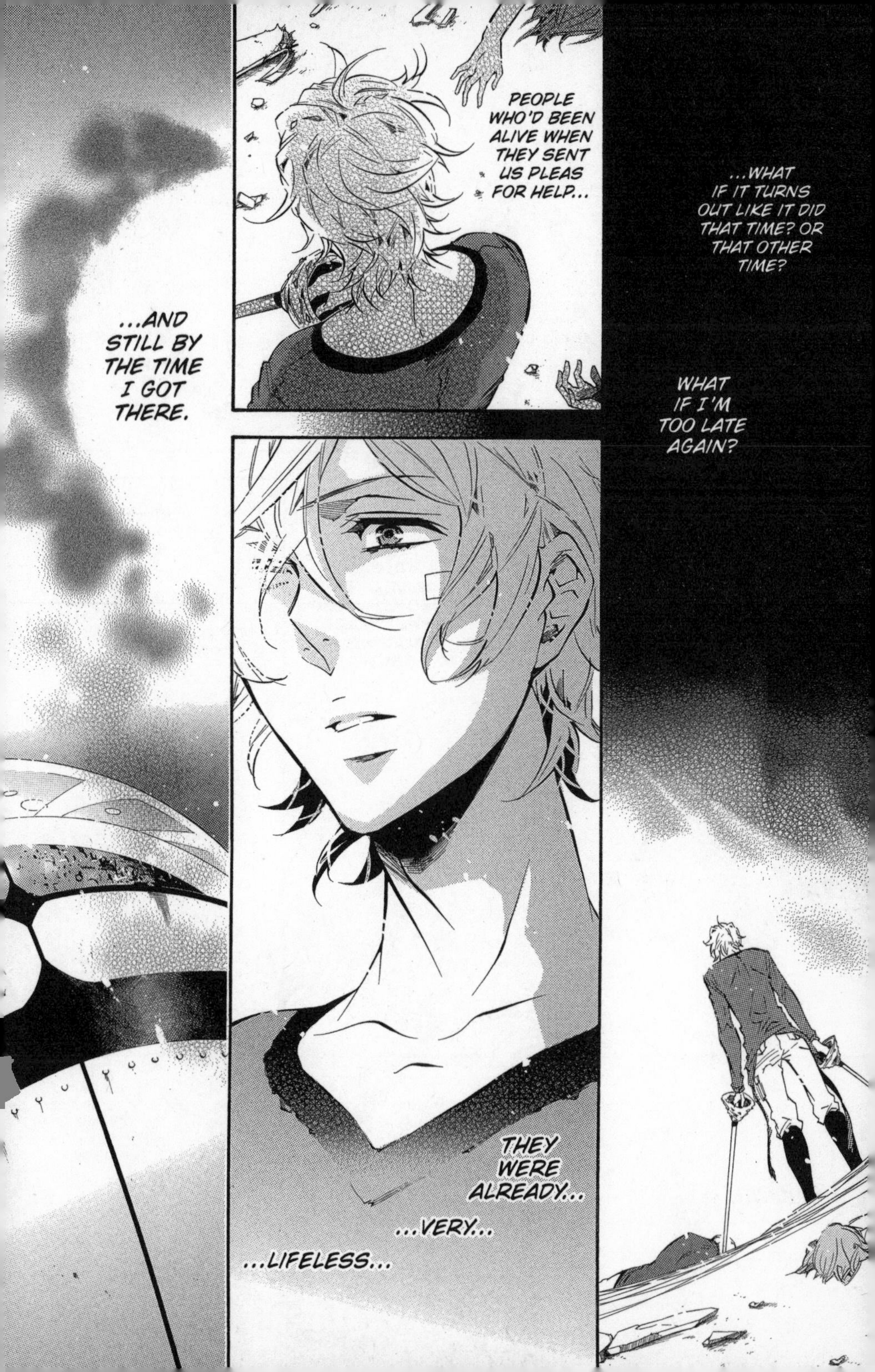
...WHAT IF IT TURNS OUT LIKE IT DID THAT TIME? OR THAT OTHER TIME?
WHAT IF I'M TOO LATE AGAIN?
PEOPLE WHO'D BEEN ALIVE WHEN THEY SENT US PLEAS FOR HELP...
...AND STILL BY THE TIME I GOT THERE.
THEY WERE ALREADY...
...VERY...
...LIFELESS...

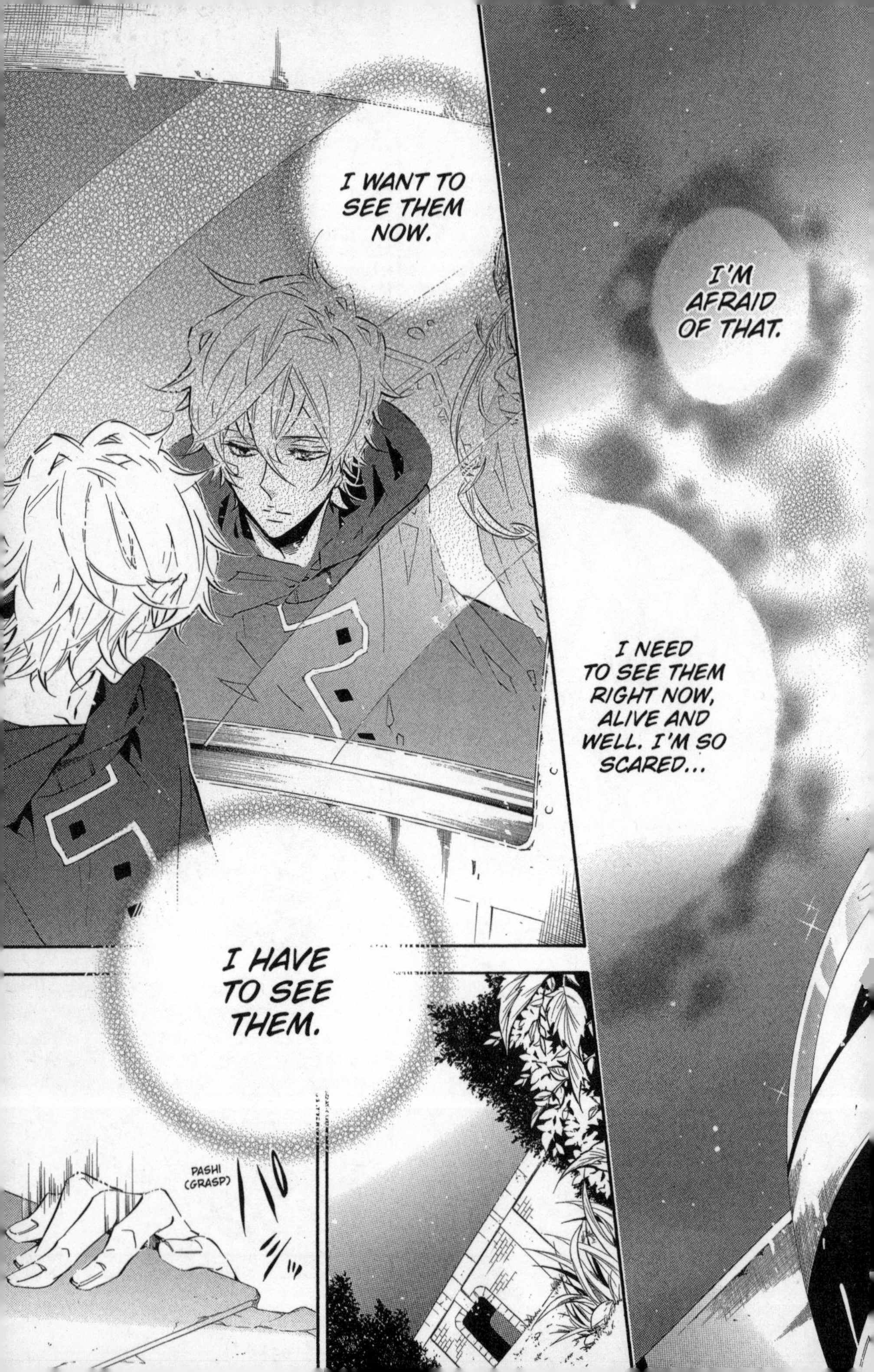
I'M AFRAID OF THAT.
I NEED TO SEE THEM RIGHT NOW, ALIVE AND WELL. I'M SO SCARED...
I WANT TO SEE THEM NOW.
I HAVE TO SEE THEM.
DASHI (GRASP)

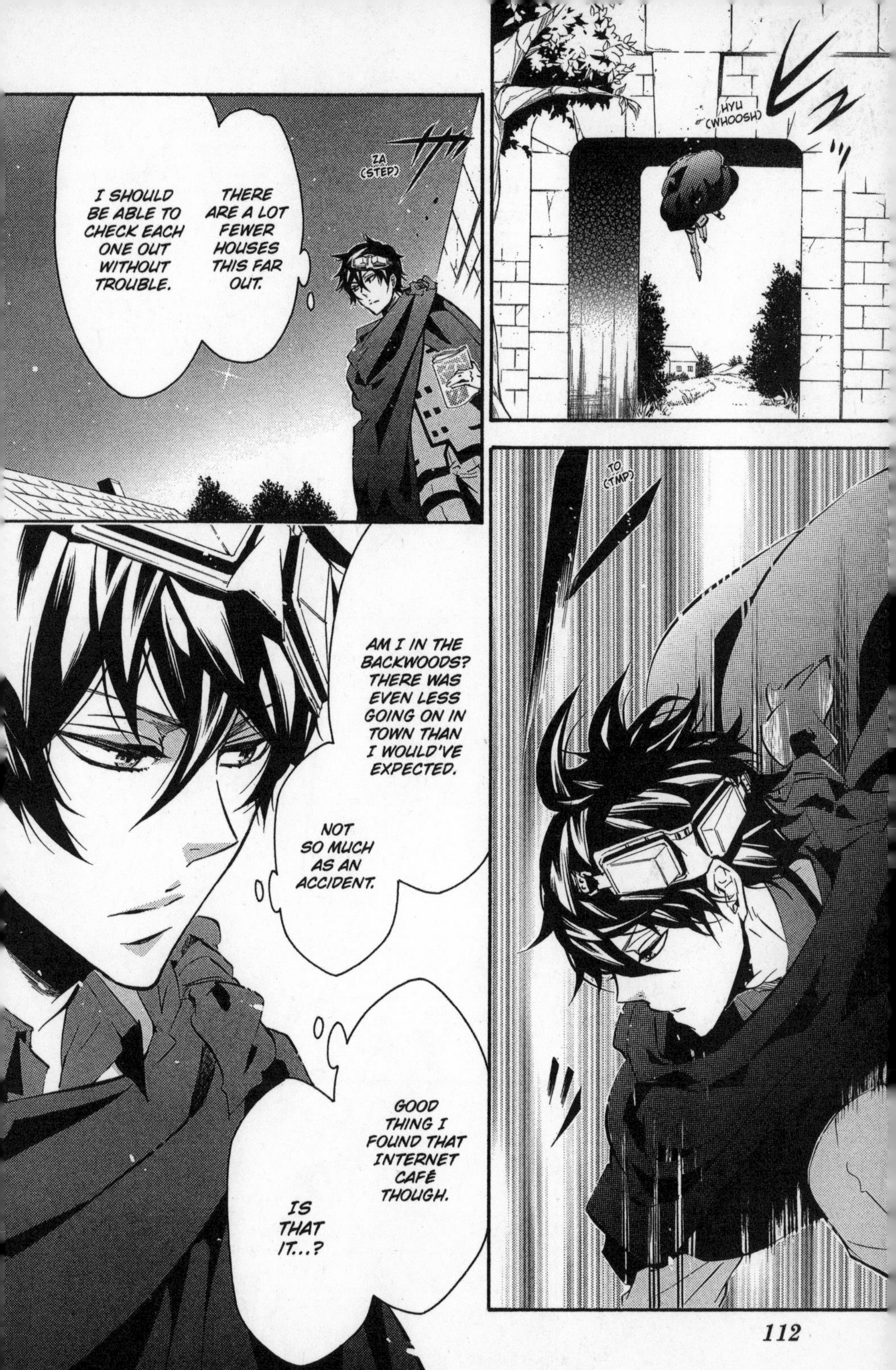
HYU (WHOOSH)
ZA (STEP)
THERE ARE A LOT FEWER HOUSES THIS FAR OUT.
I SHOULD BE ABLE TO CHECK EACH ONE OUT WITHOUT TROUBLE.
TO (TMP)
AM I IN THE BACKWOODS? THERE WAS EVEN LESS GOING ON IN TOWN THAN I WOULD'VE EXPECTED.
NOT SO MUCH AS AN ACCIDENT.
GOOD THING I FOUND THAT INTERNET CAFÉ THOUGH.
IS THAT IT...?

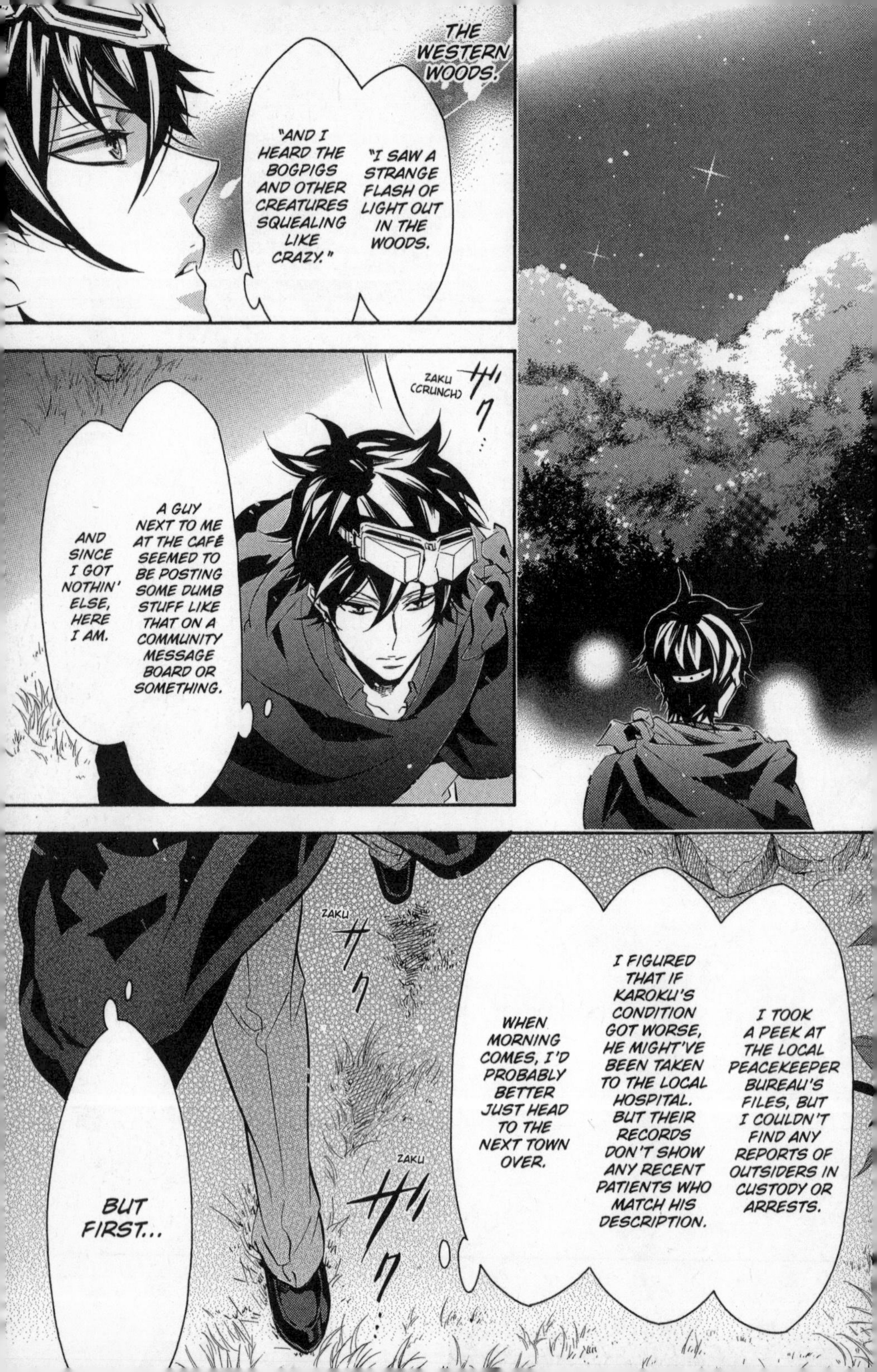
THE WESTERN WOODS.
"I SAW A STRANGE FLASH OF LIGHT OUT IN THE WOODS.
"AND I HEARD THE BOGPIGS AND OTHER CREATURES SQUEALING LIKE CRAZY."
ZAKU (CRUNCH)
A GUY NEXT TO ME AT THE CAFÉ SEEMED TO BE POSTING SOME DUMB STUFF LIKE THAT ON A COMMUNITY MESSAGE BOARD OR SOMETHING.
AND SINCE I GOT NOTHIN' ELSE, HERE I AM.
I TOOK A PEEK AT THE LOCAL PEACEKEEPER BUREAU'S FILES, BUT I COULDN'T FIND ANY REPORTS OF OUTSIDERS IN CUSTODY OR ARRESTS.
I FIGURED THAT IF KAROKU'S CONDITION GOT WORSE, HE MIGHT'VE BEEN TAKEN TO THE LOCAL HOSPITAL. BUT THEIR RECORDS DON'T SHOW ANY RECENT PATIENTS WHO MATCH HIS DESCRIPTION.
WHEN MORNING COMES, I'D PROBABLY BETTER JUST HEAD TO THE NEXT TOWN OVER.
ZAKU
ZAKU
BUT FIRST...

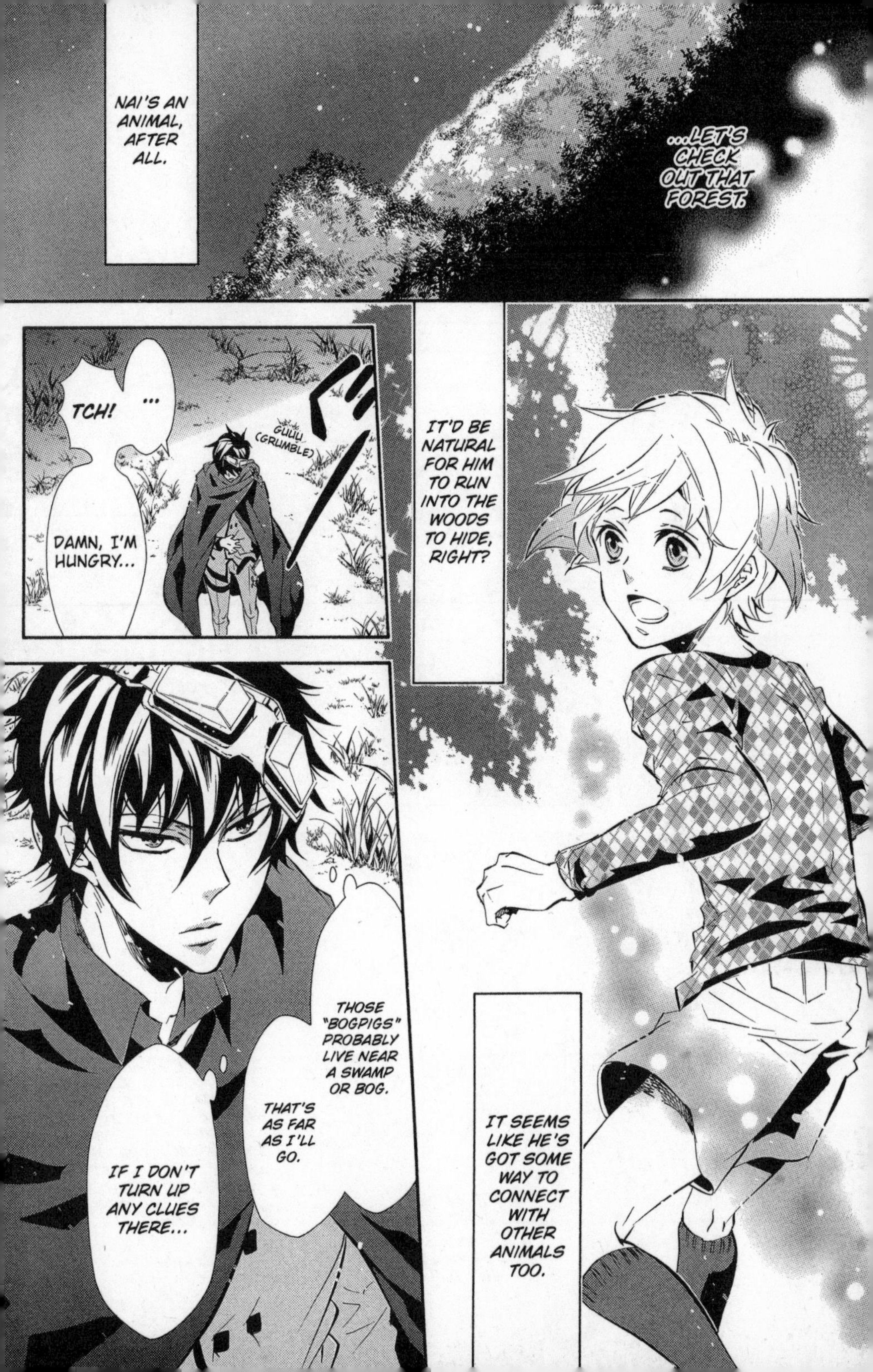
NAI'S AN ANIMAL, AFTER ALL.
...LET'S CHECK OUT THAT FOREST.
IT'D BE NATURAL FOR HIM TO RUN INTO THE WOODS TO HIDE, RIGHT?
IT SEEMS LIKE HE'S GOT SOME WAY TO CONNECT WITH OTHER ANIMALS TOO.
...
TCH!
GUUU (GRUMBLE)
DAMN, I'M HUNGRY...
THOSE "BOGPIGS" PROBABLY LIVE NEAR A SWAMP OR BOG.
THAT'S AS FAR AS I'LL GO.
IF I DON'T TURN UP ANY CLUES THERE...

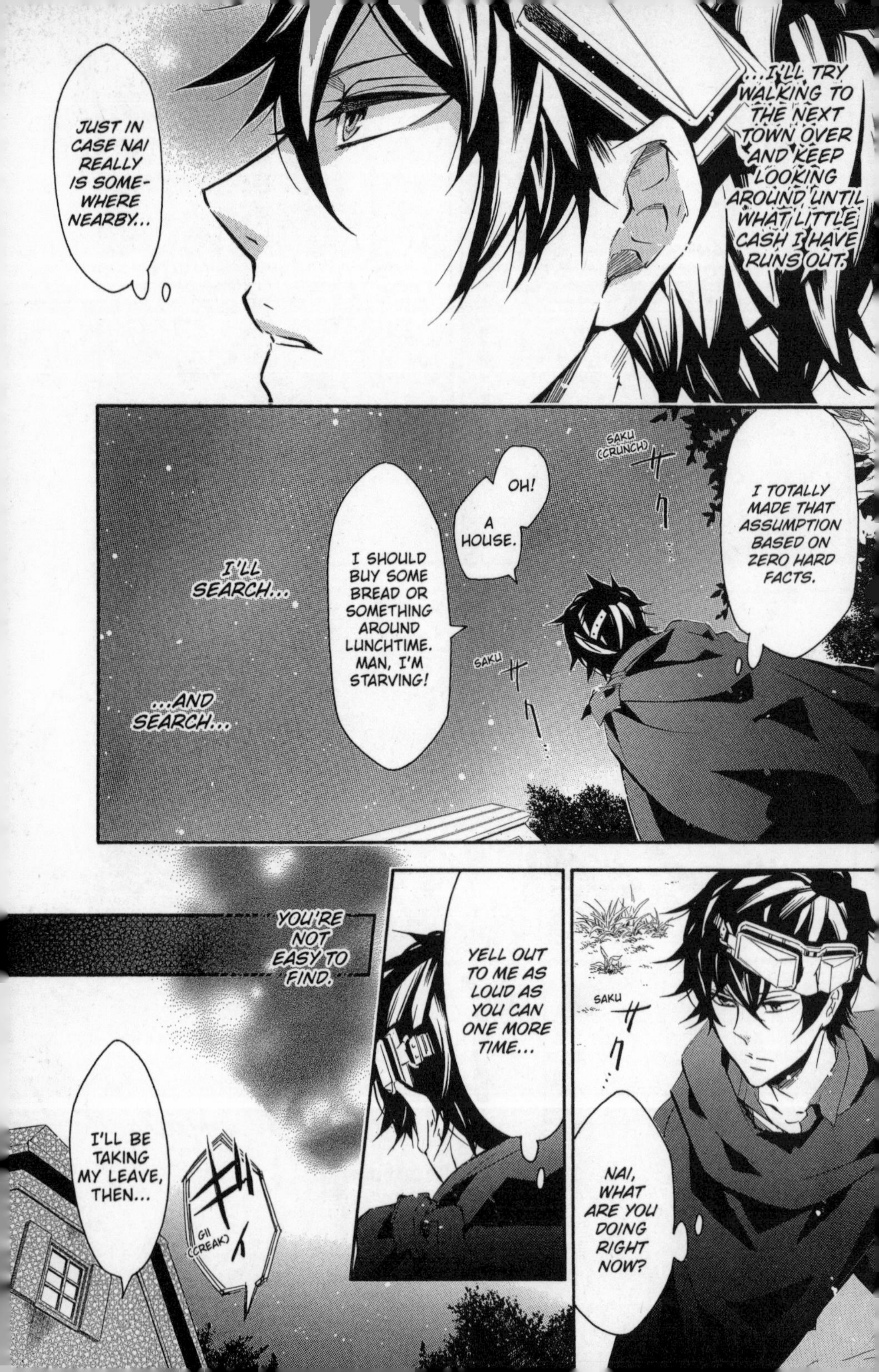
...I'LL TRY WALKING TO THE NEXT TOWN OVER AND KEEP LOOKING AROUND UNTIL WHAT LITTLE CASH I HAVE RUNS OUT.
JUST IN CASE NAI REALLY IS SOME-WHERE NEARBY...
I TOTALLY MADE THAT ASSUMPTION BASED ON ZERO HARD FACTS.
SAKU (CRUNCH)
OH! A HOUSE.
I SHOULD BUY SOME BREAD OR SOMETHING AROUND LUNCHTIME. MAN, I'M STARVING!
SAKU
I'LL SEARCH...
...AND SEARCH...
SAKU
NAI, WHAT ARE YOU DOING RIGHT NOW?
YELL OUT TO ME AS LOUD AS YOU CAN ONE MORE TIME...
YOU'RE NOT EASY TO FIND.
GII (CREAK)
I'LL BE TAKING MY LEAVE, THEN...

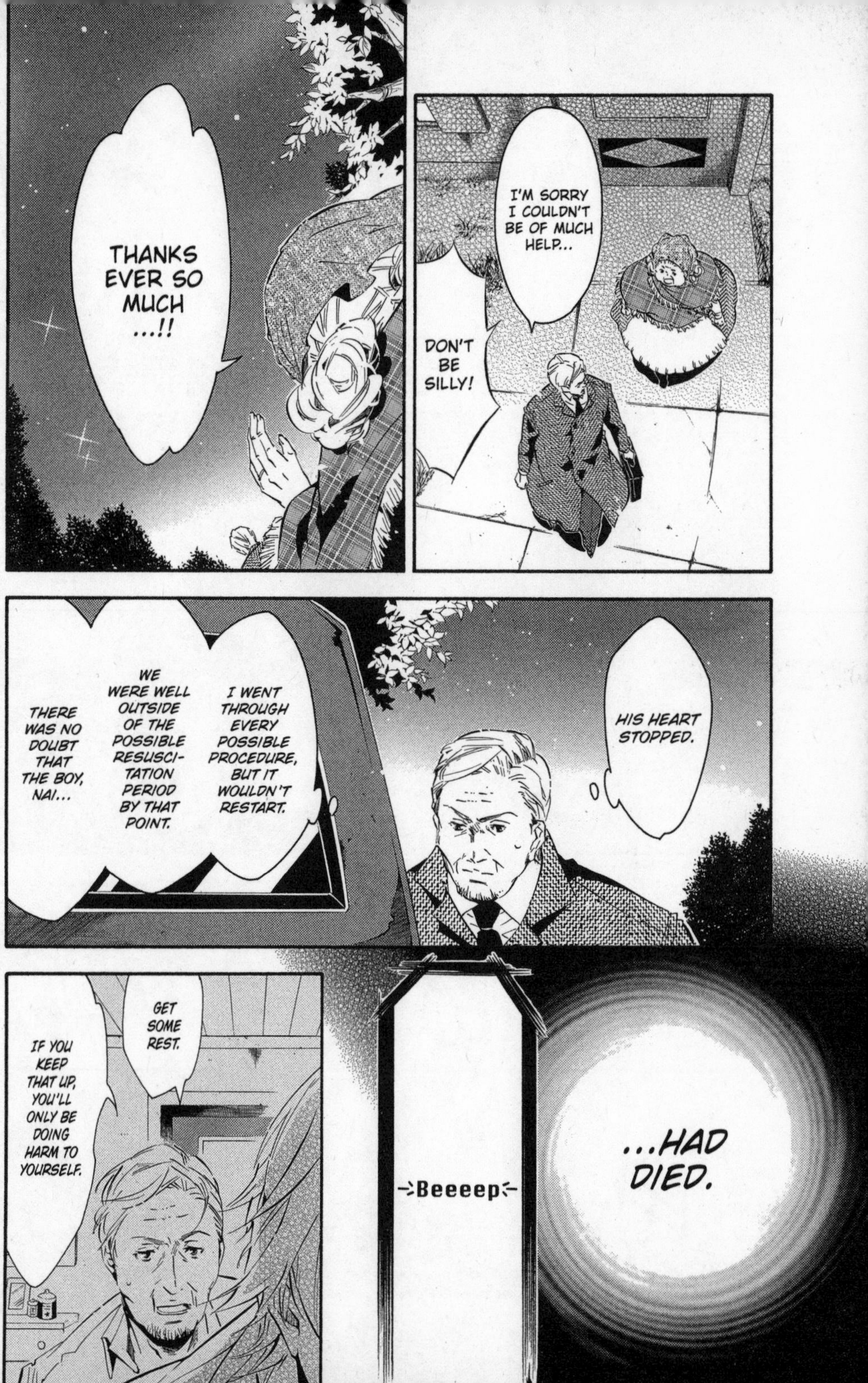
I'M SORRY I COULDN'T BE OF MUCH HELP...
DON'T BE SILLY!
THANKS EVER SO MUCH ...!!
HIS HEART STOPPED.
I WENT THROUGH EVERY POSSIBLE PROCEDURE, BUT IT WOULDN'T RESTART.
WE WERE WELL OUTSIDE OF THE POSSIBLE RESUSCITATION PERIOD BY THAT POINT.
THERE WAS NO DOUBT THAT THE BOY, NAI...
...HAD DIED.
Beeeep
GET SOME REST.
IF YOU KEEP THAT UP, YOU'LL ONLY BE DOING HARM TO YOURSELF.

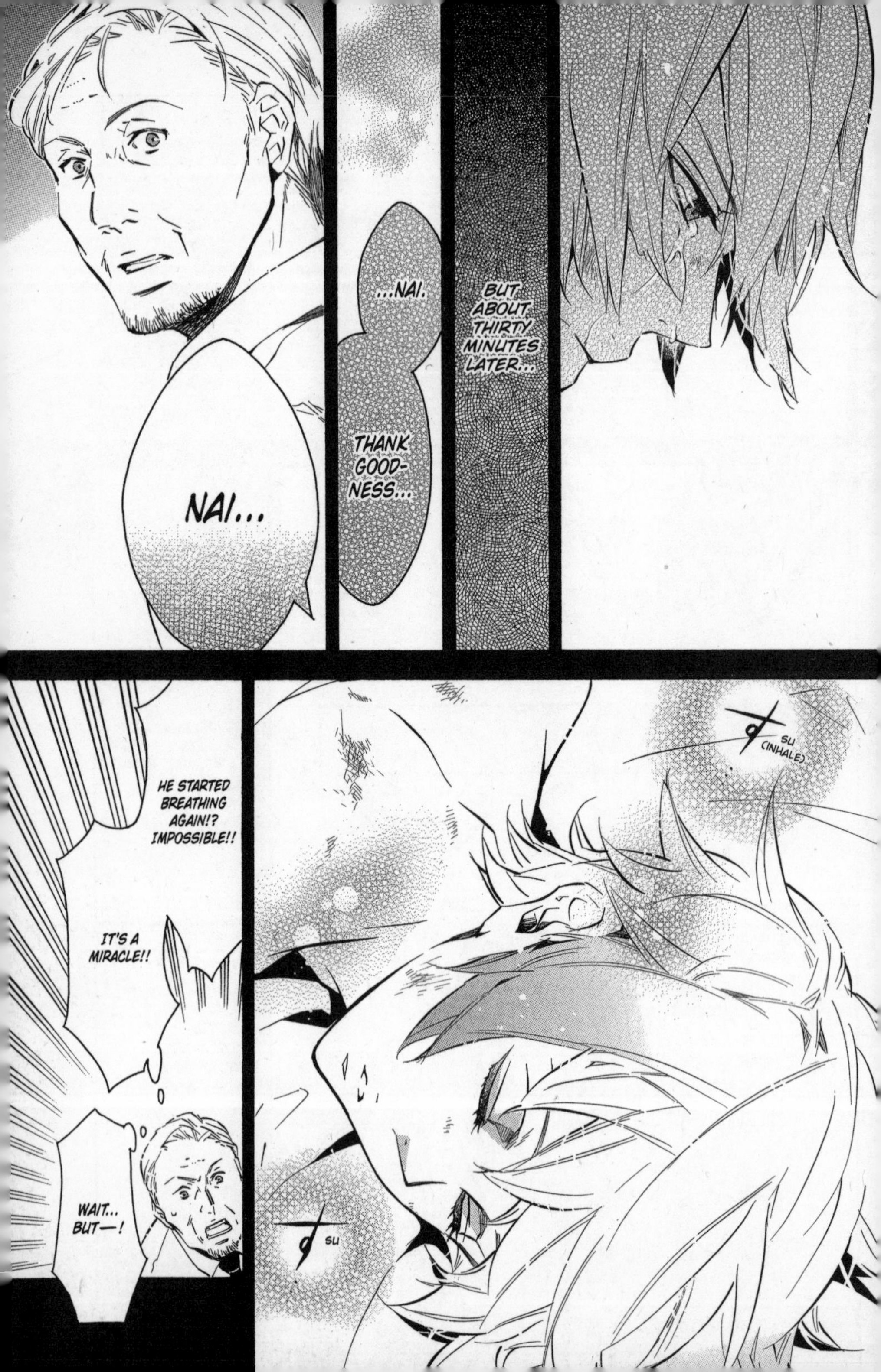
BUT ABOUT THIRTY MINUTES LATER...
...NAI.
THANK GOODNESS...
NAI...
SU (INHALE)
SU
HE STARTED BREATHING AGAIN!? IMPOSSIBLE!!
IT'S A MIRACLE!!
WAIT... BUT—!

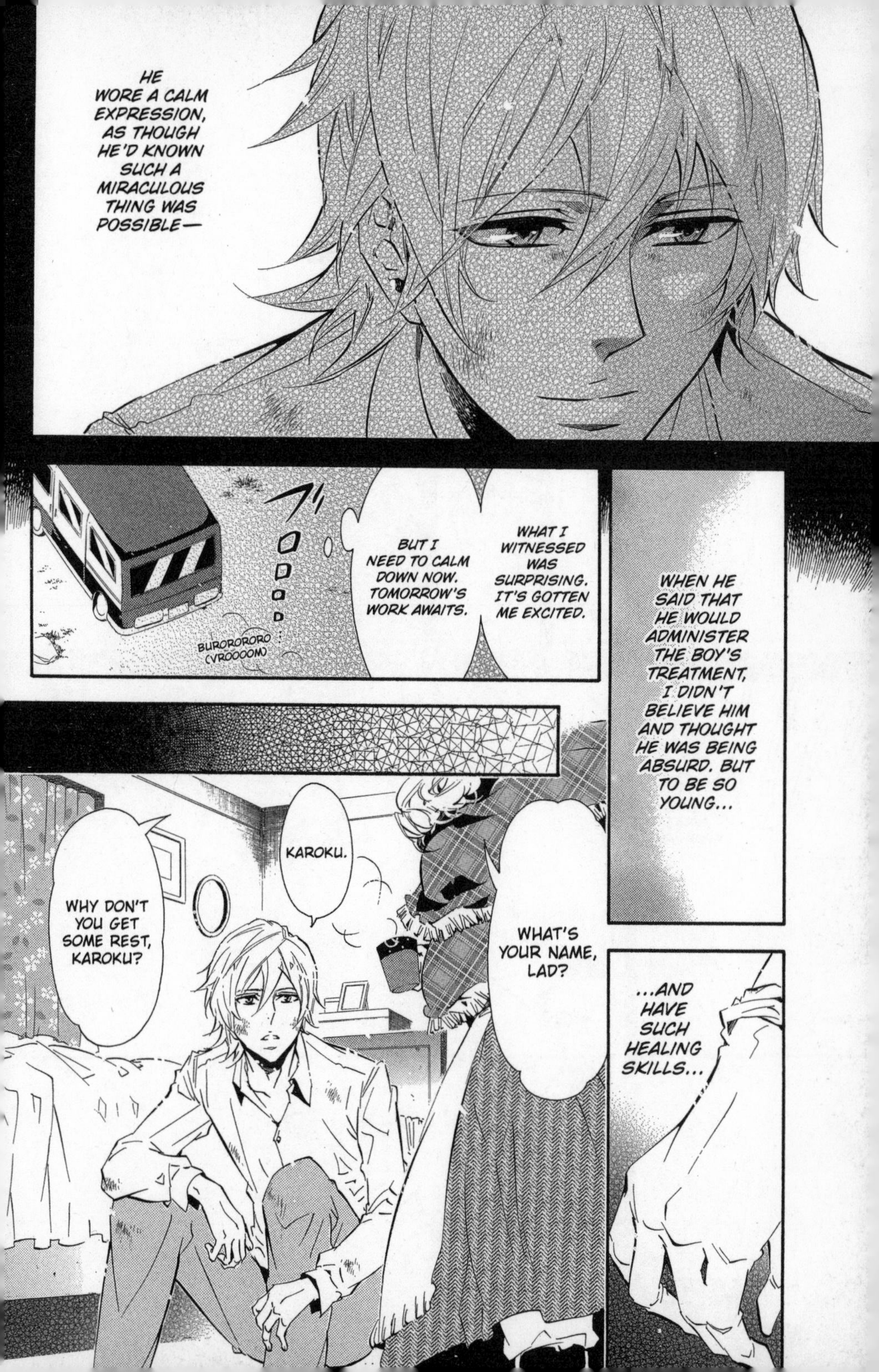
HE WORE A CALM EXPRESSION, AS THOUGH HE'D KNOWN SUCH A MIRACULOUS THING WAS POSSIBLE—
WHEN HE SAID THAT HE WOULD ADMINISTER THE BOY'S TREATMENT, I DIDN'T BELIEVE HIM AND THOUGHT HE WAS BEING ABSURD. BUT TO BE SO YOUNG...
WHAT I WITNESSED WAS SURPRISING. IT'S GOTTEN ME EXCITED.
BUT I NEED TO CALM DOWN NOW. TOMORROW'S WORK AWAITS.
BUROROROROO... (VROOOOM)
...AND HAVE SUCH HEALING SKILLS...
WHAT'S YOUR NAME, LAD?
KAROKU.
WHY DON'T YOU GET SOME REST, KAROKU?

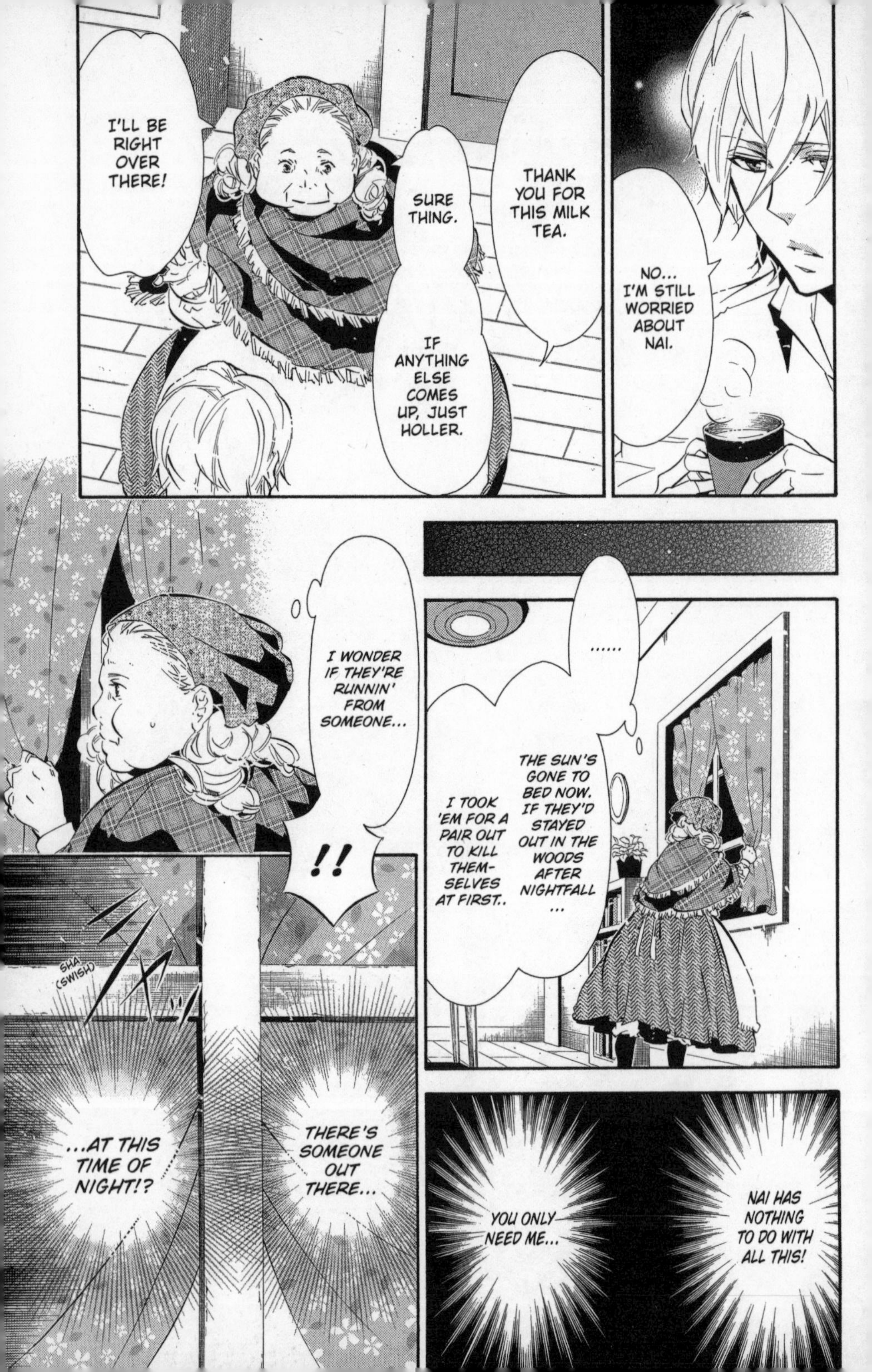
NO... I'M STILL WORRIED ABOUT NAI.
THANK YOU FOR THIS MILK TEA.
SURE THING.
IF ANYTHING ELSE COMES UP, JUST HOLLER.
I'LL BE RIGHT OVER THERE!
......
THE SUN'S GONE TO BED NOW. IF THEY'D STAYED OUT IN THE WOODS AFTER NIGHTFALL ...
I TOOK 'EM FOR A PAIR OUT TO KILL THEM-SELVES AT FIRST..
I WONDER IF THEY'RE RUNNIN' FROM SOMEONE...
!!
SHA (SWISH)
NAI HAS NOTHING TO DO WITH ALL THIS!
YOU ONLY NEED ME...
THERE'S SOMEONE OUT THERE...
...AT THIS TIME OF NIGHT!?

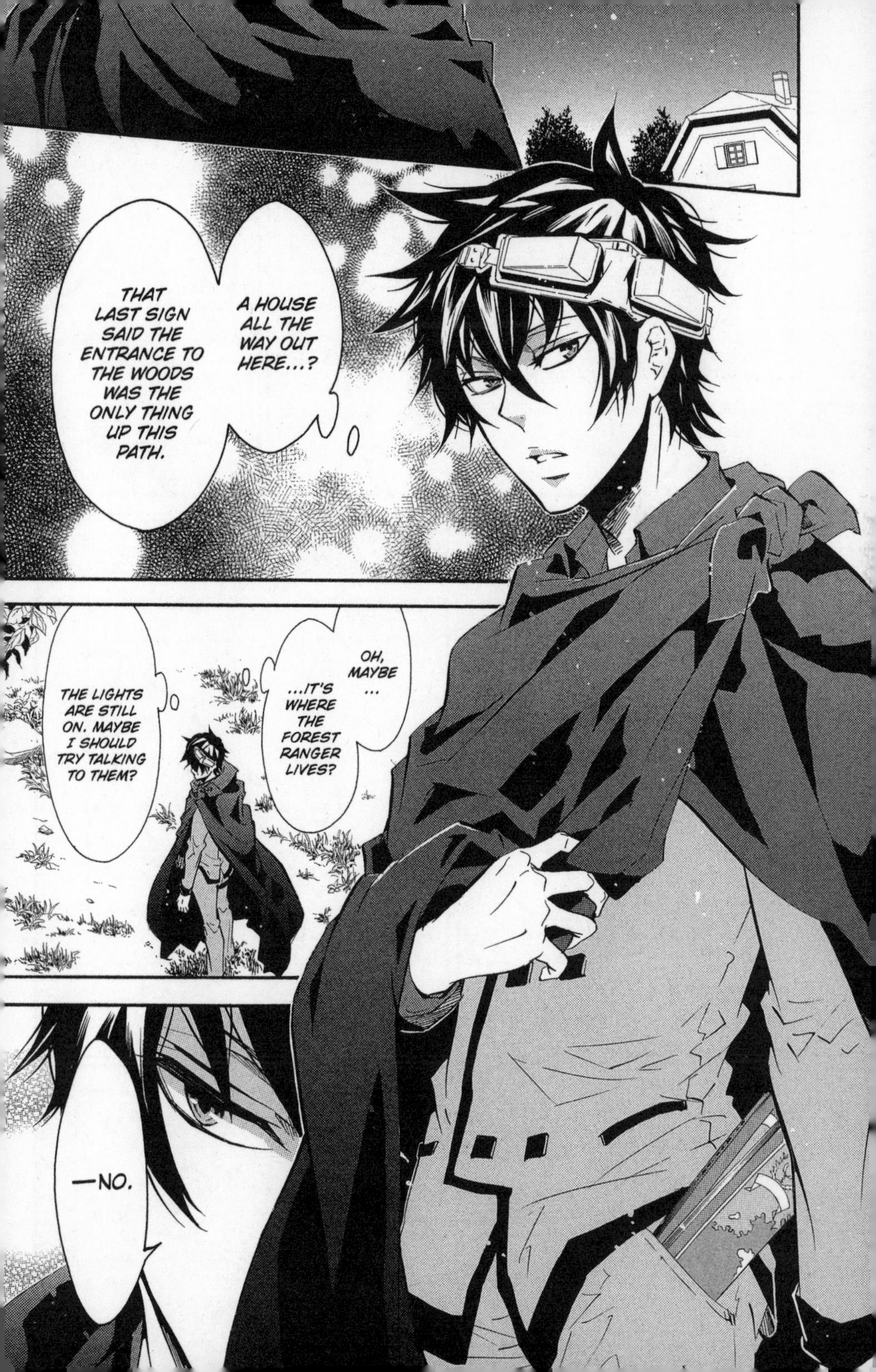
A HOUSE ALL THE WAY OUT HERE...?
THAT LAST SIGN SAID THE ENTRANCE TO THE WOODS WAS THE ONLY THING UP THIS PATH.
OH, MAYBE ...
...IT'S WHERE THE FOREST RANGER LIVES?
THE LIGHTS ARE STILL ON. MAYBE I SHOULD TRY TALKING TO THEM?
—NO.

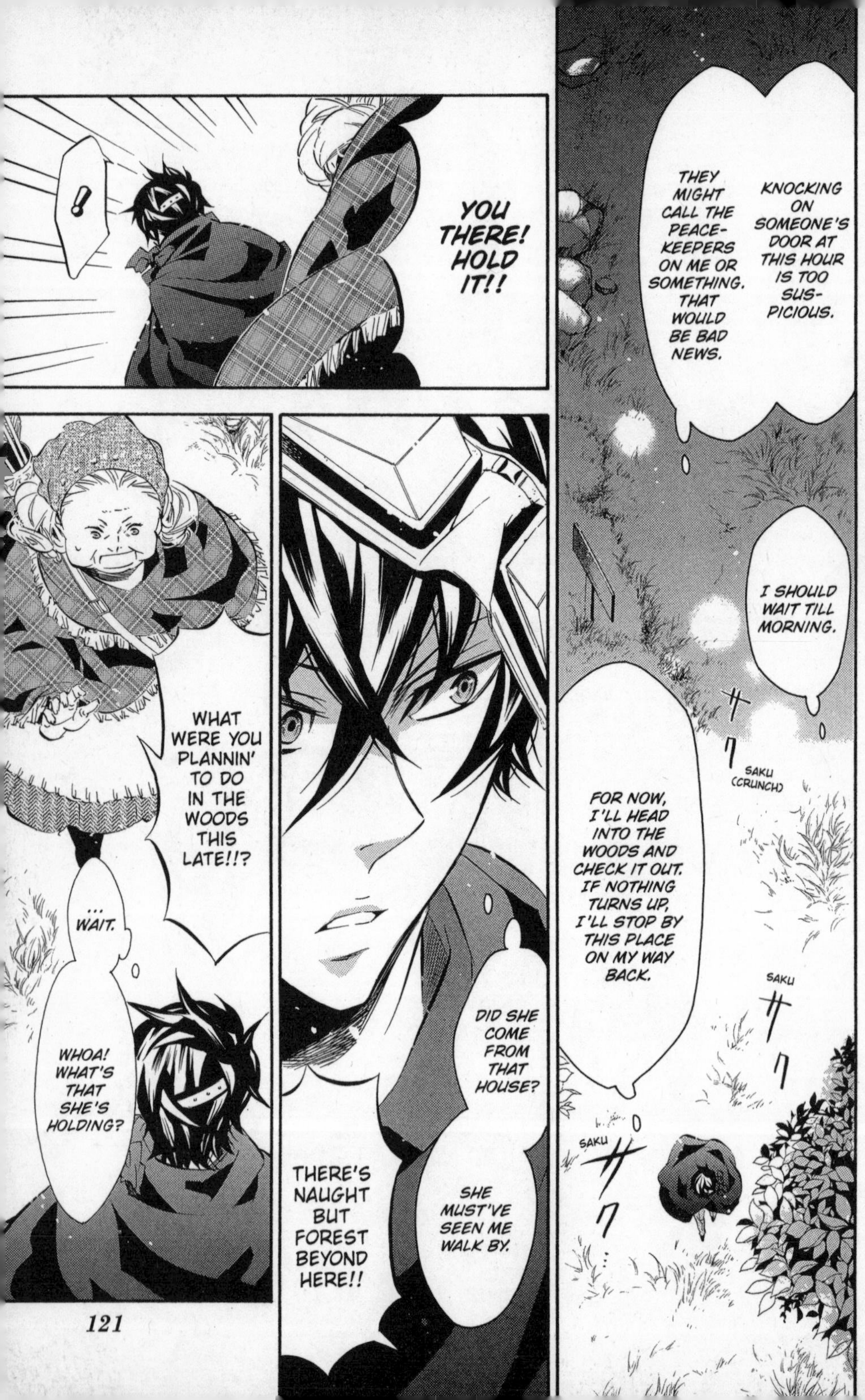
KNOCKING ON SOMEONE'S DOOR AT THIS HOUR IS TOO SUS-PICIOUS.
THEY MIGHT CALL THE PEACE-KEEPERS ON ME OR SOMETHING. THAT WOULD BE BAD NEWS.
I SHOULD WAIT TILL MORNING.
SAKU (CRUNCH)
FOR NOW, I'LL HEAD INTO THE WOODS AND CHECK IT OUT. IF NOTHING TURNS UP, I'LL STOP BY THIS PLACE ON MY WAY BACK.
SAKU
SAKU
YOU THERE! HOLD IT!!
!
DID SHE COME FROM THAT HOUSE?
SHE MUST'VE SEEN ME WALK BY.
THERE'S NAUGHT BUT FOREST BEYOND HERE!!
WHAT WERE YOU PLANNIN' TO DO IN THE WOODS THIS LATE!!?
... WAIT.
WHOA! WHAT'S THAT SHE'S HOLDING?

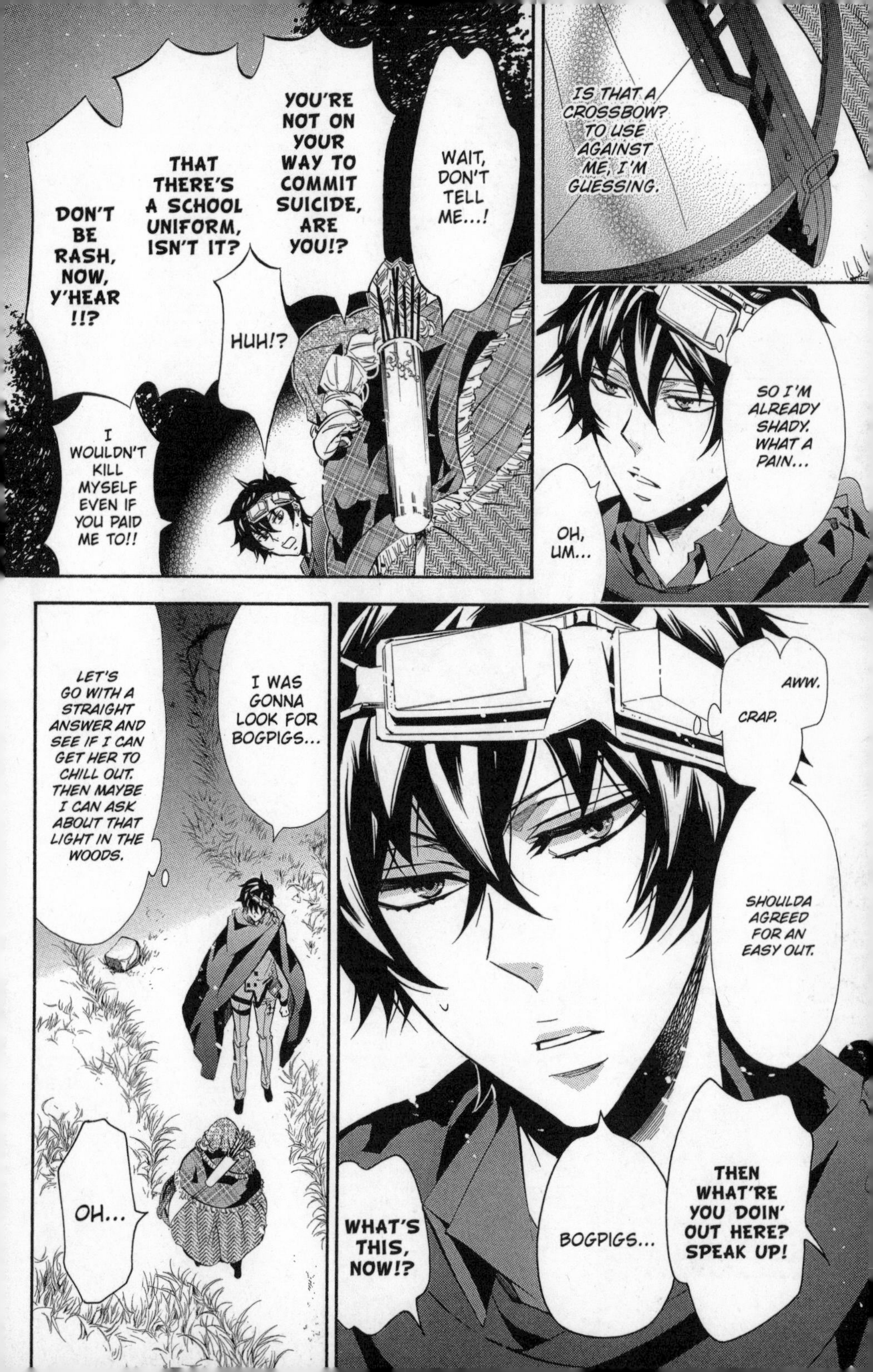
IS THAT A CROSSBOW? TO USE AGAINST ME, I'M GUESSING.
SO I'M ALREADY SHADY. WHAT A PAIN...
OH, UM...
WAIT, DON'T TELL ME...!
YOU'RE NOT ON YOUR WAY TO COMMIT SUICIDE, ARE YOU!?
THAT THERE'S A SCHOOL UNIFORM, ISN'T IT?
DON'T BE RASH, NOW, Y'HEAR!!?
HUH!?
I WOULDN'T KILL MYSELF EVEN IF YOU PAID ME TO!!
AWW.
CRAP.
SHOULDA AGREED FOR AN EASY OUT.
THEN WHAT'RE YOU DOIN' OUT HERE? SPEAK UP!
BOGPIGS...
WHAT'S THIS, NOW!?
I WAS GONNA LOOK FOR BOGPIGS...
LET'S GO WITH A STRAIGHT ANSWER AND SEE IF I CAN GET HER TO CHILL OUT. THEN MAYBE I CAN ASK ABOUT THAT LIGHT IN THE WOODS.
OH...

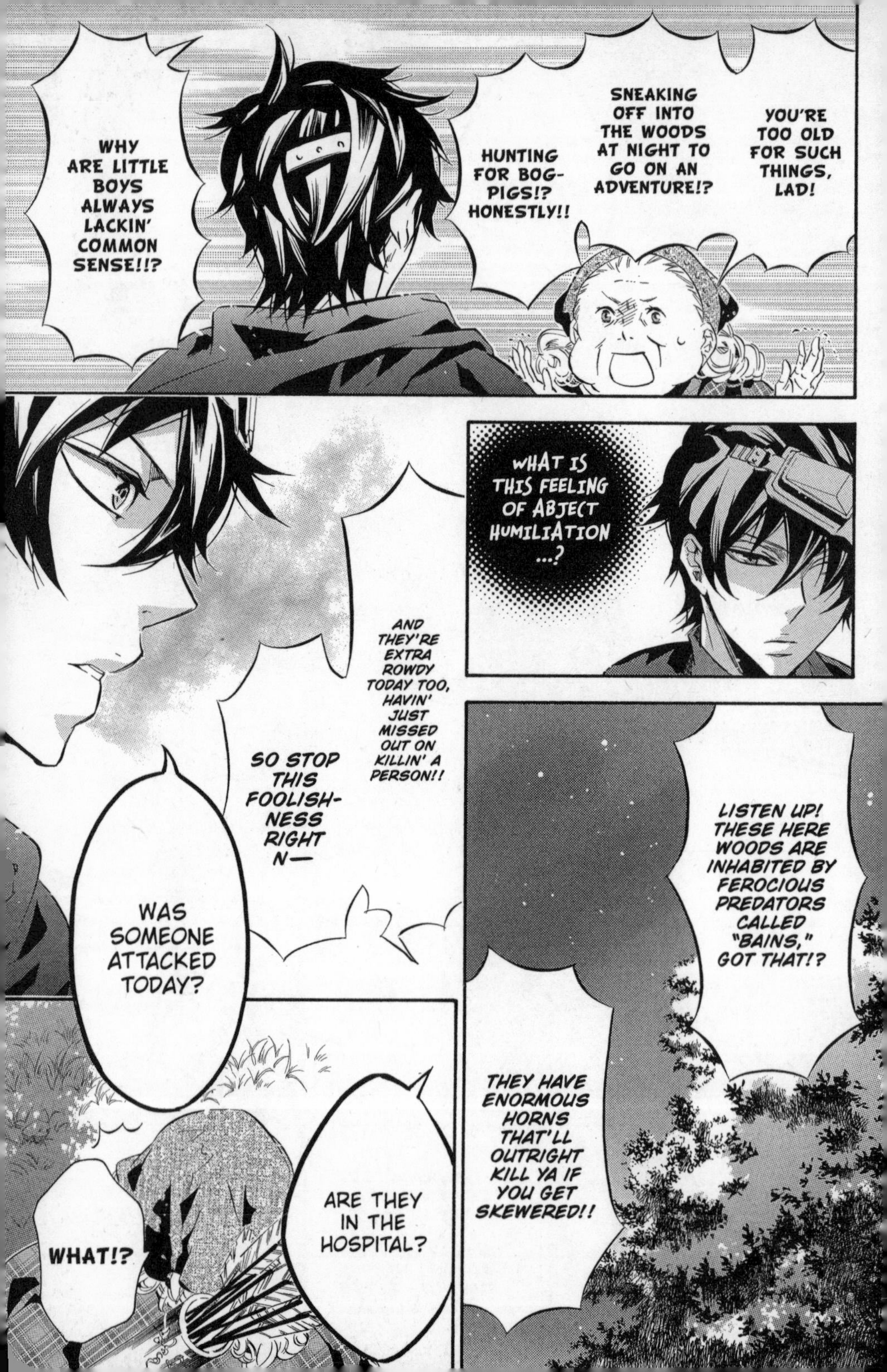
YOU'RE TOO OLD FOR SUCH THINGS, LAD!
SNEAKING OFF INTO THE WOODS AT NIGHT TO GO ON AN ADVENTURE!?
HUNTING FOR BOG-PIGS!? HONESTLY!!
WHY ARE LITTLE BOYS ALWAYS LACKIN' COMMON SENSE!!?
WHAT IS THIS FEELING OF ABJECT HUMILIATION ...?
LISTEN UP! THESE HERE WOODS ARE INHABITED BY FEROCIOUS PREDATORS CALLED "BAINS," GOT THAT!?
THEY HAVE ENORMOUS HORNS THAT'LL OUTRIGHT KILL YA IF YOU GET SKEWERED!!
AND THEY'RE EXTRA ROWDY TODAY TOO, HAVIN' JUST MISSED OUT ON KILLIN' A PERSON!!
SO STOP THIS FOOLISH-NESS RIGHT N—
WAS SOMEONE ATTACKED TODAY?
ARE THEY IN THE HOSPITAL?
WHAT!?

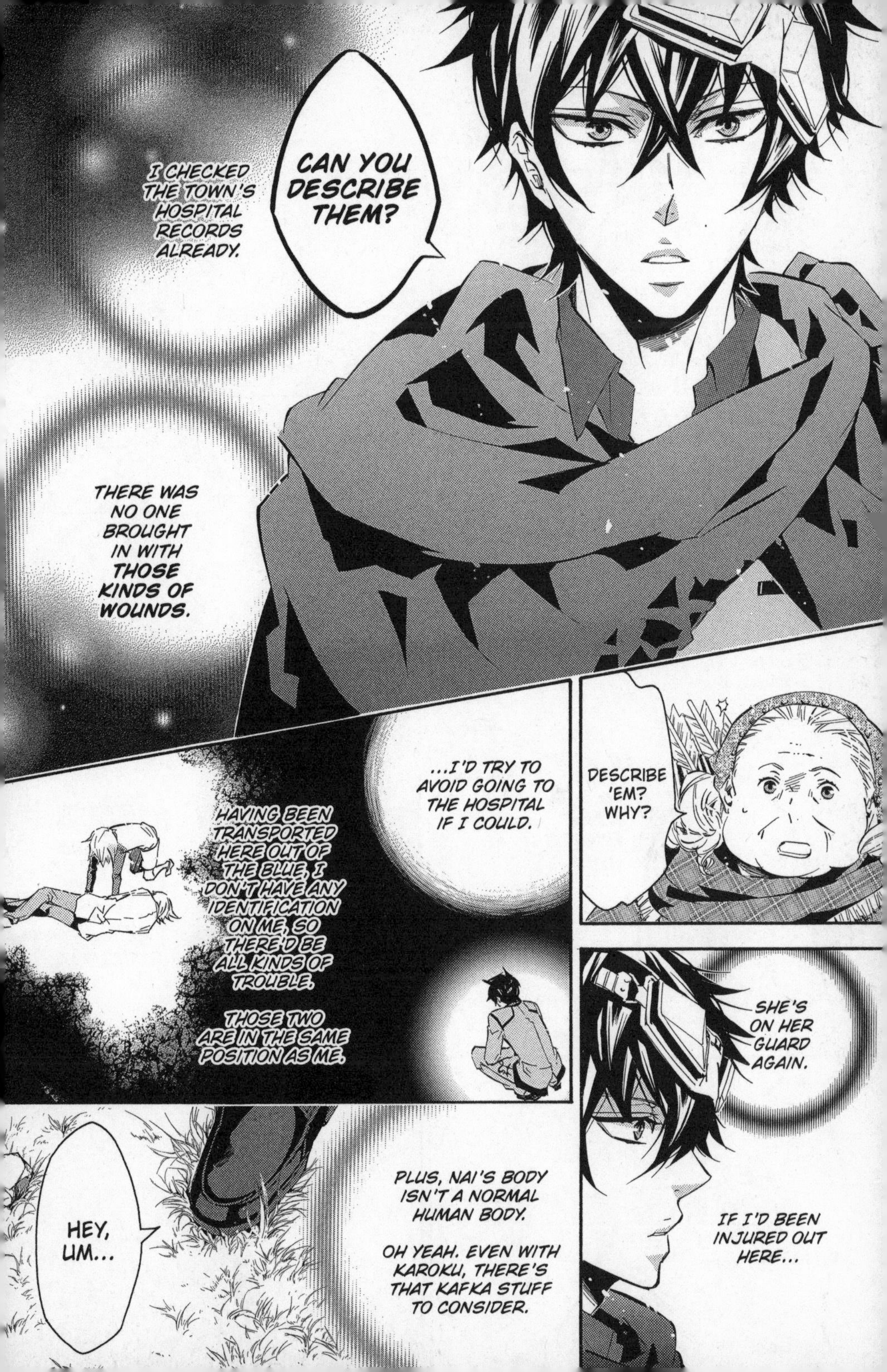

CAN YOU DESCRIBE THEM?
I CHECKED THE TOWN'S HOSPITAL RECORDS ALREADY.
THERE WAS NO ONE BROUGHT IN WITH THOSE KINDS OF WOUNDS.
DESCRIBE 'EM? WHY?
SHE'S ON HER GUARD AGAIN.
IF I'D BEEN INJURED OUT HERE...
...I'D TRY TO AVOID GOING TO THE HOSPITAL IF I COULD.
HAVING BEEN TRANSPORTED HERE OUT OF THE BLUE, I DON'T HAVE ANY IDENTIFICATION ON ME, SO THERE'D BE ALL KINDS OF TROUBLE.
THOSE TWO ARE IN THE SAME POSITION AS ME.
PLUS, NAI'S BODY ISN'T A NORMAL HUMAN BODY.
OH YEAH. EVEN WITH KAROKU, THERE'S THAT KAFKA STUFF TO CONSIDER.
HEY, UM...

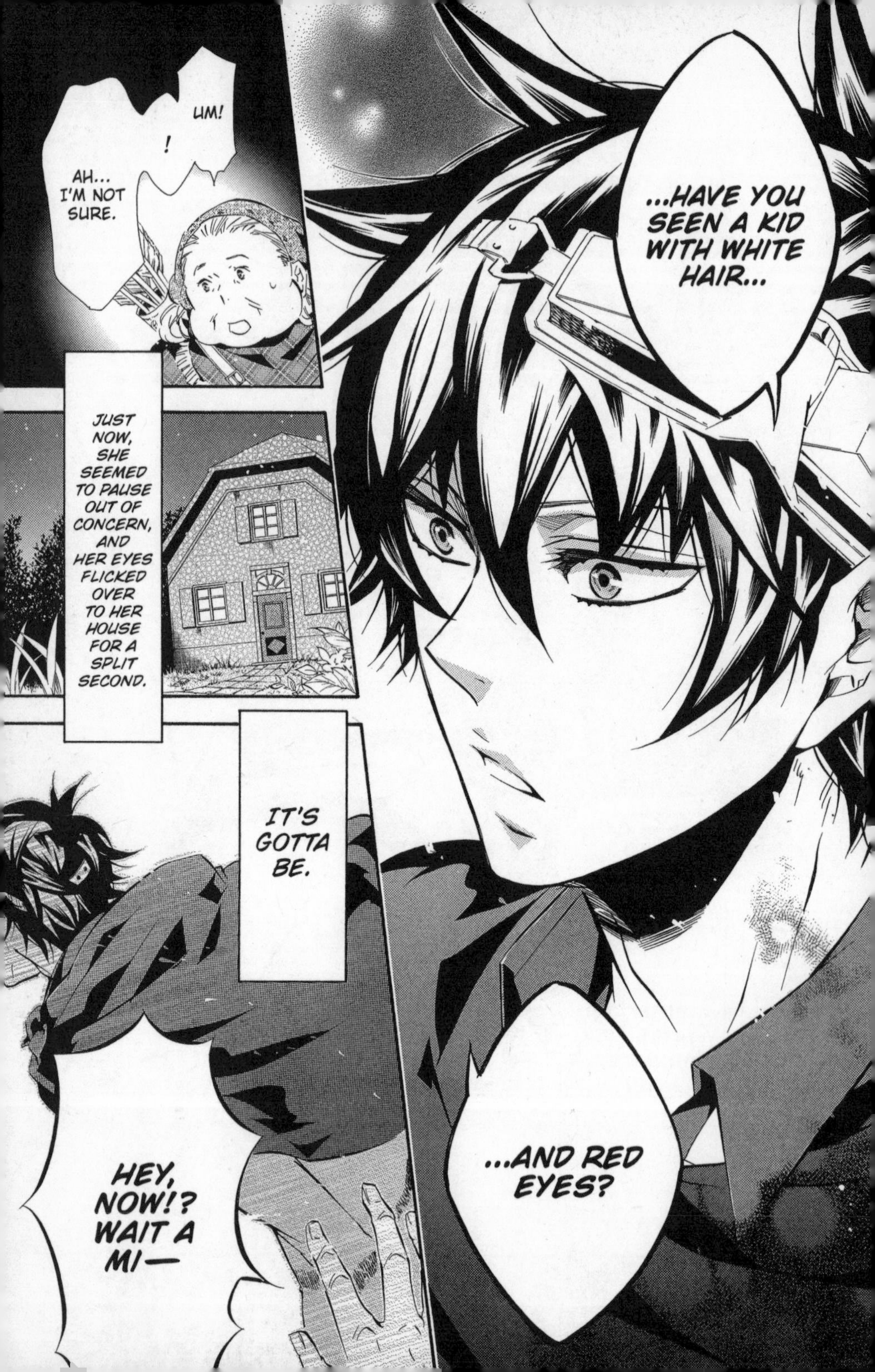
...HAVE YOU SEEN A KID WITH WHITE HAIR...
...AND RED EYES?
UM!
!
AH... I'M NOT SURE.
JUST NOW, SHE SEEMED TO PAUSE OUT OF CONCERN, AND HER EYES FLICKED OVER TO HER HOUSE FOR A SPLIT SECOND.
IT'S GOTTA BE.
HEY, NOW!? WAIT A MI—

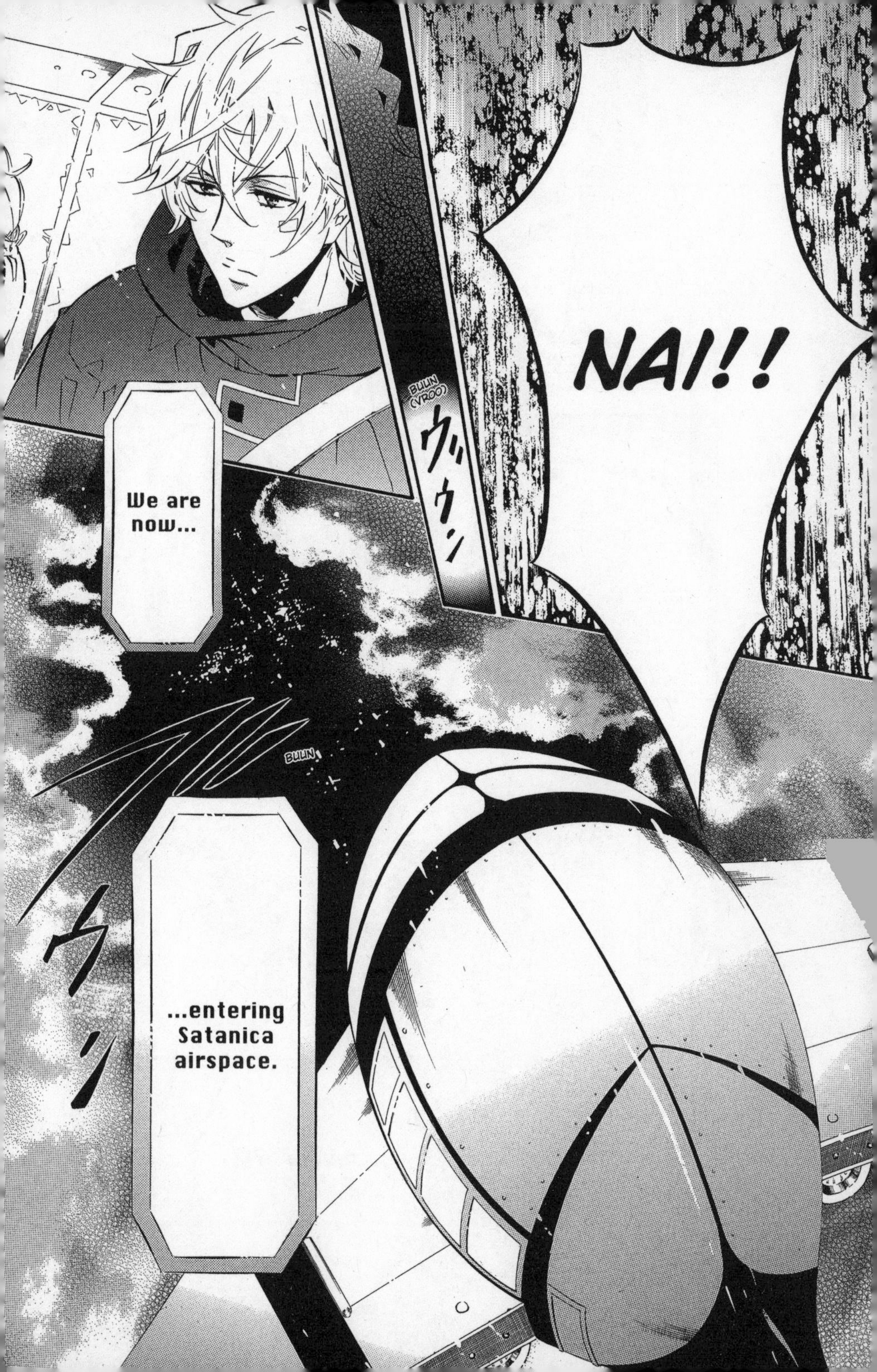
NAI!!
BUUN (VROO)
ヴゥン
We are now...
BUUN
...entering Satanica airspace.

KARNEVAL

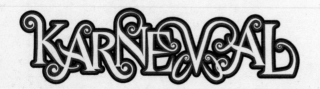

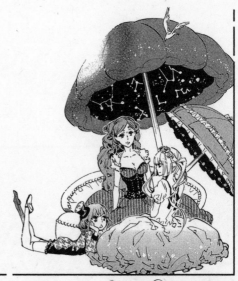

KARNEVAL

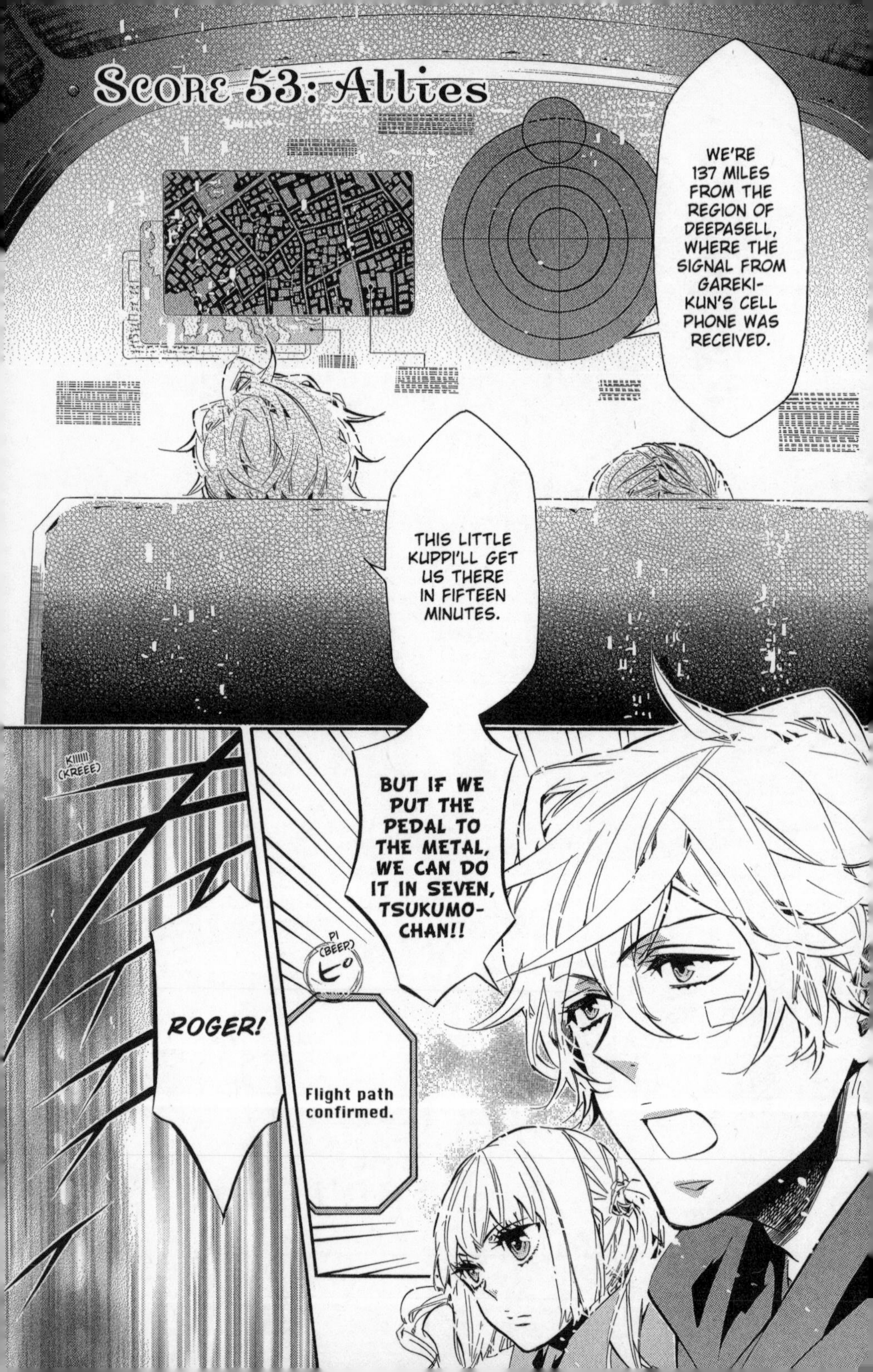

Score 53: Allies
WE'RE 137 MILES FROM THE REGION OF DEEPASELL, WHERE THE SIGNAL FROM GAREKI-KUN'S CELL PHONE WAS RECEIVED.
THIS LITTLE KUPPI'LL GET US THERE IN FIFTEEN MINUTES.
BUT IF WE PUT THE PEDAL TO THE METAL, WE CAN DO IT IN SEVEN, TSUKUMO-CHAN!!
PI (BEEP)
Flight path confirmed.
KIIIII (KREEE)
ROGER!

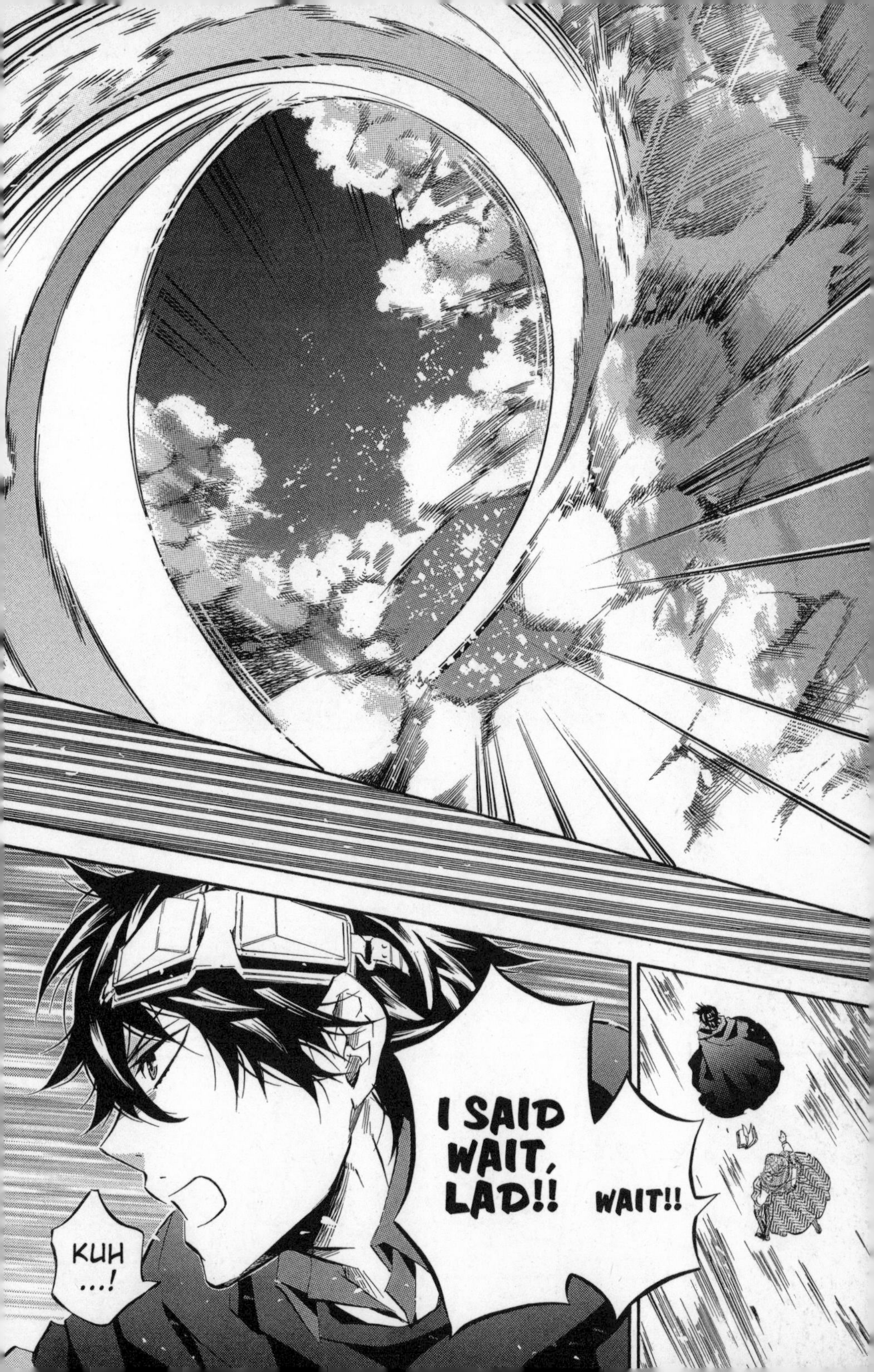
I SAID WAIT, LAD!!
WAIT!!
KUH ...!

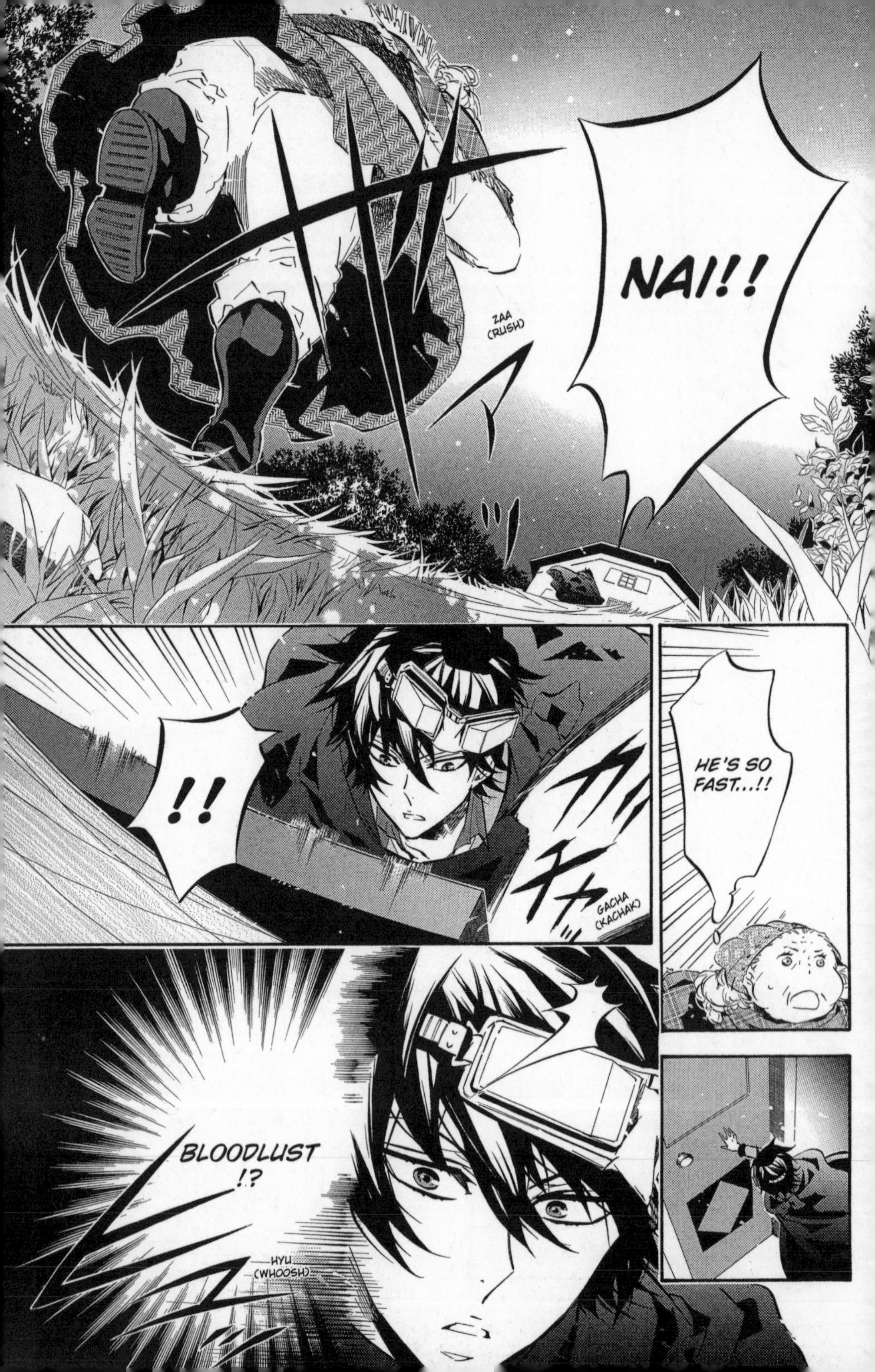
NAI!!
ZAA (RUSH)
HE'S SO FAST...!!
!!
GACHA (KACHAK)
BLOODLUST !?
HYU (WHOOSH)

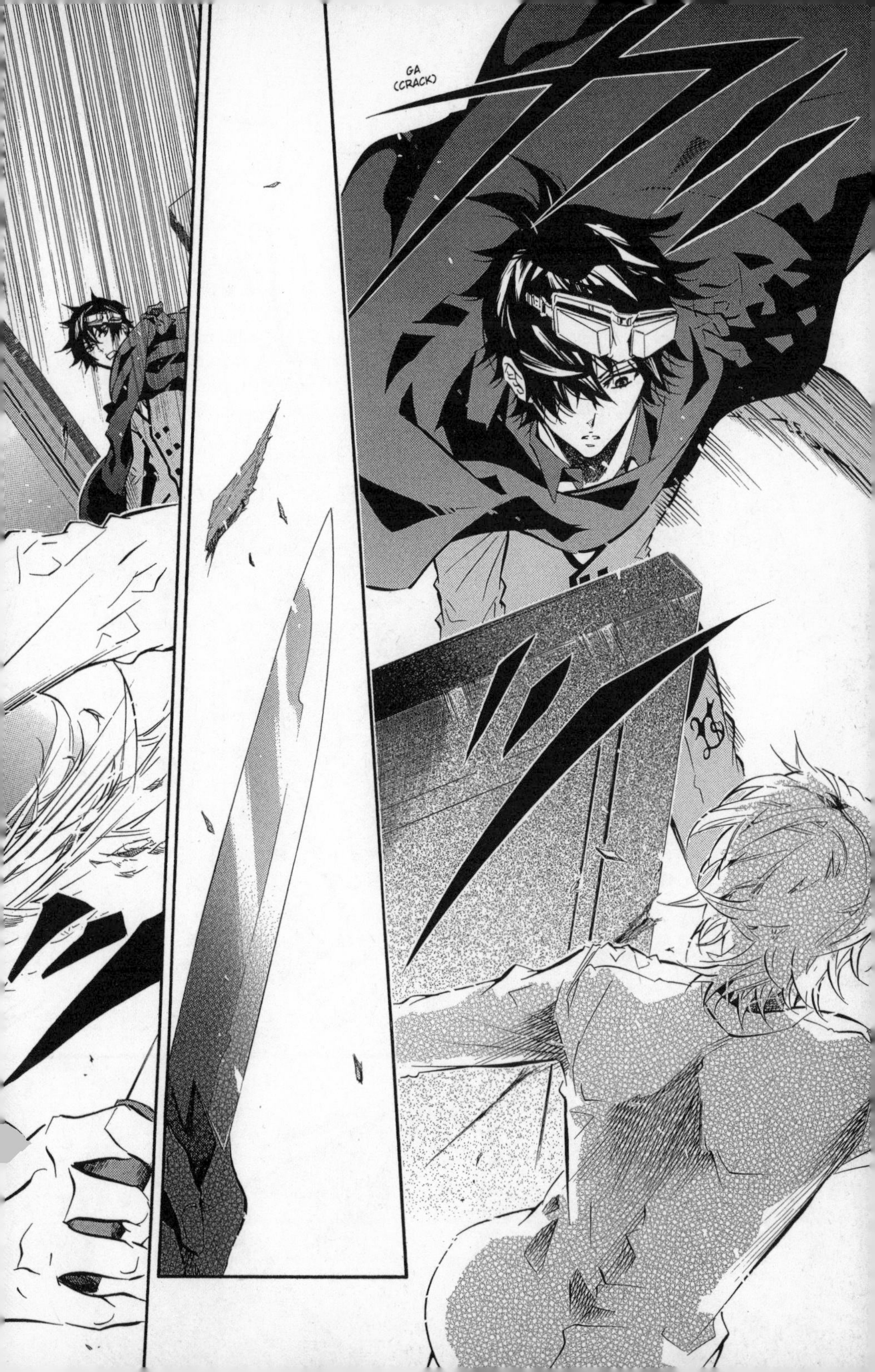
GA
(CRACK)

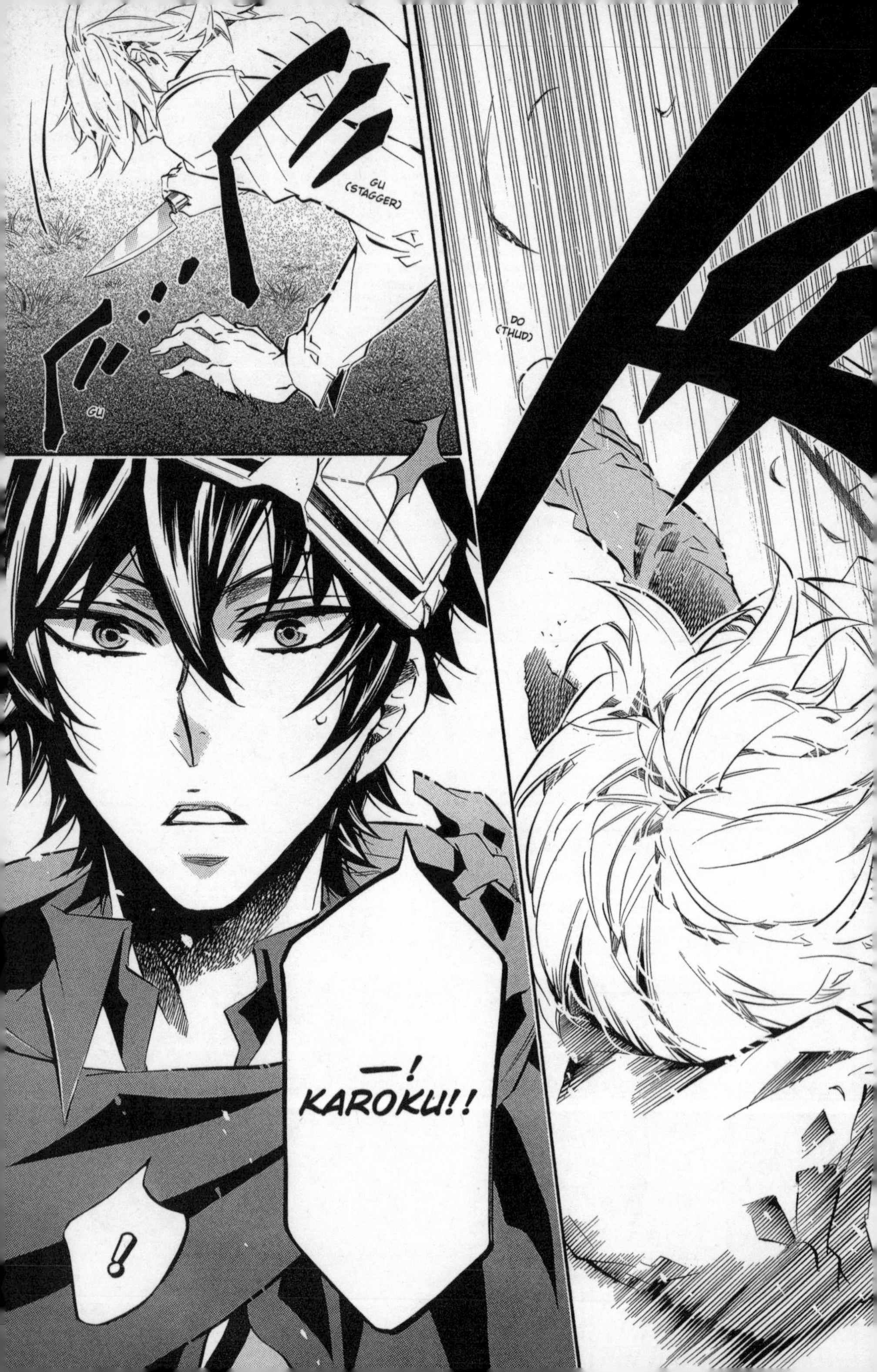
DO (THUD)
GU (STAGGER)
GU
—! KAROKU!!
!

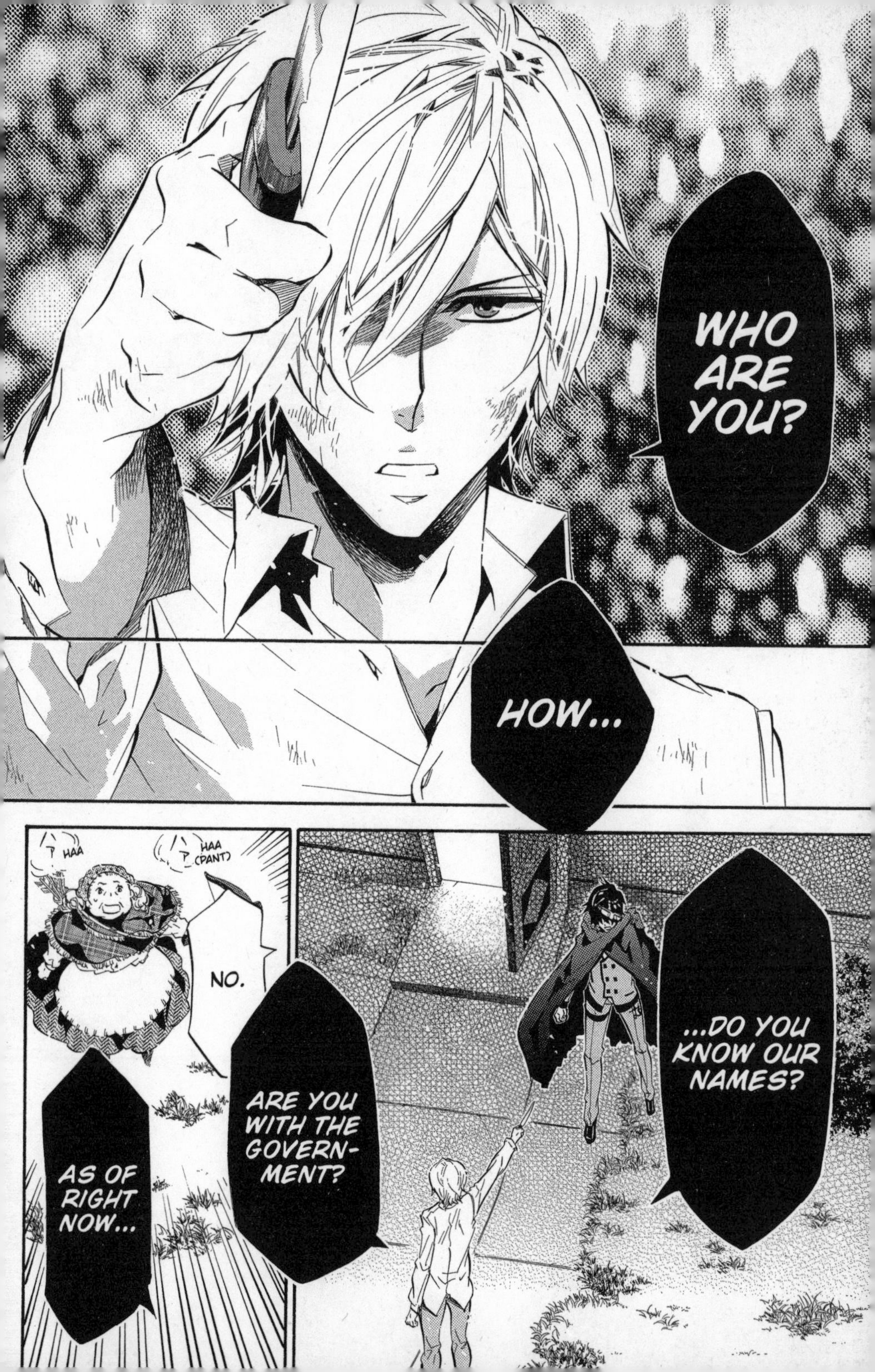
WHO ARE YOU?
HOW...
...DO YOU KNOW OUR NAMES?
ARE YOU WITH THE GOVERN-MENT?
HAA
HAA (PANT)
NO.
AS OF RIGHT NOW...

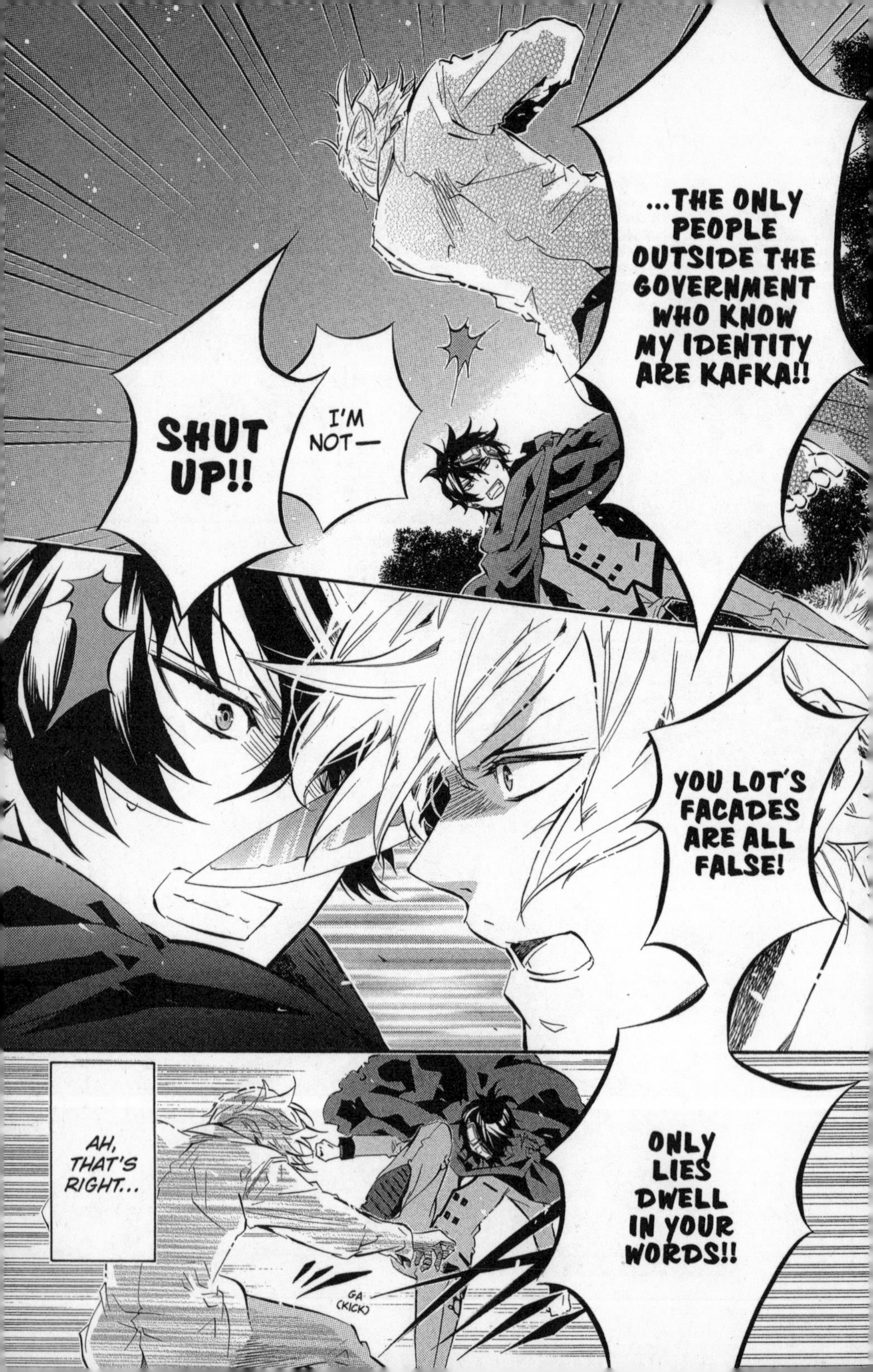
...THE ONLY PEOPLE OUTSIDE THE GOVERNMENT WHO KNOW MY IDENTITY ARE KAFKA!!
I'M NOT—
SHUT UP!!
YOU LOT'S FACADES ARE ALL FALSE!
ONLY LIES DWELL IN YOUR WORDS!!
GA (KICK)
AH, THAT'S RIGHT...

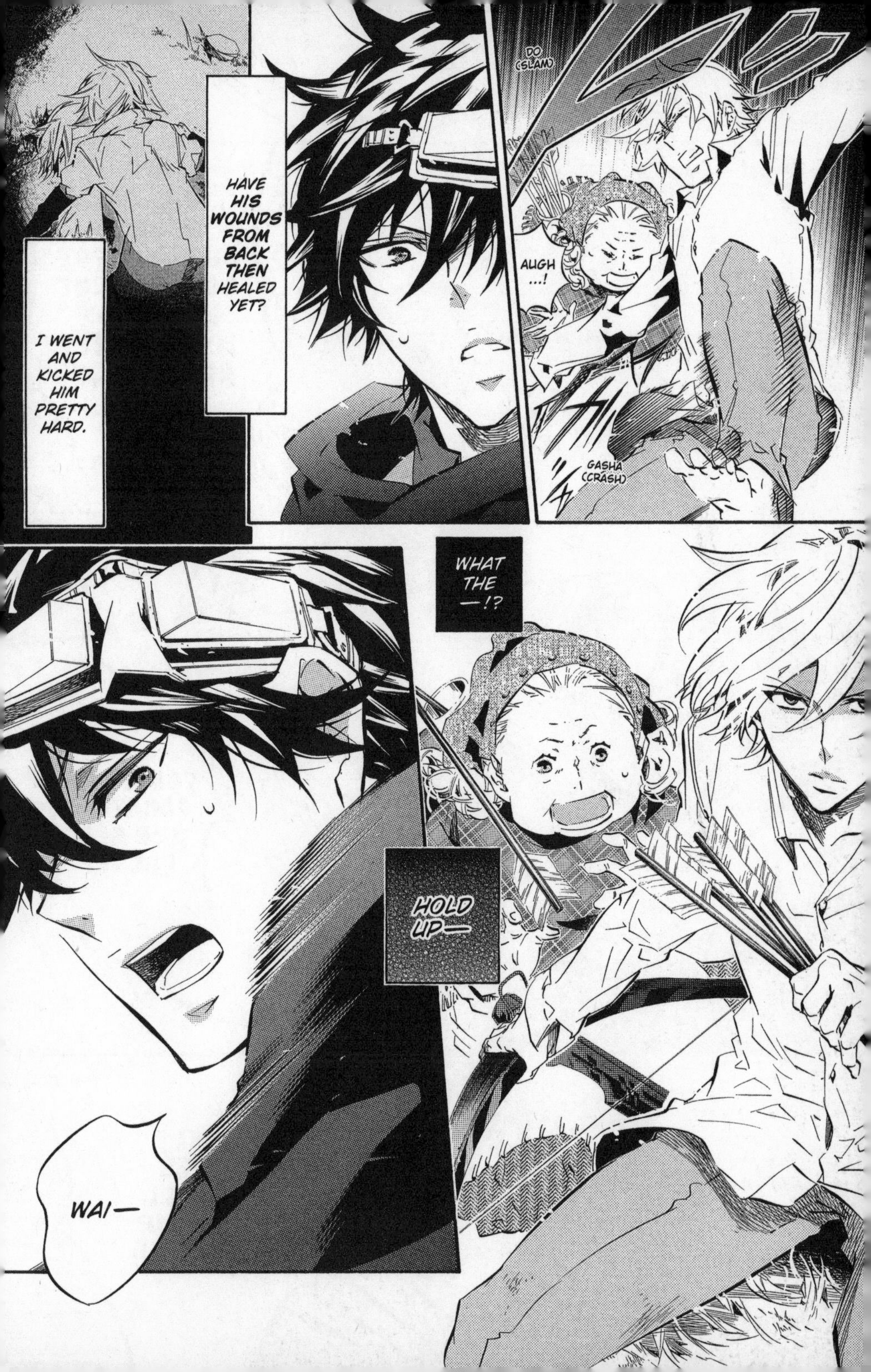
DO (SLAM)
AUGH ...!
GASHA (CRASH)
HAVE HIS WOUNDS FROM BACK THEN HEALED YET?
I WENT AND KICKED HIM PRETTY HARD.
WHAT THE —!?
HOLD UP—
WAI—

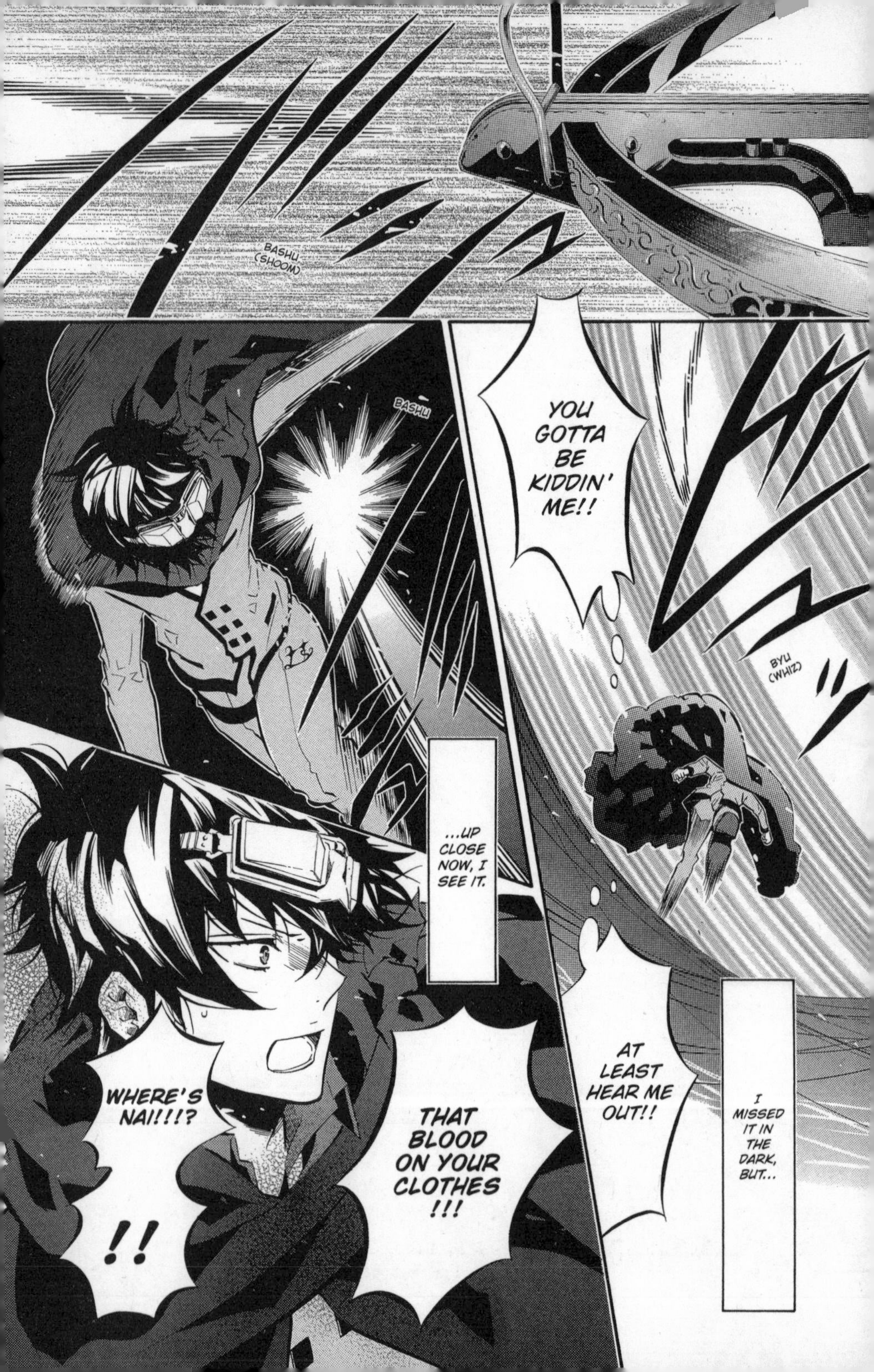
BASHU (SHOOM)
YOU GOTTA BE KIDDIN' ME!!
BYU (WHIZ)
AT LEAST HEAR ME OUT!!
I MISSED IT IN THE DARK, BUT...
BASHU
...UP CLOSE NOW, I SEE IT.
THAT BLOOD ON YOUR CLOTHES!!!
WHERE'S NAI!!!?
!!

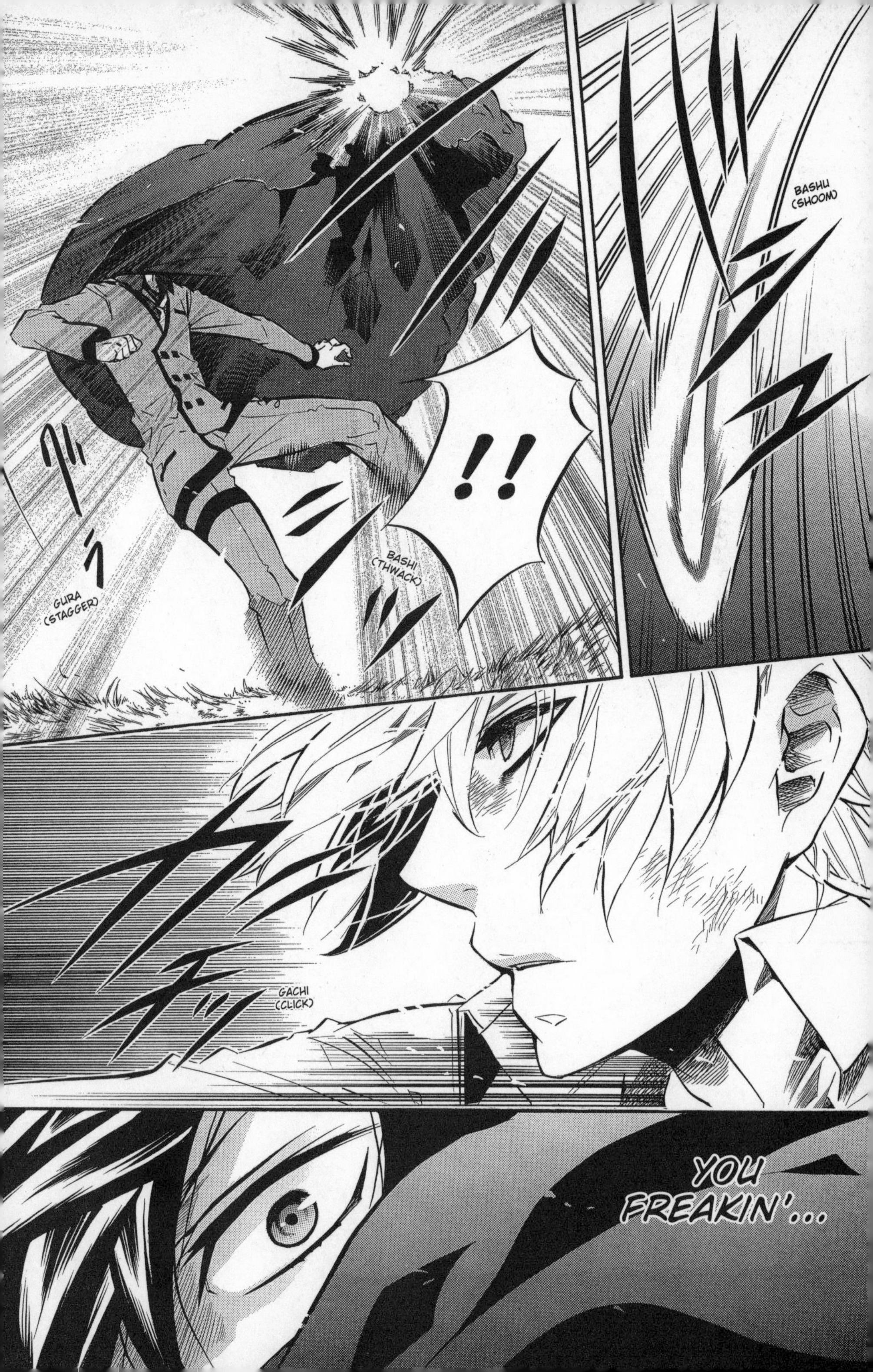
BASHU
(SHOOM)
!!
BASHI
(THWACK)
GURA
(STAGGER)
GACHI
(CLICK)
YOU FREAKIN'...

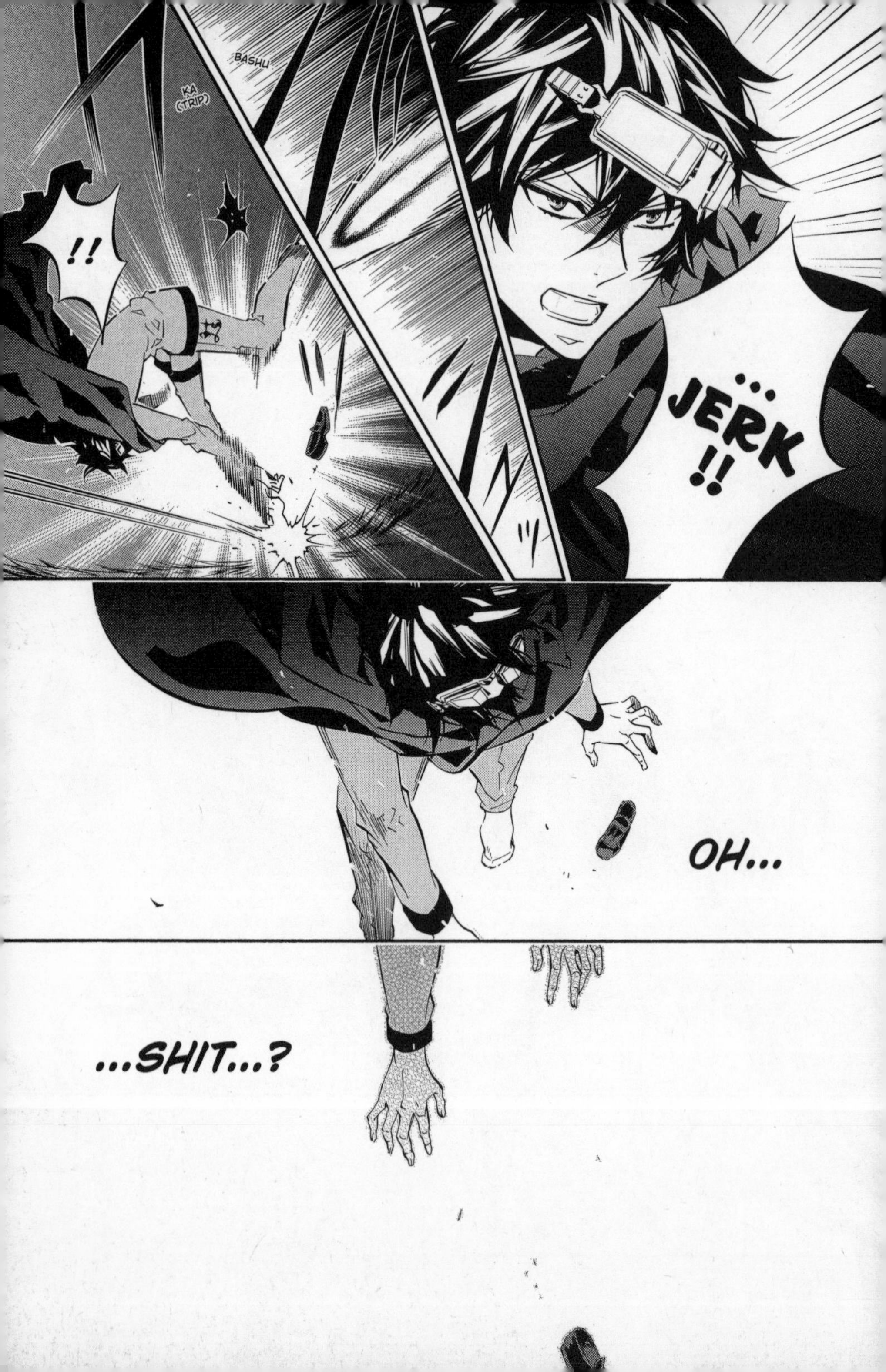
...JERK!!
BASHU
KA (TRIP)
!!
OH...
...SHIT...?

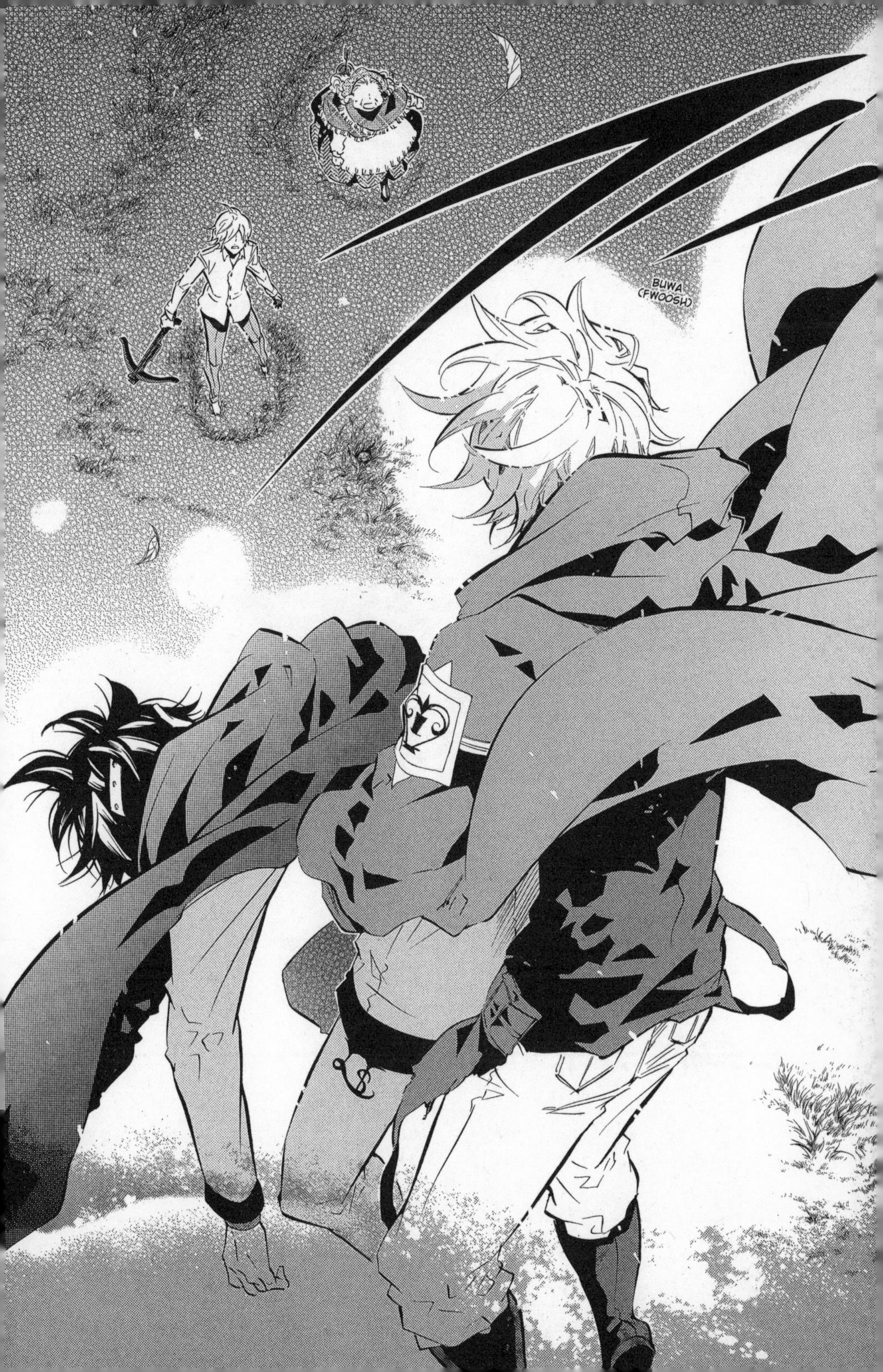
BUWA
(FWOOSH)

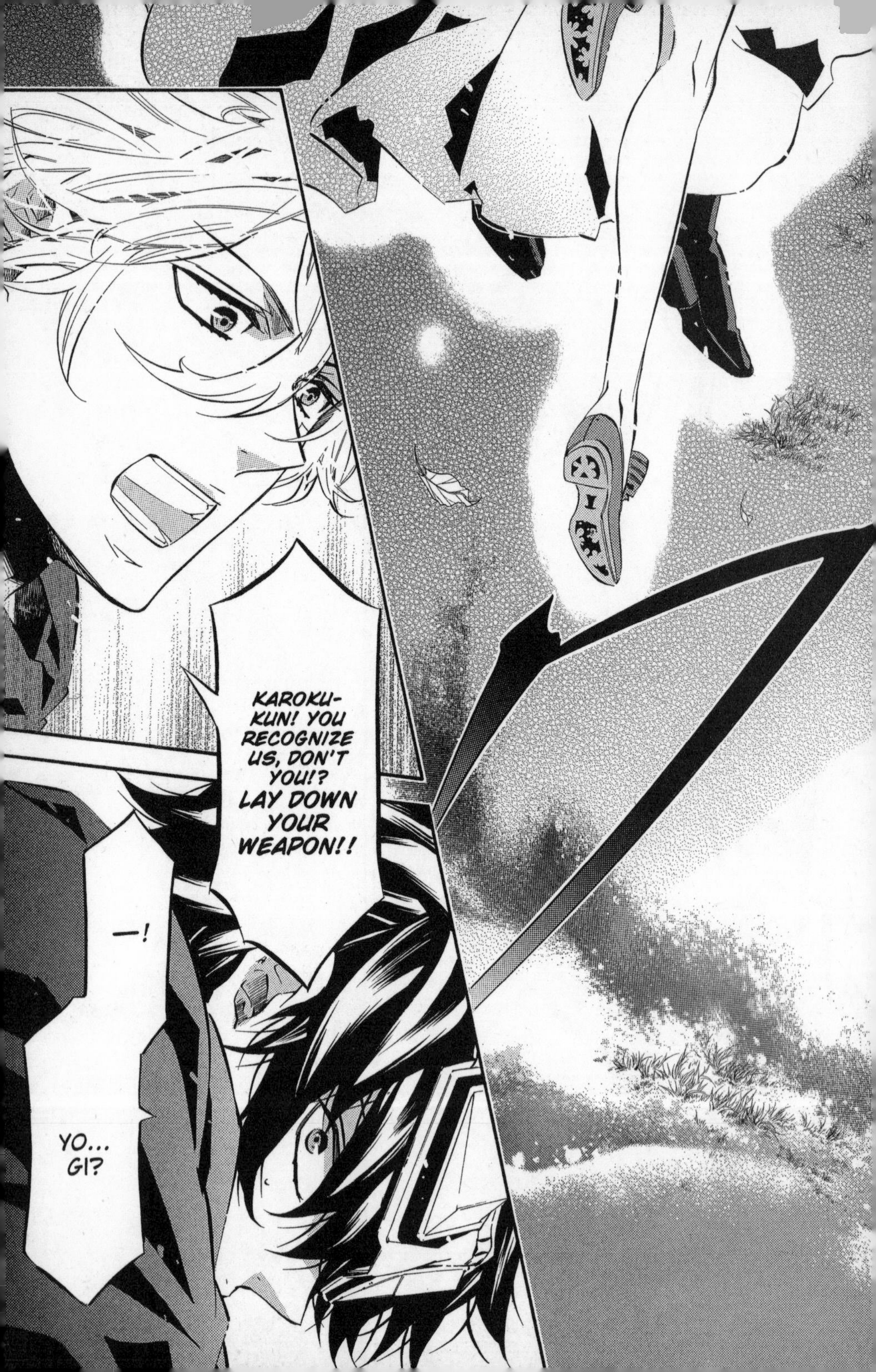
KAROKU-KUN! YOU RECOGNIZE US, DON'T YOU!? LAY DOWN YOUR WEAPON!!
—!
YO... GI?

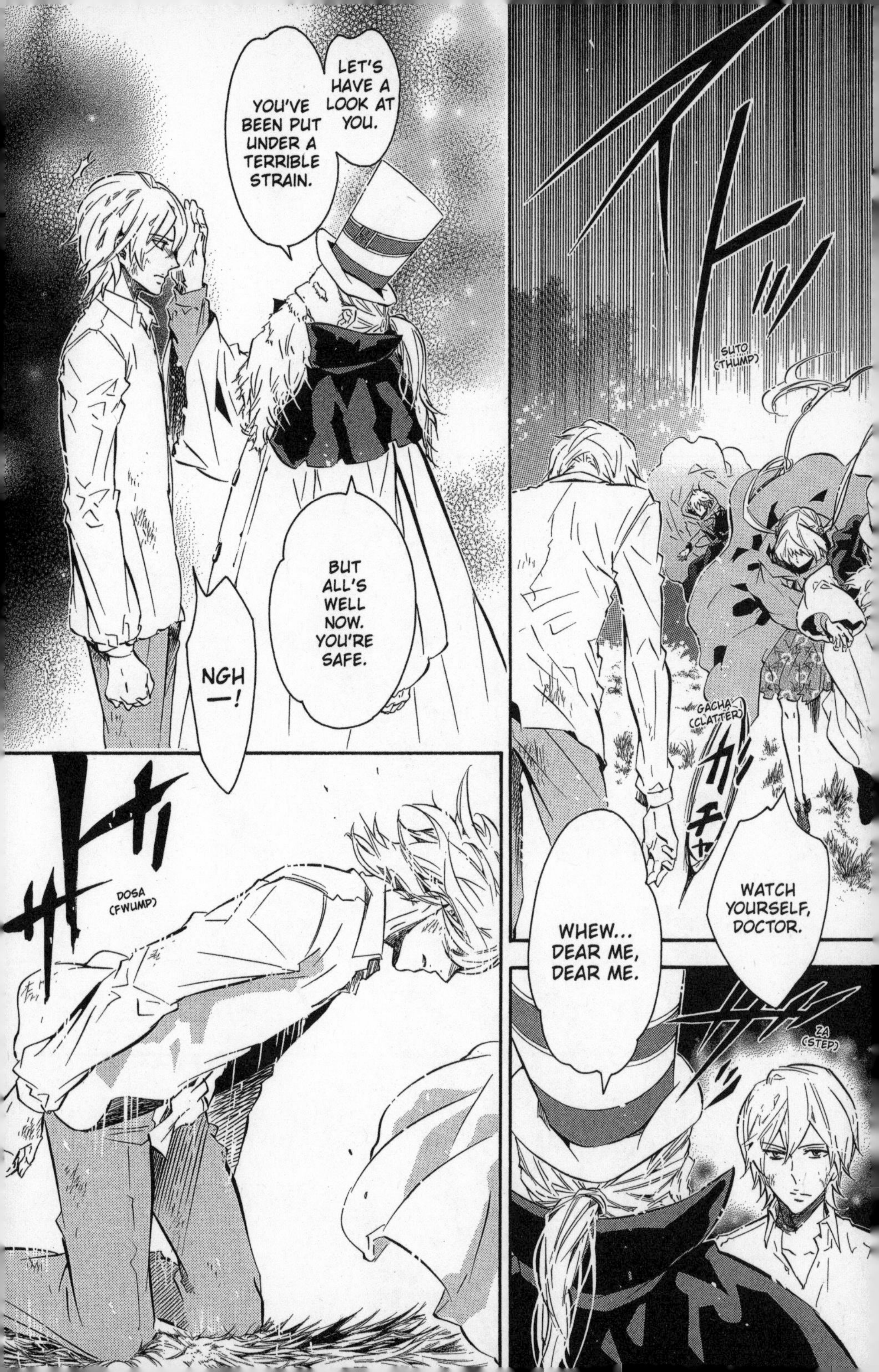
SUTO (THUMP)
GACHA (CLATTER)
WATCH YOURSELF, DOCTOR.
LET'S HAVE A LOOK AT YOU.
YOU'VE BEEN PUT UNDER A TERRIBLE STRAIN.
BUT ALL'S WELL NOW. YOU'RE SAFE.
NGH—!
WHEW... DEAR ME, DEAR ME.
ZA (STEP)
DOSA (FWUMP)

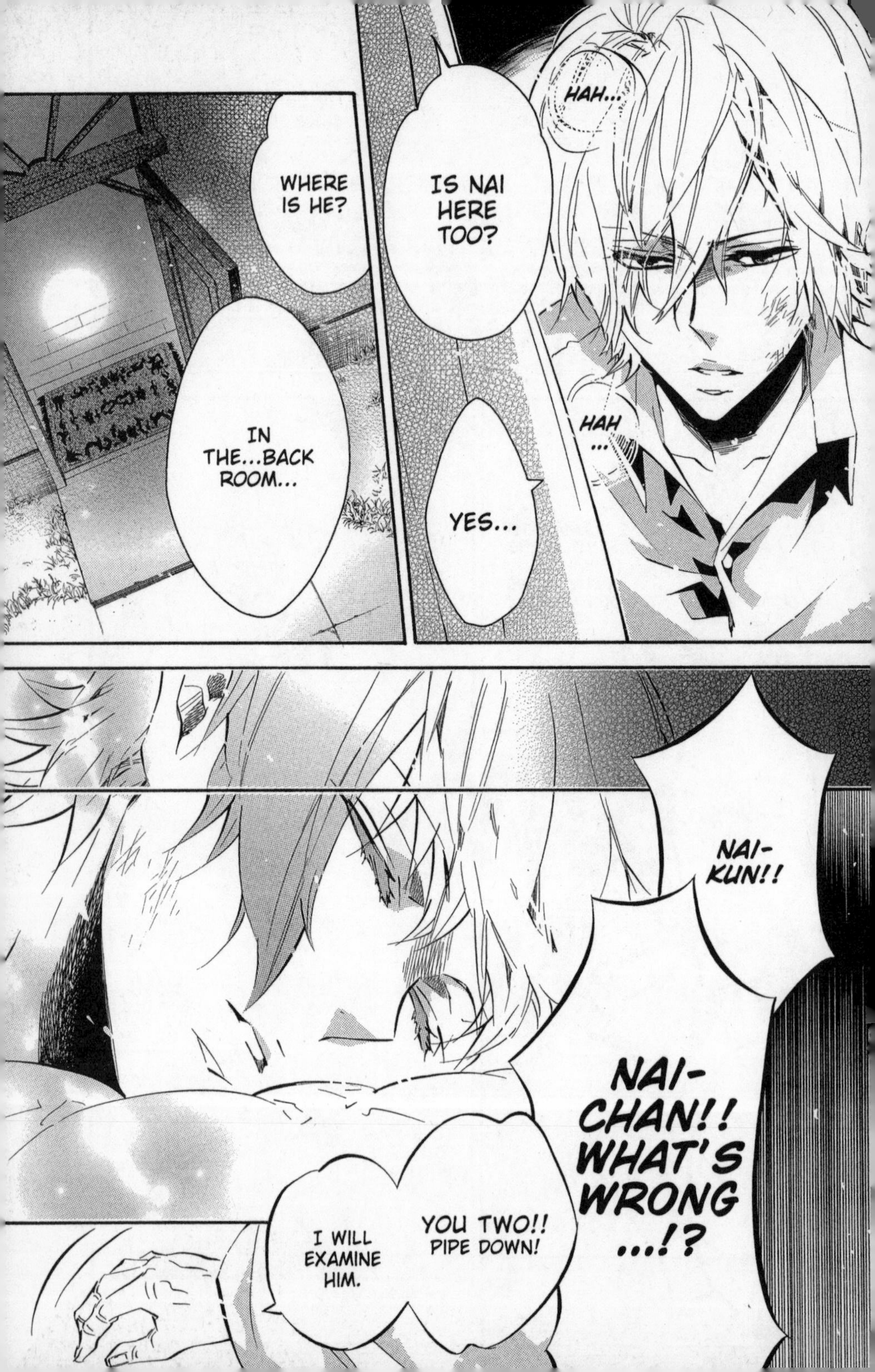
HAH...
IS NAI HERE TOO?
HAH ...
YES...
WHERE IS HE?
IN THE...BACK ROOM...
NAI-KUN!!
NAI-CHAN!! WHAT'S WRONG ...!?
YOU TWO!! PIPE DOWN!
I WILL EXAMINE HIM.

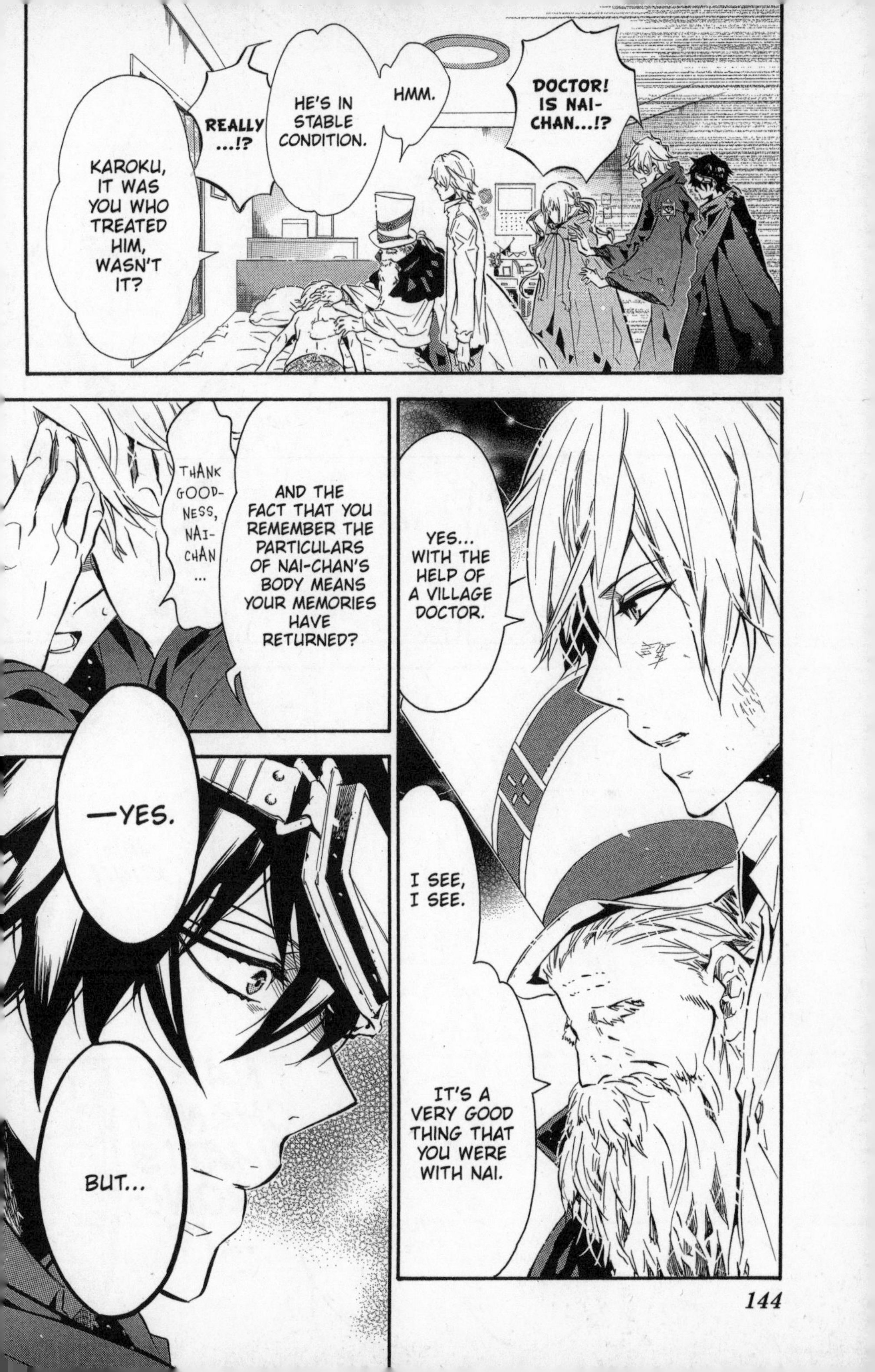
DOCTOR! IS NAI-CHAN...!?
HMM.
HE'S IN STABLE CONDITION.
REALLY ...!?
KAROKU, IT WAS YOU WHO TREATED HIM, WASN'T IT?
YES... WITH THE HELP OF A VILLAGE DOCTOR.
I SEE, I SEE.
IT'S A VERY GOOD THING THAT YOU WERE WITH NAI.
AND THE FACT THAT YOU REMEMBER THE PARTICULARS OF NAI-CHAN'S BODY MEANS YOUR MEMORIES HAVE RETURNED?
THANK GOODNESS, NAI-CHAN ...
—YES.
BUT...

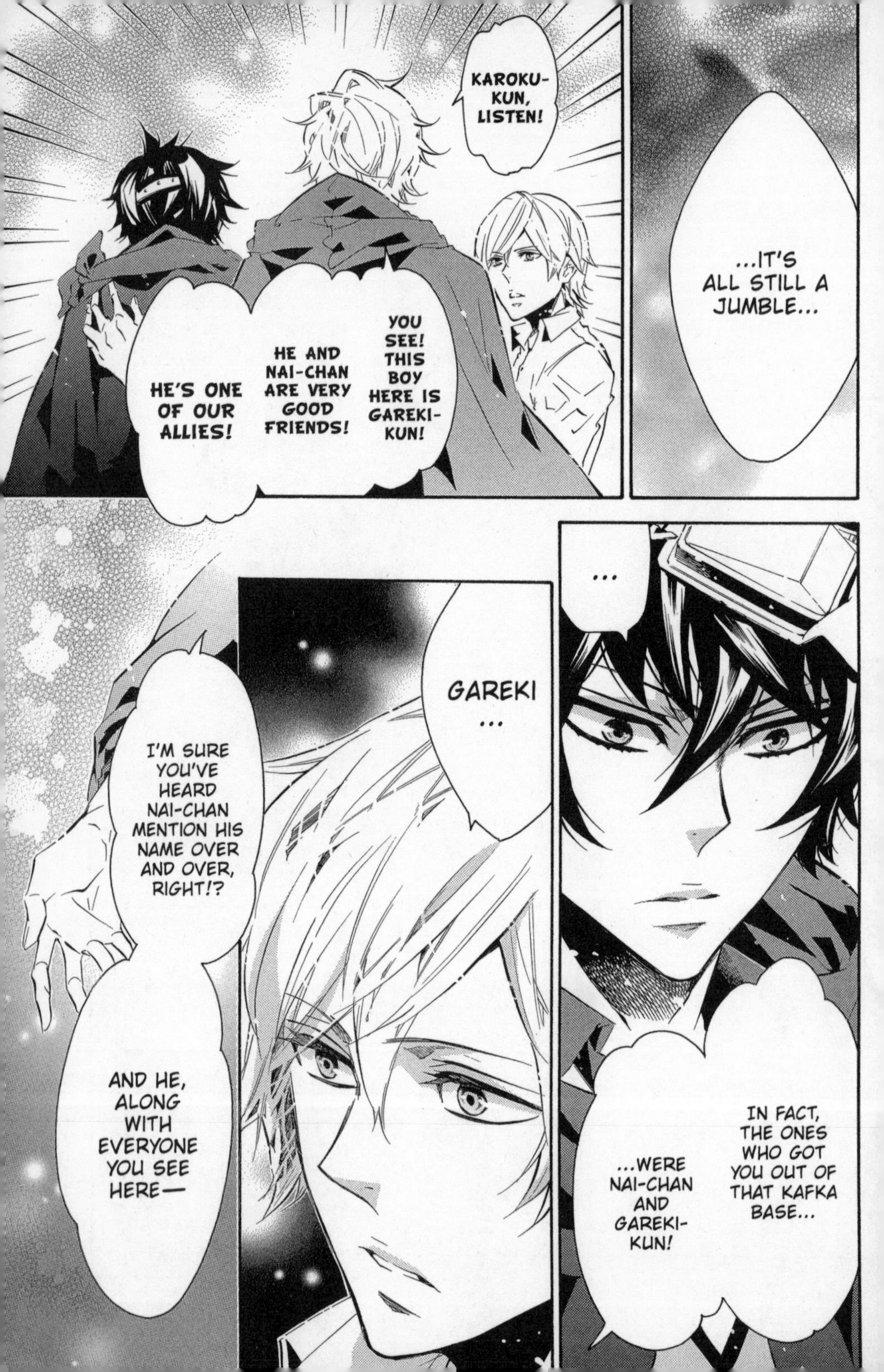
...IT'S ALL STILL A JUMBLE...
KAROKU-KUN, LISTEN!
YOU SEE! THIS BOY HERE IS GAREKI-KUN!
HE AND NAI-CHAN ARE VERY GOOD FRIENDS!
HE'S ONE OF OUR ALLIES!
...
GAREKI ...
I'M SURE YOU'VE HEARD NAI-CHAN MENTION HIS NAME OVER AND OVER, RIGHT!?
AND HE, ALONG WITH EVERYONE YOU SEE HERE—
IN FACT, THE ONES WHO GOT YOU OUT OF THAT KAFKA BASE...
...WERE NAI-CHAN AND GAREKI-KUN!

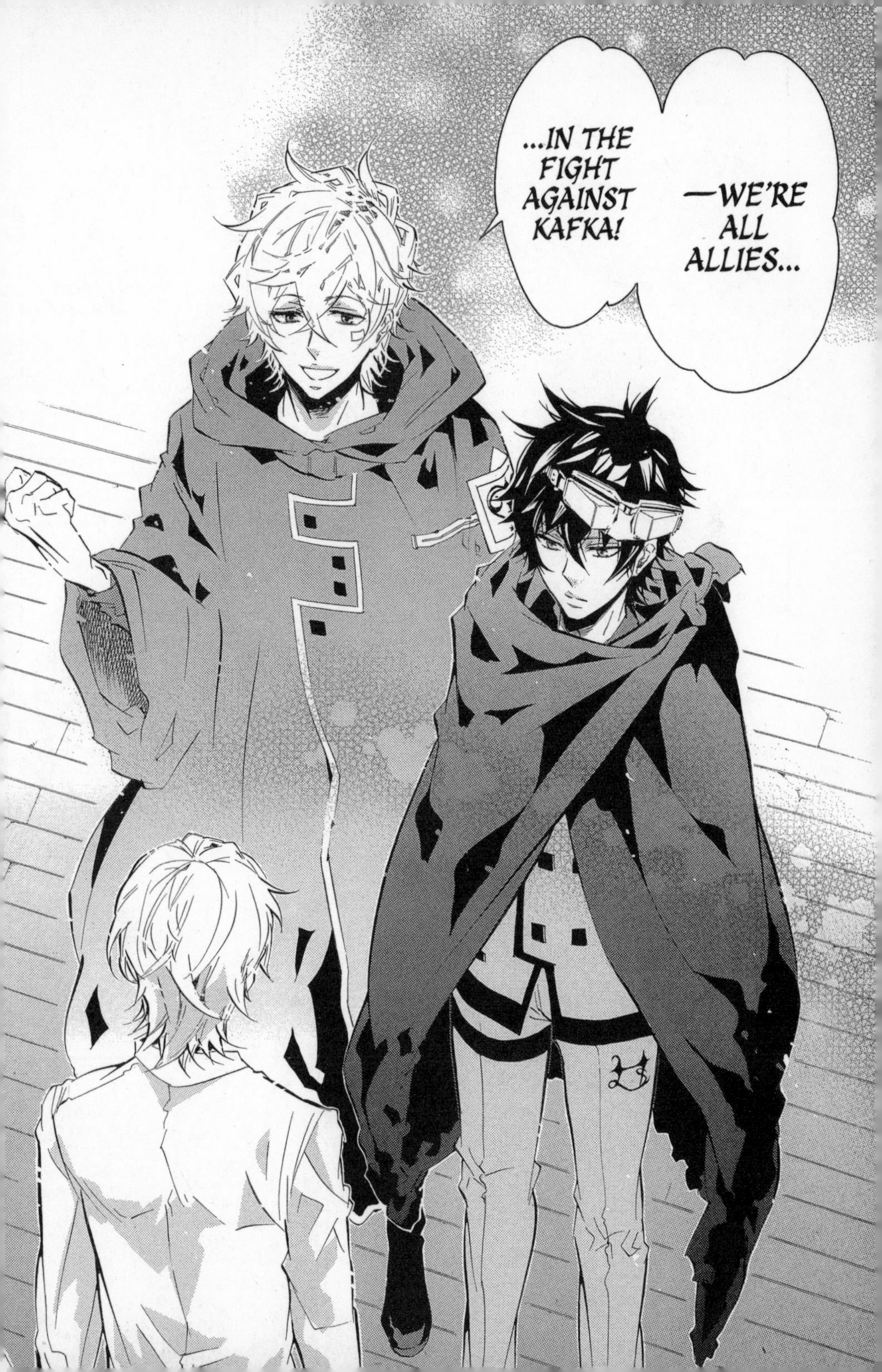
—WE'RE ALL ALLIES...
...IN THE FIGHT AGAINST KAFKA!

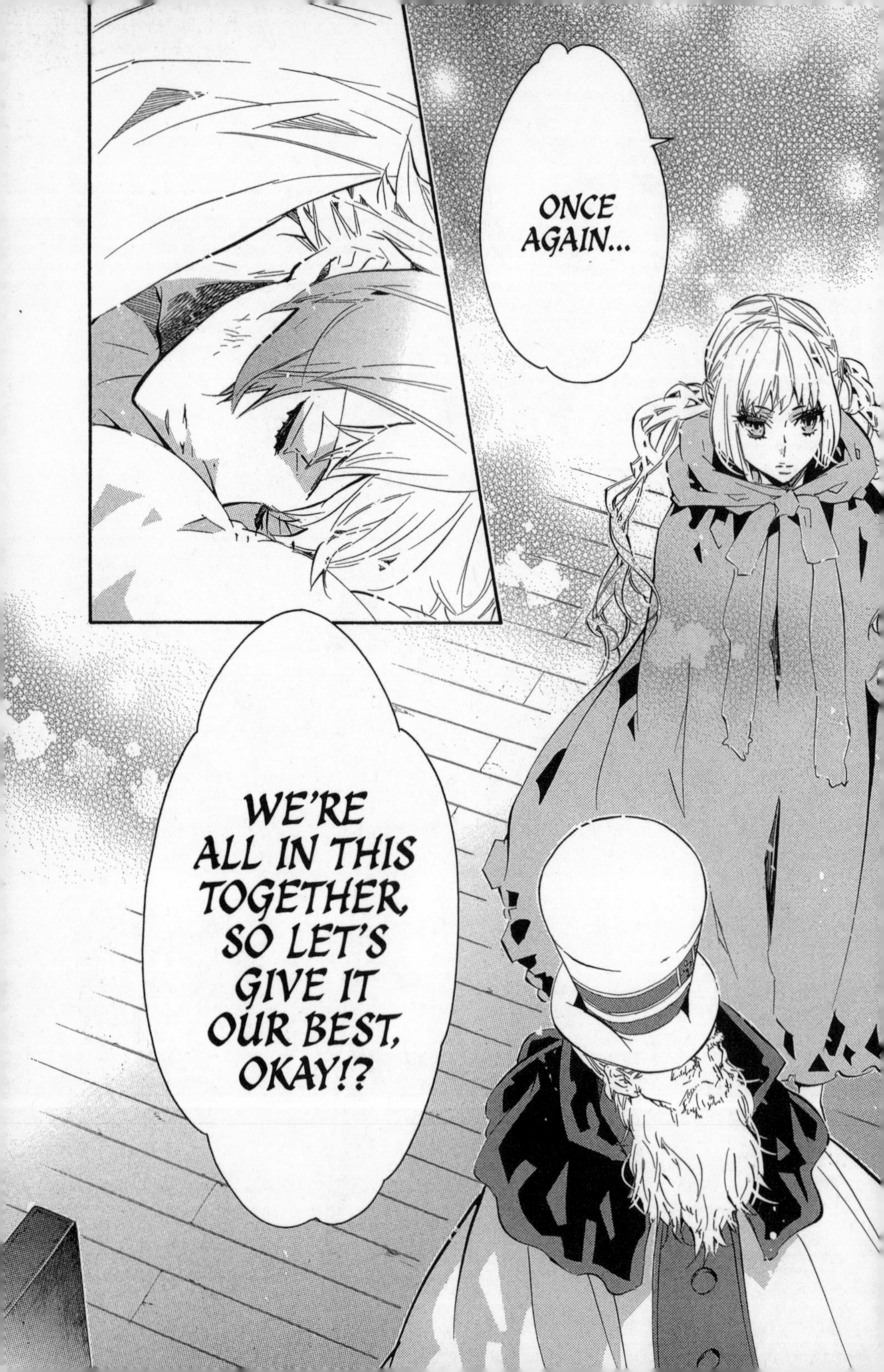
ONCE AGAIN...
WE'RE ALL IN THIS TOGETHER, SO LET'S GIVE IT OUR BEST, OKAY!?

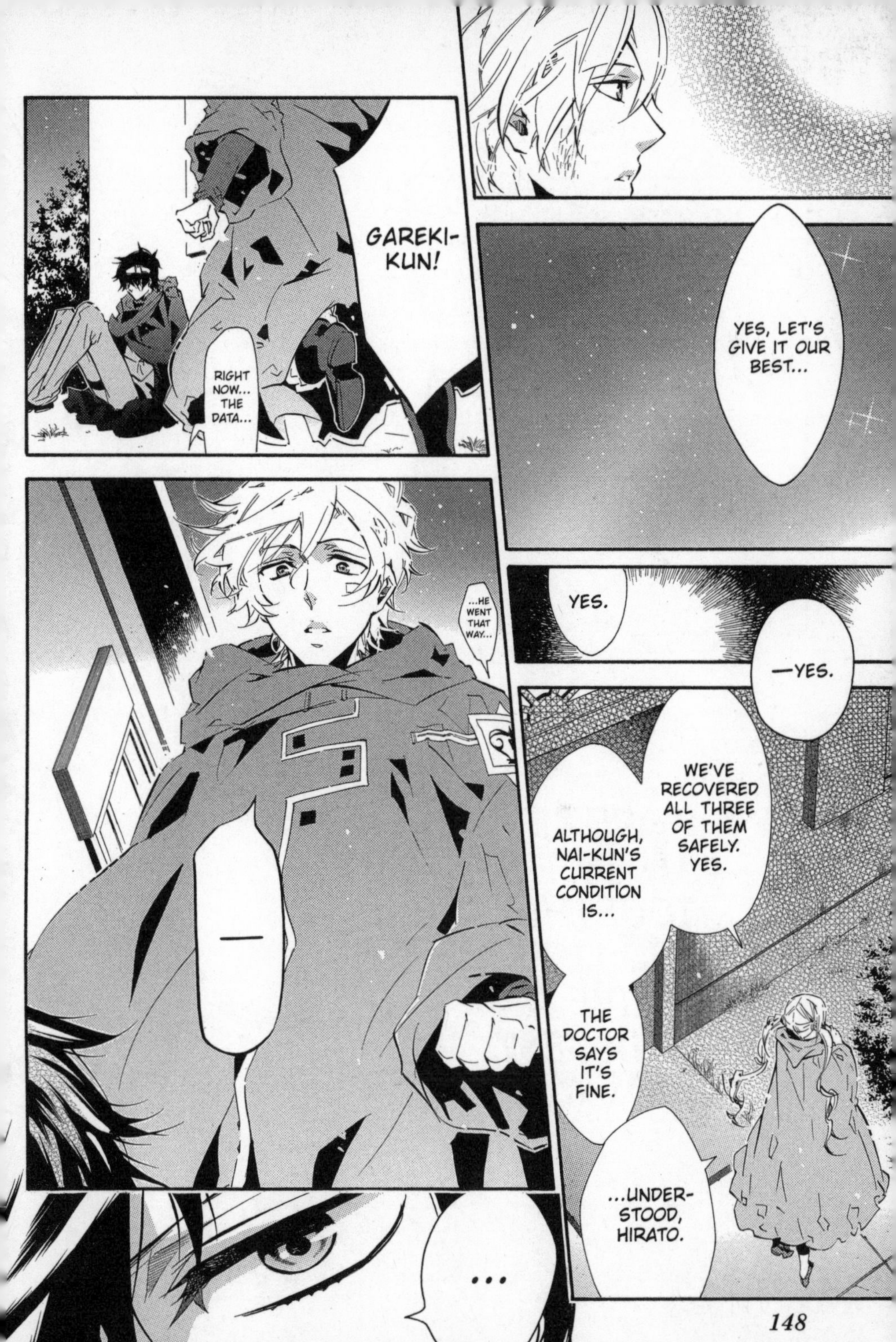
YES, LET'S GIVE IT OUR BEST...
YES.
—YES.
WE'VE RECOVERED ALL THREE OF THEM SAFELY. YES.
ALTHOUGH, NAI-KUN'S CURRENT CONDITION IS...
THE DOCTOR SAYS IT'S FINE.
...UNDER-STOOD, HIRATO.
GAREKI-KUN!
RIGHT NOW... THE DATA...
...HE WENT THAT WAY...
—
...

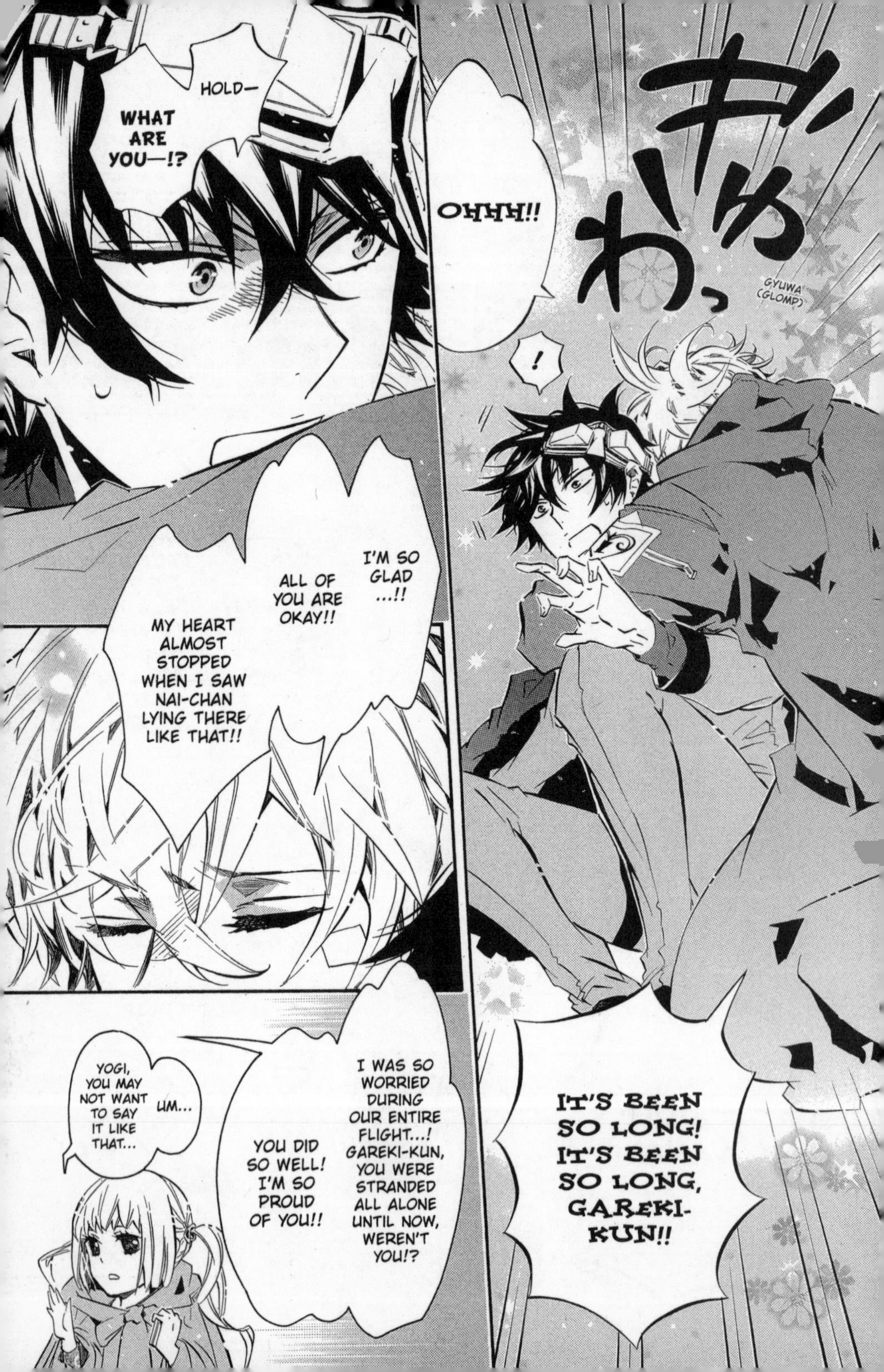

ぎゅわっ
GYUWA (GLOMP)
OHHH!!
!
IT'S BEEN SO LONG! IT'S BEEN SO LONG, GAREKI-KUN!!
HOLD—
WHAT ARE YOU—!?
I'M SO GLAD ...!!
ALL OF YOU ARE OKAY!!
MY HEART ALMOST STOPPED WHEN I SAW NAI-CHAN LYING THERE LIKE THAT!!
I WAS SO WORRIED DURING OUR ENTIRE FLIGHT...! GAREKI-KUN, YOU WERE STRANDED ALL ALONE UNTIL NOW, WEREN'T YOU!?
YOU DID SO WELL! I'M SO PROUD OF YOU!!
UM...
YOGI, YOU MAY NOT WANT TO SAY IT LIKE THAT...

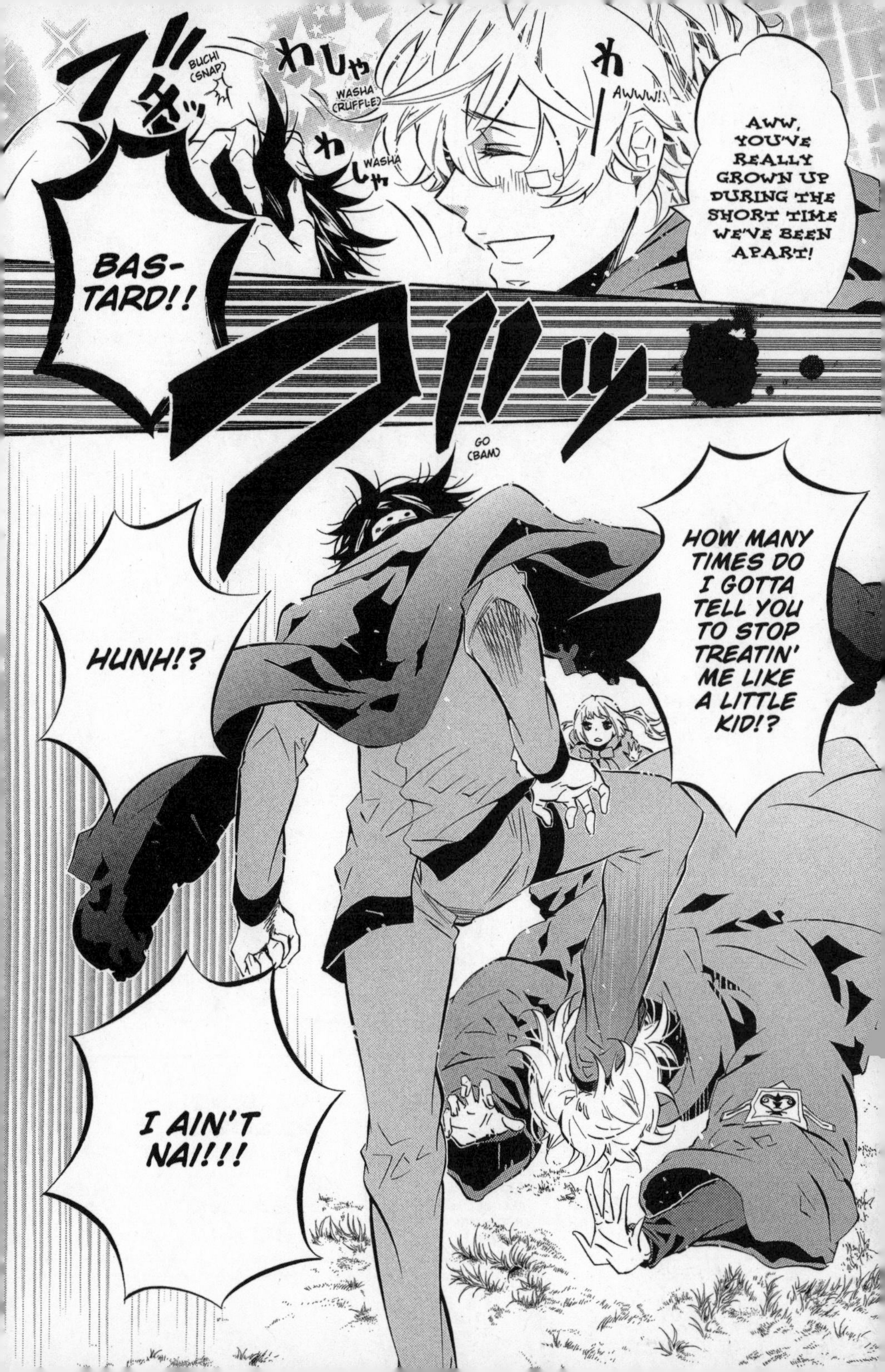
AWW, YOU'VE REALLY GROWN UP DURING THE SHORT TIME WE'VE BEEN APART!
AWWW!
WASHA (RUFFLE)
WASHA
BUCHI (SNAP)
BAS-TARD!!
GO (BAM)
HOW MANY TIMES DO I GOTTA TELL YOU TO STOP TREATIN' ME LIKE A LITTLE KID!?
HUNH!?
I AIN'T NAI!!!

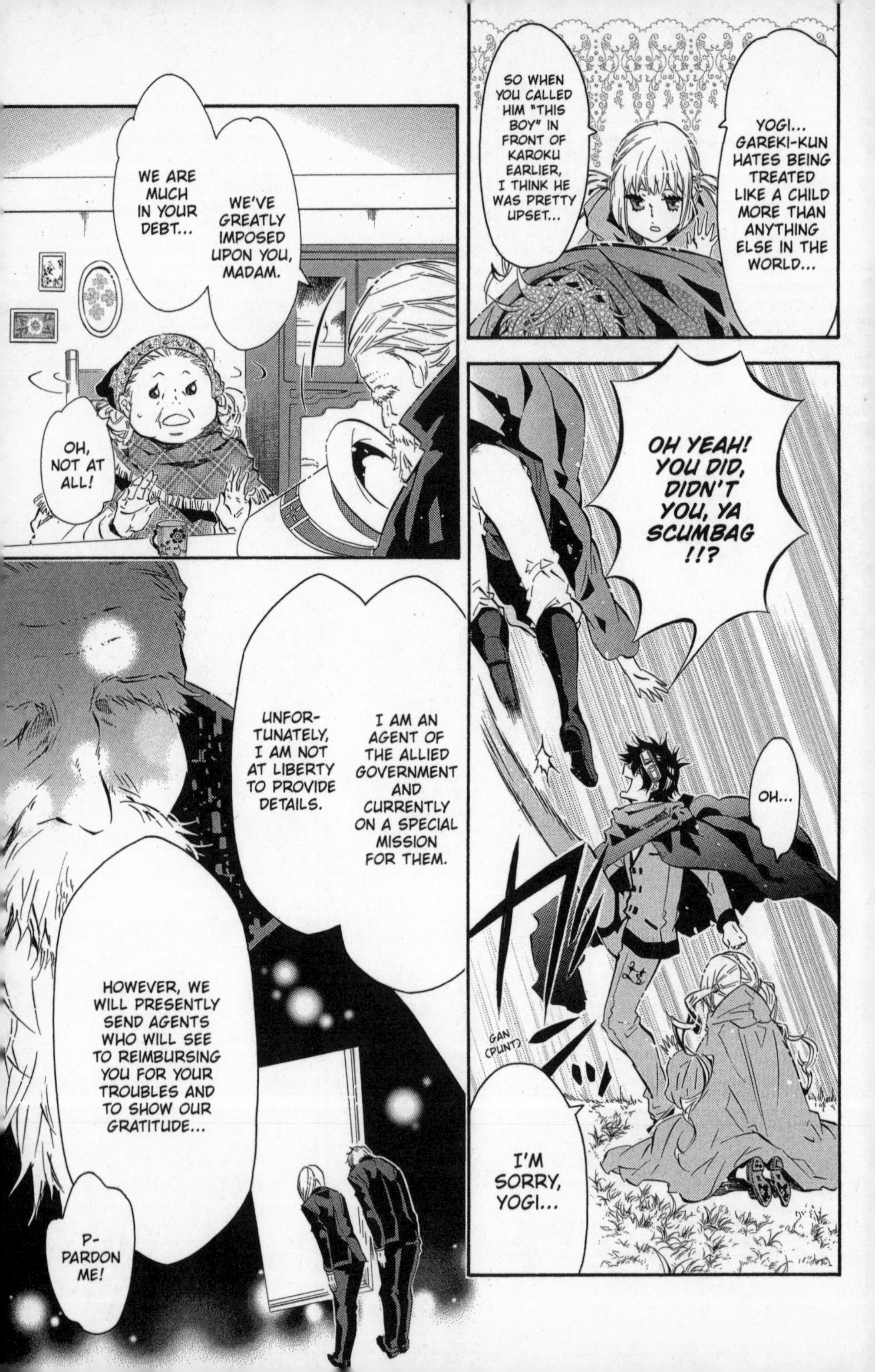
YOGI... GAREKI-KUN HATES BEING TREATED LIKE A CHILD MORE THAN ANYTHING ELSE IN THE WORLD...
SO WHEN YOU CALLED HIM "THIS BOY" IN FRONT OF KAROKU EARLIER, I THINK HE WAS PRETTY UPSET...
WE'VE GREATLY IMPOSED UPON YOU, MADAM.
WE ARE MUCH IN YOUR DEBT...
OH, NOT AT ALL!
OH YEAH! YOU DID, DIDN'T YOU, YA SCUMBAG!!?
OH...
GAN (PUNT)
I'M SORRY, YOGI...
I AM AN AGENT OF THE ALLIED GOVERNMENT AND CURRENTLY ON A SPECIAL MISSION FOR THEM.
UNFOR-TUNATELY, I AM NOT AT LIBERTY TO PROVIDE DETAILS.
HOWEVER, WE WILL PRESENTLY SEND AGENTS WHO WILL SEE TO REIMBURSING YOU FOR YOUR TROUBLES AND TO SHOW OUR GRATITUDE...
P-PARDON ME!

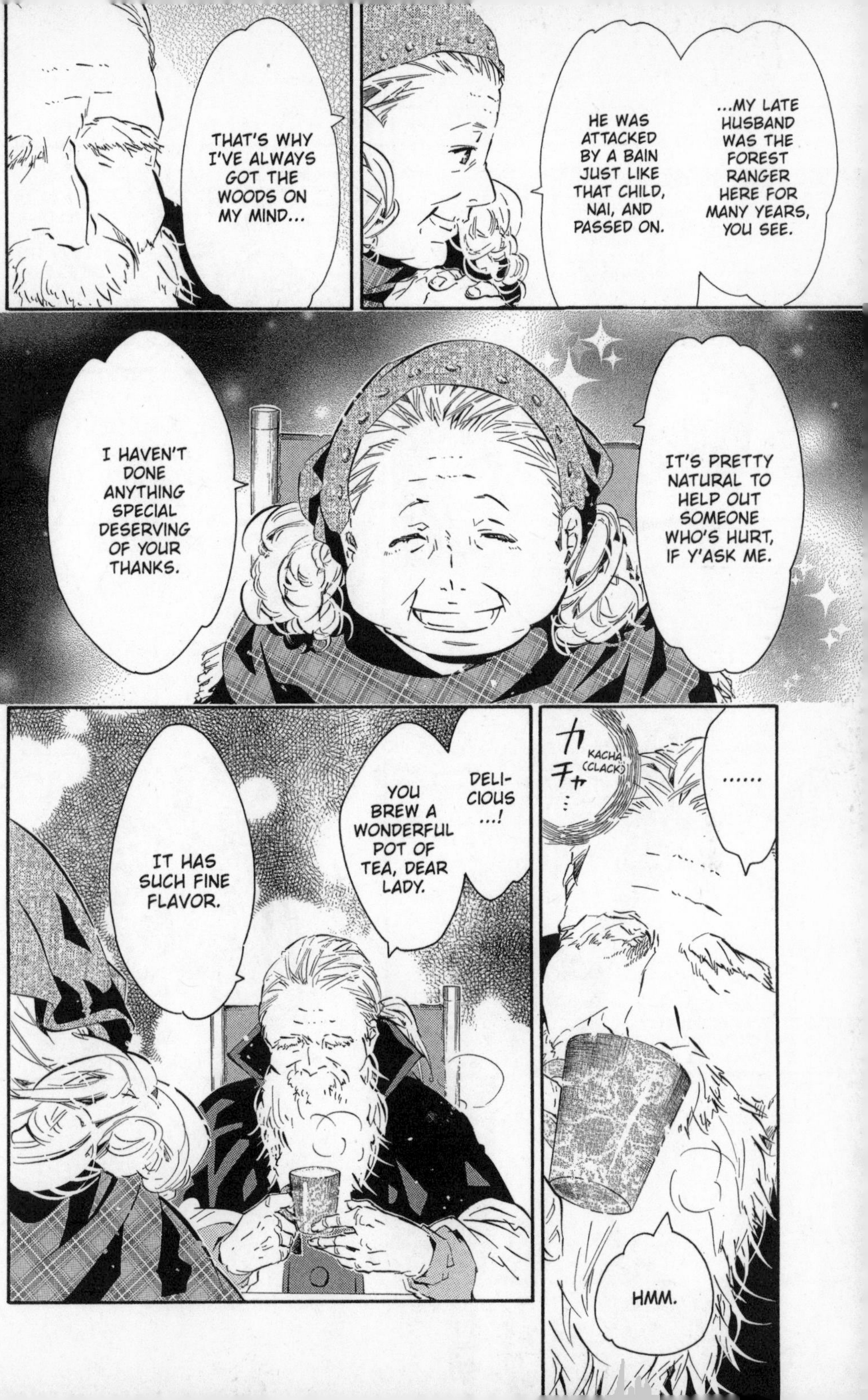
...MY LATE HUSBAND WAS THE FOREST RANGER HERE FOR MANY YEARS, YOU SEE.
HE WAS ATTACKED BY A BAIN JUST LIKE THAT CHILD, NAI, AND PASSED ON.
THAT'S WHY I'VE ALWAYS GOT THE WOODS ON MY MIND...
IT'S PRETTY NATURAL TO HELP OUT SOMEONE WHO'S HURT, IF Y'ASK ME.
I HAVEN'T DONE ANYTHING SPECIAL DESERVING OF YOUR THANKS.
......
カチャ…
KACHA (CLACK)
HMM.
DELI-CIOUS ...!
YOU BREW A WONDERFUL POT OF TEA, DEAR LADY.
IT HAS SUCH FINE FLAVOR.

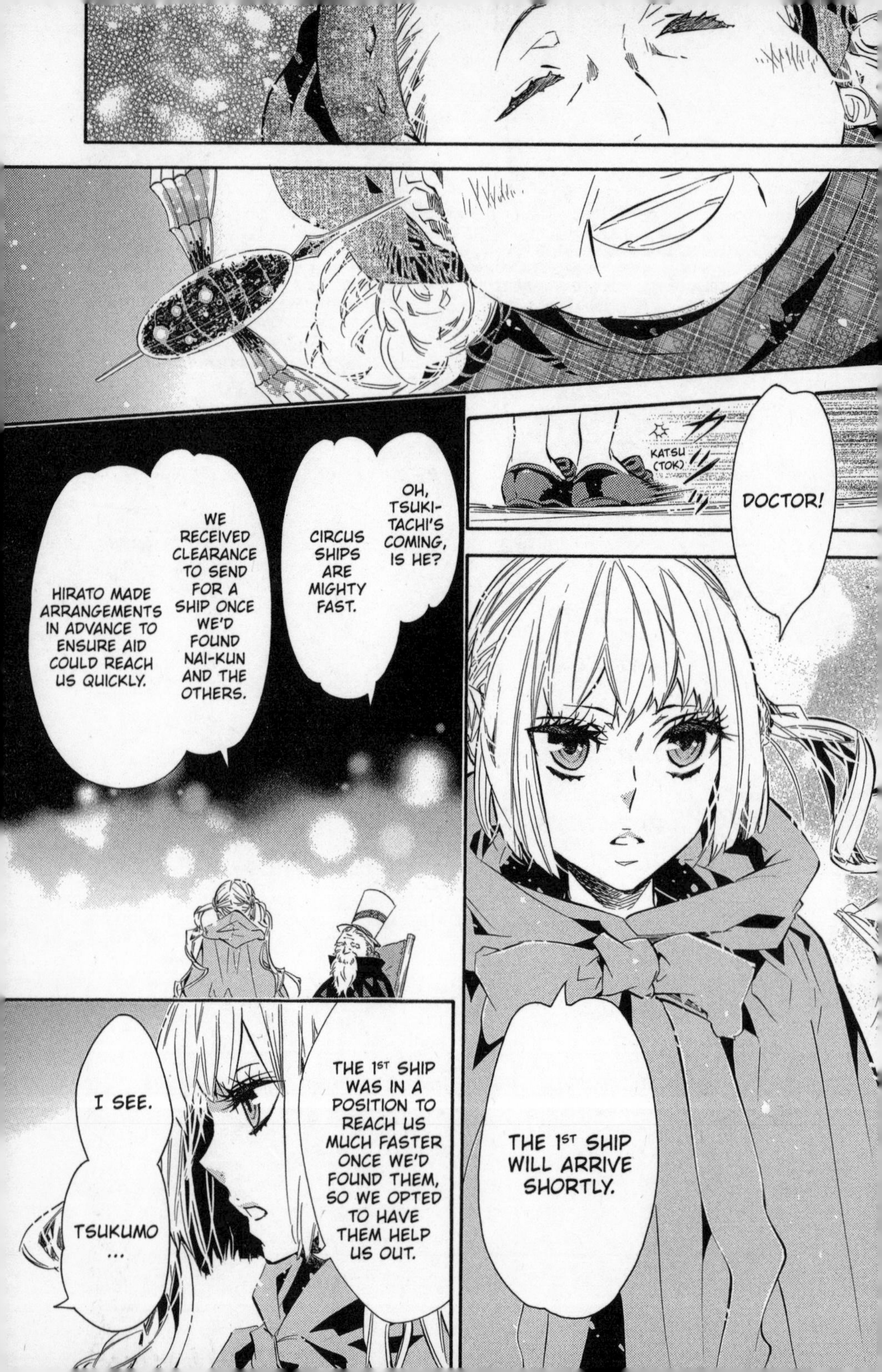
KATSU (TOK)
DOCTOR!
THE 1ST SHIP WILL ARRIVE SHORTLY.
OH, TSUKITACHI'S COMING, IS HE?
CIRCUS SHIPS ARE MIGHTY FAST.
WE RECEIVED CLEARANCE TO SEND FOR A SHIP ONCE WE'D FOUND NAI-KUN AND THE OTHERS.
HIRATO MADE ARRANGEMENTS IN ADVANCE TO ENSURE AID COULD REACH US QUICKLY.
THE 1ST SHIP WAS IN A POSITION TO REACH US MUCH FASTER ONCE WE'D FOUND THEM, SO WE OPTED TO HAVE THEM HELP US OUT.
I SEE.
TSUKUMO ...

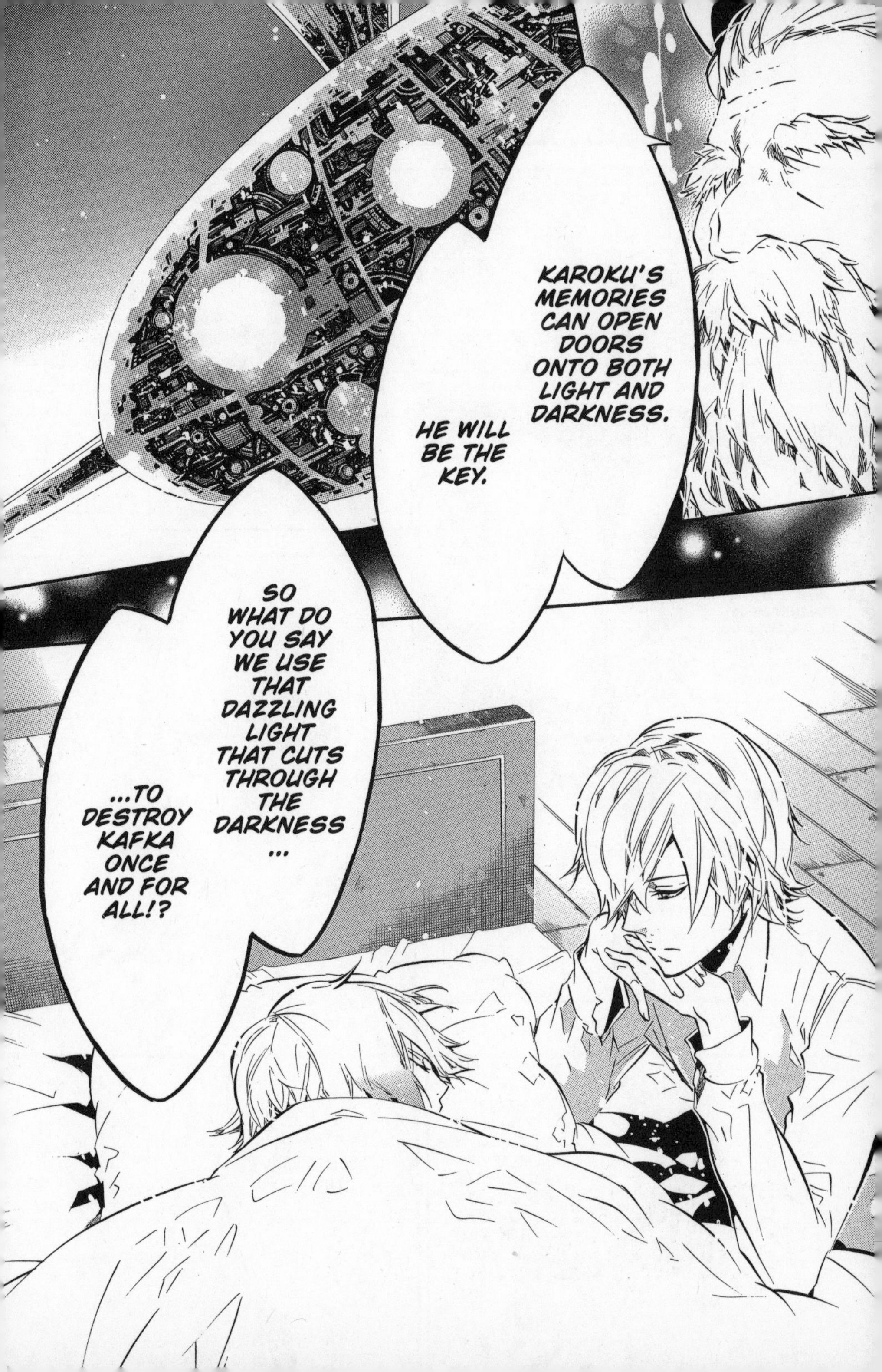
KAROKU'S MEMORIES CAN OPEN DOORS ONTO BOTH LIGHT AND DARKNESS.
HE WILL BE THE KEY.
SO WHAT DO YOU SAY WE USE THAT DAZZLING LIGHT THAT CUTS THROUGH THE DARKNESS ...
...TO DESTROY KAFKA ONCE AND FOR ALL!?

KARNEVAL

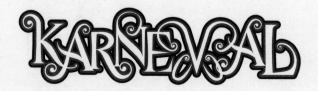

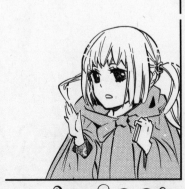

KARNEVAL

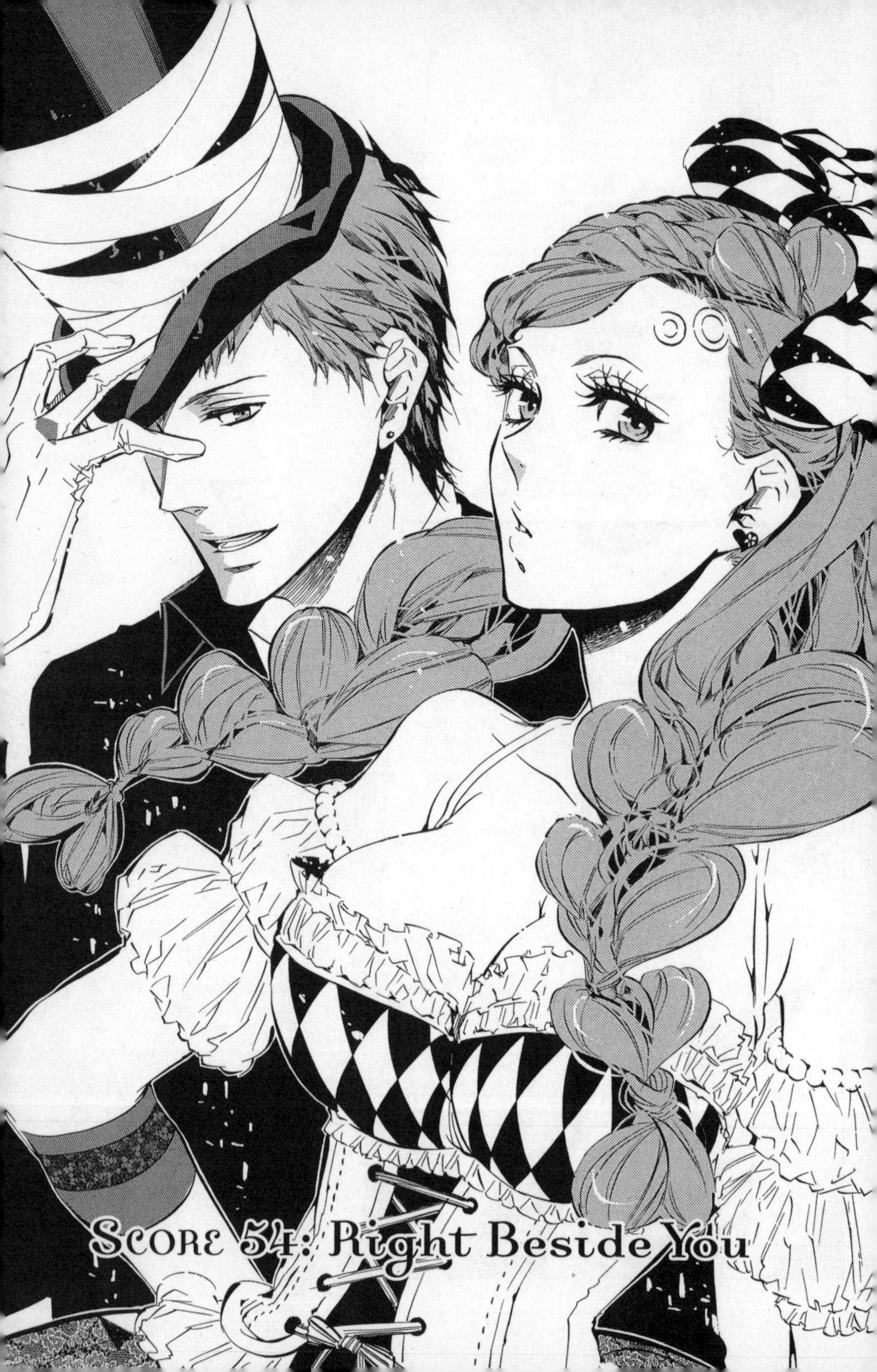
SCORE 54: Right Beside You

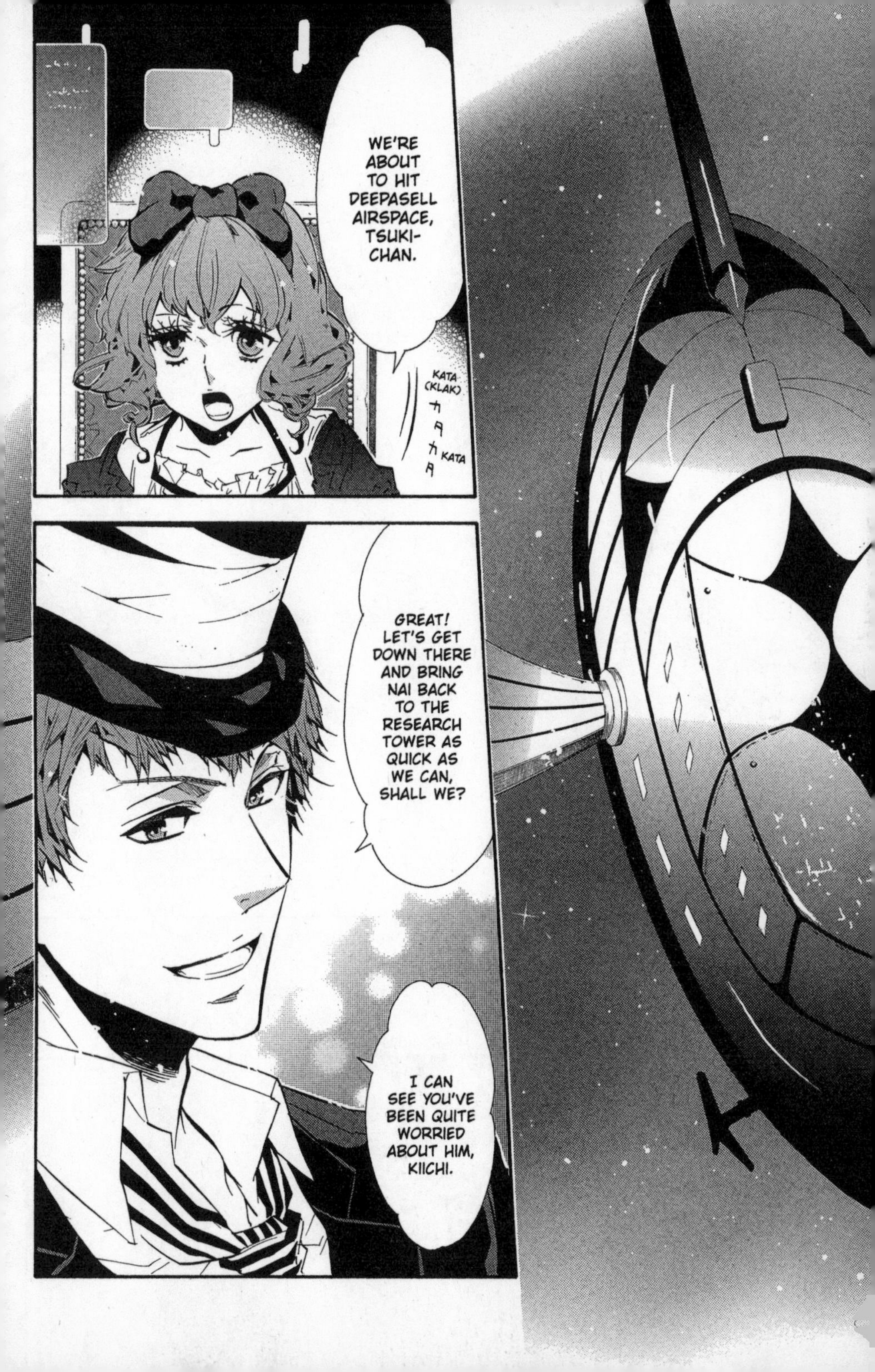
WE'RE ABOUT TO HIT DEEPASELL AIRSPACE, TSUKI-CHAN.
KATA (KLAK)
カタカタ
KATA
GREAT! LET'S GET DOWN THERE AND BRING NAI BACK TO THE RESEARCH TOWER AS QUICK AS WE CAN, SHALL WE?
I CAN SEE YOU'VE BEEN QUITE WORRIED ABOUT HIM, KIICHI.

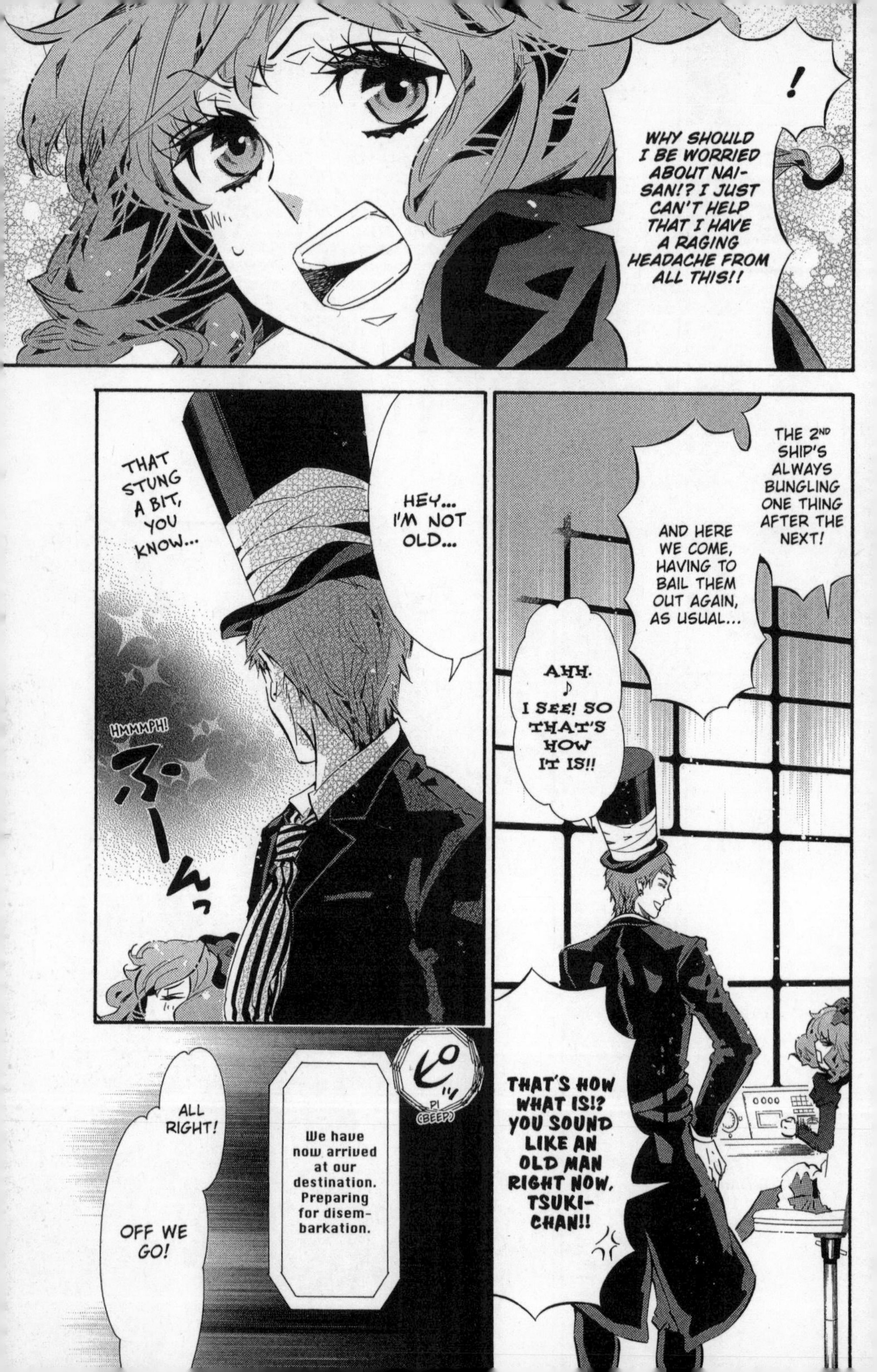
!
WHY SHOULD I BE WORRIED ABOUT NAI-SAN!? I JUST CAN'T HELP THAT I HAVE A RAGING HEADACHE FROM ALL THIS!!
THE 2ND SHIP'S ALWAYS BUNGLING ONE THING AFTER THE NEXT!
AND HERE WE COME, HAVING TO BAIL THEM OUT AGAIN, AS USUAL...
AHH. ♪ I SEE! SO THAT'S HOW IT IS!!
THAT'S HOW WHAT IS!? YOU SOUND LIKE AN OLD MAN RIGHT NOW, TSUKI-CHAN!!
HEY... I'M NOT OLD...
THAT STUNG A BIT, YOU KNOW...
HMMMPH!
ぷーんっ
ぴっ
PI (BEEP)
We have now arrived at our destination. Preparing for disem-barkation.
ALL RIGHT!
OFF WE GO!

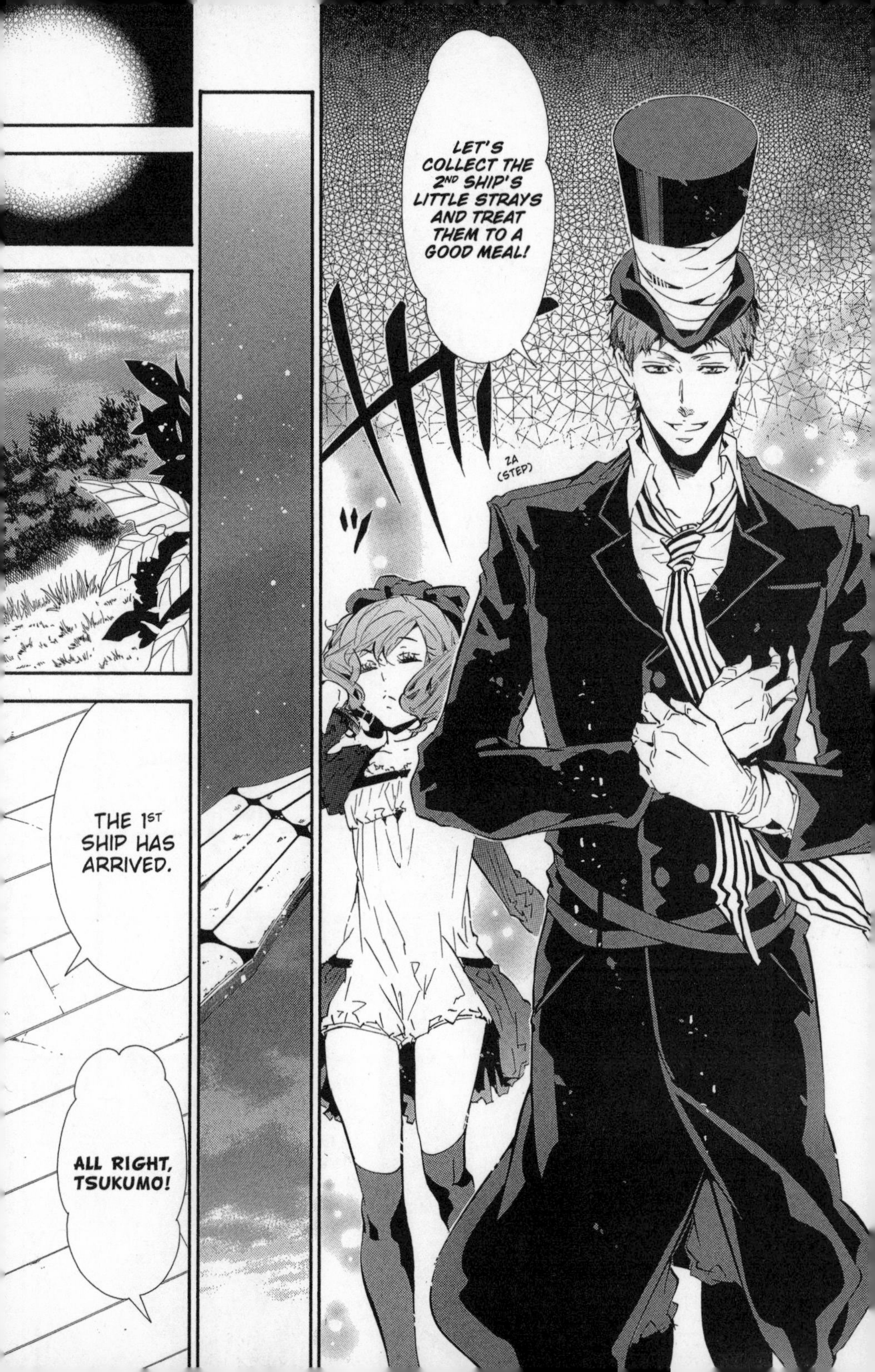
LET'S COLLECT THE 2ND SHIP'S LITTLE STRAYS AND TREAT THEM TO A GOOD MEAL!
ZA (STEP)
THE 1ST SHIP HAS ARRIVED.
ALL RIGHT, TSUKUMO!

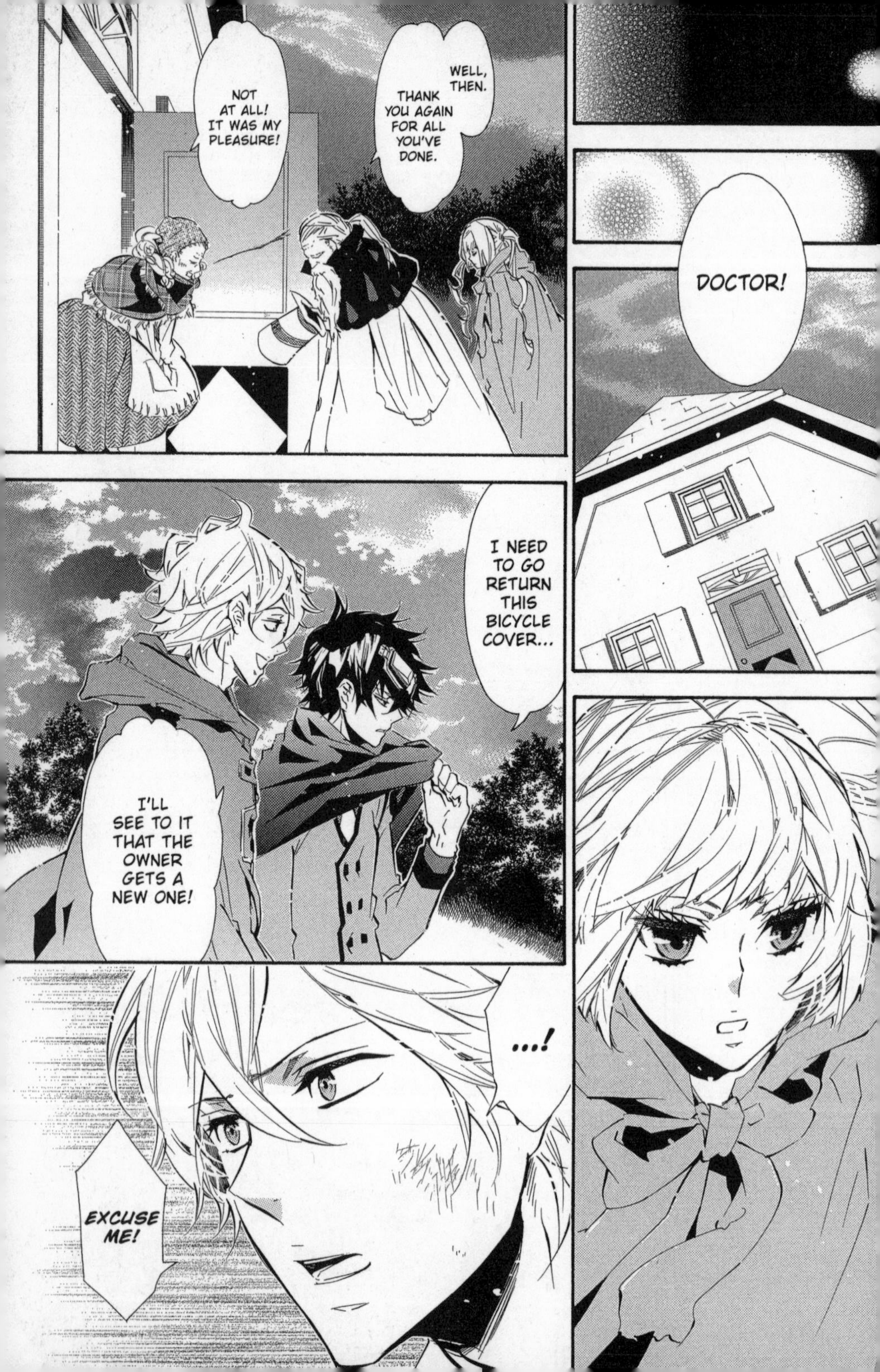
DOCTOR!
WELL, THEN. THANK YOU AGAIN FOR ALL YOU'VE DONE.
NOT AT ALL! IT WAS MY PLEASURE!
I NEED TO GO RETURN THIS BICYCLE COVER...
I'LL SEE TO IT THAT THE OWNER GETS A NEW ONE!
...!
EXCUSE ME!

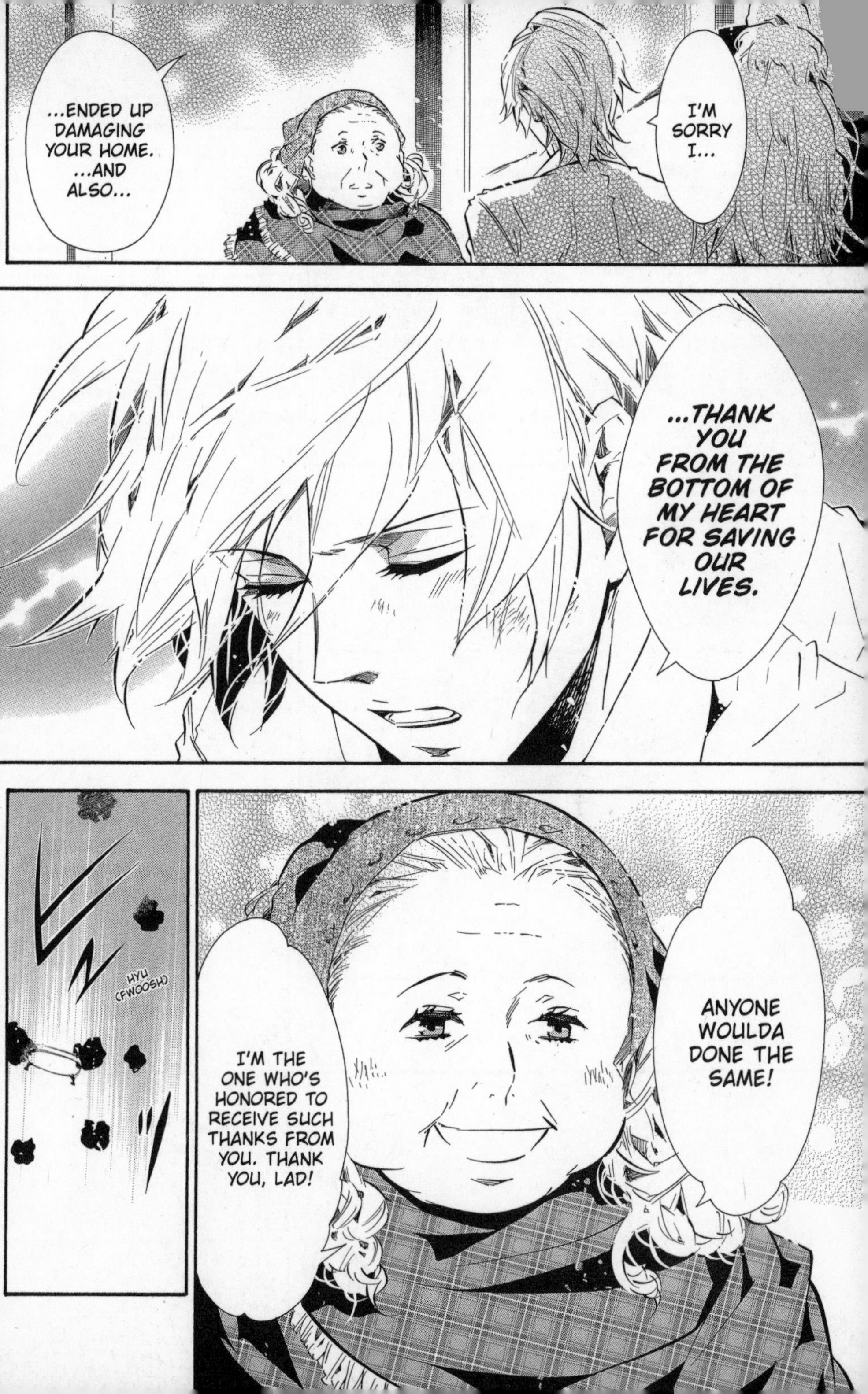
I'M SORRY I...
...ENDED UP DAMAGING YOUR HOME. ...AND ALSO...
...THANK YOU FROM THE BOTTOM OF MY HEART FOR SAVING OUR LIVES.
ANYONE WOULDA DONE THE SAME!
I'M THE ONE WHO'S HONORED TO RECEIVE SUCH THANKS FROM YOU. THANK YOU, LAD!
HYU (FWOOSH)

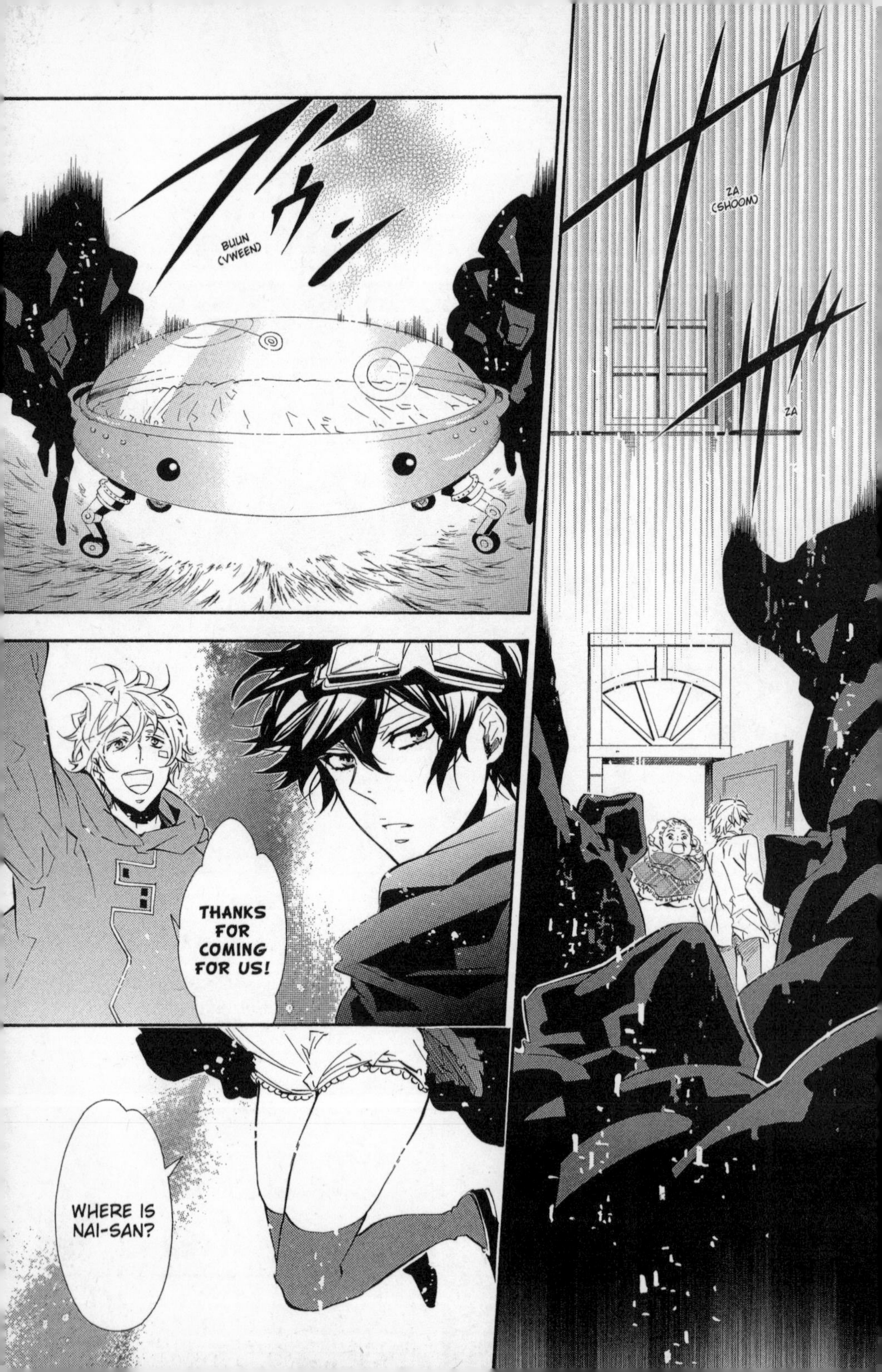
ZA (SHOOM)
ZA
BUUN (VWEEN)
THANKS FOR COMING FOR US!
WHERE IS NAI-SAN?

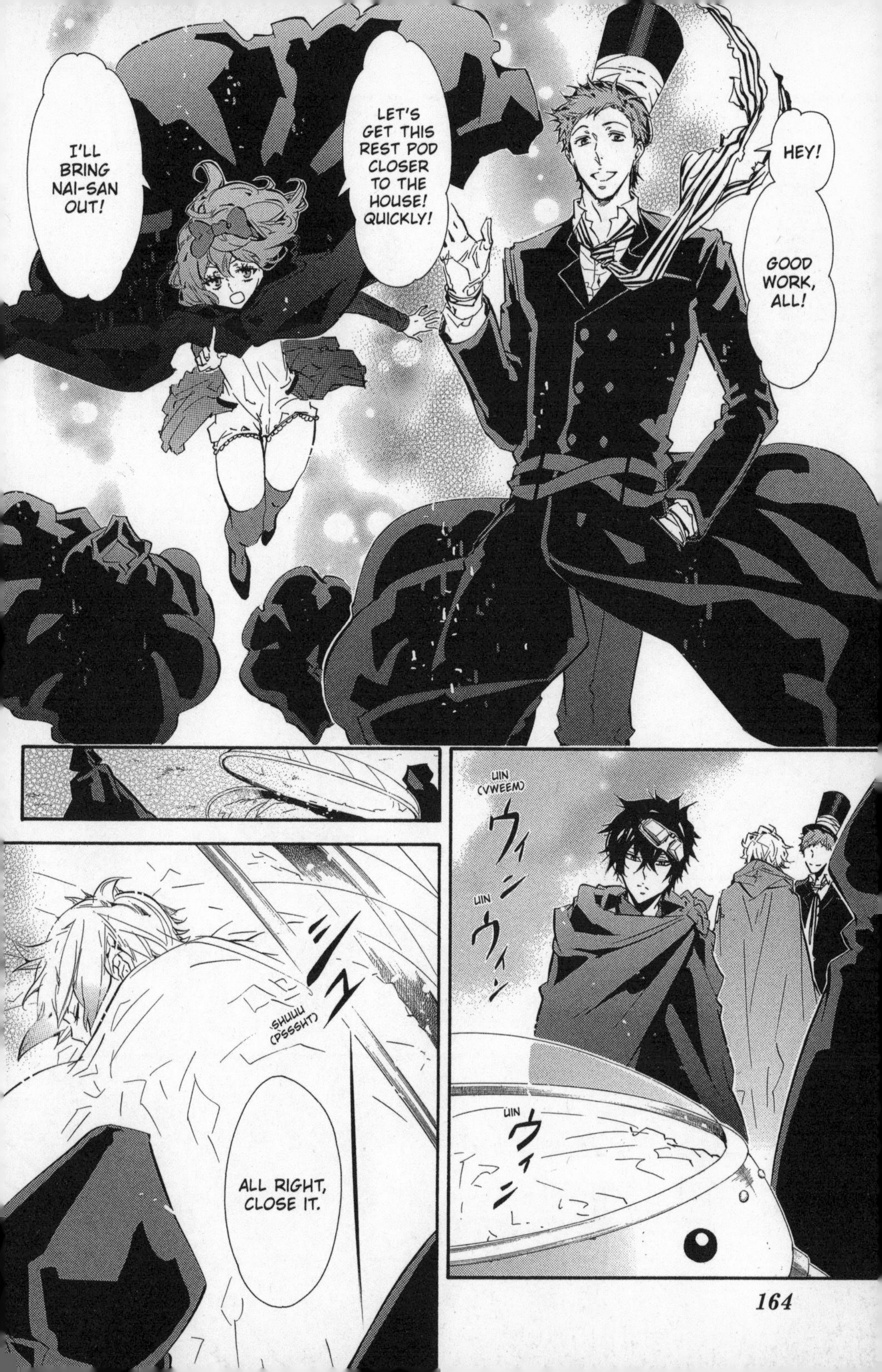
HEY!
GOOD WORK, ALL!
LET'S GET THIS REST POD CLOSER TO THE HOUSE! QUICKLY!
I'LL BRING NAI-SAN OUT!
UIN (VWEEM)
ウィン
UIN
ウィン
UIN
ウィン
SHUUU (PSSSHT)
シュ
ALL RIGHT, CLOSE IT.

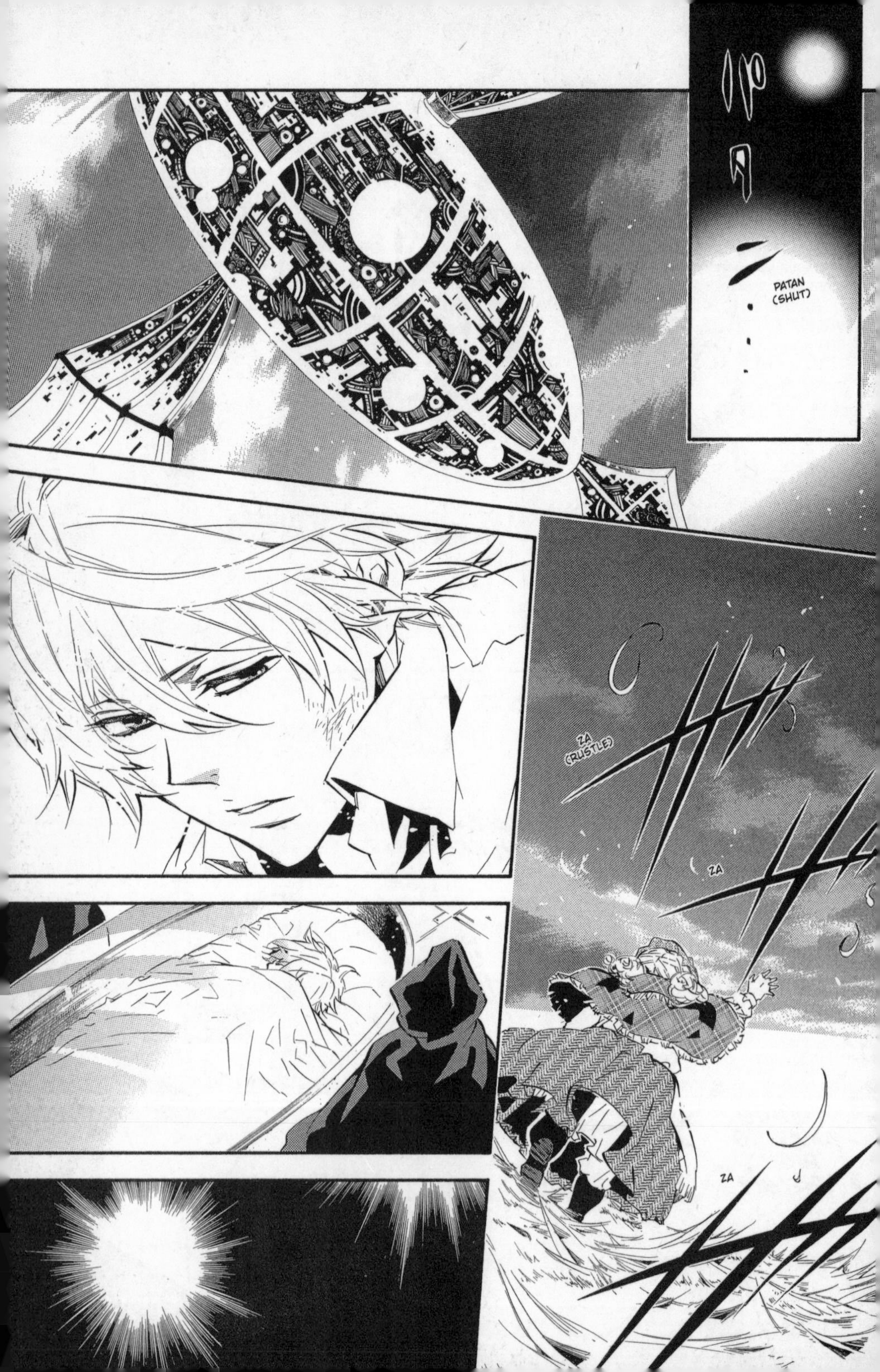
PATAN (SHUT)
ZA (RUSTLE)
ZA
ZA

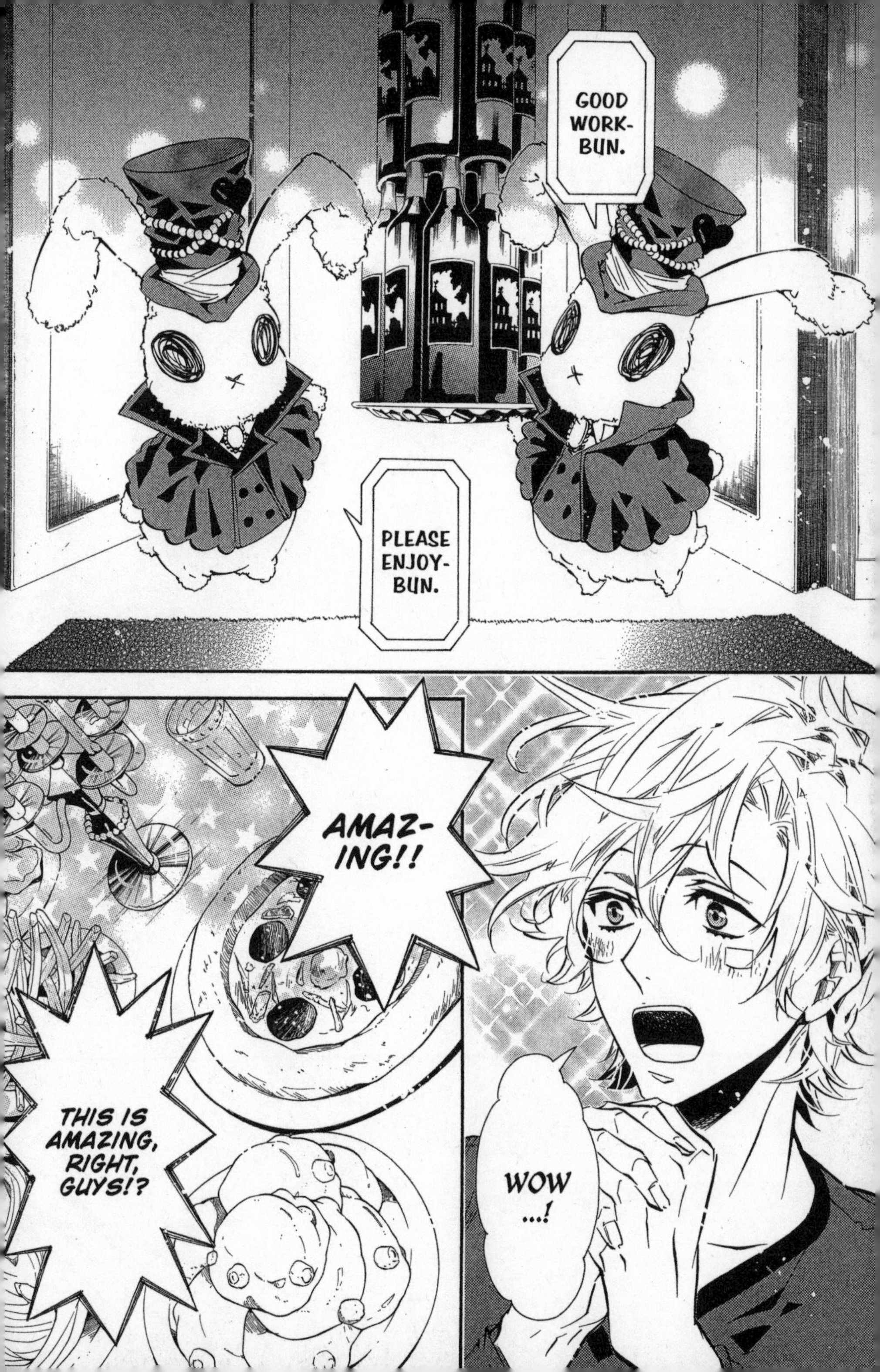
GOOD WORK-BUN.
PLEASE ENJOY-BUN.
WOW ...!
AMAZ-ING!!
THIS IS AMAZING, RIGHT, GUYS!?

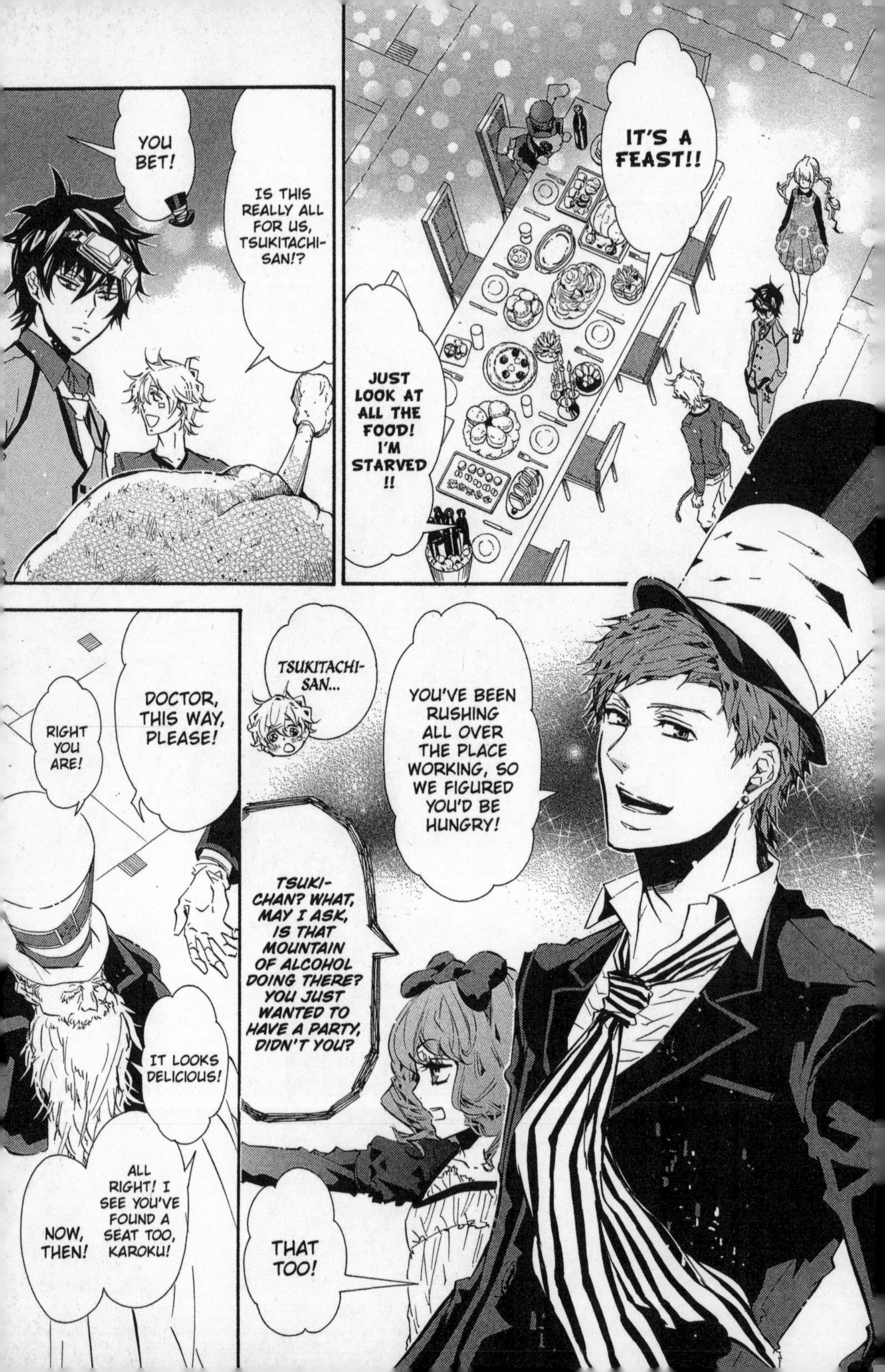
IT'S A FEAST!!
JUST LOOK AT ALL THE FOOD! I'M STARVED!!
IS THIS REALLY ALL FOR US, TSUKITACHI-SAN!?
YOU BET!
YOU'VE BEEN RUSHING ALL OVER THE PLACE WORKING, SO WE FIGURED YOU'D BE HUNGRY!
TSUKITACHI-SAN...
TSUKI-CHAN? WHAT, MAY I ASK, IS THAT MOUNTAIN OF ALCOHOL DOING THERE? YOU JUST WANTED TO HAVE A PARTY, DIDN'T YOU?
THAT TOO!
DOCTOR, THIS WAY, PLEASE!
RIGHT YOU ARE!
IT LOOKS DELICIOUS!
ALL RIGHT! I SEE YOU'VE FOUND A SEAT TOO, KAROKU!
NOW, THEN!

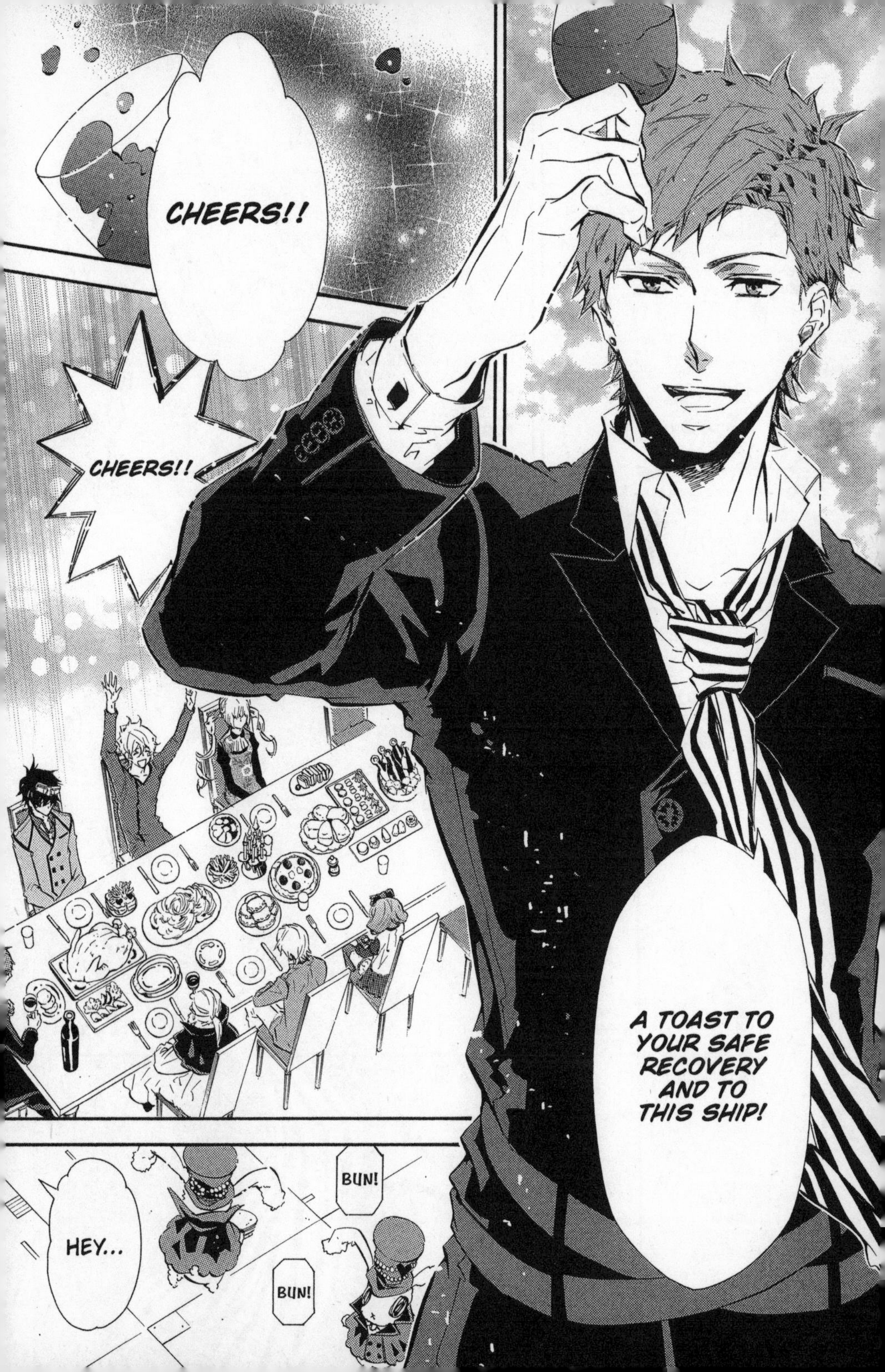
A TOAST TO YOUR SAFE RECOVERY AND TO THIS SHIP!
CHEERS!!
CHEERS!!
BUN!
BUN!
HEY...

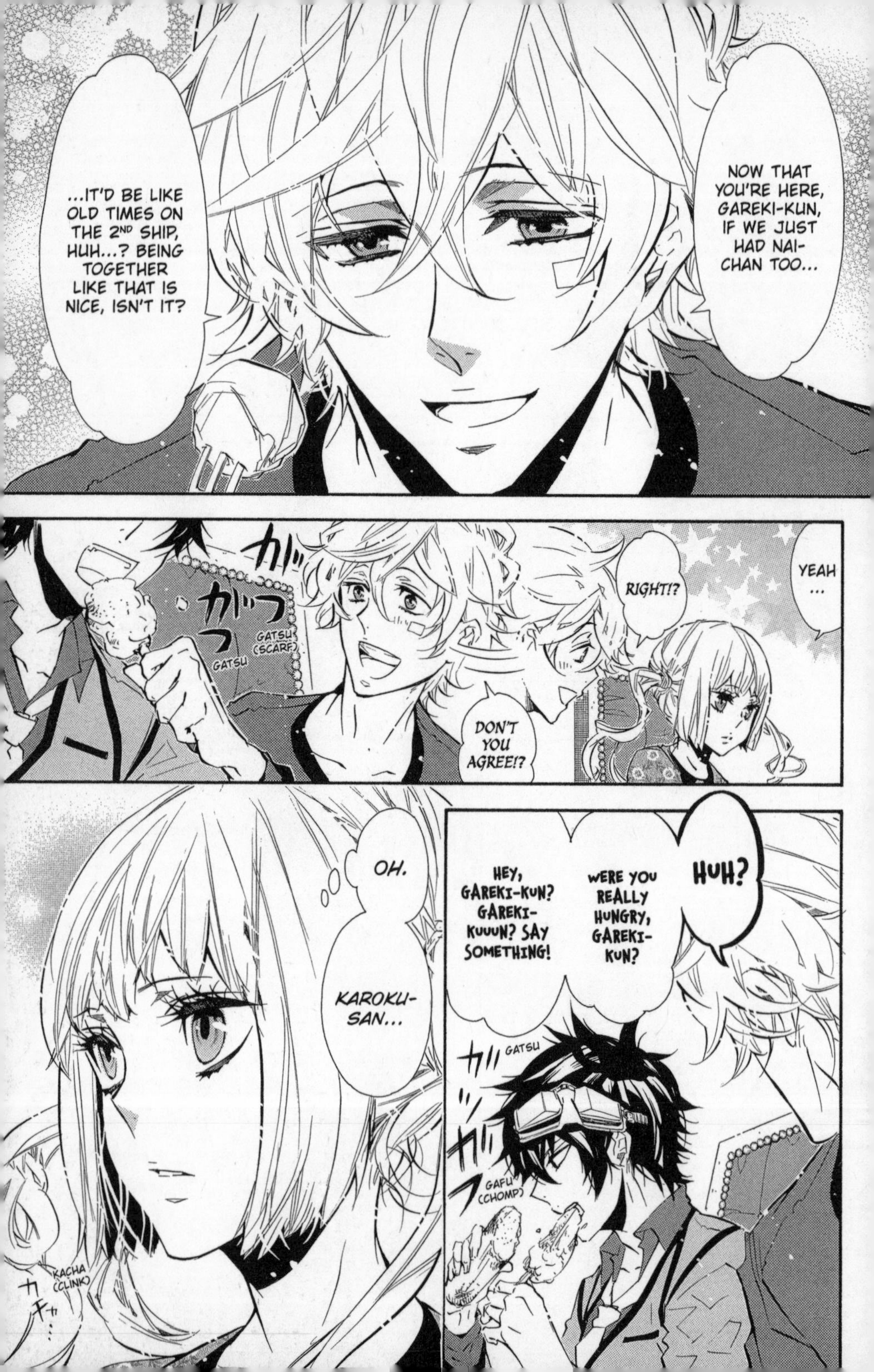
NOW THAT YOU'RE HERE, GAREKI-KUN, IF WE JUST HAD NAI-CHAN TOO...
...IT'D BE LIKE OLD TIMES ON THE 2ND SHIP, HUH...? BEING TOGETHER LIKE THAT IS NICE, ISN'T IT?
YEAH...
RIGHT!?
DON'T YOU AGREE!?
GATSU (SCARF)
GATSU
HUH?
WERE YOU REALLY HUNGRY, GAREKI-KUN?
HEY, GAREKI-KUN? GAREKI-KUUUN? SAY SOMETHING!
GATSU
GAFU (CHOMP)
OH.
KAROKU-SAN...
KACHA (CLINK)

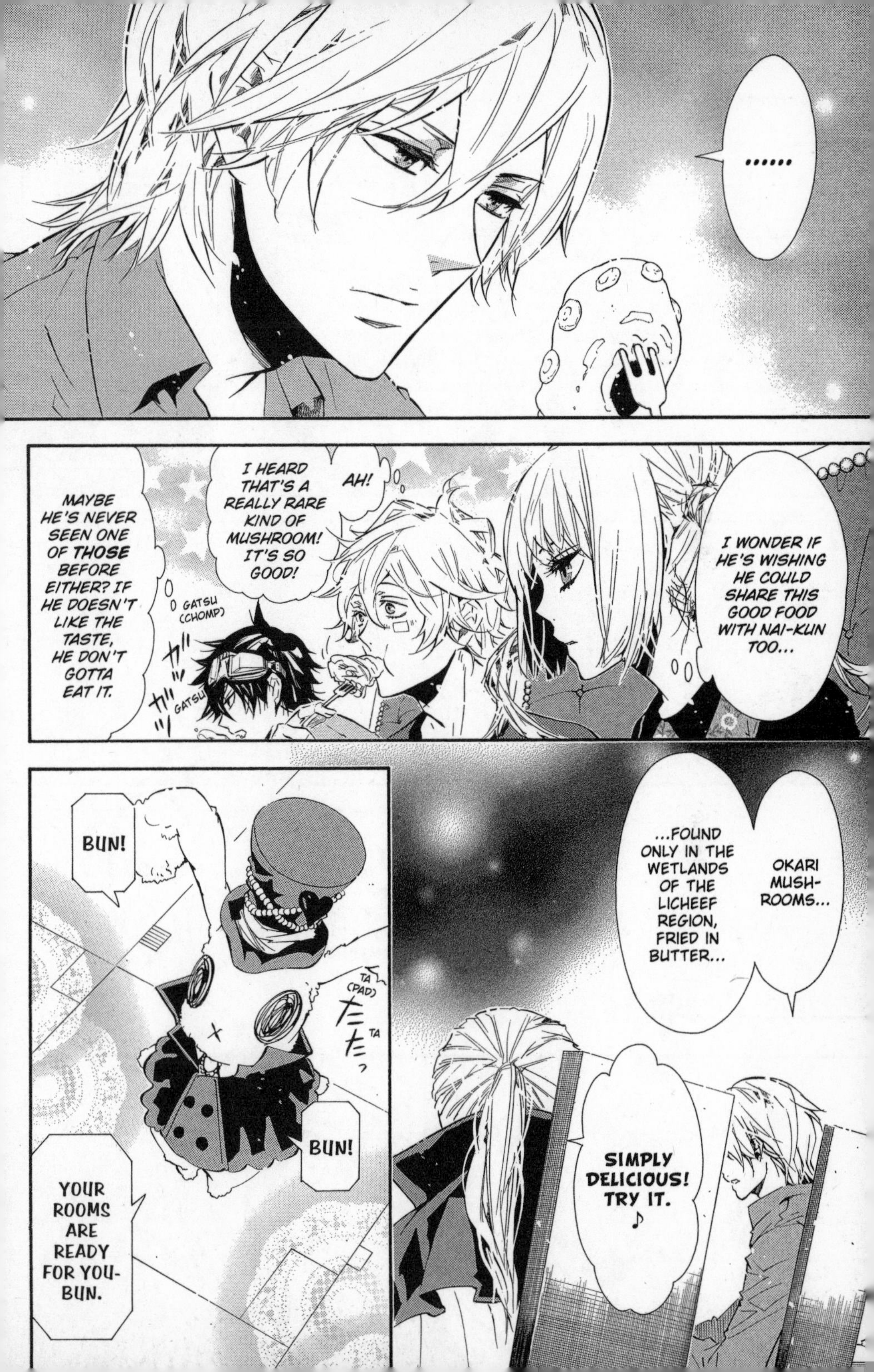
......
I WONDER IF HE'S WISHING HE COULD SHARE THIS GOOD FOOD WITH NAI-KUN TOO...
AH!
I HEARD THAT'S A REALLY RARE KIND OF MUSHROOM! IT'S SO GOOD!
GATSU (CHOMP)
GATSU
MAYBE HE'S NEVER SEEN ONE OF THOSE BEFORE EITHER? IF HE DOESN'T LIKE THE TASTE, HE DON'T GOTTA EAT IT.
OKARI MUSH-ROOMS...
...FOUND ONLY IN THE WETLANDS OF THE LICHEEF REGION, FRIED IN BUTTER...
SIMPLY DELICIOUS! TRY IT. ♪
BUN!
TA (PAD)
TA
BUN!
YOUR ROOMS ARE READY FOR YOU-BUN.

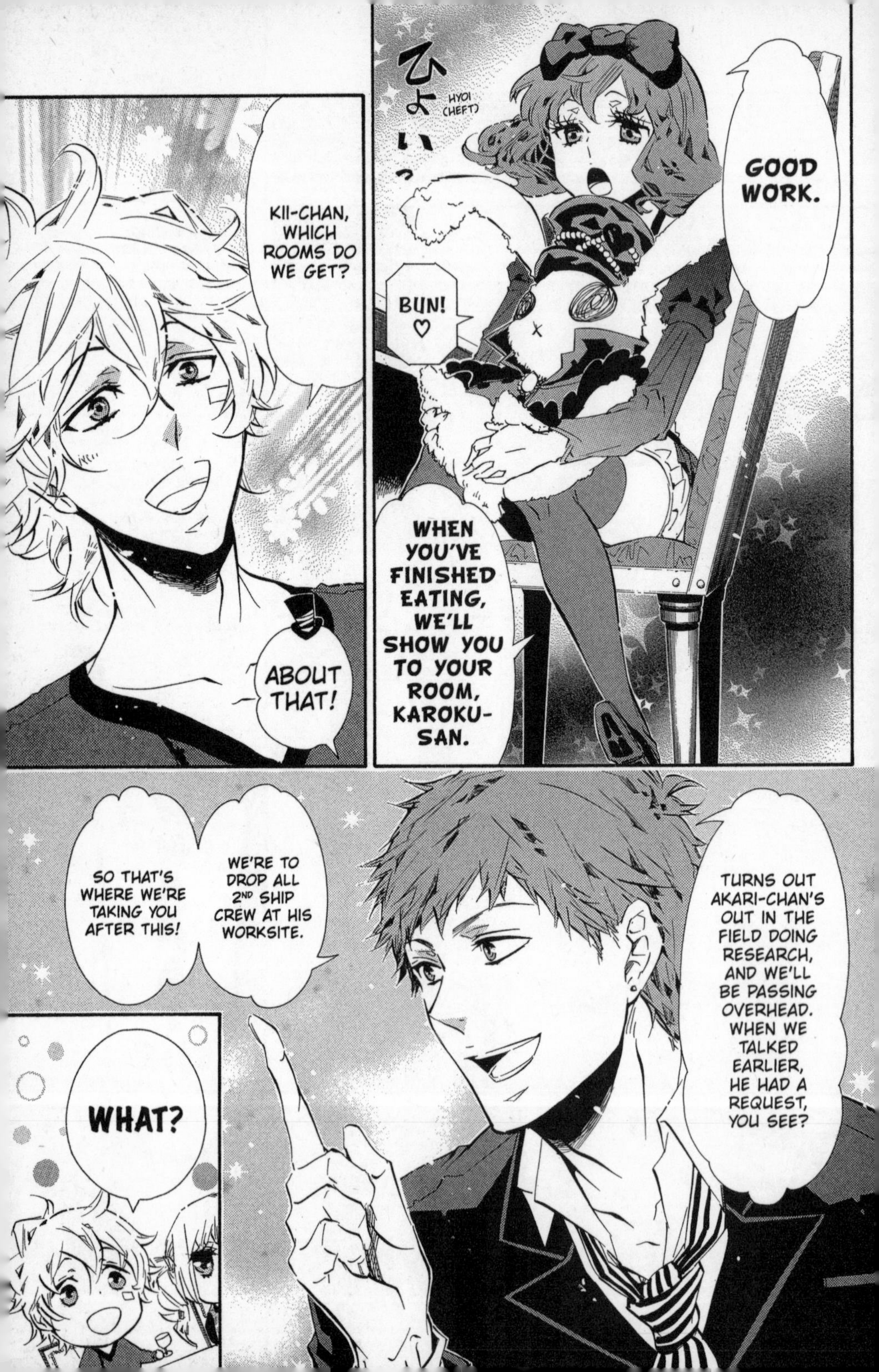
GOOD WORK.
ひょいっ
HYOI (HEFT)
BUN! ♡
WHEN YOU'VE FINISHED EATING, WE'LL SHOW YOU TO YOUR ROOM, KAROKU-SAN.
KII-CHAN, WHICH ROOMS DO WE GET?
ABOUT THAT!
TURNS OUT AKARI-CHAN'S OUT IN THE FIELD DOING RESEARCH, AND WE'LL BE PASSING OVERHEAD. WHEN WE TALKED EARLIER, HE HAD A REQUEST, YOU SEE?
WE'RE TO DROP ALL 2ND SHIP CREW AT HIS WORKSITE.
SO THAT'S WHERE WE'RE TAKING YOU AFTER THIS!
WHAT?

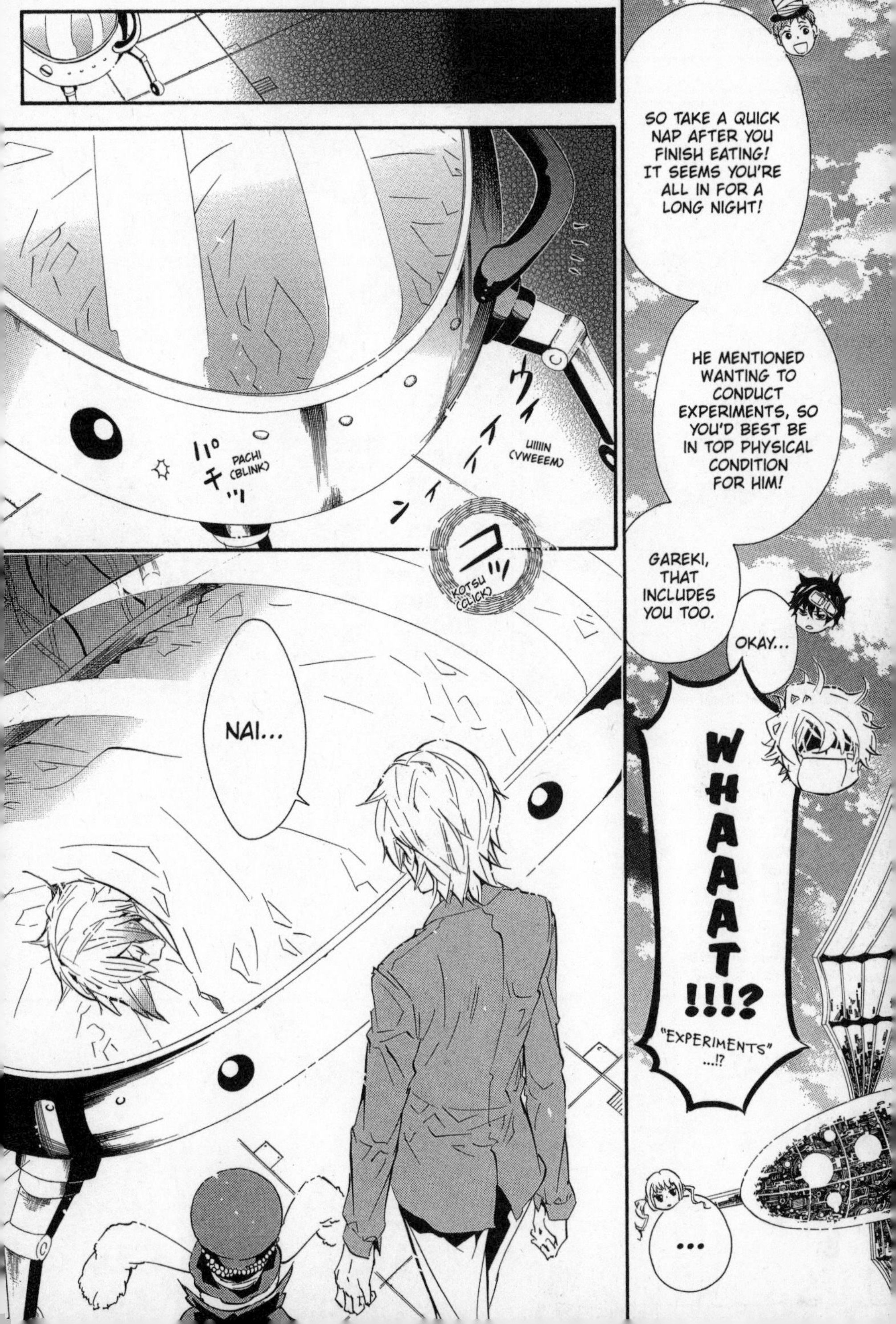
SO TAKE A QUICK NAP AFTER YOU FINISH EATING! IT SEEMS YOU'RE ALL IN FOR A LONG NIGHT!
HE MENTIONED WANTING TO CONDUCT EXPERIMENTS, SO YOU'D BEST BE IN TOP PHYSICAL CONDITION FOR HIM!
GAREKI, THAT INCLUDES YOU TOO.
OKAY...
WHAAAT!!!?
"EXPERIMENTS" ...!?
...
ヴィイイン
UIIIIN (VWEEEM)
パチッ
PACHI (BLINK)
コツ
KOTSU (CLICK)
NAI...

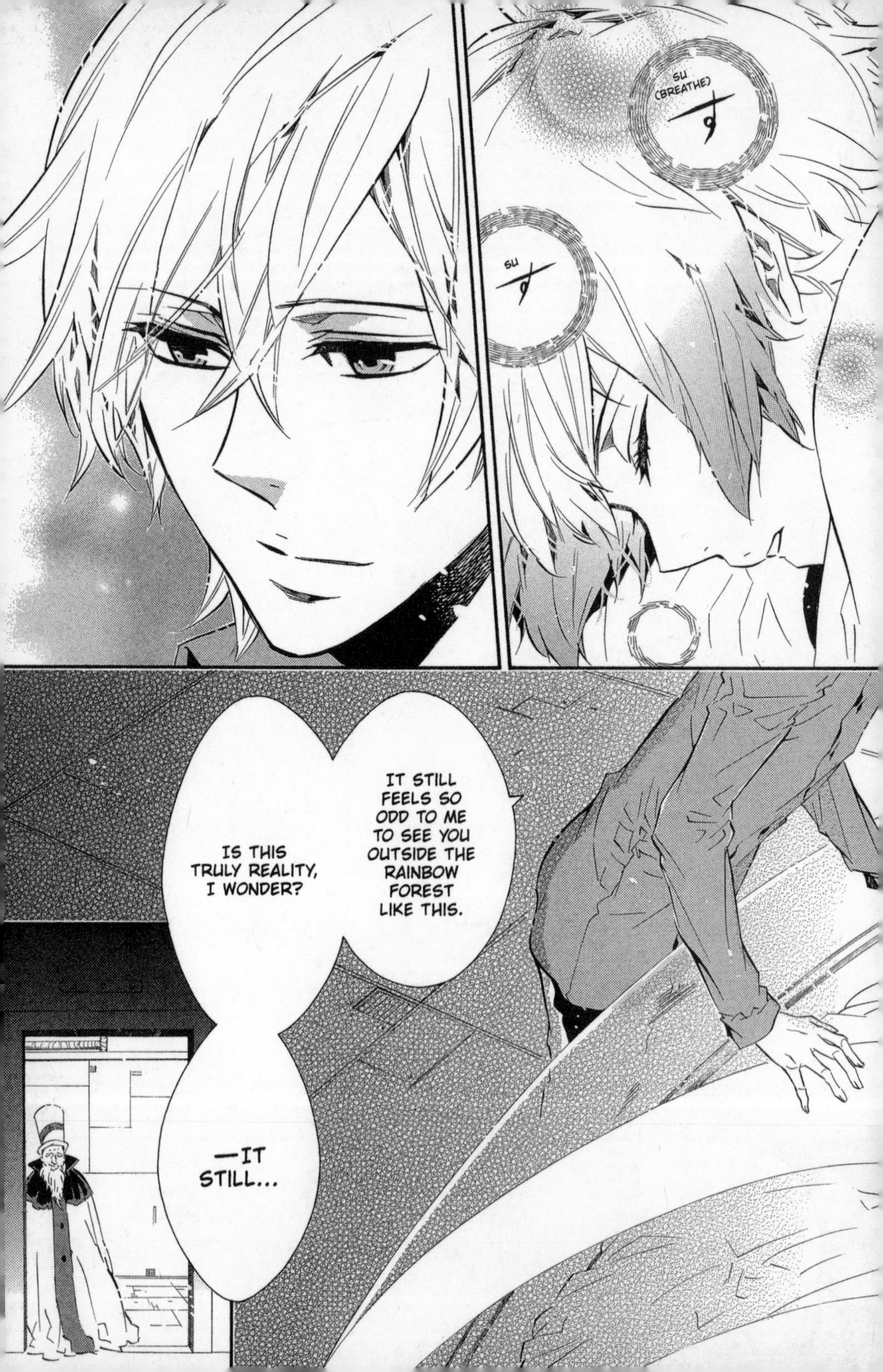
SU (BREATHE)
SU
IT STILL FEELS SO ODD TO ME TO SEE YOU OUTSIDE THE RAINBOW FOREST LIKE THIS.
IS THIS TRULY REALITY, I WONDER?
—IT STILL...

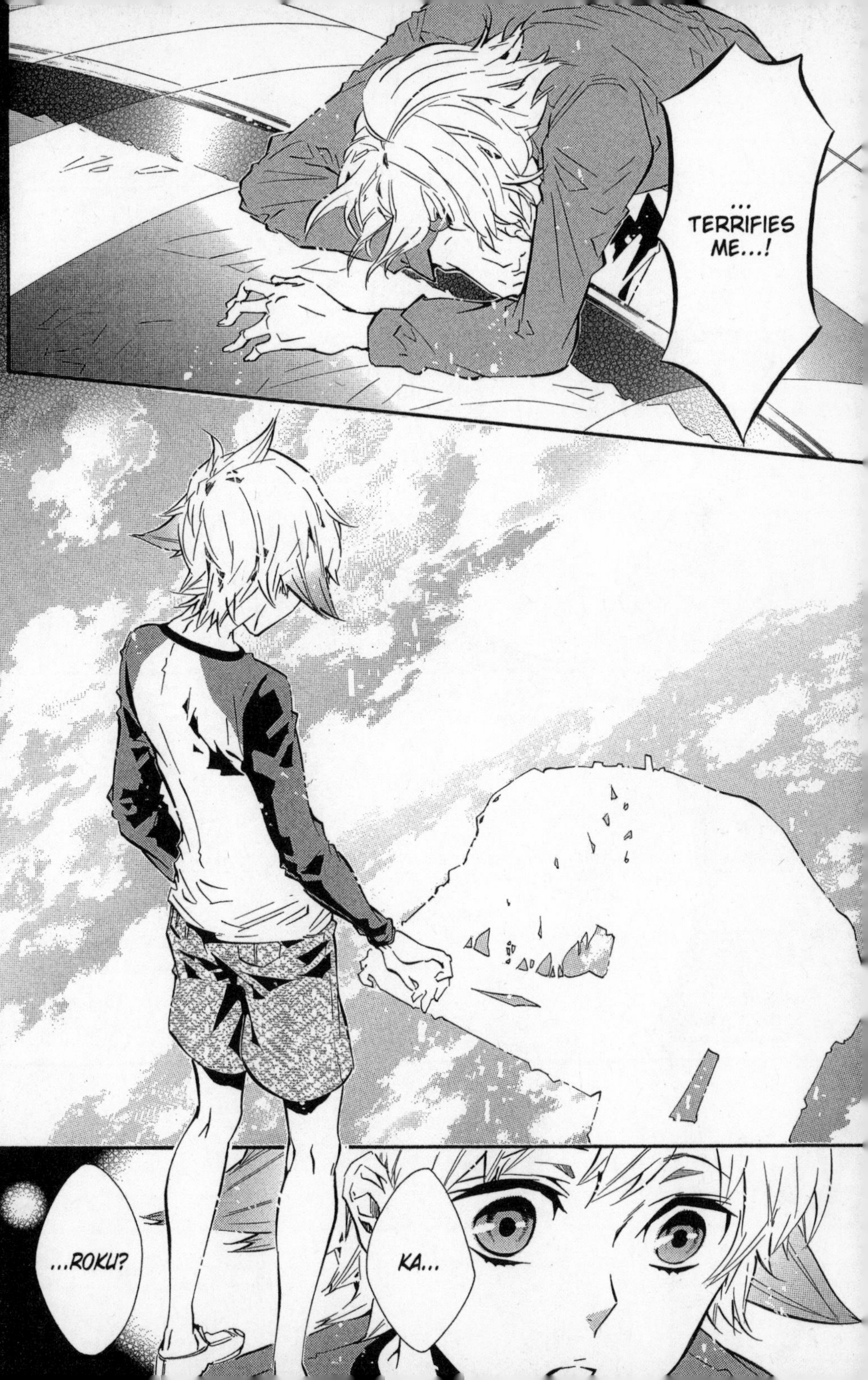
...TERRIFIES ME...!
KA...
...ROKU?

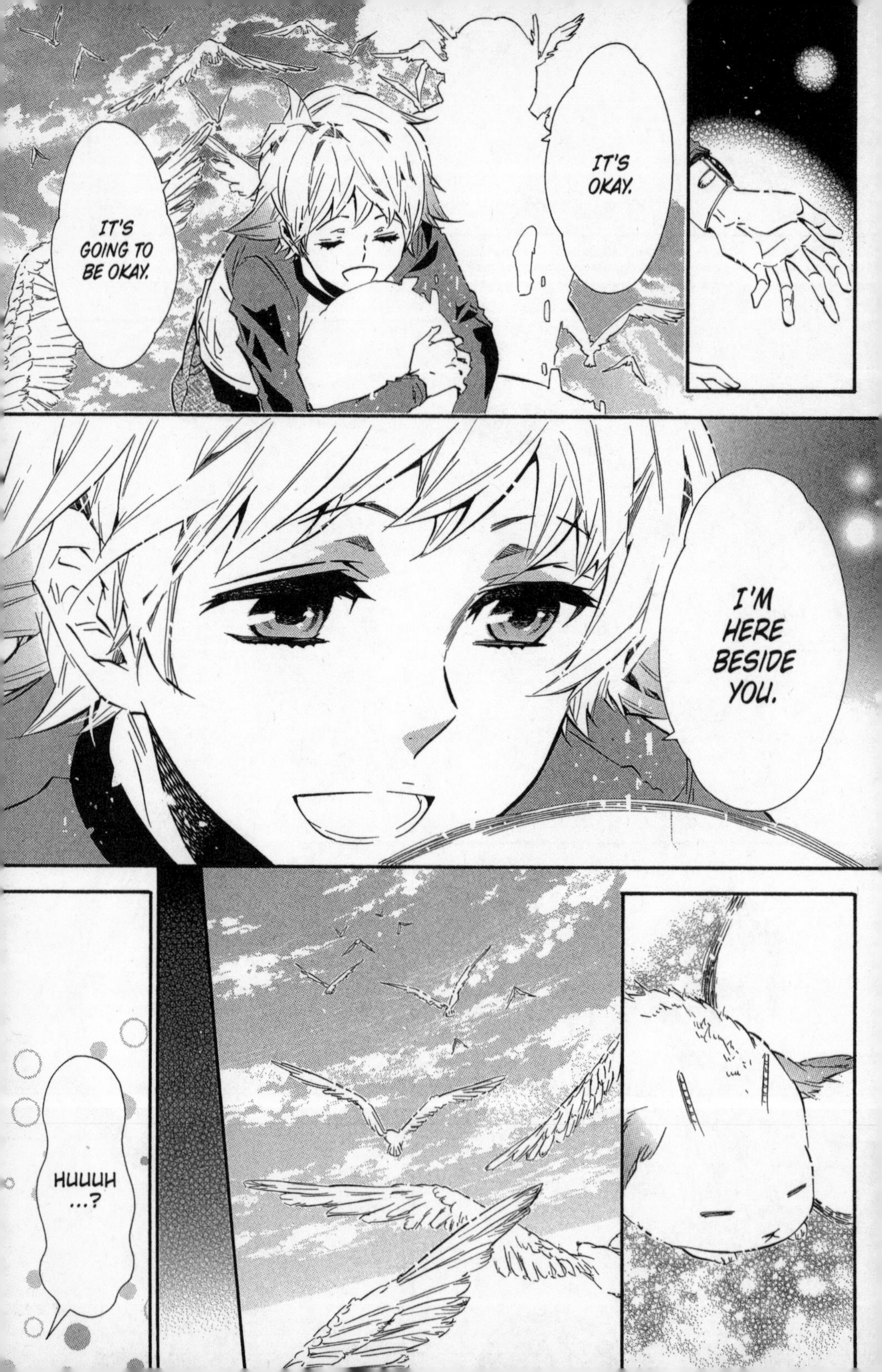
IT'S OKAY.
IT'S GOING TO BE OKAY.
I'M HERE BESIDE YOU.
HUUUH ...?

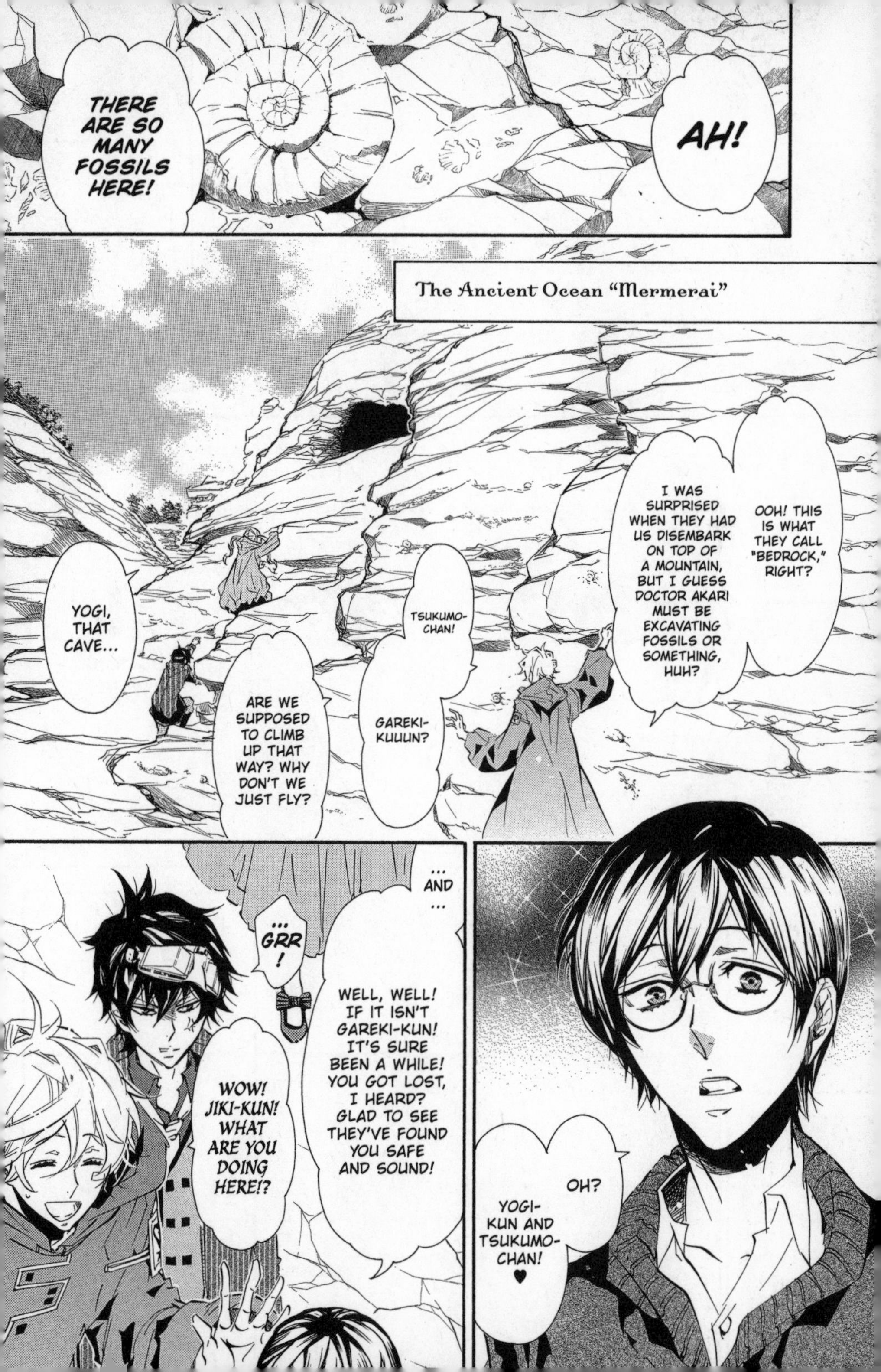
AH!
THERE ARE SO MANY FOSSILS HERE!
The Ancient Ocean "Mermerai"
OOH! THIS IS WHAT THEY CALL "BEDROCK," RIGHT?
I WAS SURPRISED WHEN THEY HAD US DISEMBARK ON TOP OF A MOUNTAIN, BUT I GUESS DOCTOR AKARI MUST BE EXCAVATING FOSSILS OR SOMETHING, HUH?
TSUKUMO-CHAN!
GAREKI-KUUUN?
ARE WE SUPPOSED TO CLIMB UP THAT WAY? WHY DON'T WE JUST FLY?
YOGI, THAT CAVE...
OH?
YOGI-KUN AND TSUKUMO-CHAN! ♥
...AND...
...GRR!
WELL, WELL! IF IT ISN'T GAREKI-KUN! IT'S SURE BEEN A WHILE! YOU GOT LOST, I HEARD? GLAD TO SEE THEY'VE FOUND YOU SAFE AND SOUND!
WOW! JIKI-KUN! WHAT ARE YOU DOING HERE!?

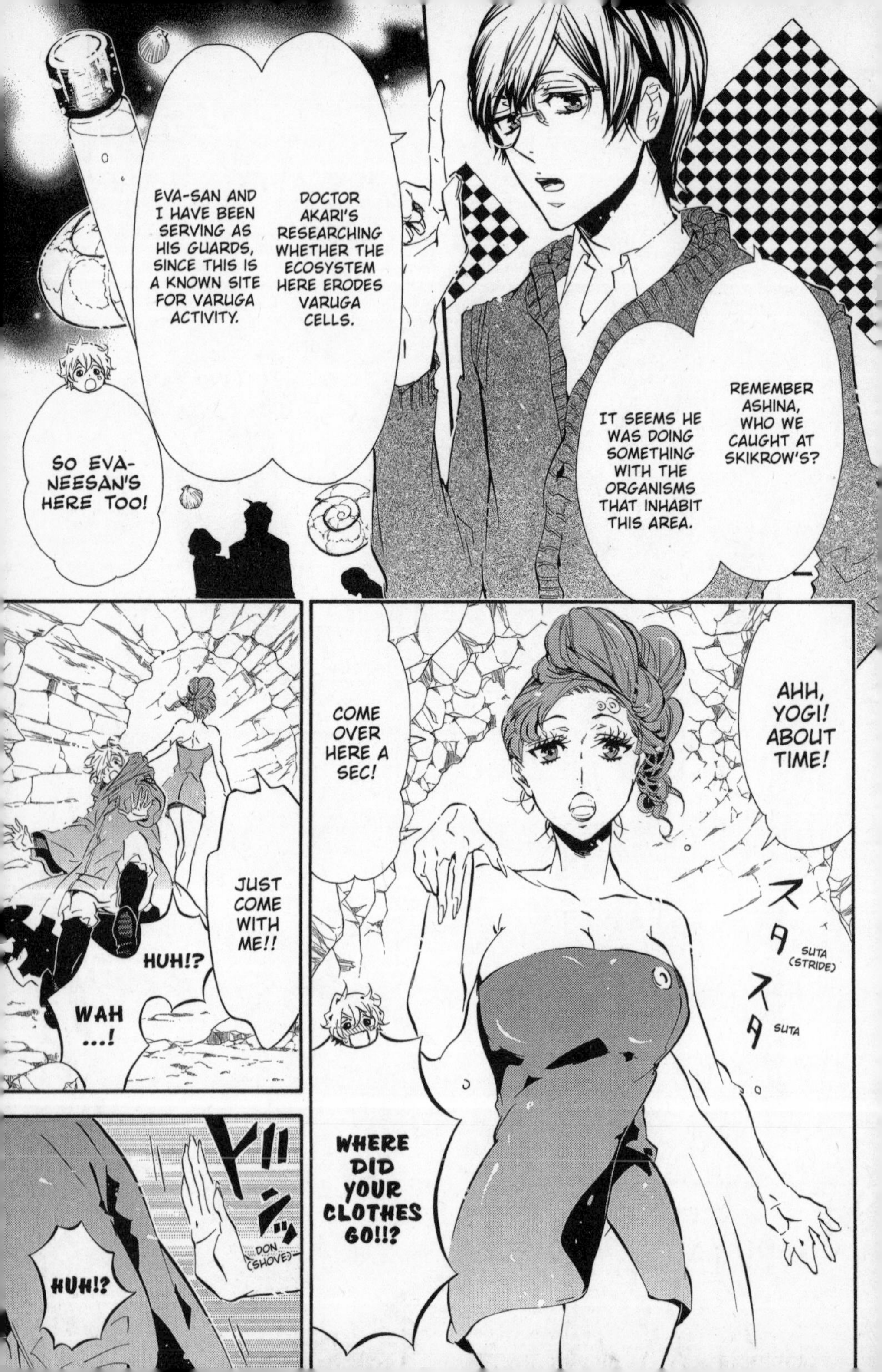
REMEMBER ASHINA, WHO WE CAUGHT AT SKIKROW'S?
IT SEEMS HE WAS DOING SOMETHING WITH THE ORGANISMS THAT INHABIT THIS AREA.
DOCTOR AKARI'S RESEARCHING WHETHER THE ECOSYSTEM HERE ERODES VARUGA CELLS.
EVA-SAN AND I HAVE BEEN SERVING AS HIS GUARDS, SINCE THIS IS A KNOWN SITE FOR VARUGA ACTIVITY.
SO EVA-NEESAN'S HERE TOO!
AHH, YOGI! ABOUT TIME!
COME OVER HERE A SEC!
スタ
SUTA (STRIDE)
スタ
SUTA
WHERE DID YOUR CLOTHES GO!!?
JUST COME WITH ME!!
HUH!?
WAH...!
DON (SHOVE)
HUH!?

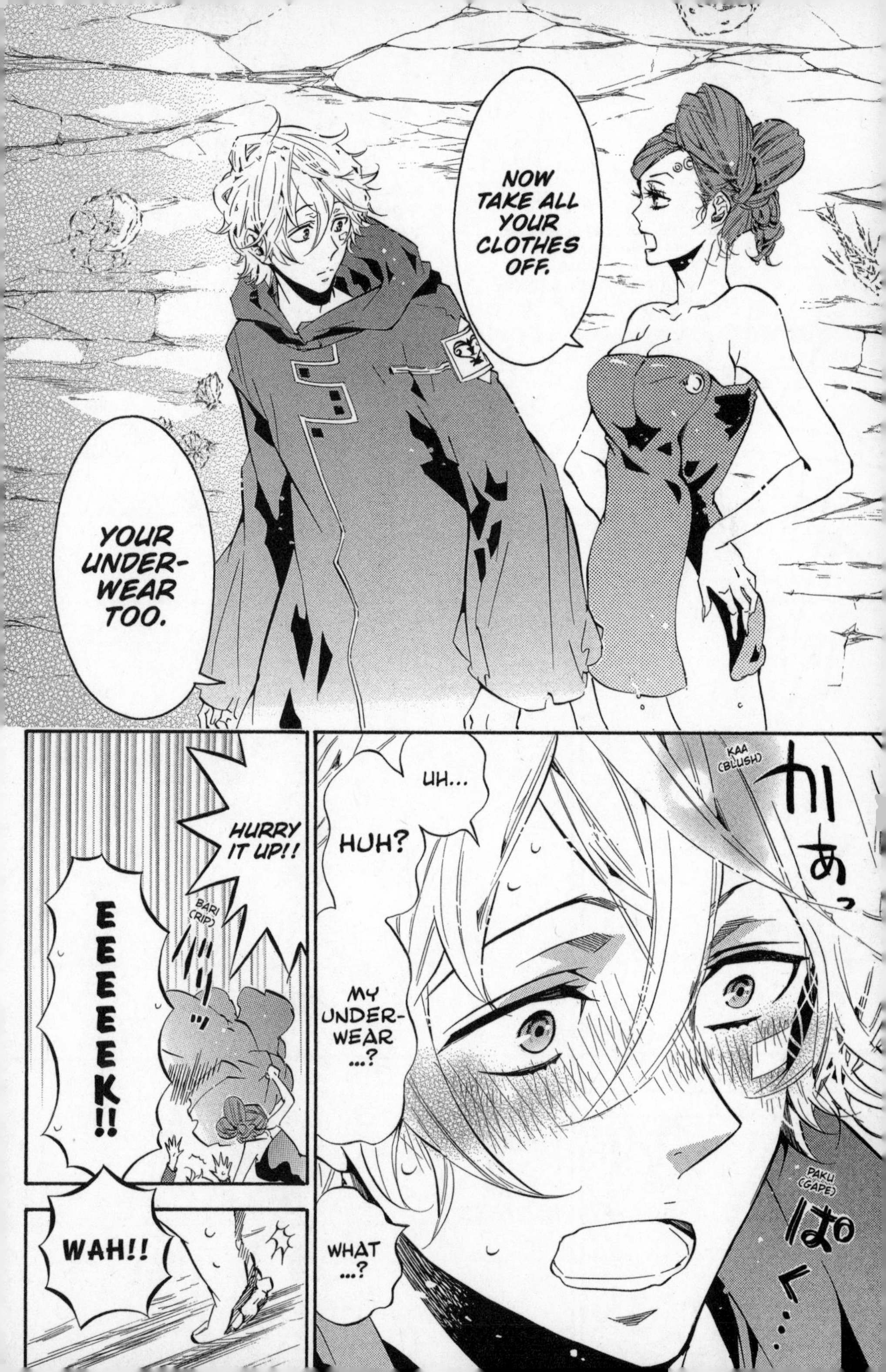
NOW TAKE ALL YOUR CLOTHES OFF.
YOUR UNDER-WEAR TOO.
KAA (BLUSH)
かあっ
UH...
HUH?
MY UNDER-WEAR ...?
PAKU (GAPE)
ぱく
WHAT ...?
HURRY IT UP!!
BARI (RIP)
バリッ
EEEEEEK!!
WAH!!

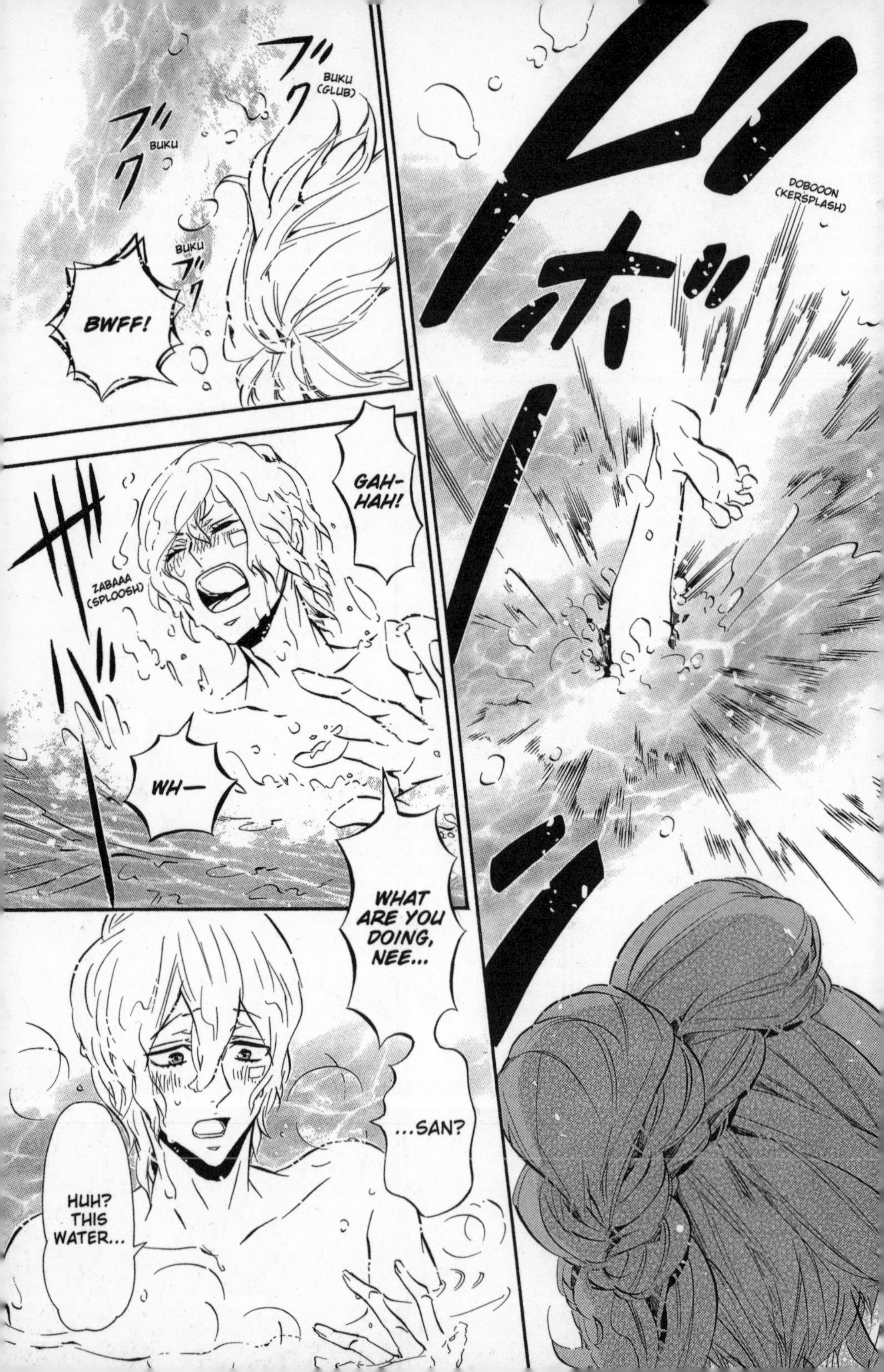
DOBOOON (KERSPLASH)
BUKU (GLUB)
BUKU
BUKU
BWFF!
GAH-HAH!
ZABAAA (SPLOOSH)
WH—
WHAT ARE YOU DOING, NEE...
...SAN?
HUH? THIS WATER...

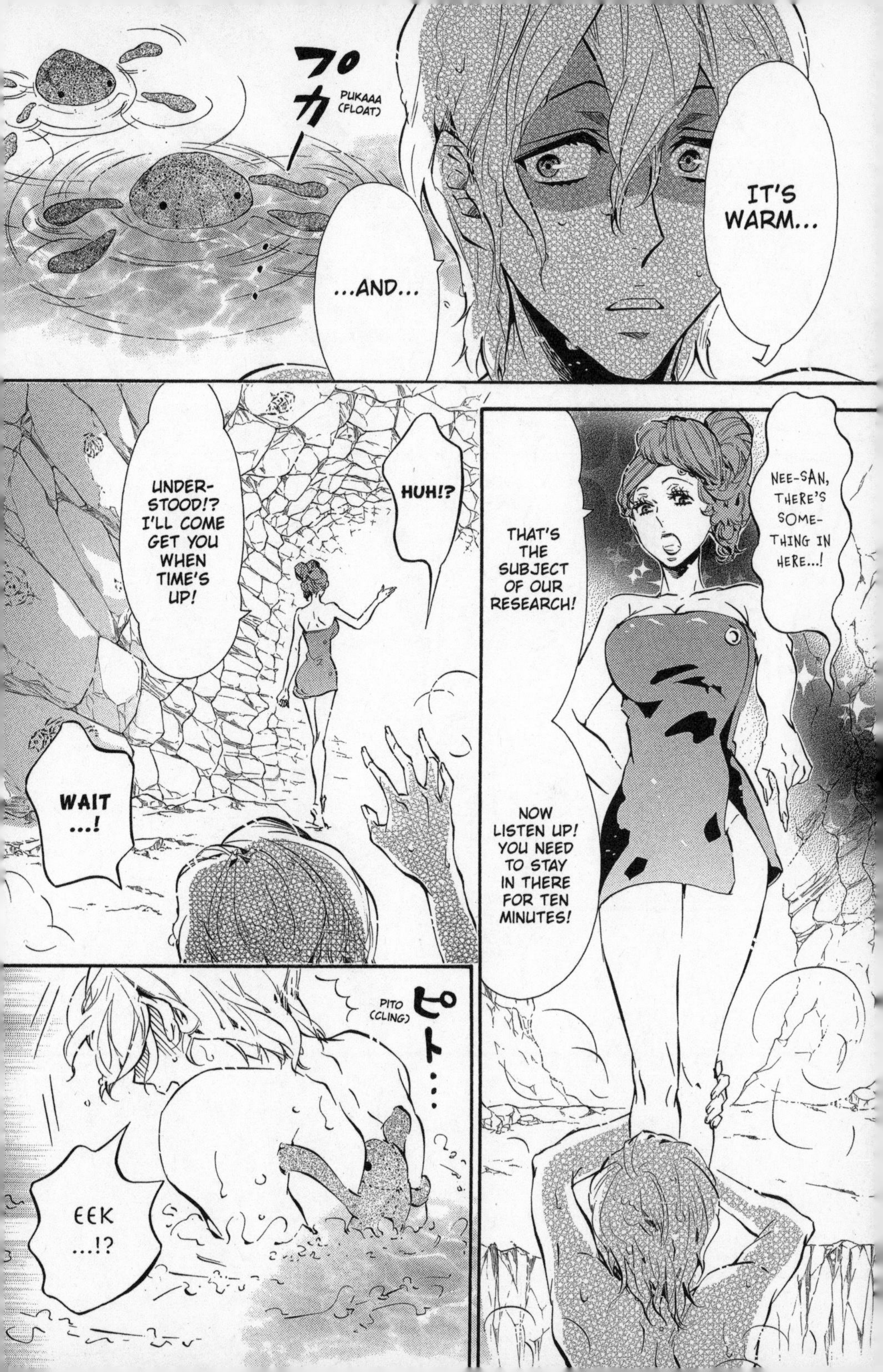

IT'S WARM...
...AND...
フカー
PUKAAA (FLOAT)
NEE-SAN, THERE'S SOME-THING IN HERE...!
THAT'S THE SUBJECT OF OUR RESEARCH!
NOW LISTEN UP! YOU NEED TO STAY IN THERE FOR TEN MINUTES!
UNDER-STOOD!? I'LL COME GET YOU WHEN TIME'S UP!
HUH!?
WAIT...!
ピト...
PITO (CLING)
EEK...!?

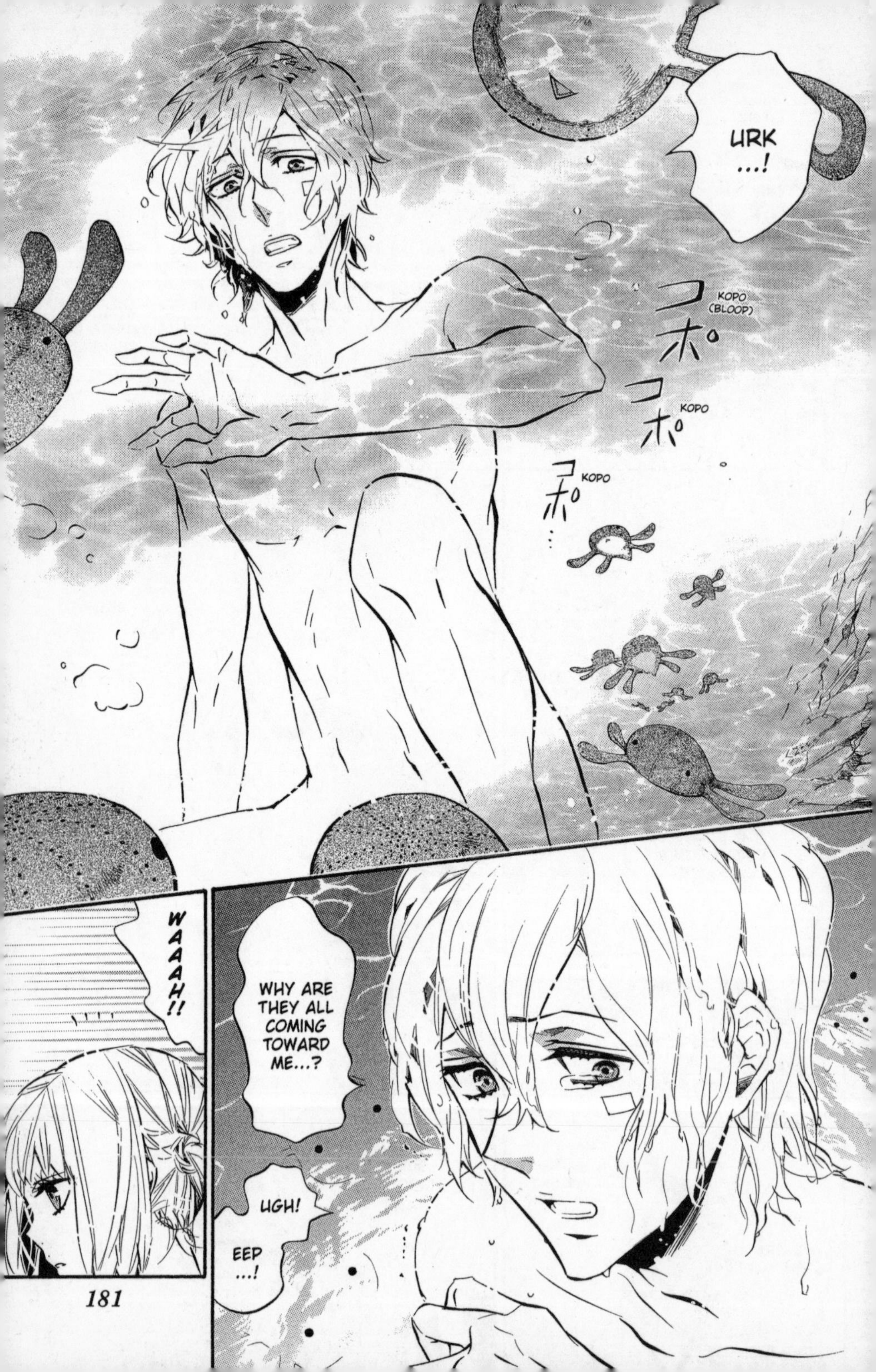
URK ...!
コポ
KOPO (BLOOP)
コポ
KOPO
コポ...
KOPO
WHY ARE THEY ALL COMING TOWARD ME...?
UGH!
EEP ...!
WAAAAH!!

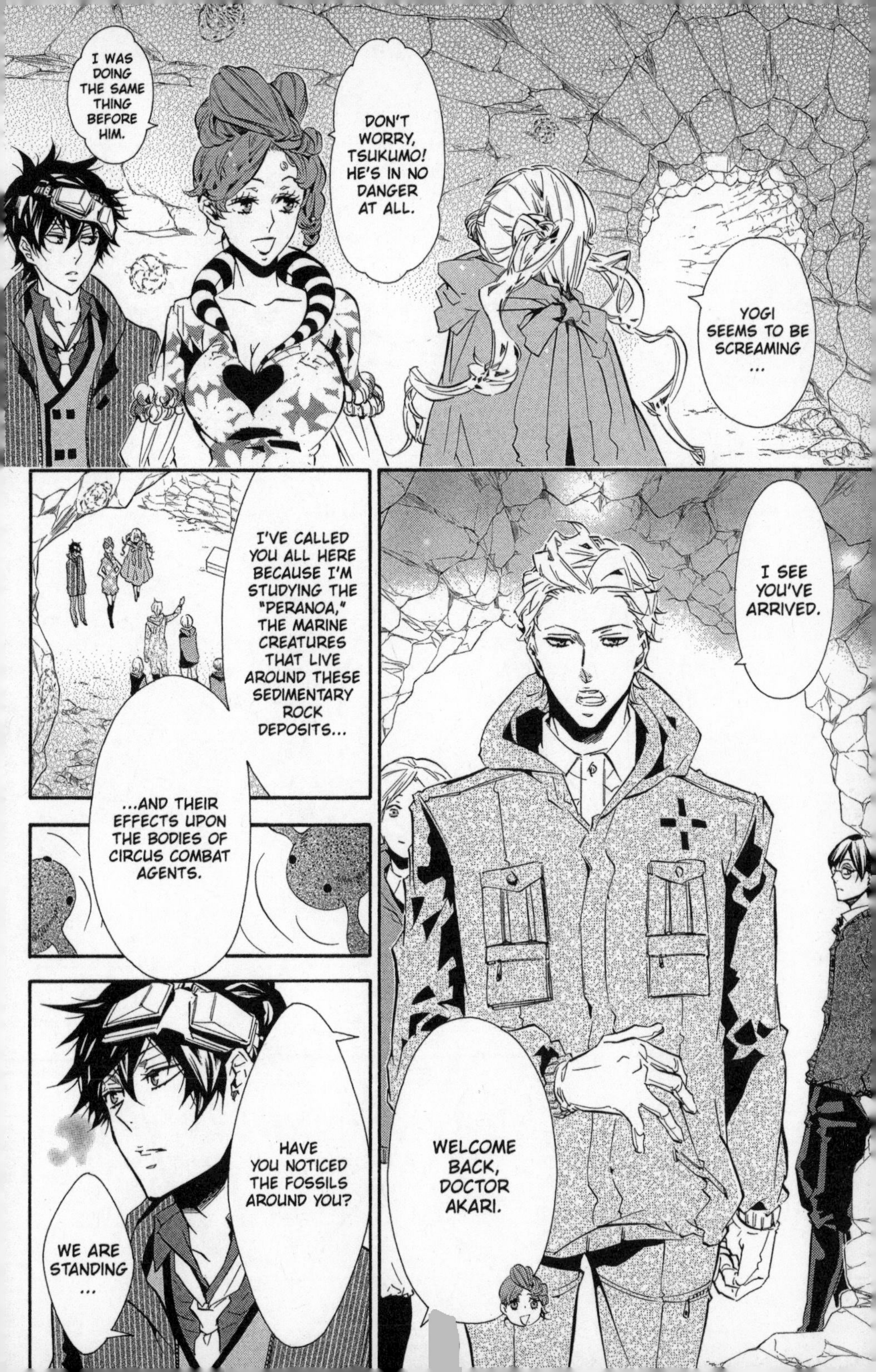
YOGI SEEMS TO BE SCREAMING ...
DON'T WORRY, TSUKUMO! HE'S IN NO DANGER AT ALL.
I WAS DOING THE SAME THING BEFORE HIM.
I SEE YOU'VE ARRIVED.
WELCOME BACK, DOCTOR AKARI.
I'VE CALLED YOU ALL HERE BECAUSE I'M STUDYING THE "PERANOA," THE MARINE CREATURES THAT LIVE AROUND THESE SEDIMENTARY ROCK DEPOSITS...
...AND THEIR EFFECTS UPON THE BODIES OF CIRCUS COMBAT AGENTS.
HAVE YOU NOTICED THE FOSSILS AROUND YOU?
WE ARE STANDING ...

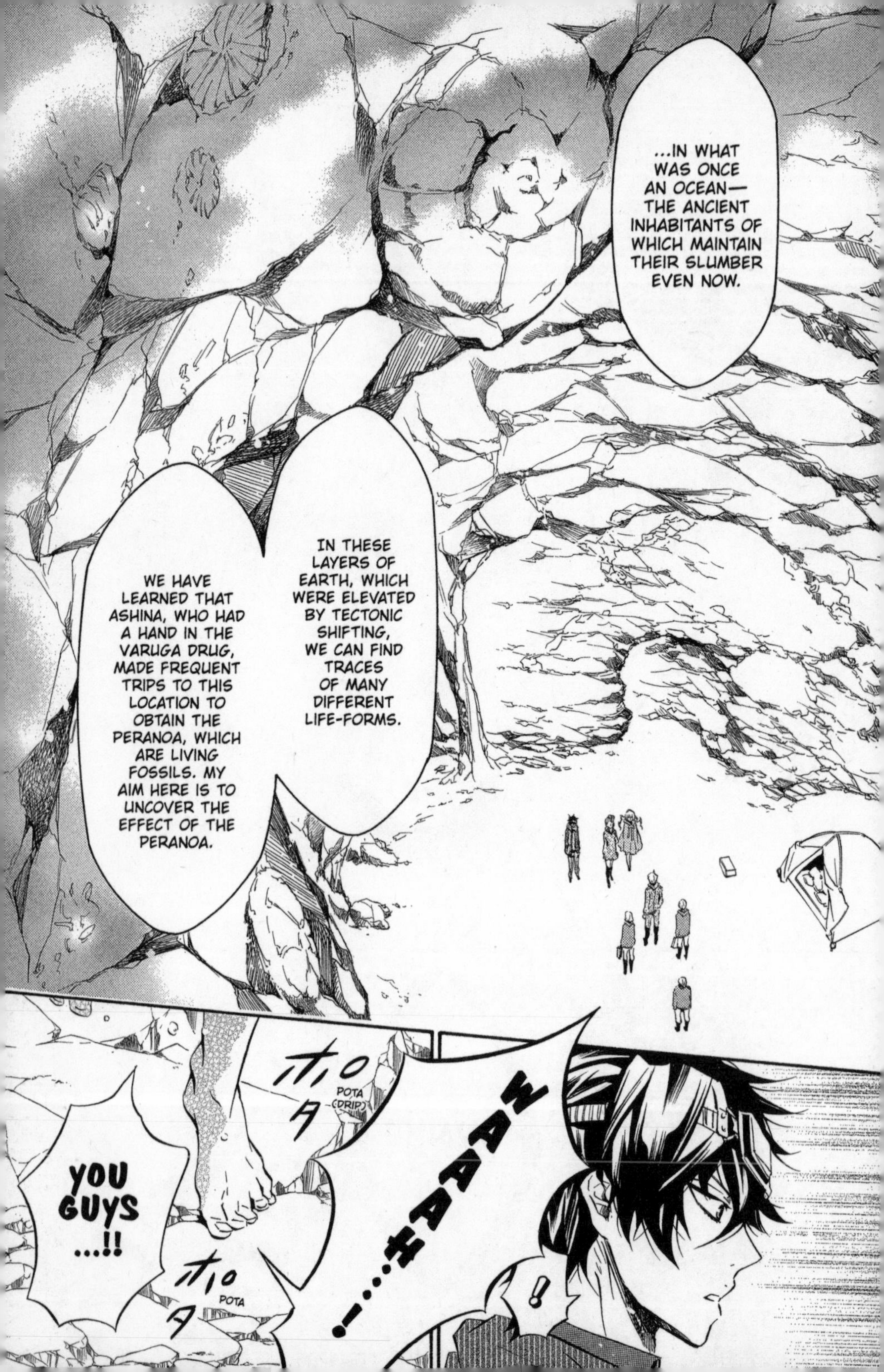
...IN WHAT WAS ONCE AN OCEAN—THE ANCIENT INHABITANTS OF WHICH MAINTAIN THEIR SLUMBER EVEN NOW.
IN THESE LAYERS OF EARTH, WHICH WERE ELEVATED BY TECTONIC SHIFTING, WE CAN FIND TRACES OF MANY DIFFERENT LIFE-FORMS.
WE HAVE LEARNED THAT ASHINA, WHO HAD A HAND IN THE VARUGA DRUG, MADE FREQUENT TRIPS TO THIS LOCATION TO OBTAIN THE PERANOA, WHICH ARE LIVING FOSSILS. MY AIM HERE IS TO UNCOVER THE EFFECT OF THE PERANOA.
WAAAAH...!!
!
ポタ
POTA (DRIP)
YOU GUYS...!!
ポタ
POTA

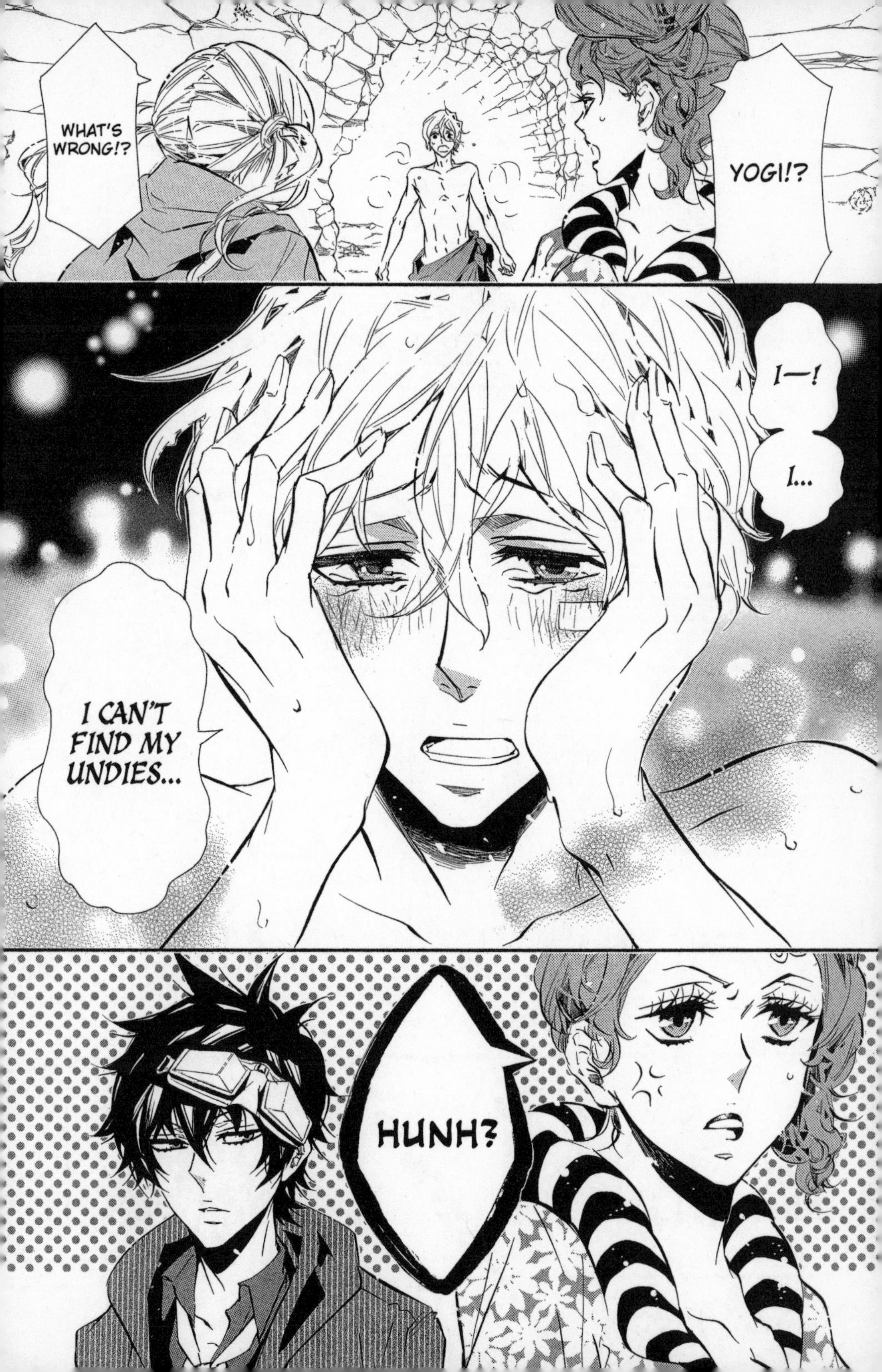
YOGI!?
WHAT'S WRONG!?
I—!
I...
I CAN'T FIND MY UNDIES...
HUNH?

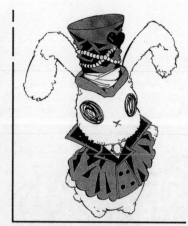

KARNEVAL

KARNEVAL

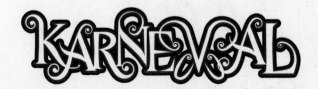

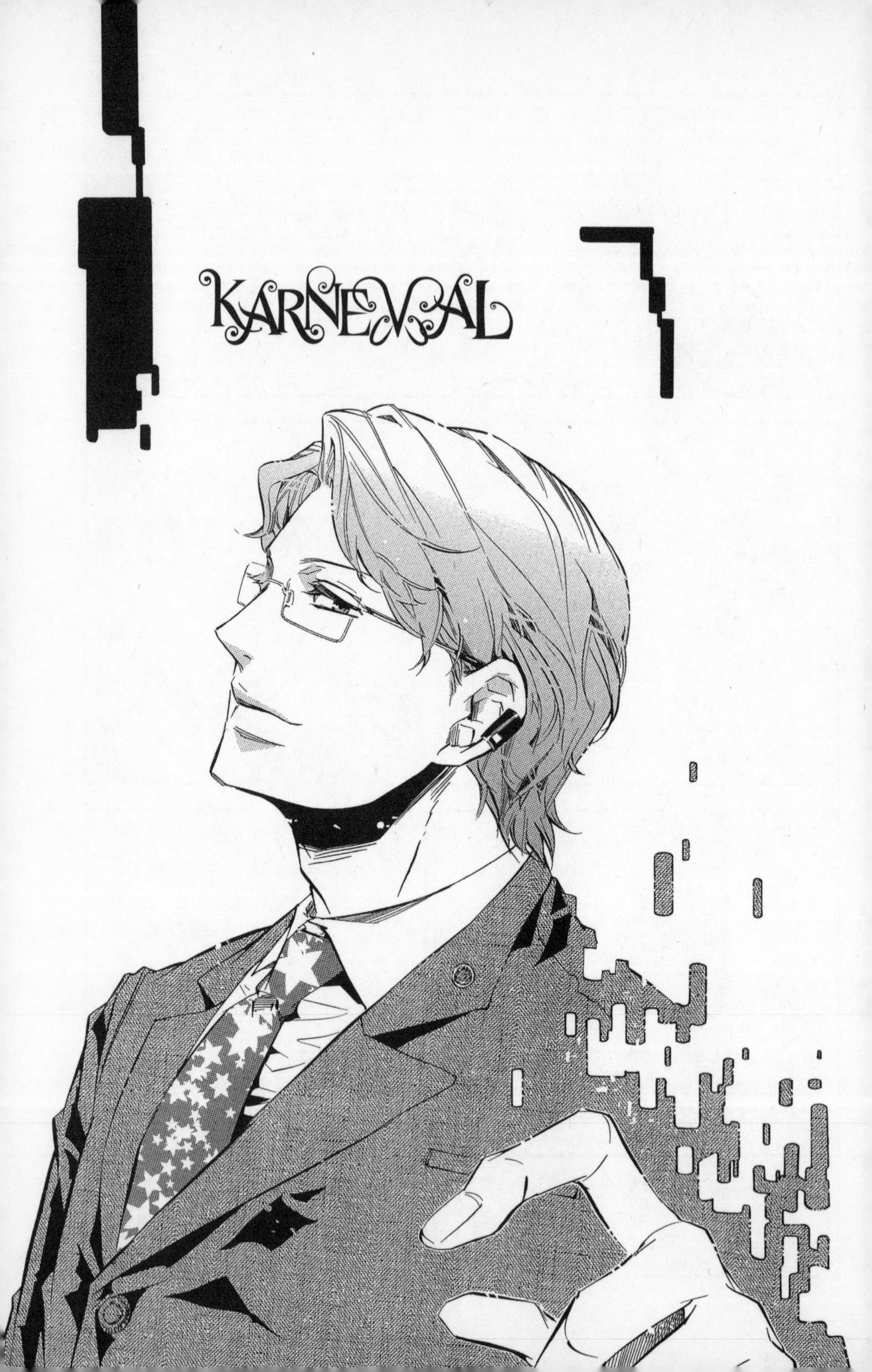
KARNEVAL

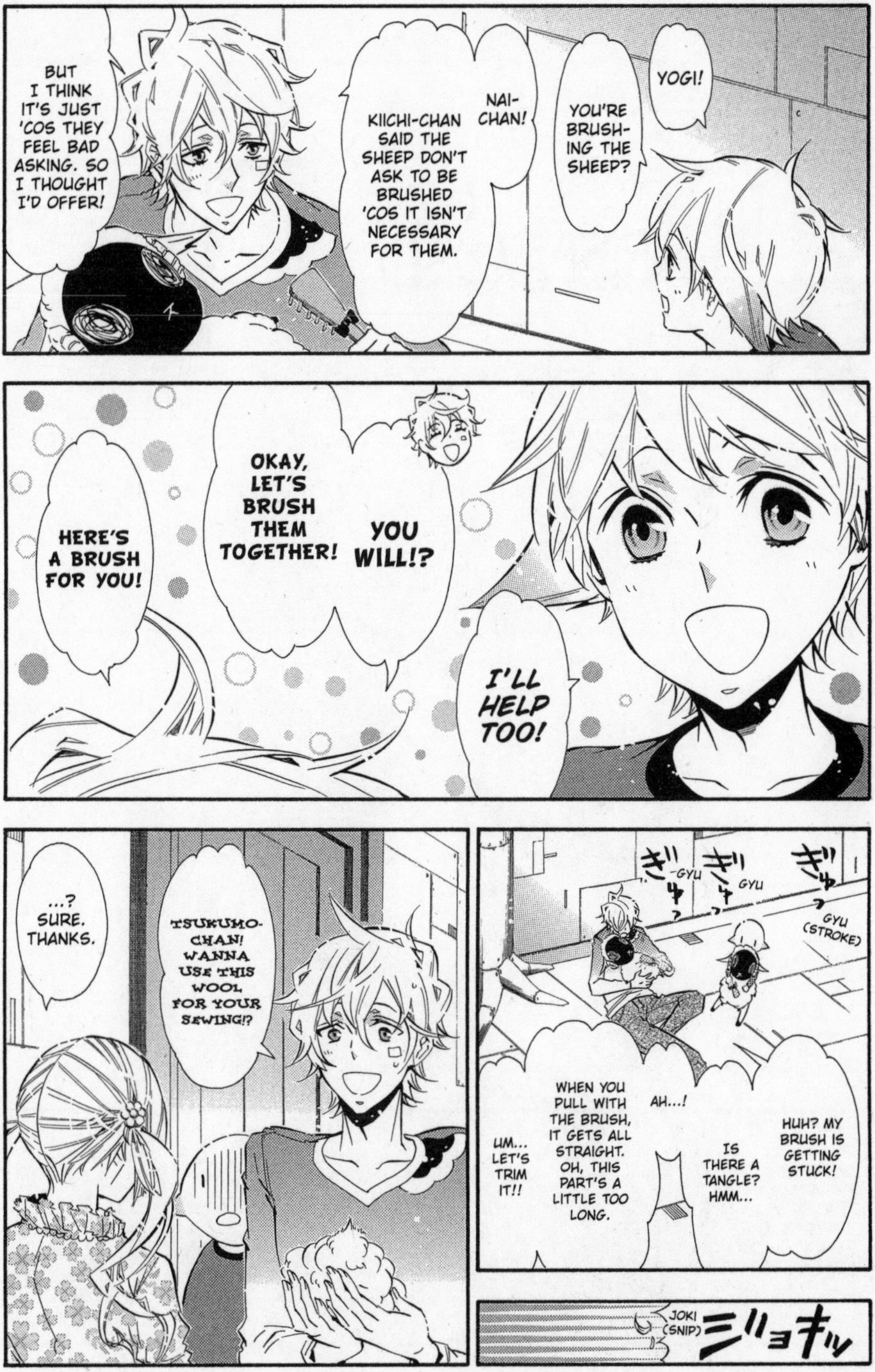
YOGI!
YOU'RE BRUSHING THE SHEEP?
NAI-CHAN!
KIICHI-CHAN SAID THE SHEEP DON'T ASK TO BE BRUSHED 'COS IT ISN'T NECESSARY FOR THEM.
BUT I THINK IT'S JUST 'COS THEY FEEL BAD ASKING. SO I THOUGHT I'D OFFER!
I'LL HELP TOO!
YOU WILL!?
OKAY, LET'S BRUSH THEM TOGETHER!
HERE'S A BRUSH FOR YOU!
ぎゅ GYU (STROKE)
ぎゅ GYU
ぎゅ GYU
HUH? MY BRUSH IS GETTING STUCK!
IS THERE A TANGLE? HMM...
AH...!
WHEN YOU PULL WITH THE BRUSH, IT GETS ALL STRAIGHT. OH, THIS PART'S A LITTLE TOO LONG.
UM... LET'S TRIM IT!!
ジョキッ JOKI (SNIP)
TSUKUMO-CHAN! WANNA USE THIS WOOL FOR YOUR SEWING!?
...? SURE. THANKS.

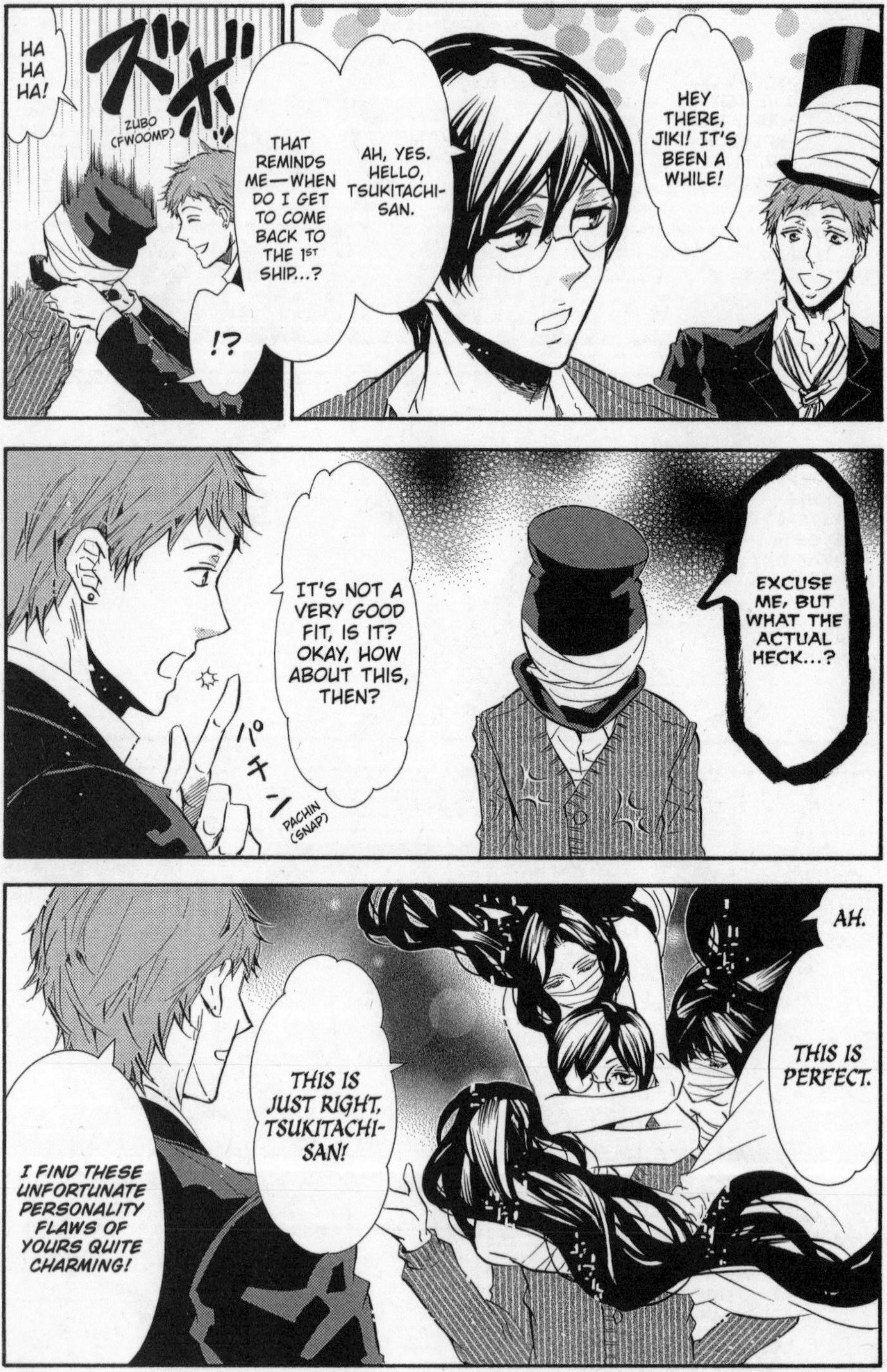
HEY THERE, JIKI! IT'S BEEN A WHILE!
AH, YES. HELLO, TSUKITACHI-SAN.
THAT REMINDS ME—WHEN DO I GET TO COME BACK TO THE 1ST SHIP...?
ズボッ
ZUBO (FWOOMP)
HA HA HA!
!?
EXCUSE ME, BUT WHAT THE ACTUAL HECK...?
IT'S NOT A VERY GOOD FIT, IS IT? OKAY, HOW ABOUT THIS, THEN?
パチン
PACHIN (SNAP)
AH.
THIS IS PERFECT.
THIS IS JUST RIGHT, TSUKITACHI-SAN!
I FIND THESE UNFORTUNATE PERSONALITY FLAWS OF YOURS QUITE CHARMING!

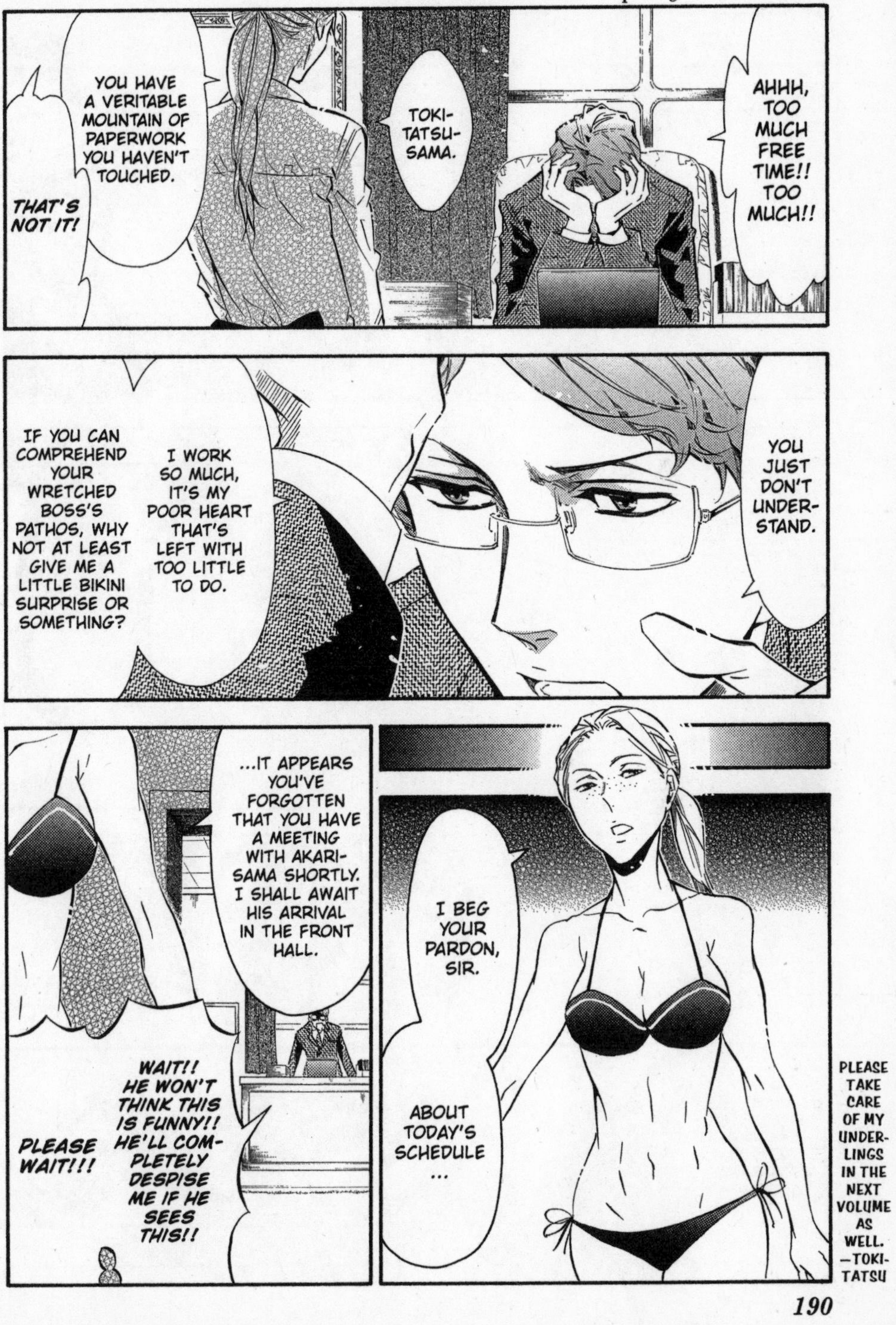
AHHH, TOO MUCH FREE TIME!! TOO MUCH!!
TOKI-TATSU-SAMA.
YOU HAVE A VERITABLE MOUNTAIN OF PAPERWORK YOU HAVEN'T TOUCHED.
THAT'S NOT IT!
YOU JUST DON'T UNDER-STAND.
I WORK SO MUCH, IT'S MY POOR HEART THAT'S LEFT WITH TOO LITTLE TO DO.
IF YOU CAN COMPREHEND YOUR WRETCHED BOSS'S PATHOS, WHY NOT AT LEAST GIVE ME A LITTLE BIKINI SURPRISE OR SOMETHING?
I BEG YOUR PARDON, SIR.
ABOUT TODAY'S SCHEDULE ...
...IT APPEARS YOU'VE FORGOTTEN THAT YOU HAVE A MEETING WITH AKARI-SAMA SHORTLY. I SHALL AWAIT HIS ARRIVAL IN THE FRONT HALL.
WAIT!! HE WON'T THINK THIS IS FUNNY!! HE'LL COM-PLETELY DESPISE ME IF HE SEES THIS!!
PLEASE WAIT!!!

PLEASE TAKE CARE OF MY UNDER-LINGS IN THE NEXT VOLUME AS WELL. —TOKI-TATSU

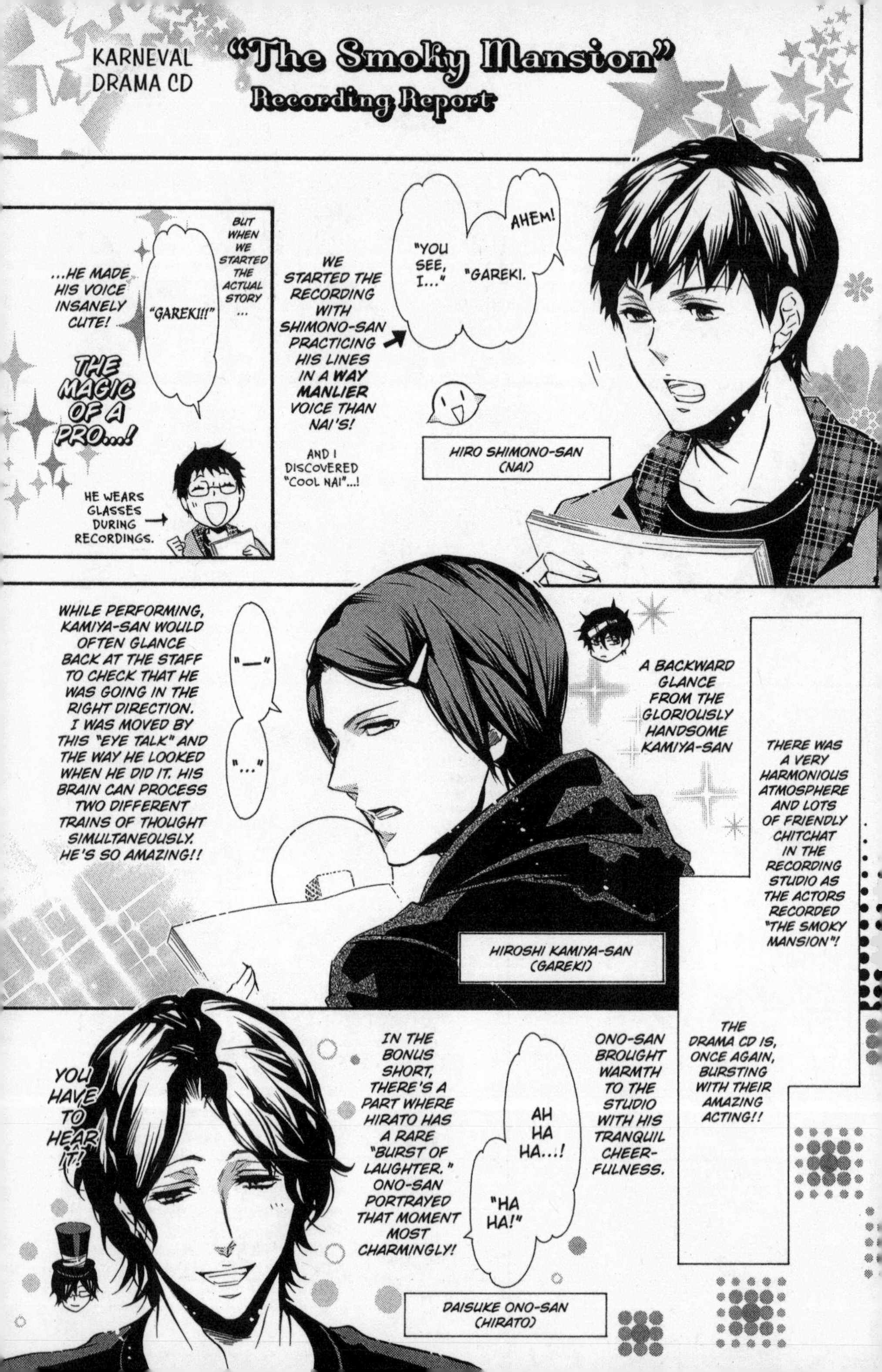
KARNEVAL DRAMA CD
"The Smoky Mansion"
Recording Report
AHEM!
"GAREKI.
"YOU SEE, I..."
WE STARTED THE RECORDING WITH SHIMONO-SAN PRACTICING HIS LINES IN A WAY MANLIER VOICE THAN NAI'S!
AND I DISCOVERED "COOL NAI"...!
HIRO SHIMONO-SAN (NAI)
BUT WHEN WE STARTED THE ACTUAL STORY...
"GAREKI!!"
...HE MADE HIS VOICE INSANELY CUTE!
THE MAGIC OF A PRO...!
HE WEARS GLASSES DURING RECORDINGS.
THERE WAS A VERY HARMONIOUS ATMOSPHERE AND LOTS OF FRIENDLY CHITCHAT IN THE RECORDING STUDIO AS THE ACTORS RECORDED "THE SMOKY MANSION"!
A BACKWARD GLANCE FROM THE GLORIOUSLY HANDSOME KAMIYA-SAN
"—"
"..."
WHILE PERFORMING, KAMIYA-SAN WOULD OFTEN GLANCE BACK AT THE STAFF TO CHECK THAT HE WAS GOING IN THE RIGHT DIRECTION. I WAS MOVED BY THIS "EYE TALK" AND THE WAY HE LOOKED WHEN HE DID IT. HIS BRAIN CAN PROCESS TWO DIFFERENT TRAINS OF THOUGHT SIMULTANEOUSLY. HE'S SO AMAZING!!
HIROSHI KAMIYA-SAN (GAREKI)
THE DRAMA CD IS, ONCE AGAIN, BURSTING WITH THEIR AMAZING ACTING!!
ONO-SAN BROUGHT WARMTH TO THE STUDIO WITH HIS TRANQUIL CHEERFULNESS.
AH HA HA...!
"HA HA!"
IN THE BONUS SHORT, THERE'S A PART WHERE HIRATO HAS A RARE "BURST OF LAUGHTER." ONO-SAN PORTRAYED THAT MOMENT MOST CHARMINGLY!
YOU HAVE TO HEAR IT!
DAISUKE ONO-SAN (HIRATO)

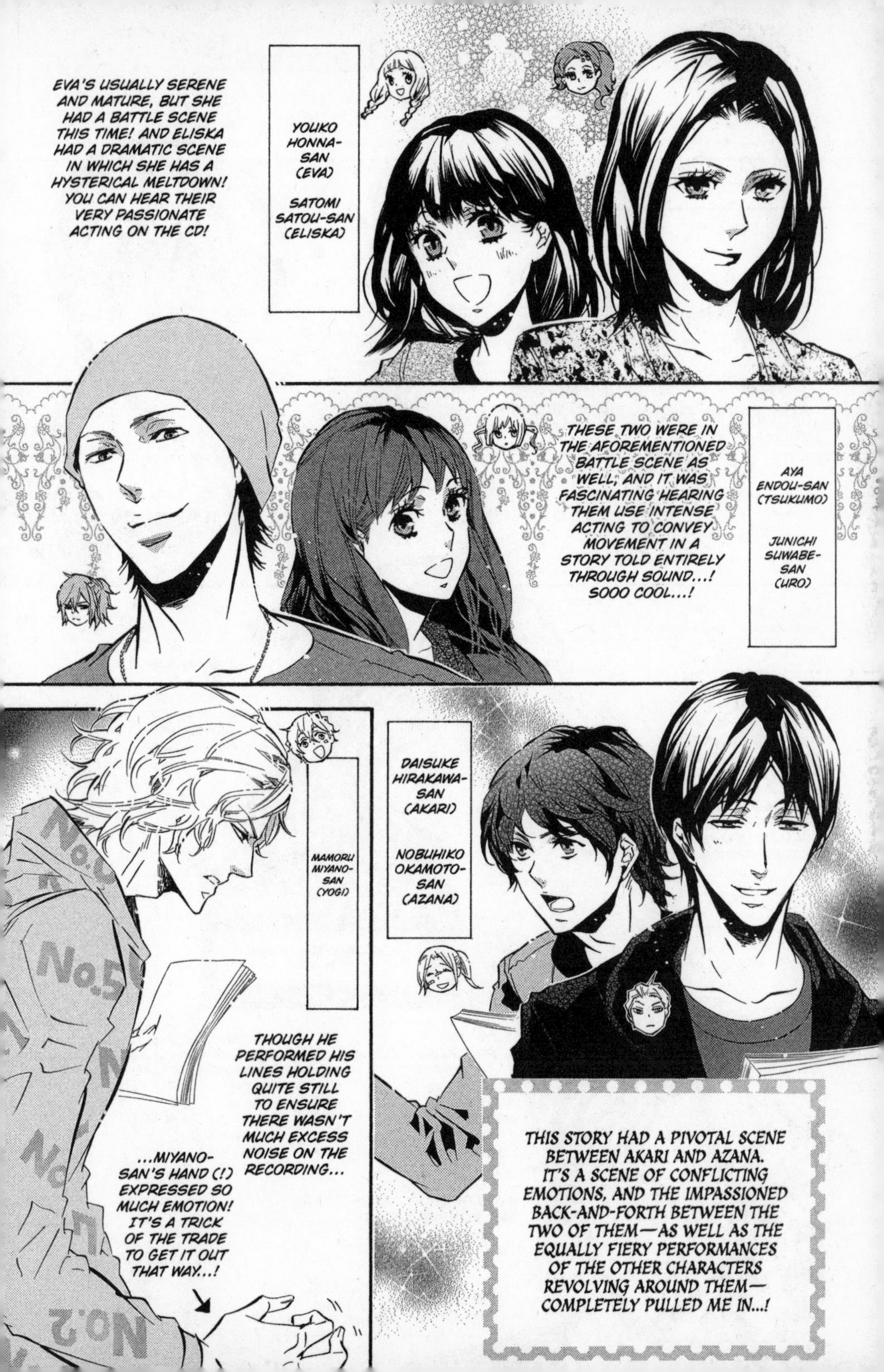
YOUKO HONNA-SAN (EVA)
SATOMI SATOU-SAN (ELISKA)
EVA'S USUALLY SERENE AND MATURE, BUT SHE HAD A BATTLE SCENE THIS TIME! AND ELISKA HAD A DRAMATIC SCENE IN WHICH SHE HAS A HYSTERICAL MELTDOWN! YOU CAN HEAR THEIR VERY PASSIONATE ACTING ON THE CD!
AYA ENDOU-SAN (TSUKUMO)
JUNICHI SUWABE-SAN (URO)
THESE TWO WERE IN THE AFOREMENTIONED BATTLE SCENE AS WELL, AND IT WAS FASCINATING HEARING THEM USE INTENSE ACTING TO CONVEY MOVEMENT IN A STORY TOLD ENTIRELY THROUGH SOUND...! SOOO COOL...!
DAISUKE HIRAKAWA-SAN (AKARI)
NOBUHIKO OKAMOTO-SAN (AZANA)
THIS STORY HAD A PIVOTAL SCENE BETWEEN AKARI AND AZANA. IT'S A SCENE OF CONFLICTING EMOTIONS, AND THE IMPASSIONED BACK-AND-FORTH BETWEEN THE TWO OF THEM—AS WELL AS THE EQUALLY FIERY PERFORMANCES OF THE OTHER CHARACTERS REVOLVING AROUND THEM—COMPLETELY PULLED ME IN...!
MAMORU MIYANO-SAN (YOGI)
THOUGH HE PERFORMED HIS LINES HOLDING QUITE STILL TO ENSURE THERE WASN'T MUCH EXCESS NOISE ON THE RECORDING...
...MIYANO-SAN'S HAND (!) EXPRESSED SO MUCH EMOTION! IT'S A TRICK OF THE TRADE TO GET IT OUT THAT WAY...!

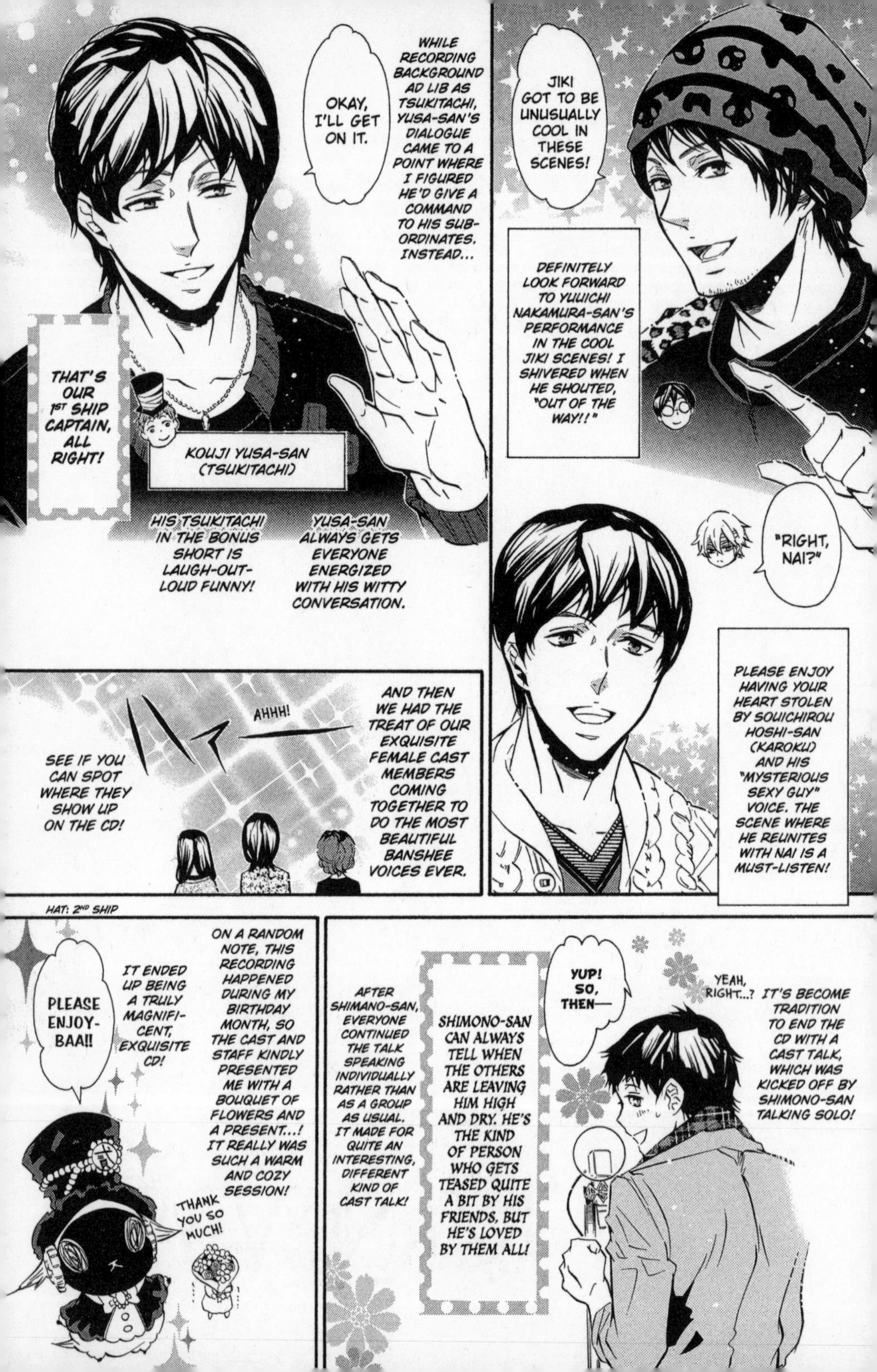
JIKI! GOT TO BE UNUSUALLY COOL IN THESE SCENES!
DEFINITELY LOOK FORWARD TO YUUICHI NAKAMURA-SAN'S PERFORMANCE IN THE COOL JIKI SCENES! I SHIVERED WHEN HE SHOUTED, "OUT OF THE WAY!!"
"RIGHT, NAI?"
PLEASE ENJOY HAVING YOUR HEART STOLEN BY SOUICHIROU HOSHI-SAN (KAROKU) AND HIS "MYSTERIOUS SEXY GUY" VOICE. THE SCENE WHERE HE REUNITES WITH NAI IS A MUST-LISTEN!
WHILE RECORDING BACKGROUND AD LIB AS TSUKITACHI, YUSA-SAN'S DIALOGUE CAME TO A POINT WHERE I FIGURED HE'D GIVE A COMMAND TO HIS SUBORDINATES. INSTEAD...
OKAY, I'LL GET ON IT.
THAT'S OUR 1ST SHIP CAPTAIN, ALL RIGHT!
KOUJI YUSA-SAN (TSUKITACHI)
YUSA-SAN ALWAYS GETS EVERYONE ENERGIZED WITH HIS WITTY CONVERSATION.
HIS TSUKITACHI IN THE BONUS SHORT IS LAUGH-OUT-LOUD FUNNY!
AND THEN WE HAD THE TREAT OF OUR EXQUISITE FEMALE CAST MEMBERS COMING TOGETHER TO DO THE MOST BEAUTIFUL BANSHEE VOICES EVER.
AHHH!
SEE IF YOU CAN SPOT WHERE THEY SHOW UP ON THE CD!
HAT: 2ND SHIP
IT'S BECOME TRADITION TO END THE CD WITH A CAST TALK, WHICH WAS KICKED OFF BY SHIMONO-SAN TALKING SOLO!
YEAH, RIGHT...?
YUP! SO, THEN—
SHIMONO-SAN CAN ALWAYS TELL WHEN THE OTHERS ARE LEAVING HIM HIGH AND DRY. HE'S THE KIND OF PERSON WHO GETS TEASED QUITE A BIT BY HIS FRIENDS, BUT HE'S LOVED BY THEM ALL!
AFTER SHIMANO-SAN, EVERYONE CONTINUED THE TALK SPEAKING INDIVIDUALLY RATHER THAN AS A GROUP AS USUAL. IT MADE FOR QUITE AN INTERESTING, DIFFERENT KIND OF CAST TALK!
ON A RANDOM NOTE, THIS RECORDING HAPPENED DURING MY BIRTHDAY MONTH, SO THE CAST AND STAFF KINDLY PRESENTED ME WITH A BOUQUET OF FLOWERS AND A PRESENT...! IT REALLY WAS SUCH A WARM AND COZY SESSION!
IT ENDED UP BEING A TRULY MAGNIFICENT, EXQUISITE CD!
PLEASE ENJOY-BAA!!
THANK YOU SO MUCH!

KARNEVAL

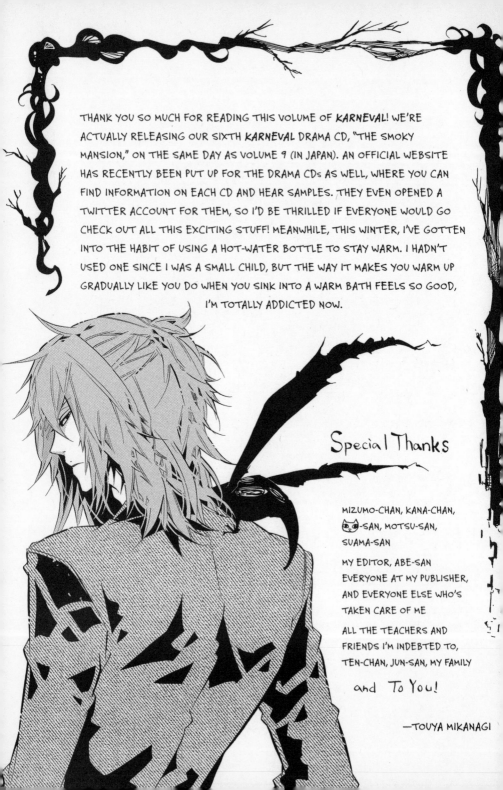

THANK YOU SO MUCH FOR READING THIS VOLUME OF *KARNEVAL*! WE'RE
ACTUALLY RELEASING OUR SIXTH *KARNEVAL* DRAMA CD, "THE SMOKY
MANSION," ON THE SAME DAY AS VOLUME 9 (IN JAPAN). AN OFFICIAL WEBSITE
HAS RECENTLY BEEN PUT UP FOR THE DRAMA CDs AS WELL, WHERE YOU CAN
FIND INFORMATION ON EACH CD AND HEAR SAMPLES. THEY EVEN OPENED A
TWITTER ACCOUNT FOR THEM, SO I'D BE THRILLED IF EVERYONE WOULD GO
CHECK OUT ALL THIS EXCITING STUFF! MEANWHILE, THIS WINTER, I'VE GOTTEN
INTO THE HABIT OF USING A HOT-WATER BOTTLE TO STAY WARM. I HADN'T
USED ONE SINCE I WAS A SMALL CHILD, BUT THE WAY IT MAKES YOU WARM UP
GRADUALLY LIKE YOU DO WHEN YOU SINK INTO A WARM BATH FEELS SO GOOD,
I'M TOTALLY ADDICTED NOW.

Special Thanks

MIZUMO-CHAN, KANA-CHAN,
🐱-SAN, MOTSU-SAN,
SUAMA-SAN

MY EDITOR, ABE-SAN
EVERYONE AT MY PUBLISHER,
AND EVERYONE ELSE WHO'S
TAKEN CARE OF ME

ALL THE TEACHERS AND
FRIENDS I'M INDEBTED TO,
TEN-CHAN, JUN-SAN, MY FAMILY

and To You!

—TOUYA MIKANAGI

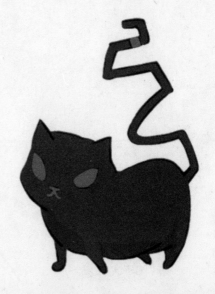

Score 55: Halo

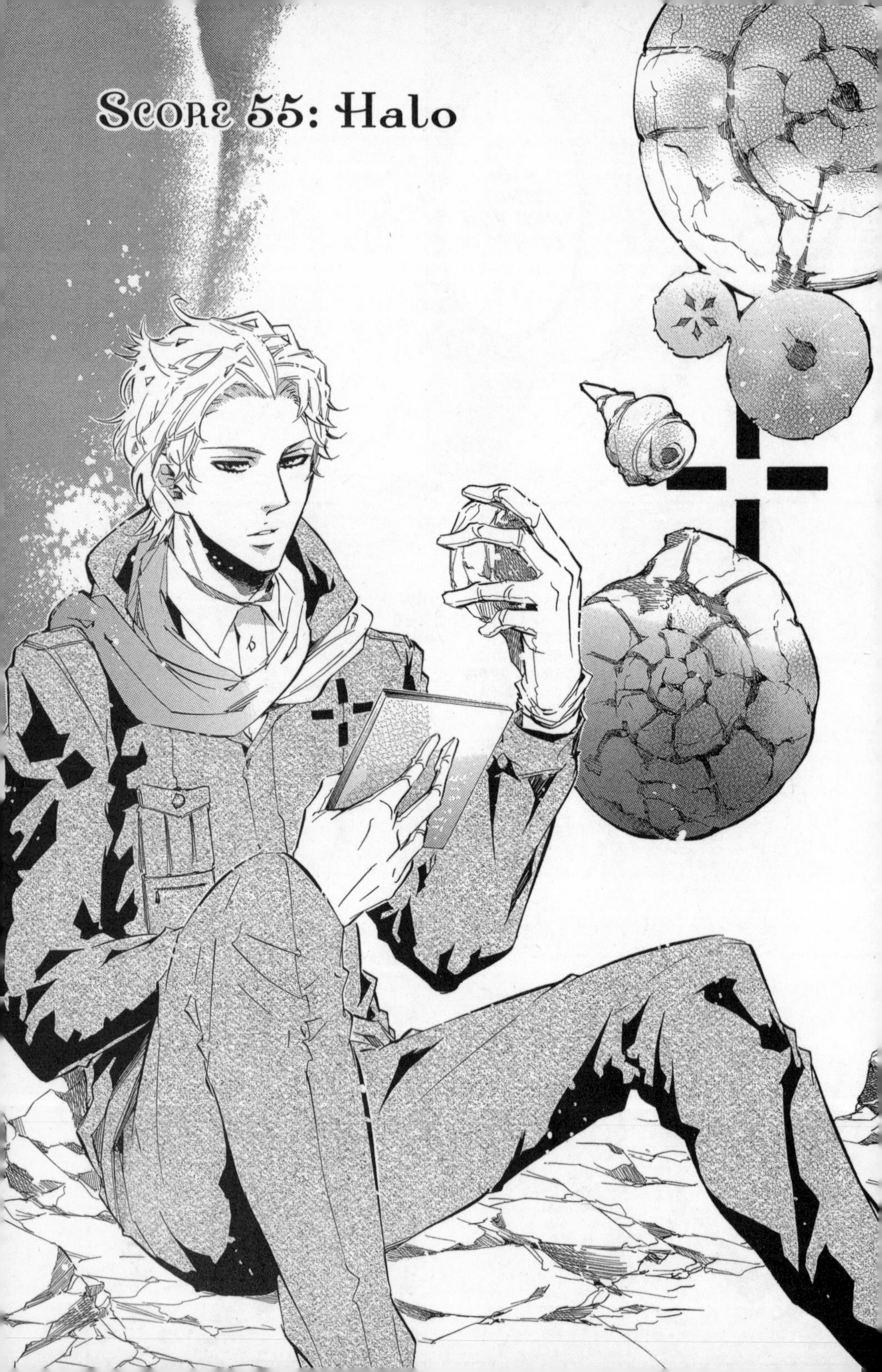

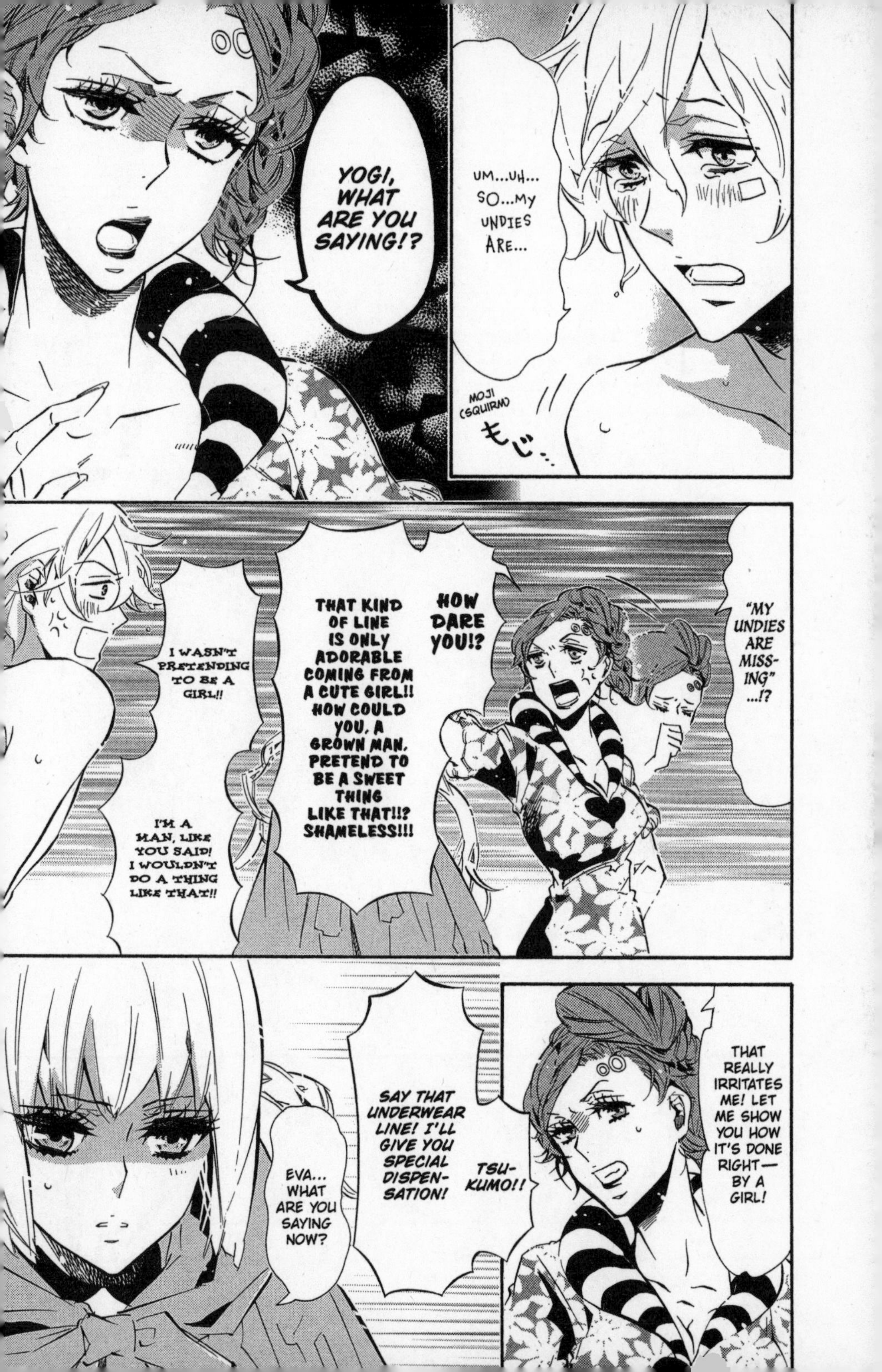
UM...UH... SO...MY UNDIES ARE...
MOJI (SQUIRM)
もじ...
YOGI, WHAT ARE YOU SAYING!?
"MY UNDIES ARE MISS-ING" ...!?
HOW DARE YOU!?
THAT KIND OF LINE IS ONLY ADORABLE COMING FROM A CUTE GIRL!! HOW COULD YOU, A GROWN MAN, PRETEND TO BE A SWEET THING LIKE THAT!!? SHAMELESS!!!
I WASN'T PRETENDING TO BE A GIRL!!
I'M A MAN, LIKE YOU SAID! I WOULDN'T DO A THING LIKE THAT!!
THAT REALLY IRRITATES ME! LET ME SHOW YOU HOW IT'S DONE RIGHT— BY A GIRL!
TSU-KUMO!!
SAY THAT UNDERWEAR LINE! I'LL GIVE YOU SPECIAL DISPEN-SATION!
EVA... WHAT ARE YOU SAYING NOW?

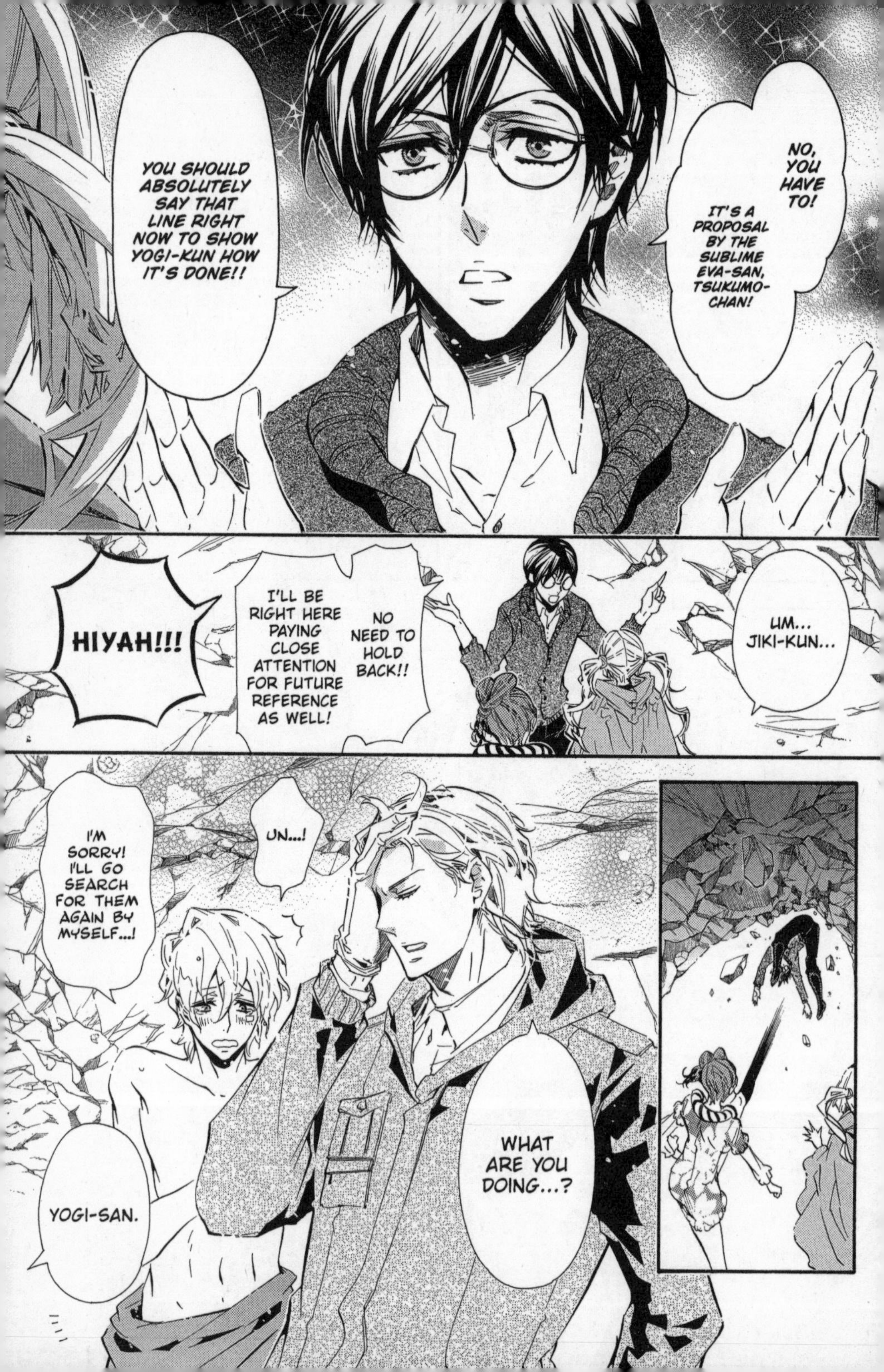
NO, YOU HAVE TO!
IT'S A PROPOSAL BY THE SUBLIME EVA-SAN, TSUKUMO-CHAN!
YOU SHOULD ABSOLUTELY SAY THAT LINE RIGHT NOW TO SHOW YOGI-KUN HOW IT'S DONE!!
UM... JIKI-KUN...
NO NEED TO HOLD BACK!!
I'LL BE RIGHT HERE PAYING CLOSE ATTENTION FOR FUTURE REFERENCE AS WELL!
HIYAH!!!
UN...!
I'M SORRY! I'LL GO SEARCH FOR THEM AGAIN BY MYSELF...!
WHAT ARE YOU DOING...?
YOGI-SAN.

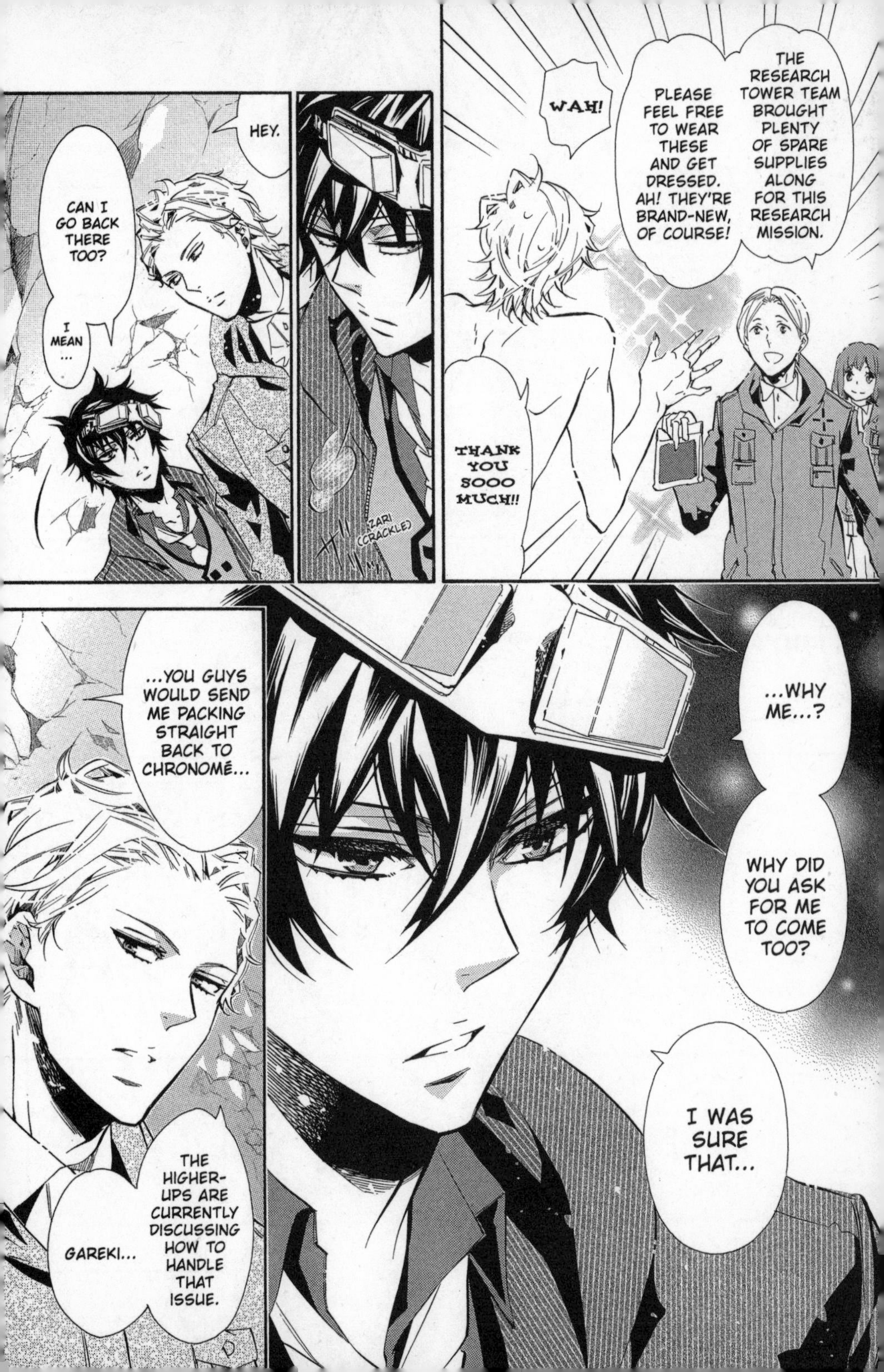
THE RESEARCH TOWER TEAM BROUGHT PLENTY OF SPARE SUPPLIES ALONG FOR THIS RESEARCH MISSION.
PLEASE FEEL FREE TO WEAR THESE AND GET DRESSED. AH! THEY'RE BRAND-NEW, OF COURSE!
WAH!
THANK YOU SOOO MUCH!!
ZARI (CRACKLE)
HEY.
CAN I GO BACK THERE TOO?
I MEAN ...
...WHY ME...?
WHY DID YOU ASK FOR ME TO COME TOO?
I WAS SURE THAT...
...YOU GUYS WOULD SEND ME PACKING STRAIGHT BACK TO CHRONOMÉ...
THE HIGHER-UPS ARE CURRENTLY DISCUSSING HOW TO HANDLE THAT ISSUE.
GAREKI...

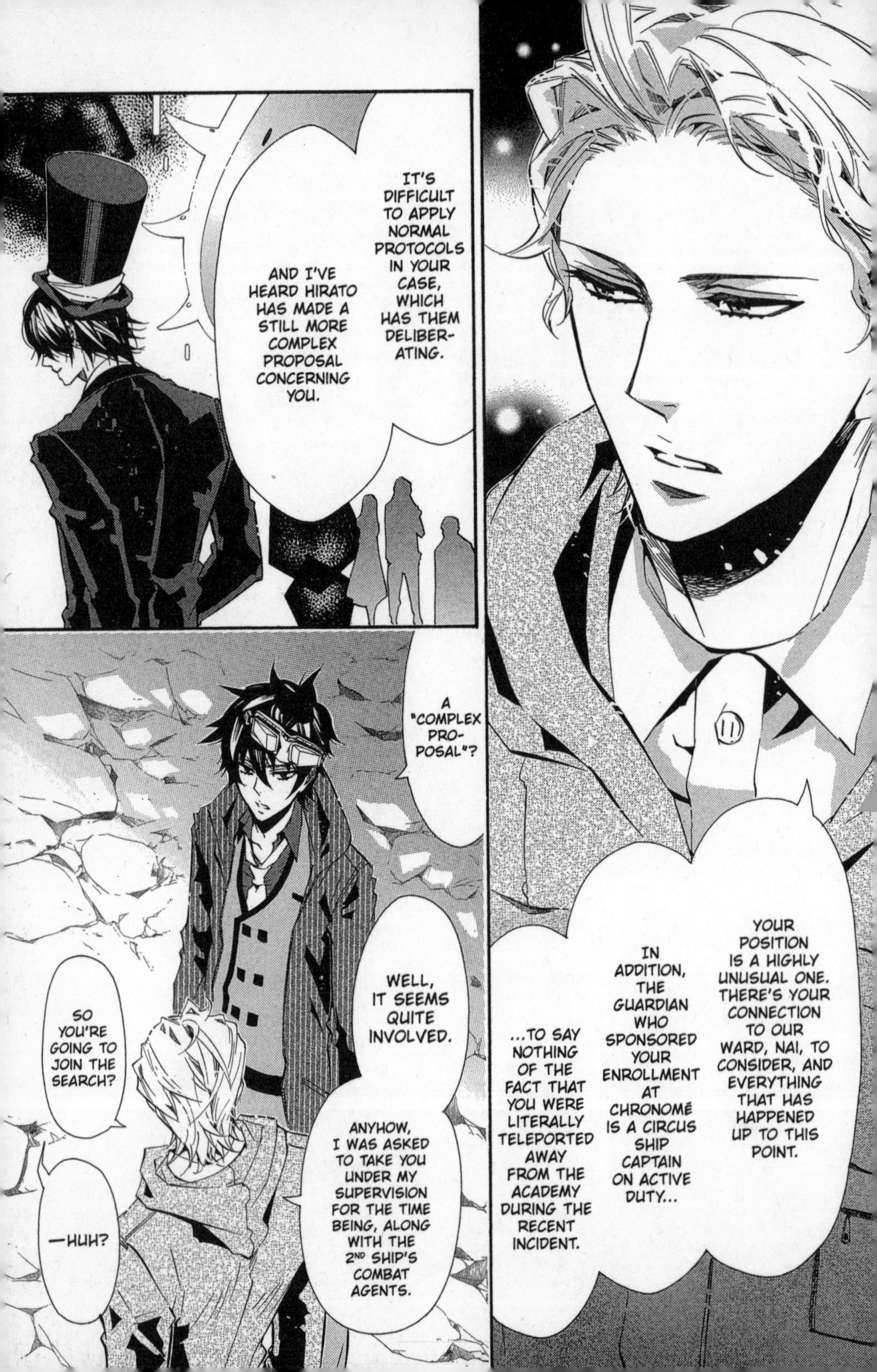
YOUR POSITION IS A HIGHLY UNUSUAL ONE. THERE'S YOUR CONNECTION TO OUR WARD, NAI, TO CONSIDER, AND EVERYTHING THAT HAS HAPPENED UP TO THIS POINT.
IN ADDITION, THE GUARDIAN WHO SPONSORED YOUR ENROLLMENT AT CHRONOMÉ IS A CIRCUS SHIP CAPTAIN ON ACTIVE DUTY...
...TO SAY NOTHING OF THE FACT THAT YOU WERE LITERALLY TELEPORTED AWAY FROM THE ACADEMY DURING THE RECENT INCIDENT.
IT'S DIFFICULT TO APPLY NORMAL PROTOCOLS IN YOUR CASE, WHICH HAS THEM DELIBER-ATING.
AND I'VE HEARD HIRATO HAS MADE A STILL MORE COMPLEX PROPOSAL CONCERNING YOU.
A "COMPLEX PRO-POSAL"?
WELL, IT SEEMS QUITE INVOLVED.
ANYHOW, I WAS ASKED TO TAKE YOU UNDER MY SUPERVISION FOR THE TIME BEING, ALONG WITH THE 2ND SHIP'S COMBAT AGENTS.
—HUH?
SO YOU'RE GOING TO JOIN THE SEARCH?

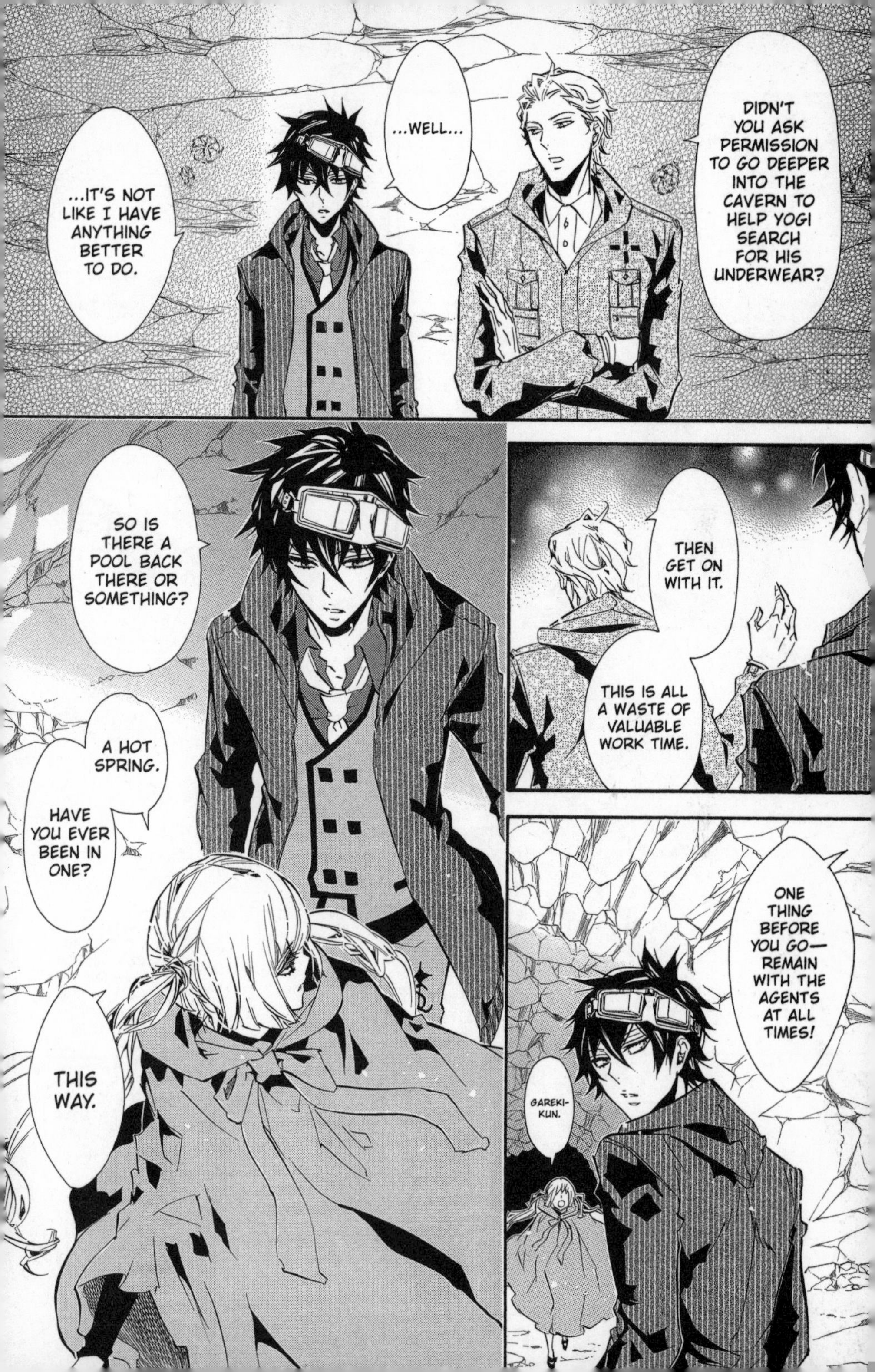
DIDN'T YOU ASK PERMISSION TO GO DEEPER INTO THE CAVERN TO HELP YOGI SEARCH FOR HIS UNDERWEAR?
...WELL...
...IT'S NOT LIKE I HAVE ANYTHING BETTER TO DO.
THEN GET ON WITH IT.
THIS IS ALL A WASTE OF VALUABLE WORK TIME.
ONE THING BEFORE YOU GO—REMAIN WITH THE AGENTS AT ALL TIMES!
GAREKI-KUN.
SO IS THERE A POOL BACK THERE OR SOMETHING?
A HOT SPRING.
HAVE YOU EVER BEEN IN ONE?
THIS WAY.

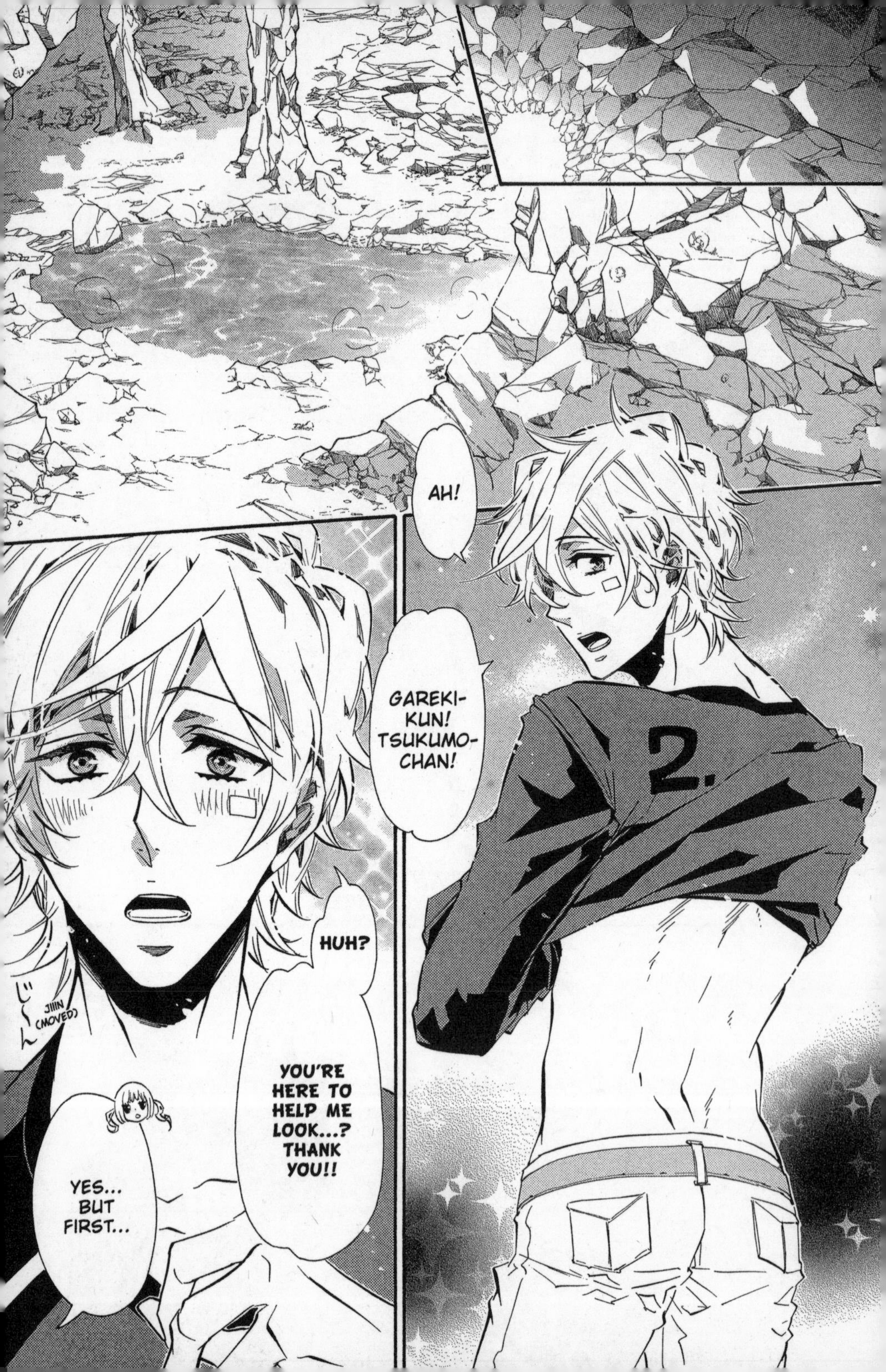
AH!
GAREKI-KUN! TSUKUMO-CHAN!
HUH?
じ～ん
JIIIN (MOVED)
YOU'RE HERE TO HELP ME LOOK...? THANK YOU!!
YES... BUT FIRST...

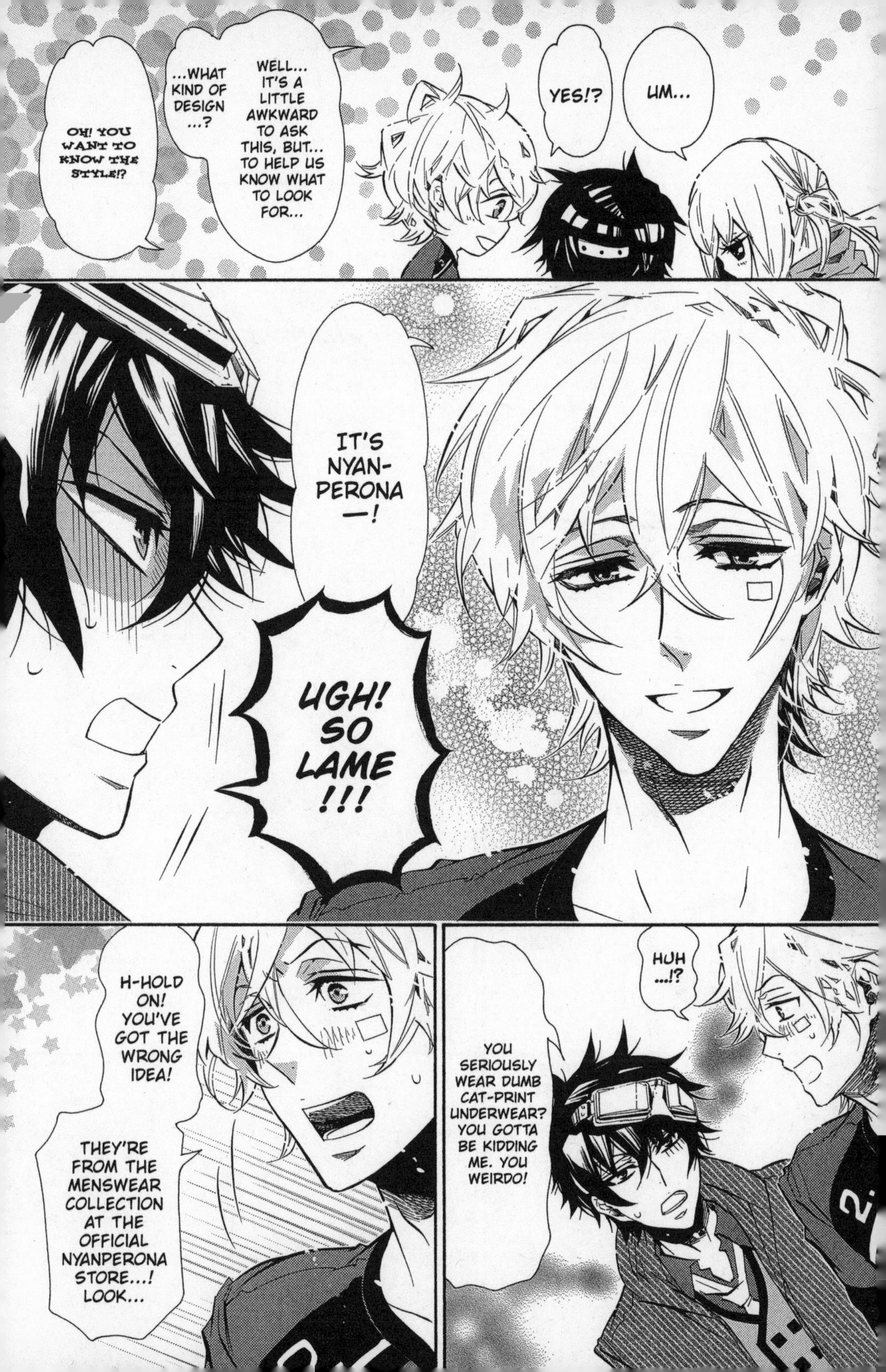
UM...
YES!?
WELL... IT'S A LITTLE AWKWARD TO ASK THIS, BUT... TO HELP US KNOW WHAT TO LOOK FOR...
...WHAT KIND OF DESIGN ...?
OH! YOU WANT TO KNOW THE STYLE!?
IT'S NYAN-PERONA—!
UGH! SO LAME !!!
HUH ...!?
YOU SERIOUSLY WEAR DUMB CAT-PRINT UNDERWEAR? YOU GOTTA BE KIDDING ME. YOU WEIRDO!
H-HOLD ON! YOU'VE GOT THE WRONG IDEA!
THEY'RE FROM THE MENSWEAR COLLECTION AT THE OFFICIAL NYANPERONA STORE...! LOOK...

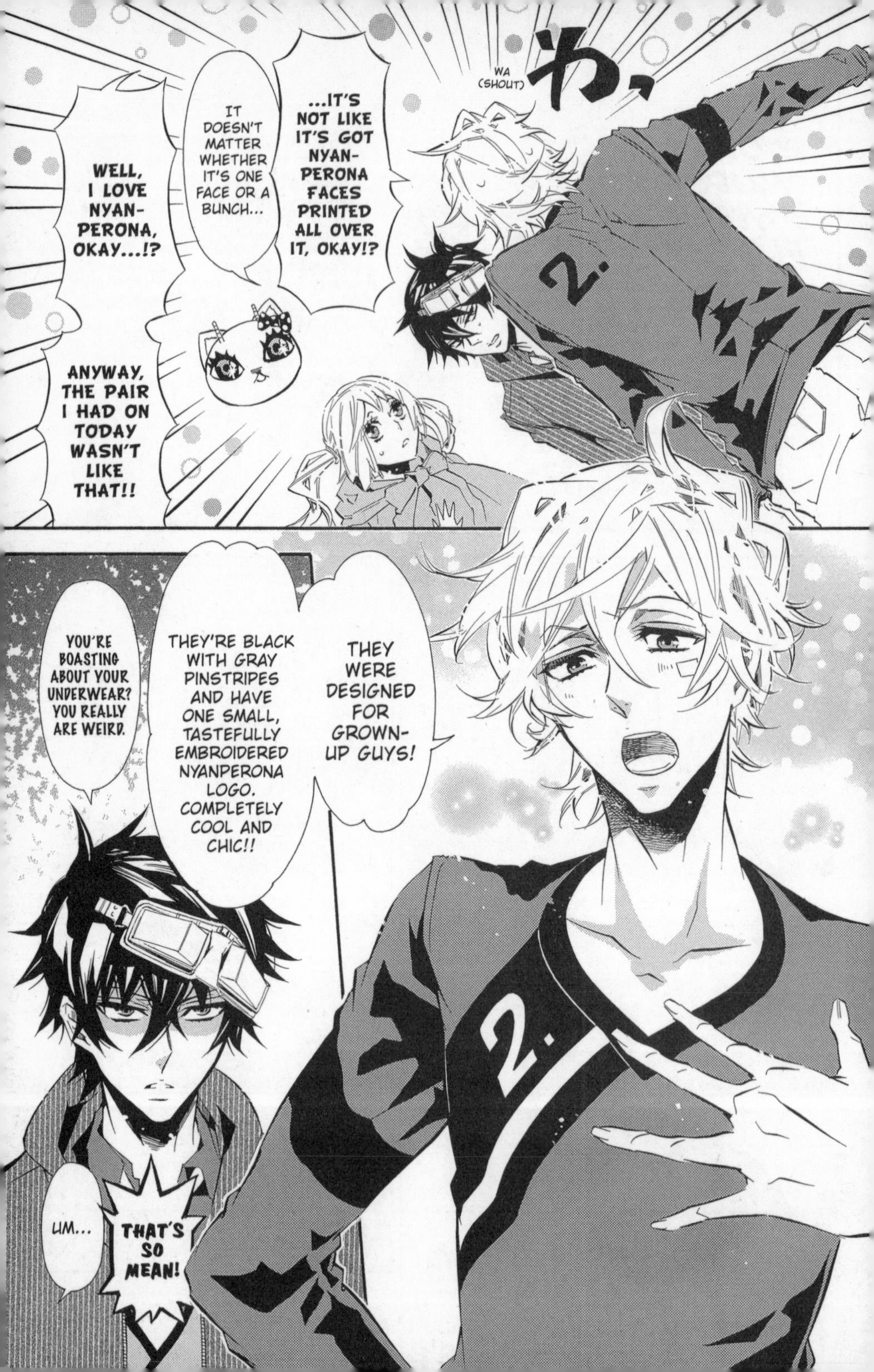

わ
WA (SHOUT)
...IT'S NOT LIKE IT'S GOT NYAN-PERONA FACES PRINTED ALL OVER IT, OKAY!?
IT DOESN'T MATTER WHETHER IT'S ONE FACE OR A BUNCH...
WELL, I LOVE NYAN-PERONA, OKAY...!?
ANYWAY, THE PAIR I HAD ON TODAY WASN'T LIKE THAT!!
THEY WERE DESIGNED FOR GROWN-UP GUYS!
THEY'RE BLACK WITH GRAY PINSTRIPES AND HAVE ONE SMALL, TASTEFULLY EMBROIDERED NYANPERONA LOGO. COMPLETELY COOL AND CHIC!!
YOU'RE BOASTING ABOUT YOUR UNDERWEAR? YOU REALLY ARE WEIRD.
THAT'S SO MEAN!
UM...

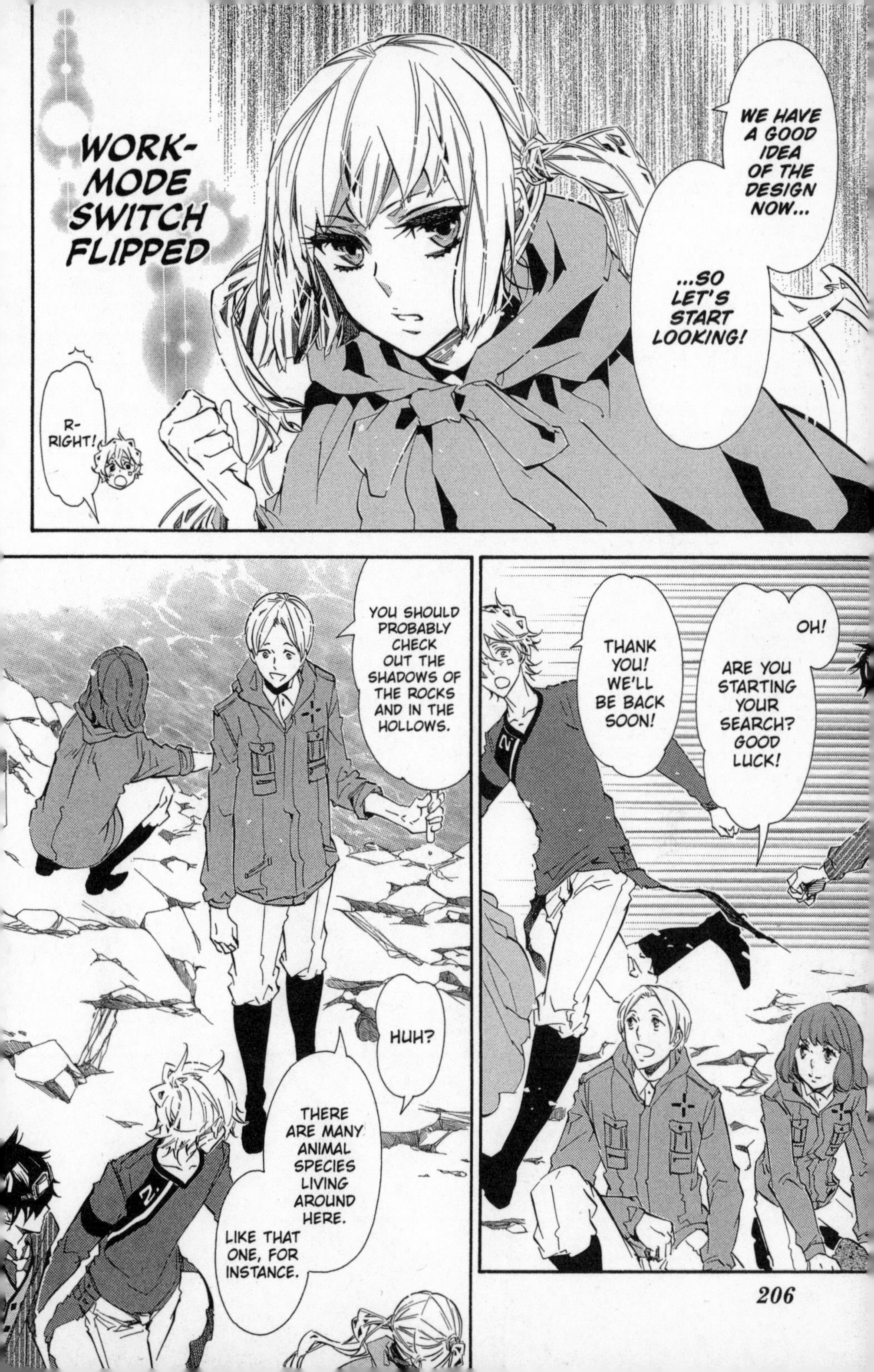
WE HAVE A GOOD IDEA OF THE DESIGN NOW...
...SO LET'S START LOOKING!
WORK-MODE SWITCH FLIPPED
R-RIGHT!
OH!
ARE YOU STARTING YOUR SEARCH? GOOD LUCK!
THANK YOU! WE'LL BE BACK SOON!
YOU SHOULD PROBABLY CHECK OUT THE SHADOWS OF THE ROCKS AND IN THE HOLLOWS.
HUH?
THERE ARE MANY ANIMAL SPECIES LIVING AROUND HERE.
LIKE THAT ONE, FOR INSTANCE.

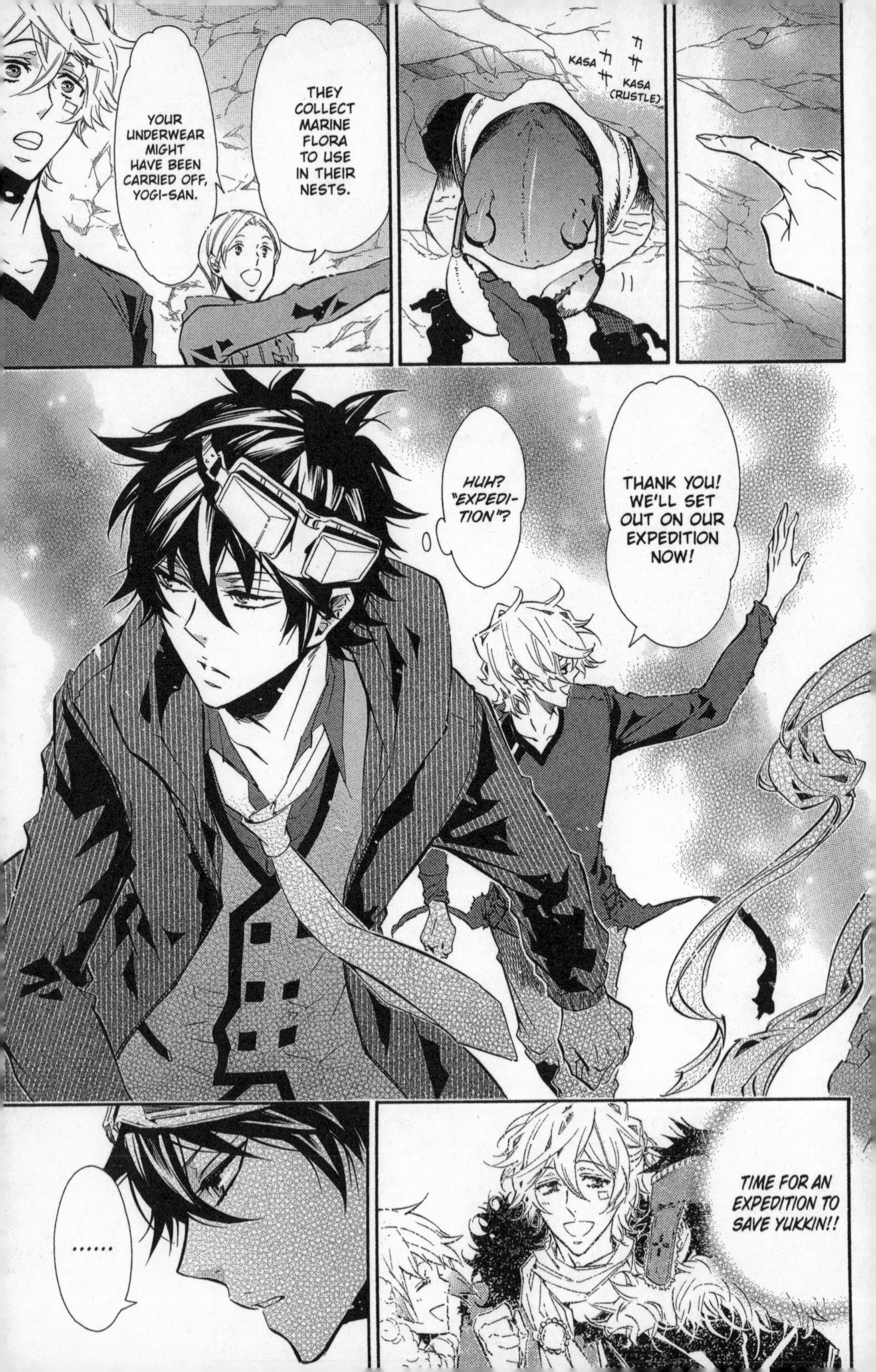
KASA
KASA (RUSTLE)
THEY COLLECT MARINE FLORA TO USE IN THEIR NESTS.
YOUR UNDERWEAR MIGHT HAVE BEEN CARRIED OFF, YOGI-SAN.
THANK YOU! WE'LL SET OUT ON OUR EXPEDITION NOW!
HUH? "EXPEDITION"?
TIME FOR AN EXPEDITION TO SAVE YUKKIN!!
......

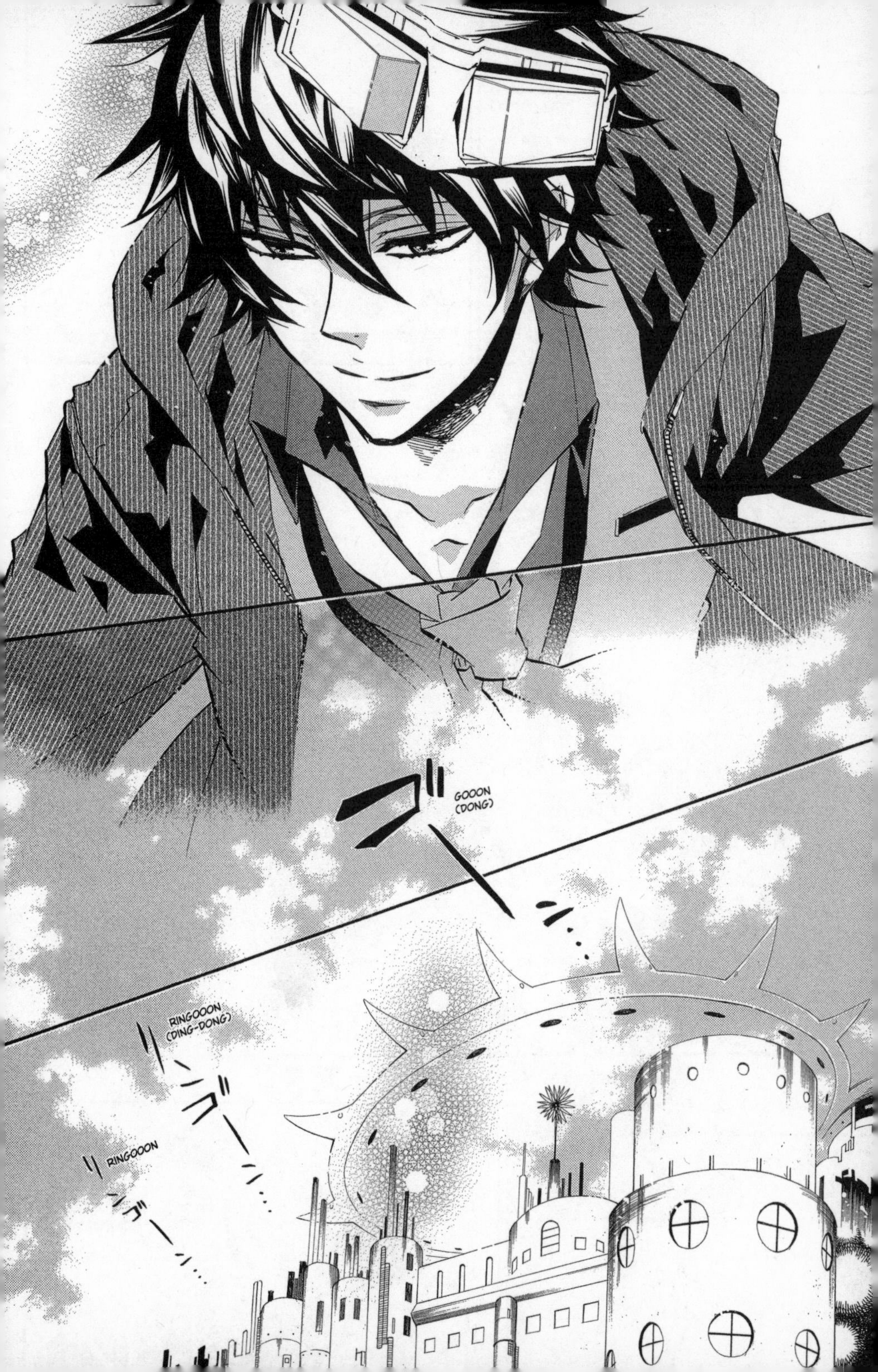
ゴーン…
GOOON (DONG)
リンゴーン…
RINGOOON (DING-DONG)
リンゴーン…
RINGOOON

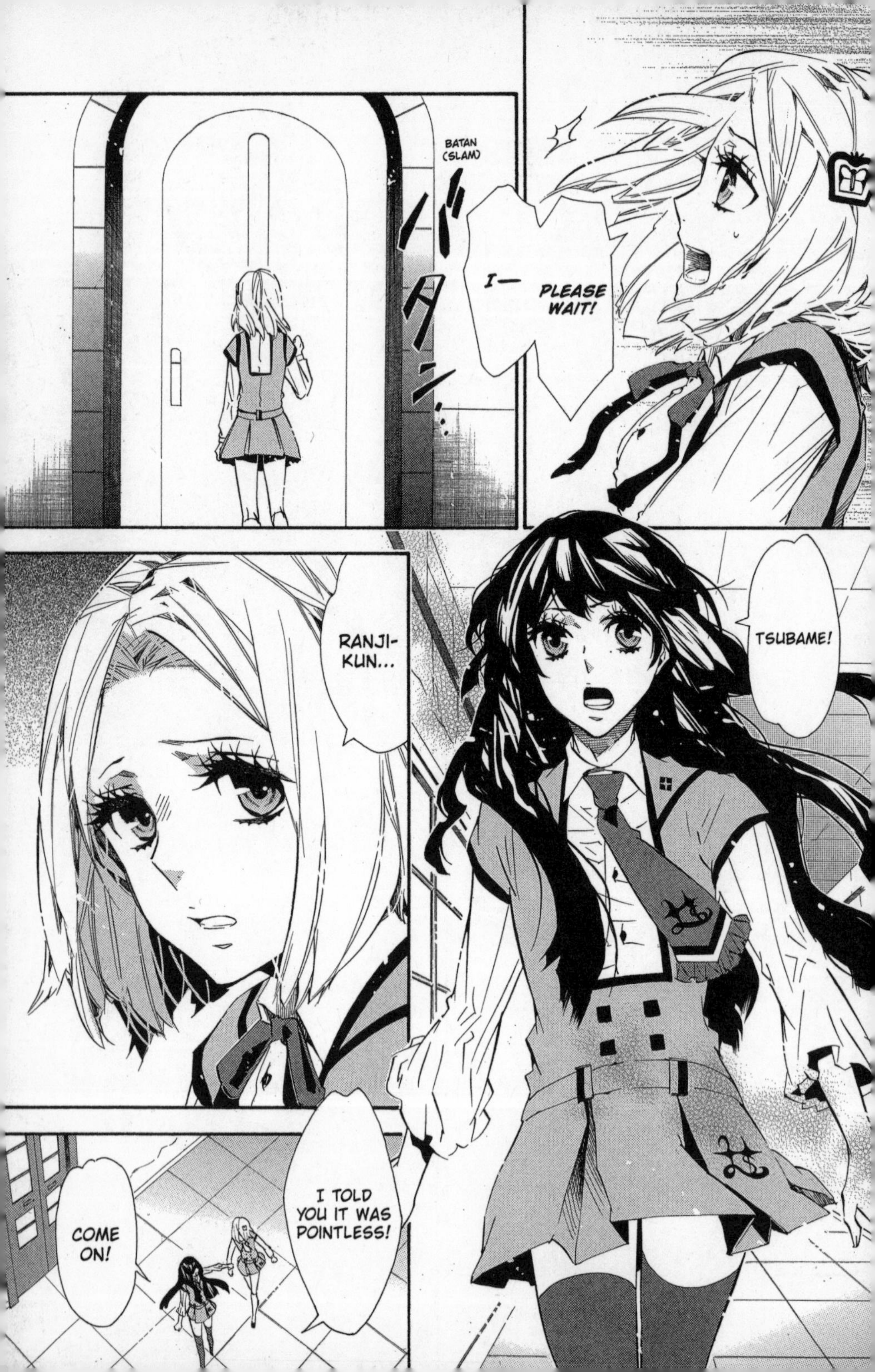
I— PLEASE WAIT!
BATAN (SLAM)
TSUBAME!
RANJI-KUN...
I TOLD YOU IT WAS POINTLESS!
COME ON!

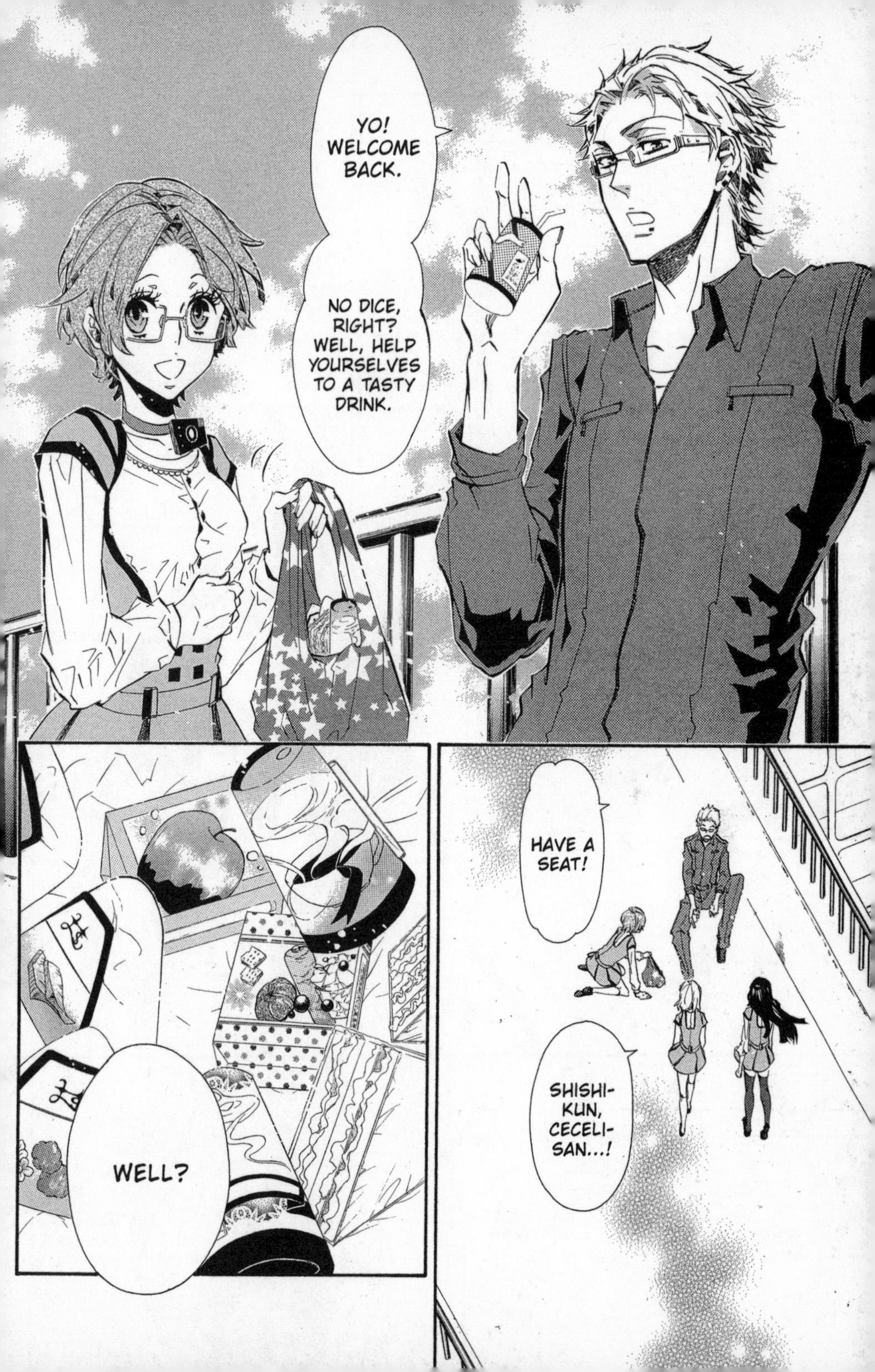
YO! WELCOME BACK.
NO DICE, RIGHT? WELL, HELP YOURSELVES TO A TASTY DRINK.
HAVE A SEAT!
SHISHI-KUN, CECELI-SAN...!
WELL?

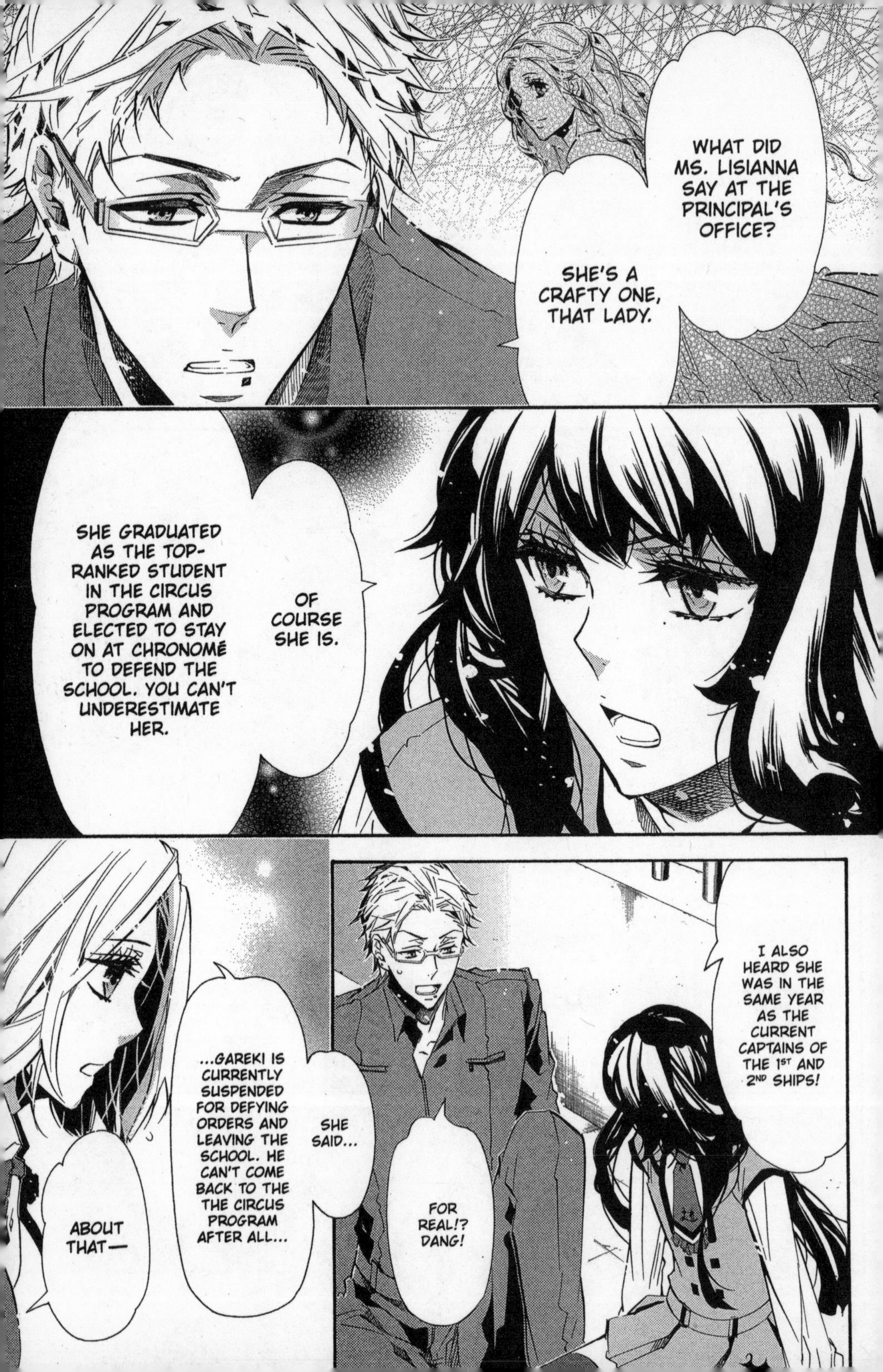
WHAT DID MS. LISIANNA SAY AT THE PRINCIPAL'S OFFICE?
SHE'S A CRAFTY ONE, THAT LADY.
OF COURSE SHE IS.
SHE GRADUATED AS THE TOP-RANKED STUDENT IN THE CIRCUS PROGRAM AND ELECTED TO STAY ON AT CHRONOMÉ TO DEFEND THE SCHOOL. YOU CAN'T UNDERESTIMATE HER.
I ALSO HEARD SHE WAS IN THE SAME YEAR AS THE CURRENT CAPTAINS OF THE 1ST AND 2ND SHIPS!
FOR REAL!? DANG!
ABOUT THAT—
SHE SAID...
...GAREKI IS CURRENTLY SUSPENDED FOR DEFYING ORDERS AND LEAVING THE SCHOOL. HE CAN'T COME BACK TO THE THE CIRCUS PROGRAM AFTER ALL...

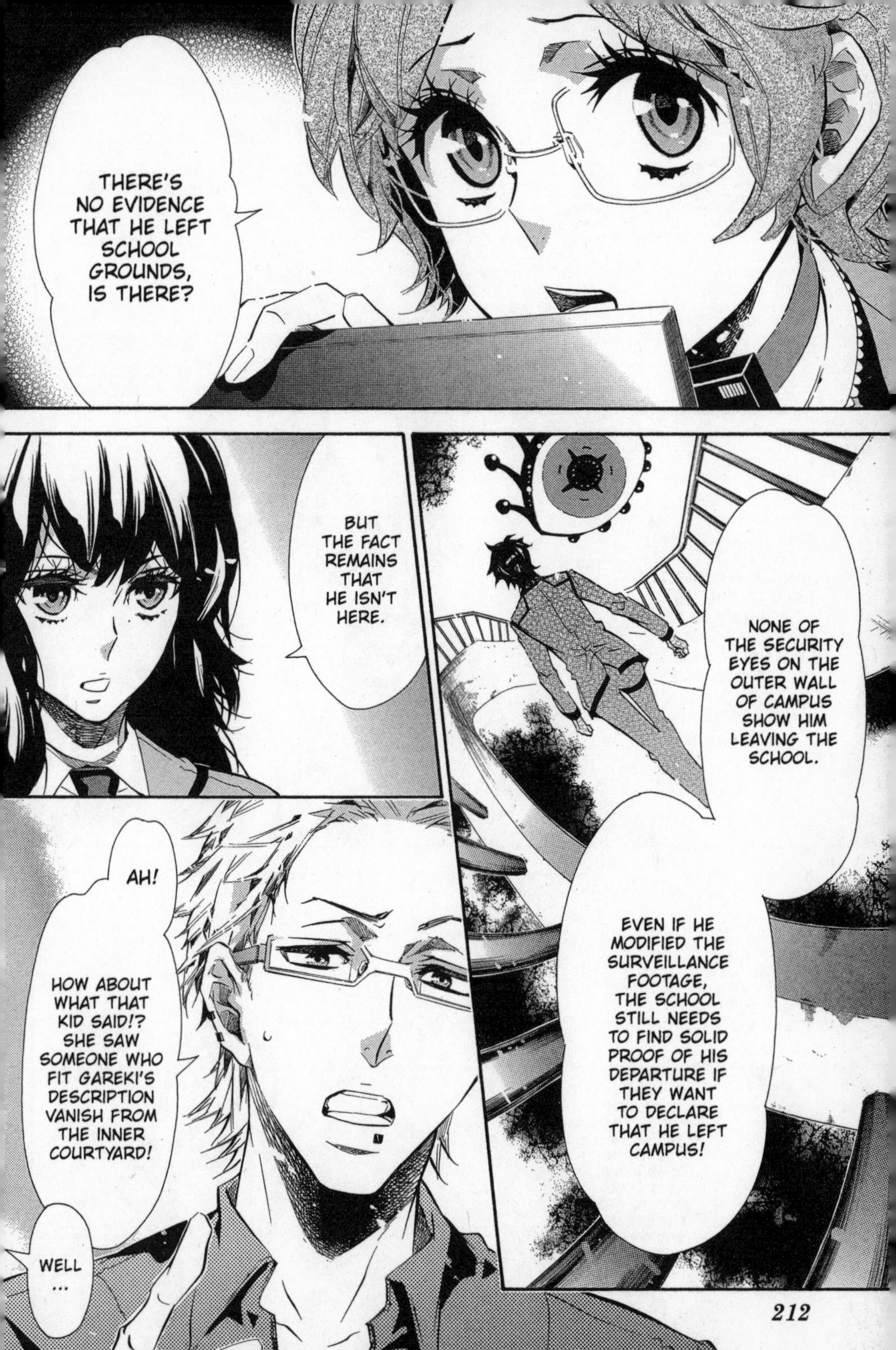
THERE'S NO EVIDENCE THAT HE LEFT SCHOOL GROUNDS, IS THERE?
NONE OF THE SECURITY EYES ON THE OUTER WALL OF CAMPUS SHOW HIM LEAVING THE SCHOOL.
EVEN IF HE MODIFIED THE SURVEILLANCE FOOTAGE, THE SCHOOL STILL NEEDS TO FIND SOLID PROOF OF HIS DEPARTURE IF THEY WANT TO DECLARE THAT HE LEFT CAMPUS!
BUT THE FACT REMAINS THAT HE ISN'T HERE.
AH!
HOW ABOUT WHAT THAT KID SAID!? SHE SAW SOMEONE WHO FIT GAREKI'S DESCRIPTION VANISH FROM THE INNER COURTYARD!
WELL ...

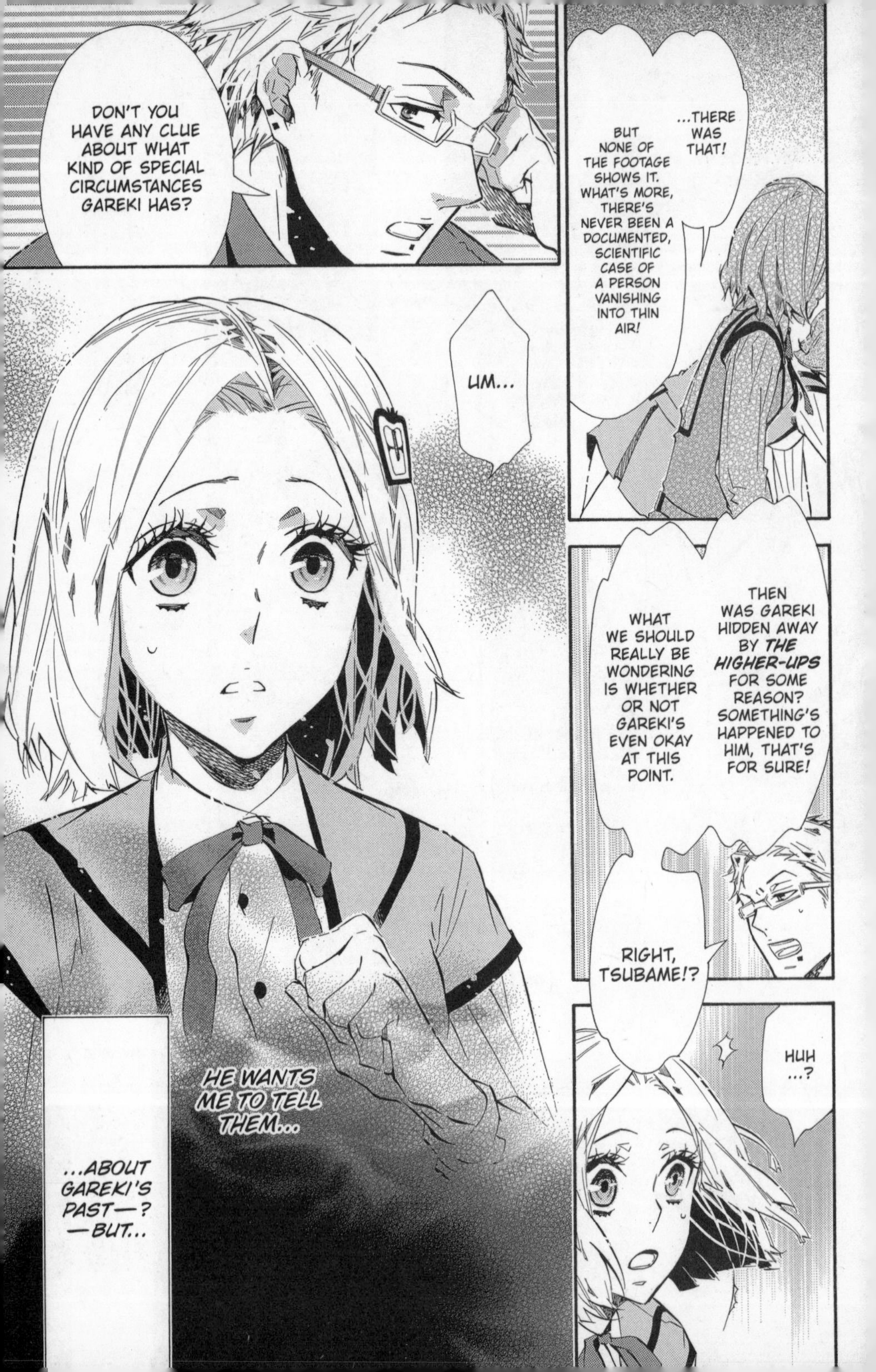

...THERE WAS THAT!
BUT NONE OF THE FOOTAGE SHOWS IT. WHAT'S MORE, THERE'S NEVER BEEN A DOCUMENTED, SCIENTIFIC CASE OF A PERSON VANISHING INTO THIN AIR!
DON'T YOU HAVE ANY CLUE ABOUT WHAT KIND OF SPECIAL CIRCUMSTANCES GAREKI HAS?
THEN WAS GAREKI HIDDEN AWAY BY *THE HIGHER-UPS* FOR SOME REASON? SOMETHING'S HAPPENED TO HIM, THAT'S FOR SURE!
WHAT WE SHOULD REALLY BE WONDERING IS WHETHER OR NOT GAREKI'S EVEN OKAY AT THIS POINT.
RIGHT, TSUBAME!?
HUH ...?
UM...
HE WANTS ME TO TELL THEM...
...ABOUT GAREKI'S PAST—? —BUT...

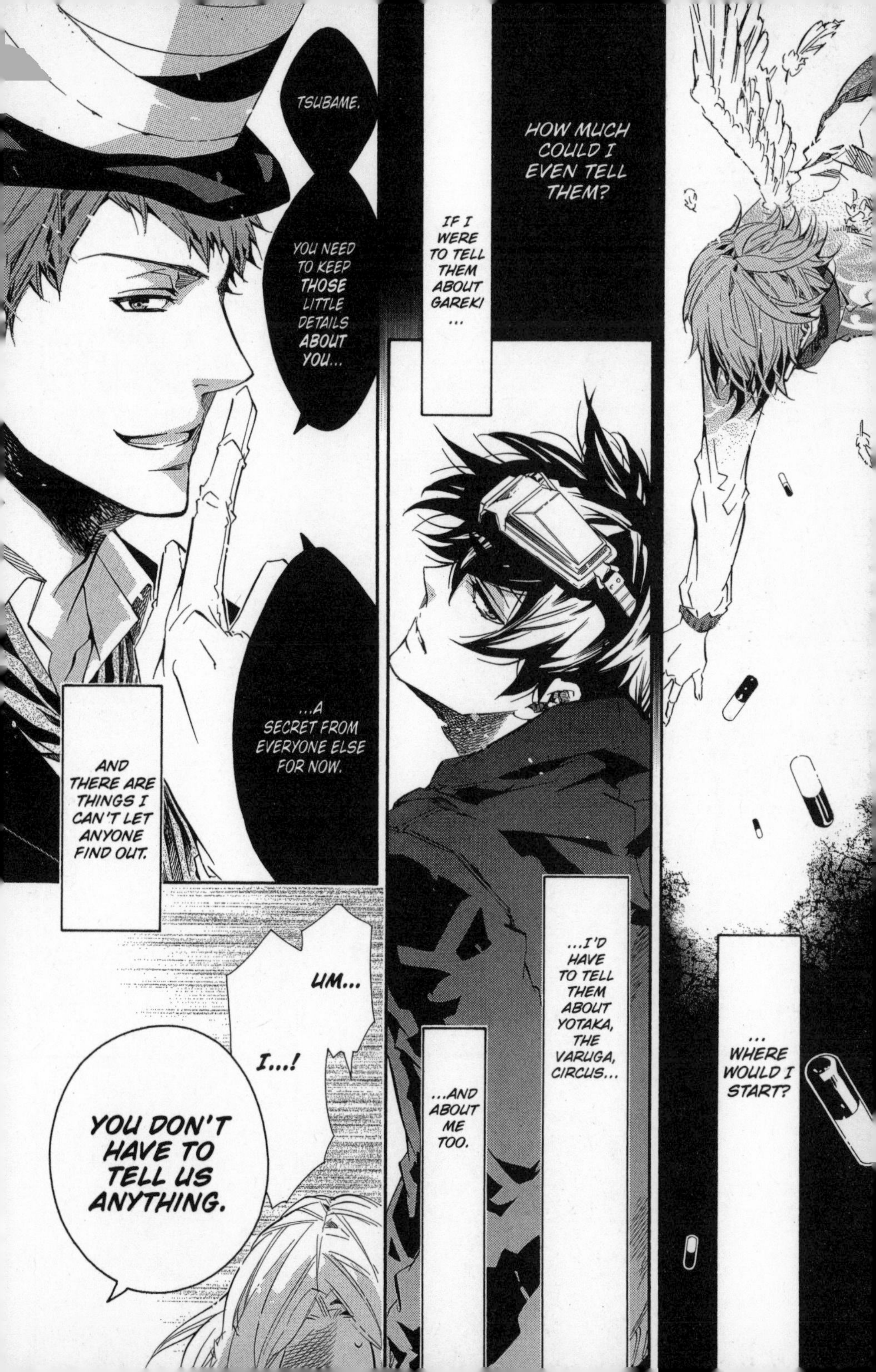
HOW MUCH COULD I EVEN TELL THEM?
IF I WERE TO TELL THEM ABOUT GAREKI...
...I'D HAVE TO TELL THEM ABOUT YOTAKA, THE VARUGA, CIRCUS...
...AND ABOUT ME TOO.
... WHERE WOULD I START?
TSUBAME.
YOU NEED TO KEEP THOSE LITTLE DETAILS ABOUT YOU...
...A SECRET FROM EVERYONE ELSE FOR NOW.
AND THERE ARE THINGS I CAN'T LET ANYONE FIND OUT.
UM...
I...!
YOU DON'T HAVE TO TELL US ANYTHING.

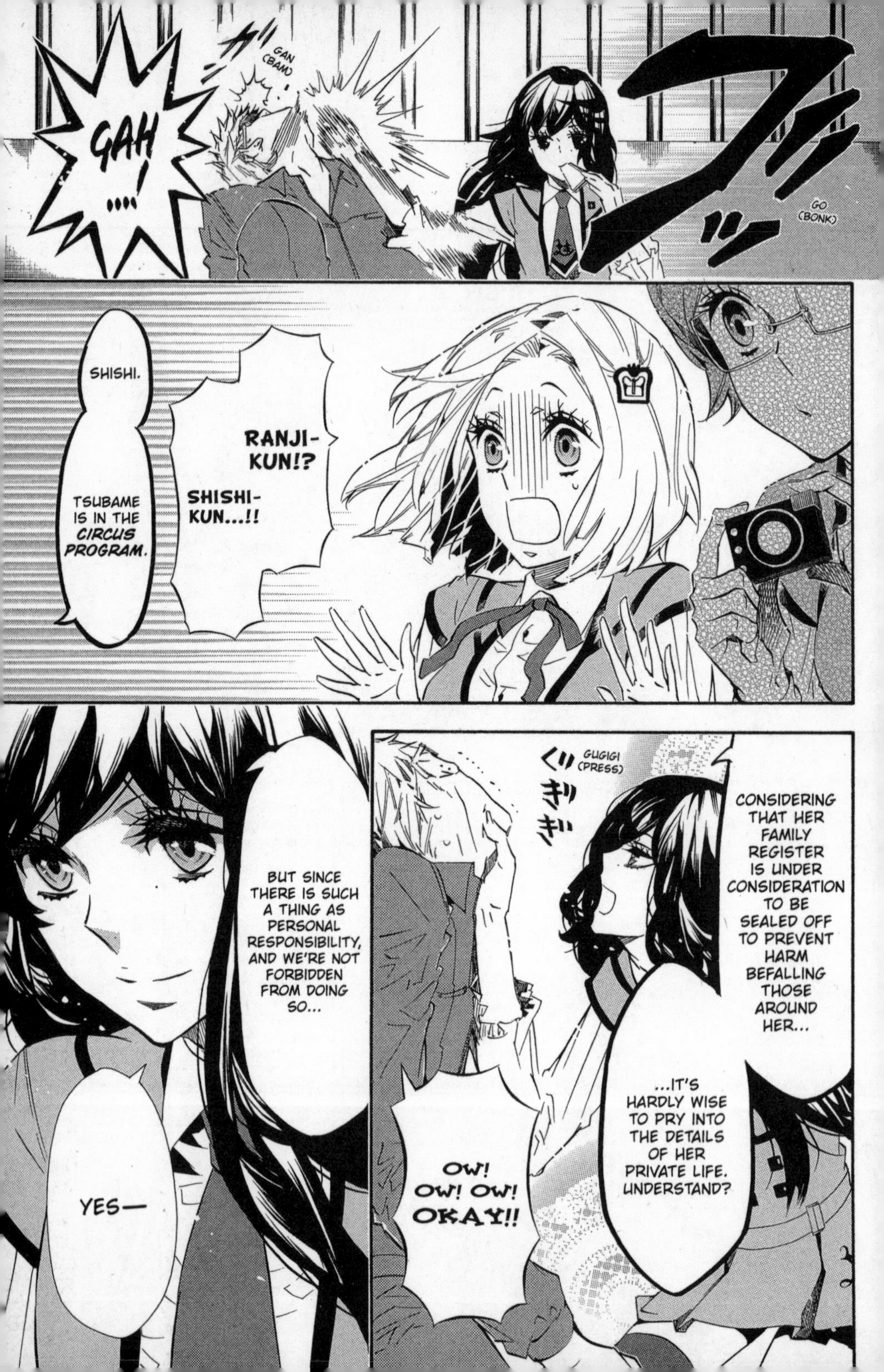
GO (BONK)
GAN (BAM)
GAH...!
RANJI-KUN!? SHISHI-KUN...!!
SHISHI.
TSUBAME IS IN THE CIRCUS PROGRAM.
GUGIGI (PRESS)
CONSIDERING THAT HER FAMILY REGISTER IS UNDER CONSIDERATION TO BE SEALED OFF TO PREVENT HARM BEFALLING THOSE AROUND HER...
...IT'S HARDLY WISE TO PRY INTO THE DETAILS OF HER PRIVATE LIFE. UNDERSTAND?
OW! OW! OW! OKAY!!
BUT SINCE THERE IS SUCH A THING AS PERSONAL RESPONSIBILITY, AND WE'RE NOT FORBIDDEN FROM DOING SO...
YES—

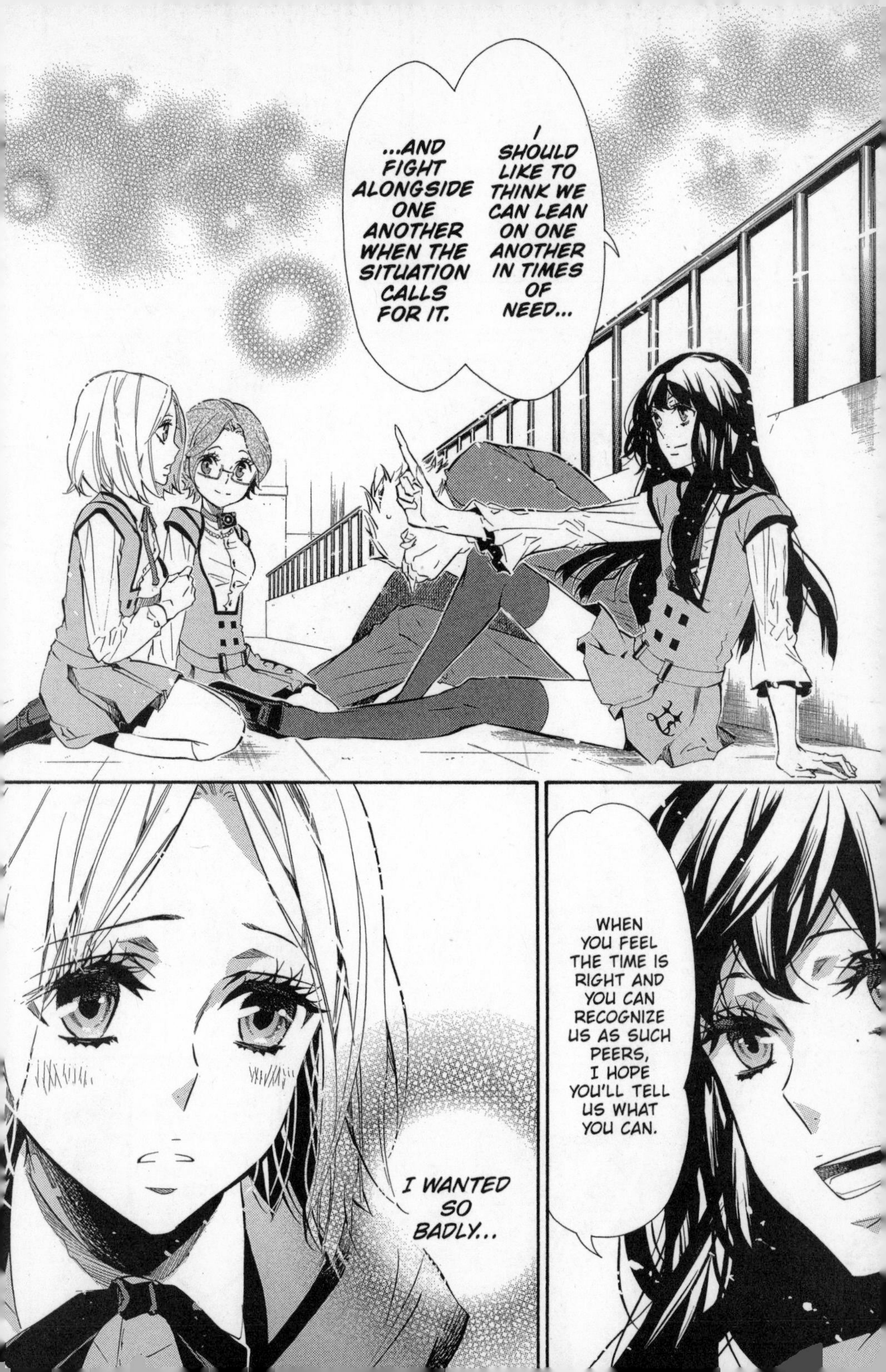
I SHOULD LIKE TO THINK WE CAN LEAN ON ONE ANOTHER IN TIMES OF NEED...
...AND FIGHT ALONGSIDE ONE ANOTHER WHEN THE SITUATION CALLS FOR IT.
WHEN YOU FEEL THE TIME IS RIGHT AND YOU CAN RECOGNIZE US AS SUCH PEERS, I HOPE YOU'LL TELL US WHAT YOU CAN.
I WANTED SO BADLY...

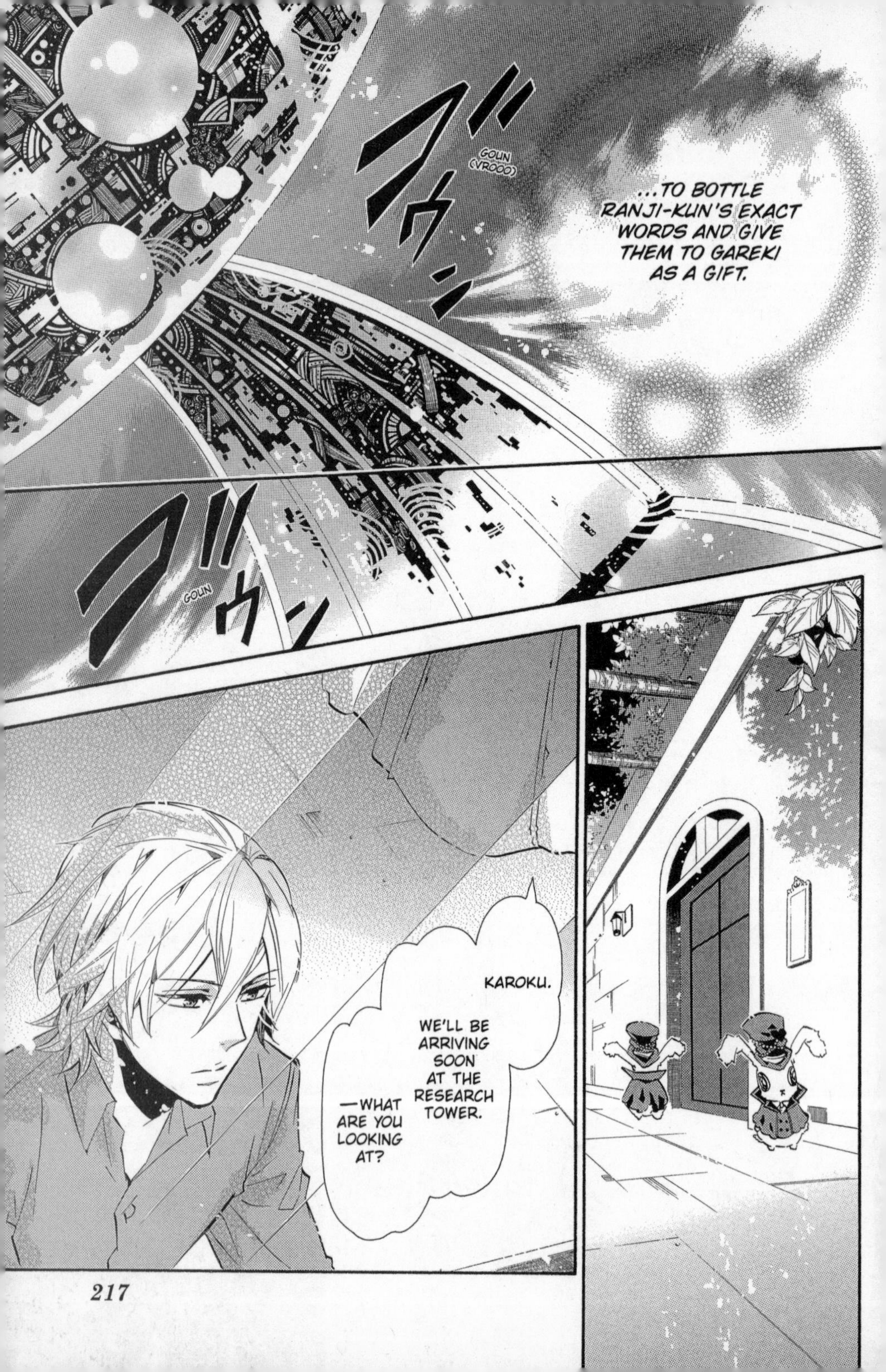
...TO BOTTLE RANJI-KUN'S EXACT WORDS AND GIVE THEM TO GAREKI AS A GIFT.
GOUN (VROOO)
GOUN
KAROKU.
WE'LL BE ARRIVING SOON AT THE RESEARCH TOWER.
—WHAT ARE YOU LOOKING AT?

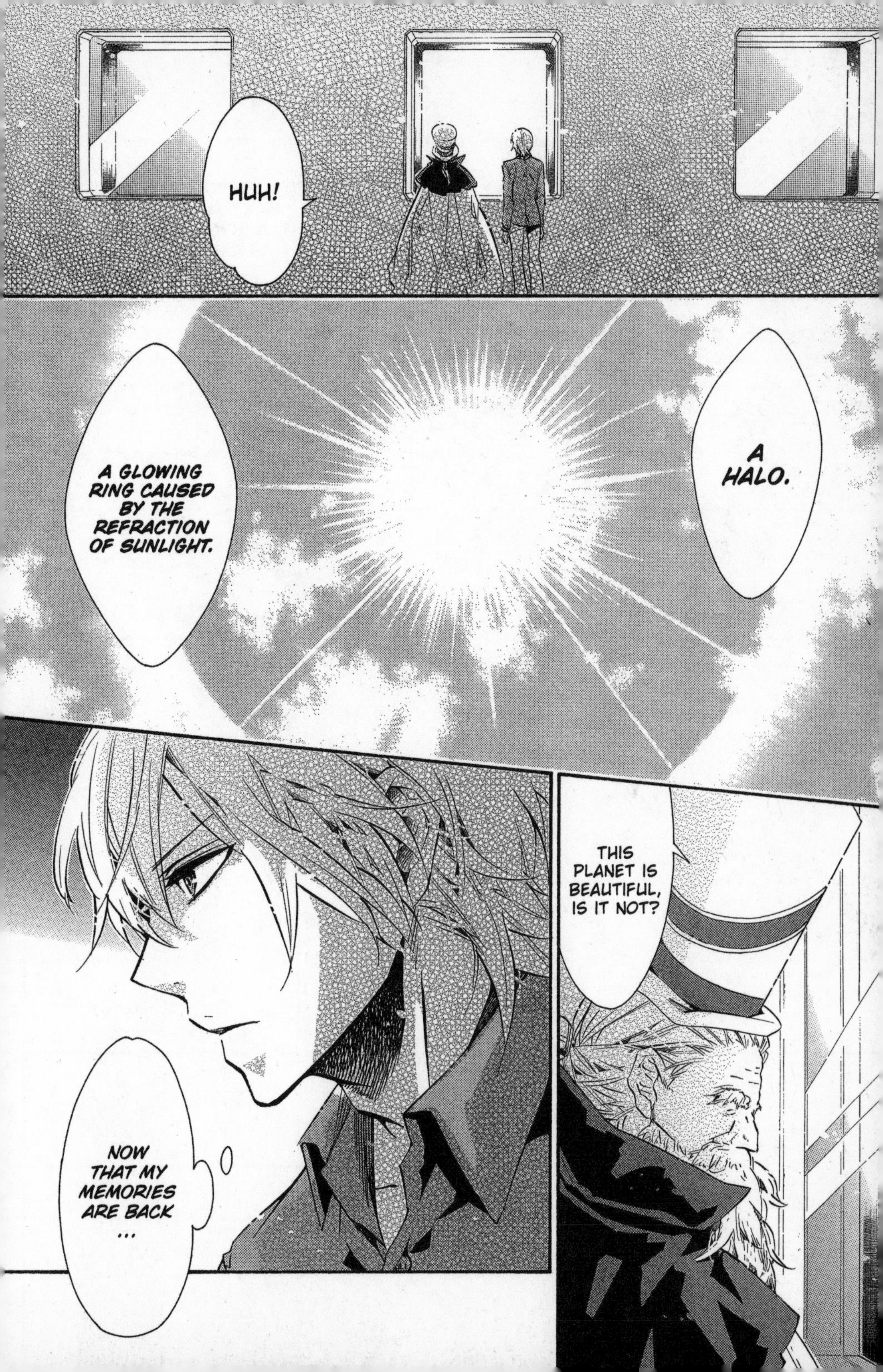
HUH!
A HALO.
A GLOWING RING CAUSED BY THE REFRACTION OF SUNLIGHT.
THIS PLANET IS BEAUTIFUL, IS IT NOT?
NOW THAT MY MEMORIES ARE BACK ...

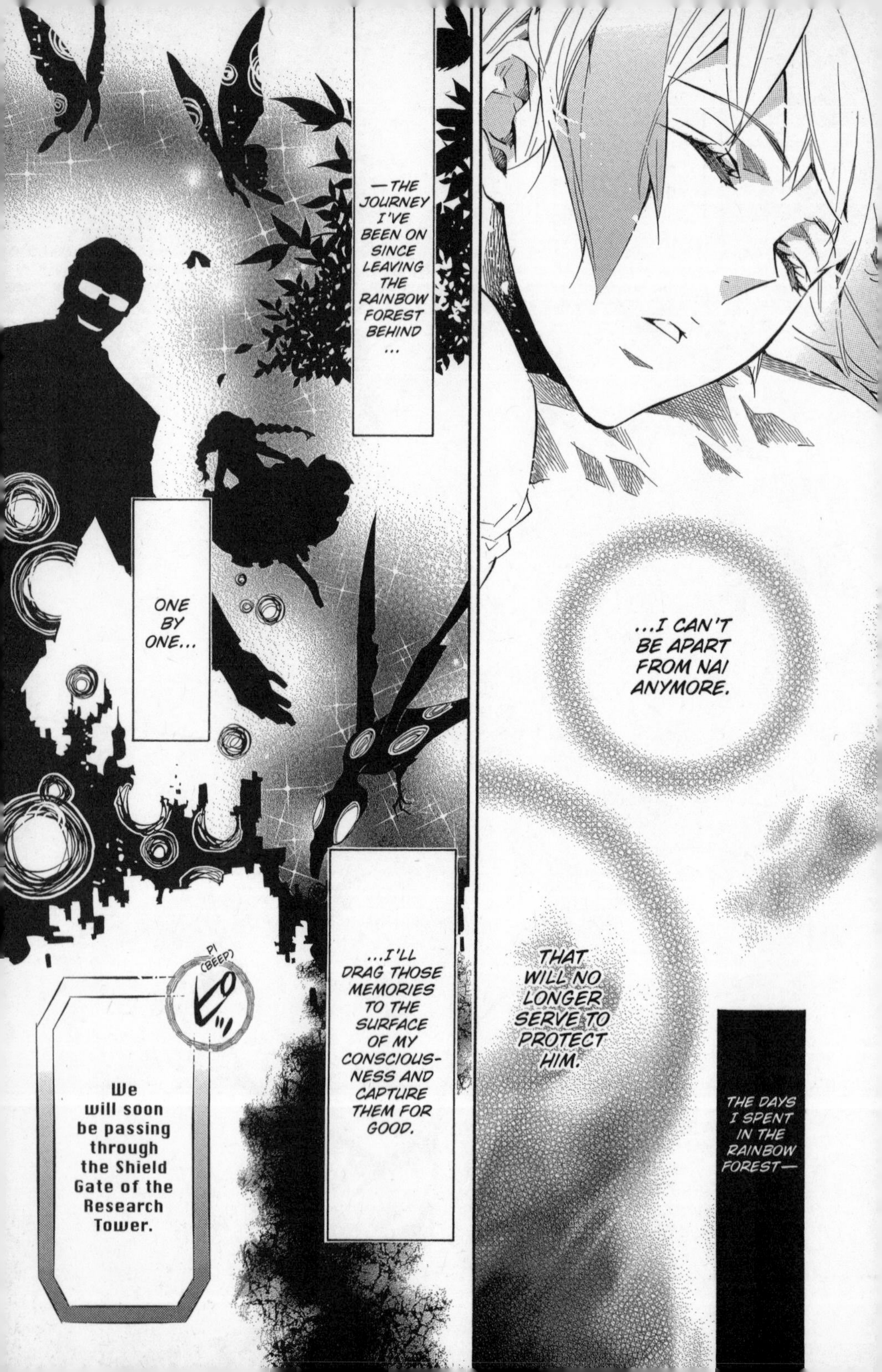
...I CAN'T BE APART FROM NAI ANYMORE.
THE DAYS I SPENT IN THE RAINBOW FOREST—
THAT WILL NO LONGER SERVE TO PROTECT HIM.
—THE JOURNEY I'VE BEEN ON SINCE LEAVING THE RAINBOW FOREST BEHIND ...
ONE BY ONE...
...I'LL DRAG THOSE MEMORIES TO THE SURFACE OF MY CONSCIOUS-NESS AND CAPTURE THEM FOR GOOD.
PI (BEEP)
We will soon be passing through the Shield Gate of the Research Tower.

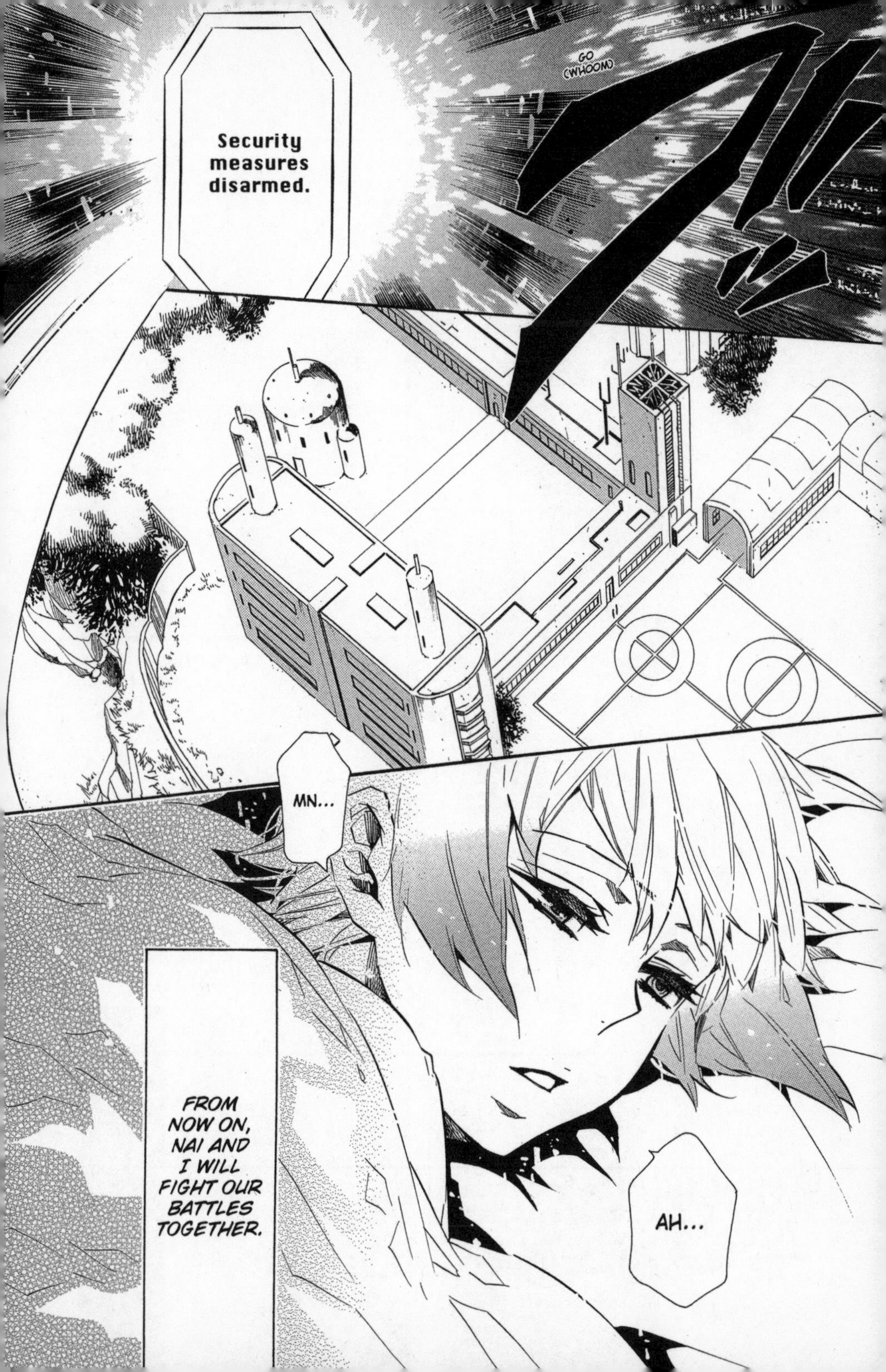
GO
(WHOOM)
Security measures disarmed.
MN...
FROM NOW ON, NAI AND I WILL FIGHT OUR BATTLES TOGETHER.
AH...

KARNEVAL

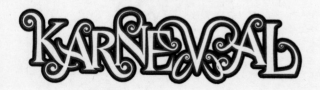

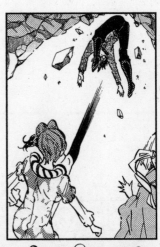

KARNEVAL

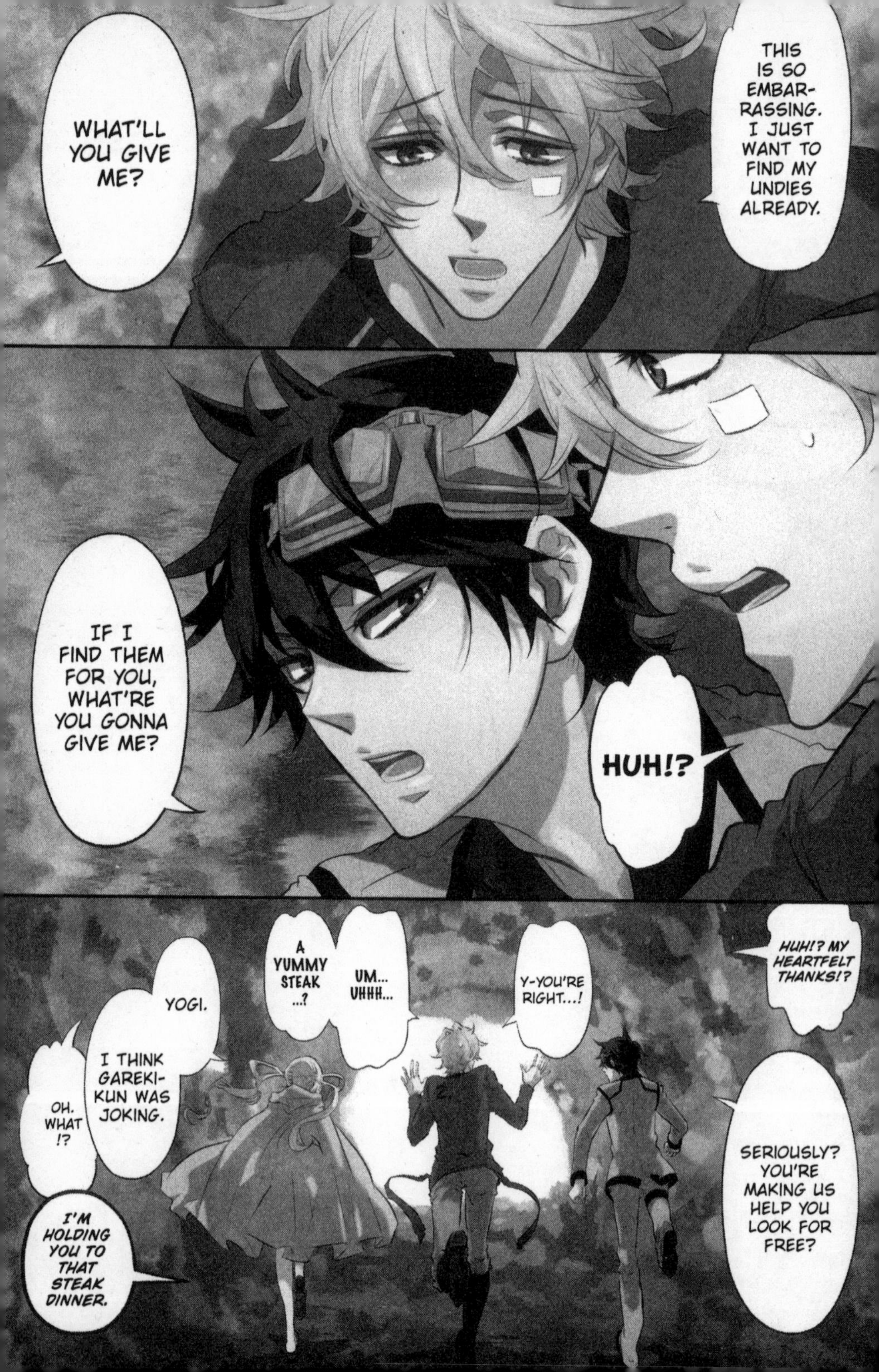
THIS IS SO EMBARRASSING. I JUST WANT TO FIND MY UNDIES ALREADY.
WHAT'LL YOU GIVE ME?
IF I FIND THEM FOR YOU, WHAT'RE YOU GONNA GIVE ME?
HUH!?
HUH!? MY HEARTFELT THANKS!?
SERIOUSLY? YOU'RE MAKING US HELP YOU LOOK FOR FREE?
Y-YOU'RE RIGHT...!
UM... UHHH...
A YUMMY STEAK ...?
YOGI.
I THINK GAREKI-KUN WAS JOKING.
OH. WHAT !?
I'M HOLDING YOU TO THAT STEAK DINNER.

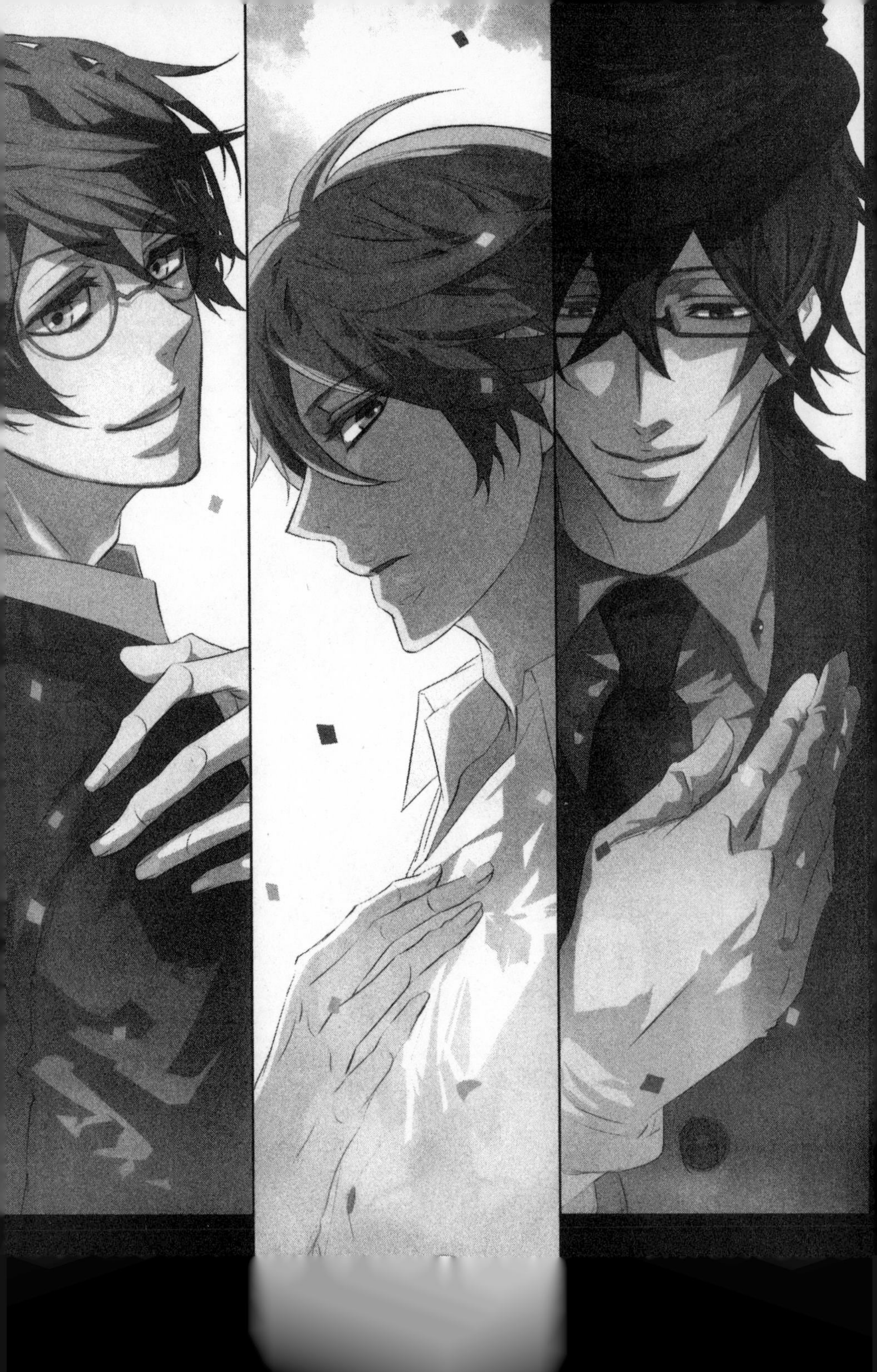

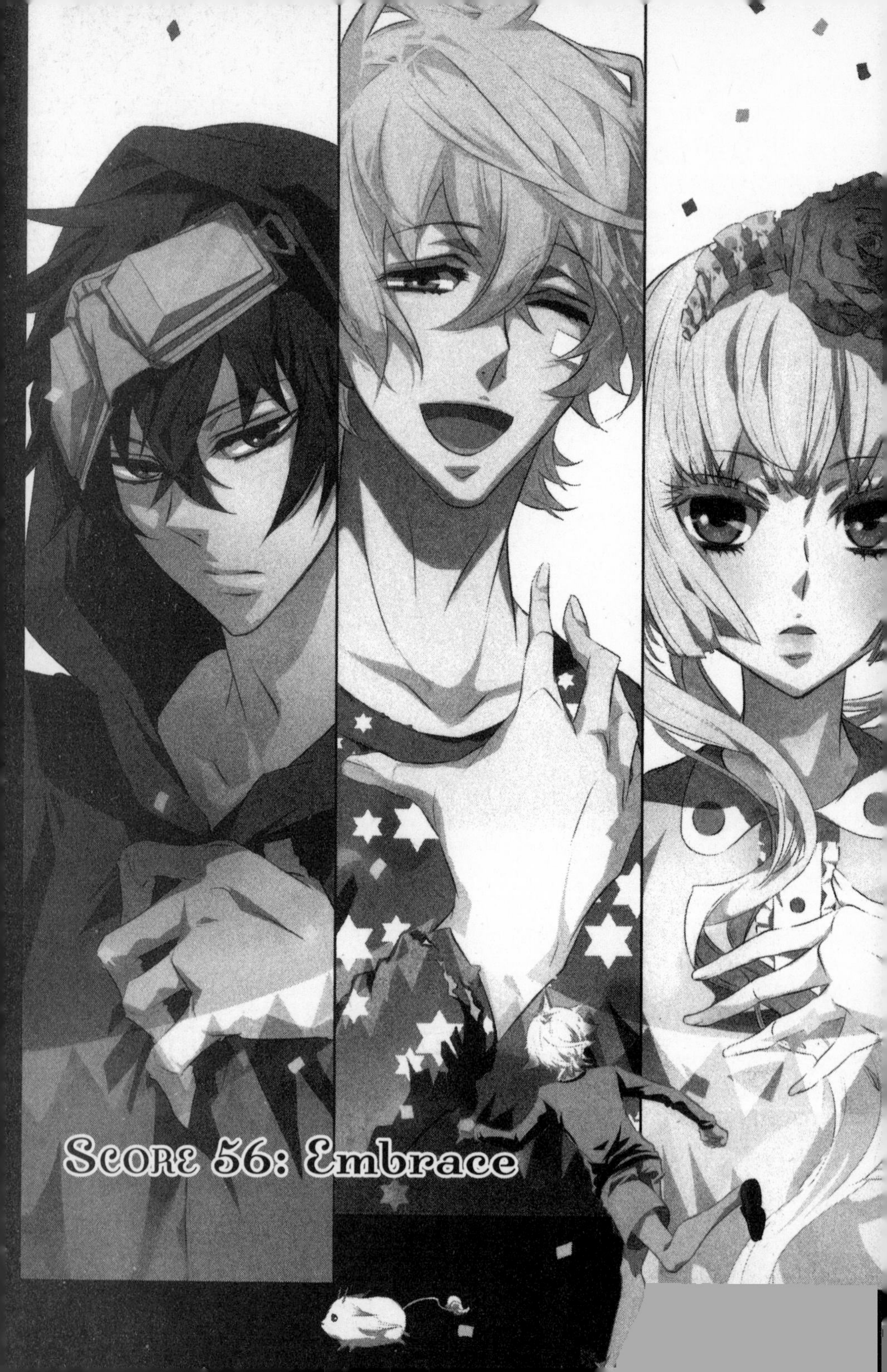
Score 56: Embrace

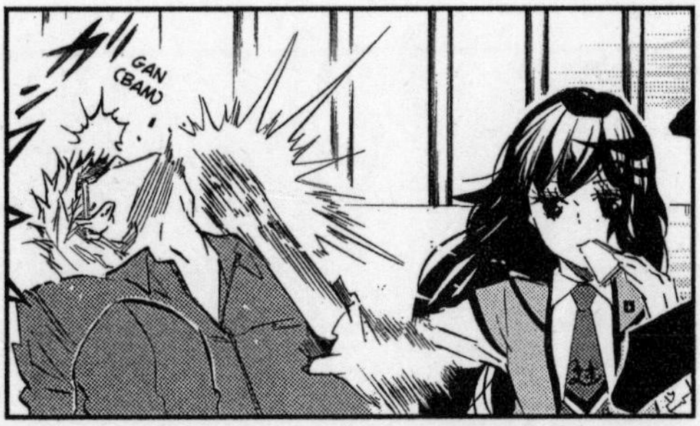
GAN
(BAM)

KARNEVAL

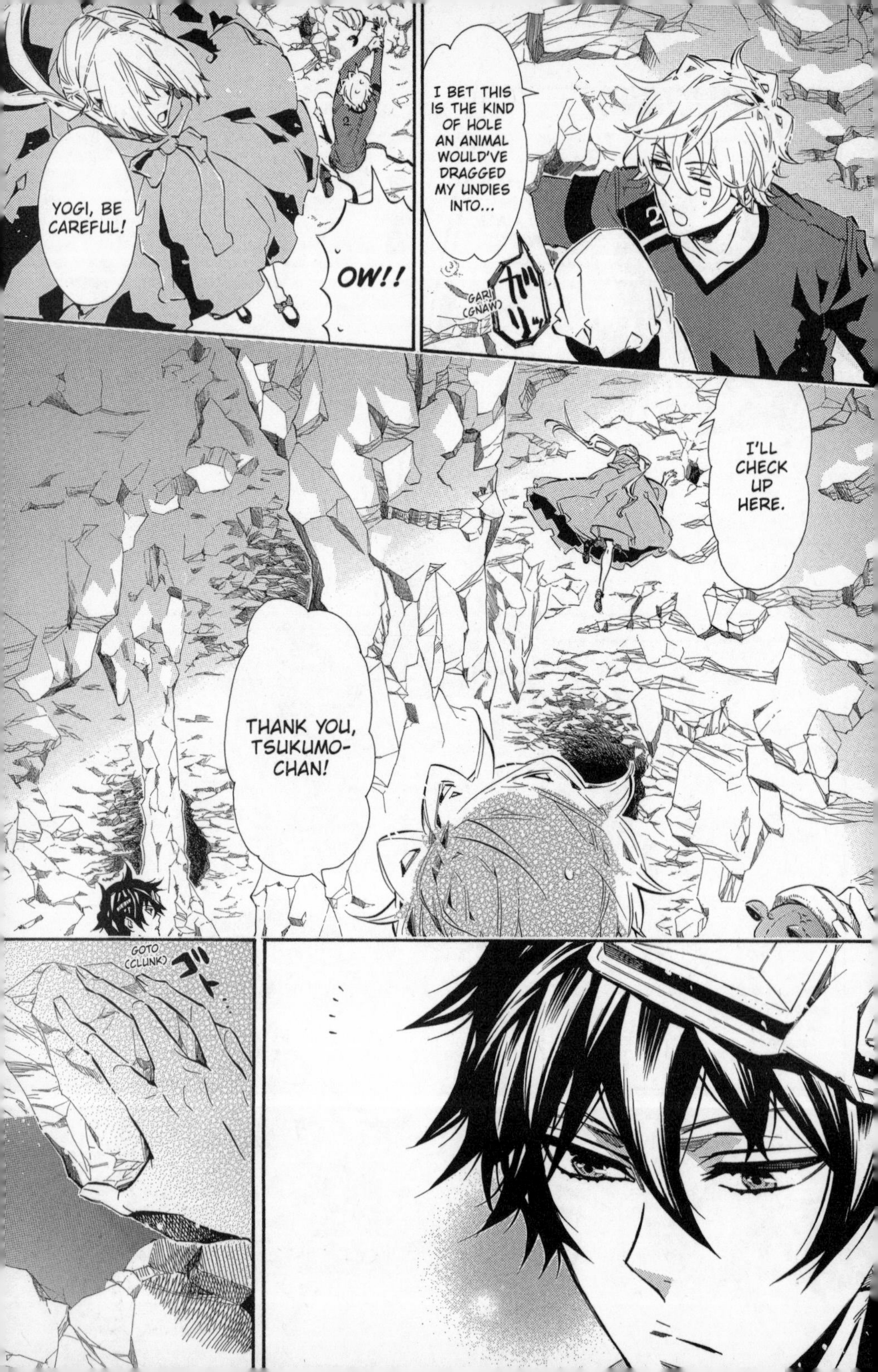
I BET THIS IS THE KIND OF HOLE AN ANIMAL WOULD'VE DRAGGED MY UNDIES INTO...
GARI (GNAW)
OW!!
YOGI, BE CAREFUL!
I'LL CHECK UP HERE.
THANK YOU, TSUKUMO-CHAN!
...
GOTO (CLUNK)

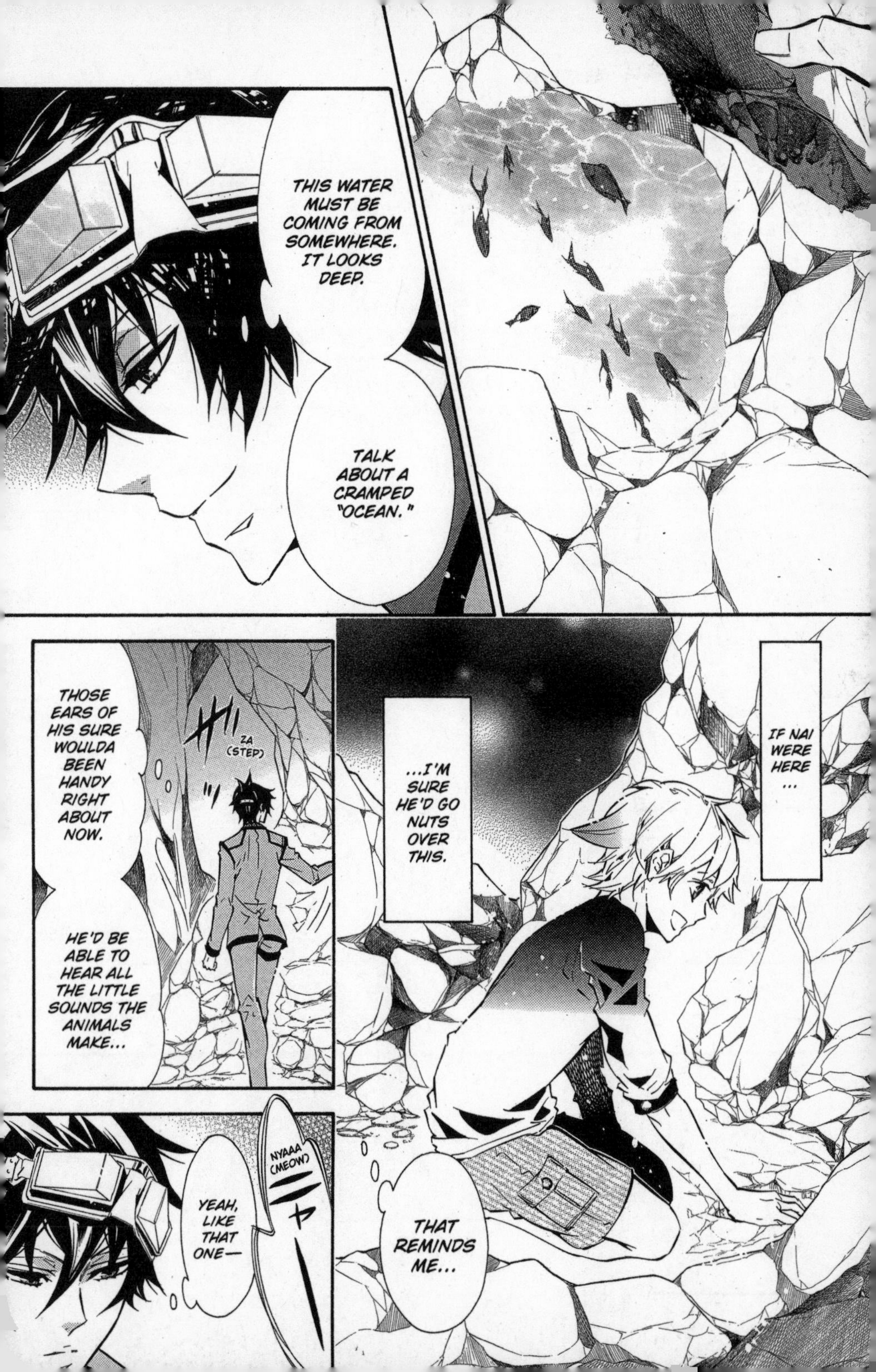
THIS WATER MUST BE COMING FROM SOMEWHERE. IT LOOKS DEEP.
TALK ABOUT A CRAMPED "OCEAN."
IF NAI WERE HERE...
...I'M SURE HE'D GO NUTS OVER THIS.
THAT REMINDS ME...
THOSE EARS OF HIS SURE WOULDA BEEN HANDY RIGHT ABOUT NOW.
ZA (STEP)
HE'D BE ABLE TO HEAR ALL THE LITTLE SOUNDS THE ANIMALS MAKE...
NYAAA (MEOW)
YEAH, LIKE THAT ONE—

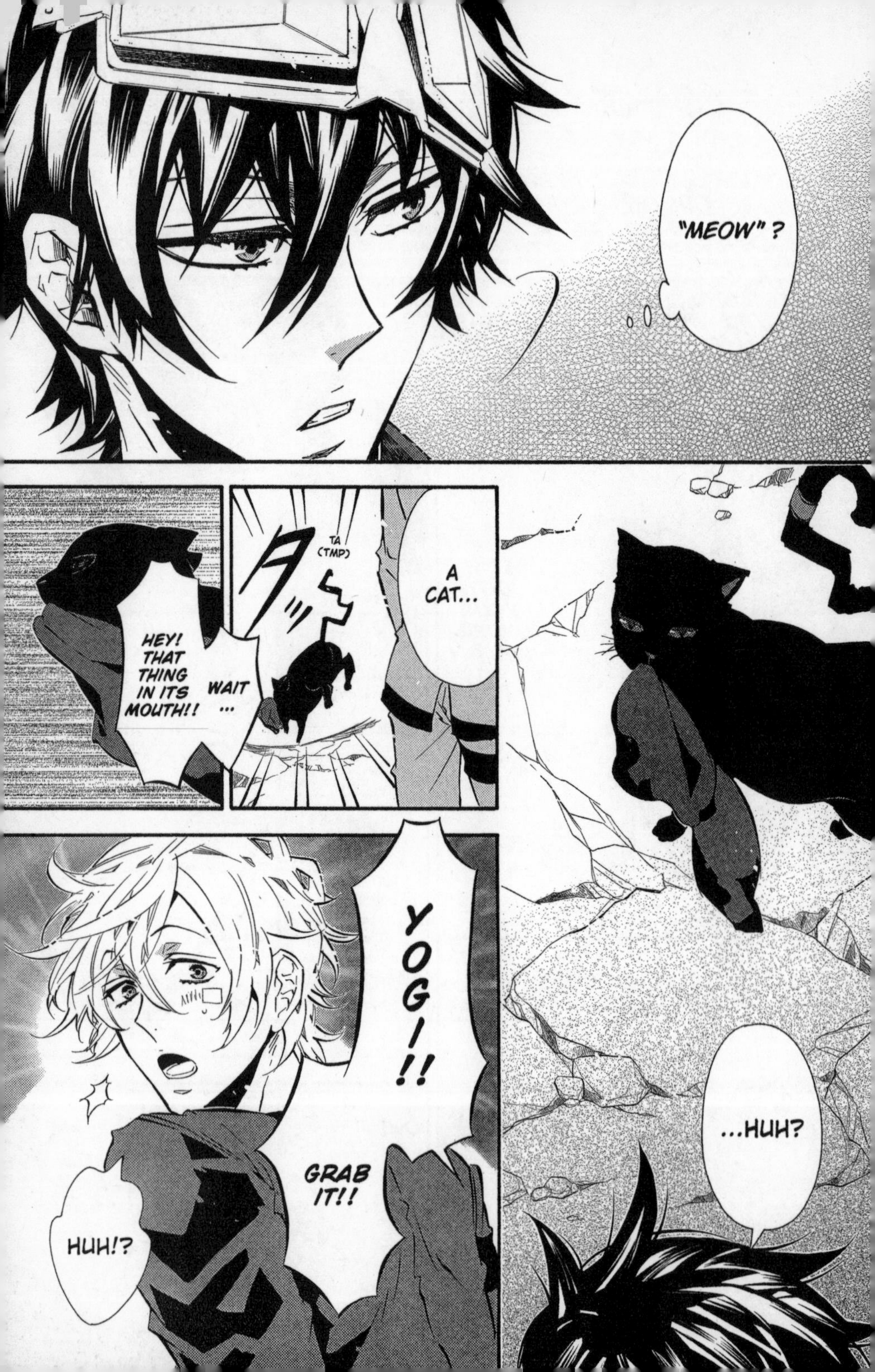
"MEOW" ?
...HUH?
TA (TMP)
A CAT...
WAIT ...
HEY! THAT THING IN ITS MOUTH!!
YOGI!!
GRAB IT!!
HUH!?

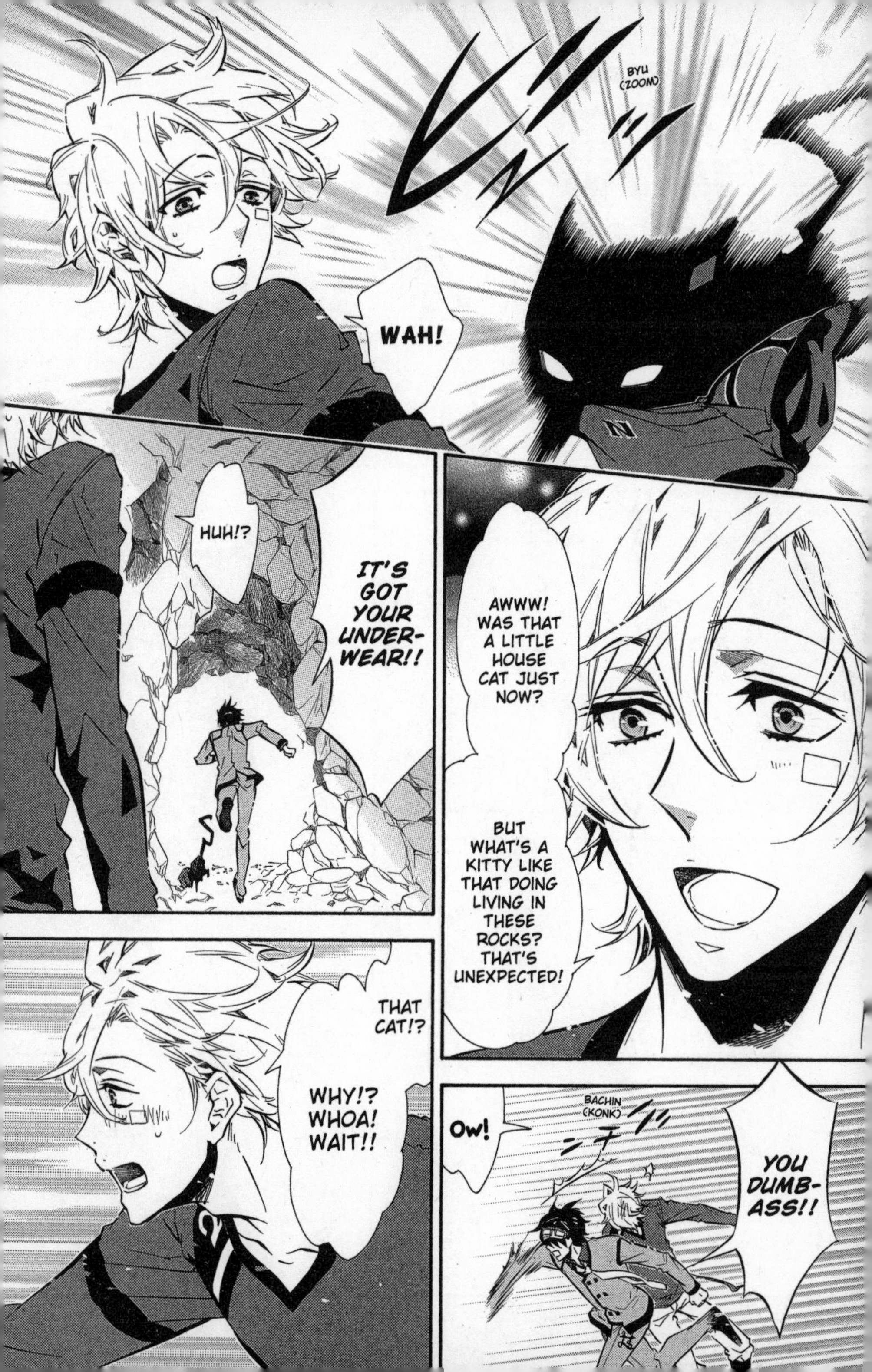

BYU (ZOOM)
WAH!
AWWW! WAS THAT A LITTLE HOUSE CAT JUST NOW?
BUT WHAT'S A KITTY LIKE THAT DOING LIVING IN THESE ROCKS? THAT'S UNEXPECTED!
IT'S GOT YOUR UNDER-WEAR!!
HUH!?
YOU DUMB-ASS!!
BACHIN (KONK)
Ow!
THAT CAT!?
WHY!? WHOA! WAIT!!

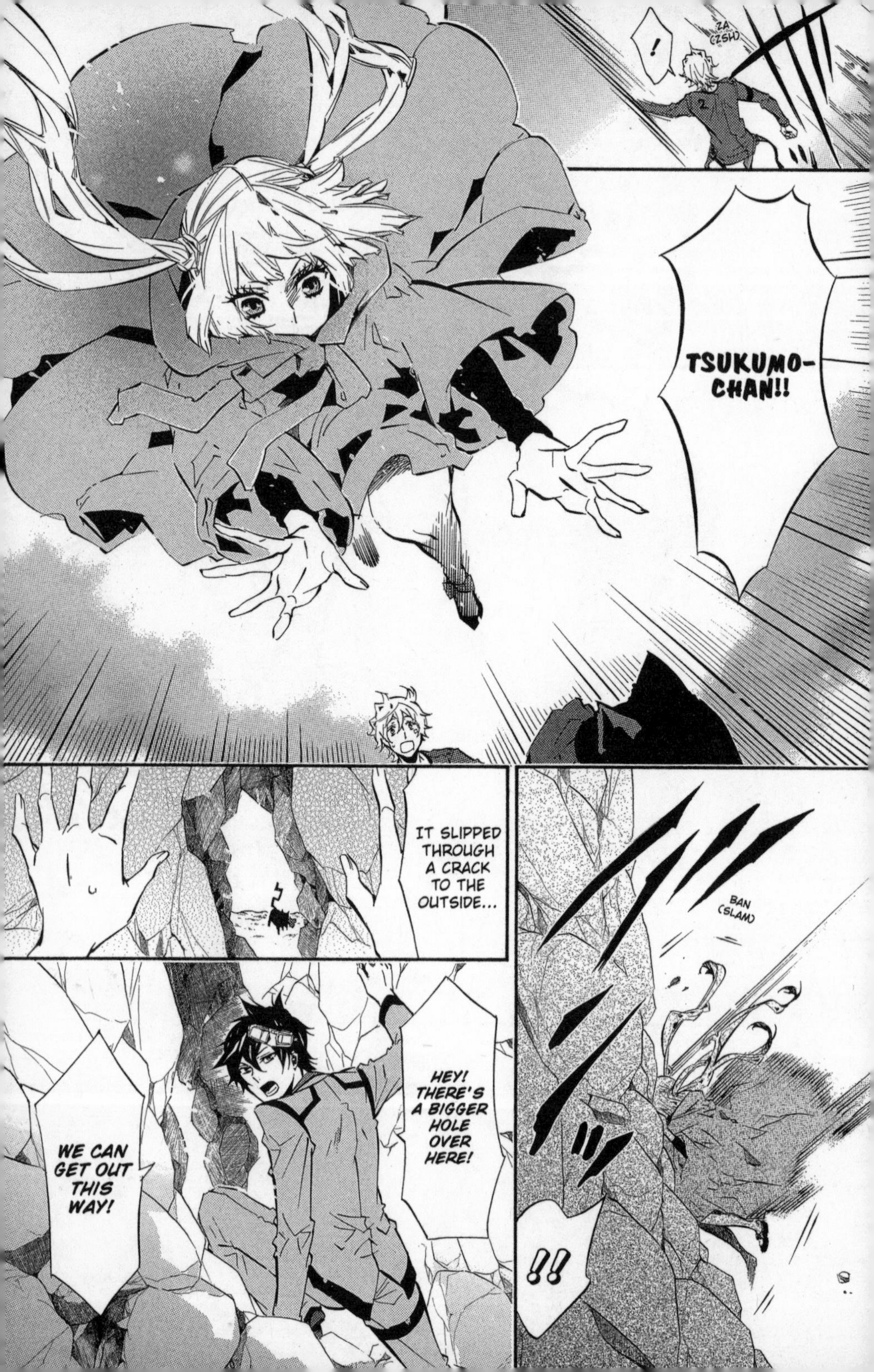
!
ZA (ZSH)
TSUKUMO-CHAN!!
BAN (SLAM)
!!
IT SLIPPED THROUGH A CRACK TO THE OUTSIDE...
HEY! THERE'S A BIGGER HOLE OVER HERE!
WE CAN GET OUT THIS WAY!

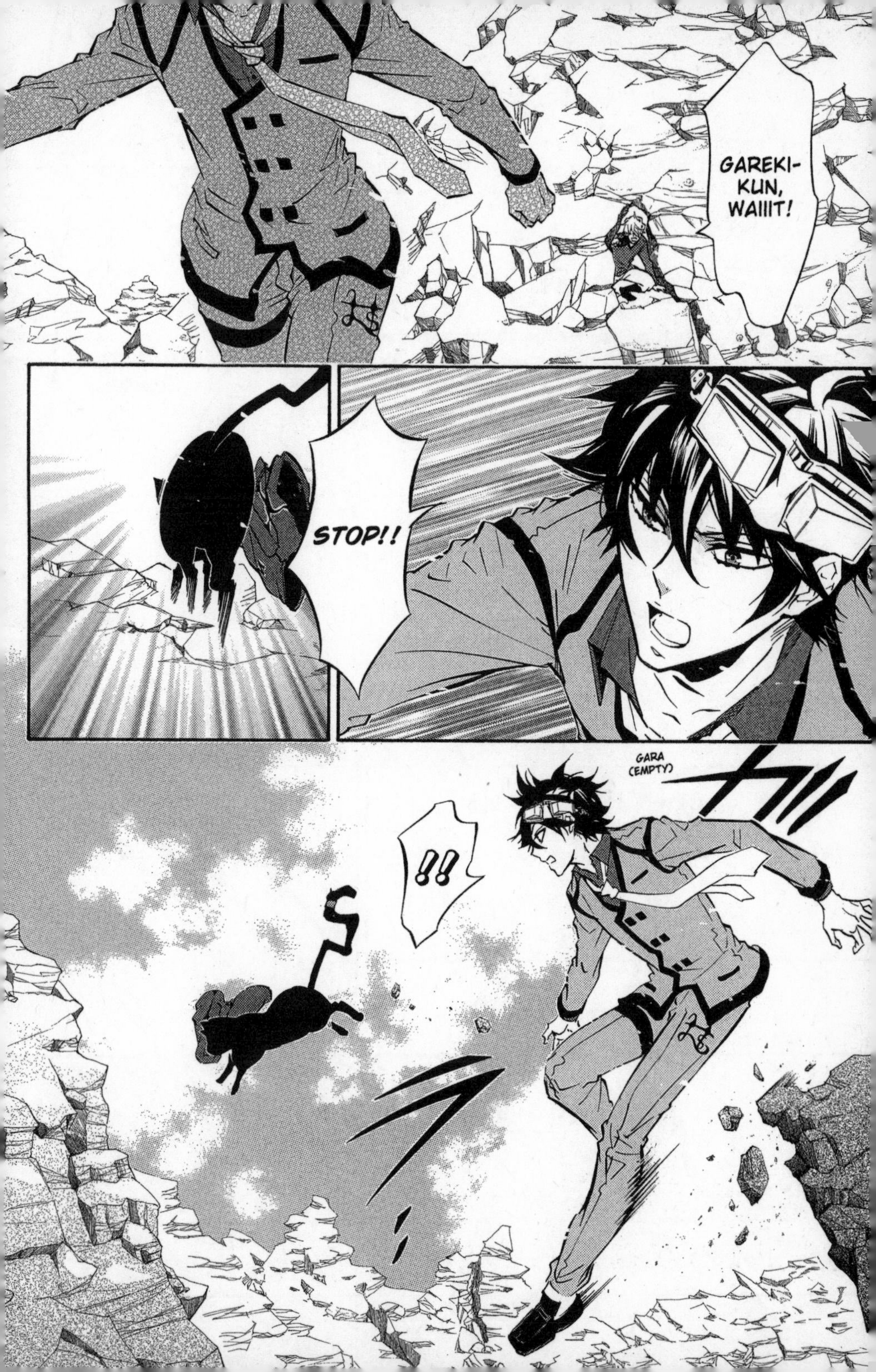
GAREKI-KUN, WAIIIT!
STOP!!
GARA (EMPTY)
!!

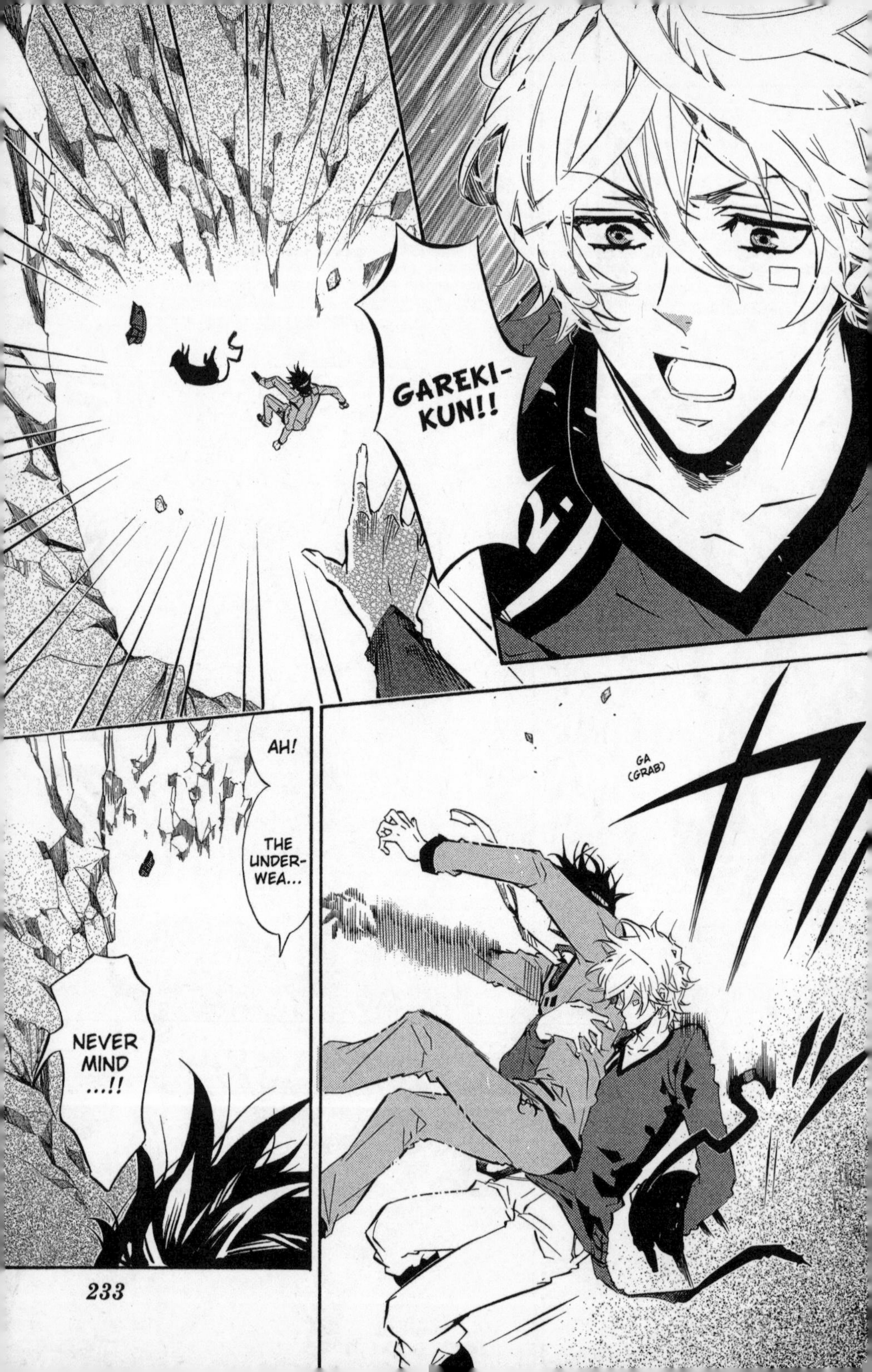
GAREKI-KUN!!
GA (GRAB)
AH!
THE UNDER-WEA...
NEVER MIND ...!!

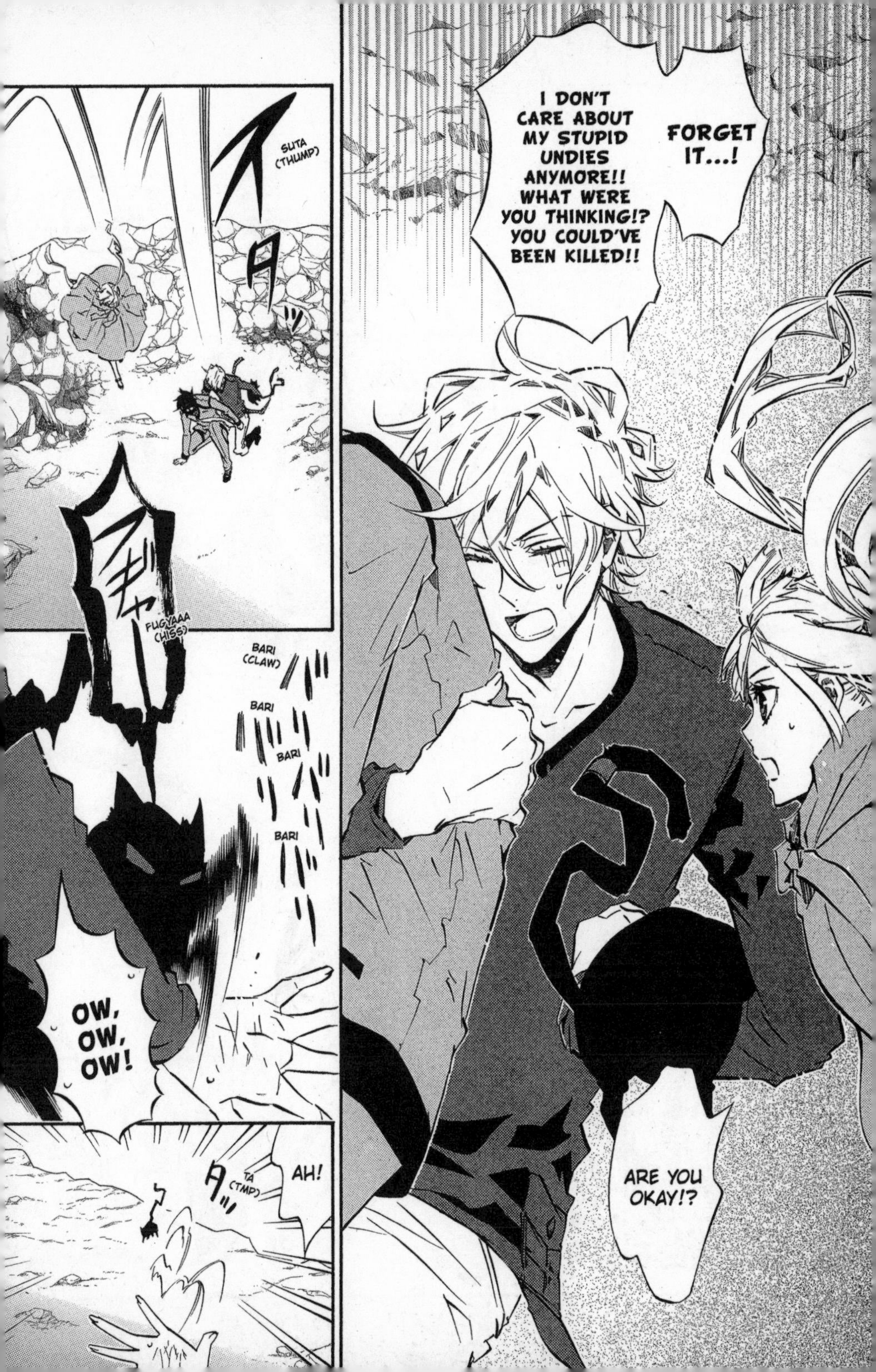
FORGET IT...!
I DON'T CARE ABOUT MY STUPID UNDIES ANYMORE!! WHAT WERE YOU THINKING!? YOU COULD'VE BEEN KILLED!!
ARE YOU OKAY!?
SUTA (THUMP)
FUGYAAA (HISS)
BARI (CLAW)
BARI
BARI
BARI
OW, OW, OW!
AH!
TA (TMP)

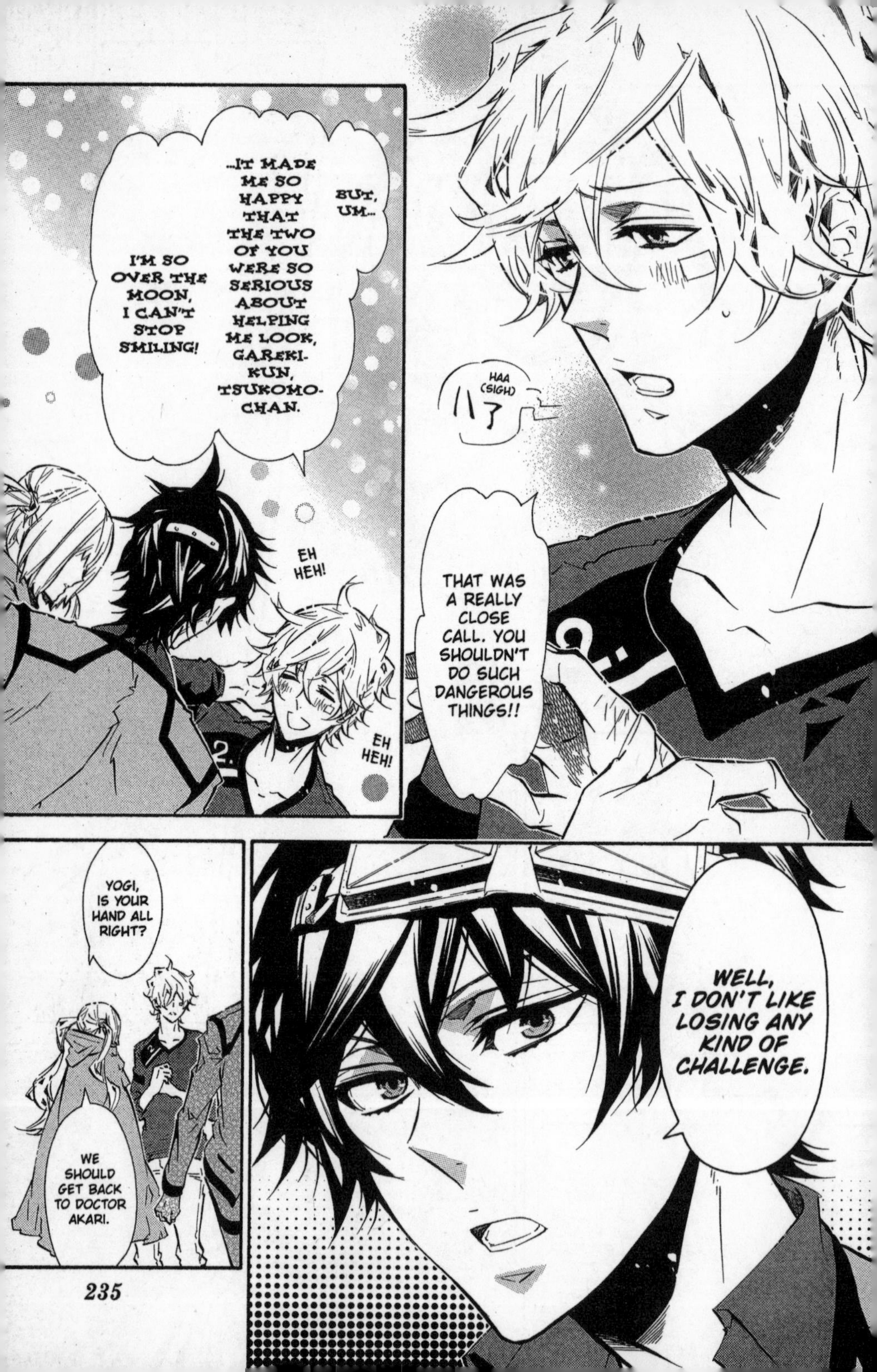
ハァ
HAA (SIGH)
THAT WAS A REALLY CLOSE CALL. YOU SHOULDN'T DO SUCH DANGEROUS THINGS!!
BUT, UM...
...IT MADE ME SO HAPPY THAT THE TWO OF YOU WERE SO SERIOUS ABOUT HELPING ME LOOK, GAREKI-KUN, TSUKOMO-CHAN.
I'M SO OVER THE MOON, I CAN'T STOP SMILING!
EH HEH!
EH HEH!
WELL, I DON'T LIKE LOSING ANY KIND OF CHALLENGE.
YOGI, IS YOUR HAND ALL RIGHT?
WE SHOULD GET BACK TO DOCTOR AKARI.

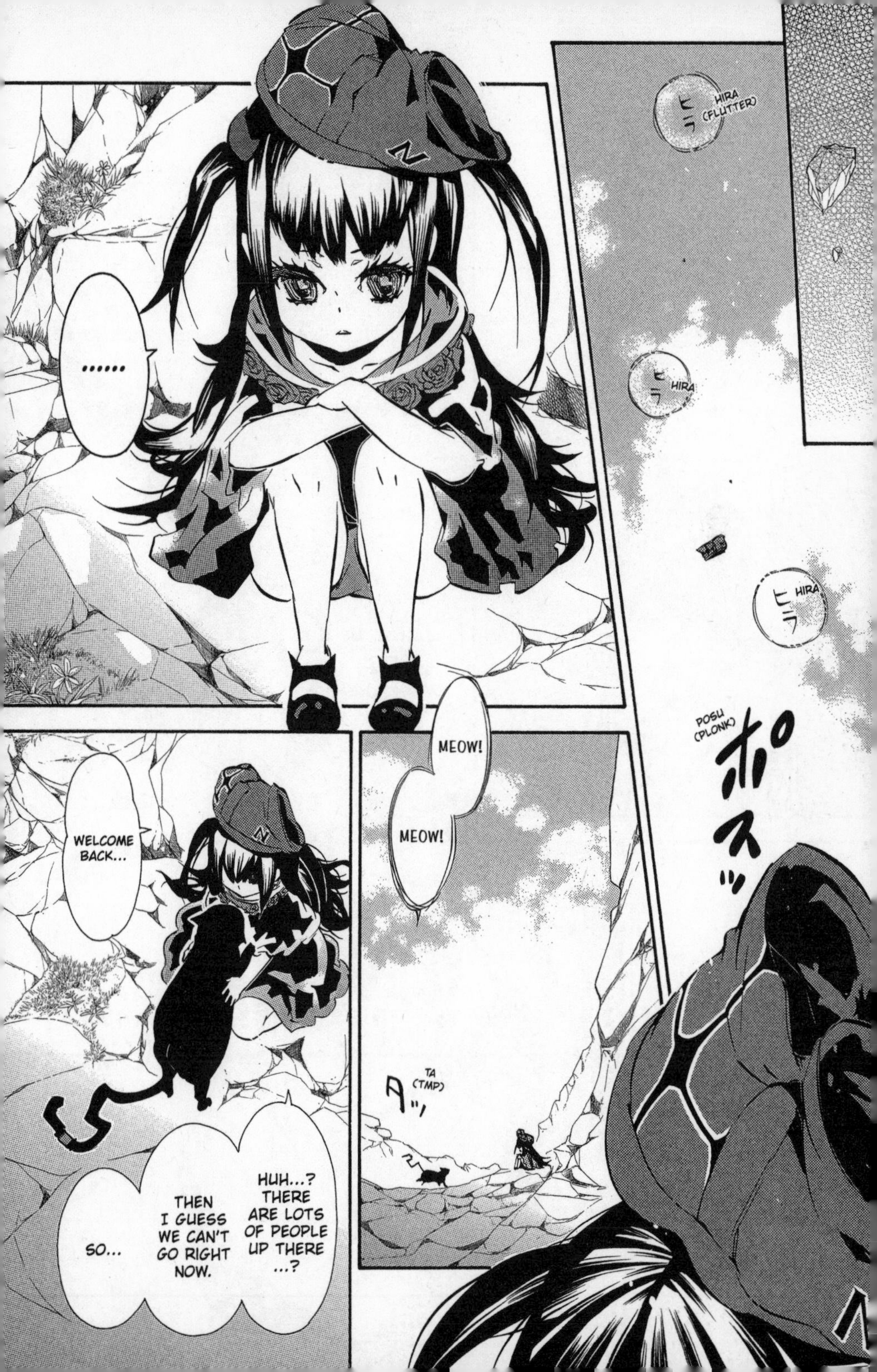

HIRA (FLUTTER)
HIRA
HIRA
POSU (PLONK)
......
MEOW!
MEOW!
TA (TMP)
WELCOME BACK...
HUH...? THERE ARE LOTS OF PEOPLE UP THERE ...?
THEN I GUESS WE CAN'T GO RIGHT NOW.
SO...

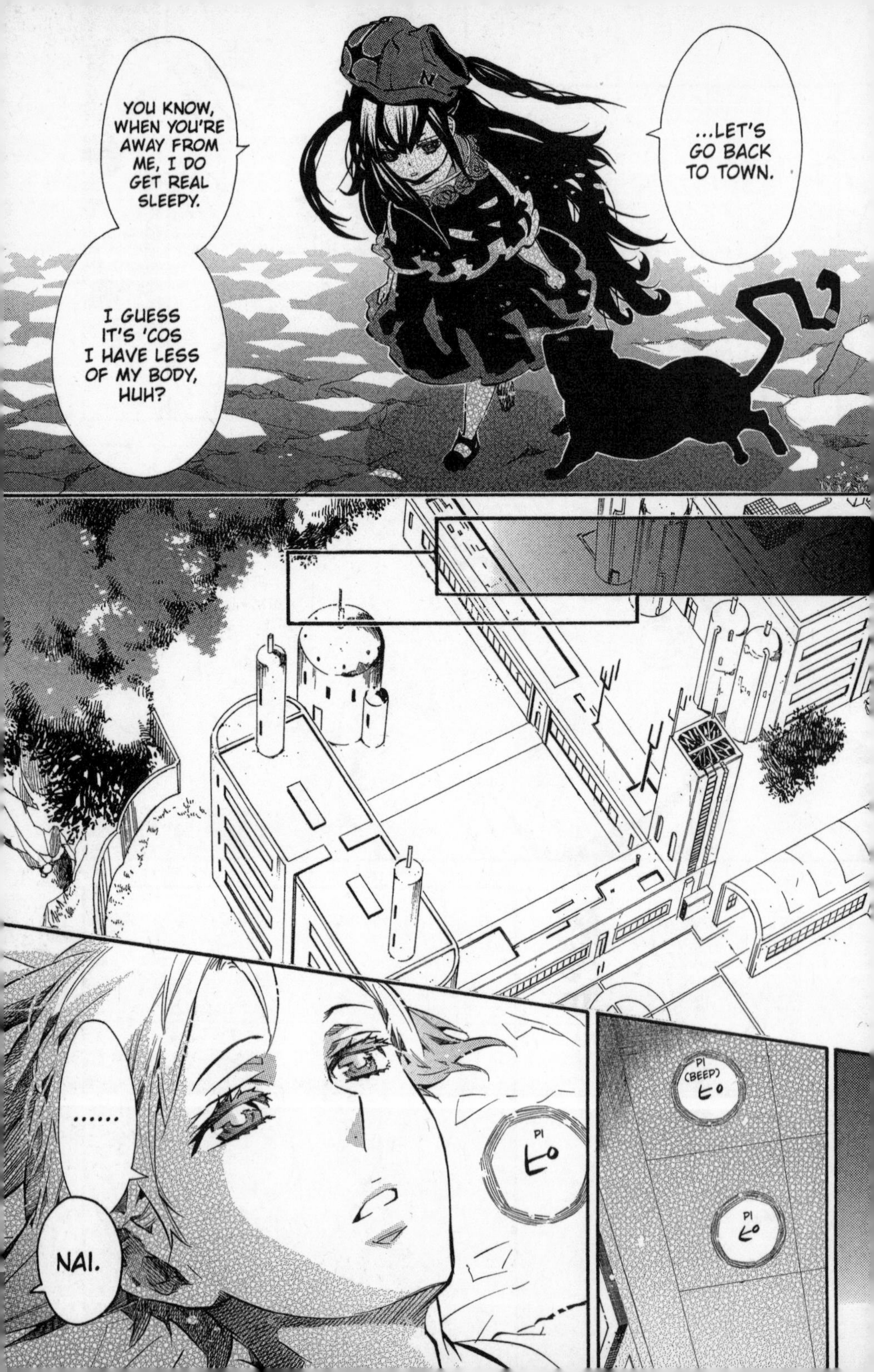
...LET'S GO BACK TO TOWN.
YOU KNOW, WHEN YOU'RE AWAY FROM ME, I DO GET REAL SLEEPY.
I GUESS IT'S 'COS I HAVE LESS OF MY BODY, HUH?
PI (BEEP) ピ
PI ピ
PI ピ
......
NAI.

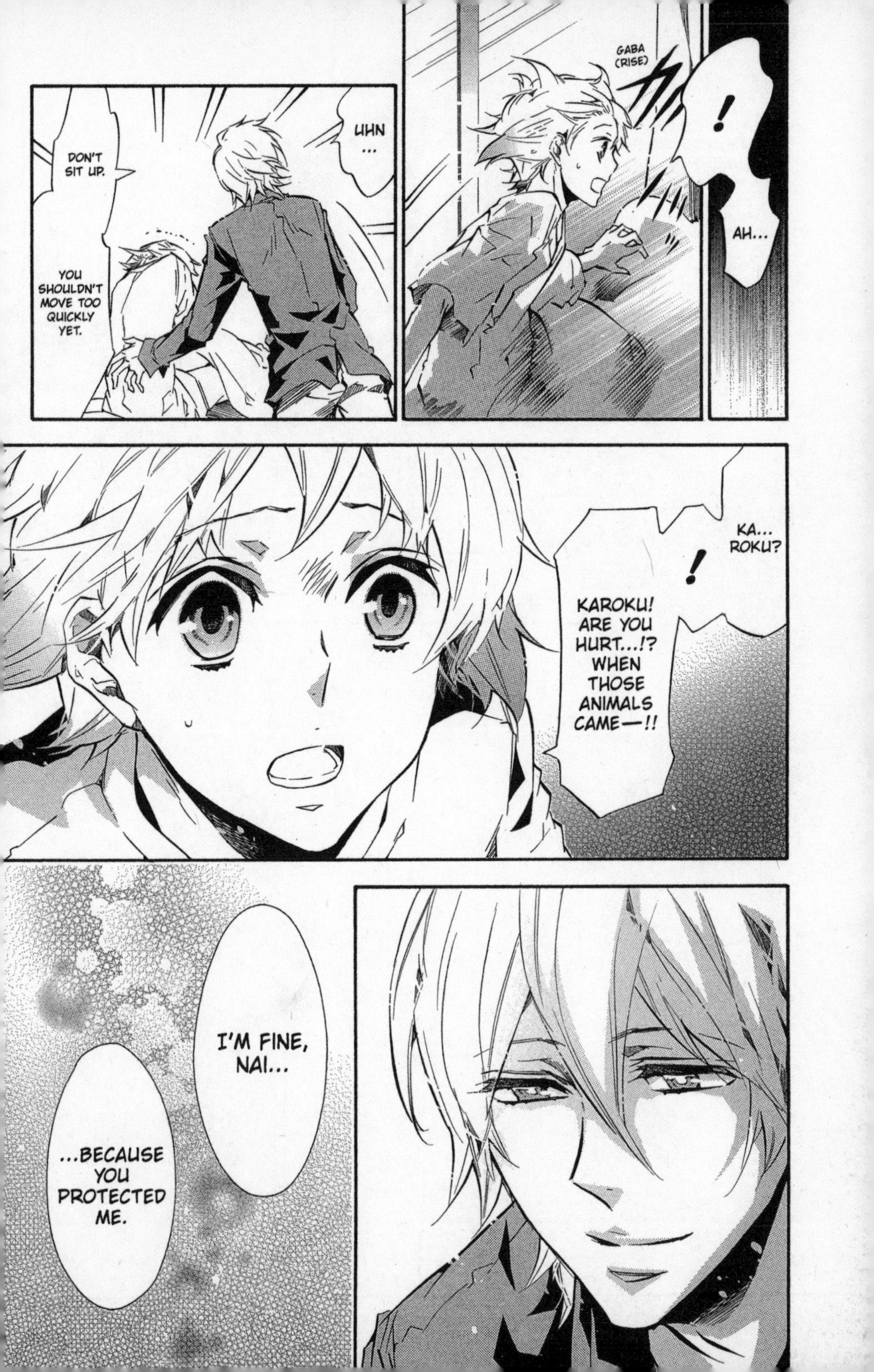
!
AH...
GABA (RISE)
UHN ...
DON'T SIT UP.
YOU SHOULDN'T MOVE TOO QUICKLY YET.
KA... ROKU?
!
KAROKU! ARE YOU HURT...!? WHEN THOSE ANIMALS CAME—!!
I'M FINE, NAI...
...BECAUSE YOU PROTECTED ME.

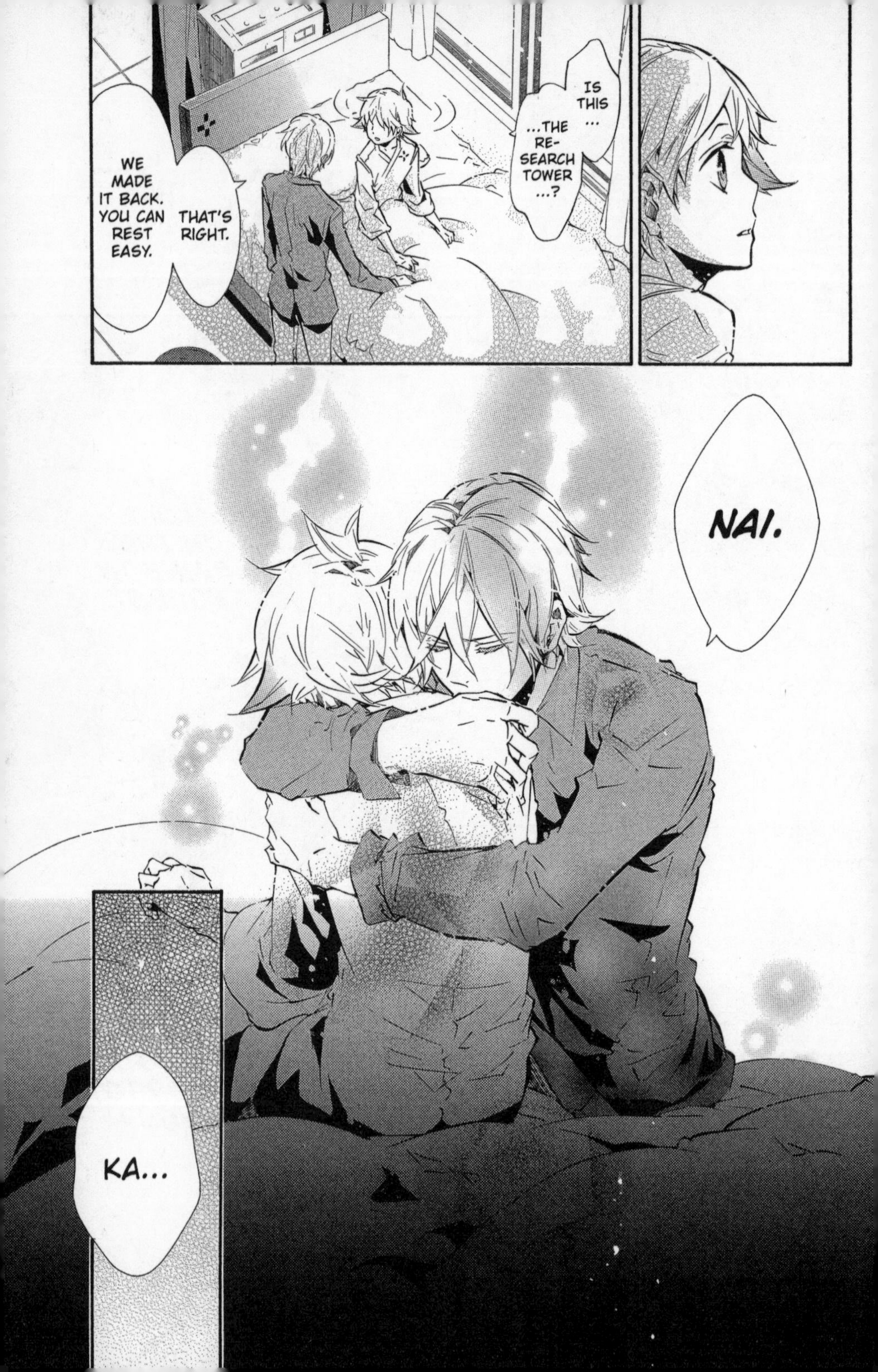
IS THIS ...
...THE RE-SEARCH TOWER ...?
THAT'S RIGHT.
WE MADE IT BACK. YOU CAN REST EASY.
NAI.
KA...

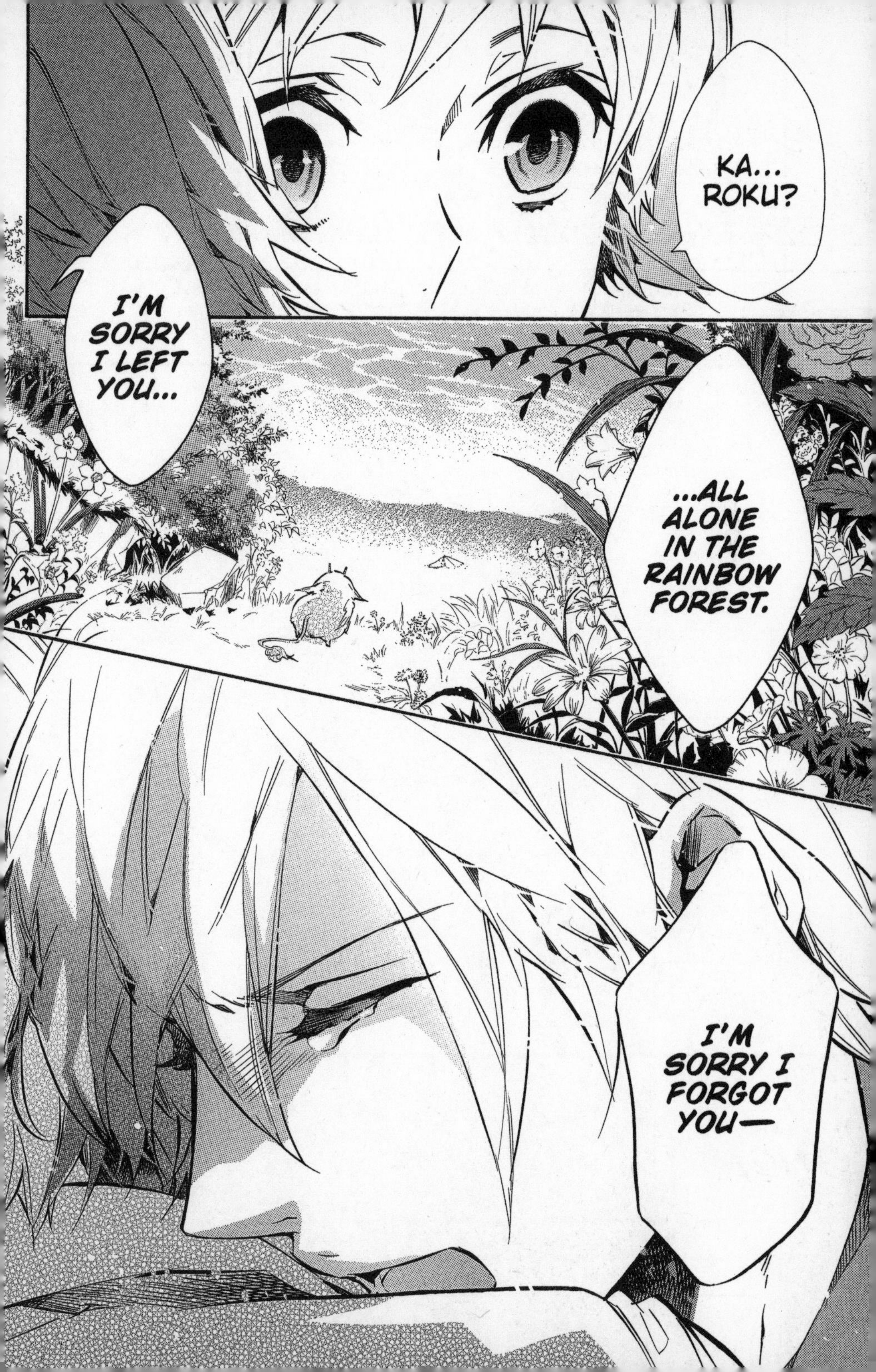
KA... ROKU?
I'M SORRY I LEFT YOU...
...ALL ALONE IN THE RAINBOW FOREST.
I'M SORRY I FORGOT YOU—

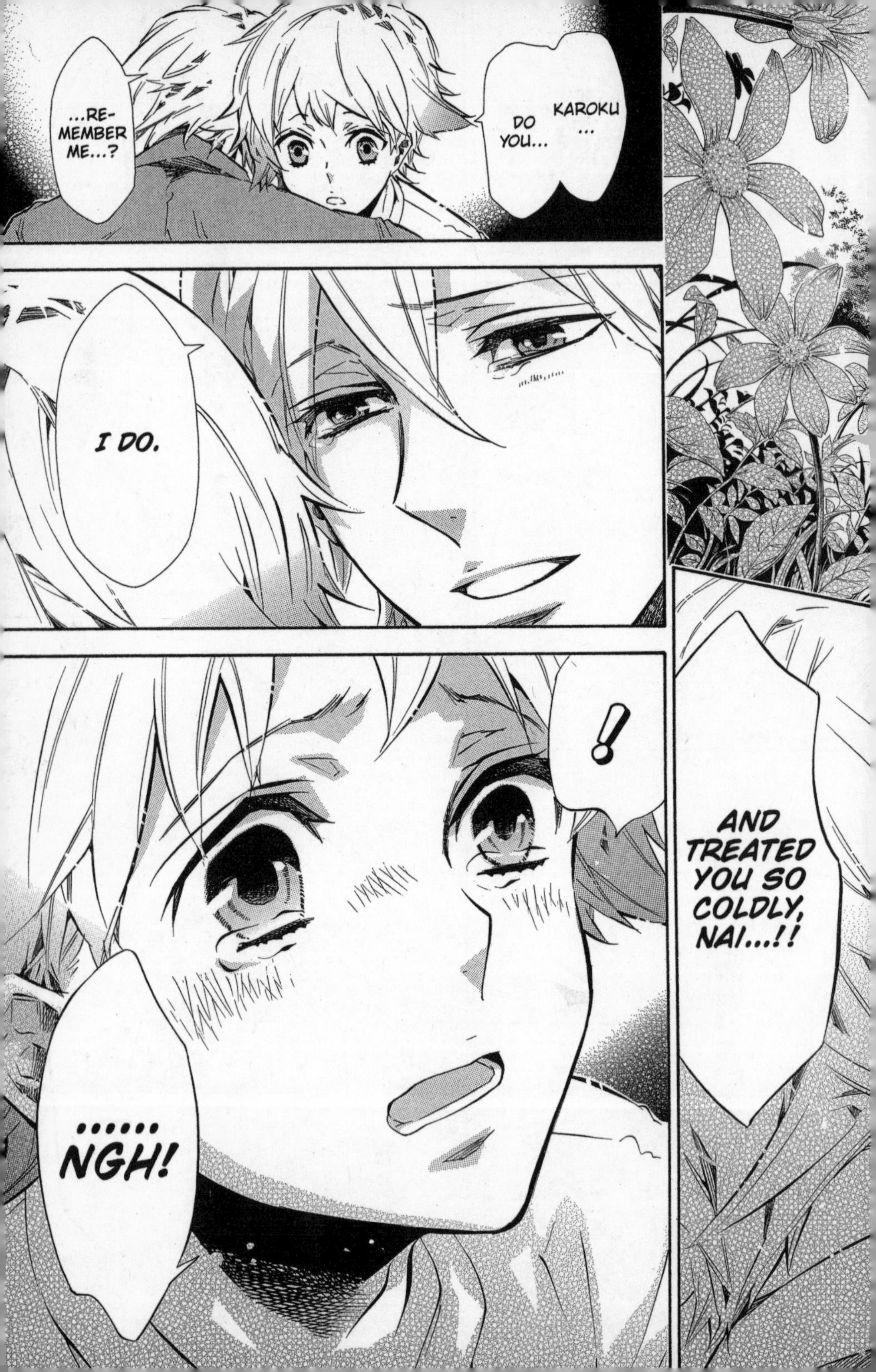
KAROKU... DO YOU...
...RE-MEMBER ME...?
I DO.
AND TREATED YOU SO COLDLY, NAI...!!
!
......NGH!

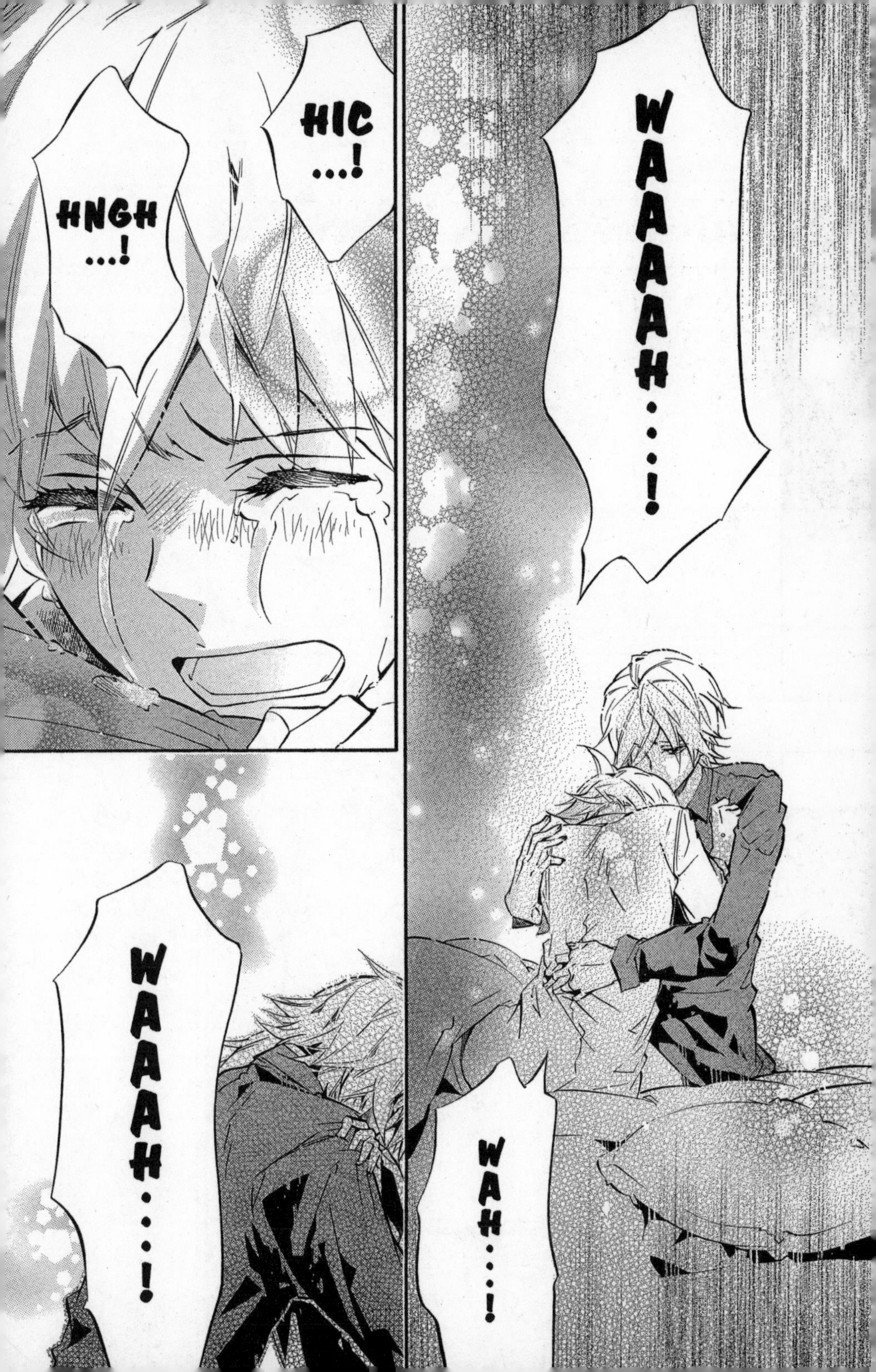
WAAAAH…!
WAH…!
HIC…!
HNGH…!
WAAAAH…!

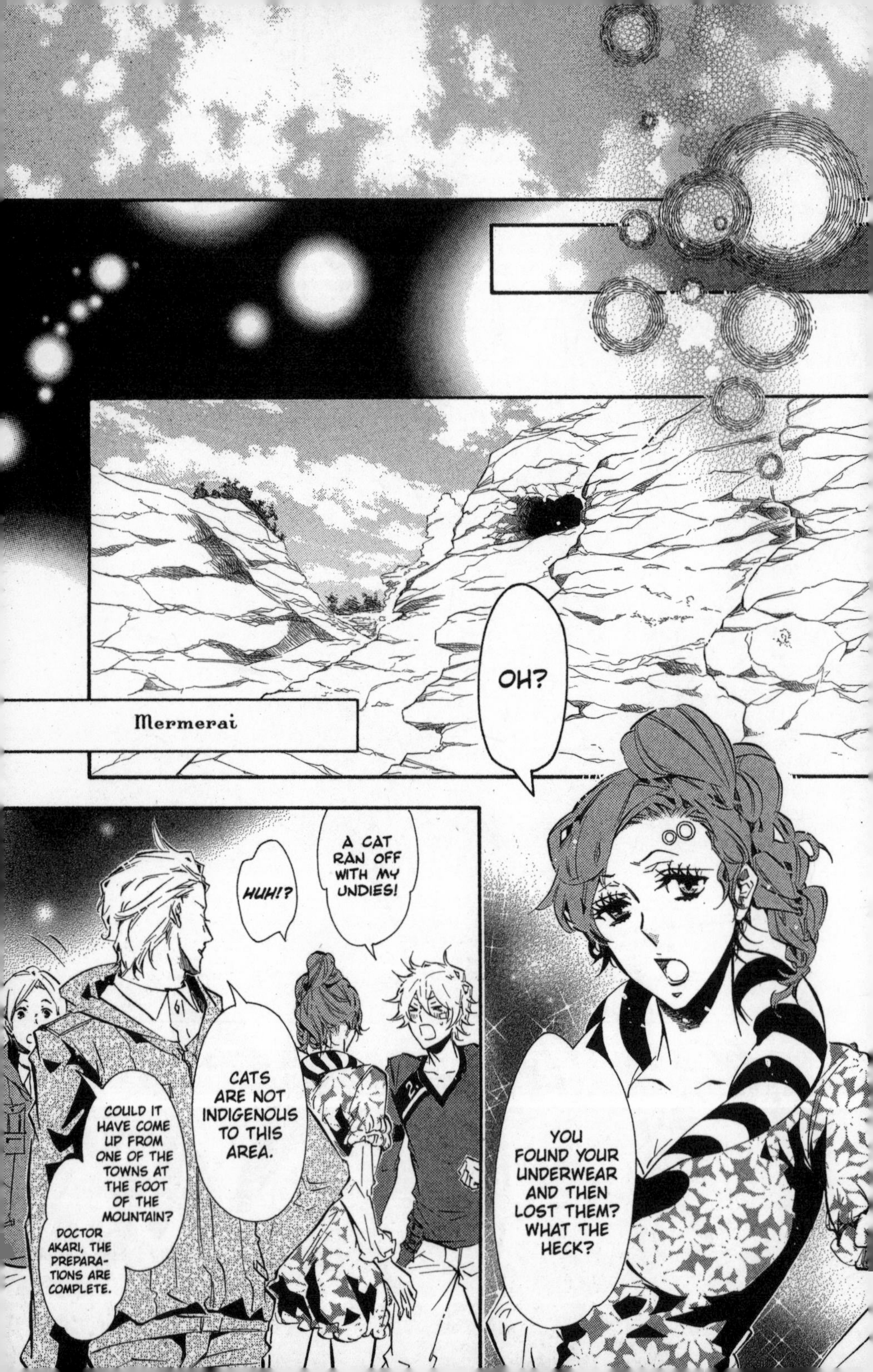
Mermerai
OH?
YOU FOUND YOUR UNDERWEAR AND THEN LOST THEM? WHAT THE HECK?
A CAT RAN OFF WITH MY UNDIES!
HUH!?
CATS ARE NOT INDIGENOUS TO THIS AREA.
COULD IT HAVE COME UP FROM ONE OF THE TOWNS AT THE FOOT OF THE MOUNTAIN?
DOCTOR AKARI, THE PREPARATIONS ARE COMPLETE.

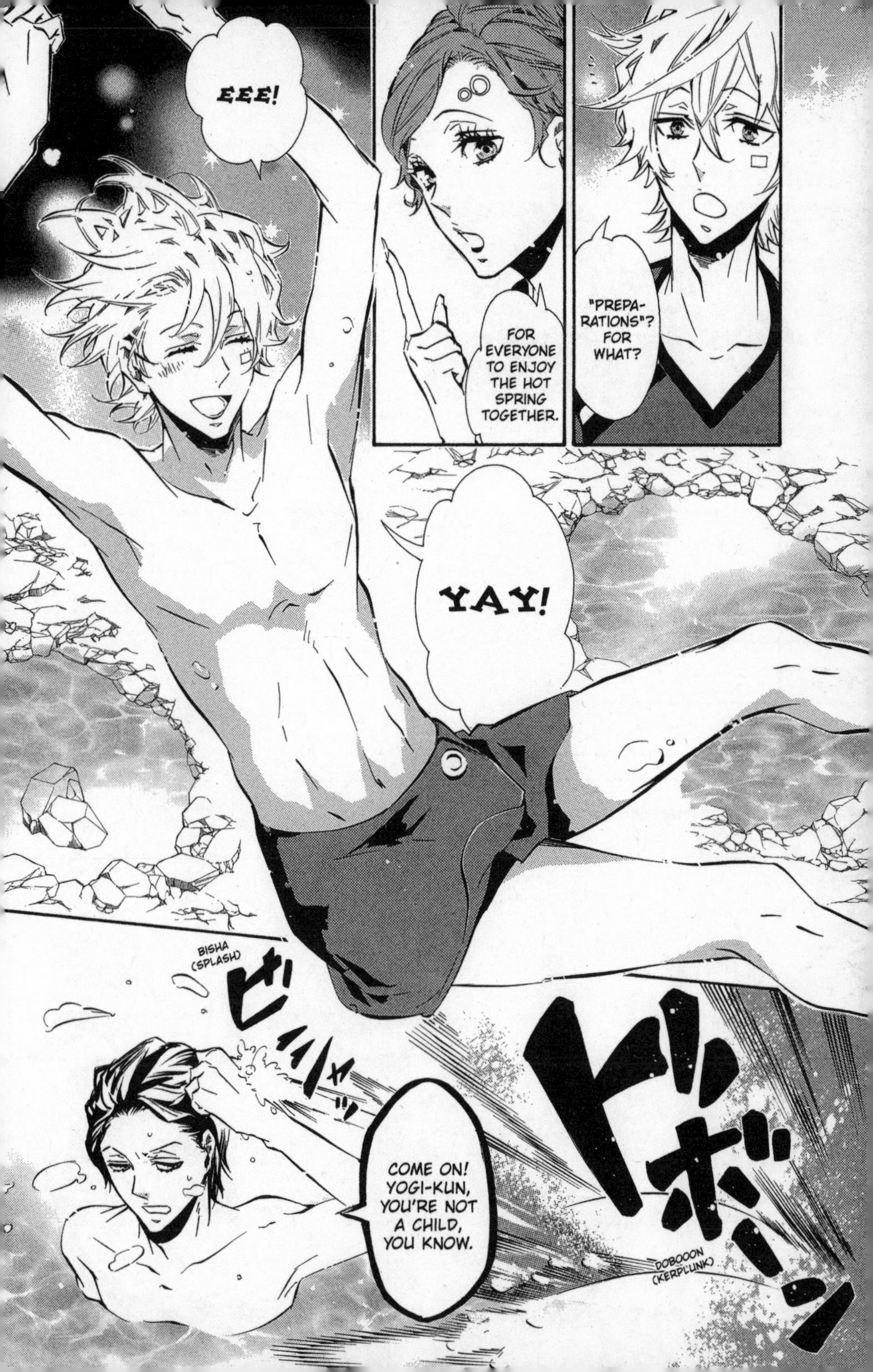

"PREPA-RATIONS"? FOR WHAT?
FOR EVERYONE TO ENJOY THE HOT SPRING TOGETHER.
EEE!
YAY!
DOBOOON (KERPLUNK)
BISHA (SPLASH)
COME ON! YOGI-KUN, YOU'RE NOT A CHILD, YOU KNOW.

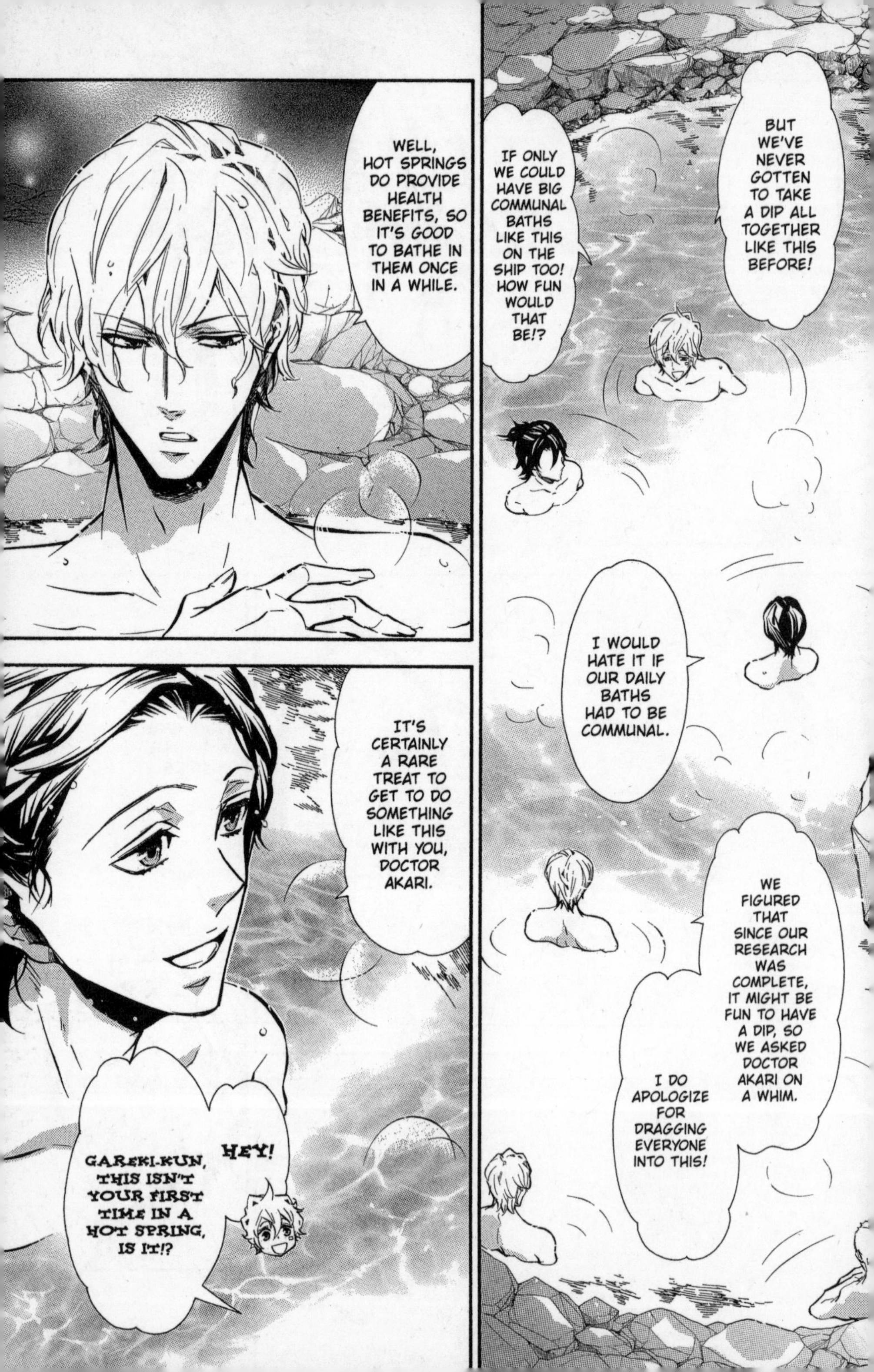
BUT WE'VE NEVER GOTTEN TO TAKE A DIP ALL TOGETHER LIKE THIS BEFORE!
IF ONLY WE COULD HAVE BIG COMMUNAL BATHS LIKE THIS ON THE SHIP TOO! HOW FUN WOULD THAT BE!?
I WOULD HATE IT IF OUR DAILY BATHS HAD TO BE COMMUNAL.
WE FIGURED THAT SINCE OUR RESEARCH WAS COMPLETE, IT MIGHT BE FUN TO HAVE A DIP, SO WE ASKED DOCTOR AKARI ON A WHIM.
I DO APOLOGIZE FOR DRAGGING EVERYONE INTO THIS!
WELL, HOT SPRINGS DO PROVIDE HEALTH BENEFITS, SO IT'S GOOD TO BATHE IN THEM ONCE IN A WHILE.
IT'S CERTAINLY A RARE TREAT TO GET TO DO SOMETHING LIKE THIS WITH YOU, DOCTOR AKARI.
HEY!
GAREKI-KUN, THIS ISN'T YOUR FIRST TIME IN A HOT SPRING, IS IT!?

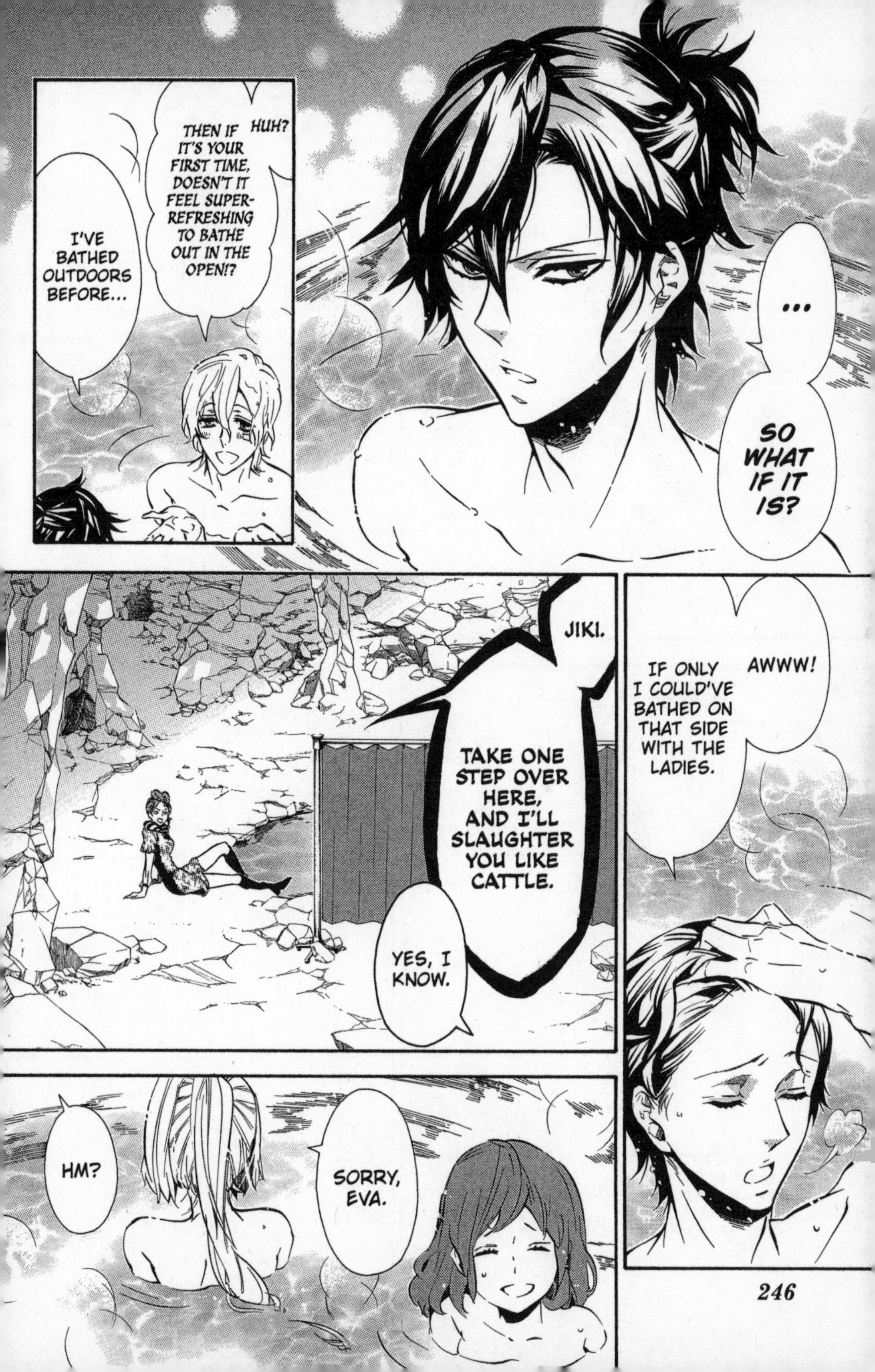
...
SO WHAT IF IT IS?
HUH?
THEN IF IT'S YOUR FIRST TIME, DOESN'T IT FEEL SUPER-REFRESHING TO BATHE OUT IN THE OPEN!?
I'VE BATHED OUTDOORS BEFORE...
AWWW!
IF ONLY I COULD'VE BATHED ON THAT SIDE WITH THE LADIES.
JIKI.
TAKE ONE STEP OVER HERE, AND I'LL SLAUGHTER YOU LIKE CATTLE.
YES, I KNOW.
SORRY, EVA.
HM?

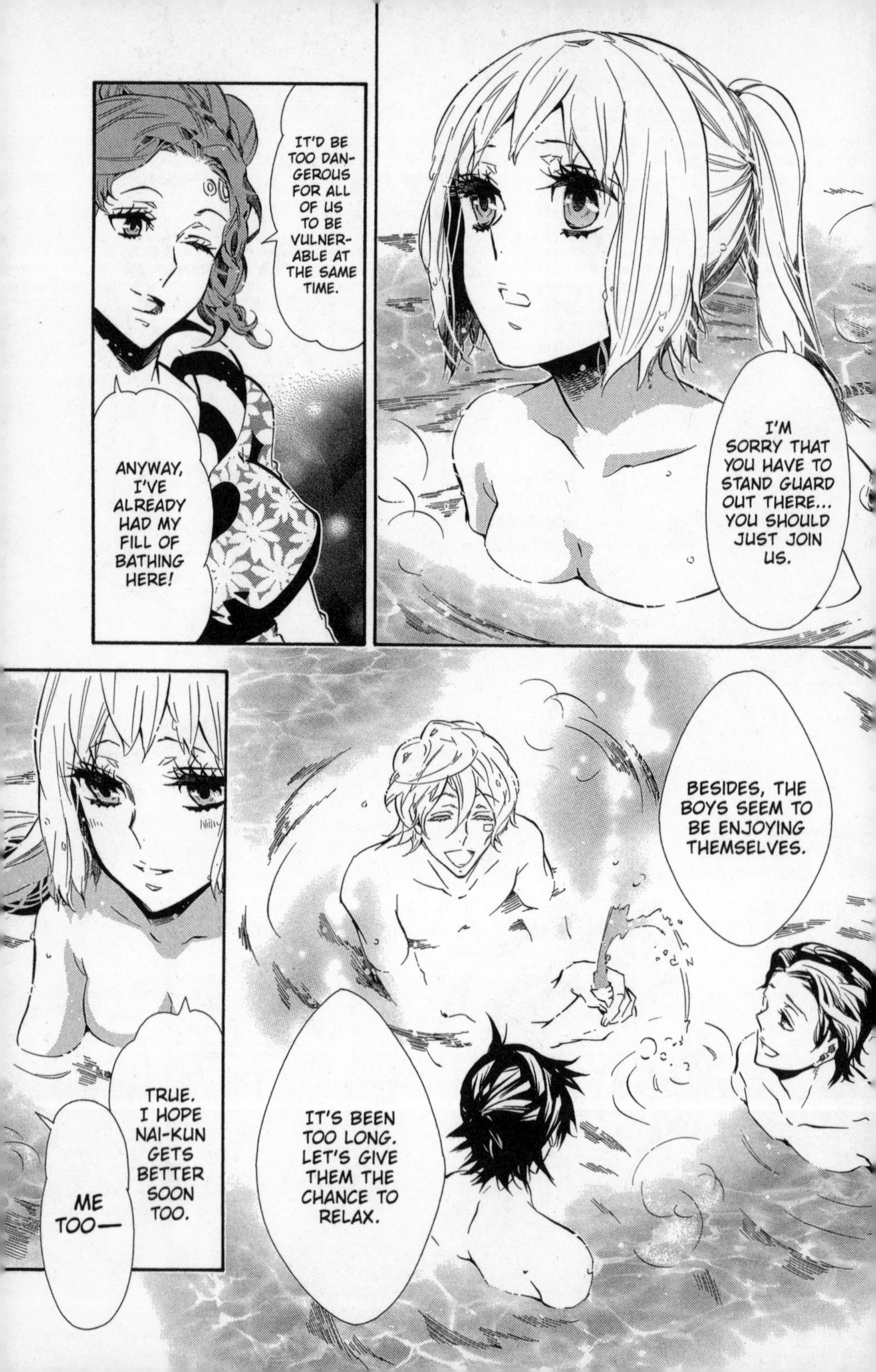
I'M SORRY THAT YOU HAVE TO STAND GUARD OUT THERE... YOU SHOULD JUST JOIN US.
IT'D BE TOO DANGEROUS FOR ALL OF US TO BE VULNERABLE AT THE SAME TIME.
ANYWAY, I'VE ALREADY HAD MY FILL OF BATHING HERE!
BESIDES, THE BOYS SEEM TO BE ENJOYING THEMSELVES.
IT'S BEEN TOO LONG. LET'S GIVE THEM THE CHANCE TO RELAX.
TRUE. I HOPE NAI-KUN GETS BETTER SOON TOO.
ME TOO—

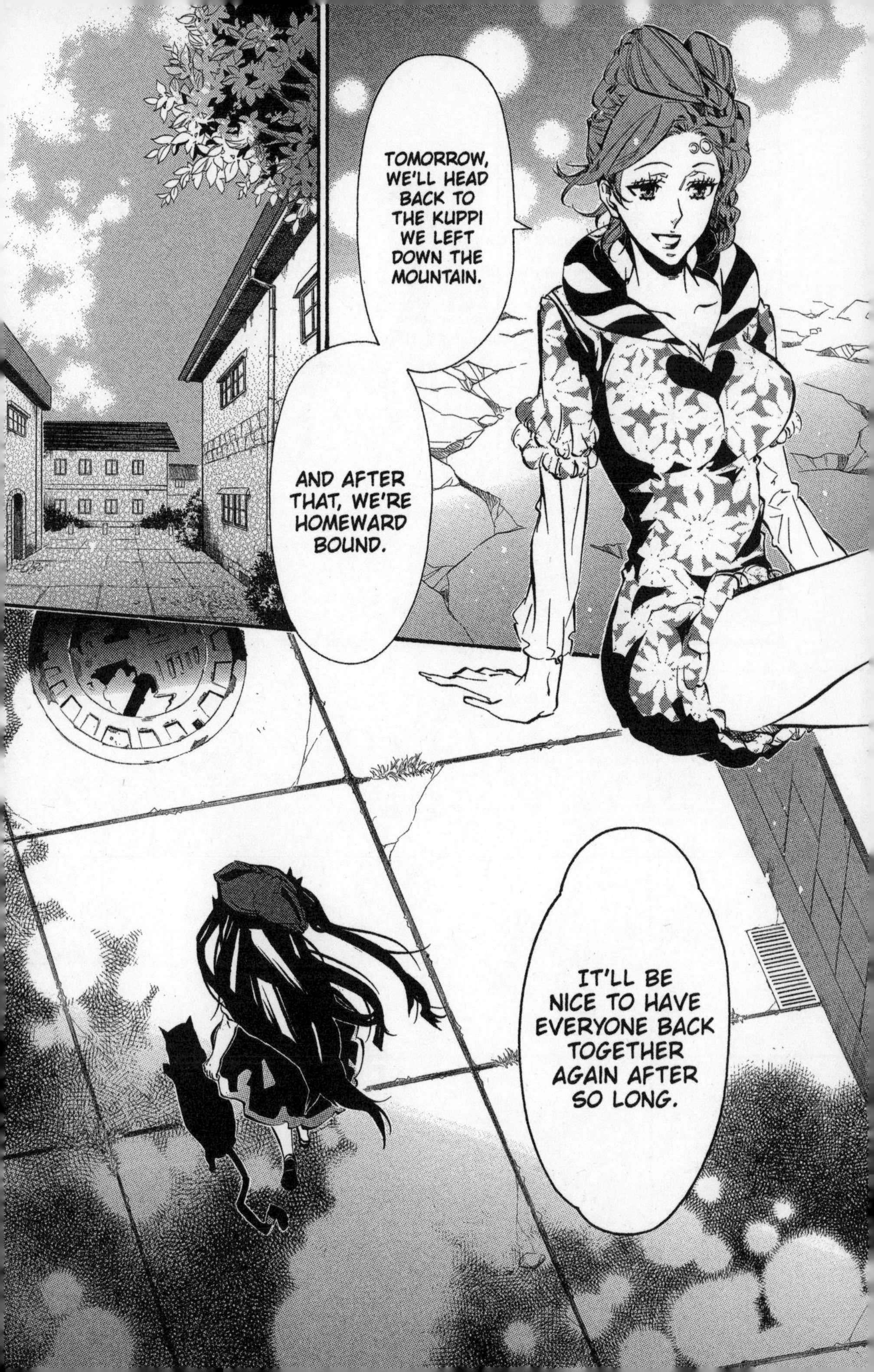
TOMORROW, WE'LL HEAD BACK TO THE KUPPI WE LEFT DOWN THE MOUNTAIN.
AND AFTER THAT, WE'RE HOMEWARD BOUND.
IT'LL BE NICE TO HAVE EVERYONE BACK TOGETHER AGAIN AFTER SO LONG.

KARNEVAL

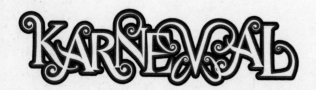

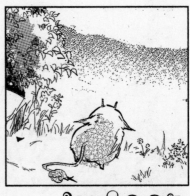

KARNEVAL

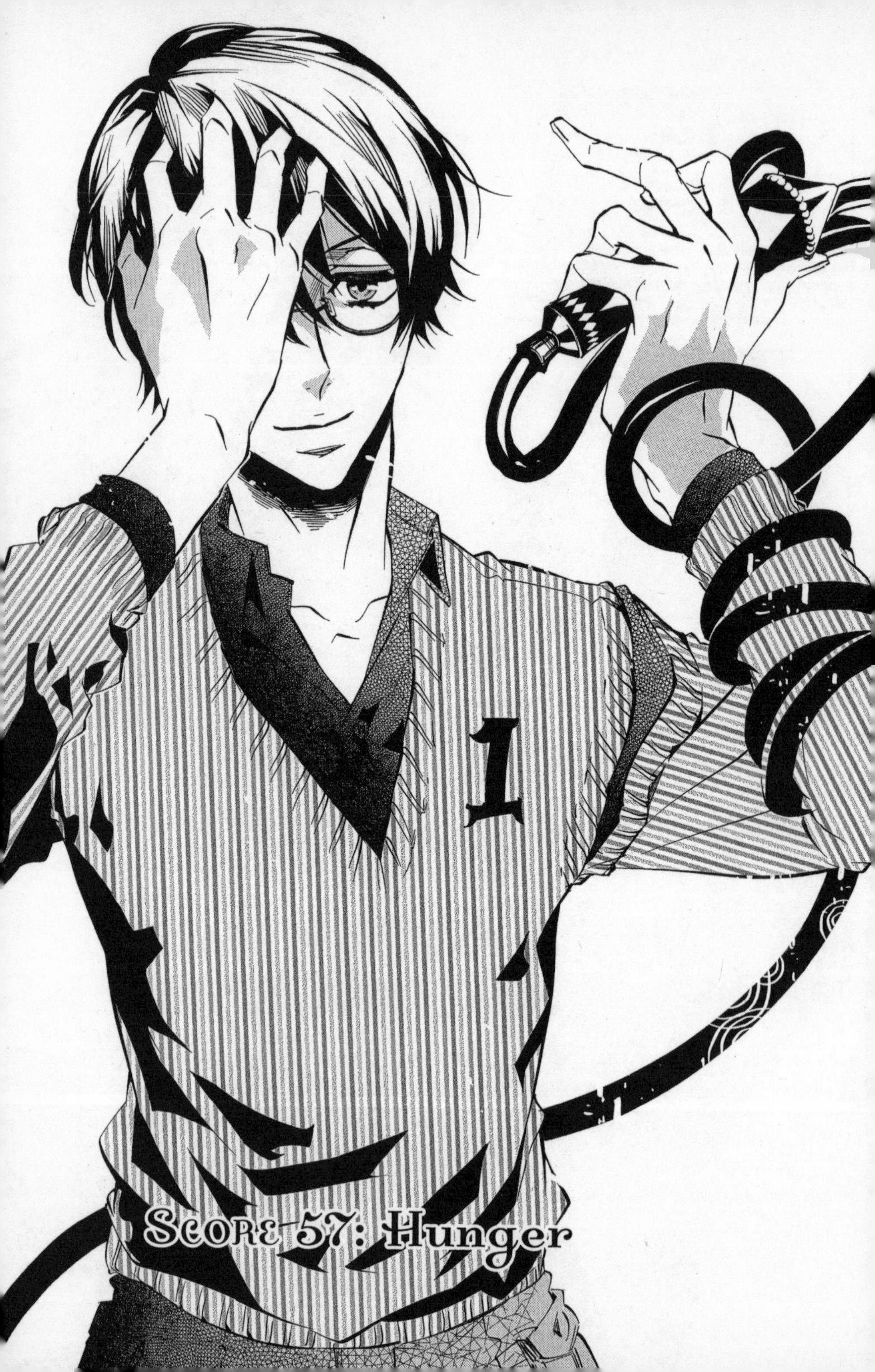
Score 57: Hunger

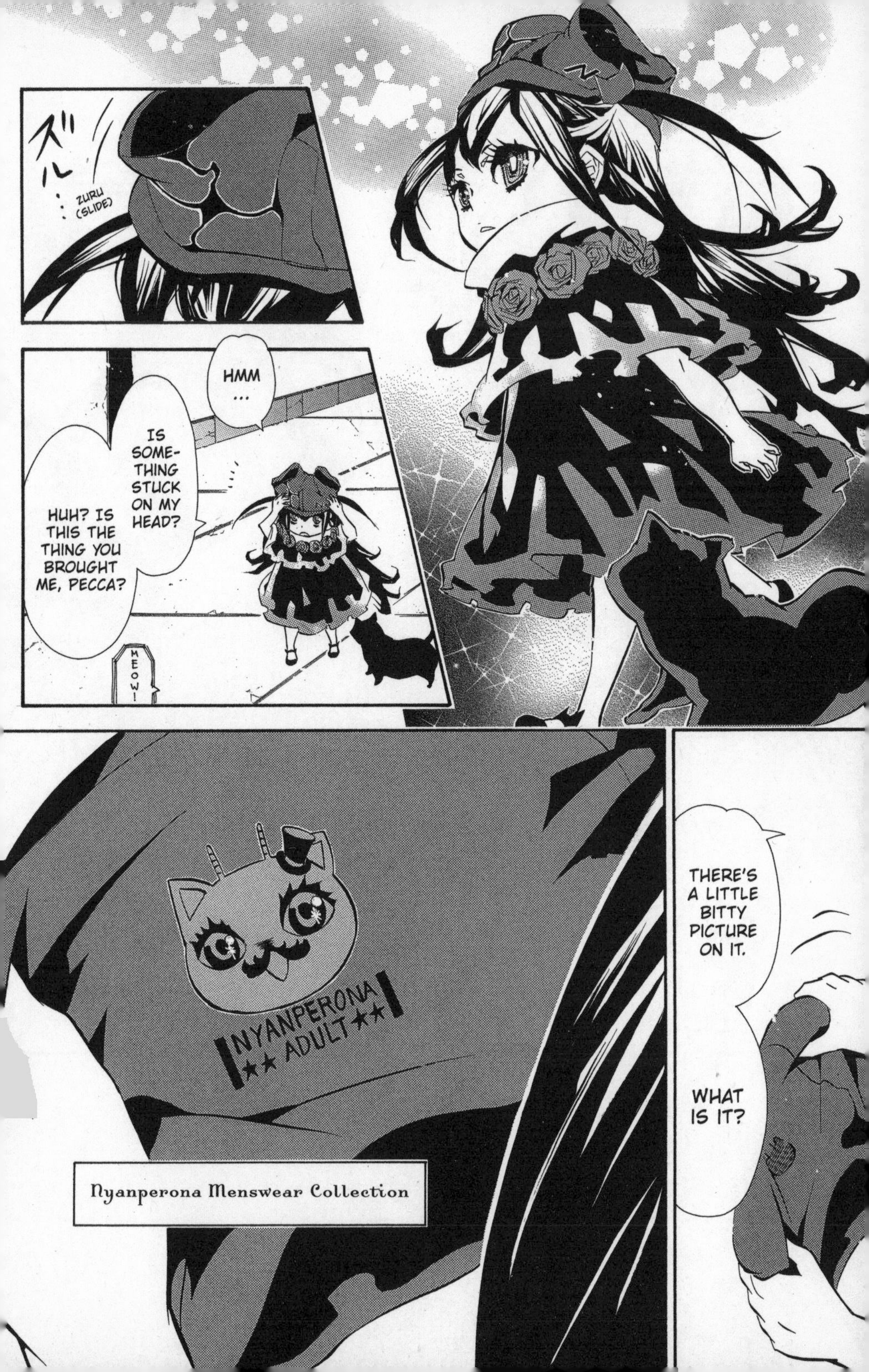
ズル…
ZURU (SLIDE)
HMM…
IS SOMETHING STUCK ON MY HEAD?
HUH? IS THIS THE THING YOU BROUGHT ME, PECCA?
MEOW!
THERE'S A LITTLE BITTY PICTURE ON IT.
WHAT IS IT?
★★ NYANPERONA ADULT ★★
Nyanperona Menswear Collection

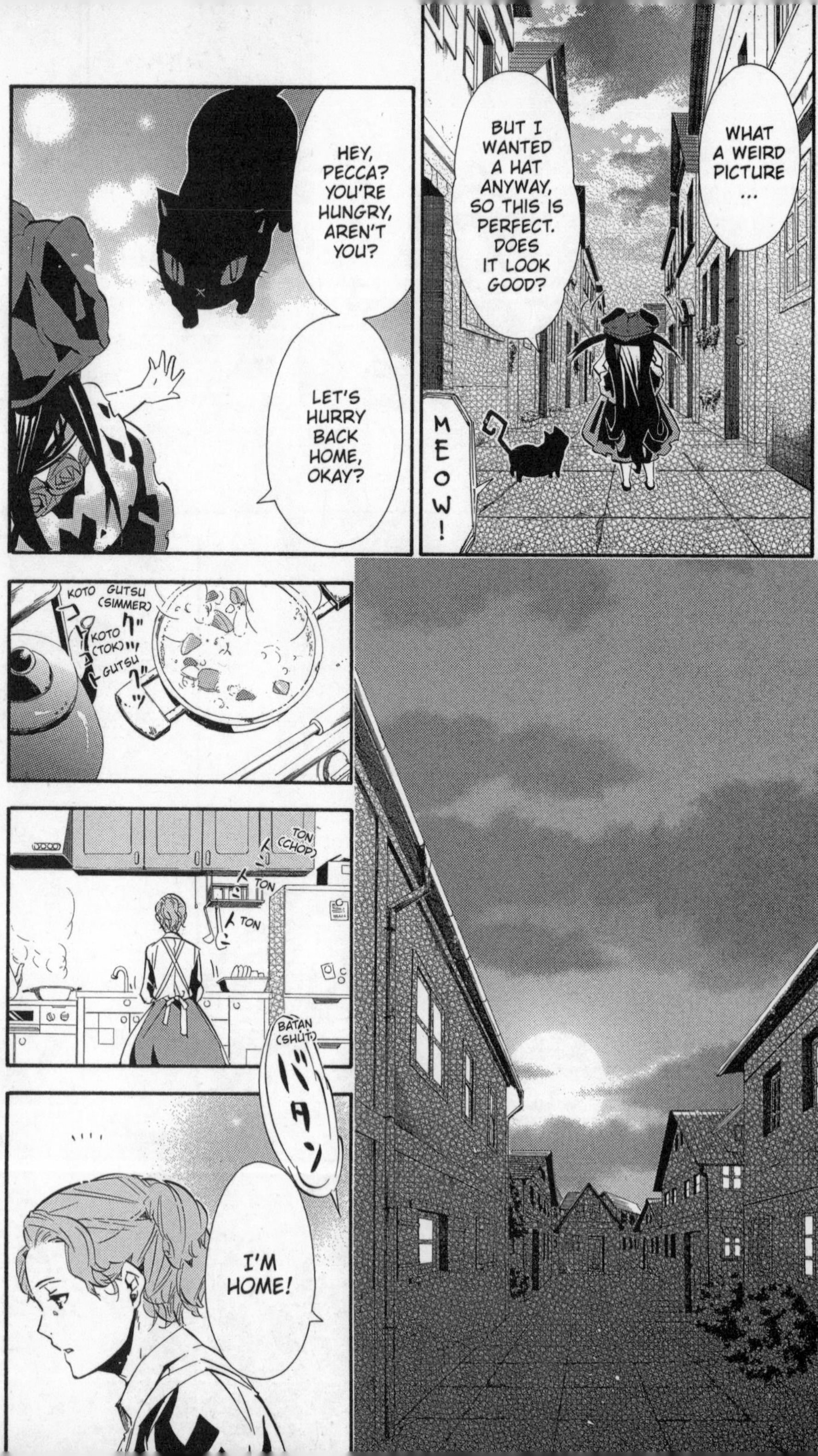
WHAT A WEIRD PICTURE ...
BUT I WANTED A HAT ANYWAY, SO THIS IS PERFECT. DOES IT LOOK GOOD?
MEOW!
HEY, PECCA? YOU'RE HUNGRY, AREN'T YOU?
LET'S HURRY BACK HOME, OKAY?
KOTO GUTSU (SIMMER)
KOTO (TOK)
GUTSU
TON (CHOP)
TON
TON
BATAN (SHUT)
I'M HOME!

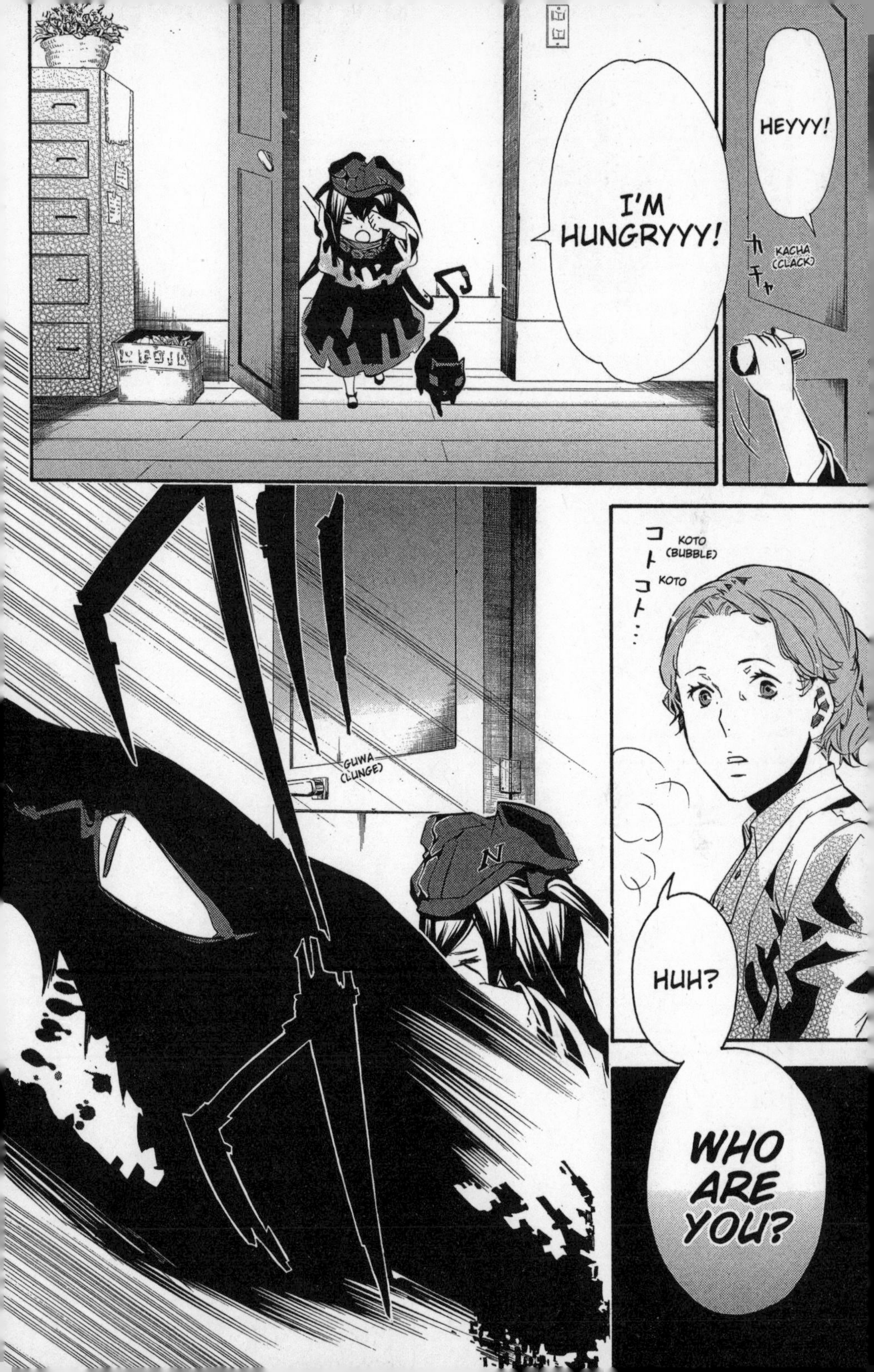
HEYYY!
カチャ
KACHA (CLACK)
I'M HUNGRYYY!
コトコト…
KOTO (BUBBLE) KOTO
HUH?
GUWA (LUNGE)
WHO ARE YOU?

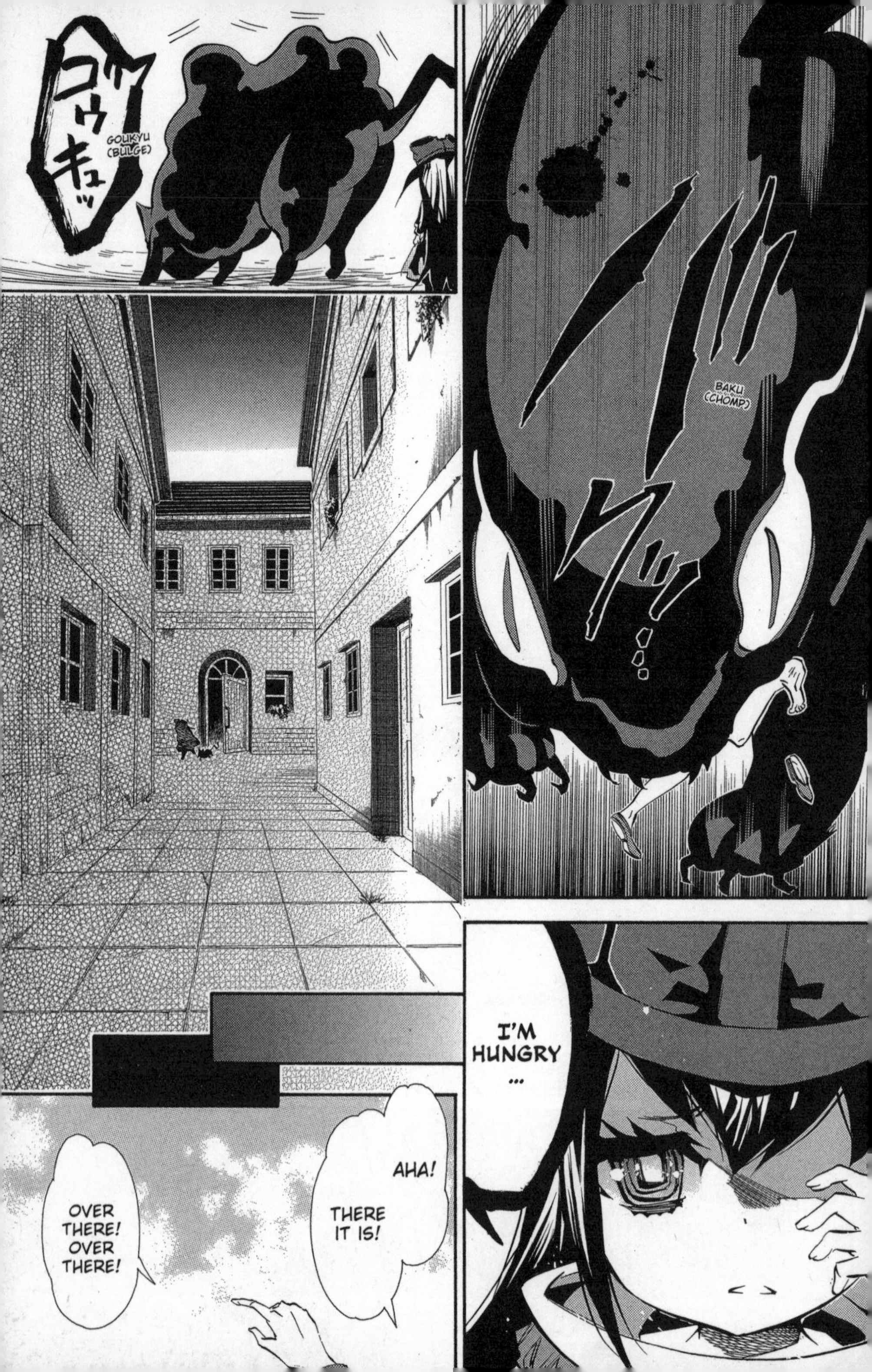
BAKU (CHOMP)
GOUKYU (BULGE)
I'M HUNGRY ...
AHA! THERE IT IS!
OVER THERE! OVER THERE!

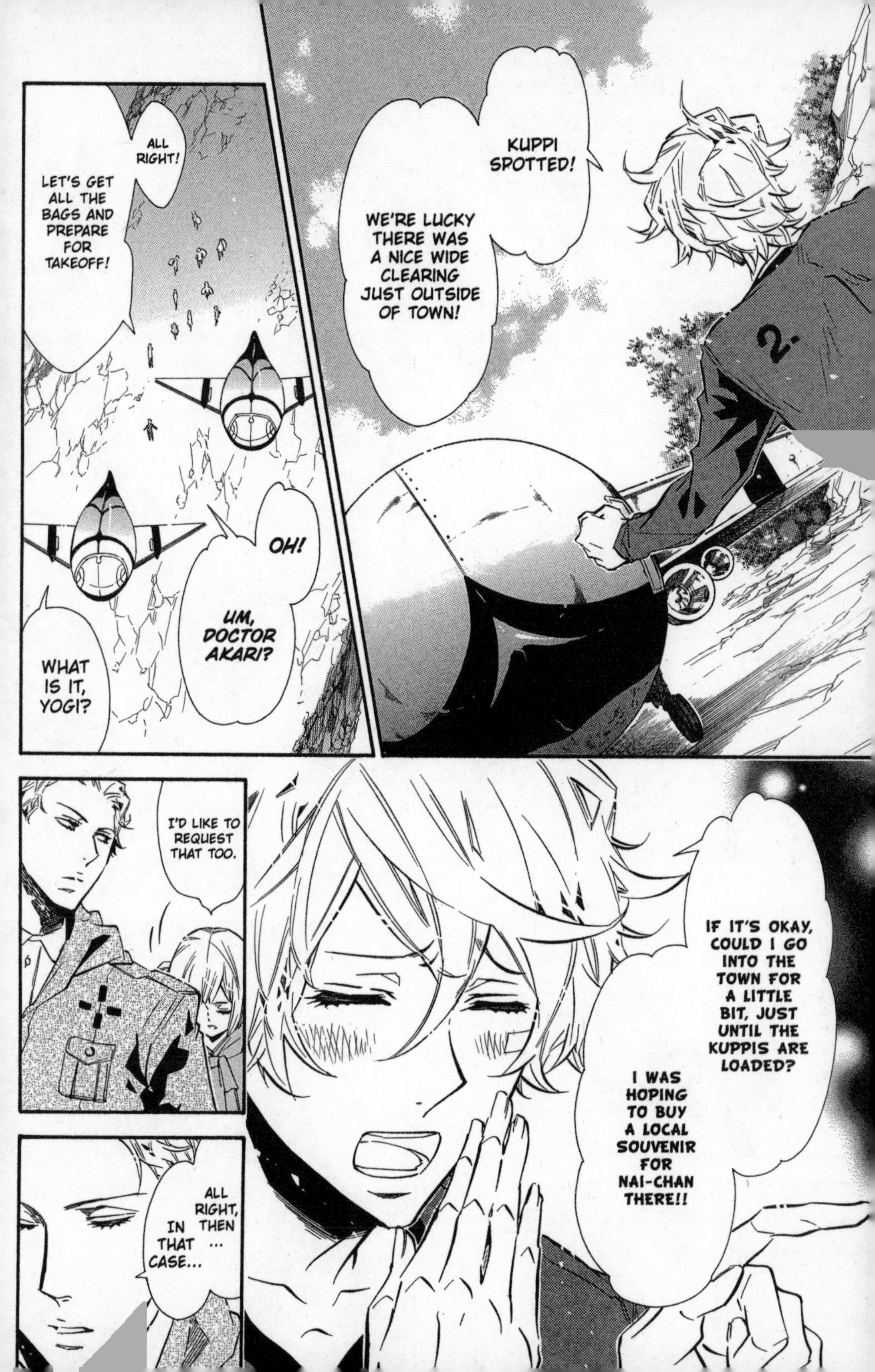
KUPPI SPOTTED!
WE'RE LUCKY THERE WAS A NICE WIDE CLEARING JUST OUTSIDE OF TOWN!
ALL RIGHT!
LET'S GET ALL THE BAGS AND PREPARE FOR TAKEOFF!
OH!
UM, DOCTOR AKARI?
WHAT IS IT, YOGI?
IF IT'S OKAY, COULD I GO INTO THE TOWN FOR A LITTLE BIT, JUST UNTIL THE KUPPIS ARE LOADED?
I WAS HOPING TO BUY A LOCAL SOUVENIR FOR NAI-CHAN THERE!!
I'D LIKE TO REQUEST THAT TOO.
ALL RIGHT, THEN ...
IN THAT CASE...

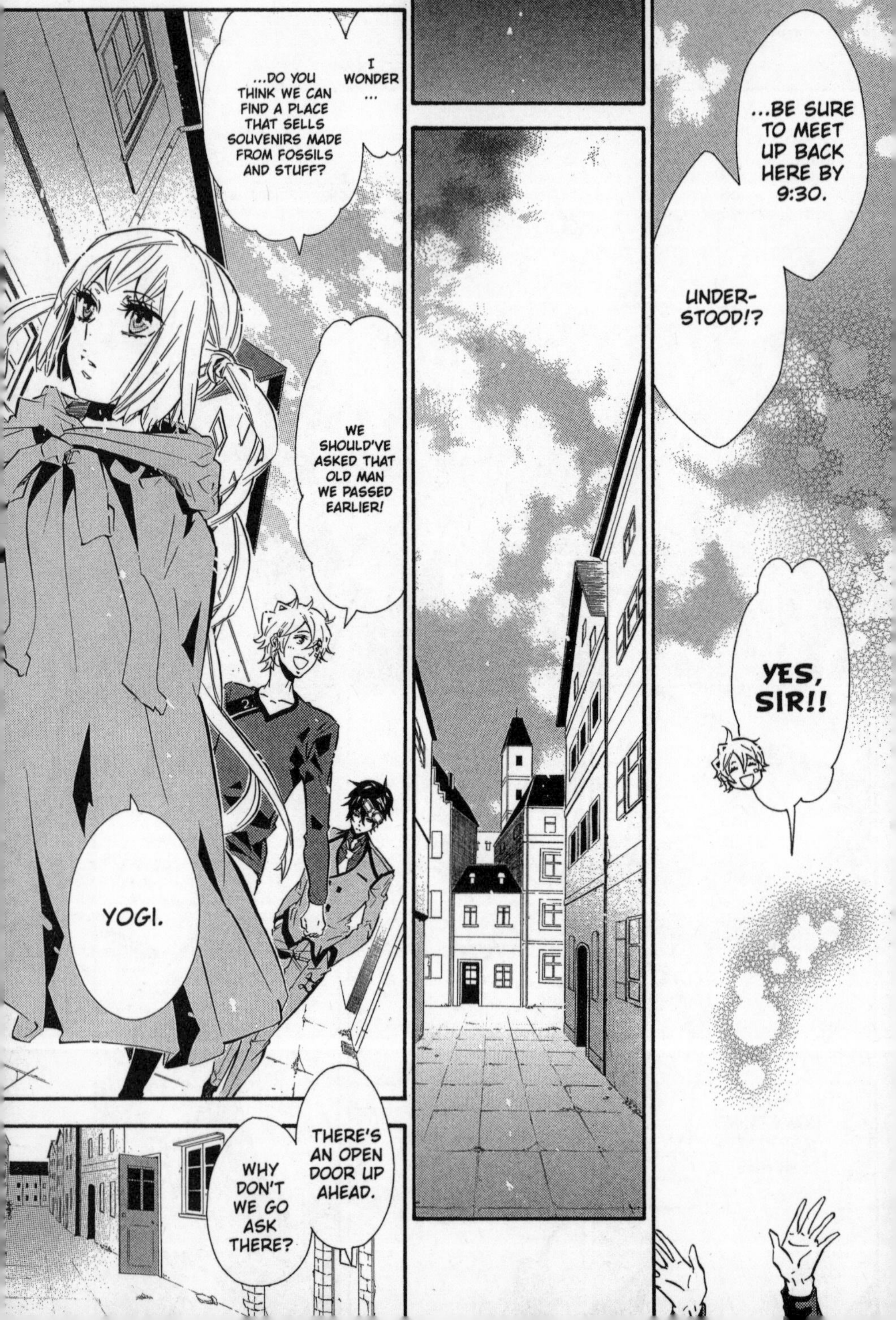
...BE SURE TO MEET UP BACK HERE BY 9:30.
UNDER-STOOD!?
YES, SIR!!
I WONDER ...
...DO YOU THINK WE CAN FIND A PLACE THAT SELLS SOUVENIRS MADE FROM FOSSILS AND STUFF?
WE SHOULD'VE ASKED THAT OLD MAN WE PASSED EARLIER!
YOGI.
THERE'S AN OPEN DOOR UP AHEAD.
WHY DON'T WE GO ASK THERE?

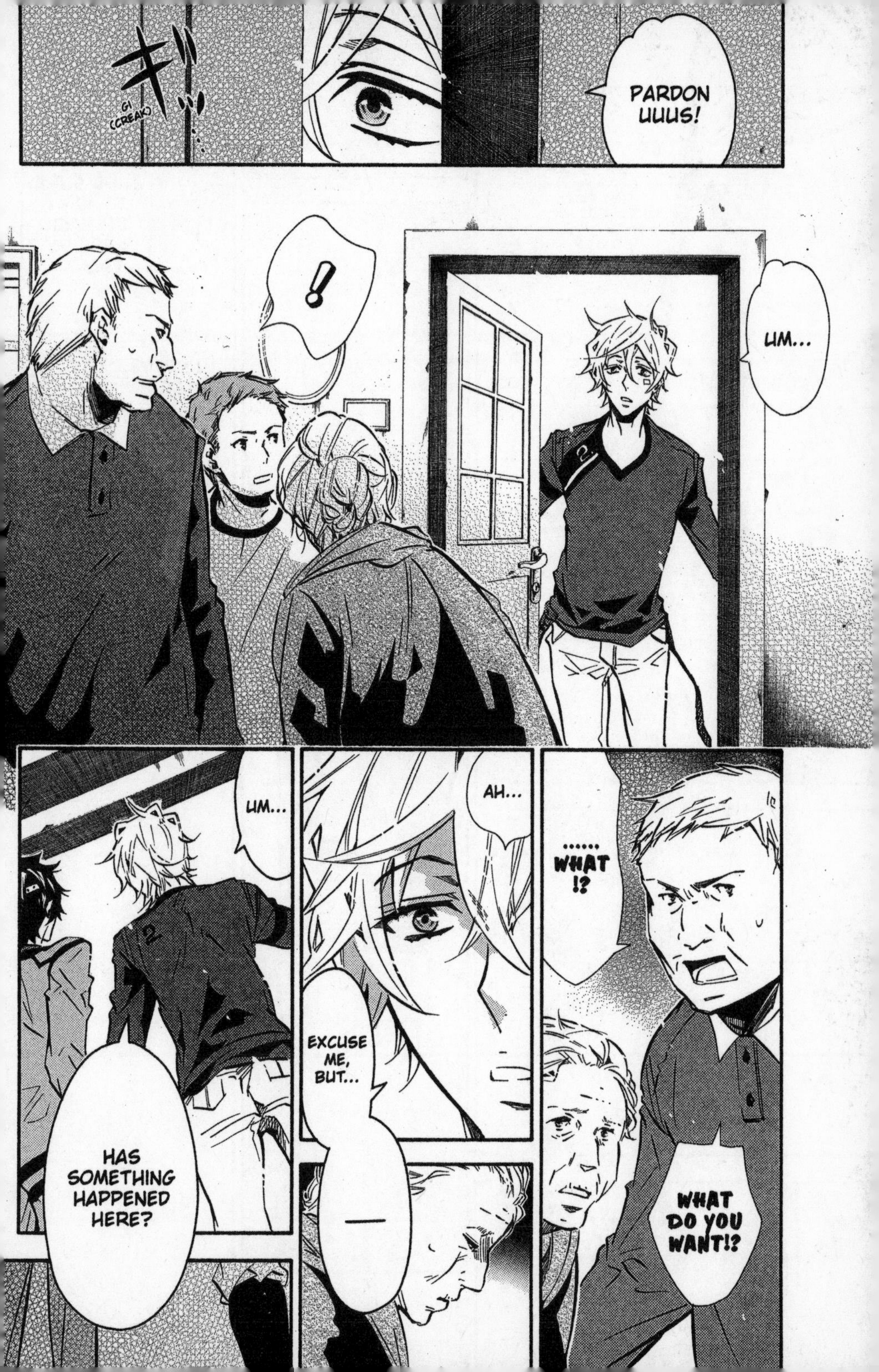
PARDON UUUS!
GI (CREAK)
UM...
!
......WHAT!?
WHAT DO YOU WANT!?
AH...
EXCUSE ME, BUT...
—
UM...
HAS SOMETHING HAPPENED HERE?

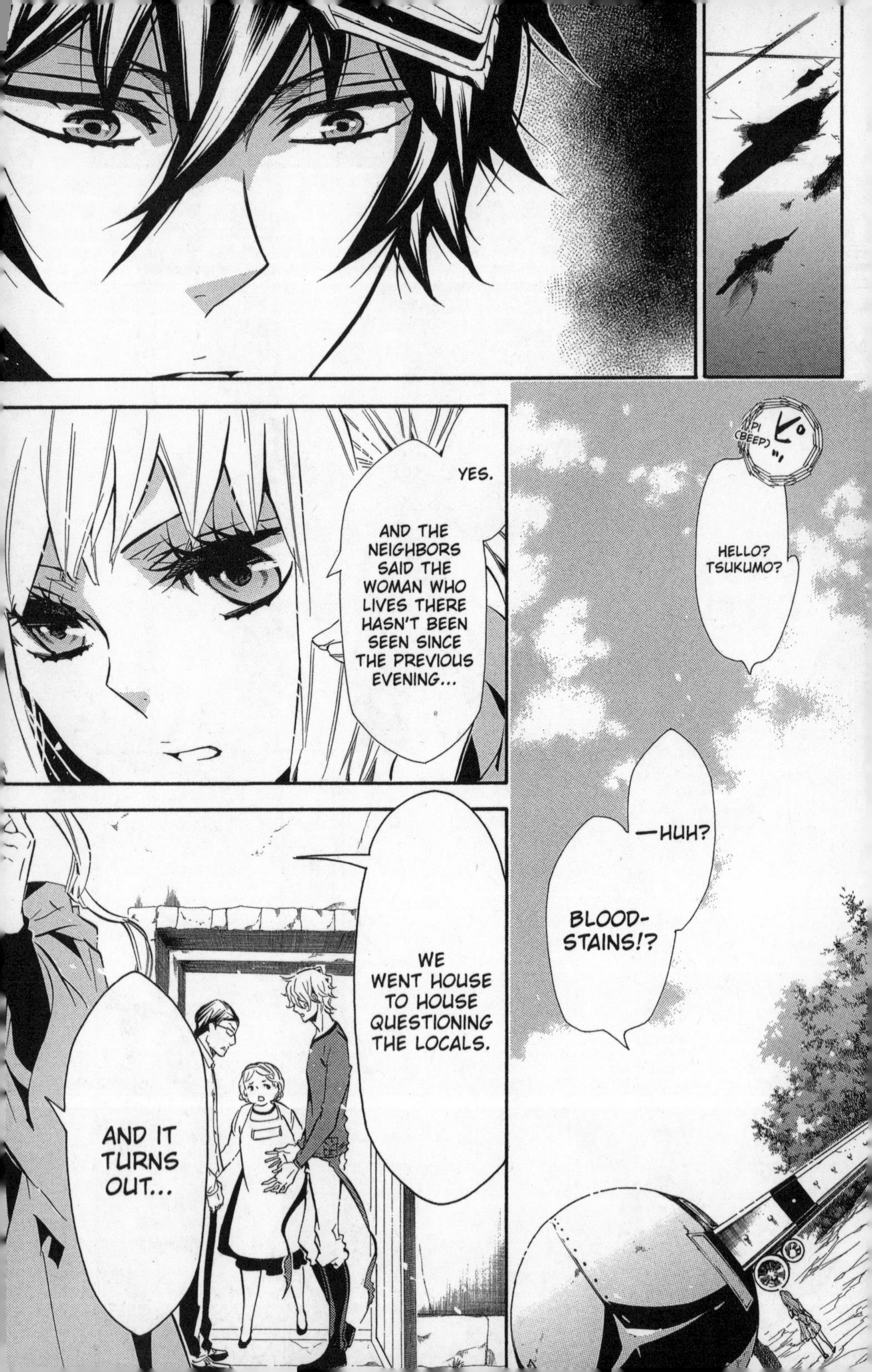
PI
(BEEP)
HELLO? TSUKUMO?
—HUH?
BLOOD-STAINS!?
YES.
AND THE NEIGHBORS SAID THE WOMAN WHO LIVES THERE HASN'T BEEN SEEN SINCE THE PREVIOUS EVENING...
WE WENT HOUSE TO HOUSE QUESTIONING THE LOCALS.
AND IT TURNS OUT...

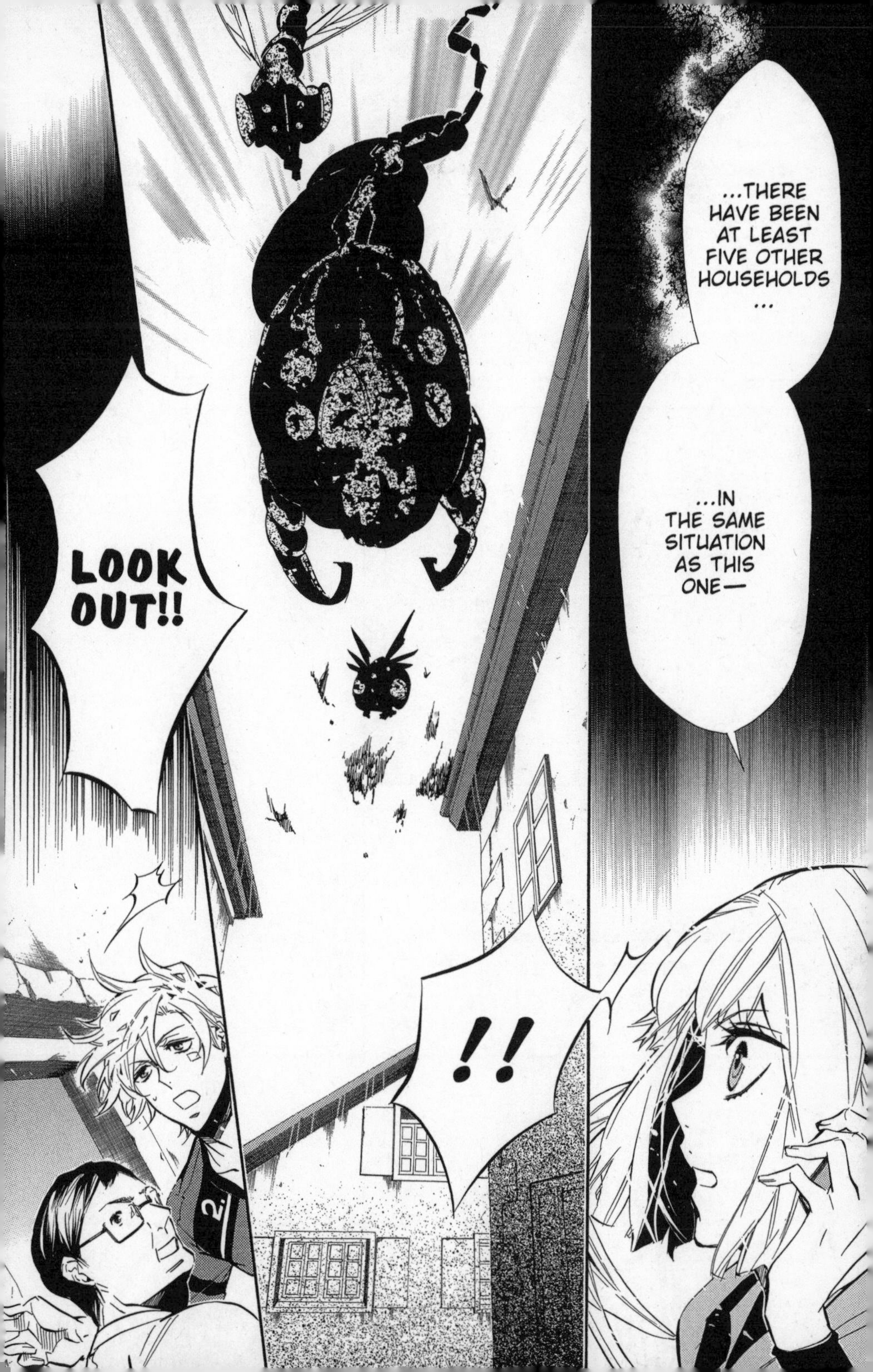
...THERE HAVE BEEN AT LEAST FIVE OTHER HOUSEHOLDS ...
...IN THE SAME SITUATION AS THIS ONE—
LOOK OUT!!
!!

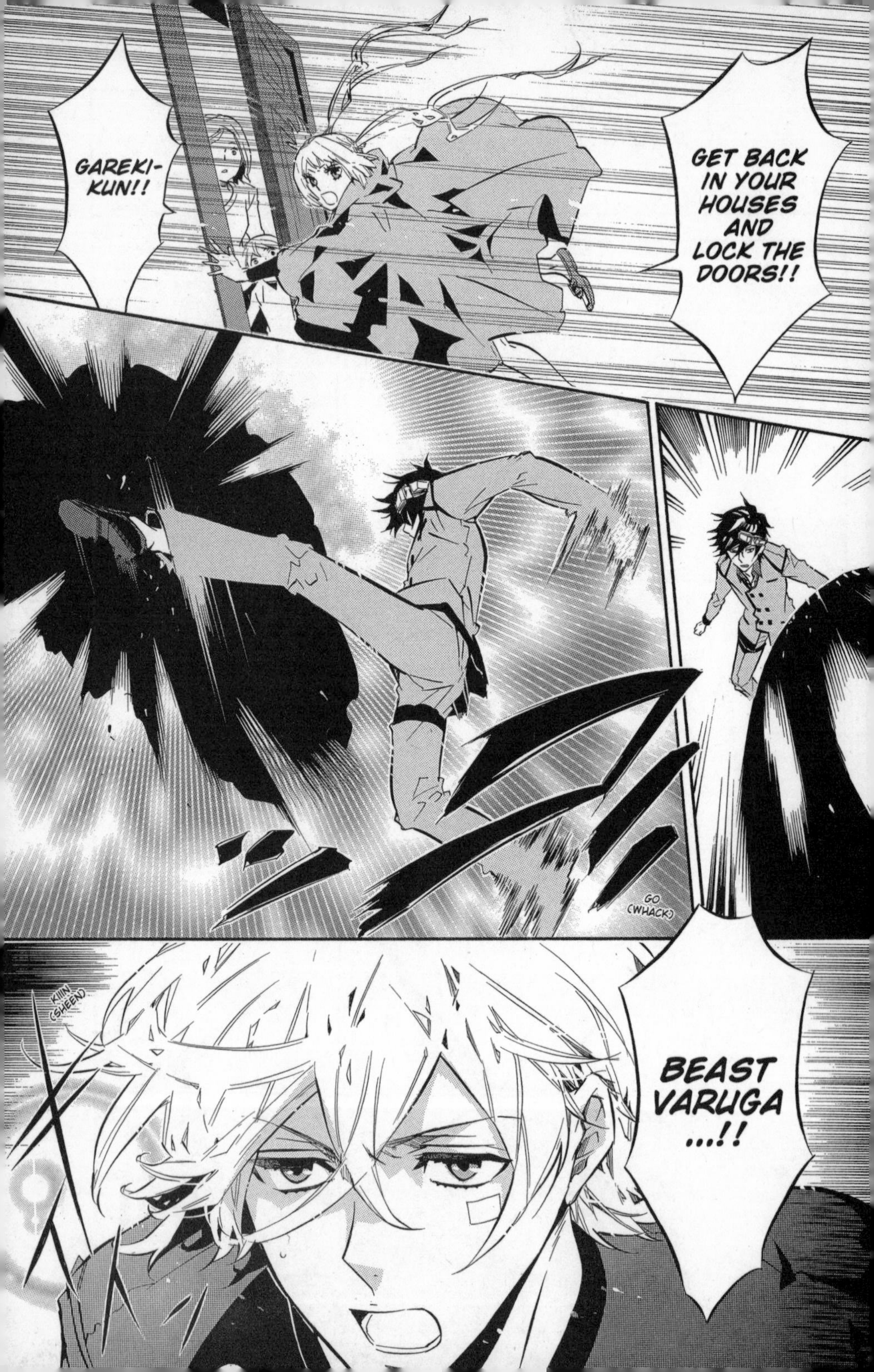
GET BACK IN YOUR HOUSES AND LOCK THE DOORS!!
GAREKI-KUN!!
GO (WHACK)
BEAST VARUGA ...!!
KIIN (SHEEN)

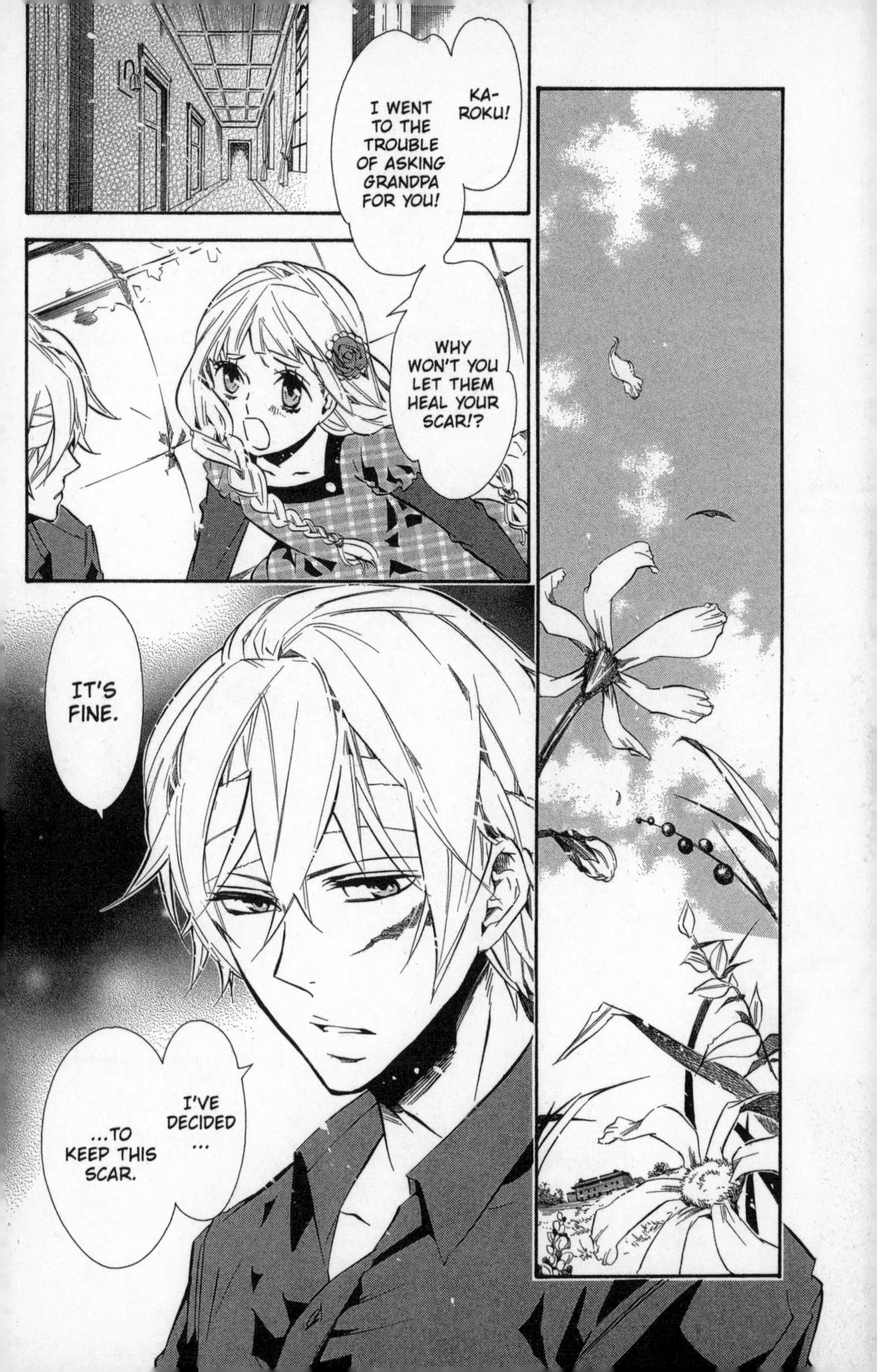
KA-ROKU!
I WENT TO THE TROUBLE OF ASKING GRANDPA FOR YOU!
WHY WON'T YOU LET THEM HEAL YOUR SCAR!?
IT'S FINE.
I'VE DECIDED ...
...TO KEEP THIS SCAR.

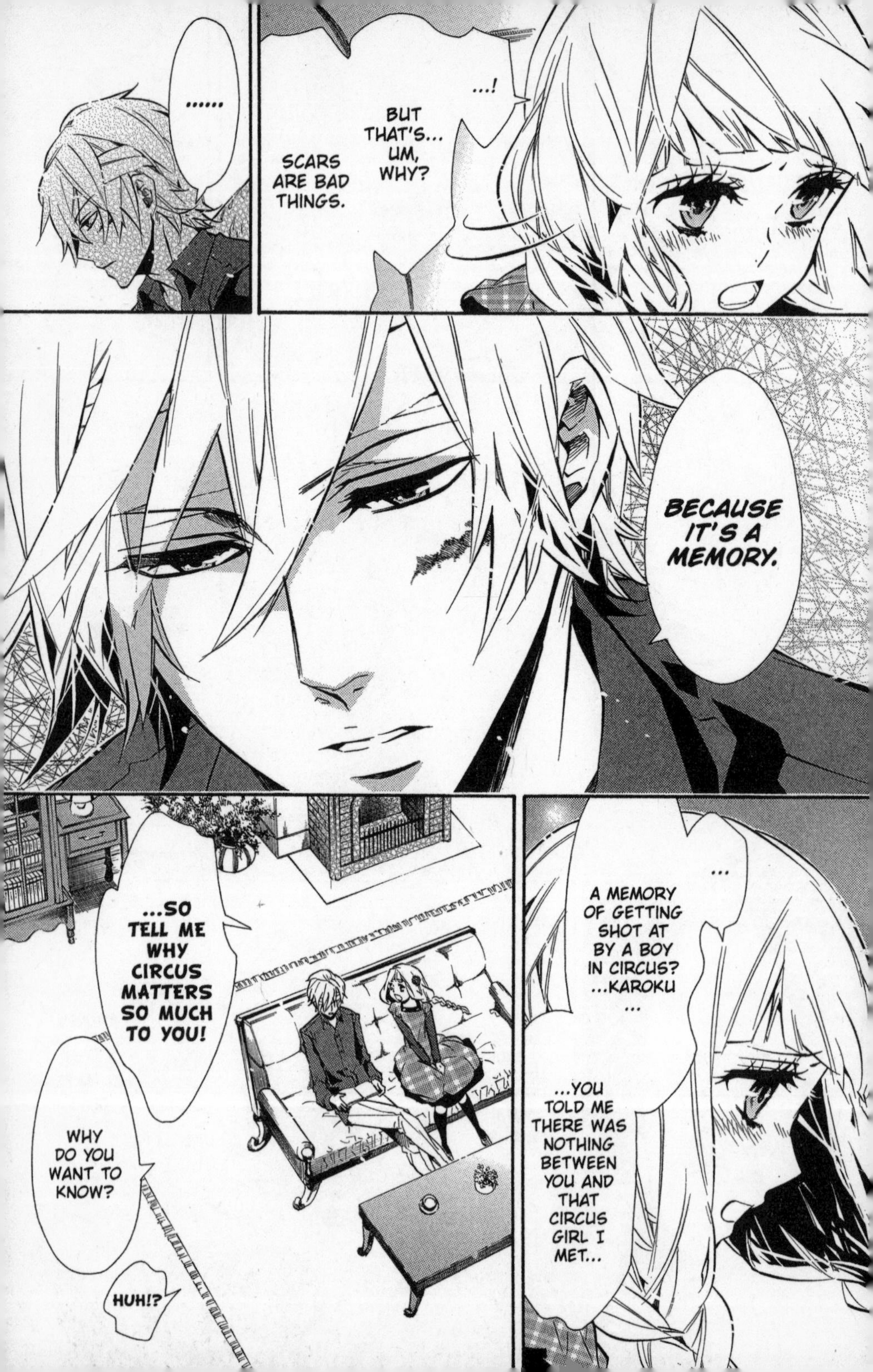

...!
BUT THAT'S... UM, WHY?
SCARS ARE BAD THINGS.
......
BECAUSE IT'S A MEMORY.
...
A MEMORY OF GETTING SHOT AT BY A BOY IN CIRCUS? ...KAROKU ...
...YOU TOLD ME THERE WAS NOTHING BETWEEN YOU AND THAT CIRCUS GIRL I MET...
...SO TELL ME WHY CIRCUS MATTERS SO MUCH TO YOU!
WHY DO YOU WANT TO KNOW?
HUH!?

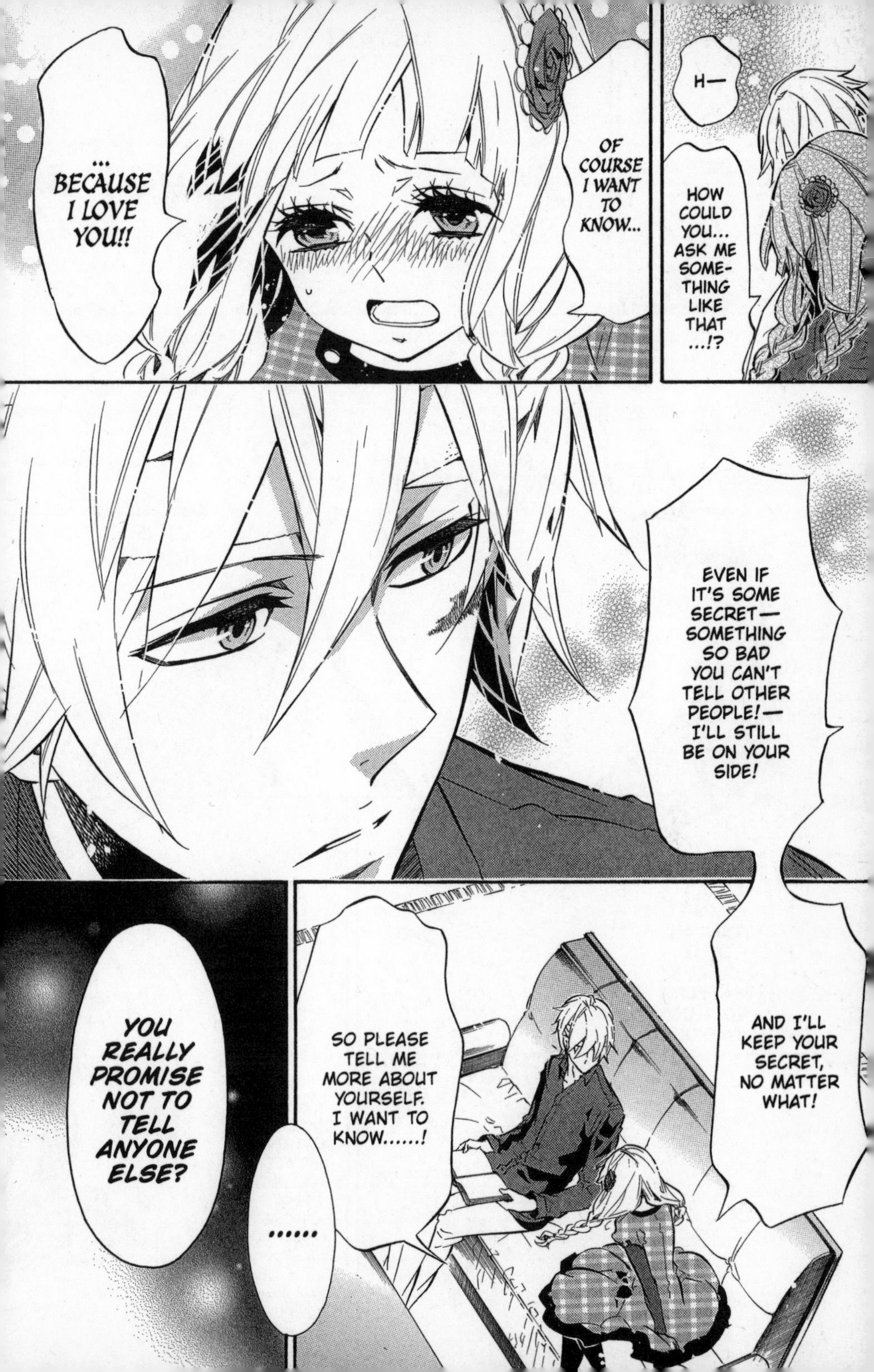
H—
HOW COULD YOU... ASK ME SOME-THING LIKE THAT ...!?
OF COURSE I WANT TO KNOW...
...BECAUSE I LOVE YOU!!
EVEN IF IT'S SOME SECRET—SOMETHING SO BAD YOU CAN'T TELL OTHER PEOPLE!—I'LL STILL BE ON YOUR SIDE!
AND I'LL KEEP YOUR SECRET, NO MATTER WHAT!
SO PLEASE TELL ME MORE ABOUT YOURSELF. I WANT TO KNOW......!
YOU REALLY PROMISE NOT TO TELL ANYONE ELSE?
......

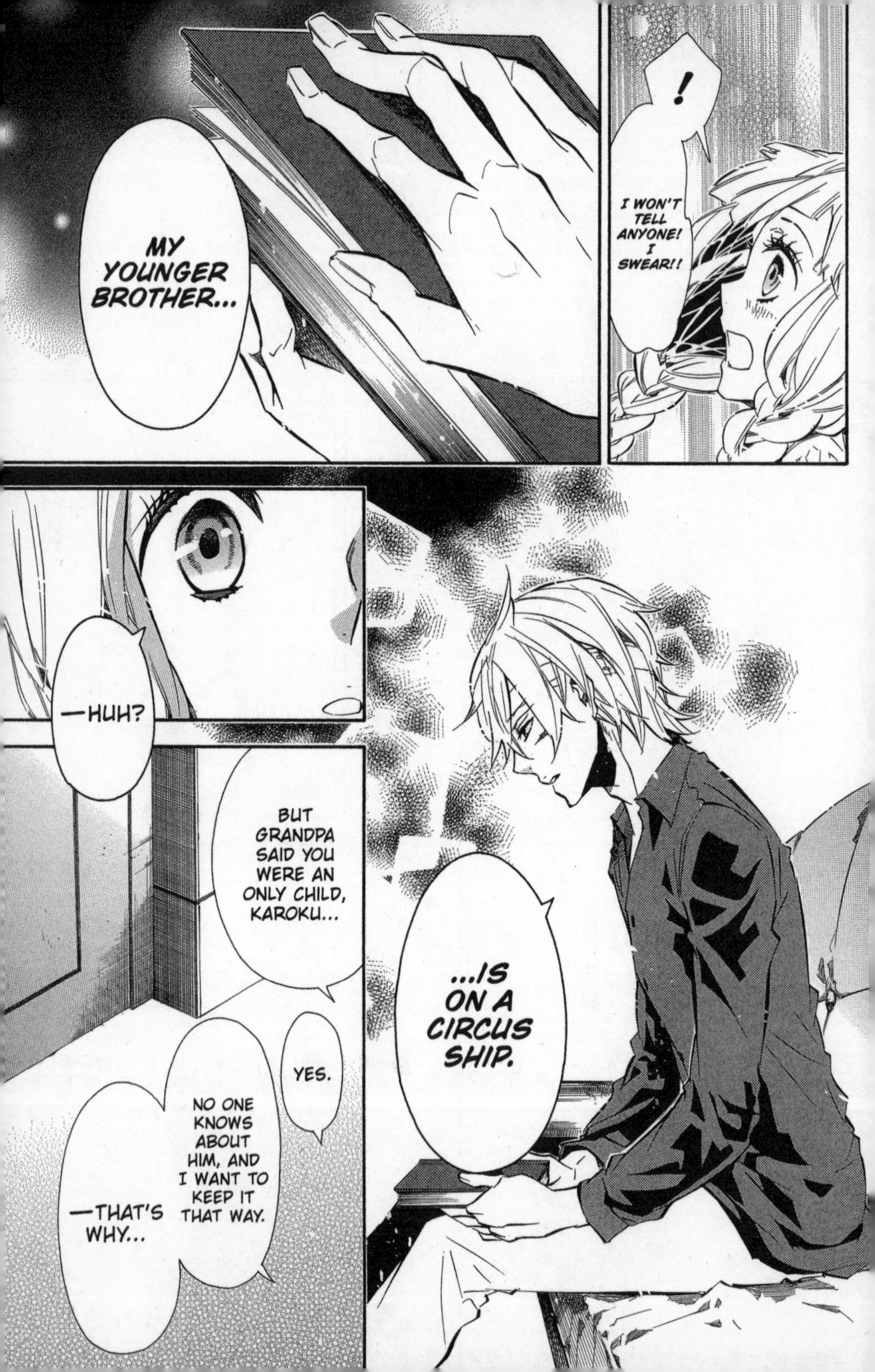
!
I WON'T TELL ANYONE! I SWEAR!!
MY YOUNGER BROTHER...
...IS ON A CIRCUS SHIP.
—HUH?
BUT GRANDPA SAID YOU WERE AN ONLY CHILD, KAROKU...
YES.
NO ONE KNOWS ABOUT HIM, AND I WANT TO KEEP IT THAT WAY.
—THAT'S WHY...

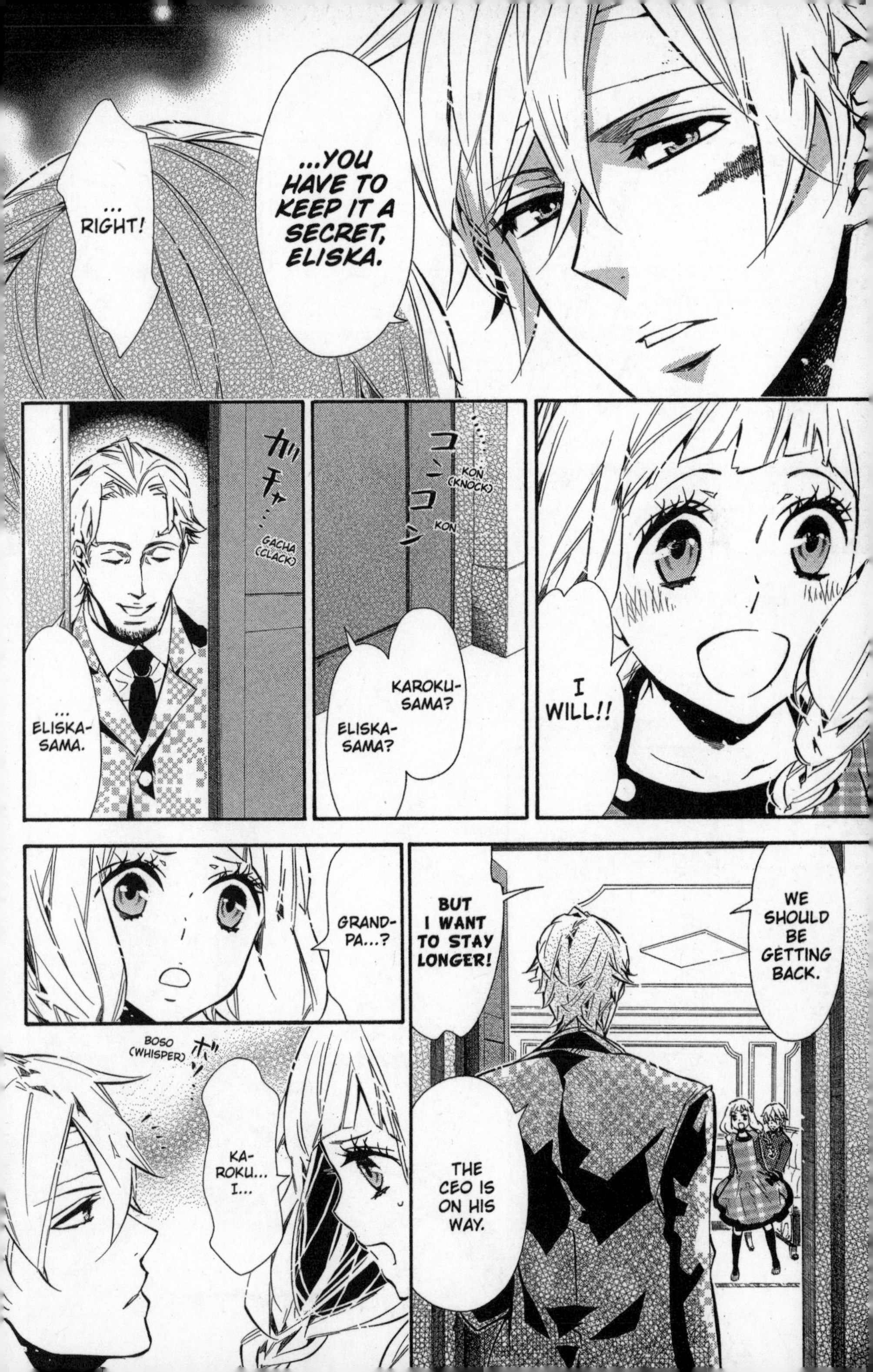
...YOU HAVE TO KEEP IT A SECRET, ELISKA.
...RIGHT!
I WILL!!
KON (KNOCK)
KON
KAROKU-SAMA?
ELISKA-SAMA?
GACHA (CLACK)
...ELISKA-SAMA.
WE SHOULD BE GETTING BACK.
BUT I WANT TO STAY LONGER!
THE CEO IS ON HIS WAY.
GRAND-PA...?
BOSO (WHISPER)
KA-ROKU... I...

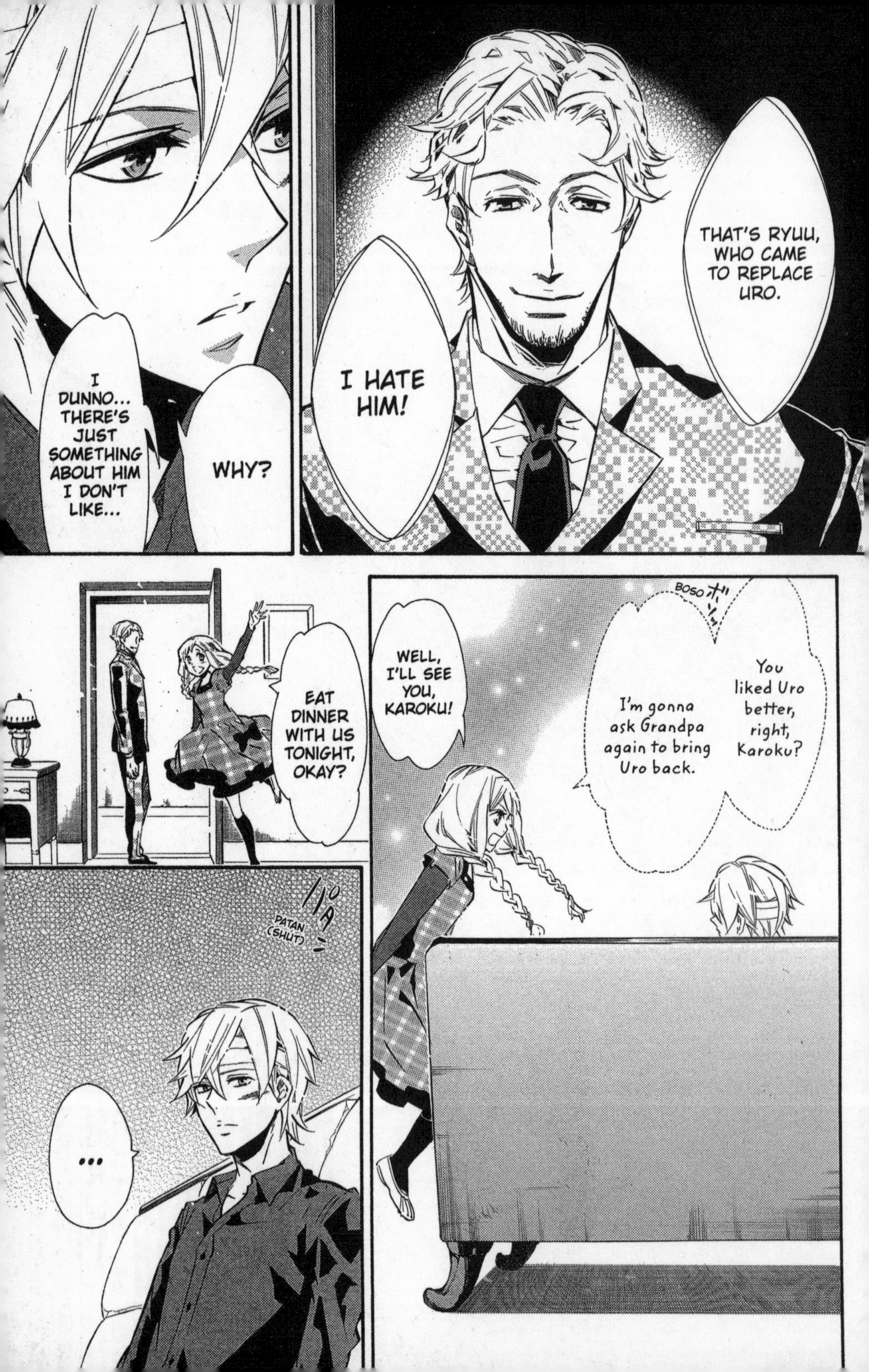
THAT'S RYUU, WHO CAME TO REPLACE URO.
I HATE HIM!
WHY?
I DUNNO... THERE'S JUST SOMETHING ABOUT HIM I DON'T LIKE...
BOSO
You liked Uro better, right, Karoku?
I'm gonna ask Grandpa again to bring Uro back.
WELL, I'LL SEE YOU, KAROKU!
EAT DINNER WITH US TONIGHT, OKAY?
PATAN (SHUT)
...

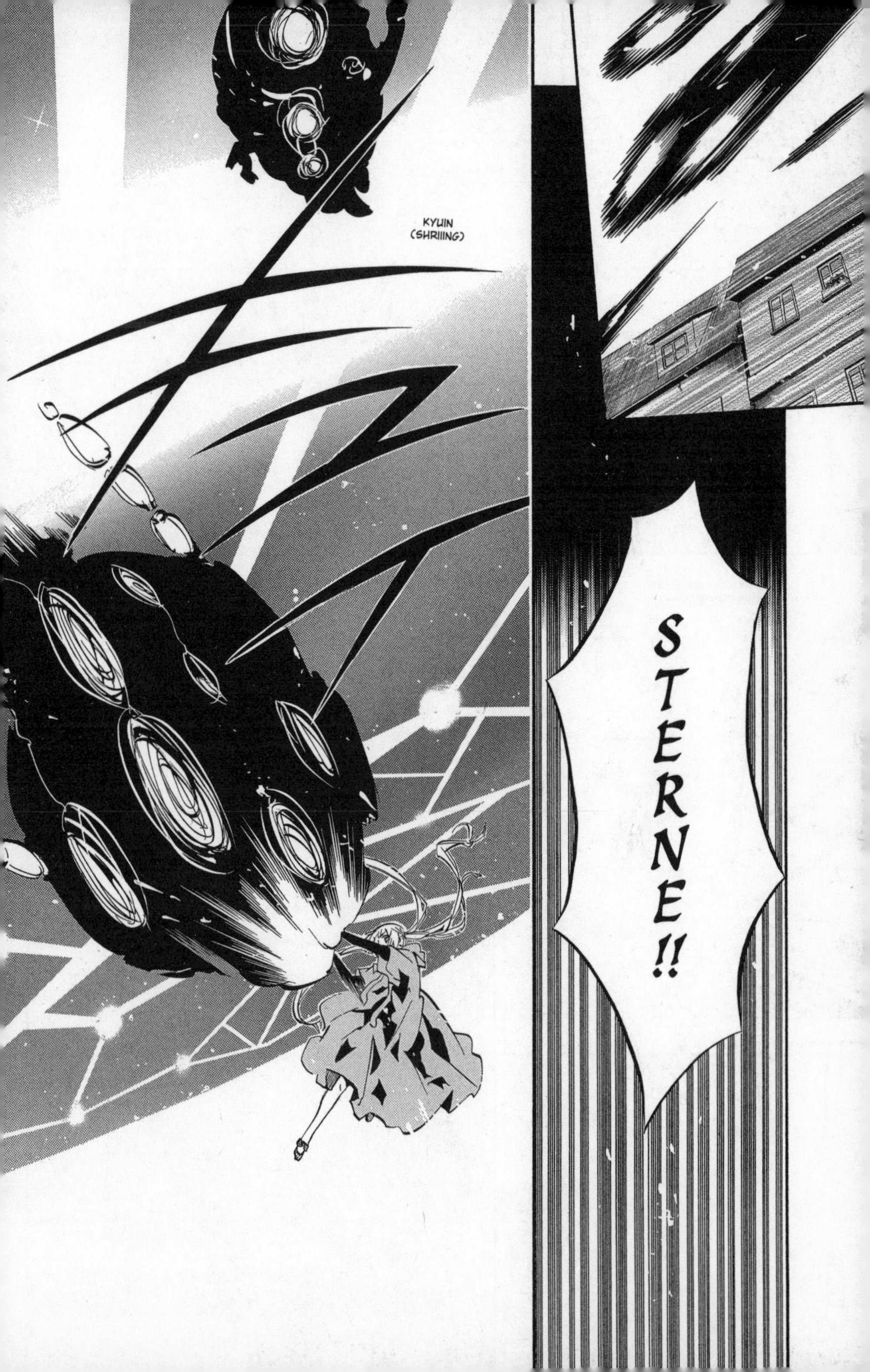
STERNE!!
KYUIN
(SHRIIING)

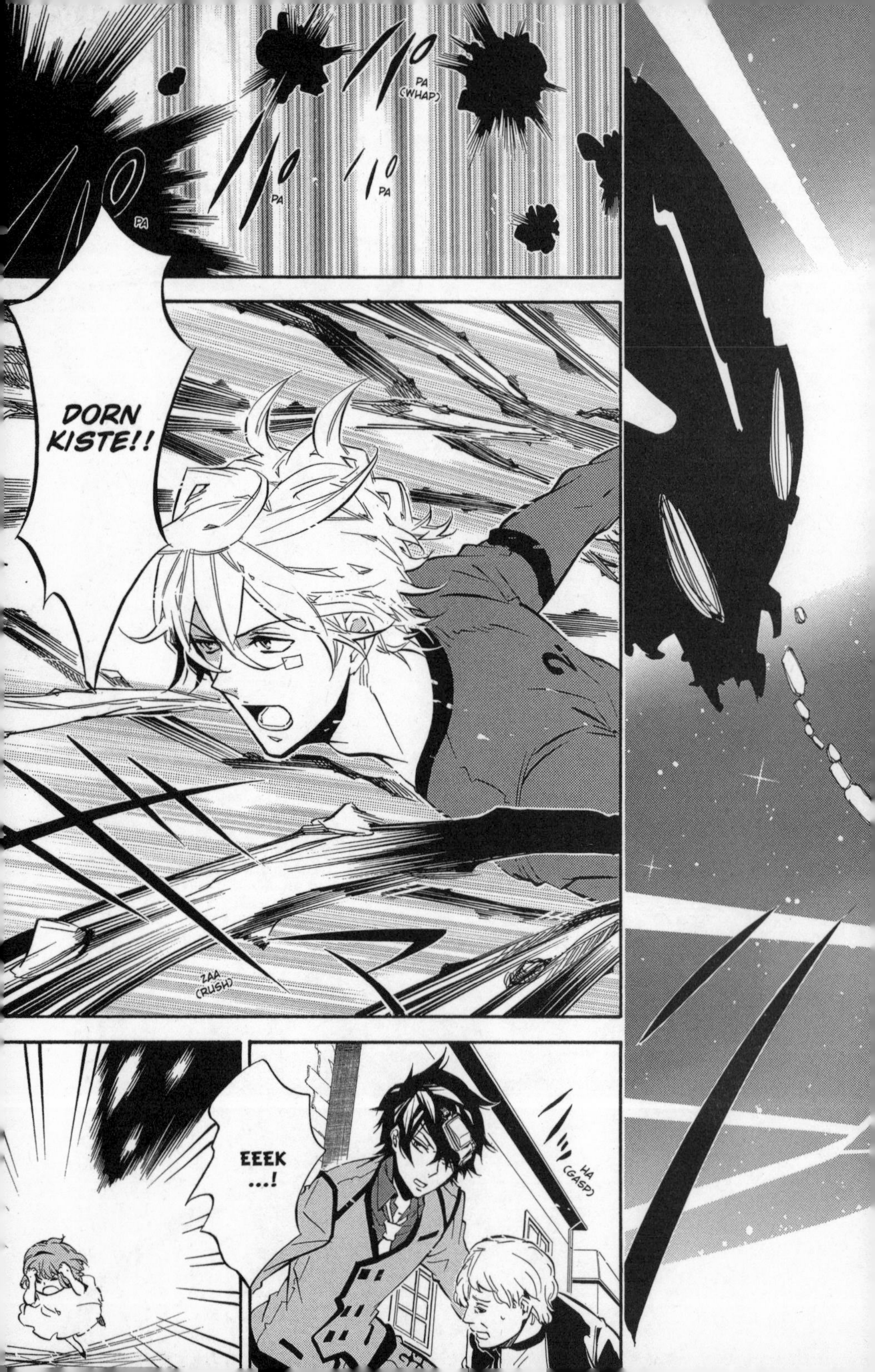
PA
(WHAP)
PA
PA
PA
DORN KISTE!!
ZAA
(RUSH)
HA
(GASP)
EEEK ...!

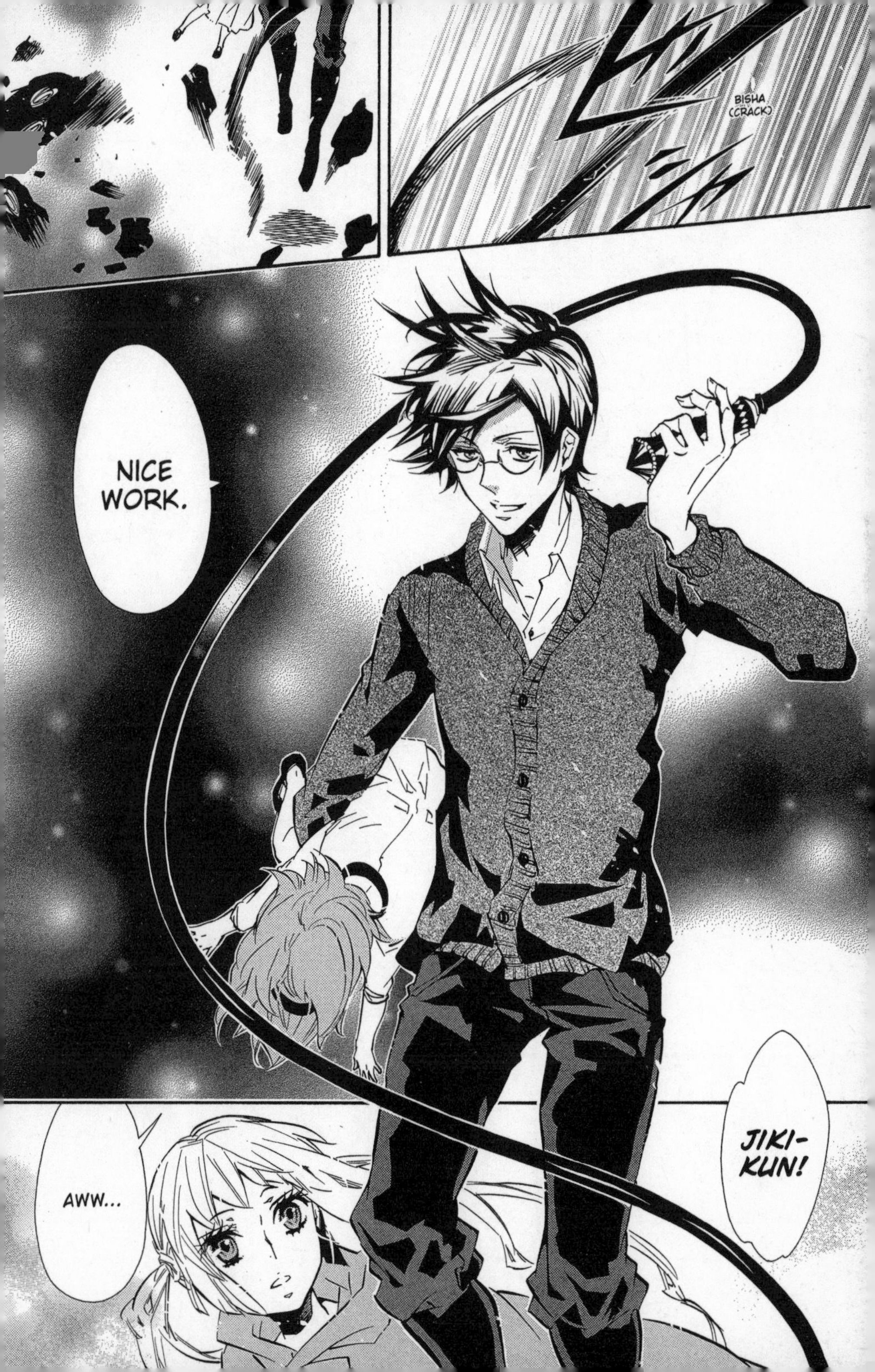
BISHA (CRACK)
NICE WORK.
JIKI-KUN!
AWW...

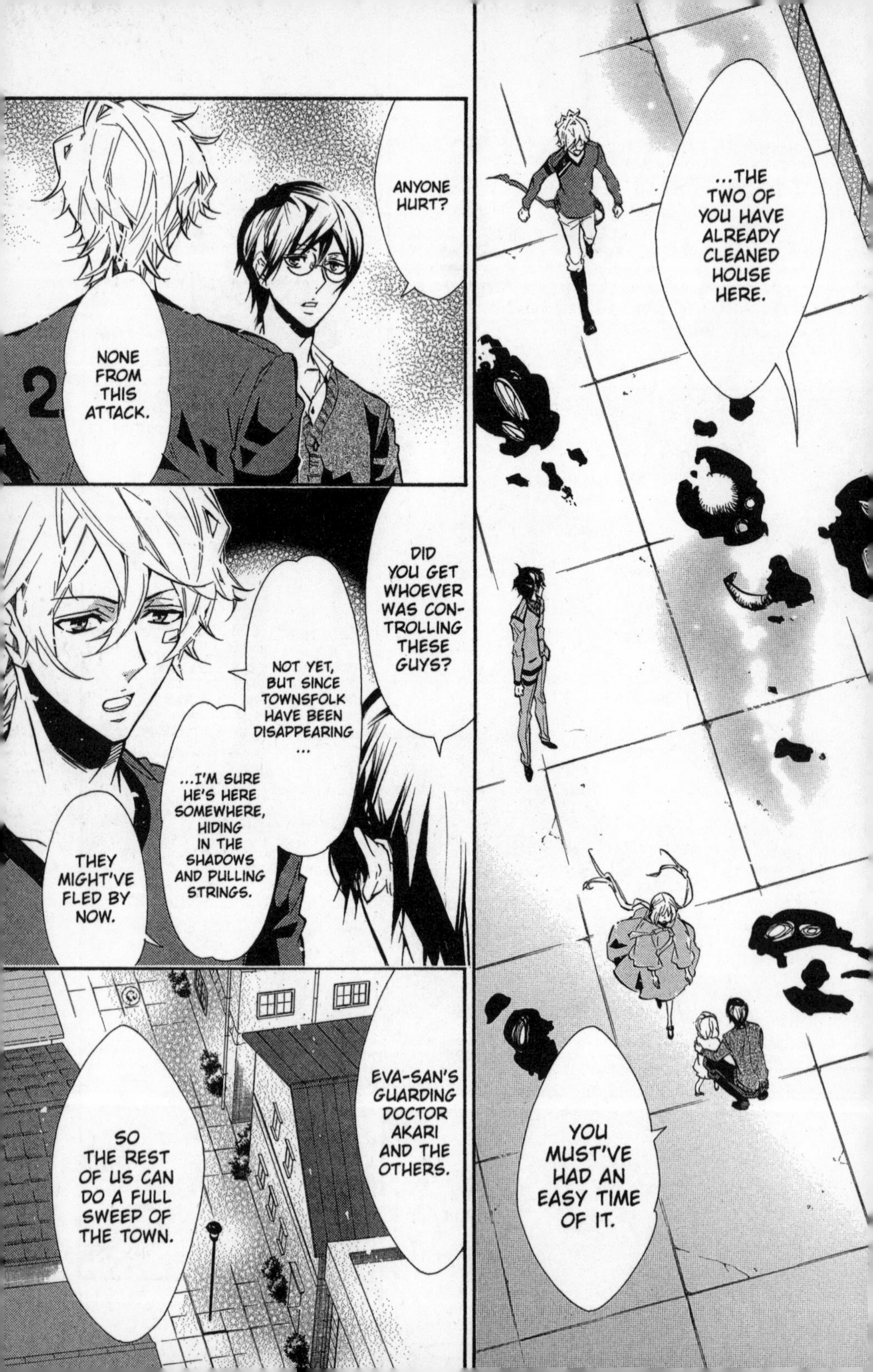
...THE TWO OF YOU HAVE ALREADY CLEANED HOUSE HERE.
YOU MUST'VE HAD AN EASY TIME OF IT.
ANYONE HURT?
NONE FROM THIS ATTACK.
DID YOU GET WHOEVER WAS CON-TROLLING THESE GUYS?
NOT YET, BUT SINCE TOWNSFOLK HAVE BEEN DISAPPEARING ...
...I'M SURE HE'S HERE SOMEWHERE, HIDING IN THE SHADOWS AND PULLING STRINGS.
THEY MIGHT'VE FLED BY NOW.
EVA-SAN'S GUARDING DOCTOR AKARI AND THE OTHERS.
SO THE REST OF US CAN DO A FULL SWEEP OF THE TOWN.

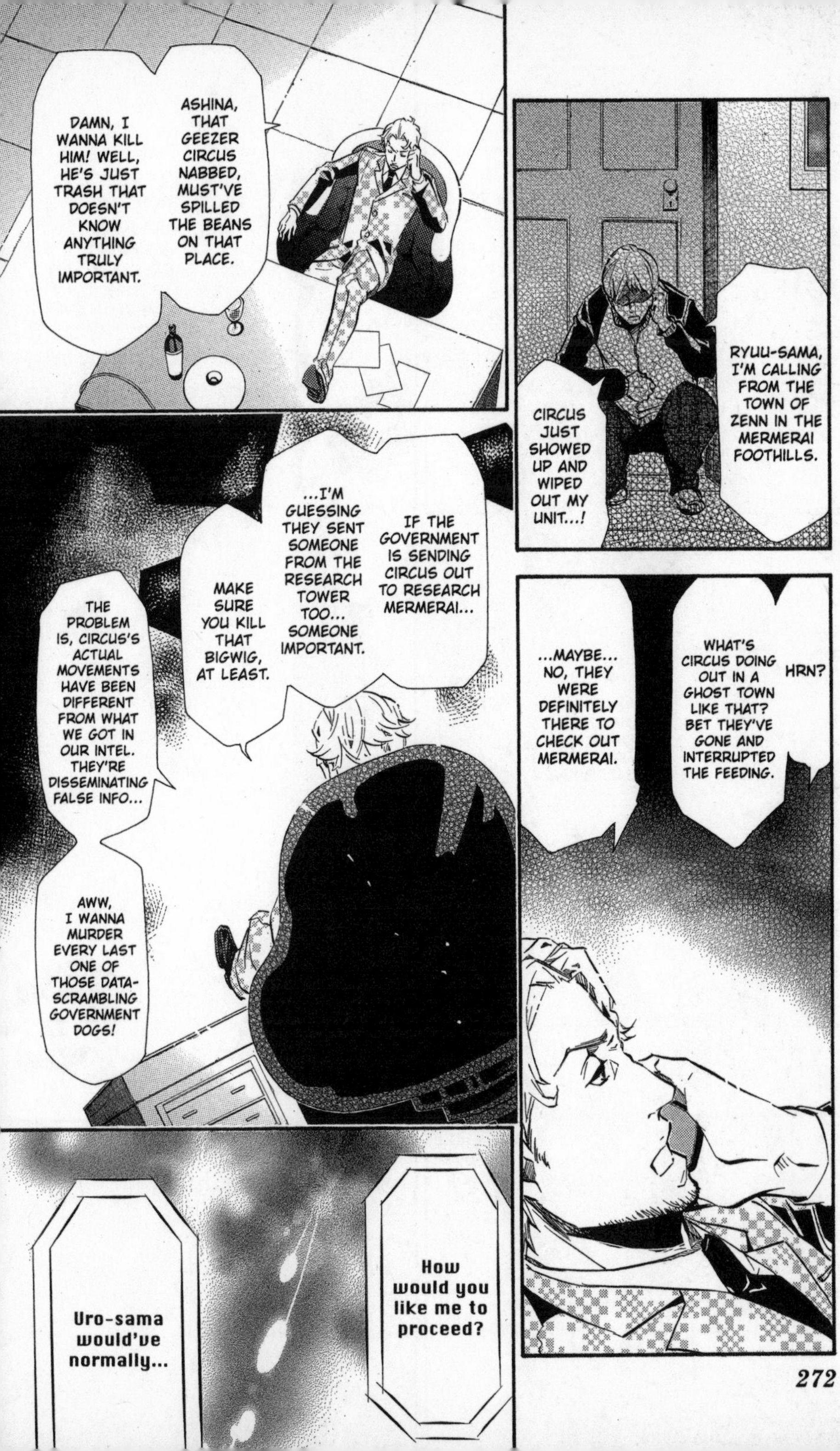
RYUU-SAMA, I'M CALLING FROM THE TOWN OF ZENN IN THE MERMERAI FOOTHILLS.
CIRCUS JUST SHOWED UP AND WIPED OUT MY UNIT...!
ASHINA, THAT GEEZER CIRCUS NABBED, MUST'VE SPILLED THE BEANS ON THAT PLACE.
DAMN, I WANNA KILL HIM! WELL, HE'S JUST TRASH THAT DOESN'T KNOW ANYTHING TRULY IMPORTANT.
HRN?
WHAT'S CIRCUS DOING OUT IN A GHOST TOWN LIKE THAT? BET THEY'VE GONE AND INTERRUPTED THE FEEDING.
...MAYBE... NO, THEY WERE DEFINITELY THERE TO CHECK OUT MERMERAI.
IF THE GOVERNMENT IS SENDING CIRCUS OUT TO RESEARCH MERMERAI...
...I'M GUESSING THEY SENT SOMEONE FROM THE RESEARCH TOWER TOO... SOMEONE IMPORTANT.
MAKE SURE YOU KILL THAT BIGWIG, AT LEAST.
THE PROBLEM IS, CIRCUS'S ACTUAL MOVEMENTS HAVE BEEN DIFFERENT FROM WHAT WE GOT IN OUR INTEL. THEY'RE DISSEMINATING FALSE INFO...
AWW, I WANNA MURDER EVERY LAST ONE OF THOSE DATA-SCRAMBLING GOVERNMENT DOGS!
How would you like me to proceed?
Uro-sama would've normally...

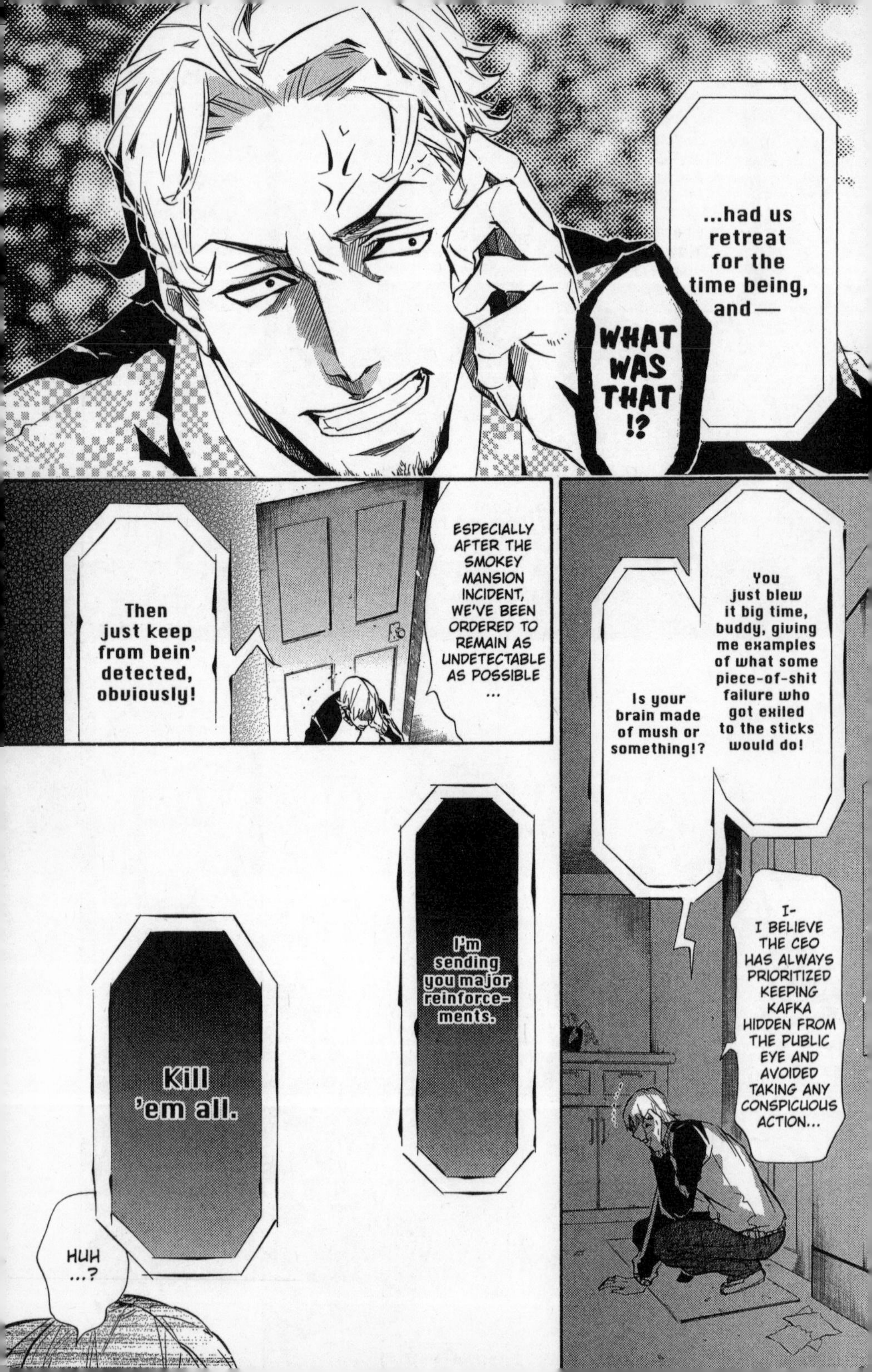
...had us retreat for the time being, and—
WHAT WAS THAT !?
You just blew it big time, buddy, giving me examples of what some piece-of-shit failure who got exiled to the sticks would do!
Is your brain made of mush or something!?
I- I BELIEVE THE CEO HAS ALWAYS PRIORITIZED KEEPING KAFKA HIDDEN FROM THE PUBLIC EYE AND AVOIDED TAKING ANY CONSPICUOUS ACTION...
ESPECIALLY AFTER THE SMOKEY MANSION INCIDENT, WE'VE BEEN ORDERED TO REMAIN AS UNDETECTABLE AS POSSIBLE ...
Then just keep from bein' detected, obviously!
I'm sending you major reinforcements.
Kill 'em all.
HUH ...?

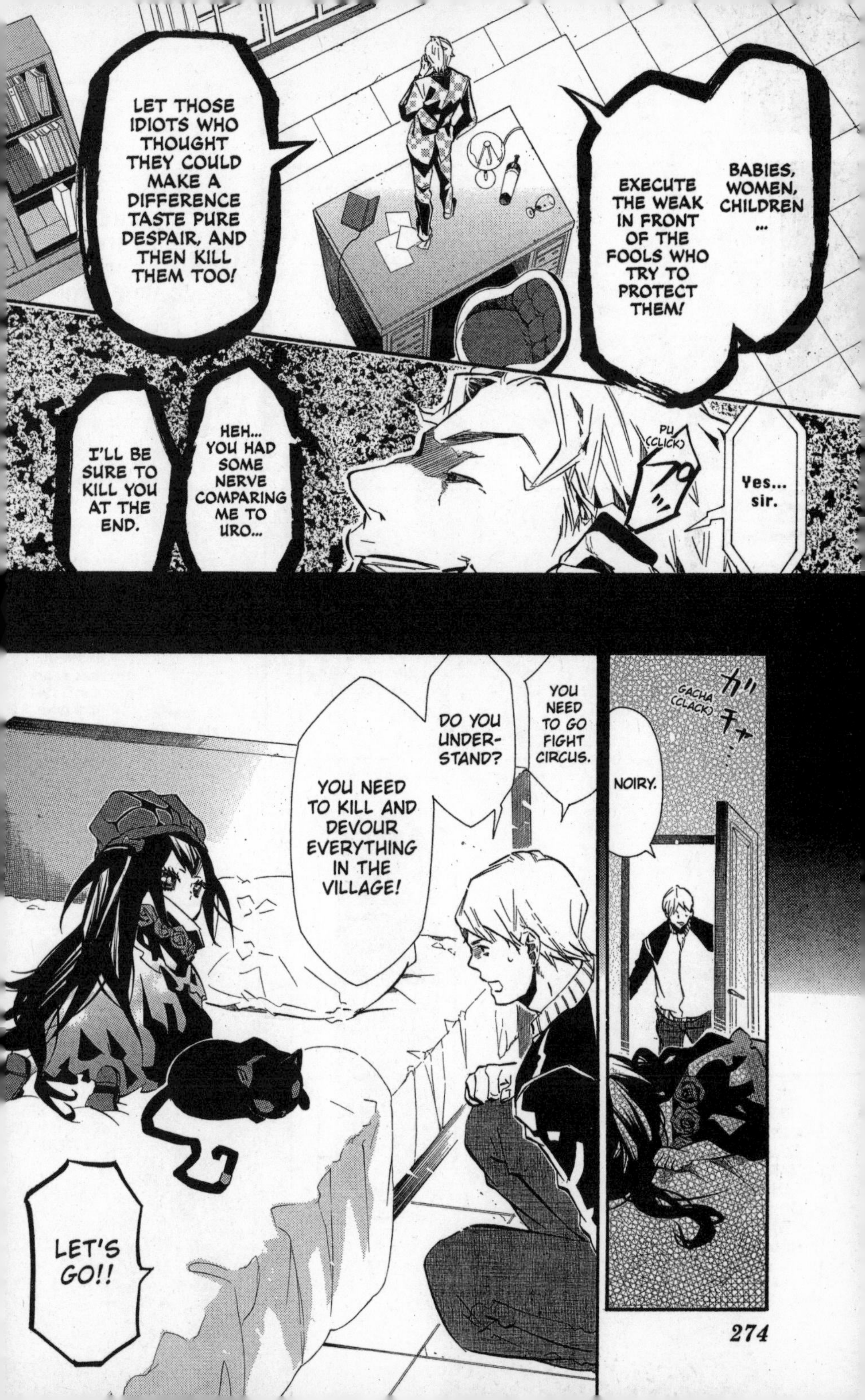
BABIES, WOMEN, CHILDREN ...
EXECUTE THE WEAK IN FRONT OF THE FOOLS WHO TRY TO PROTECT THEM!
LET THOSE IDIOTS WHO THOUGHT THEY COULD MAKE A DIFFERENCE TASTE PURE DESPAIR, AND THEN KILL THEM TOO!
Yes... sir.
PU (CLICK)
HEH... YOU HAD SOME NERVE COMPARING ME TO URO...
I'LL BE SURE TO KILL YOU AT THE END.
GACHA (CLACK)
NOIRY.
YOU NEED TO GO FIGHT CIRCUS.
DO YOU UNDER-STAND?
YOU NEED TO KILL AND DEVOUR EVERYTHING IN THE VILLAGE!
LET'S GO!!

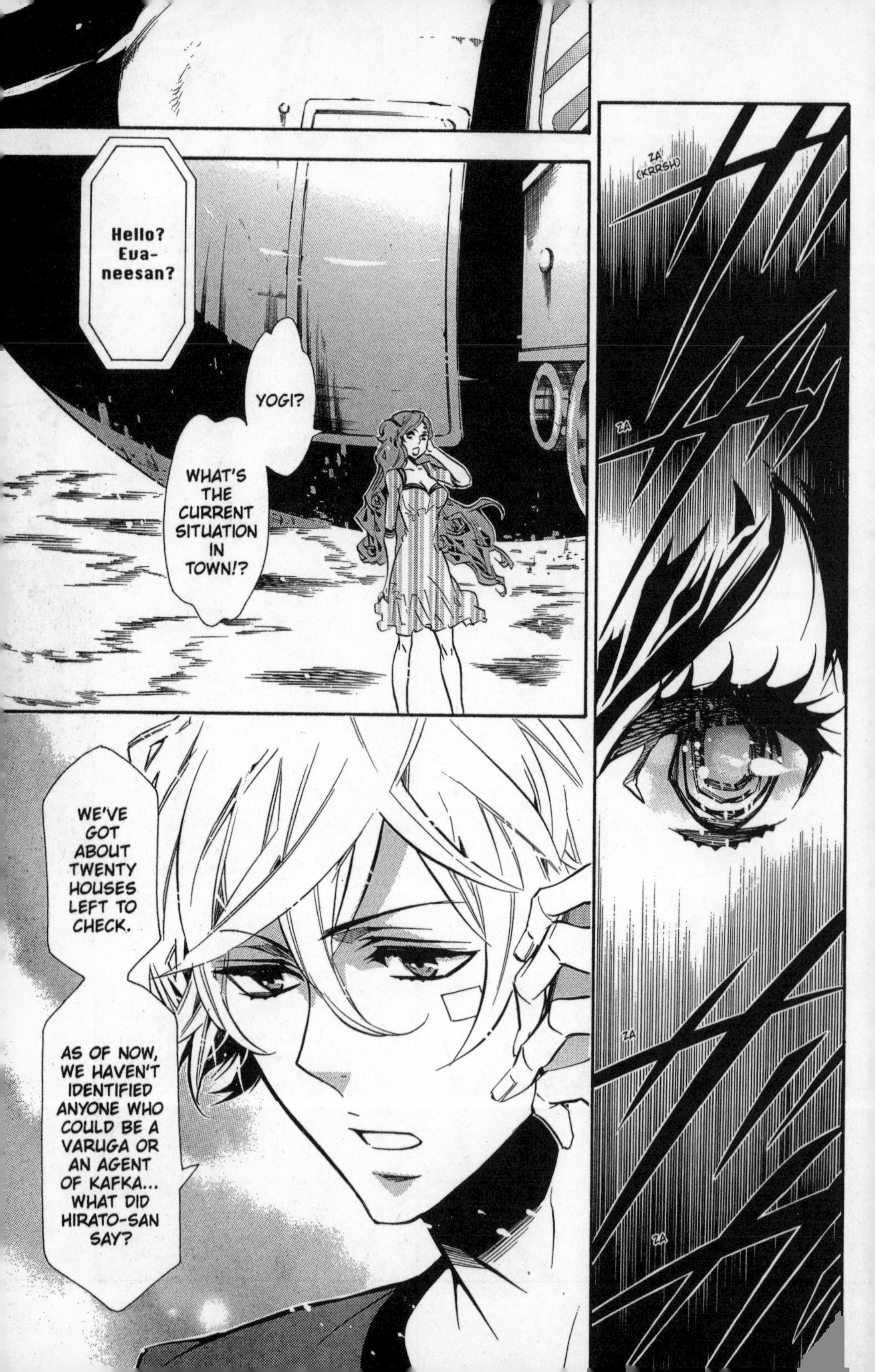
ZA (KRRSH)
ZA
ZA
ZA
Hello? Eva-neesan?
YOGI?
WHAT'S THE CURRENT SITUATION IN TOWN!?
WE'VE GOT ABOUT TWENTY HOUSES LEFT TO CHECK.
AS OF NOW, WE HAVEN'T IDENTIFIED ANYONE WHO COULD BE A VARUGA OR AN AGENT OF KAFKA... WHAT DID HIRATO-SAN SAY?

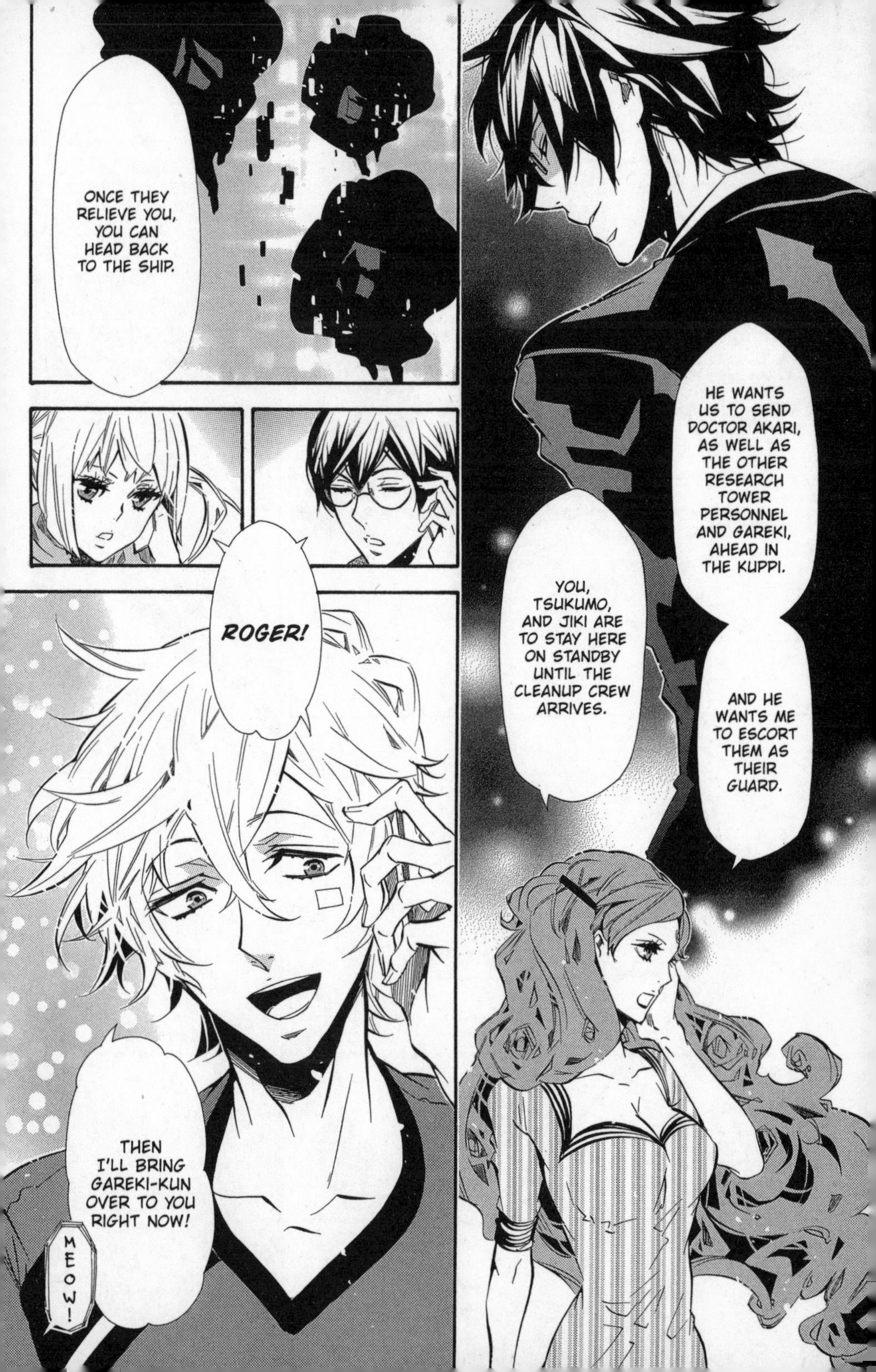
HE WANTS US TO SEND DOCTOR AKARI, AS WELL AS THE OTHER RESEARCH TOWER PERSONNEL AND GAREKI, AHEAD IN THE KUPPI.
AND HE WANTS ME TO ESCORT THEM AS THEIR GUARD.
YOU, TSUKUMO, AND JIKI ARE TO STAY HERE ON STANDBY UNTIL THE CLEANUP CREW ARRIVES.
ONCE THEY RELIEVE YOU, YOU CAN HEAD BACK TO THE SHIP.
ROGER!
THEN I'LL BRING GAREKI-KUN OVER TO YOU RIGHT NOW!
MEOW!

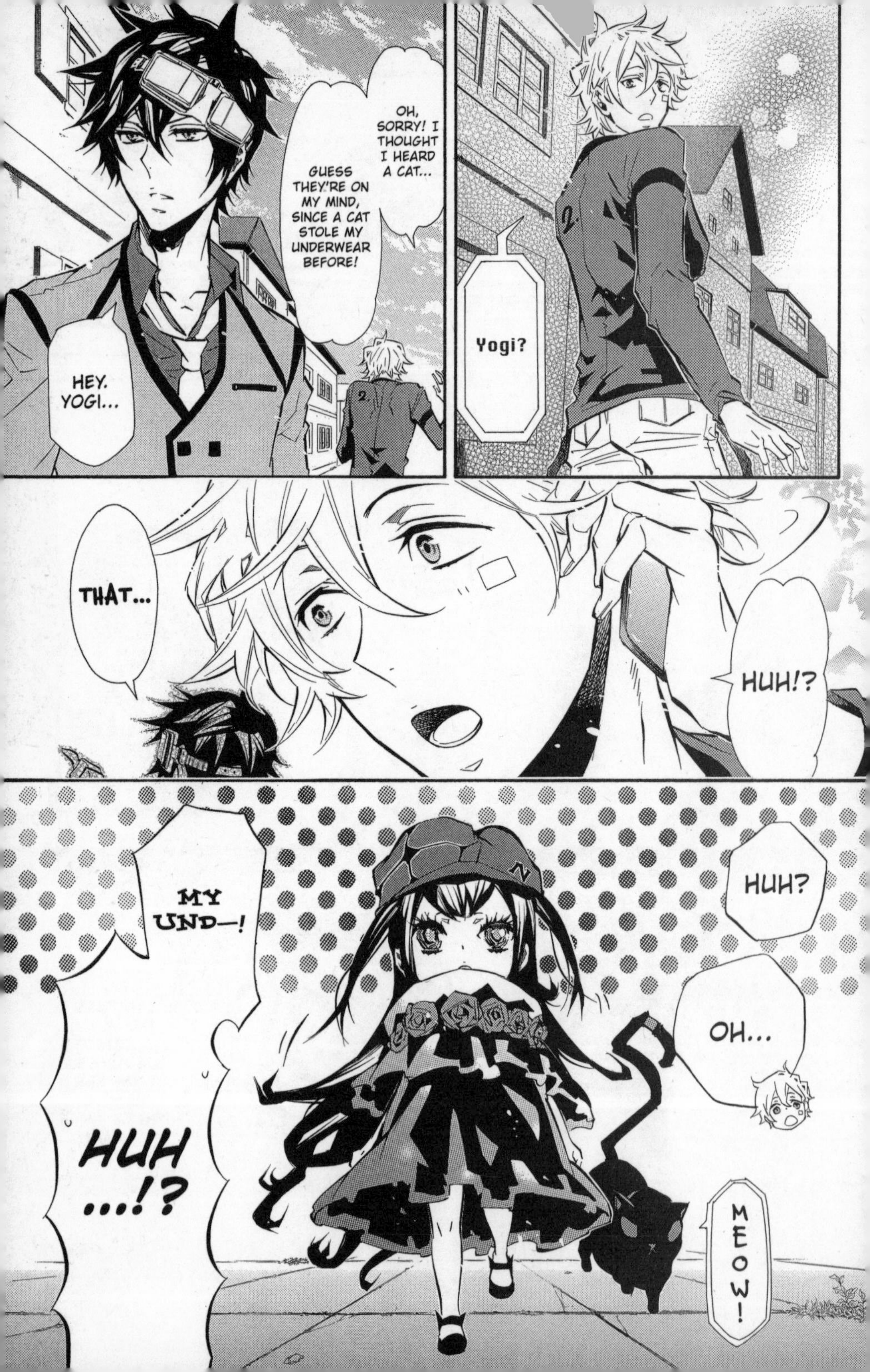
Yogi?
OH, SORRY! I THOUGHT I HEARD A CAT...
GUESS THEY'RE ON MY MIND, SINCE A CAT STOLE MY UNDERWEAR BEFORE!
HEY. YOGI...
HUH!?
THAT...
HUH?
OH...
MEOW!
MY UND—!
HUH ...!?

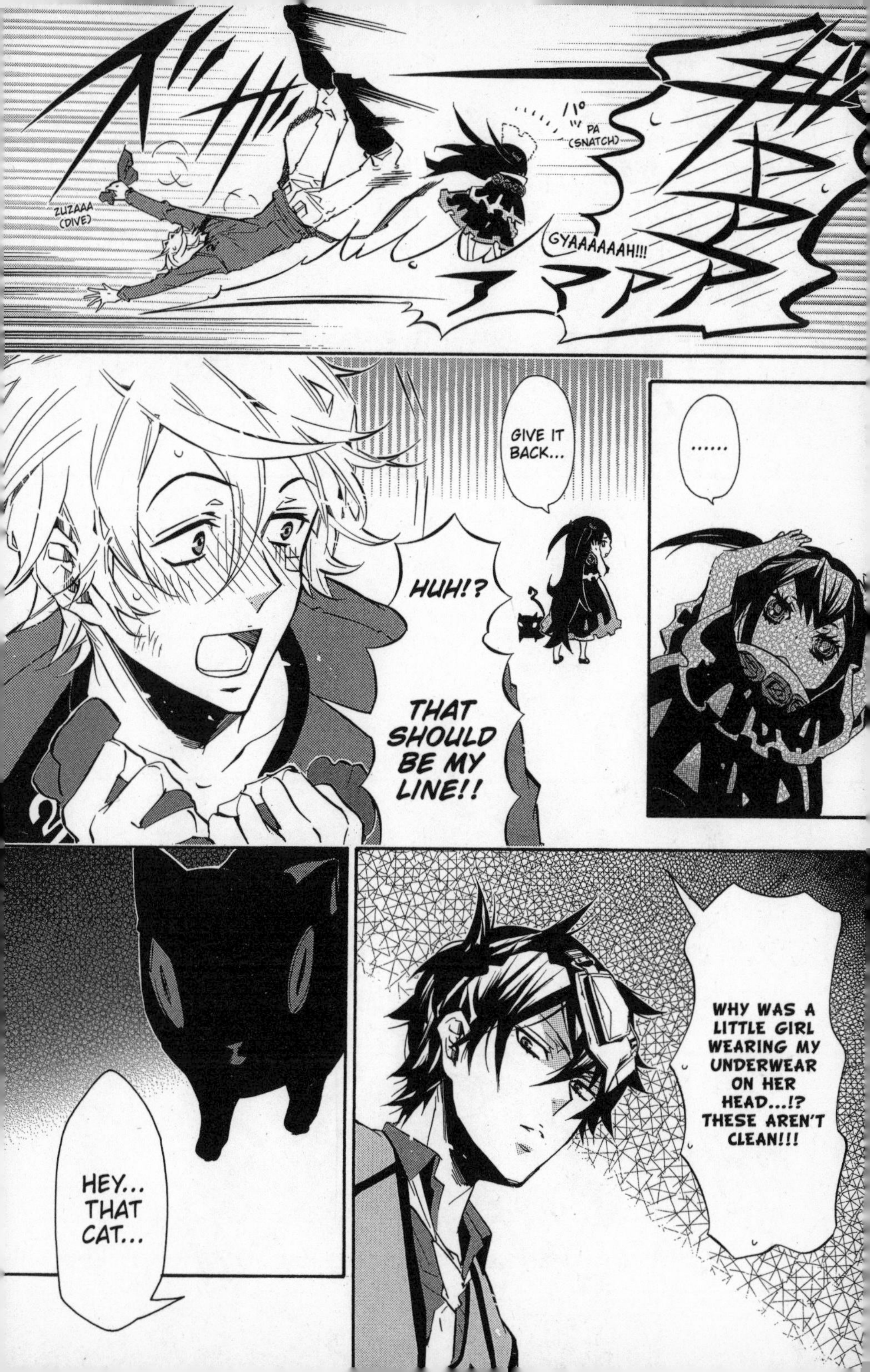
PA (SNATCH)
GYAAAAAAH!!!
ZUZAAA (DIVE)
......
GIVE IT BACK...
HUH!?
THAT SHOULD BE MY LINE!!
WHY WAS A LITTLE GIRL WEARING MY UNDERWEAR ON HER HEAD...!? THESE AREN'T CLEAN!!!
HEY... THAT CAT...

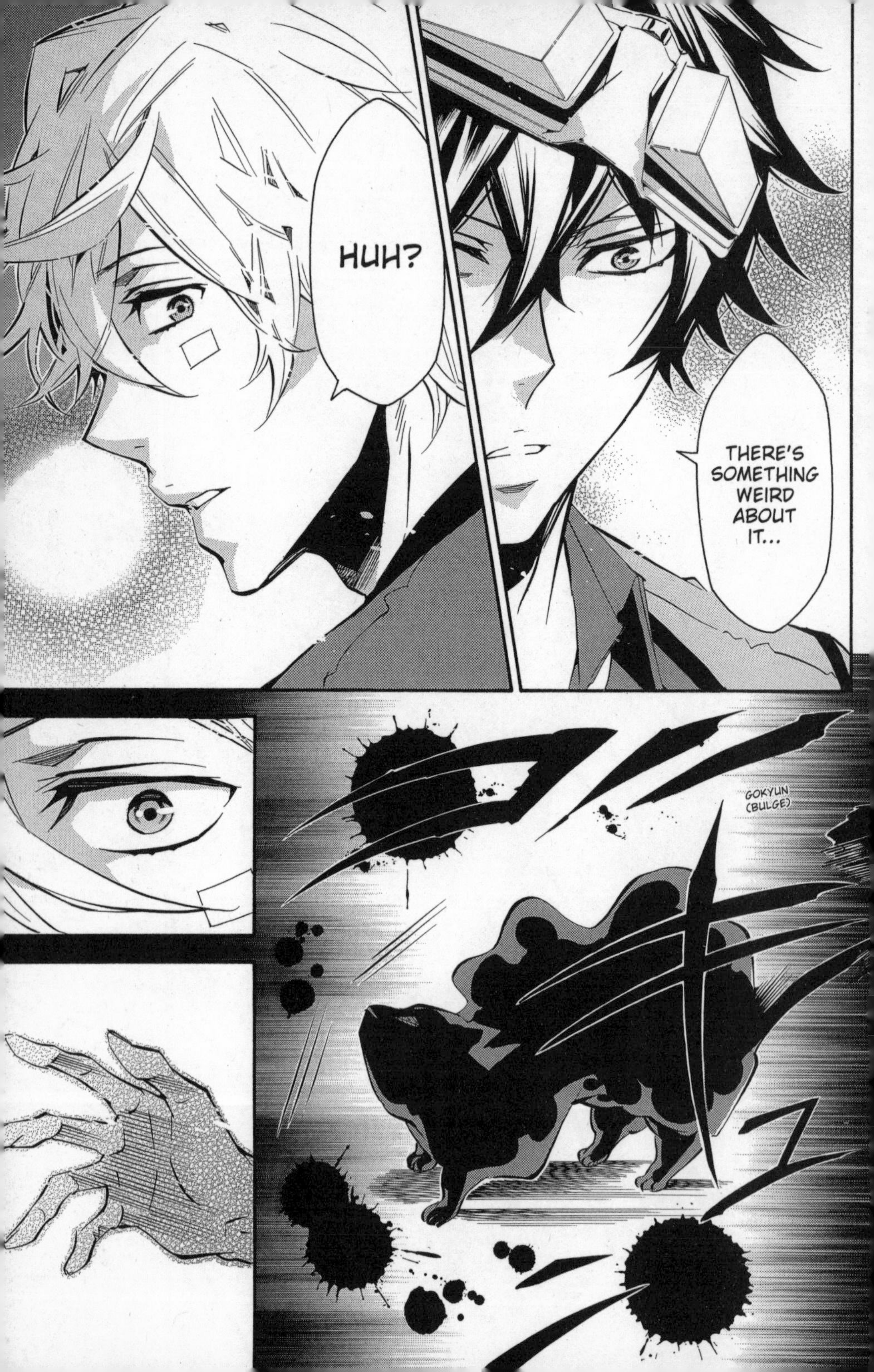

THERE'S SOMETHING WEIRD ABOUT IT...
HUH?
GOKYUN (BULGE)

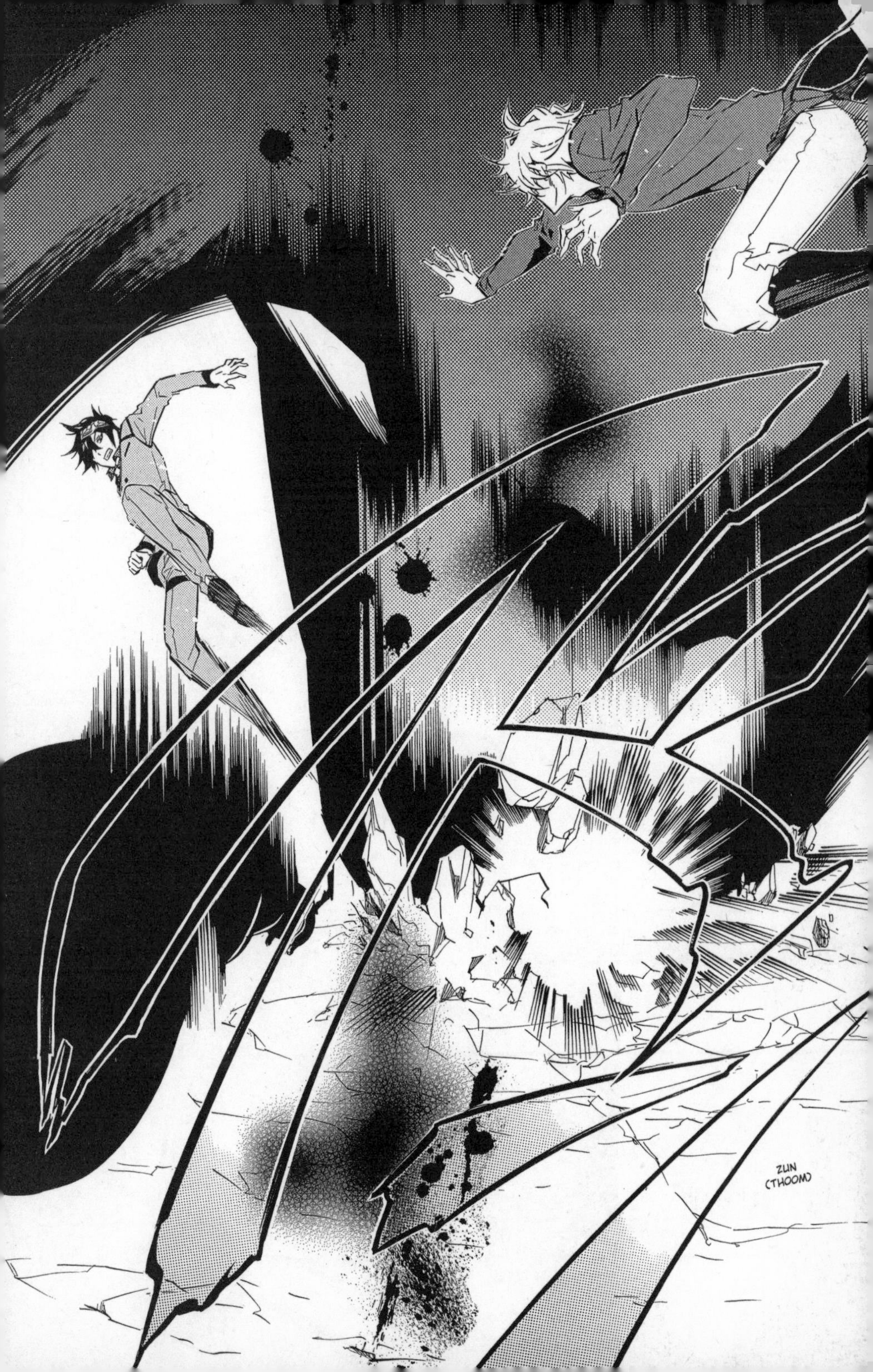
ZUN
(THOOM)

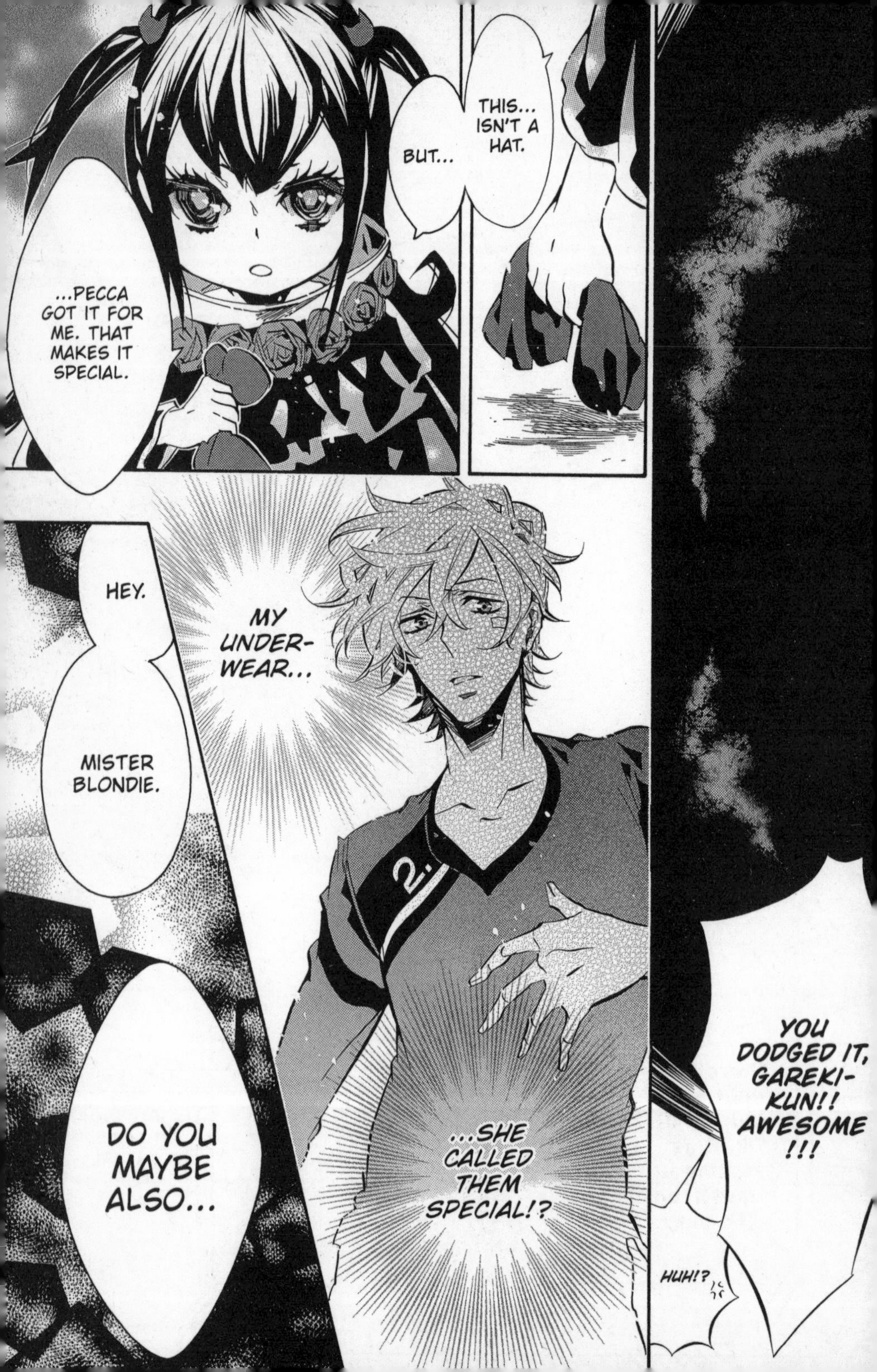
YOU DODGED IT, GAREKI-KUN!! AWESOME!!!
HUH!?
THIS... ISN'T A HAT.
BUT...
...PECCA GOT IT FOR ME. THAT MAKES IT SPECIAL.
HEY.
MISTER BLONDIE.
MY UNDER-WEAR...
...SHE CALLED THEM SPECIAL!?
DO YOU MAYBE ALSO...

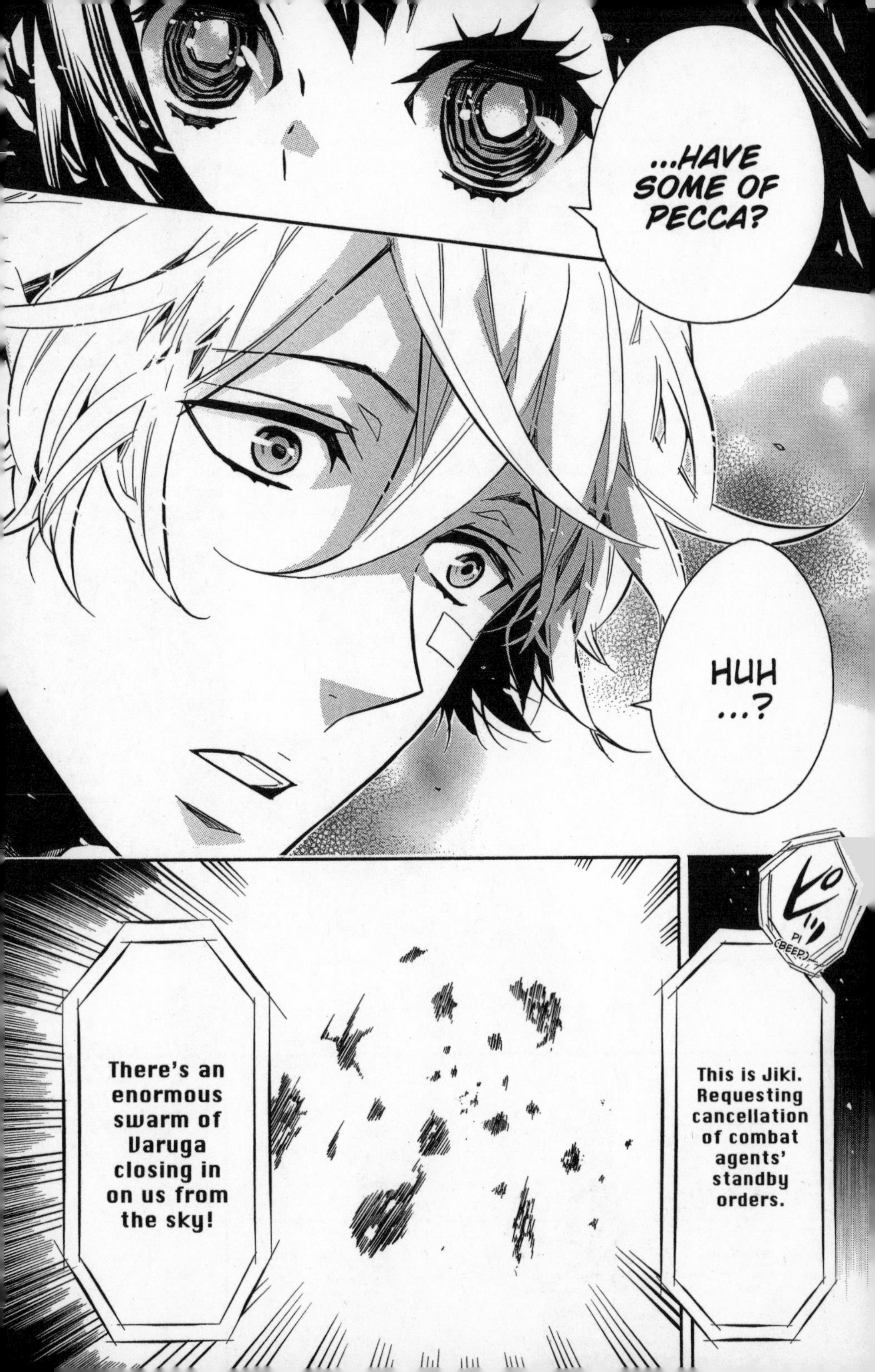
...HAVE SOME OF PECCA?
HUH ...?
PI (BEEP)
This is Jiki. Requesting cancellation of combat agents' standby orders.
There's an enormous swarm of Varuga closing in on us from the sky!

KARNEVAL

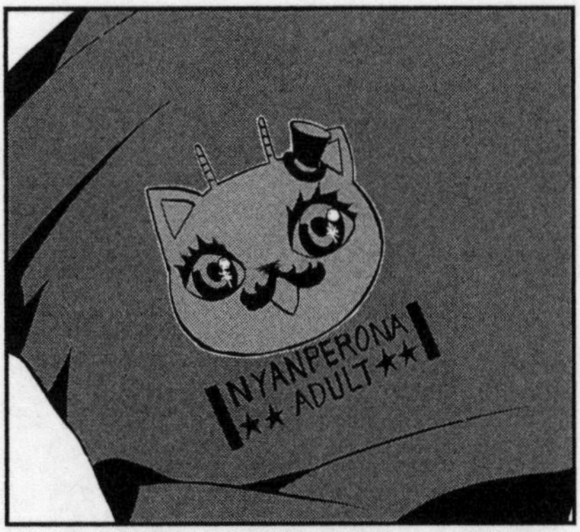
NYANPERONA
★★ ADULT ★★

KARNEVAL

Score 58: Territory

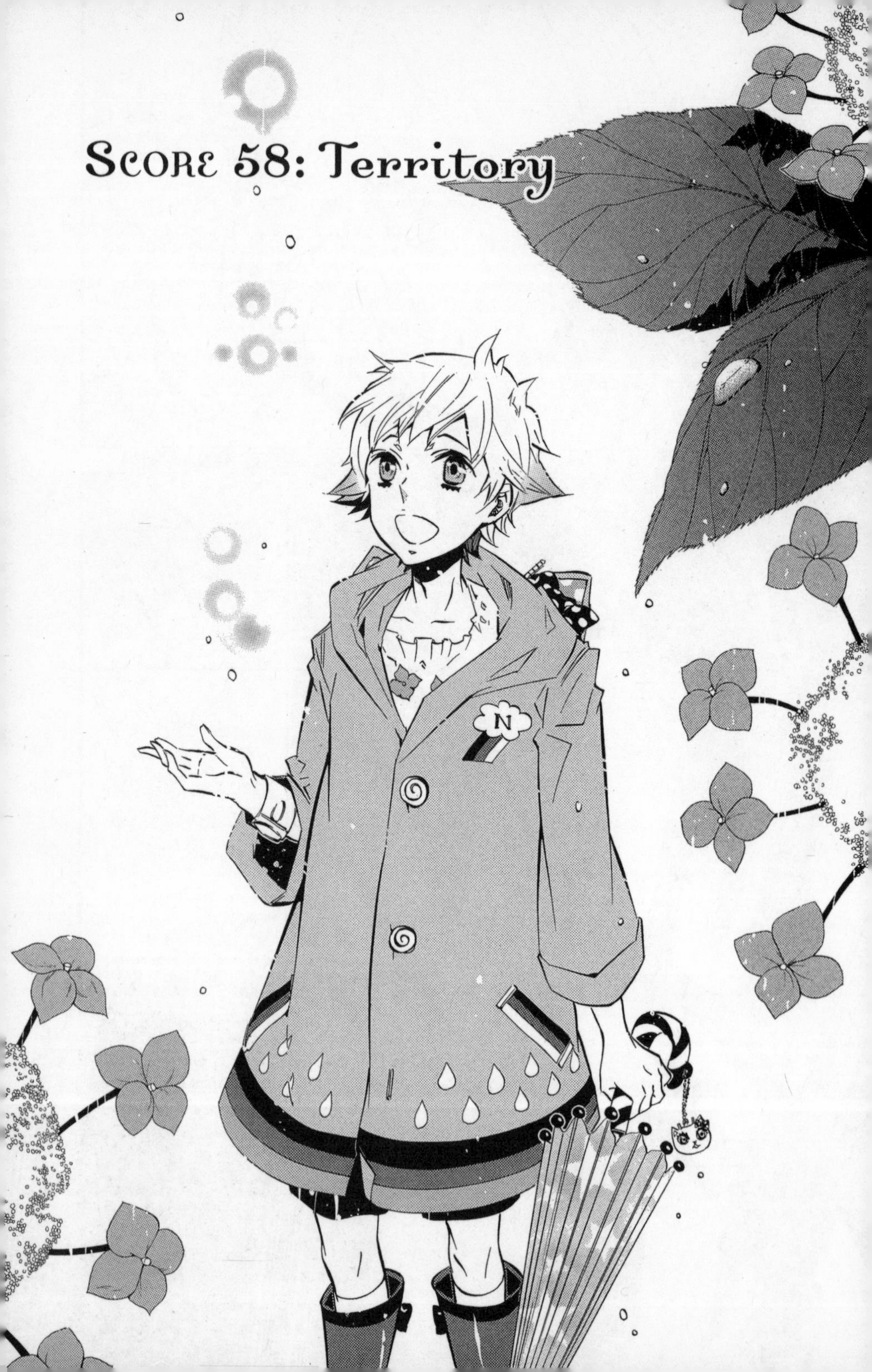

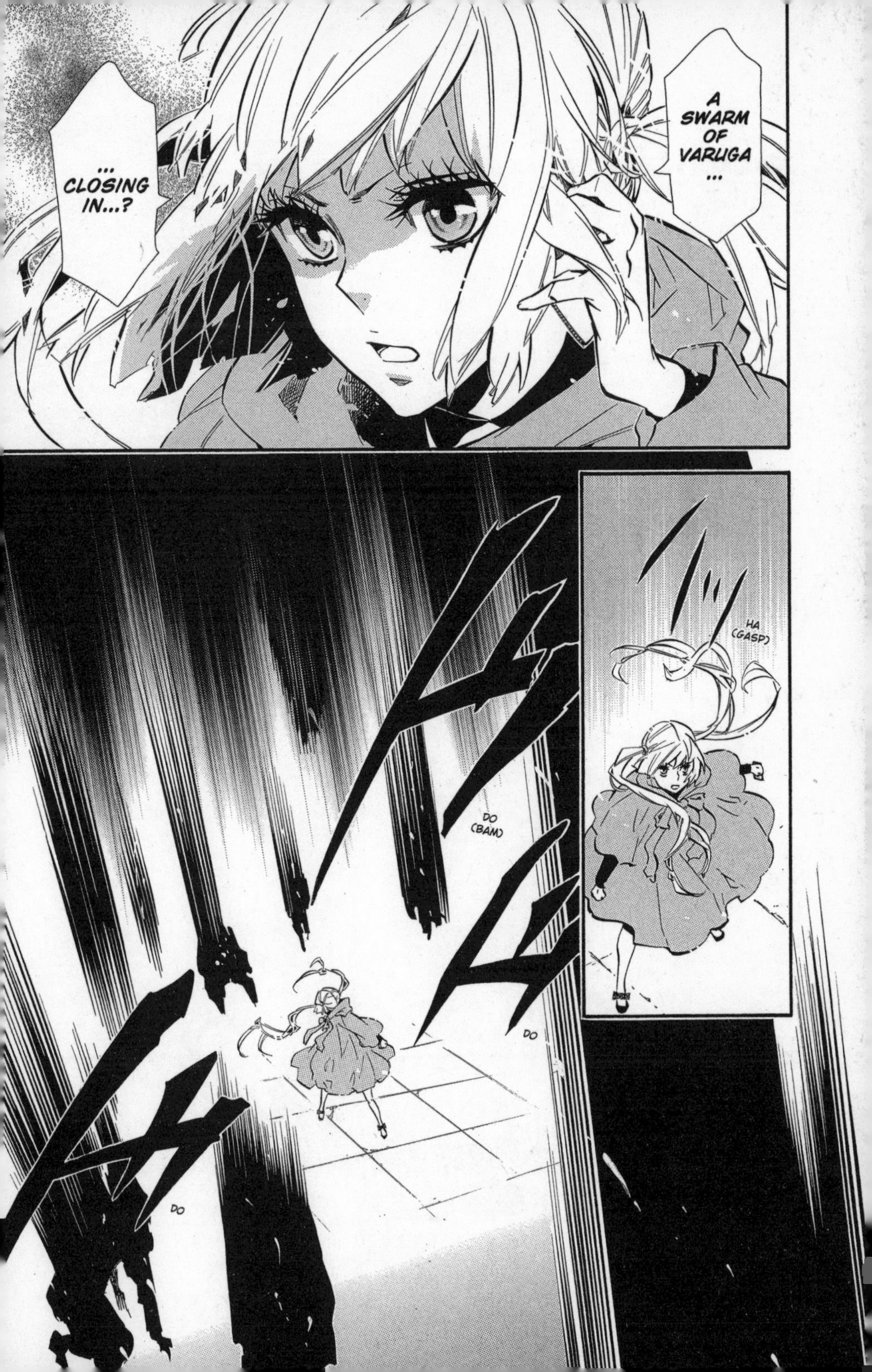
A SWARM OF VARUGA...
...CLOSING IN...?
HA (GASP)
DO (BAM)
DO
DO

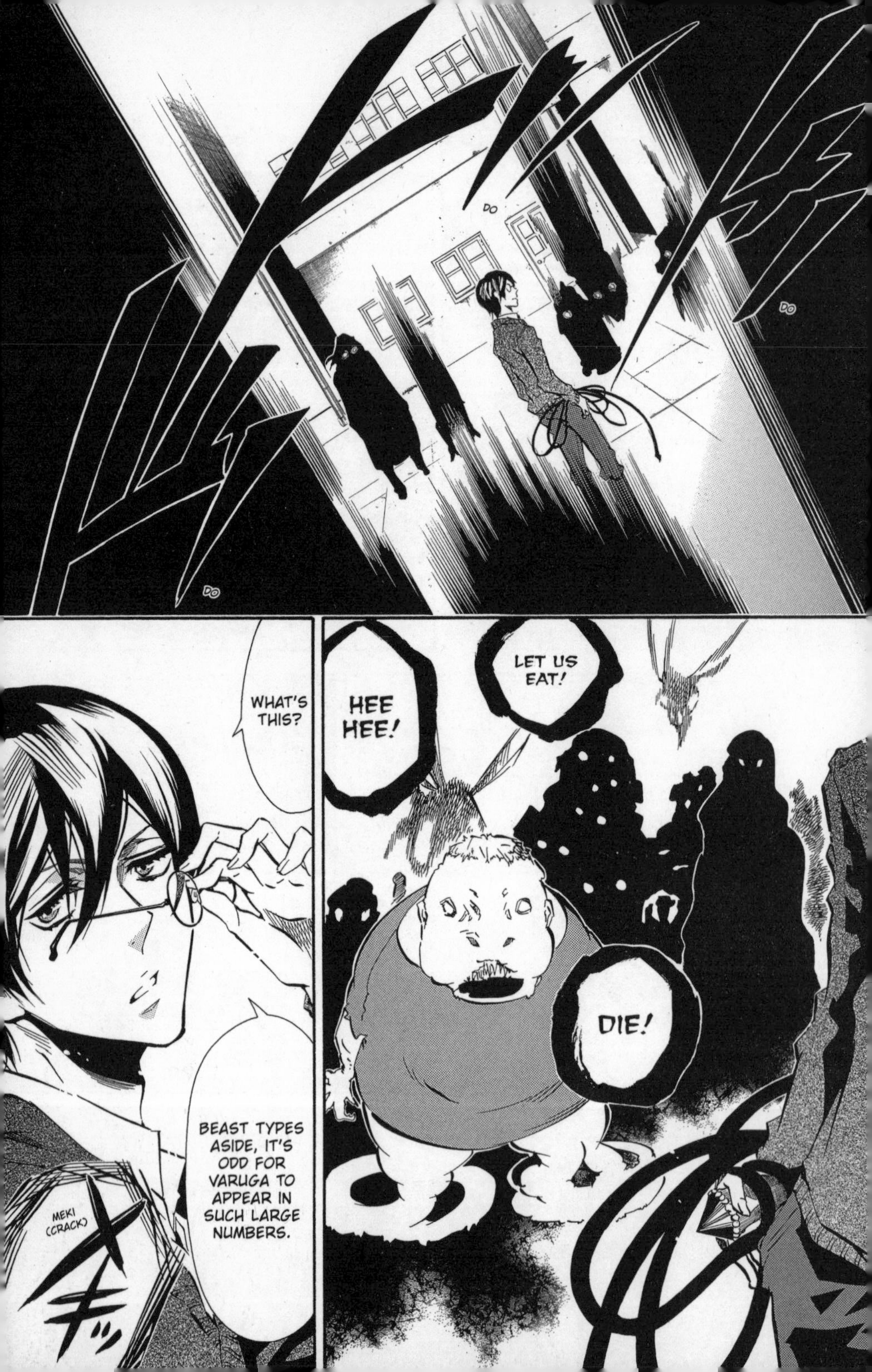
DO
DO
DO
LET US EAT!
HEE HEE!
DIE!
WHAT'S THIS?
BEAST TYPES ASIDE, IT'S ODD FOR VARUGA TO APPEAR IN SUCH LARGE NUMBERS.
MEKI (CRACK)

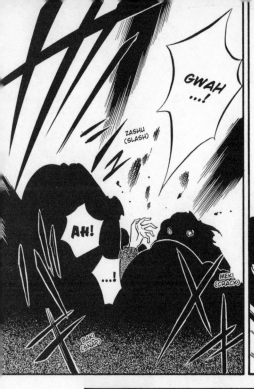

GWAH ...!

ZASHU
(SLASH)

!!

AH!

...!

MEKI
(CRACK)

BAKI
(SNAP)

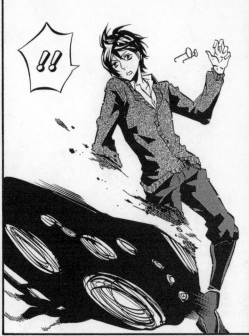

KO
(CLICK)

GATSU

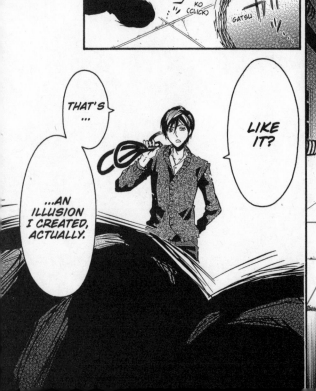

THAT'S ...

LIKE IT?

...AN ILLUSION I CREATED, ACTUALLY.

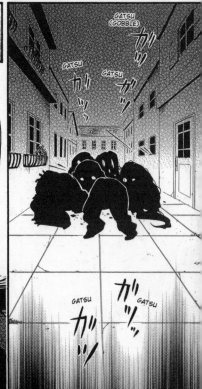

GATSU
(GOBBLE)

GATSU

GATSU

GATSU

GATSU

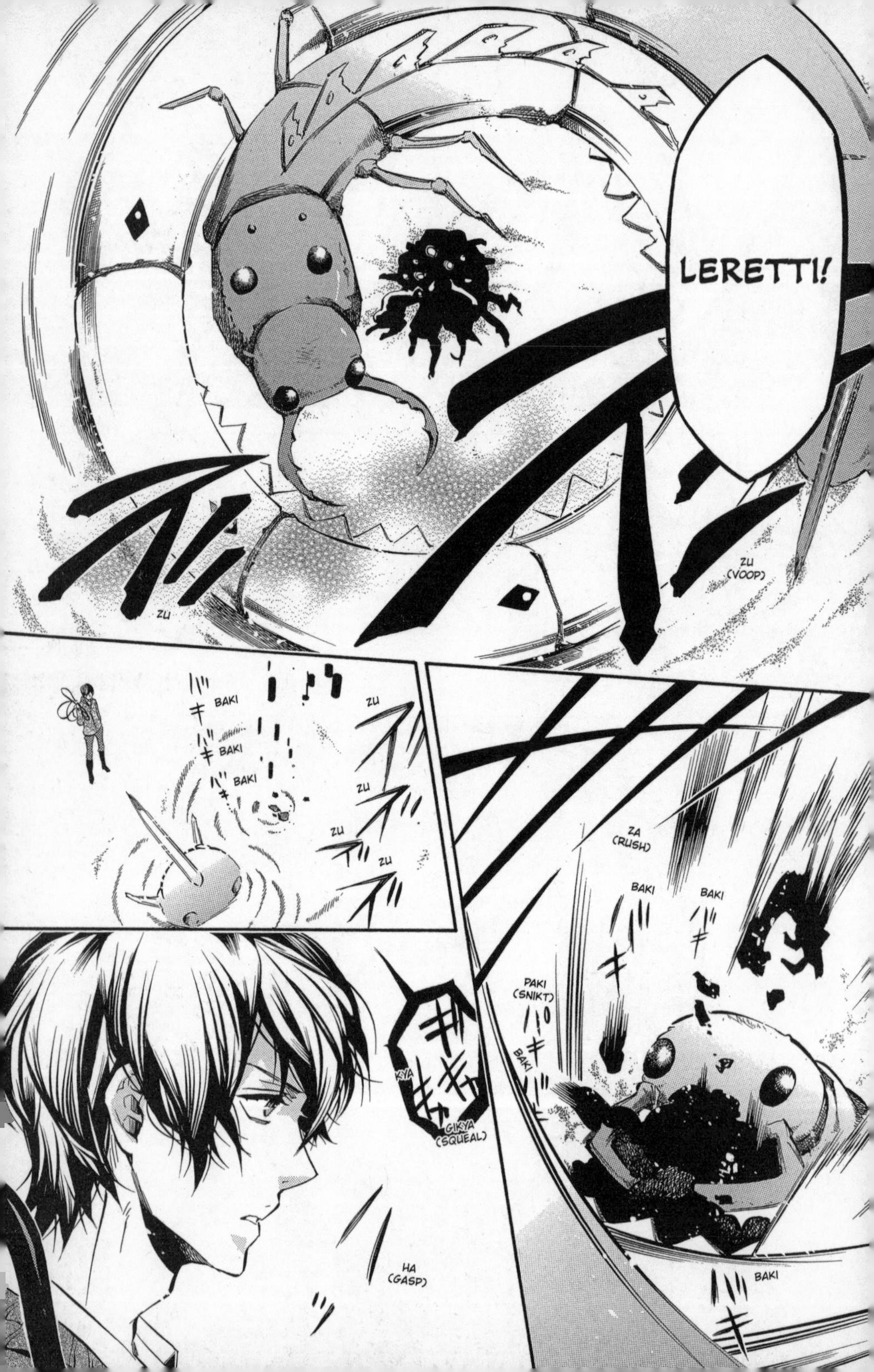
LERETTI!
ZU (VOOP)
ZU
ZA (RUSH)
BAKI
BAKI
PAKI (SNIKT)
BAKI
BAKI
ZU
ZU
ZU
ZU
BAKI
BAKI
BAKI
KYA
GIKYA (SQUEAL)
HA (GASP)

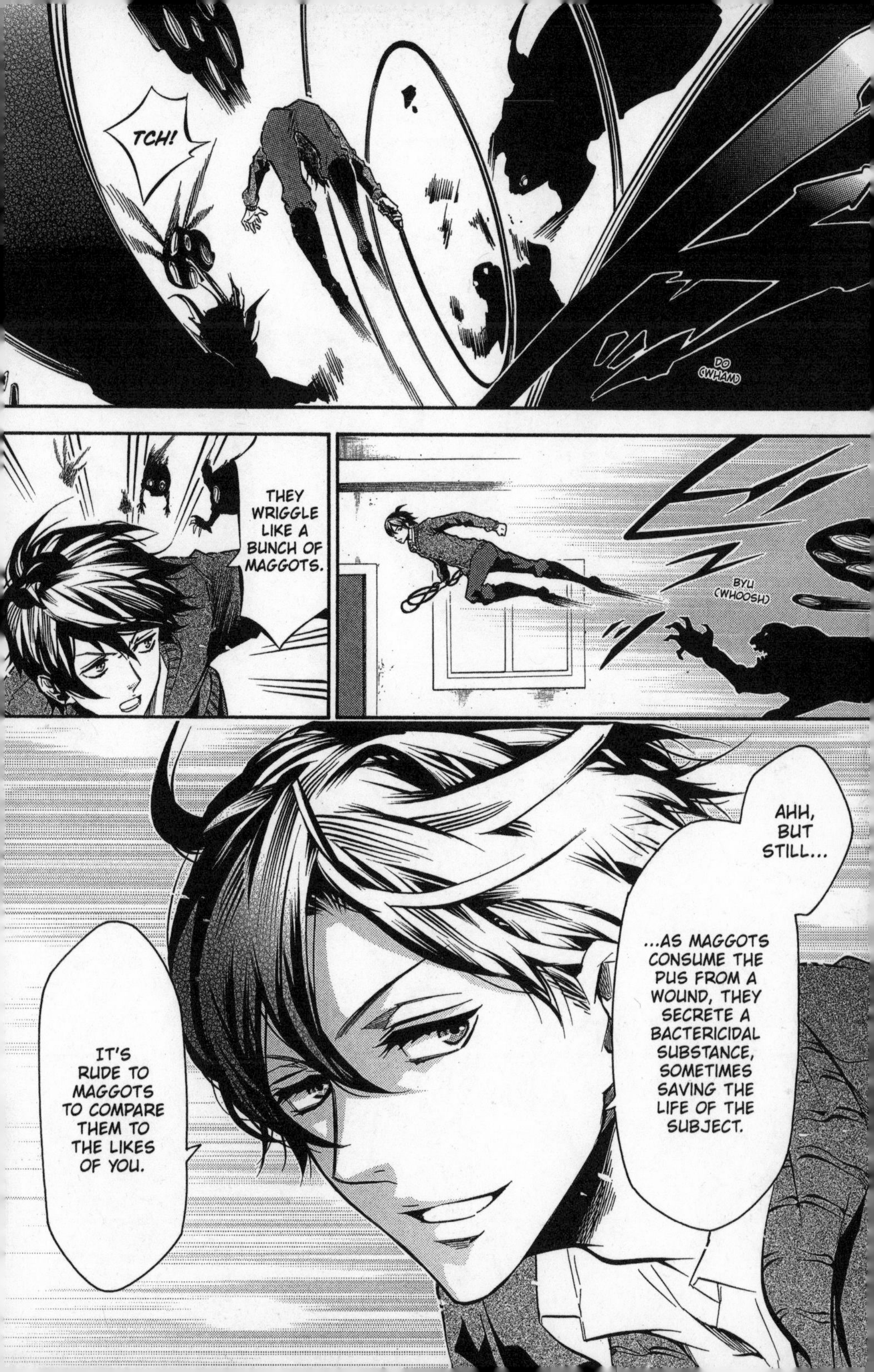
TCH!
DO (WHAM)
BYU (WHOOSH)
THEY WRIGGLE LIKE A BUNCH OF MAGGOTS.
AHH, BUT STILL...
...AS MAGGOTS CONSUME THE PUS FROM A WOUND, THEY SECRETE A BACTERICIDAL SUBSTANCE, SOMETIMES SAVING THE LIFE OF THE SUBJECT.
IT'S RUDE TO MAGGOTS TO COMPARE THEM TO THE LIKES OF YOU.

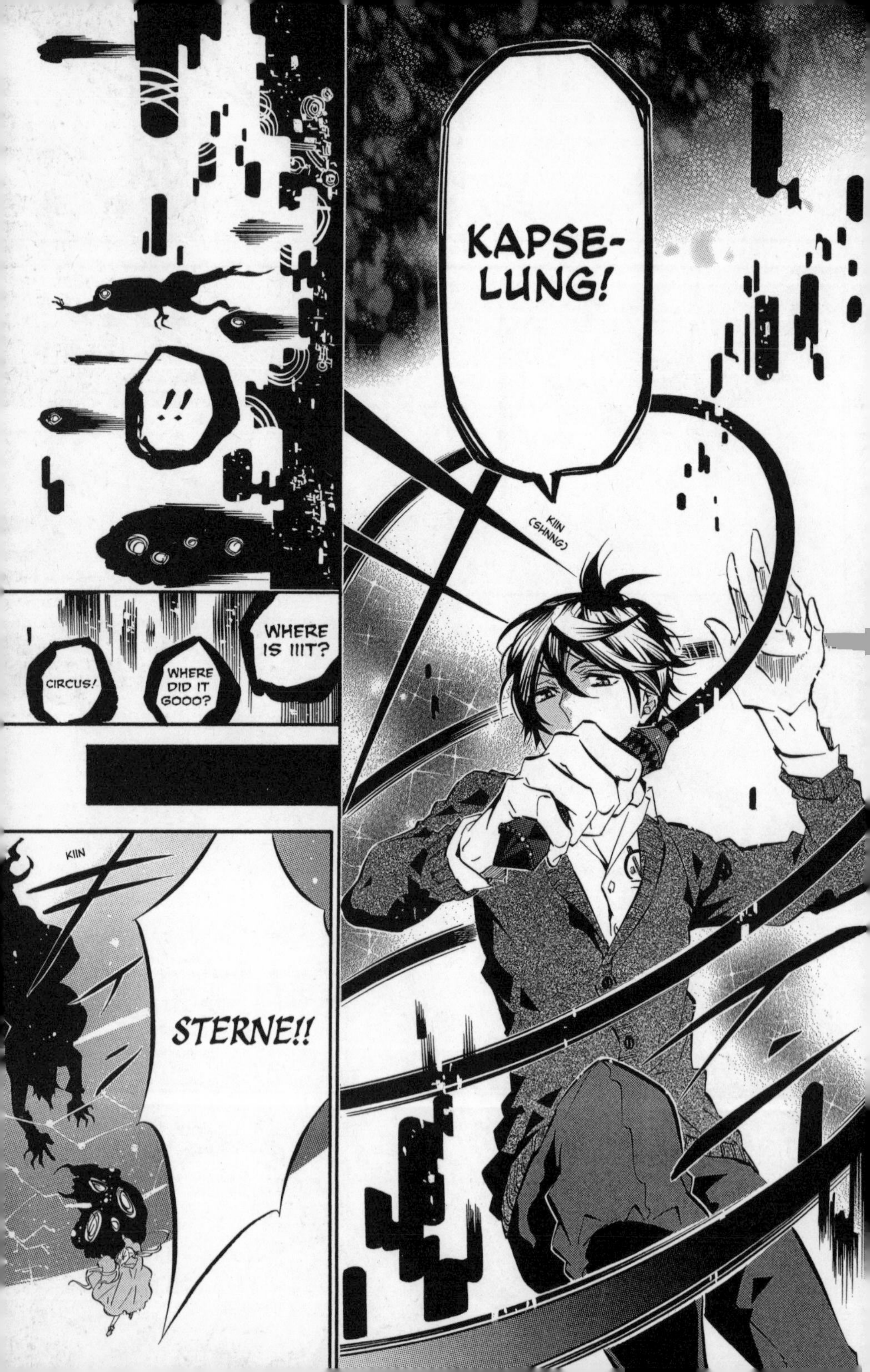
KAPSE-LUNG!
KIIN (SHNNG)
!!
WHERE IS IIIT?
WHERE DID IT GOOO?
CIRCUS!
KIIN
STERNE!!

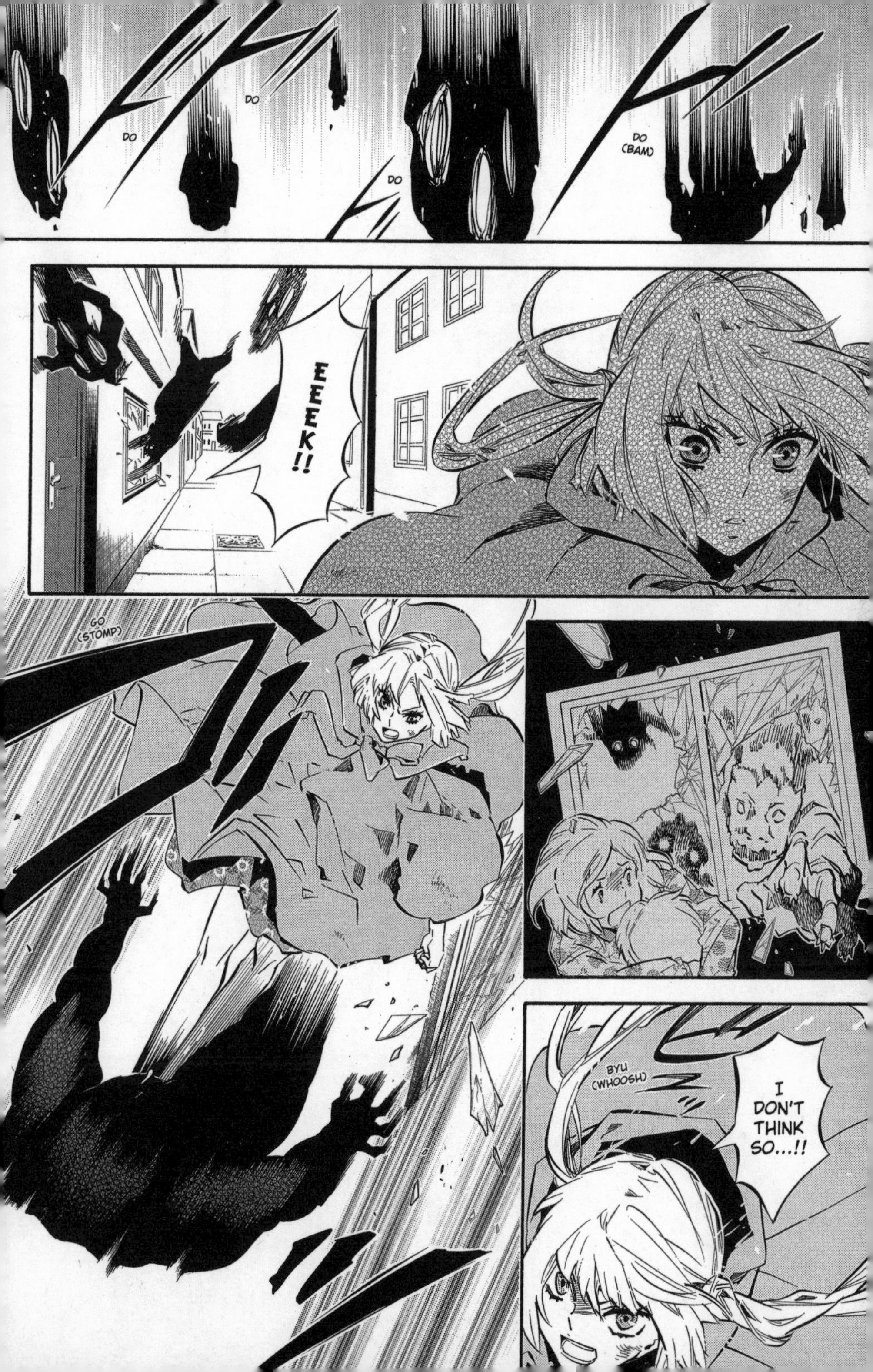
DO (BAM)
DO
DO
DO
EEEK!!
I DON'T THINK SO...!!
BYU (WHOOSH)
GO (STOMP)

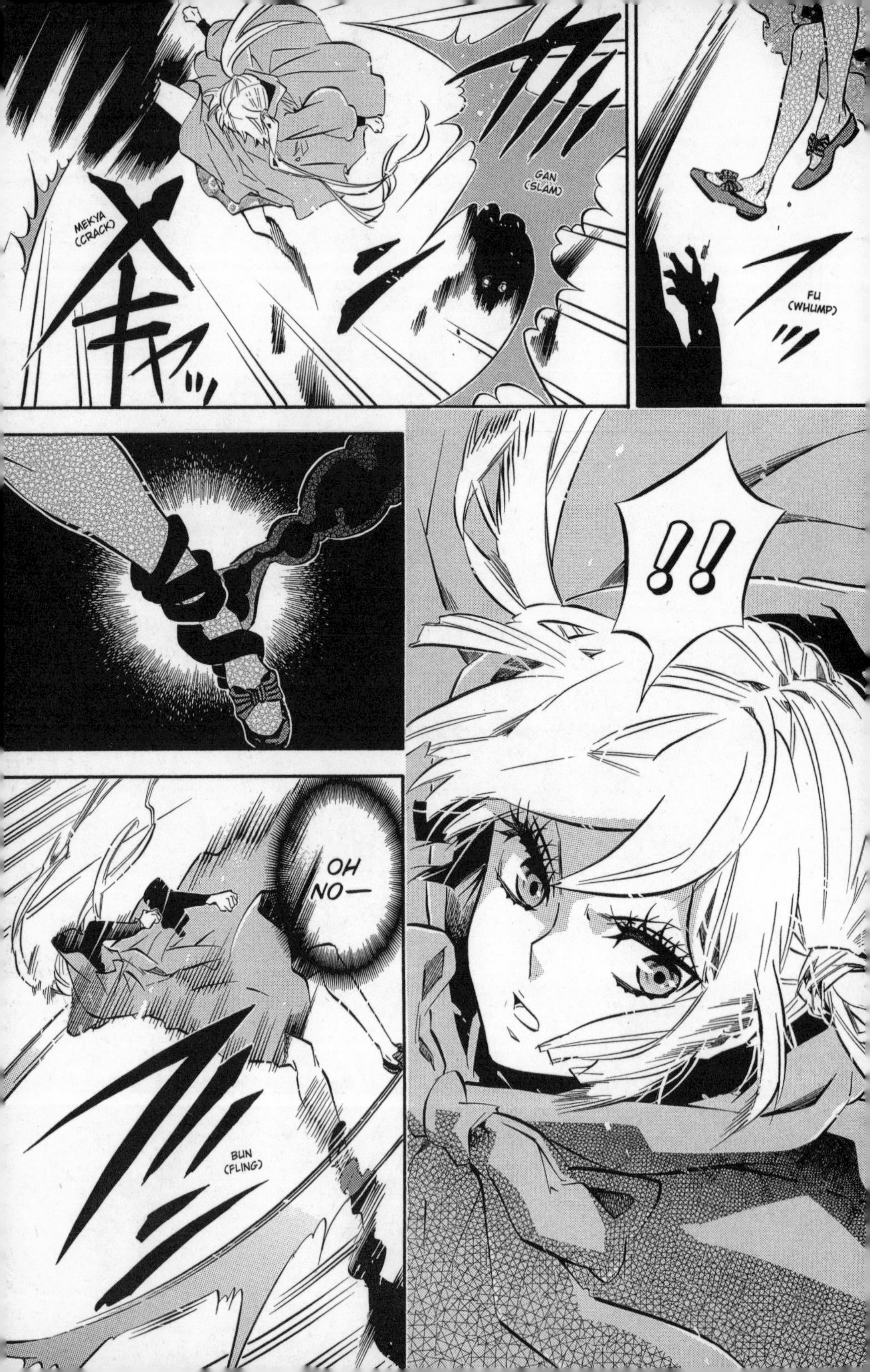
FU
(WHUMP)
GAN
(SLAM)
MEKYA
(CRACK)
!!
OH
NO—
BUN
(FLING)

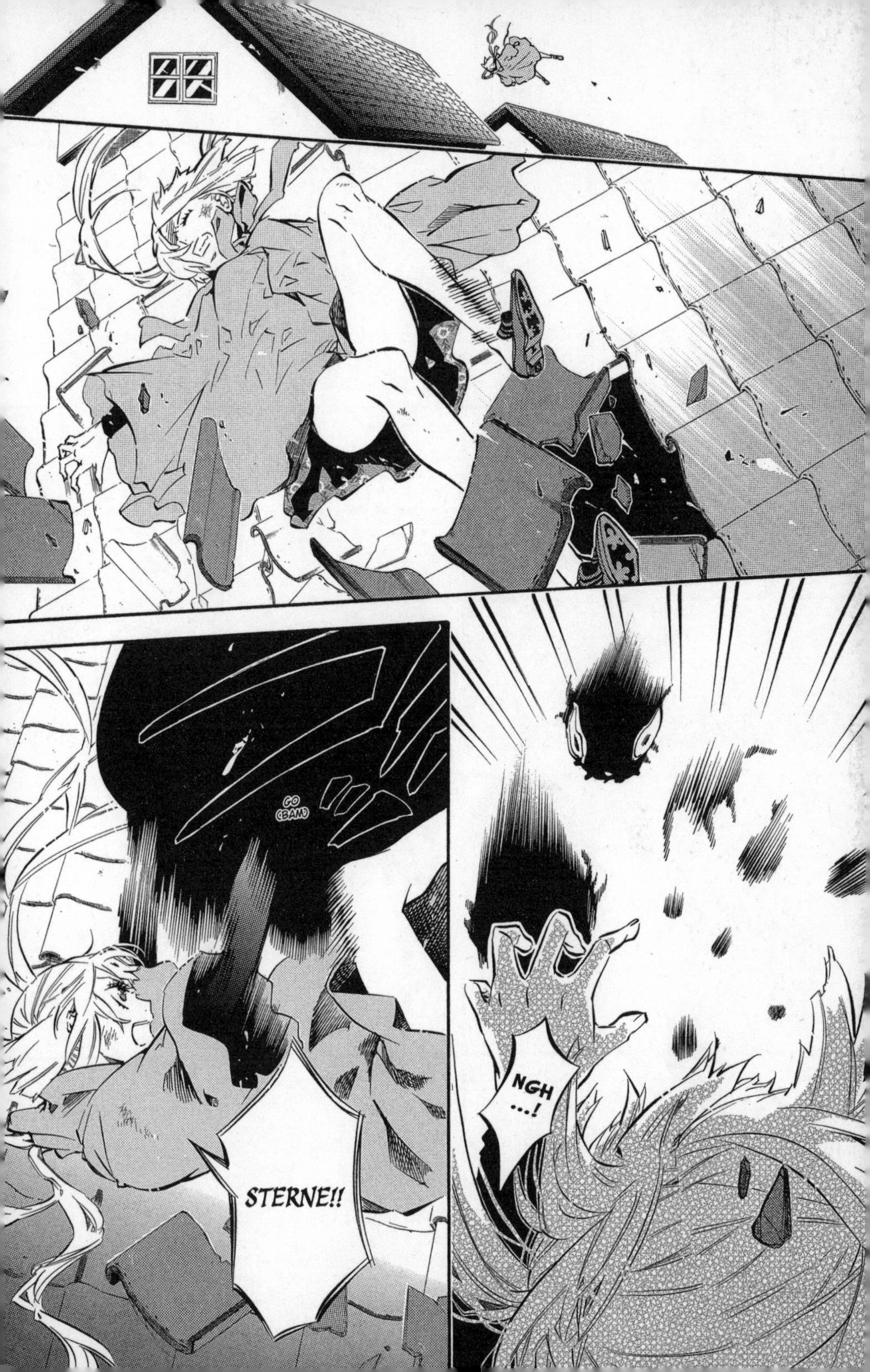
NGH ...!
GO (BAM)
STERNE!!

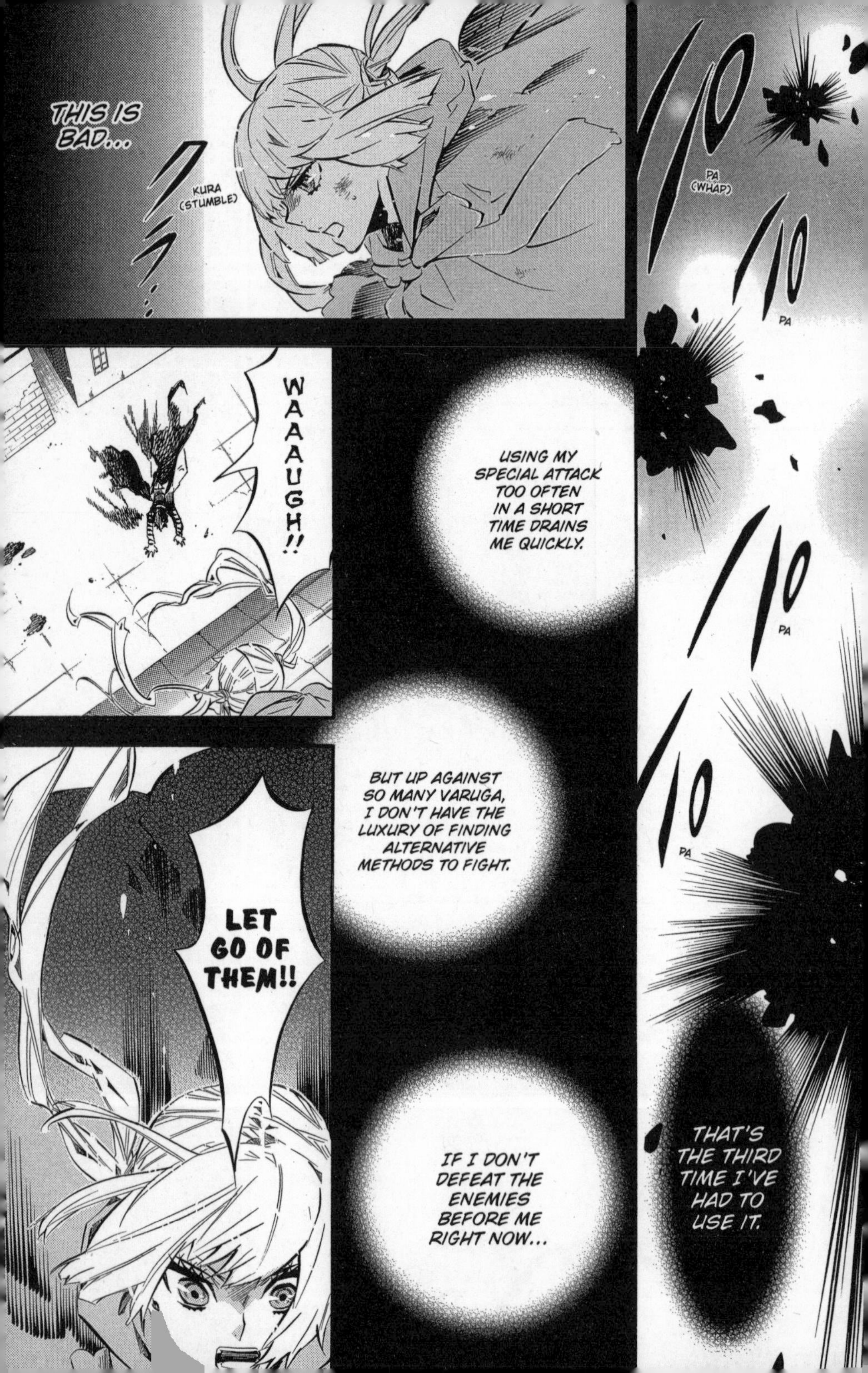
PA (WHAP)
PA
PA
PA
THAT'S THE THIRD TIME I'VE HAD TO USE IT.
KURA (STUMBLE)
THIS IS BAD...
USING MY SPECIAL ATTACK TOO OFTEN IN A SHORT TIME DRAINS ME QUICKLY.
BUT UP AGAINST SO MANY VARUGA, I DON'T HAVE THE LUXURY OF FINDING ALTERNATIVE METHODS TO FIGHT.
IF I DON'T DEFEAT THE ENEMIES BEFORE ME RIGHT NOW...
WAAAAUGH!!
LET GO OF THEM!!

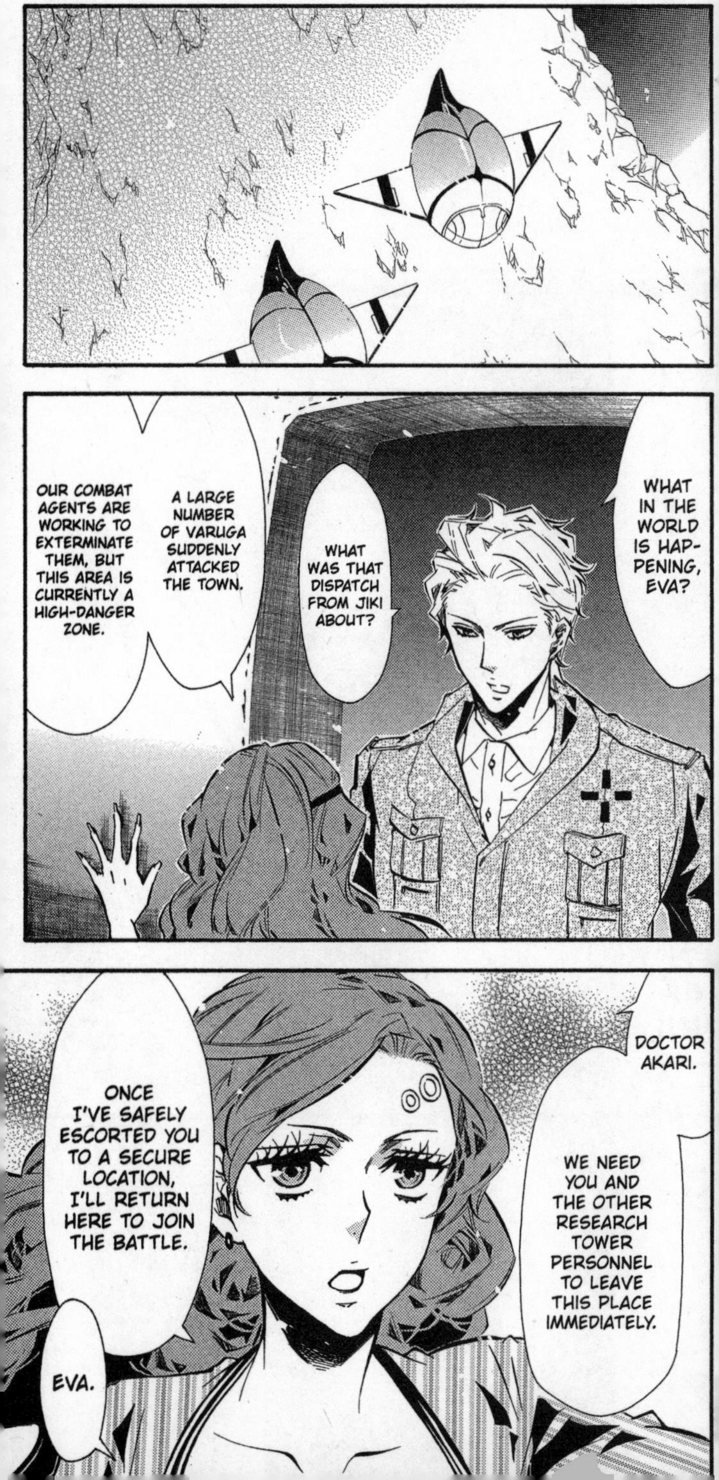
WHAT IN THE WORLD IS HAPPENING, EVA?
WHAT WAS THAT DISPATCH FROM JIKI ABOUT?
A LARGE NUMBER OF VARUGA SUDDENLY ATTACKED THE TOWN.
OUR COMBAT AGENTS ARE WORKING TO EXTERMINATE THEM, BUT THIS AREA IS CURRENTLY A HIGH-DANGER ZONE.
DOCTOR AKARI.
WE NEED YOU AND THE OTHER RESEARCH TOWER PERSONNEL TO LEAVE THIS PLACE IMMEDIATELY.
ONCE I'VE SAFELY ESCORTED YOU TO A SECURE LOCATION, I'LL RETURN HERE TO JOIN THE BATTLE.
EVA.

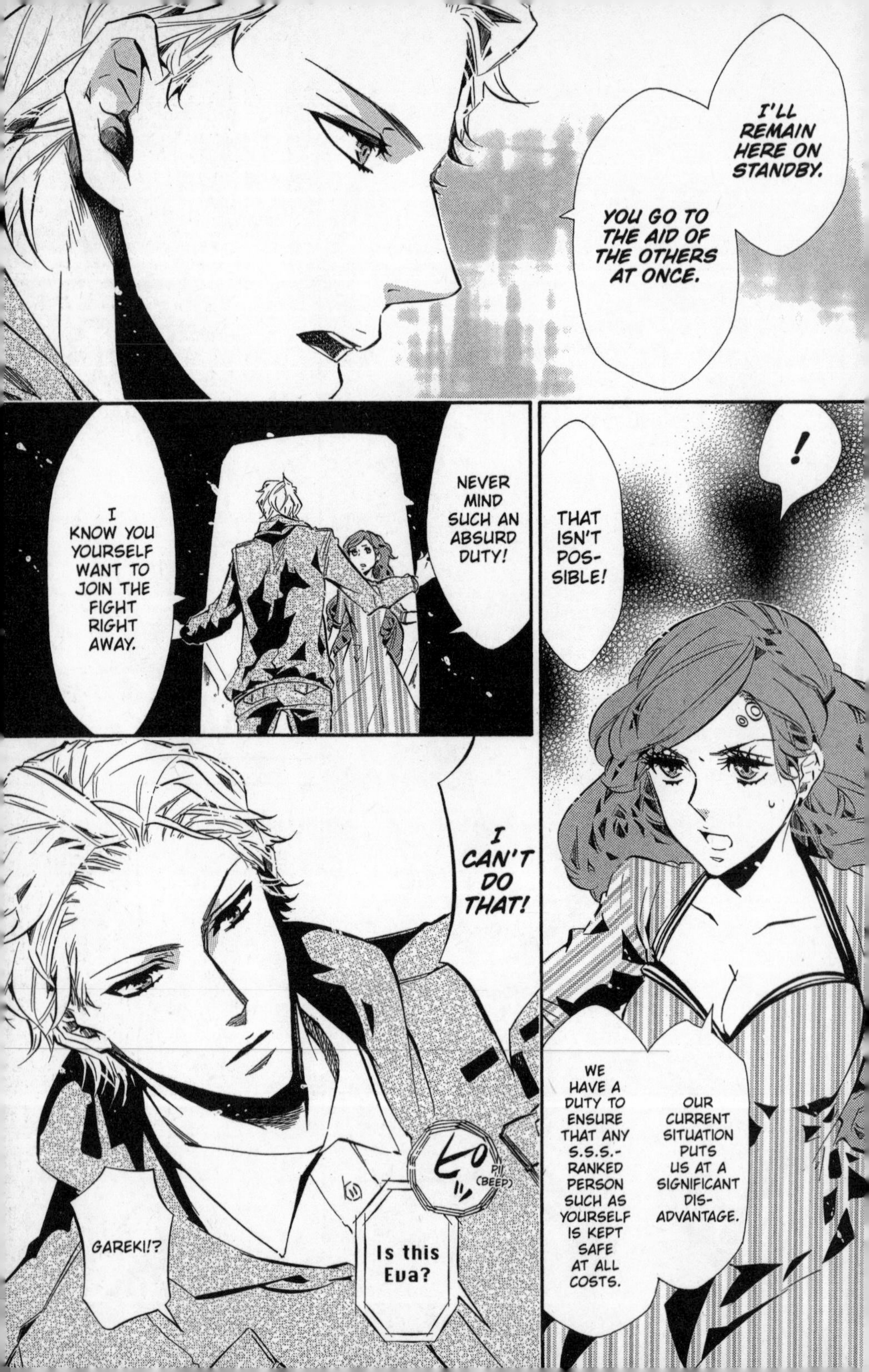
I'LL REMAIN HERE ON STANDBY.
YOU GO TO THE AID OF THE OTHERS AT ONCE.
!
THAT ISN'T POS-SIBLE!
OUR CURRENT SITUATION PUTS US AT A SIGNIFICANT DIS-ADVANTAGE.
WE HAVE A DUTY TO ENSURE THAT ANY S.S.S.-RANKED PERSON SUCH AS YOURSELF IS KEPT SAFE AT ALL COSTS.
NEVER MIND SUCH AN ABSURD DUTY!
I KNOW YOU YOURSELF WANT TO JOIN THE FIGHT RIGHT AWAY.
I CAN'T DO THAT!
PII (BEEP)
Is this Eva?
GAREKI!?

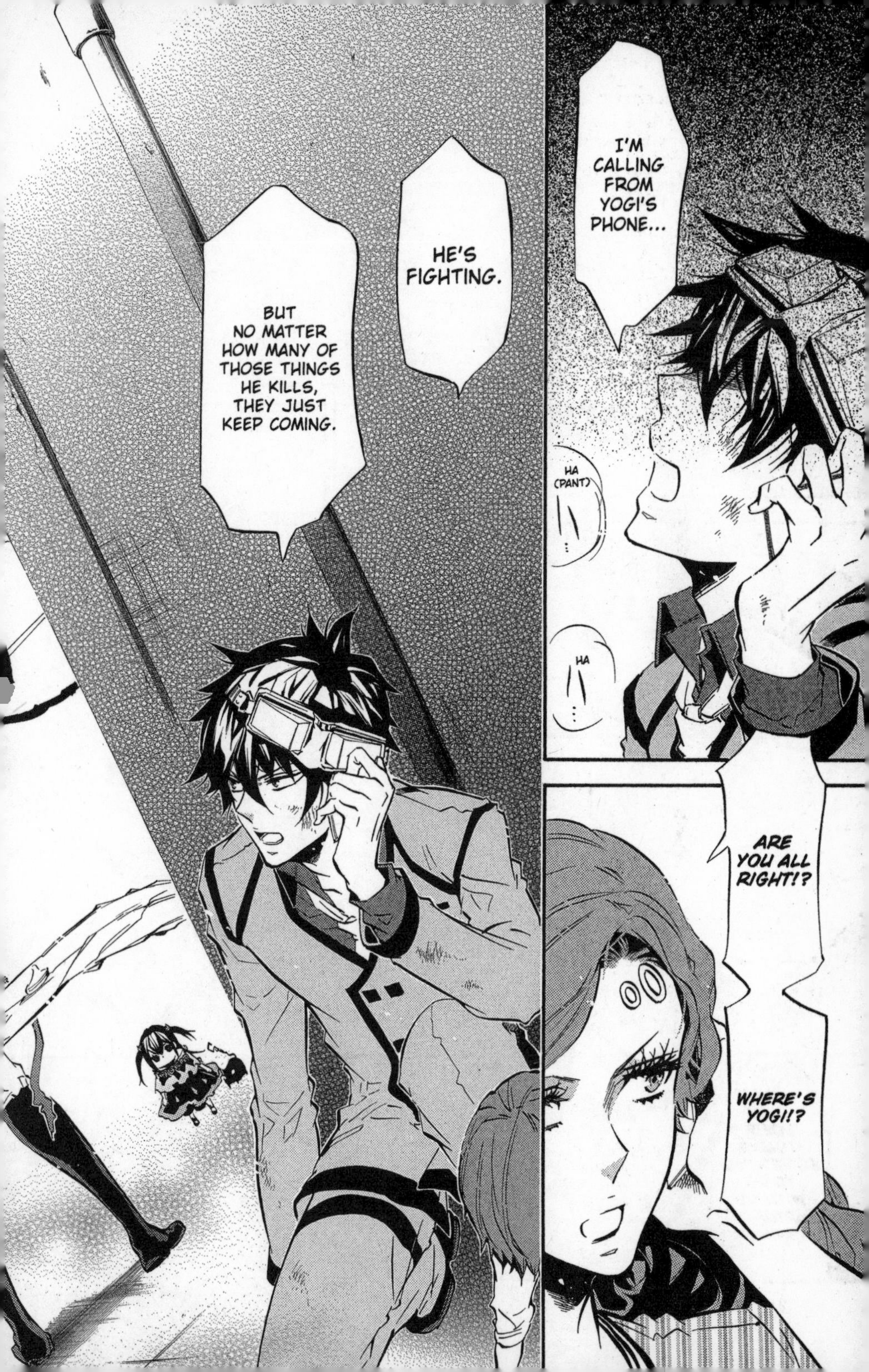
I'M CALLING FROM YOGI'S PHONE...
HA (PANT)
HA
ARE YOU ALL RIGHT!?
WHERE'S YOGI!?
HE'S FIGHTING.
BUT NO MATTER HOW MANY OF THOSE THINGS HE KILLS, THEY JUST KEEP COMING.

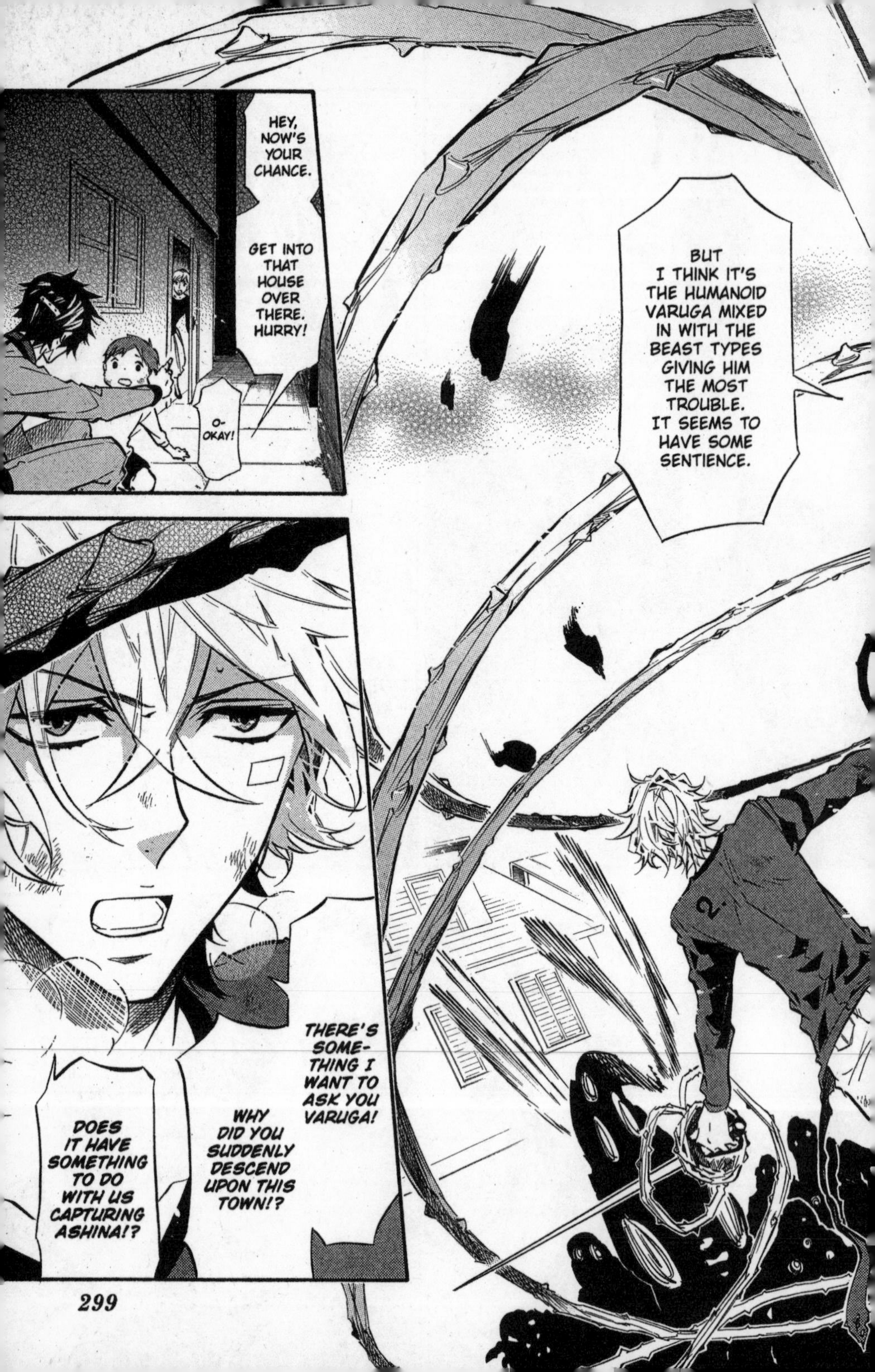
BUT I THINK IT'S THE HUMANOID VARUGA MIXED IN WITH THE BEAST TYPES GIVING HIM THE MOST TROUBLE. IT SEEMS TO HAVE SOME SENTIENCE.
HEY, NOW'S YOUR CHANCE.
GET INTO THAT HOUSE OVER THERE. HURRY!
O-OKAY!
THERE'S SOME-THING I WANT TO ASK YOU VARUGA!
WHY DID YOU SUDDENLY DESCEND UPON THIS TOWN!?
DOES IT HAVE SOMETHING TO DO WITH US CAPTURING ASHINA!?

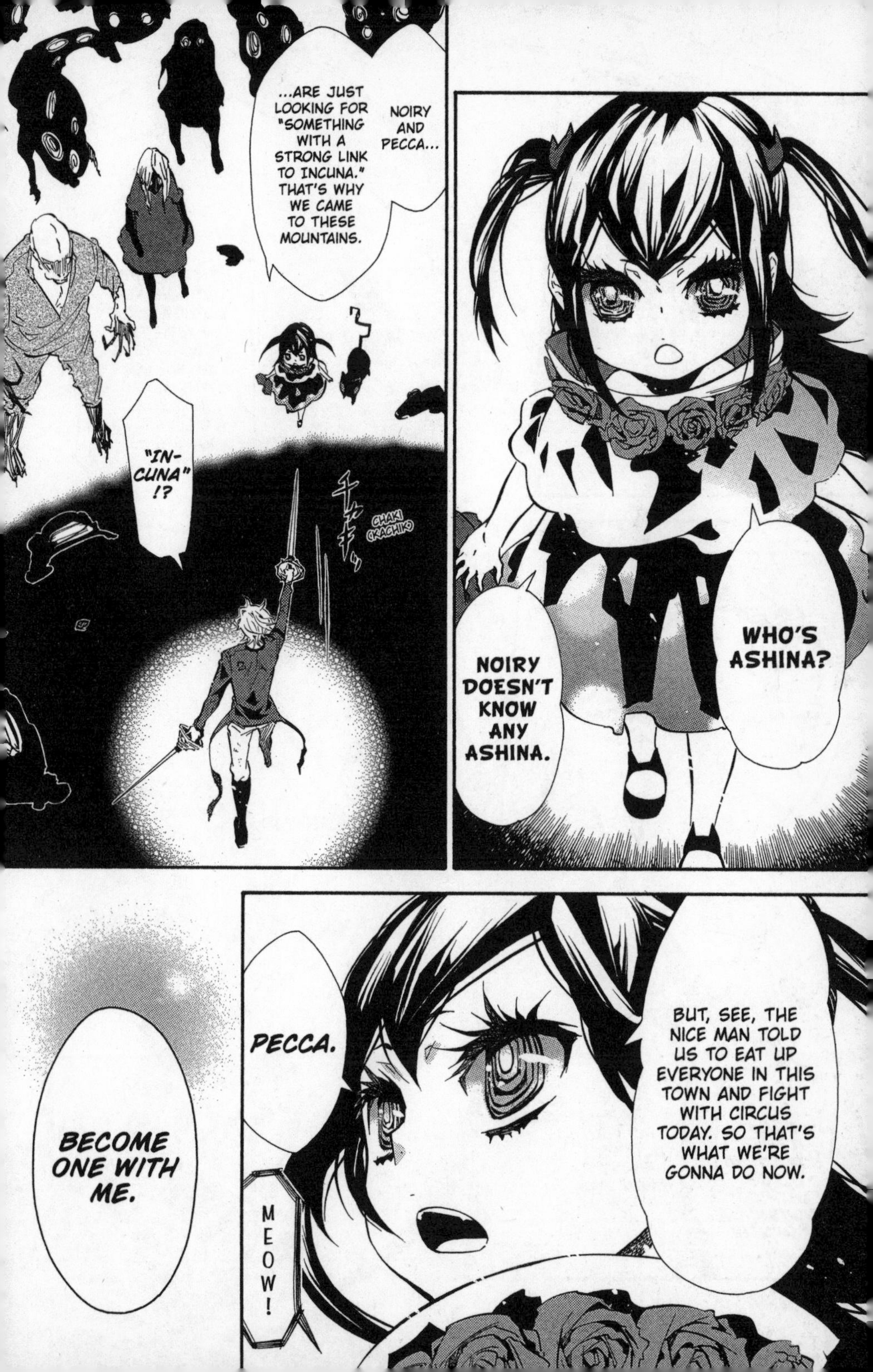
WHO'S ASHINA?
NOIRY DOESN'T KNOW ANY ASHINA.
NOIRY AND PECCA...
...ARE JUST LOOKING FOR "SOMETHING WITH A STRONG LINK TO INCUNA." THAT'S WHY WE CAME TO THESE MOUNTAINS.
"IN-CUNA" !?
CHAKI (KACHIK)
BUT, SEE, THE NICE MAN TOLD US TO EAT UP EVERYONE IN THIS TOWN AND FIGHT WITH CIRCUS TODAY. SO THAT'S WHAT WE'RE GONNA DO NOW.
PECCA.
MEOW!
BECOME ONE WITH ME.

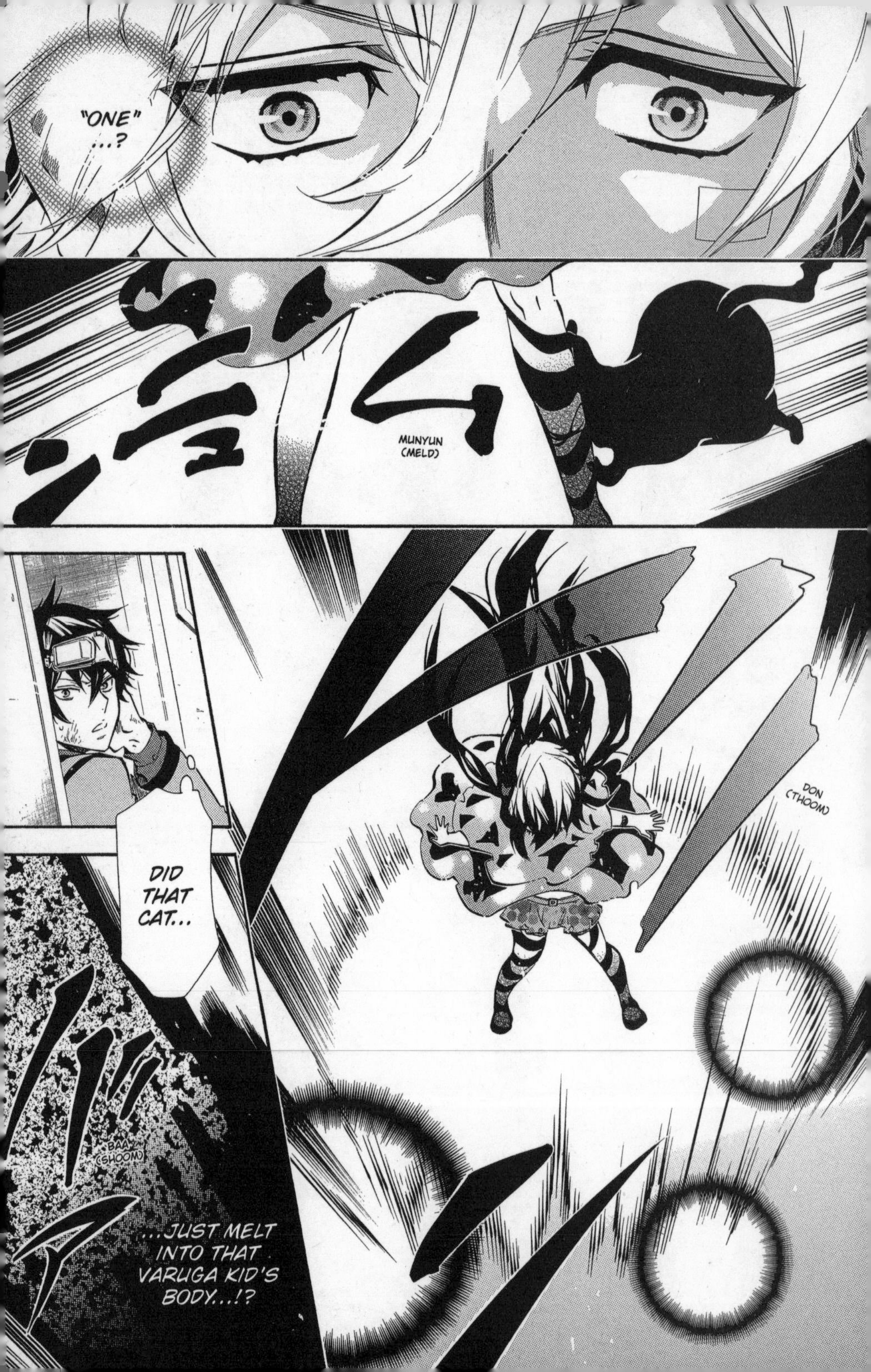
"ONE" ...?
MUNYUN (MELD)
DON (THOOM)
DID THAT CAT...
BAA (SHOON)
...JUST MELT INTO THAT VARUGA KID'S BODY...!?

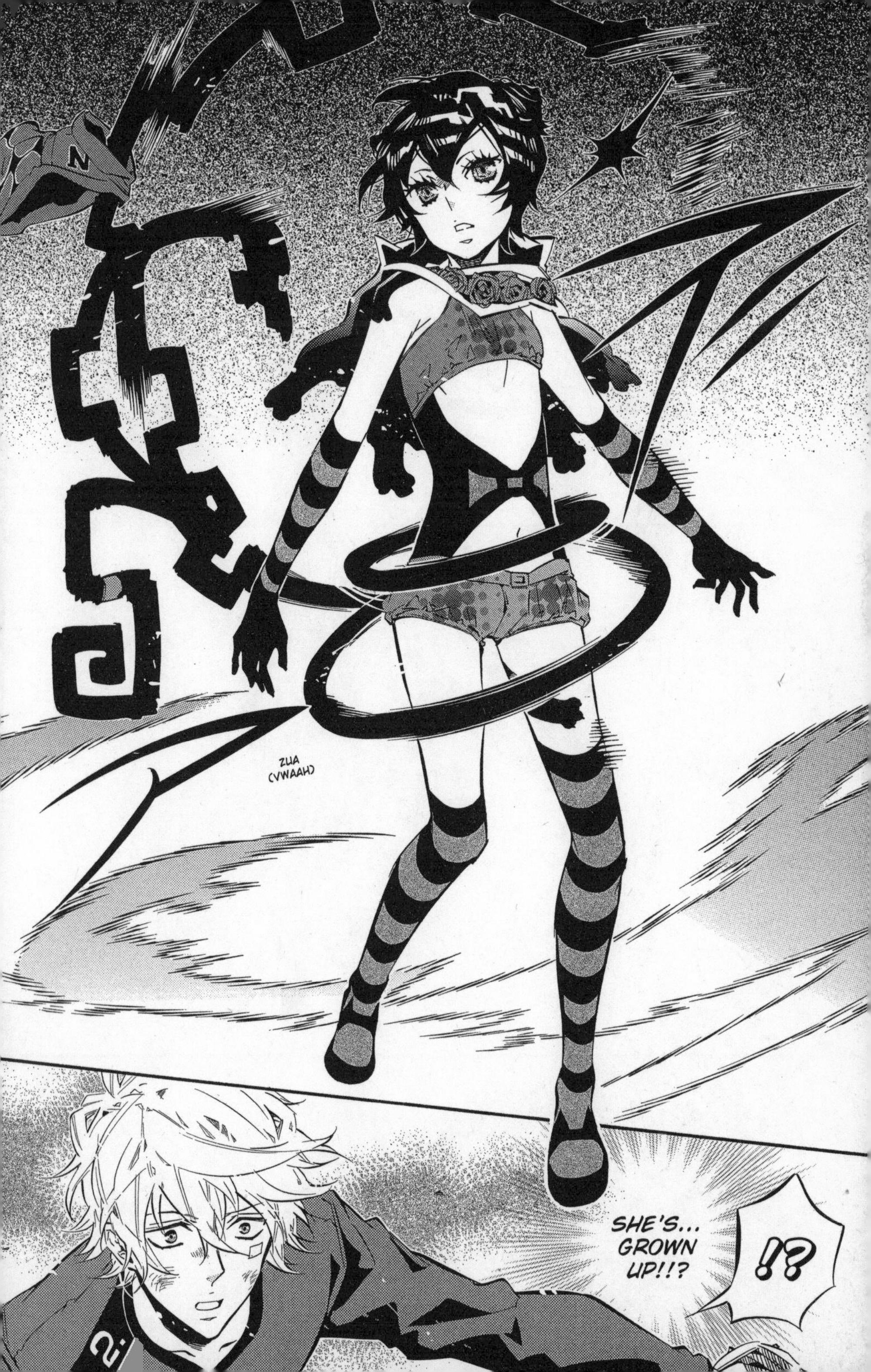
ZUA
(VWAAH)
!?
SHE'S...
GROWN
UP!!?

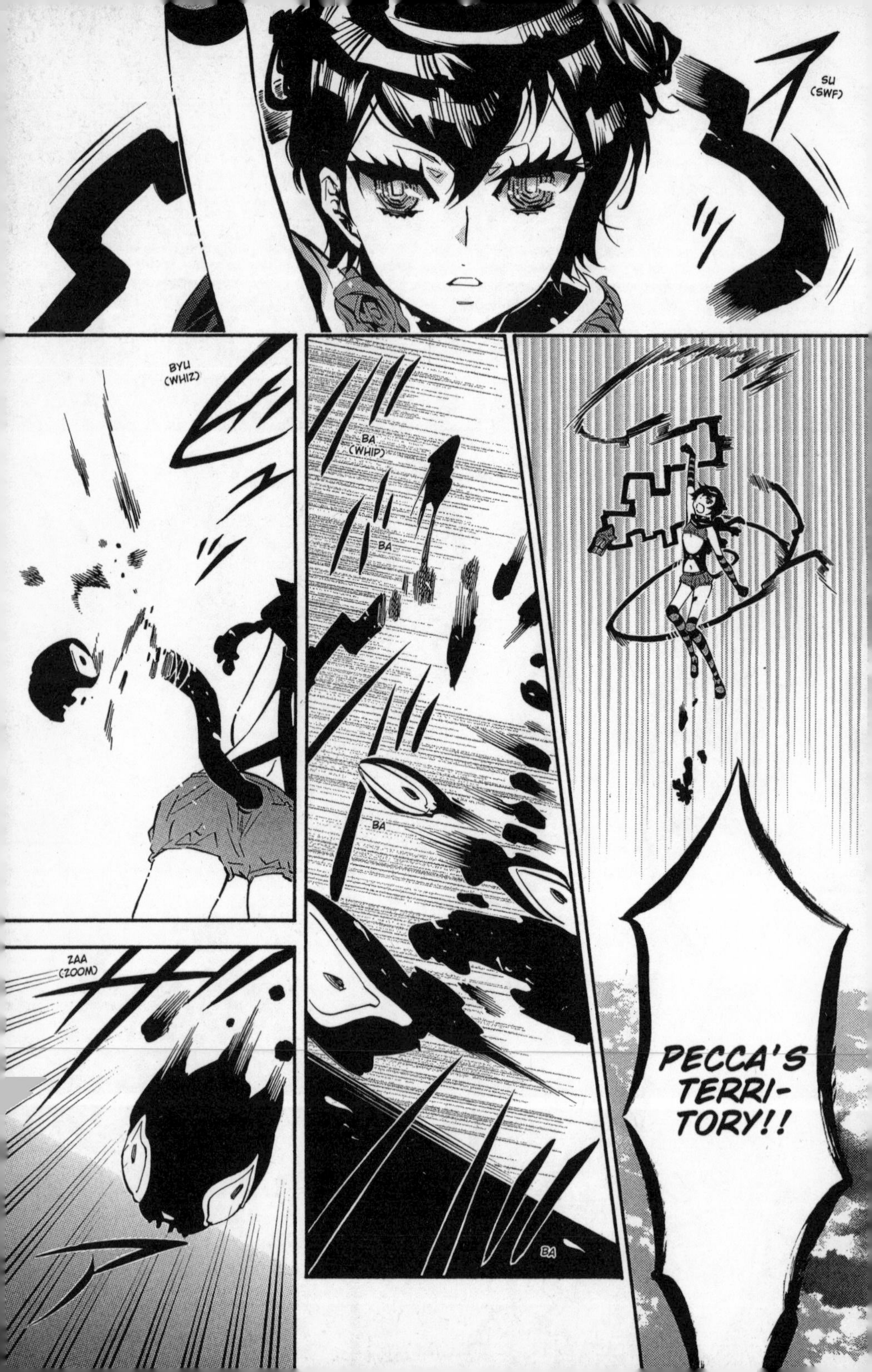
SU (SWF)
PECCA'S TERRI-TORY!!
BA (WHIP)
BA
BA
BA
BYU (WHIZ)
ZAA (ZOOM)

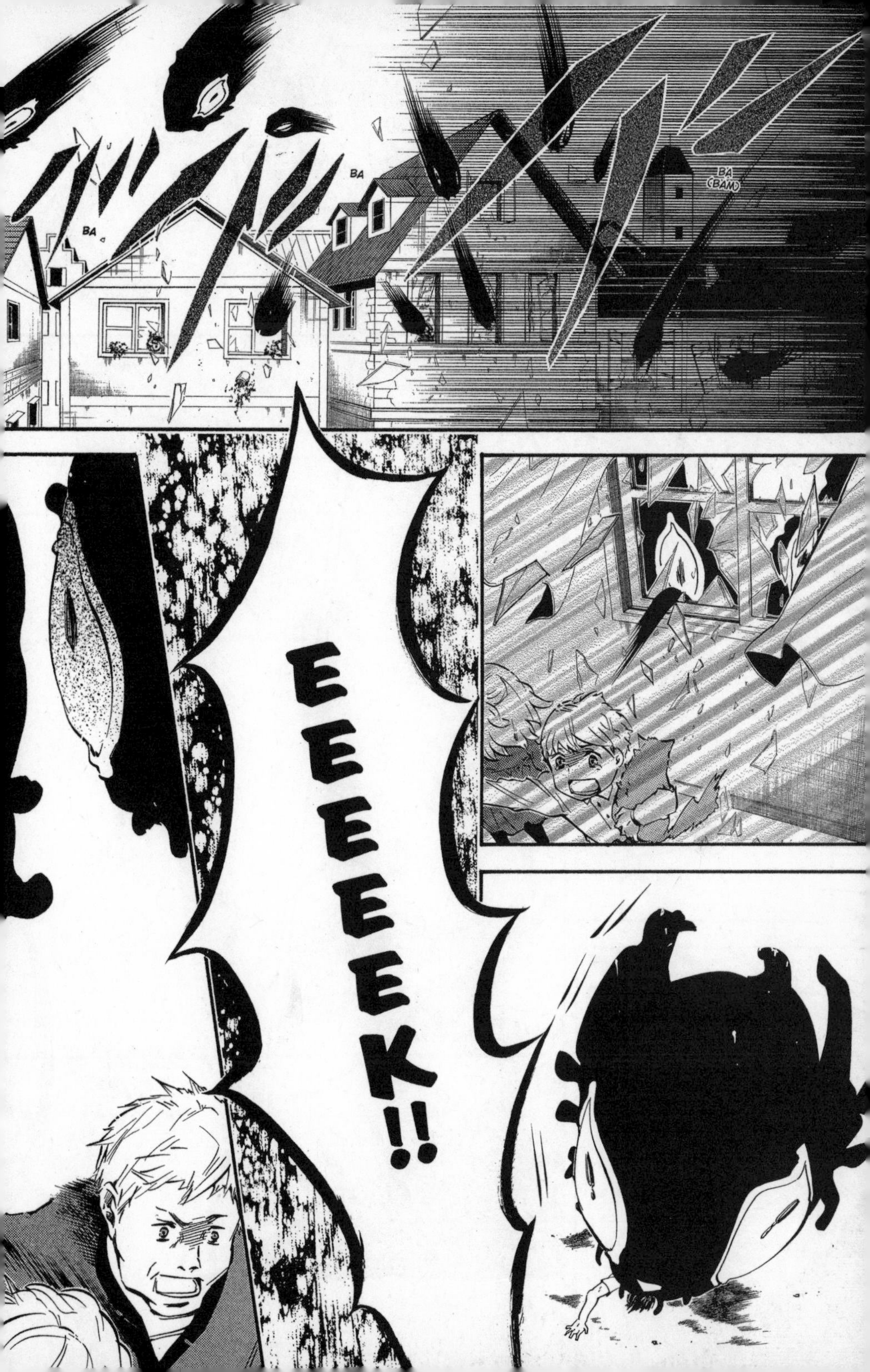
BA (BAM)
BA
BA
EEEEEK!!

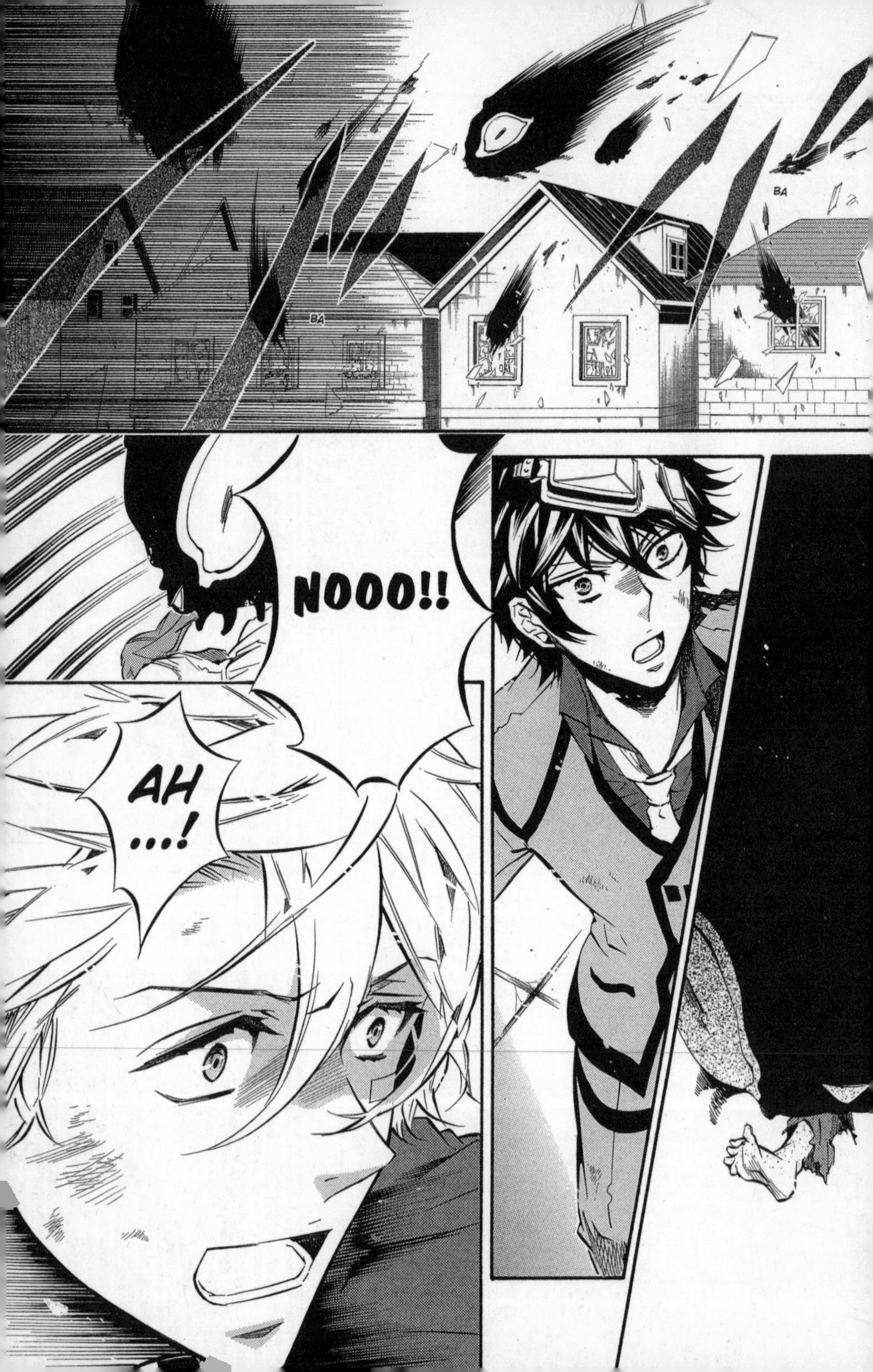
BA
BA
NOOO!!
AH ...!

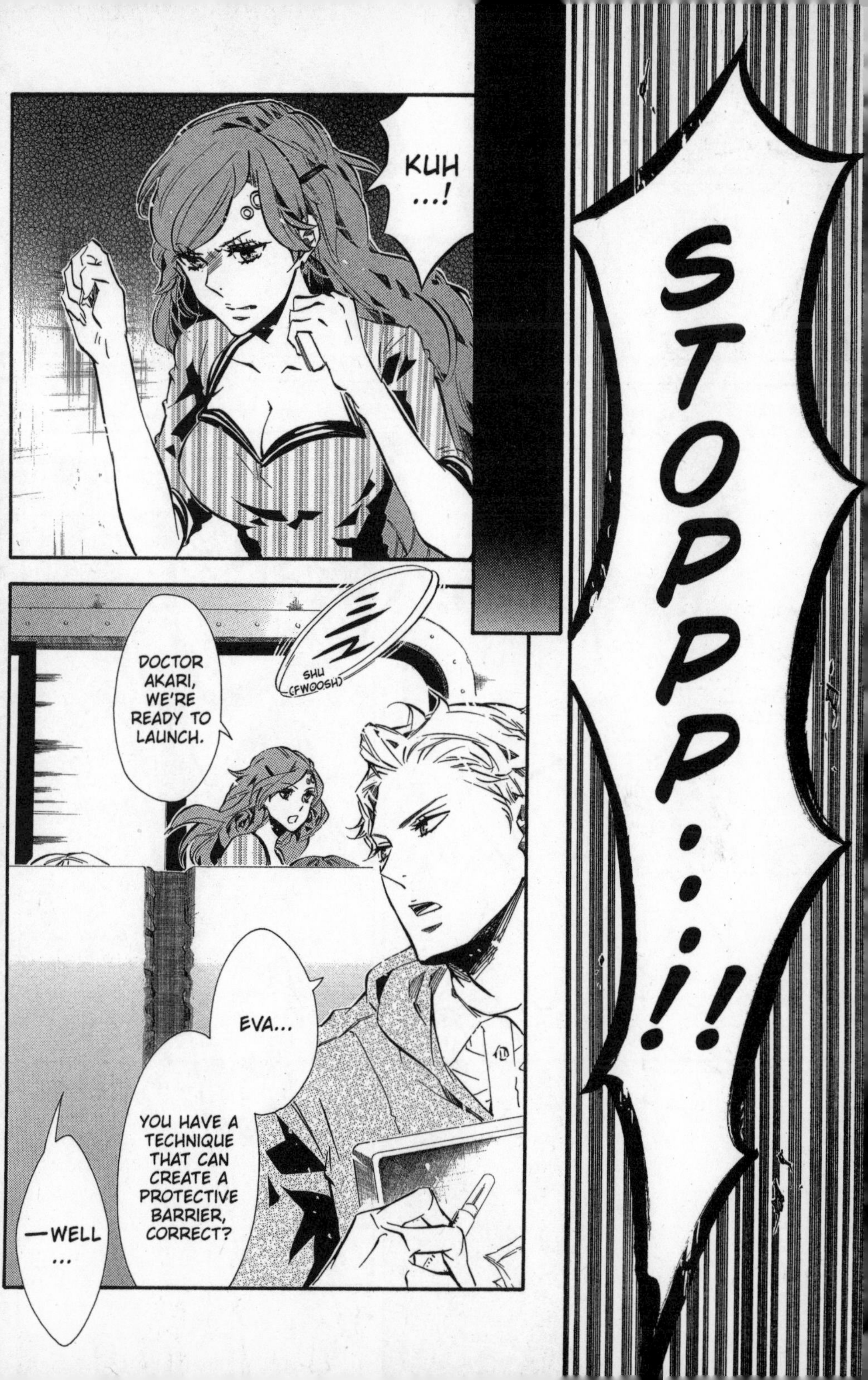
STOPP...!!
KUH ...!
SHU (FWOOSH)
DOCTOR AKARI, WE'RE READY TO LAUNCH.
EVA...
YOU HAVE A TECHNIQUE THAT CAN CREATE A PROTECTIVE BARRIER, CORRECT?
—WELL ...

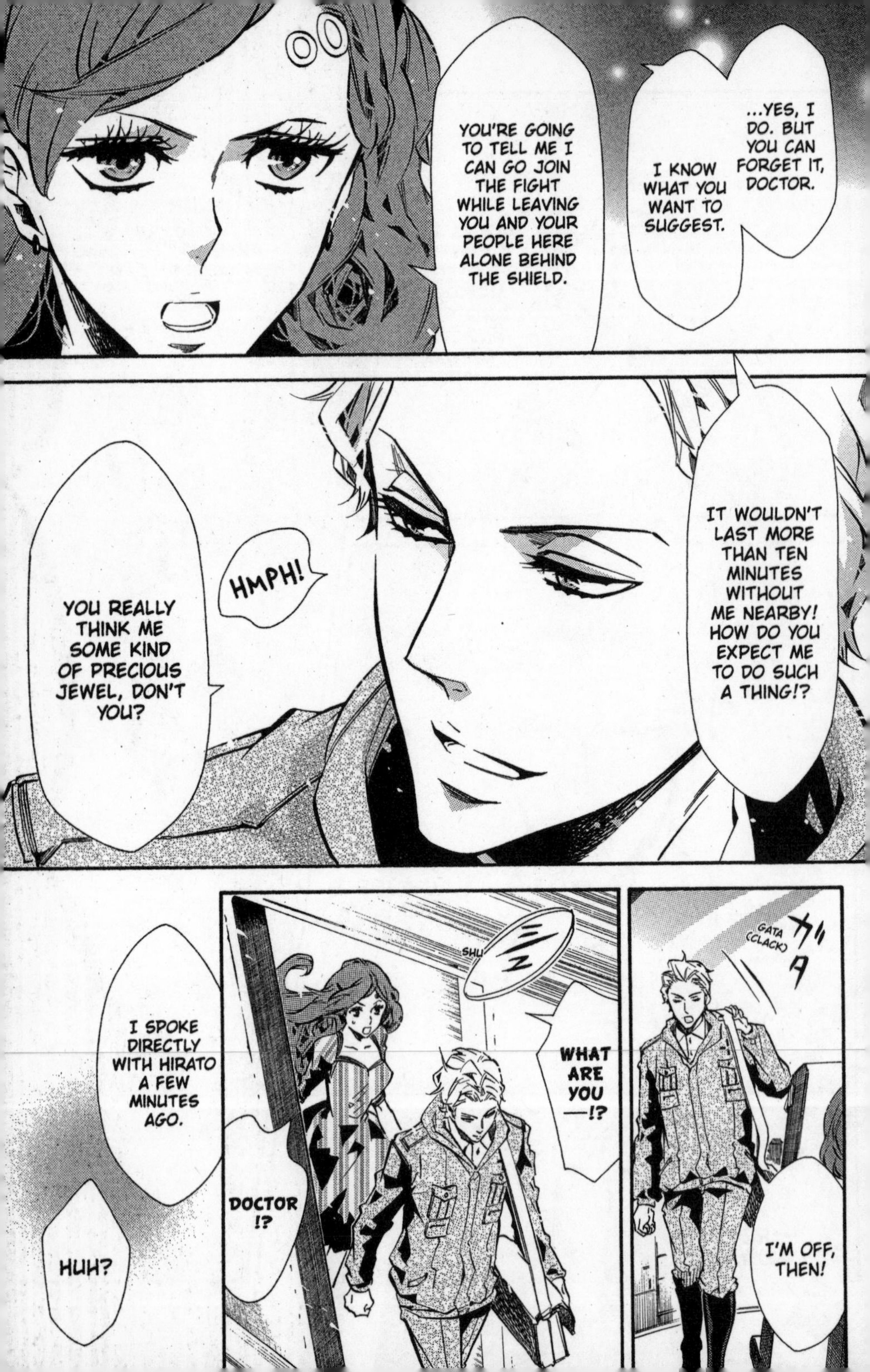
...YES, I DO. BUT YOU CAN FORGET IT, DOCTOR.
I KNOW WHAT YOU WANT TO SUGGEST.
YOU'RE GOING TO TELL ME I CAN GO JOIN THE FIGHT WHILE LEAVING YOU AND YOUR PEOPLE HERE ALONE BEHIND THE SHIELD.
IT WOULDN'T LAST MORE THAN TEN MINUTES WITHOUT ME NEARBY! HOW DO YOU EXPECT ME TO DO SUCH A THING!?
HMPH!
YOU REALLY THINK ME SOME KIND OF PRECIOUS JEWEL, DON'T YOU?
GATA (CLACK)
I'M OFF, THEN!
SHU
WHAT ARE YOU—!?
DOCTOR !?
I SPOKE DIRECTLY WITH HIRATO A FEW MINUTES AGO.
HUH?

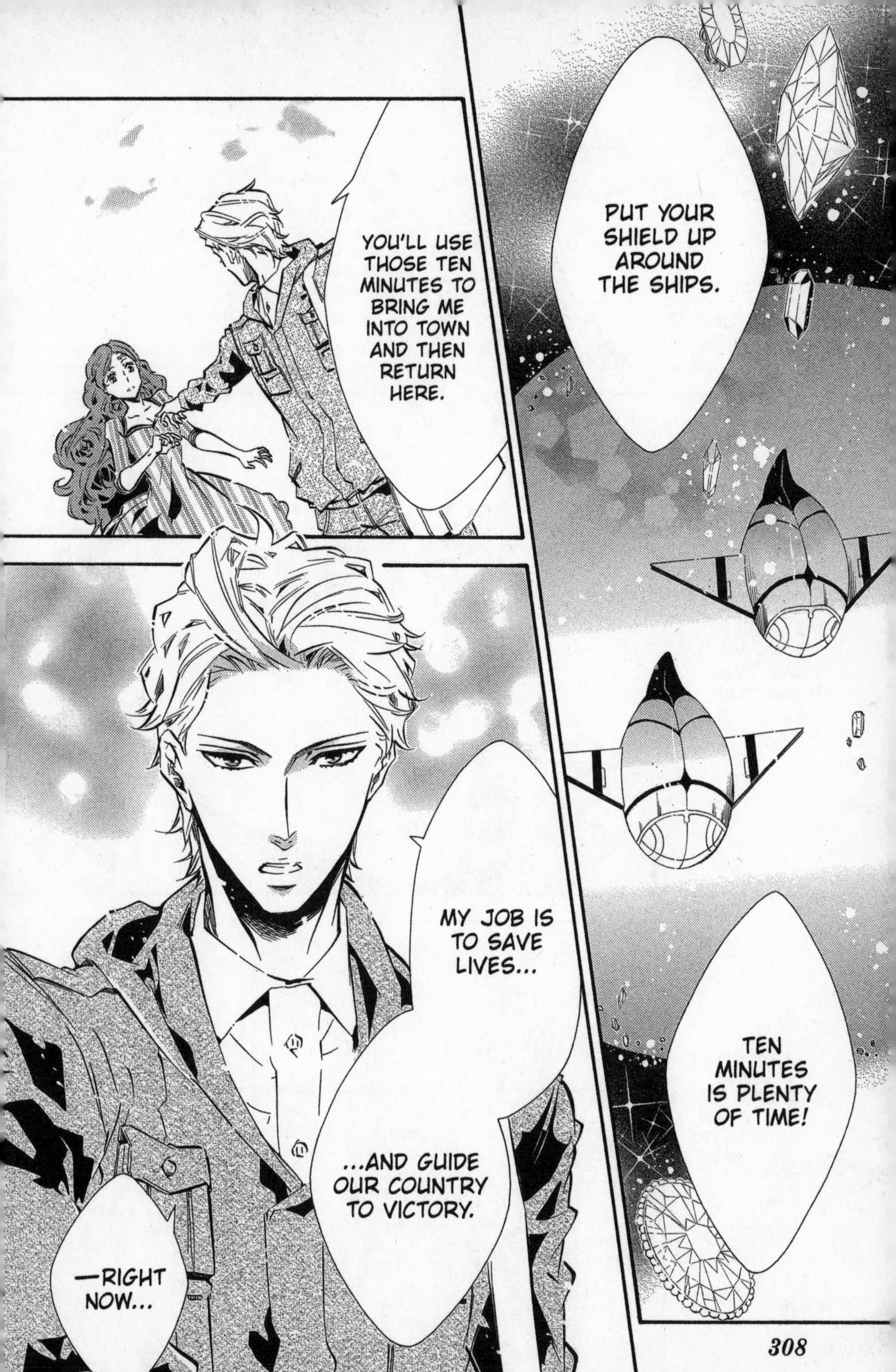
PUT YOUR SHIELD UP AROUND THE SHIPS.
TEN MINUTES IS PLENTY OF TIME!
YOU'LL USE THOSE TEN MINUTES TO BRING ME INTO TOWN AND THEN RETURN HERE.
MY JOB IS TO SAVE LIVES...
...AND GUIDE OUR COUNTRY TO VICTORY.
—RIGHT NOW...

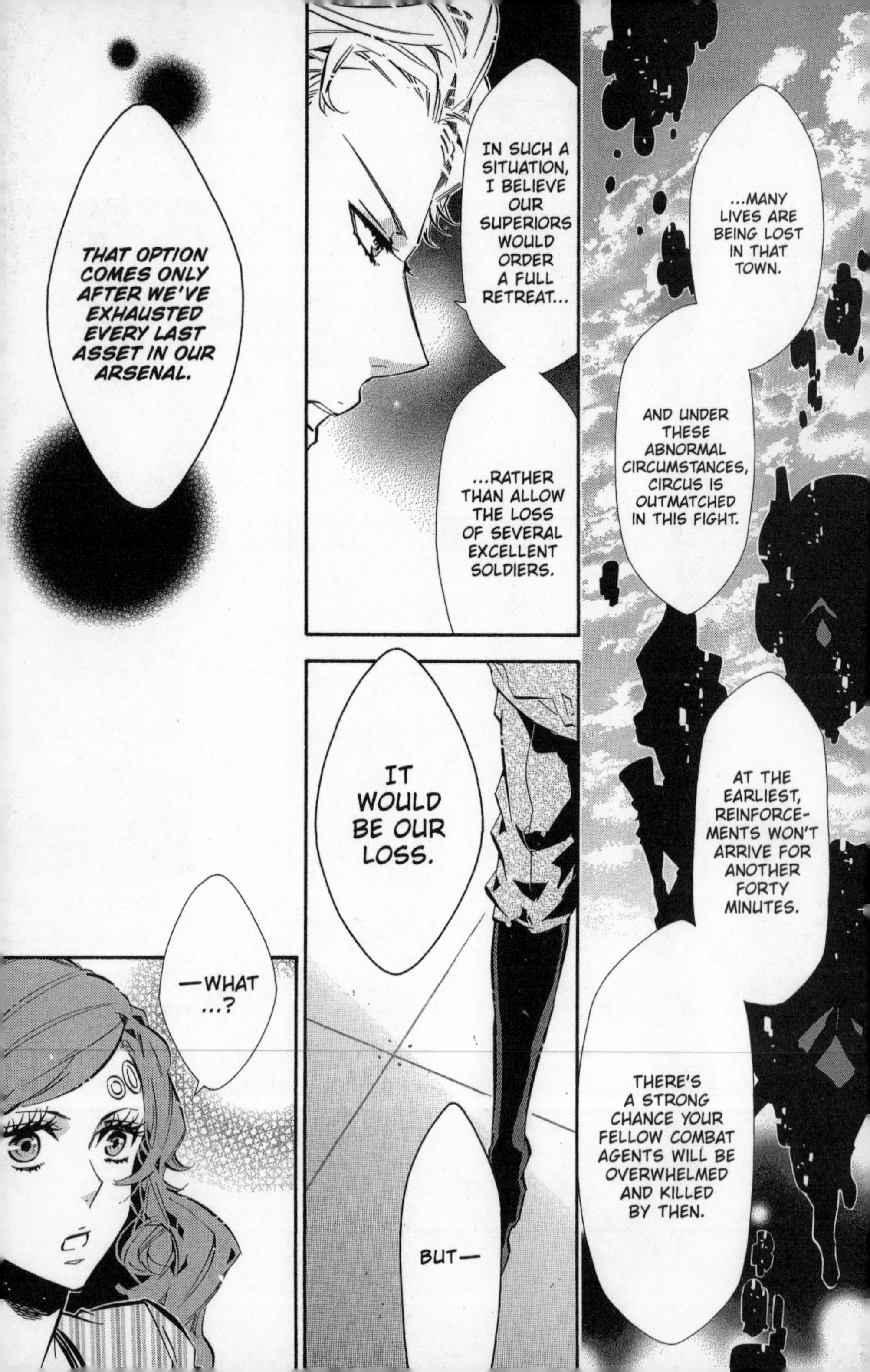
...MANY LIVES ARE BEING LOST IN THAT TOWN.
AND UNDER THESE ABNORMAL CIRCUMSTANCES, CIRCUS IS OUTMATCHED IN THIS FIGHT.
AT THE EARLIEST, REINFORCE-MENTS WON'T ARRIVE FOR ANOTHER FORTY MINUTES.
THERE'S A STRONG CHANCE YOUR FELLOW COMBAT AGENTS WILL BE OVERWHELMED AND KILLED BY THEN.
IN SUCH A SITUATION, I BELIEVE OUR SUPERIORS WOULD ORDER A FULL RETREAT...
...RATHER THAN ALLOW THE LOSS OF SEVERAL EXCELLENT SOLDIERS.
IT WOULD BE OUR LOSS.
BUT—
THAT OPTION COMES ONLY AFTER WE'VE EXHAUSTED EVERY LAST ASSET IN OUR ARSENAL.
—WHAT ...?

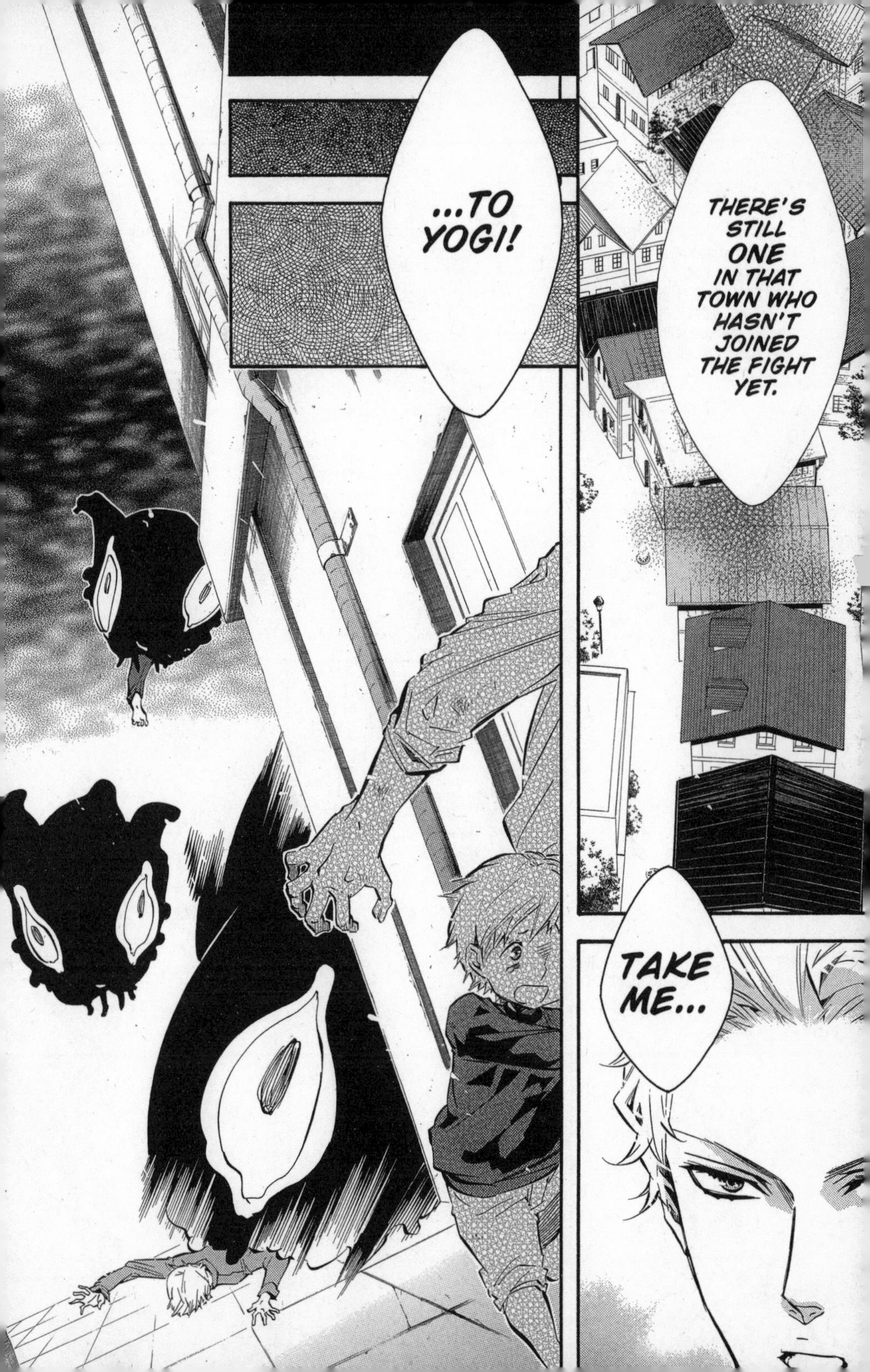
THERE'S STILL ONE IN THAT TOWN WHO HASN'T JOINED THE FIGHT YET.
TAKE ME...
...TO YOGI!

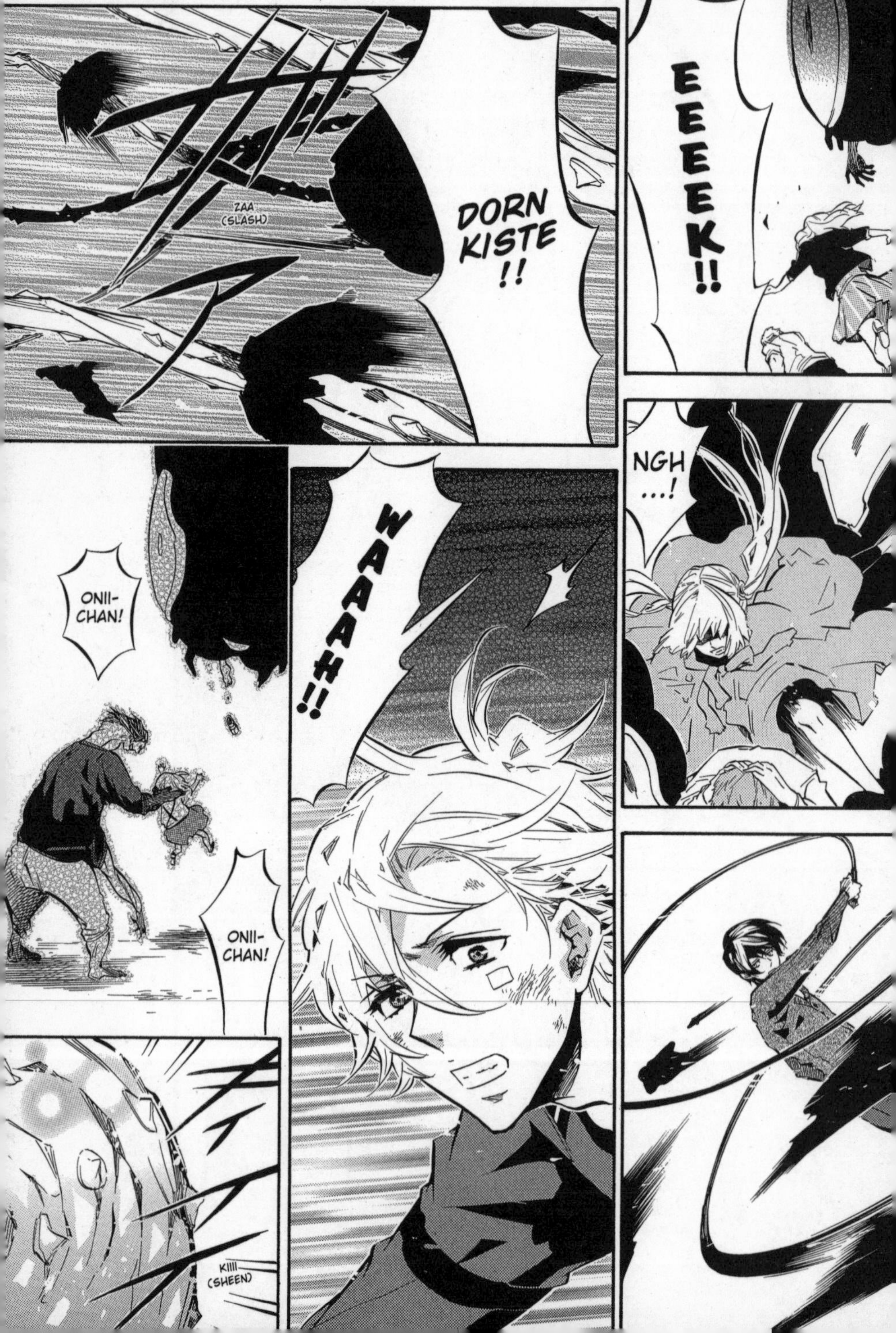
EEEEEK!!
DORN KISTE!!
ZAA (SLASH)
NGH ...!
WAAAAH!!
ONII-CHAN!
ONII-CHAN!
KIIII (SHEEN)

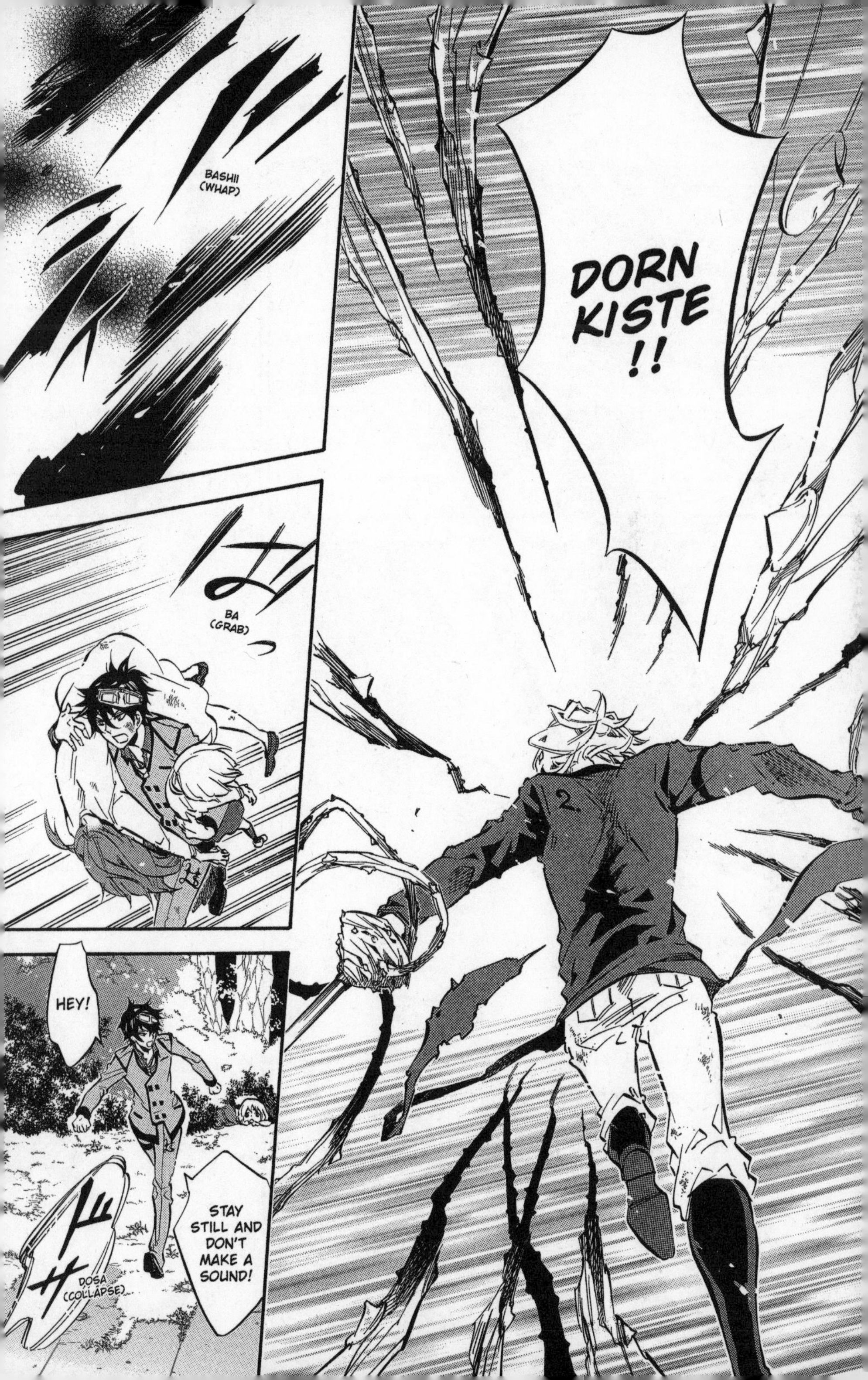
DORN KISTE!!
BASHII (WHAP)
BA (GRAB)
HEY!
STAY STILL AND DON'T MAKE A SOUND!
DOSA (COLLAPSE)

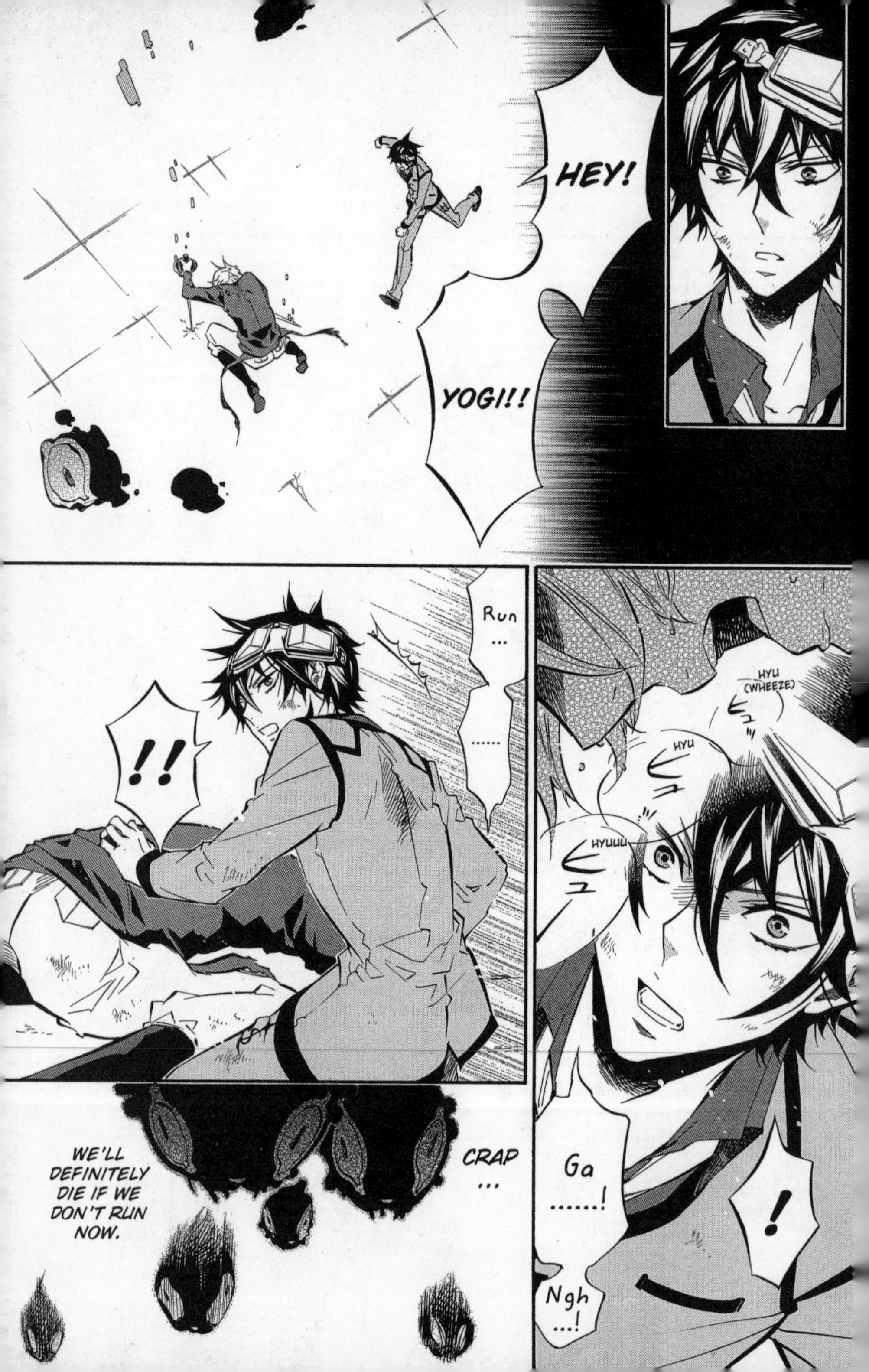
HEY!
YOGI!!
HYU (WHEEZE)
HYU
HYUUU
Ga ....!
!
Ngh ...!
Run ...
......
!!
CRAP ...
WE'LL DEFINITELY DIE IF WE DON'T RUN NOW.

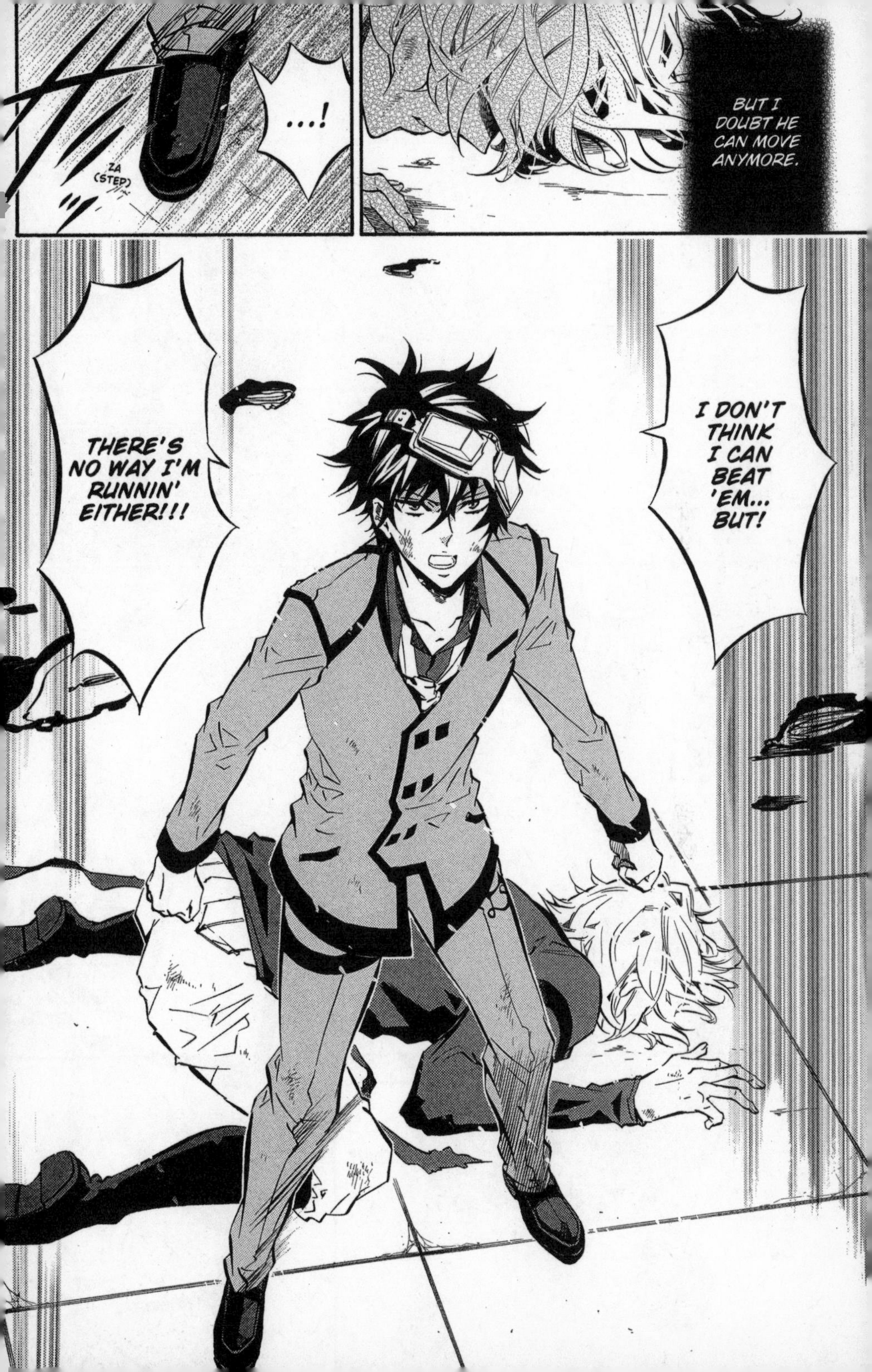
BUT I DOUBT HE CAN MOVE ANYMORE.
...!
ZA (STEP)
I DON'T THINK I CAN BEAT 'EM... BUT!
THERE'S NO WAY I'M RUNNIN' EITHER!!!

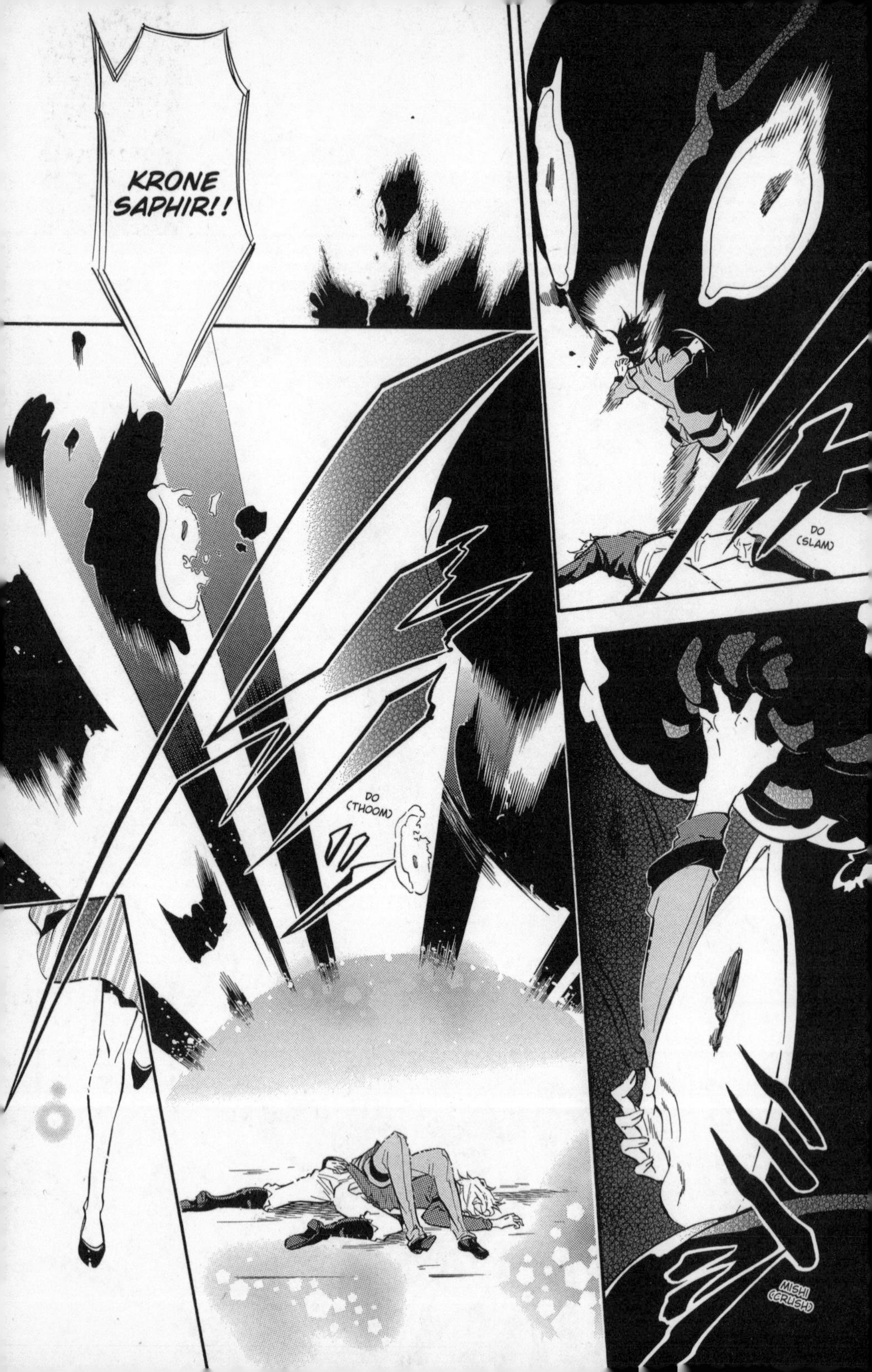
DO (SLAM)
MISHI (CRUSH)
KRONE SAPHIR!!
DO (THOOM)

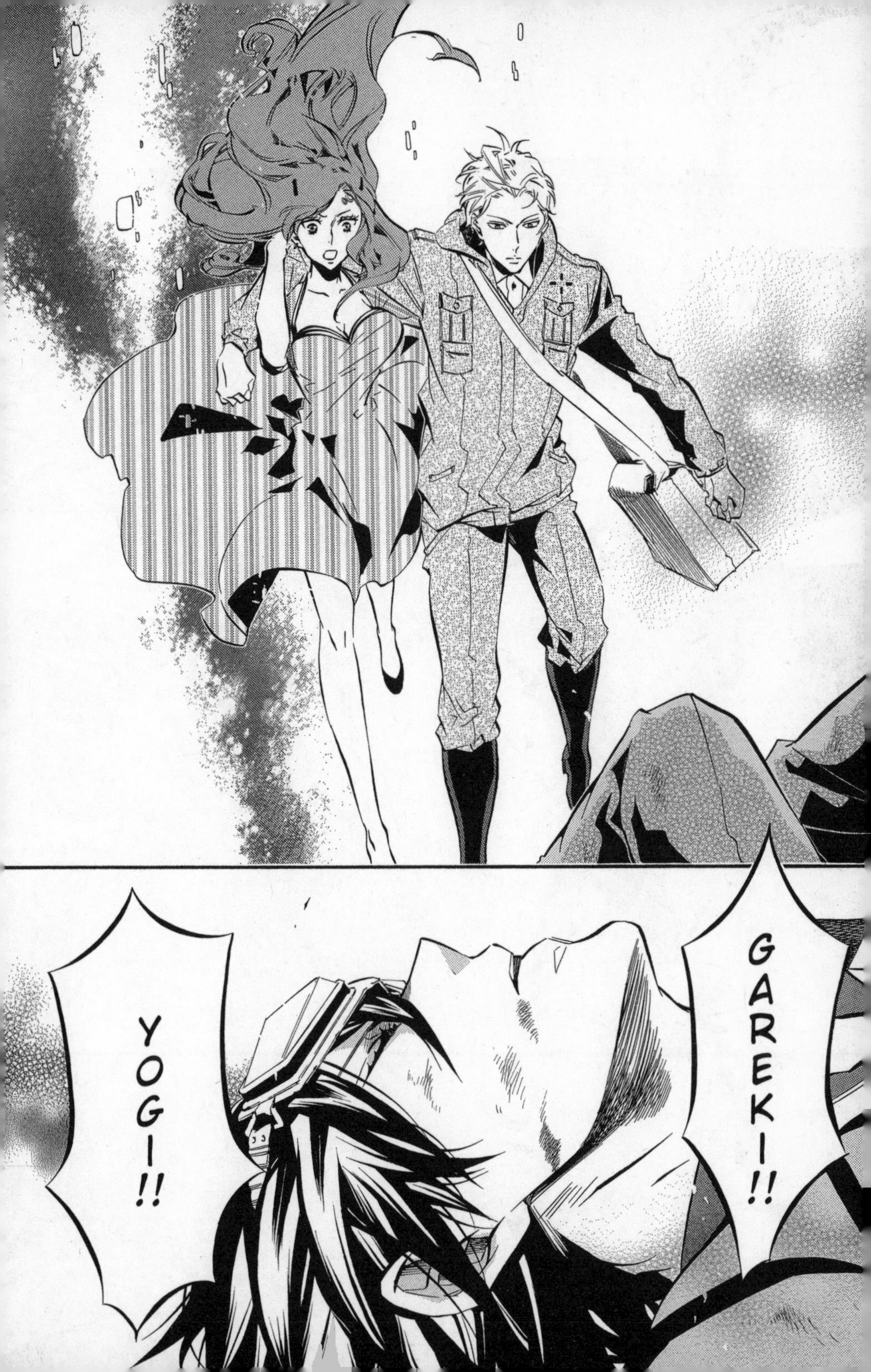
GAREKI!!
YOGI!!

Score 59: The Silver One

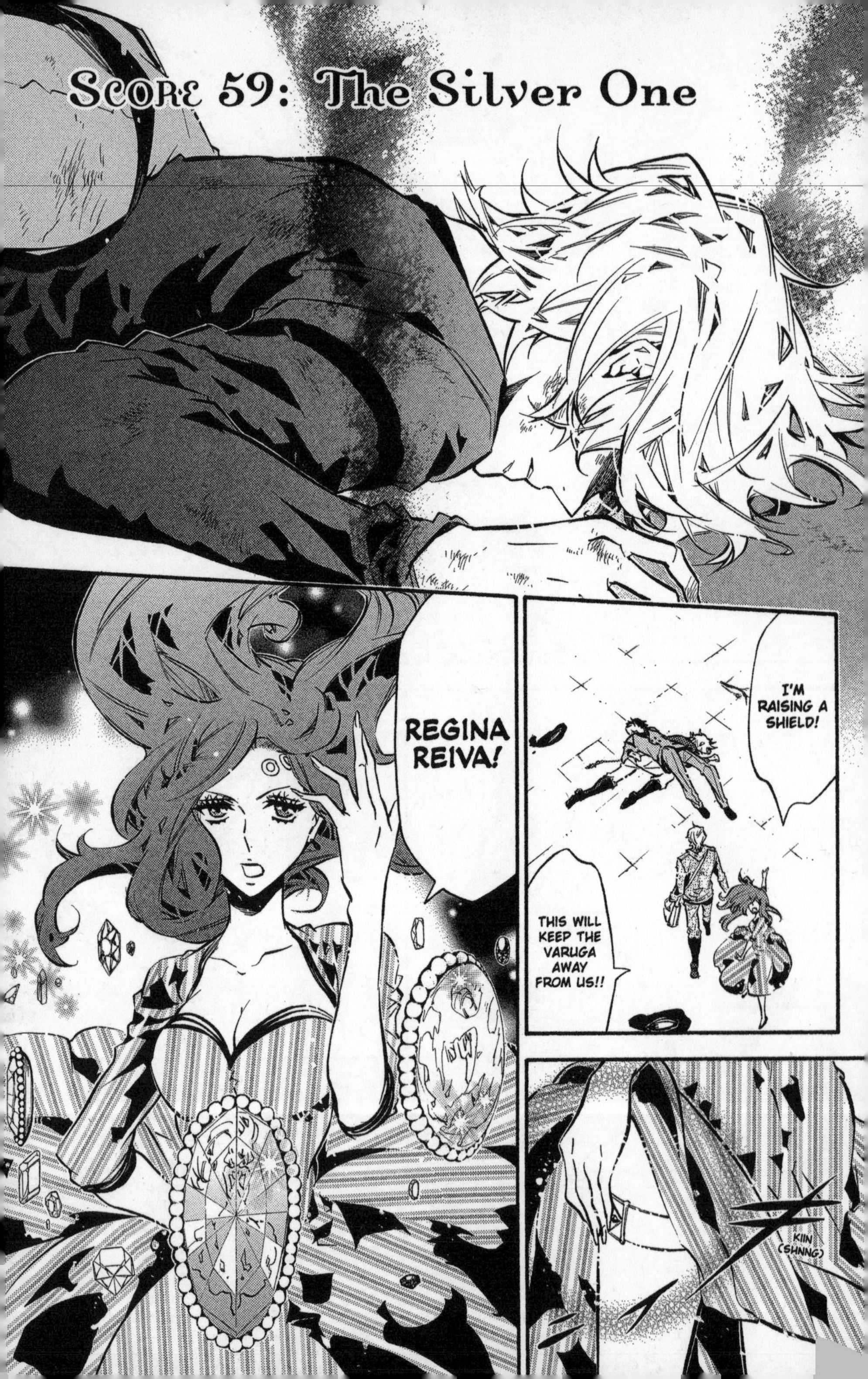

I'M RAISING A SHIELD!
THIS WILL KEEP THE VARUGA AWAY FROM US!!
KIIN (SHNNG)
REGINA REIVA!

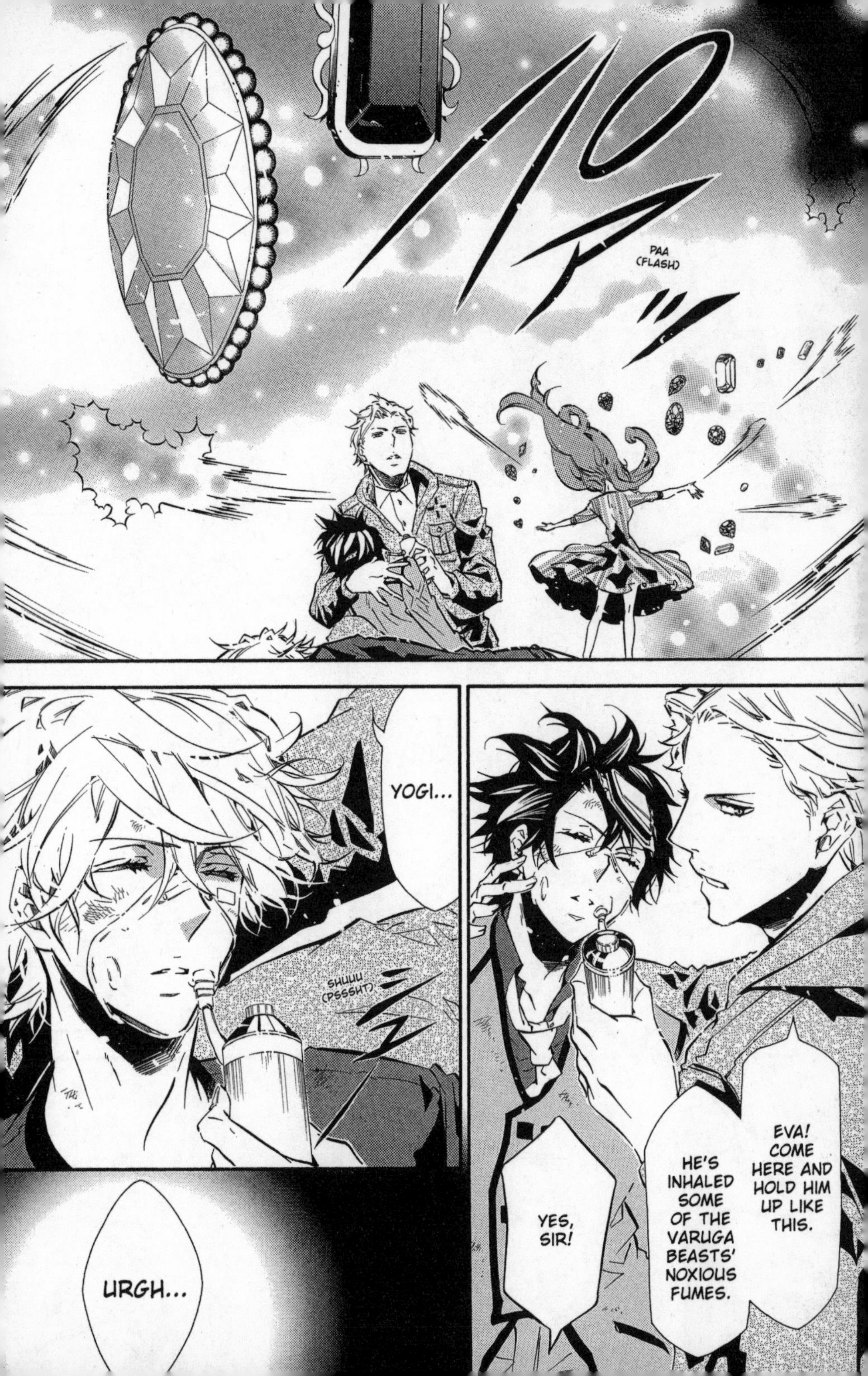
PAA (FLASH)
EVA! COME HERE AND HOLD HIM UP LIKE THIS.
HE'S INHALED SOME OF THE VARUGA BEASTS' NOXIOUS FUMES.
YES, SIR!
YOGI...
SHUUU (PSSSHT)
URGH...

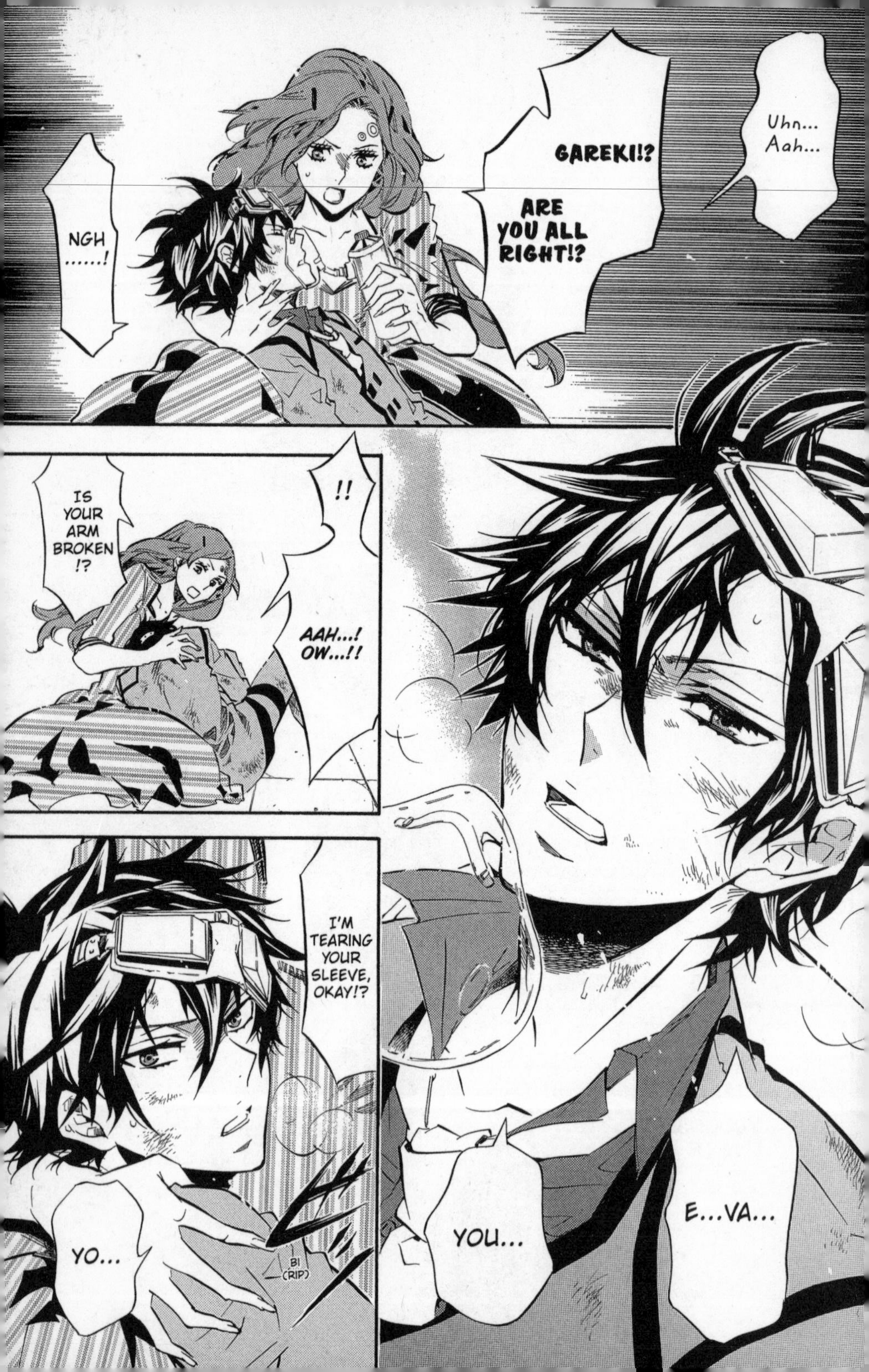
Uhn... Aah...
GAREKI!?
ARE YOU ALL RIGHT!?
NGH ......!
E...VA...
YOU...
!!
IS YOUR ARM BROKEN !?
AAH...! OW...!!
I'M TEARING YOUR SLEEVE, OKAY!?
BI (RIP)
YO...

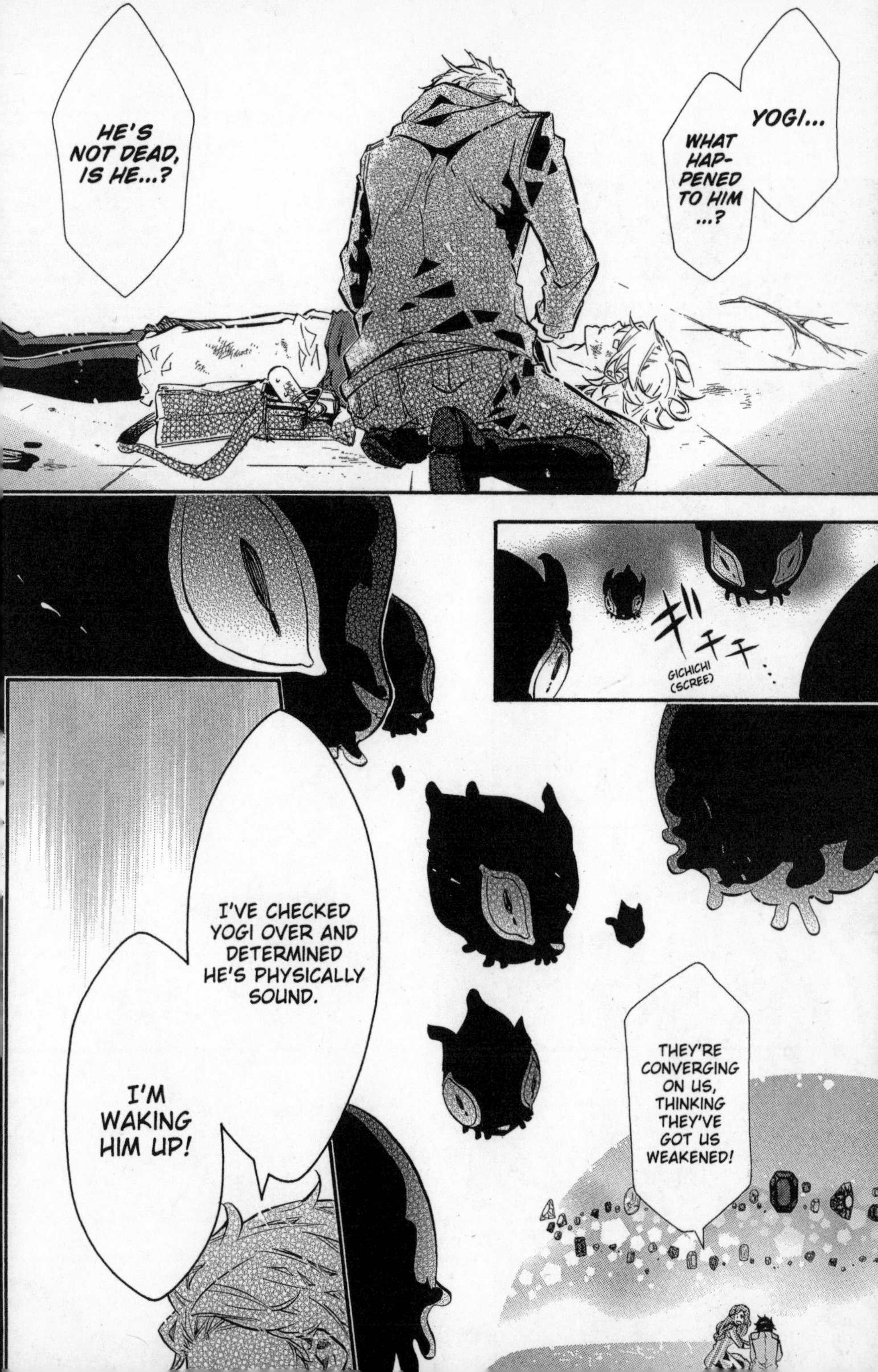
YOGI... WHAT HAP-PENED TO HIM ...?
HE'S NOT DEAD, IS HE...?
ギチチ...
GICHICHI (SCREE)
THEY'RE CONVERGING ON US, THINKING THEY'VE GOT US WEAKENED!
I'VE CHECKED YOGI OVER AND DETERMINED HE'S PHYSICALLY SOUND.
I'M WAKING HIM UP!

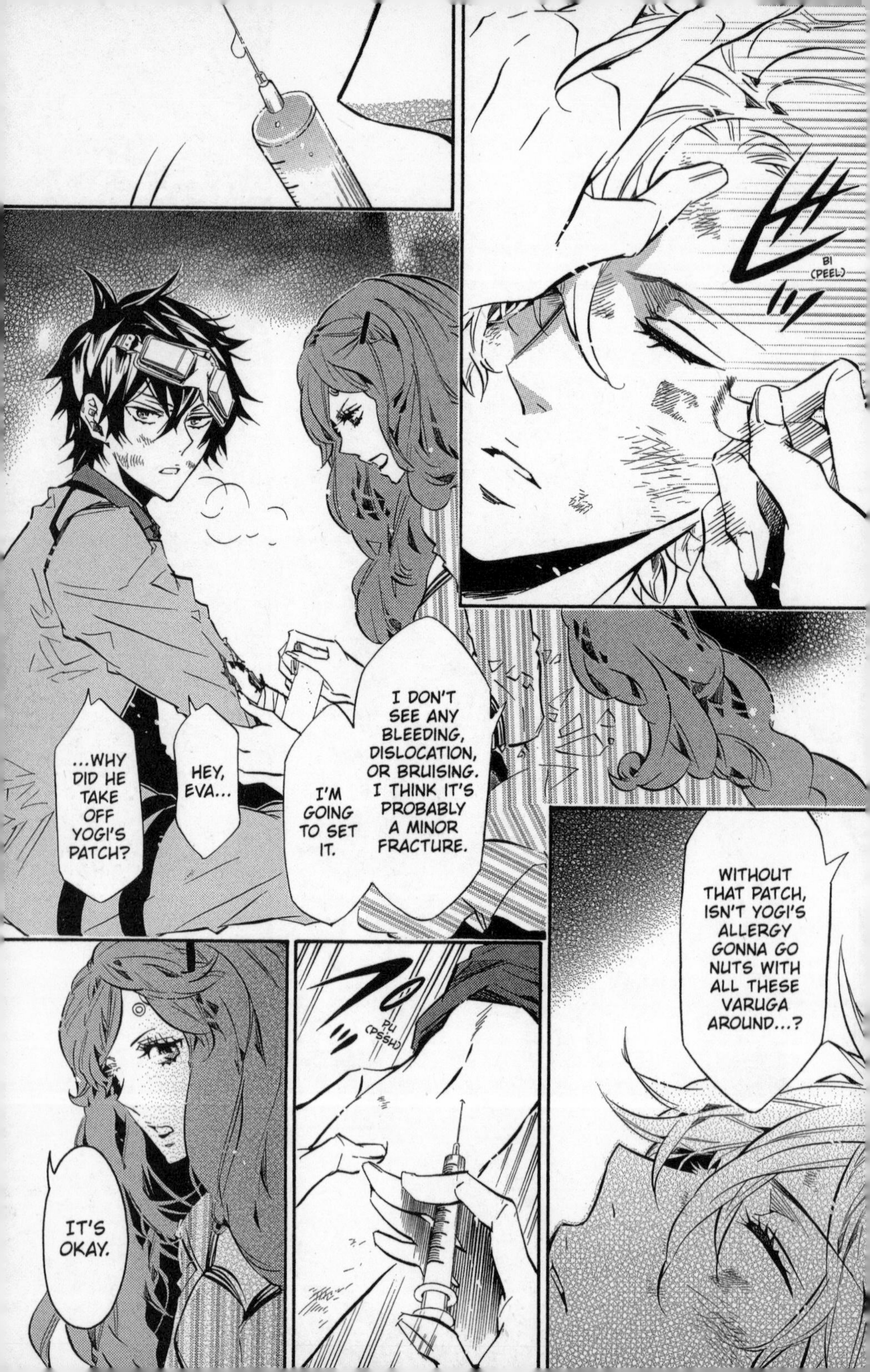
BI
(PEEL)
I DON'T SEE ANY BLEEDING, DISLOCATION, OR BRUISING. I THINK IT'S PROBABLY A MINOR FRACTURE.
I'M GOING TO SET IT.
HEY, EVA...
...WHY DID HE TAKE OFF YOGI'S PATCH?
WITHOUT THAT PATCH, ISN'T YOGI'S ALLERGY GONNA GO NUTS WITH ALL THESE VARUGA AROUND...?
PU
(PSSH)
IT'S OKAY.

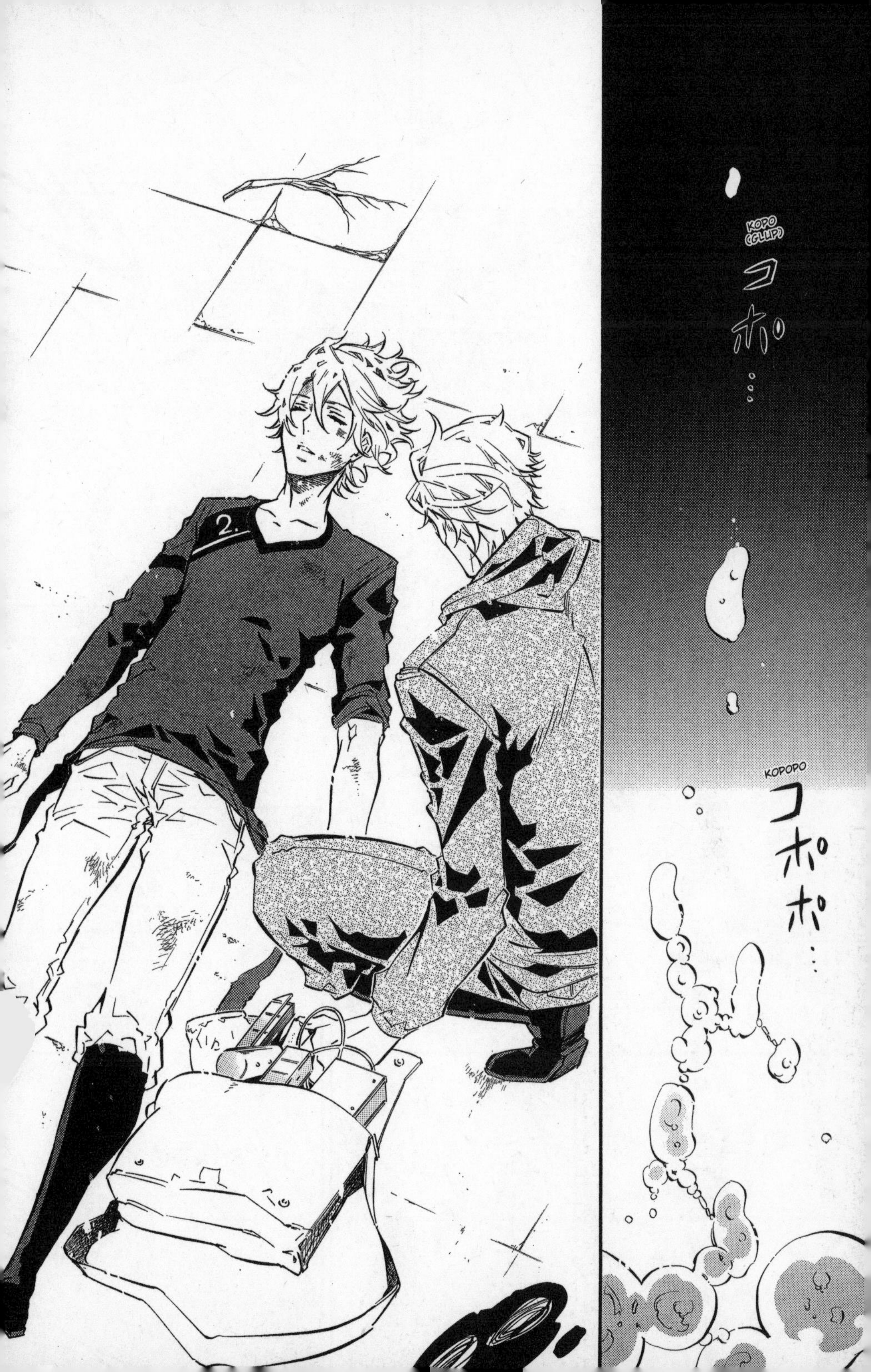
KOPO (GLUP)
コポ…
KOPOPO
コポポ…

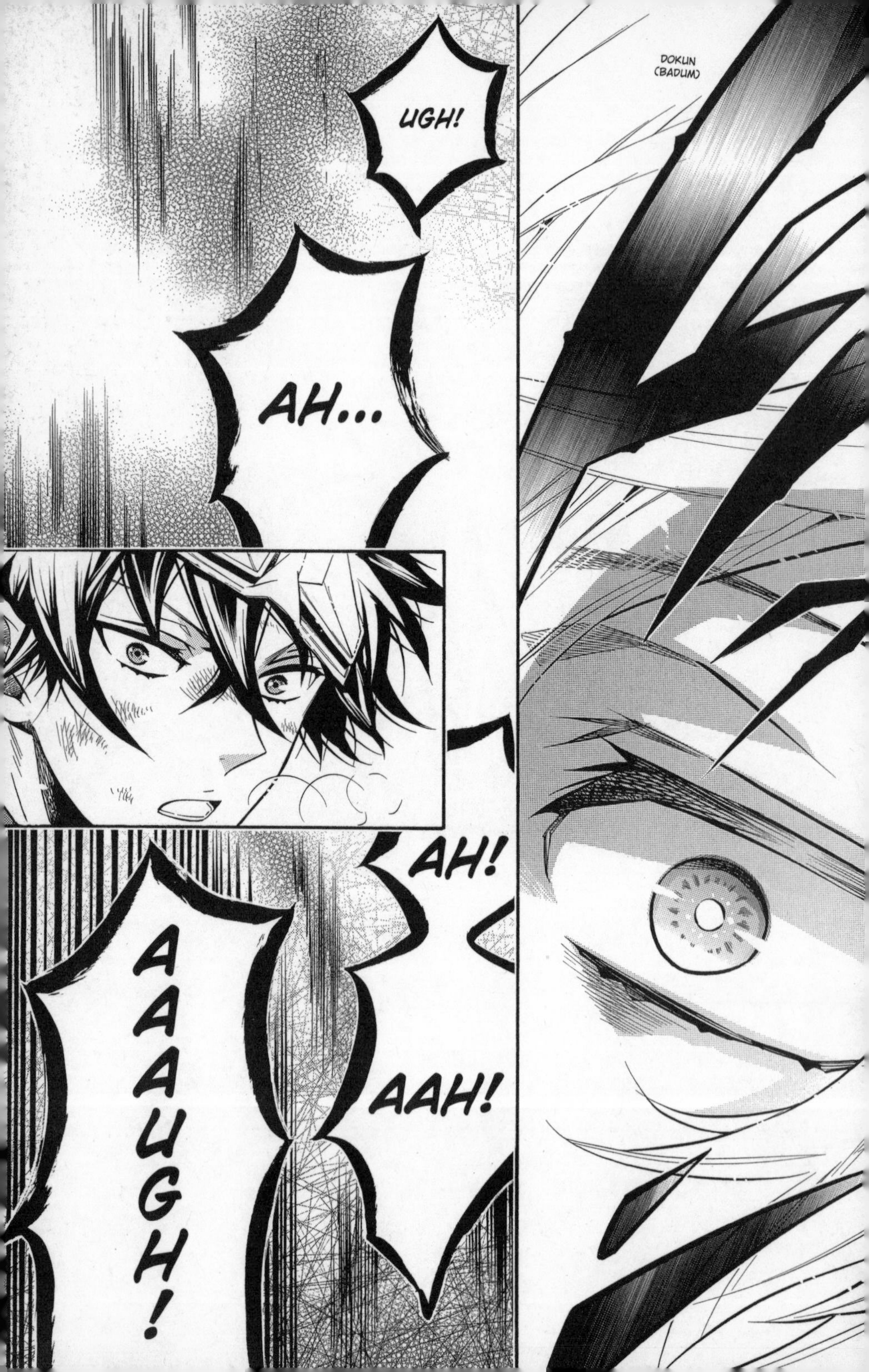
DOKUN
(BADUM)
UGH!
AH...
AH!
AAH!
AAAUGH!

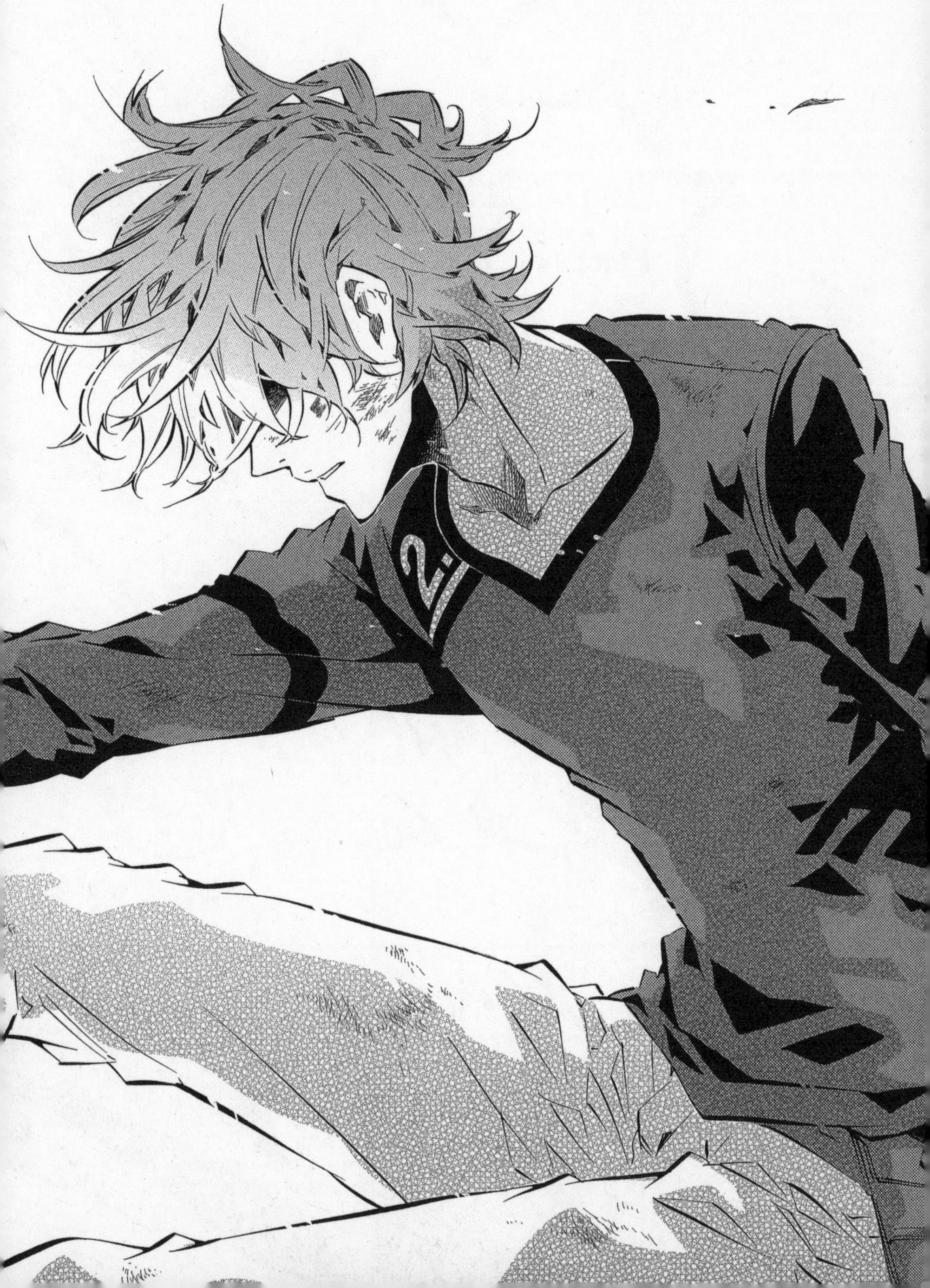

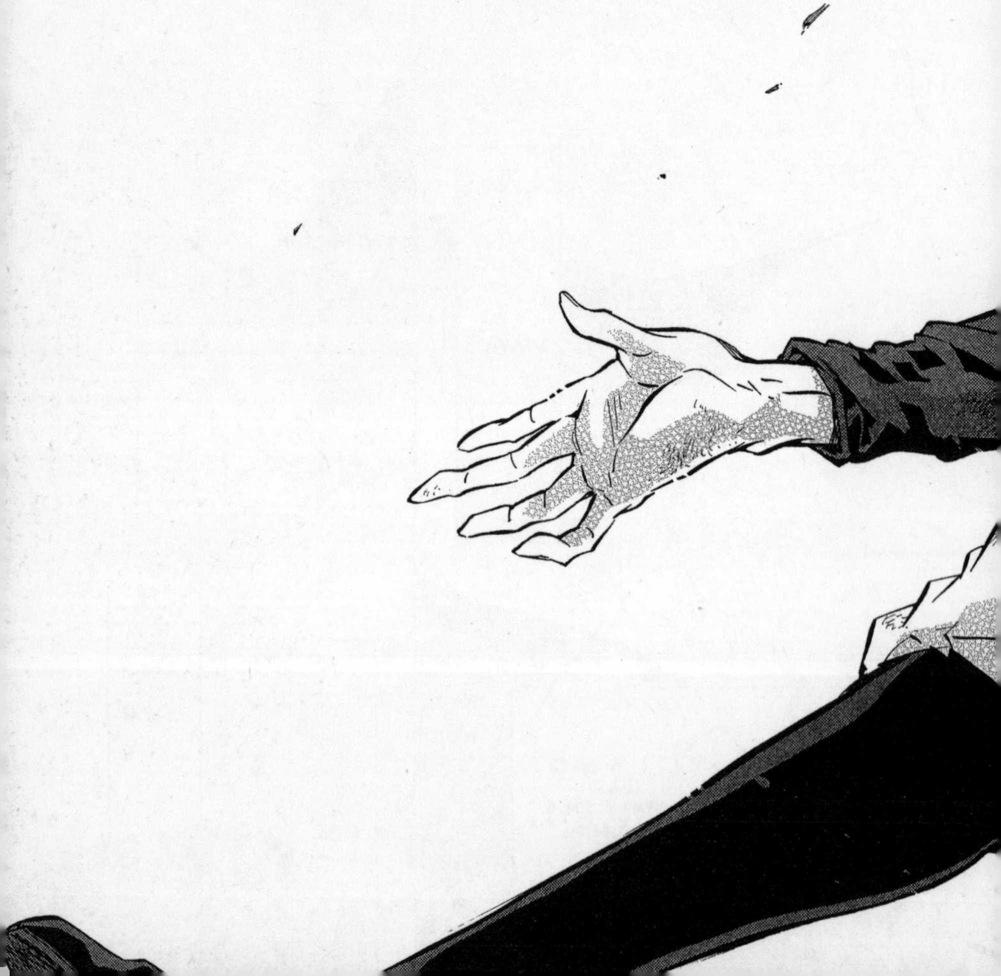

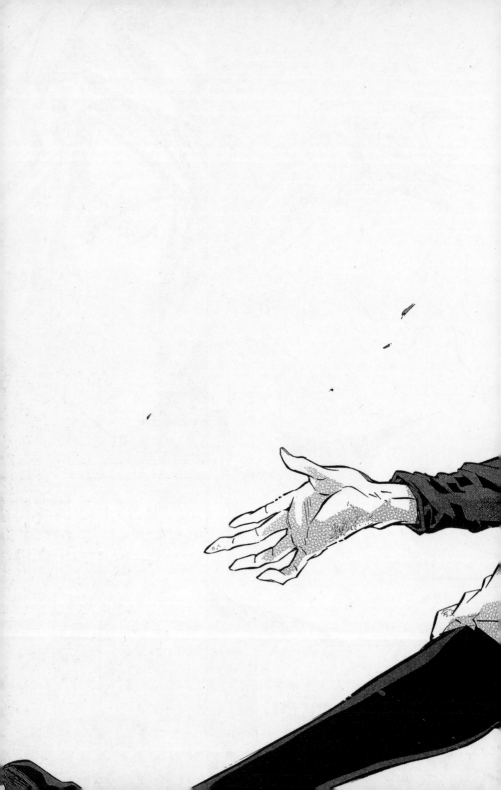

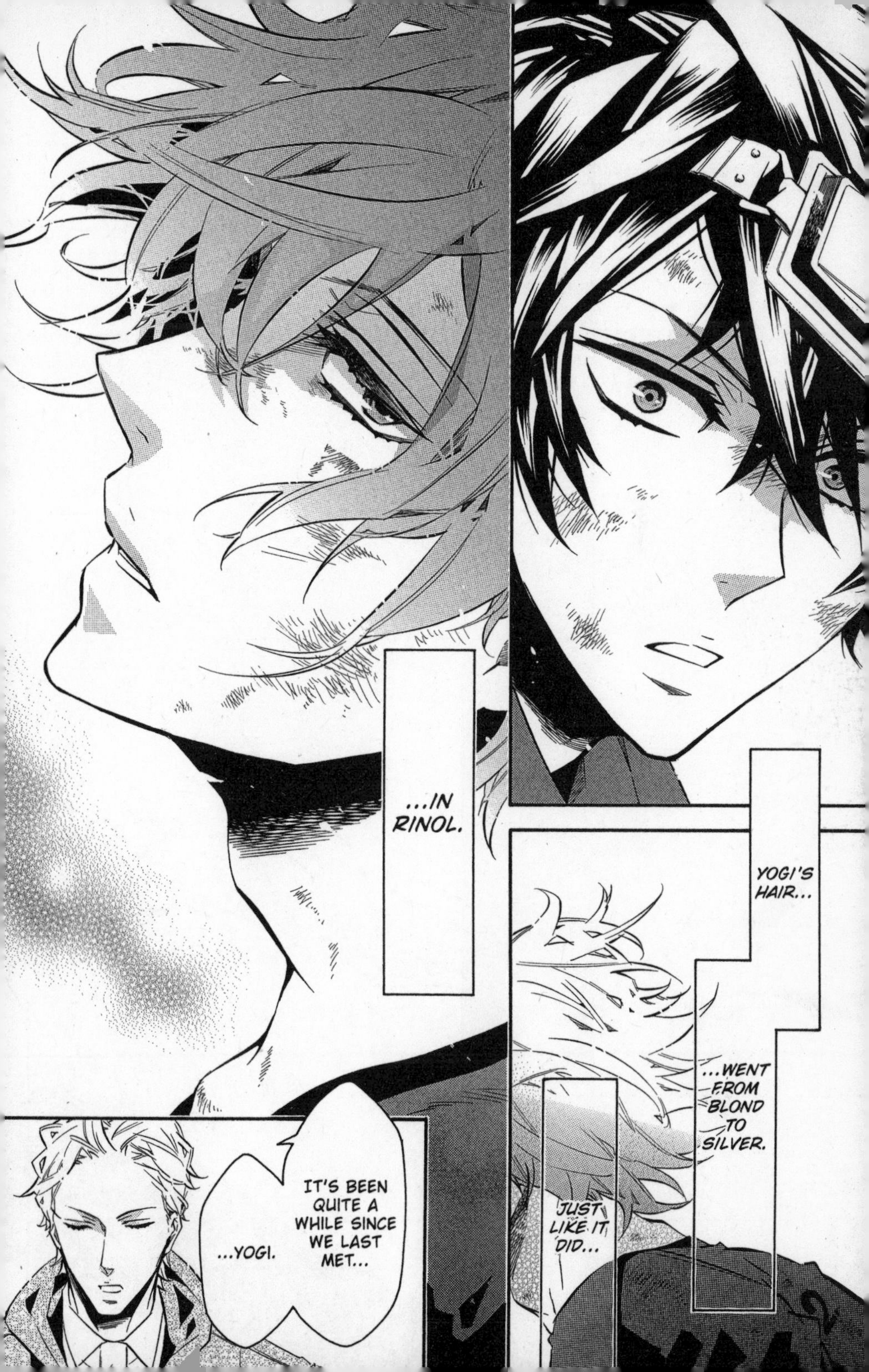
...IN RINOL.
YOGI'S HAIR...
...WENT FROM BLOND TO SILVER.
JUST LIKE IT DID...
IT'S BEEN QUITE A WHILE SINCE WE LAST MET...
...YOGI.

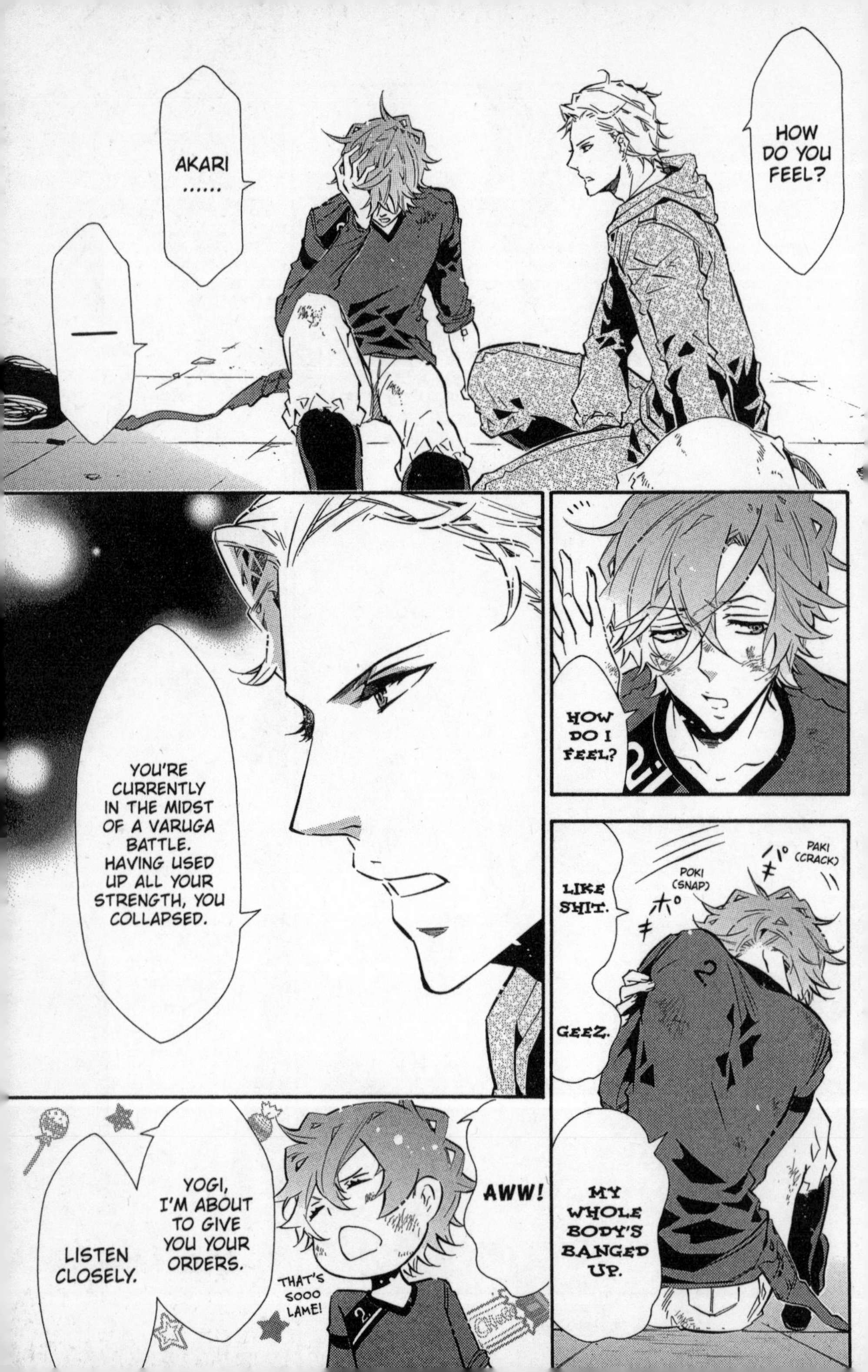
HOW DO YOU FEEL?
AKARI ......
—
HOW DO I FEEL?
PAKI (CRACK)
POKI (SNAP)
LIKE SHIT.
GEEZ.
MY WHOLE BODY'S BANGED UP.
YOU'RE CURRENTLY IN THE MIDST OF A VARUGA BATTLE. HAVING USED UP ALL YOUR STRENGTH, YOU COLLAPSED.
AWW!
THAT'S SOOO LAME!
YOGI, I'M ABOUT TO GIVE YOU YOUR ORDERS.
LISTEN CLOSELY.

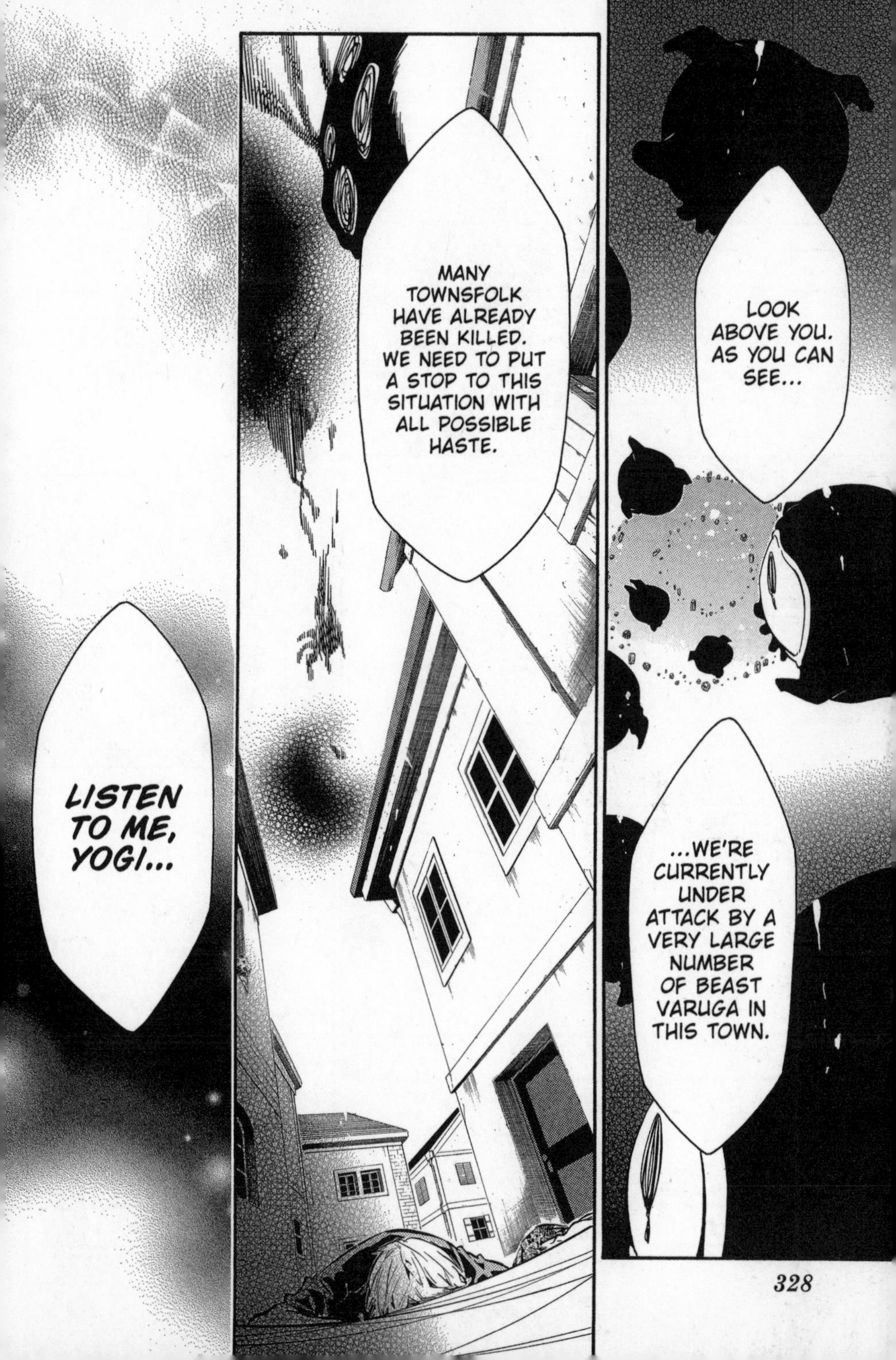
LOOK ABOVE YOU. AS YOU CAN SEE...
...WE'RE CURRENTLY UNDER ATTACK BY A VERY LARGE NUMBER OF BEAST VARUGA IN THIS TOWN.
MANY TOWNSFOLK HAVE ALREADY BEEN KILLED. WE NEED TO PUT A STOP TO THIS SITUATION WITH ALL POSSIBLE HASTE.
LISTEN TO ME, YOGI...

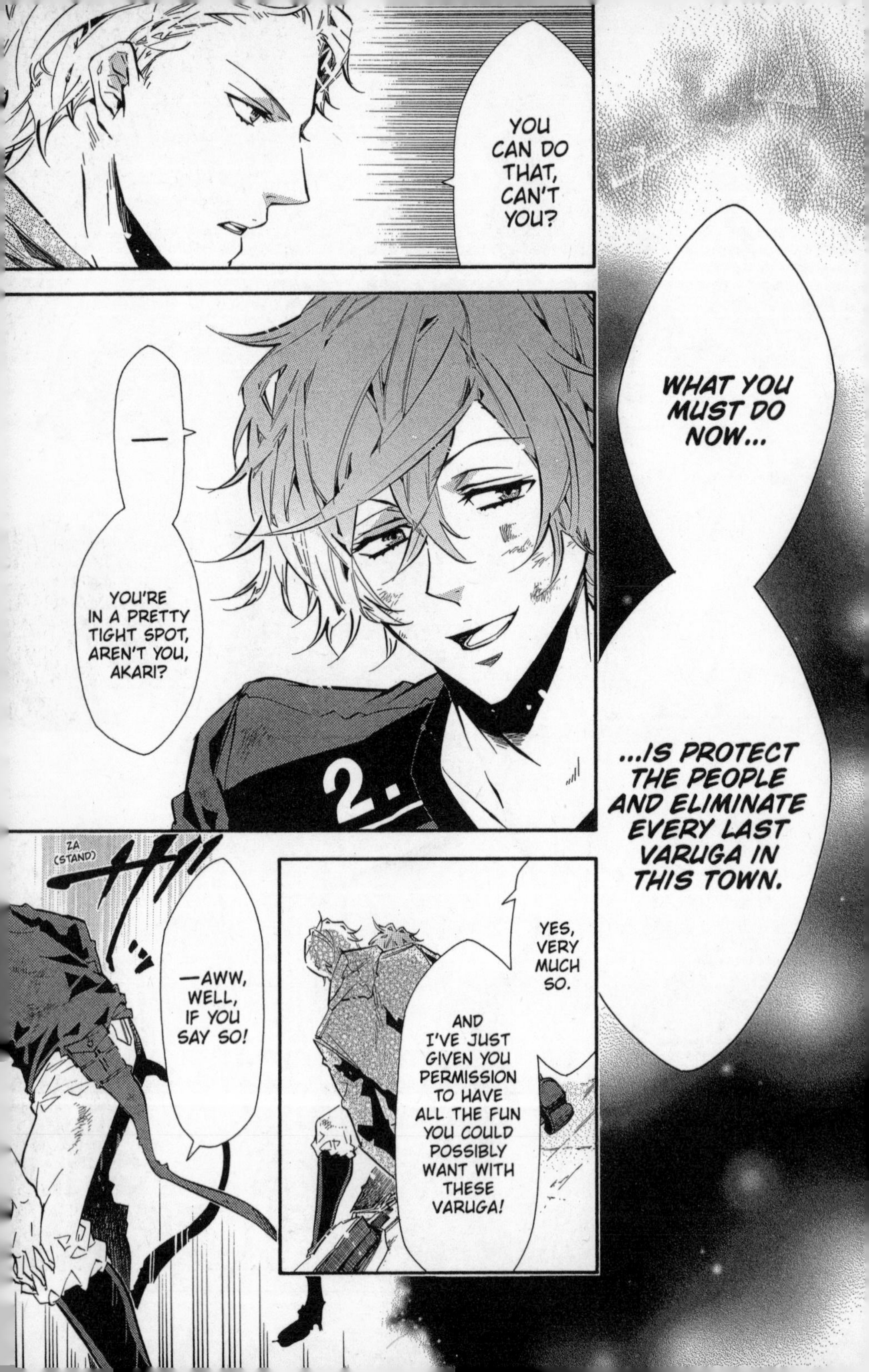
WHAT YOU MUST DO NOW...
...IS PROTECT THE PEOPLE AND ELIMINATE EVERY LAST VARUGA IN THIS TOWN.
YOU CAN DO THAT, CAN'T YOU?
—YOU'RE IN A PRETTY TIGHT SPOT, AREN'T YOU, AKARI?
YES, VERY MUCH SO.
AND I'VE JUST GIVEN YOU PERMISSION TO HAVE ALL THE FUN YOU COULD POSSIBLY WANT WITH THESE VARUGA!
ZA (STAND)
—AWW, WELL, IF YOU SAY SO!

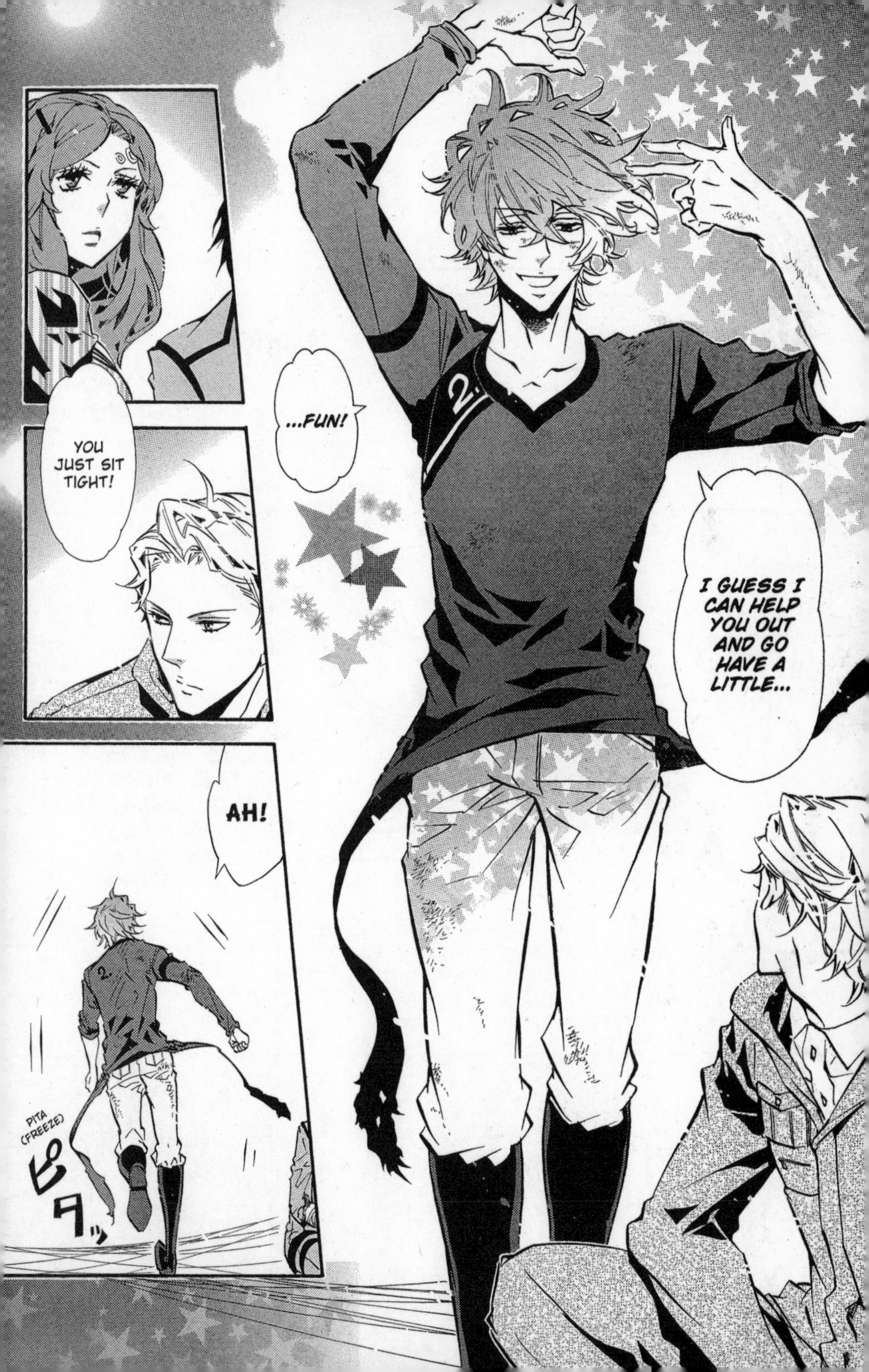
I GUESS I CAN HELP YOU OUT AND GO HAVE A LITTLE...
...FUN!
YOU JUST SIT TIGHT!
AH!
PITA (FREEZE)

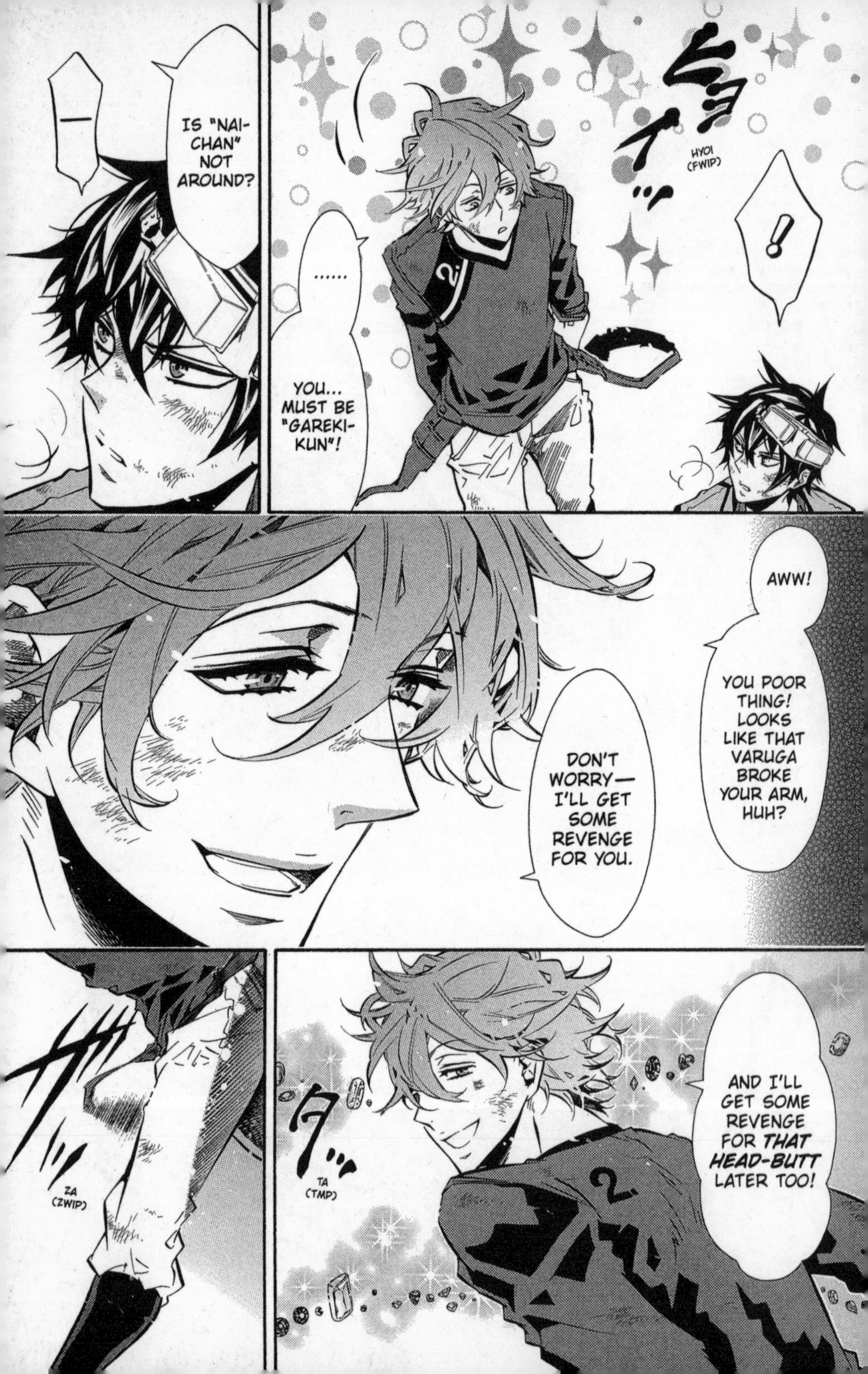
HYOI (FWIP)
!
......
YOU... MUST BE "GAREKI-KUN"!
—
IS "NAI-CHAN" NOT AROUND?
AWW!
YOU POOR THING! LOOKS LIKE THAT VARUGA BROKE YOUR ARM, HUH?
DON'T WORRY— I'LL GET SOME REVENGE FOR YOU.
AND I'LL GET SOME REVENGE FOR *THAT HEAD-BUTT* LATER TOO!
TA (TMP)
ZA (ZWIP)

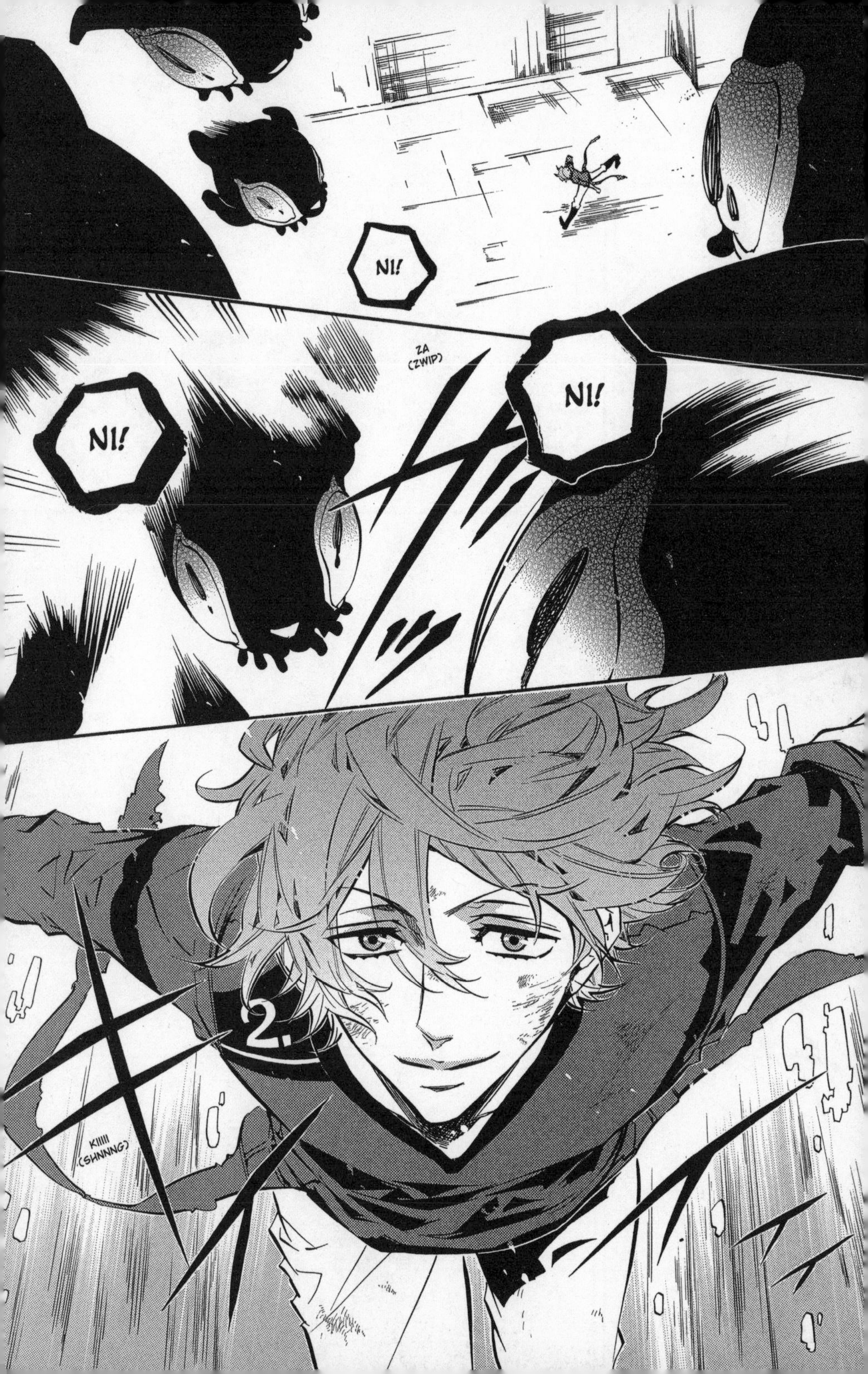
NI!
NI!
ZA (ZWIP)
NI!
2.
KIIIII (SHNNNG)

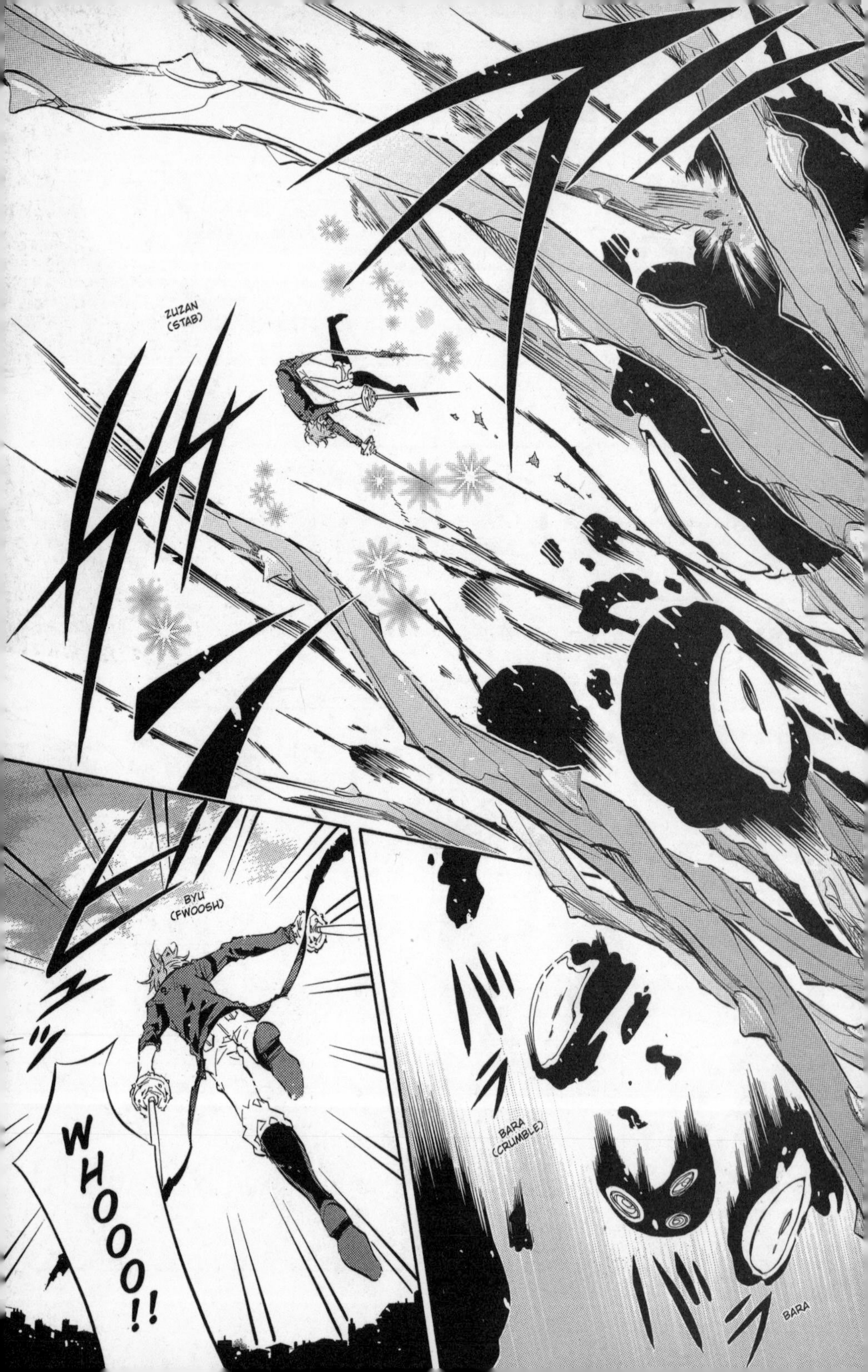
ZUZAN (STAB)
BARA (CRUMBLE)
BARA
BYU (FWOOSH)
WHOOOO!!

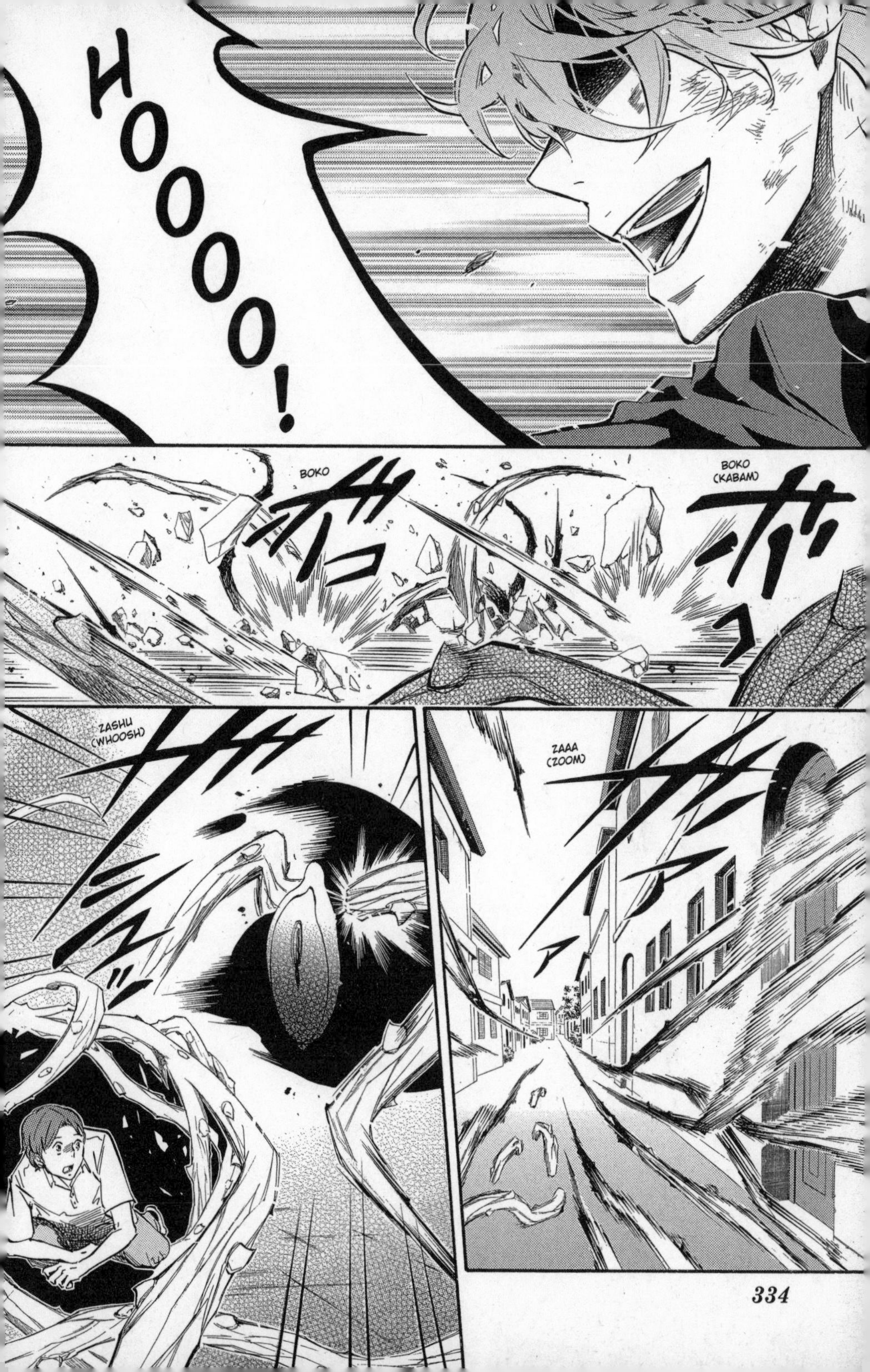
HOOOOO!
BOKO (KABAM)
BOKO
ZAAA (ZOOM)
ZASHU (WHOOSH)

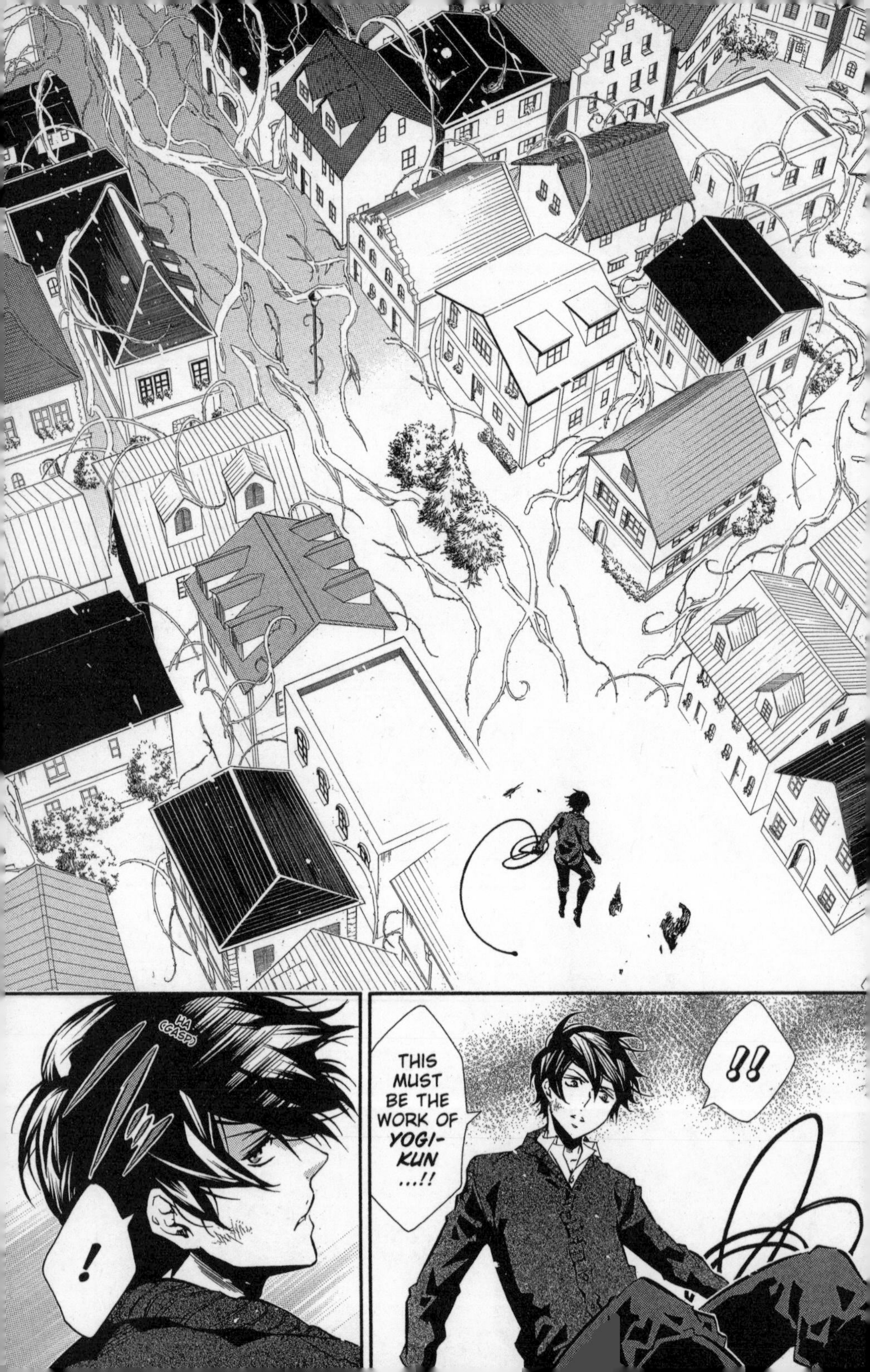
!!
THIS MUST BE THE WORK OF YOGI-KUN ...!!
HA (GASP)
!

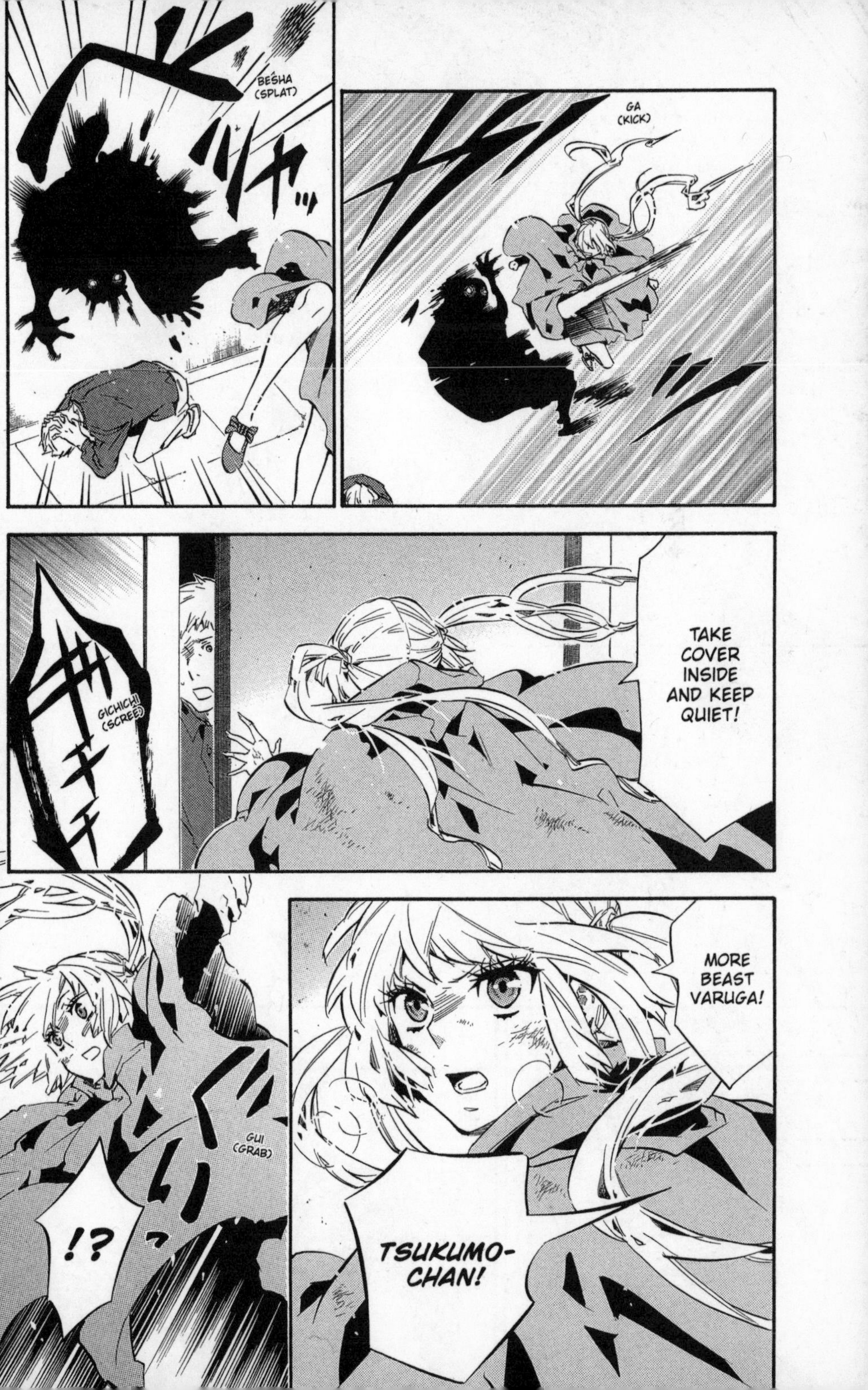
GA (KICK)
BESHA (SPLAT)
TAKE COVER INSIDE AND KEEP QUIET!
GICHICHI (SCREE)
MORE BEAST VARUGA!
TSUKUMO-CHAN!
GUI (GRAB)
!?

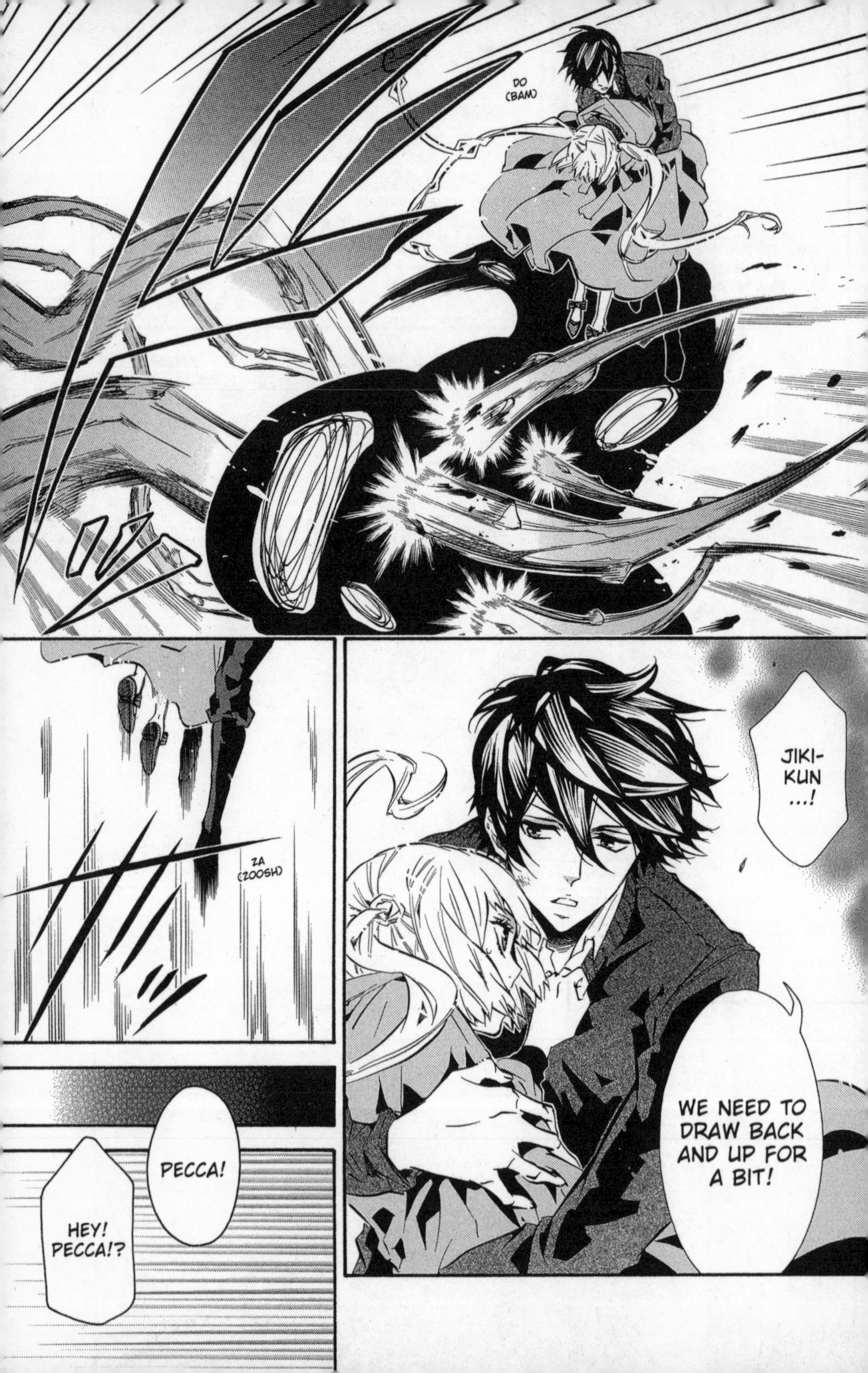
DO (BAM)
JIKI-KUN ...!
WE NEED TO DRAW BACK AND UP FOR A BIT!
ZA (ZOOSH)
PECCA!
HEY! PECCA!?

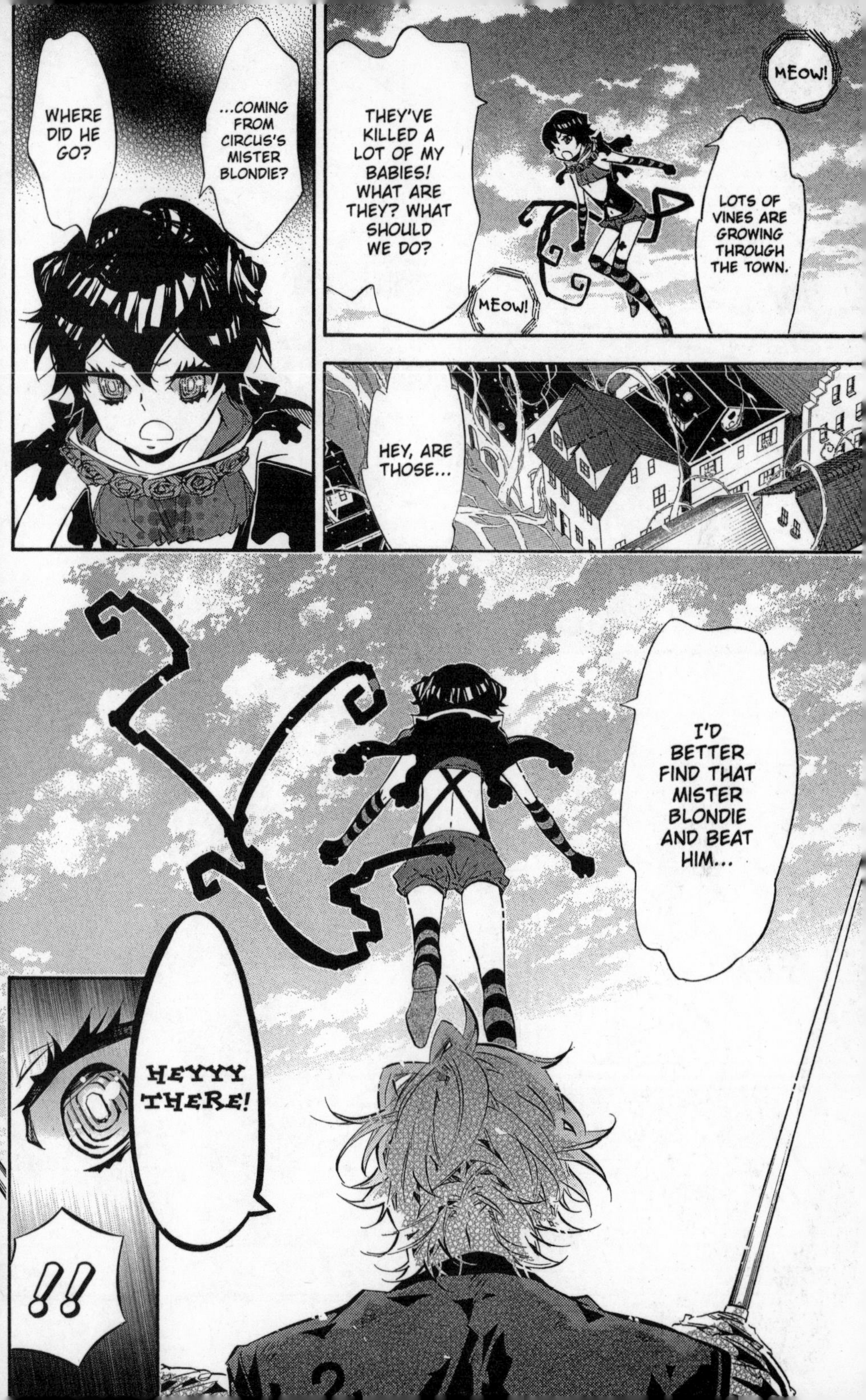
MEOW!
LOTS OF VINES ARE GROWING THROUGH THE TOWN.
THEY'VE KILLED A LOT OF MY BABIES! WHAT ARE THEY? WHAT SHOULD WE DO?
MEOW!
HEY, ARE THOSE...
...COMING FROM CIRCUS'S MISTER BLONDIE?
WHERE DID HE GO?
I'D BETTER FIND THAT MISTER BLONDIE AND BEAT HIM...
HEYYY THERE!
!!

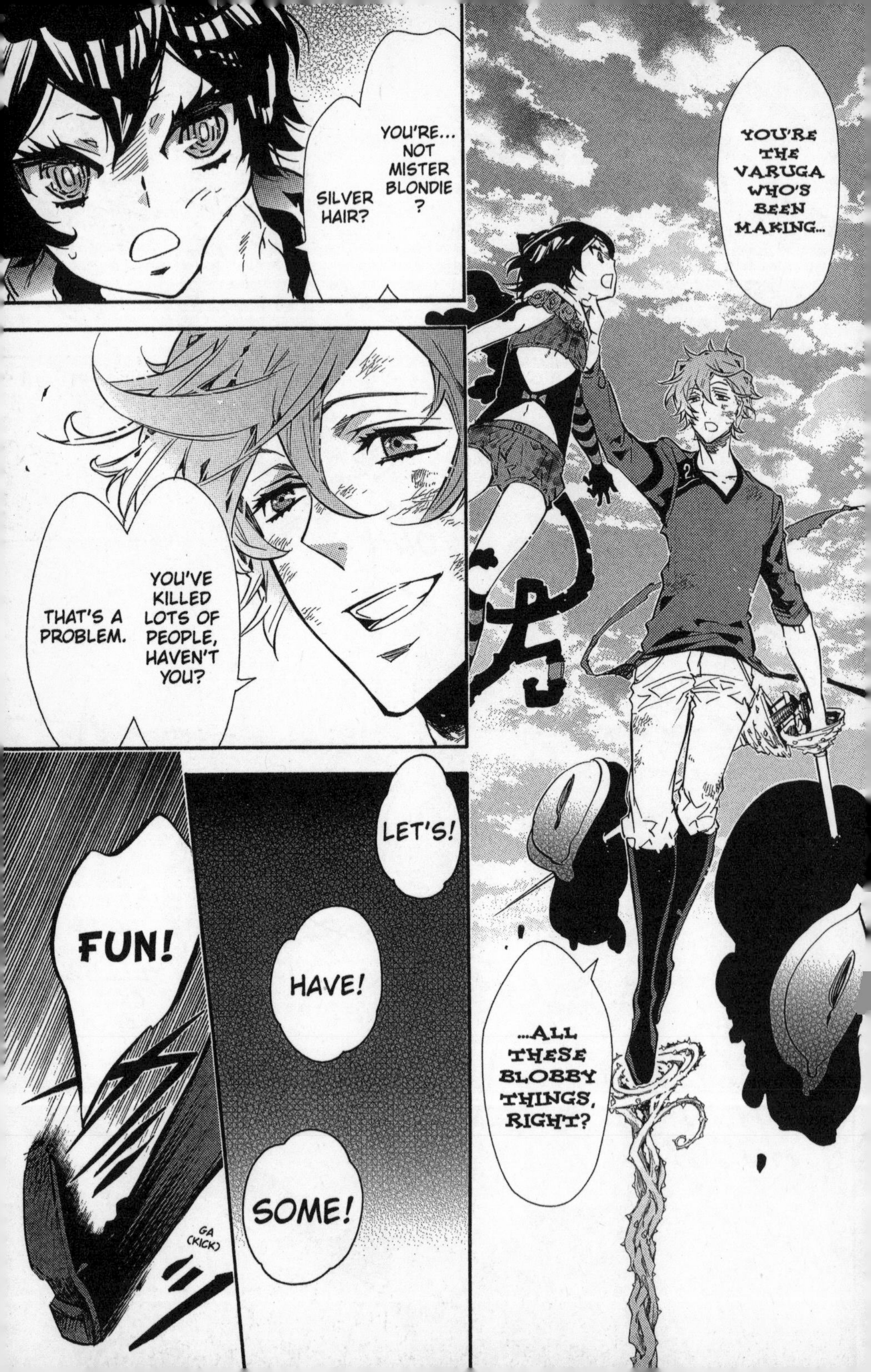
YOU'RE THE VARUGA WHO'S BEEN MAKING...
...ALL THESE BLOBBY THINGS, RIGHT?
YOU'RE... NOT MISTER BLONDIE?
SILVER HAIR?
YOU'VE KILLED LOTS OF PEOPLE, HAVEN'T YOU?
THAT'S A PROBLEM.
LET'S!
HAVE!
SOME!
FUN!
GA (KICK)

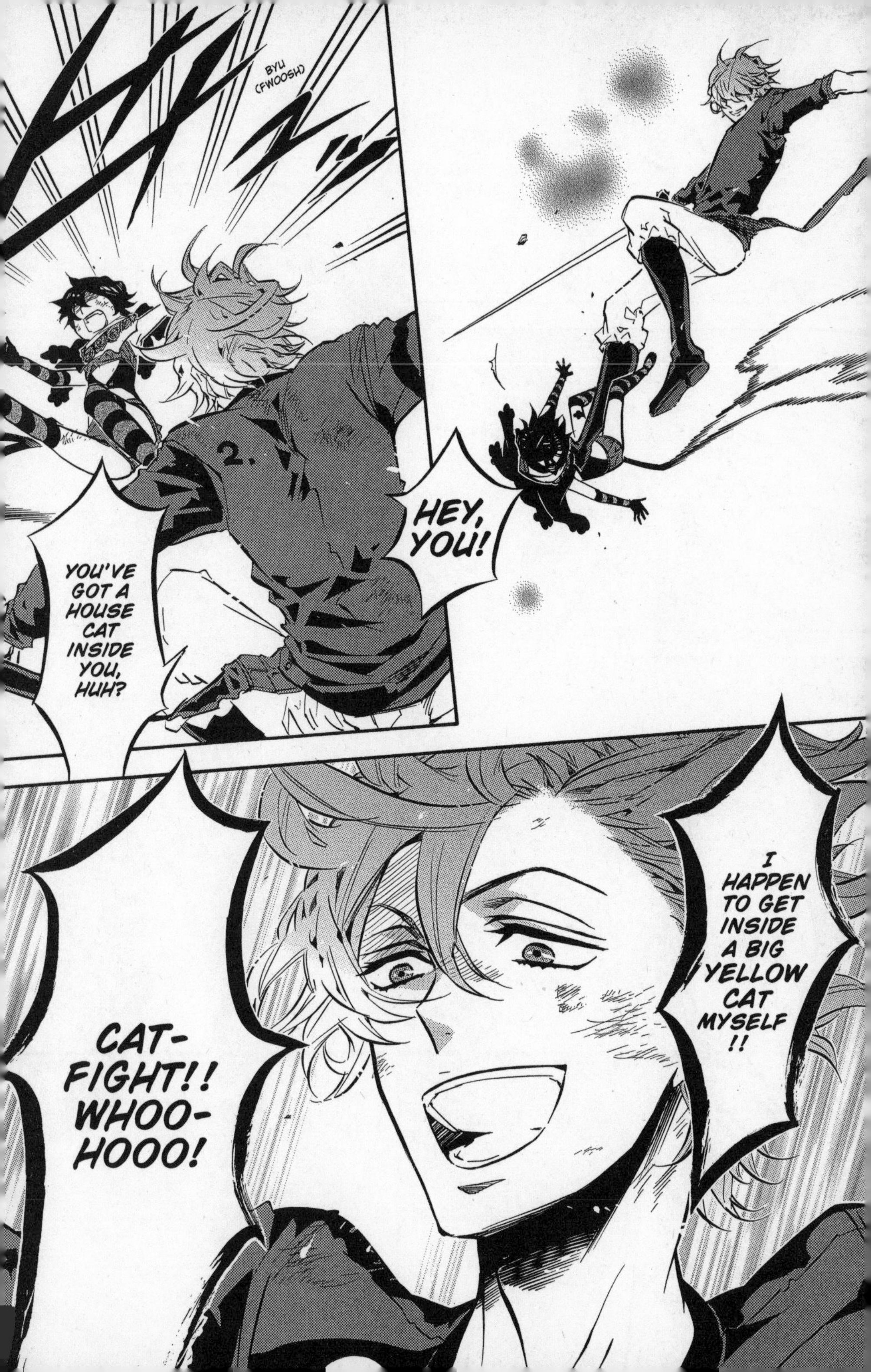
HEY, YOU!
BYU (FWOOSH)
YOU'VE GOT A HOUSE CAT INSIDE YOU, HUH?
I HAPPEN TO GET INSIDE A BIG YELLOW CAT MYSELF!!
CAT-FIGHT!! WHOO-HOOO!

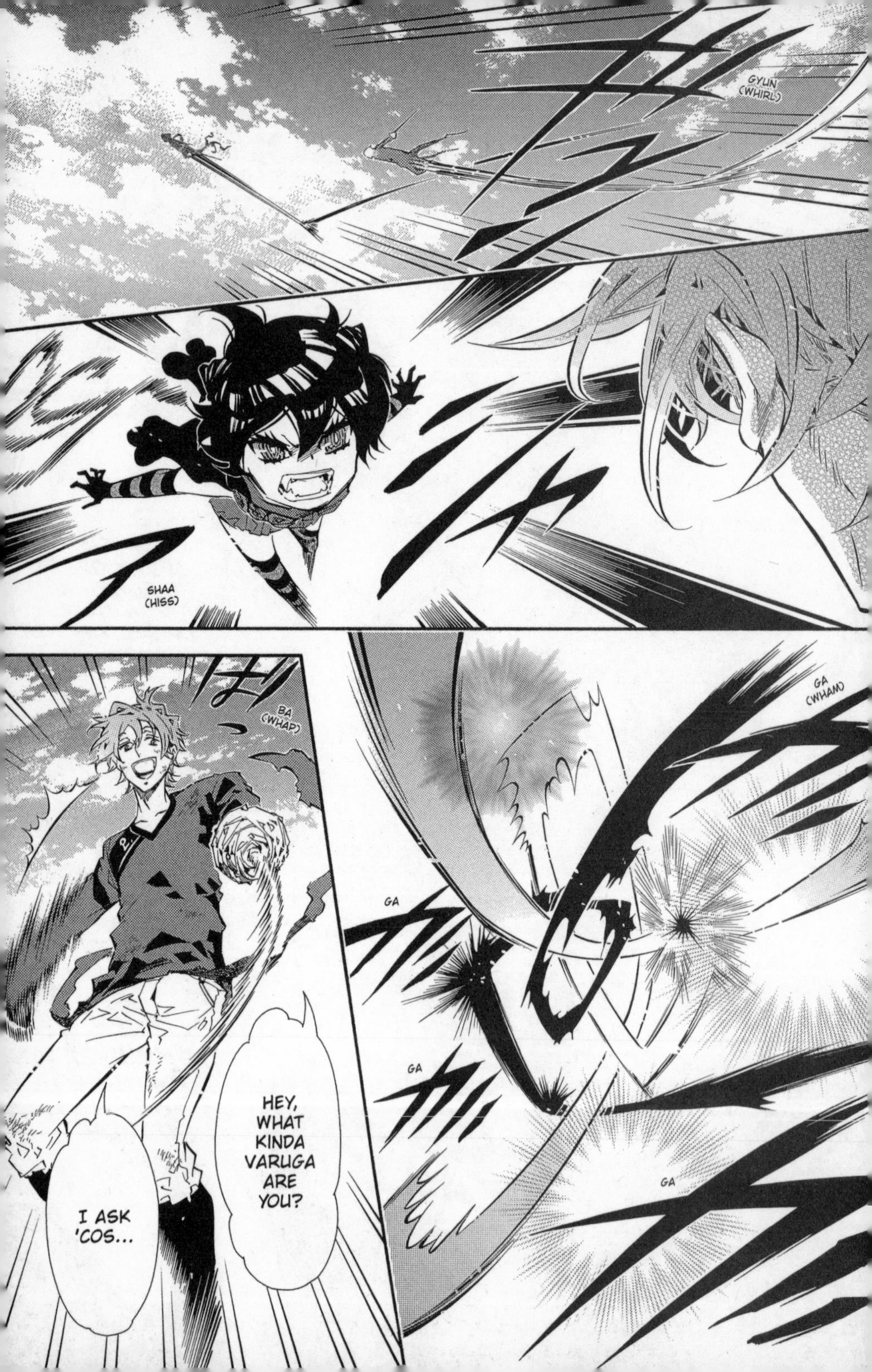
GYUN (WHIRL)
SHAA (HISS)
GA (WHAM)
GA
GA
GA
BA (WHAP)
HEY, WHAT KINDA VARUGA ARE YOU?
I ASK 'COS...

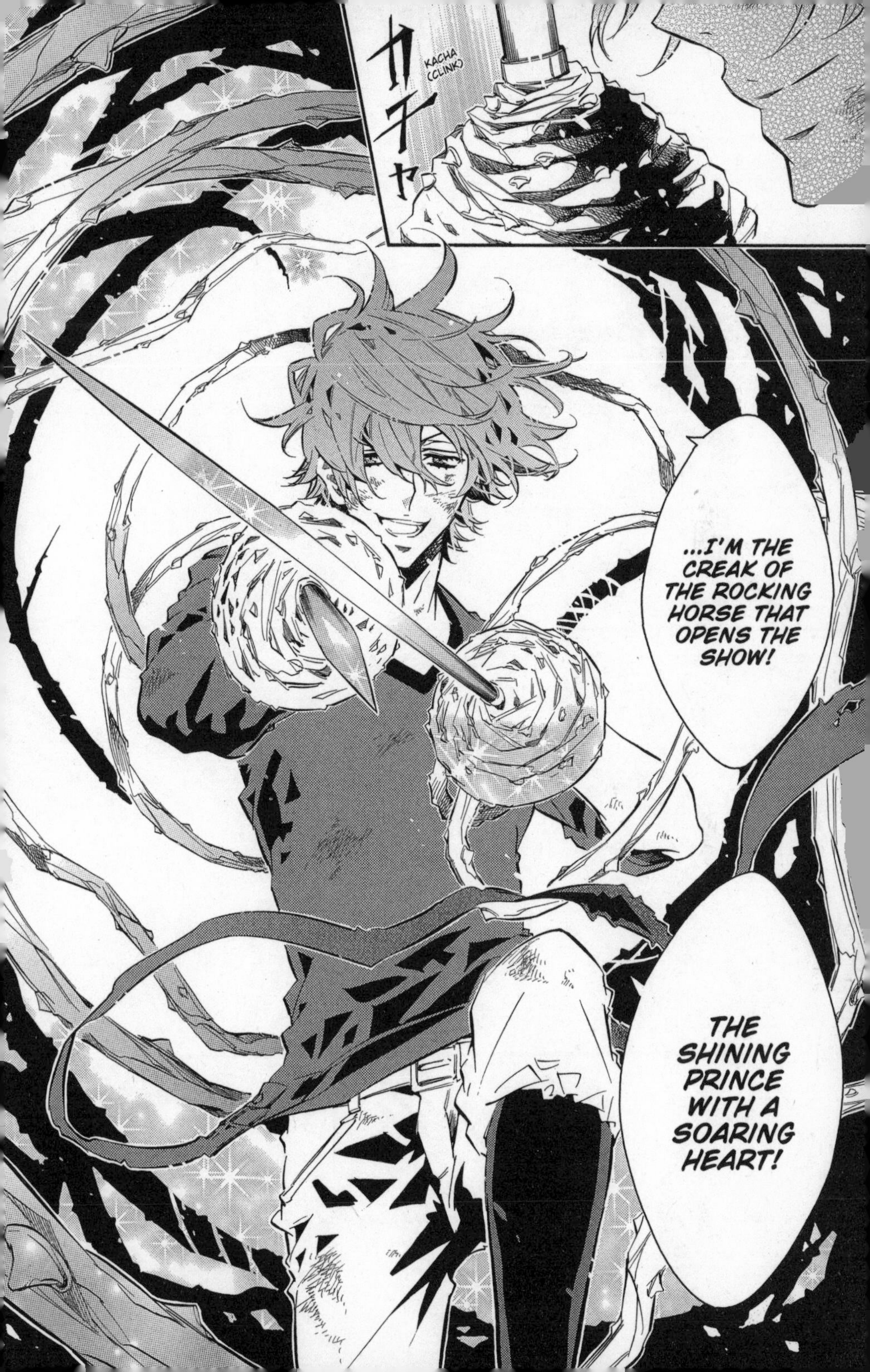
カチャ
KACHA (CLINK)
...I'M THE CREAK OF THE ROCKING HORSE THAT OPENS THE SHOW!
THE SHINING PRINCE WITH A SOARING HEART!

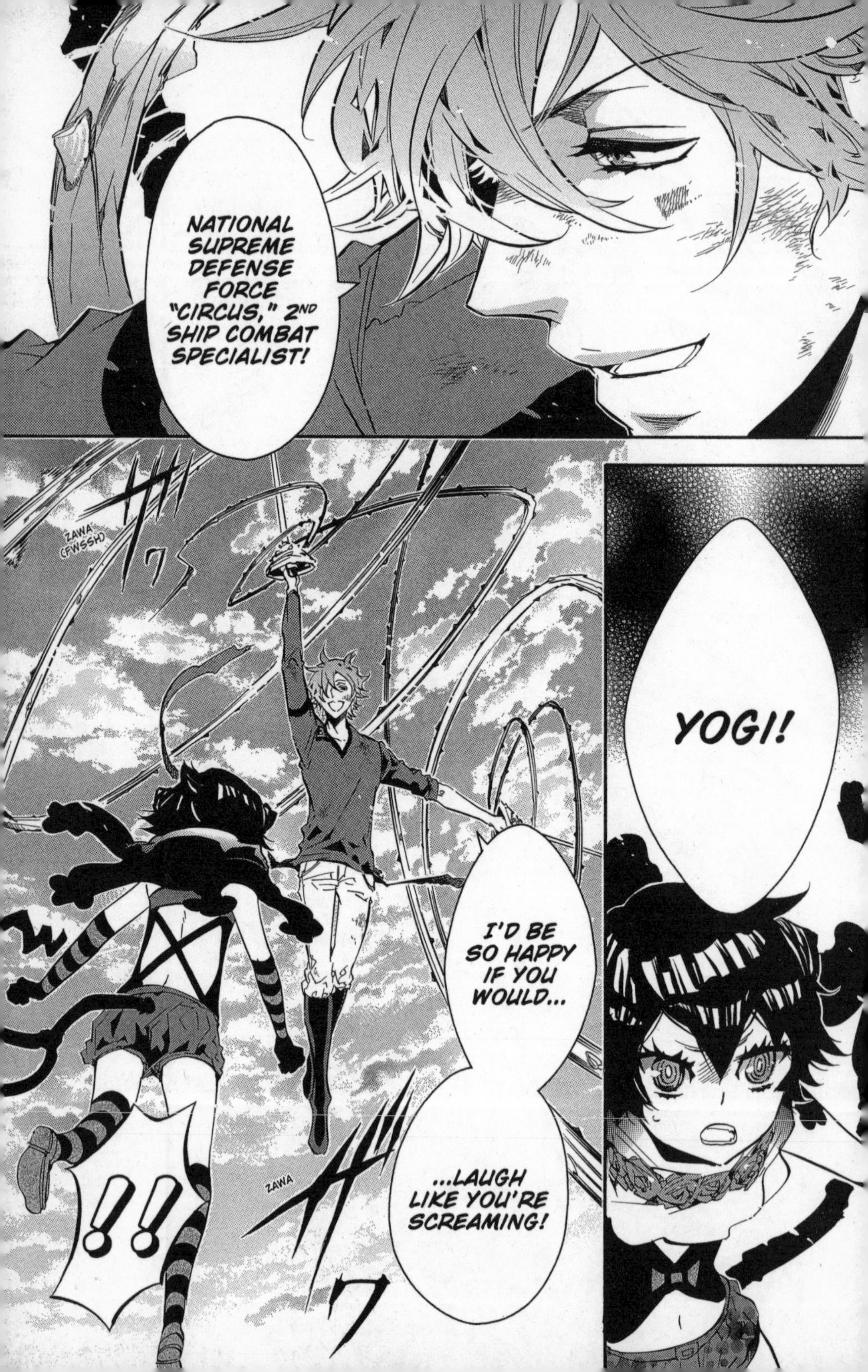
NATIONAL SUPREME DEFENSE FORCE "CIRCUS," 2ND SHIP COMBAT SPECIALIST!
YOGI!
ZAWA (FWSSH)
I'D BE SO HAPPY IF YOU WOULD...
...LAUGH LIKE YOU'RE SCREAMING!
ZAWA
!!

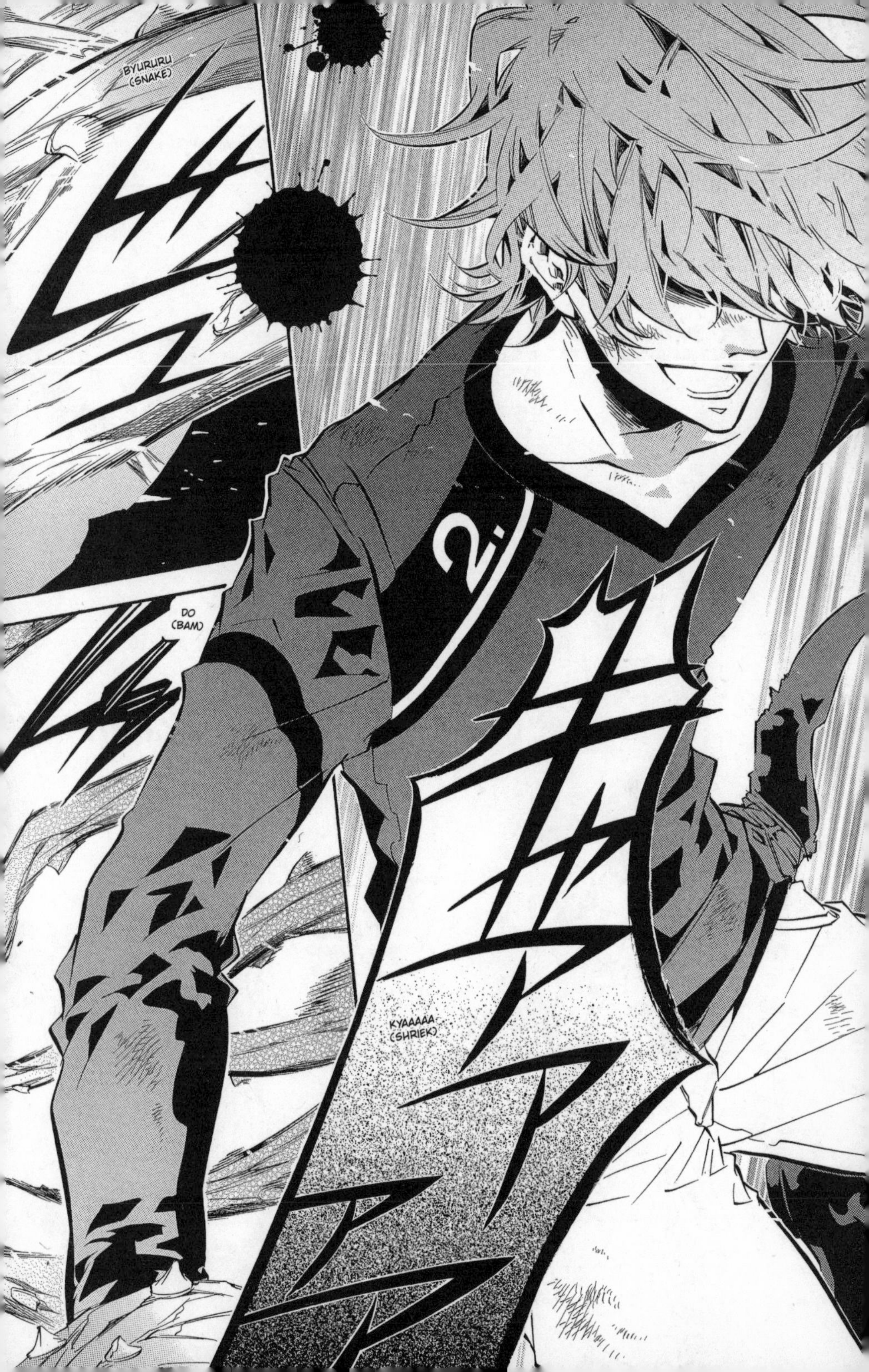
BYURURU (SNAKE)
DO (BAM)
KYAAAAA (SHRIEK)

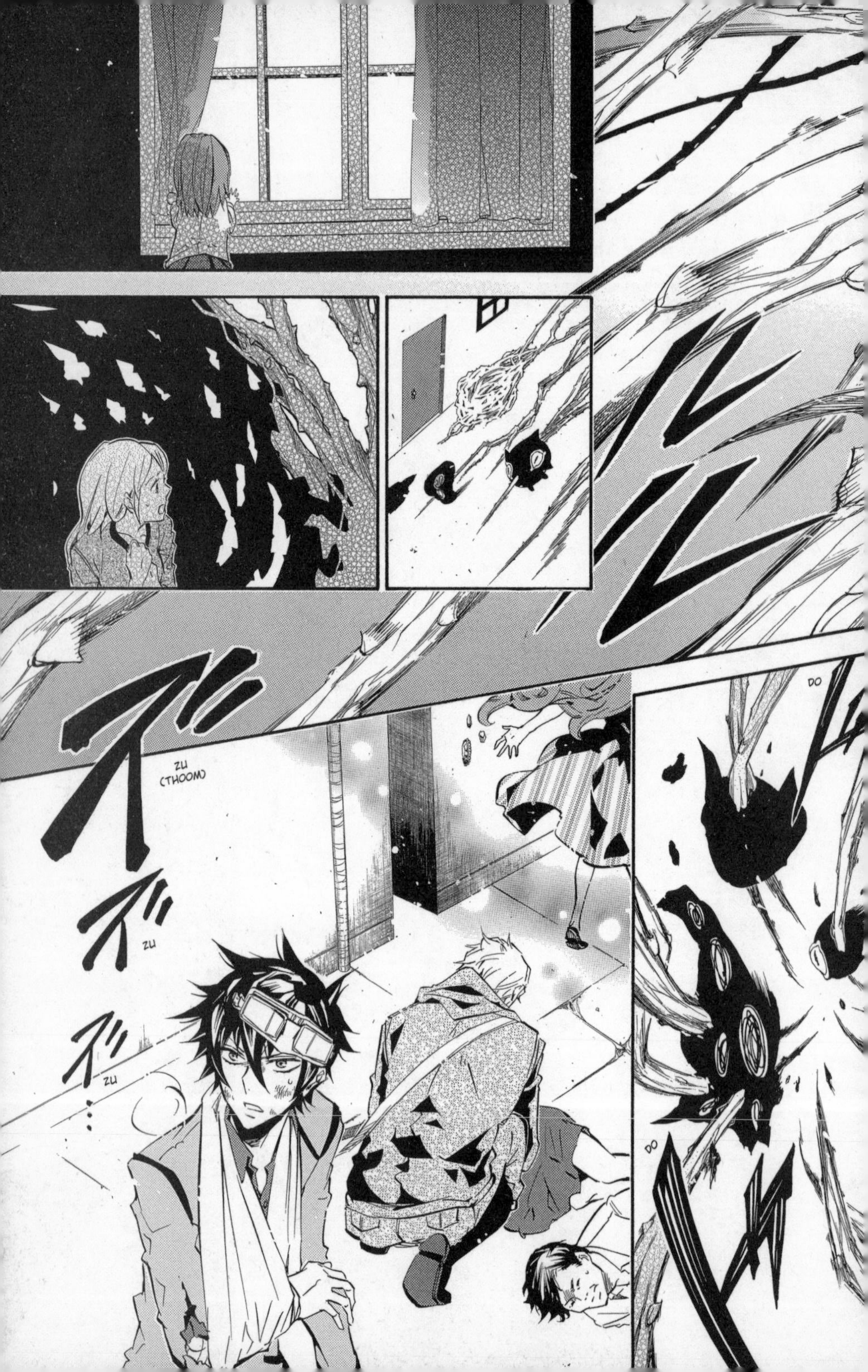
DO
DO
ZU
(THOOM)
ZU
ZU

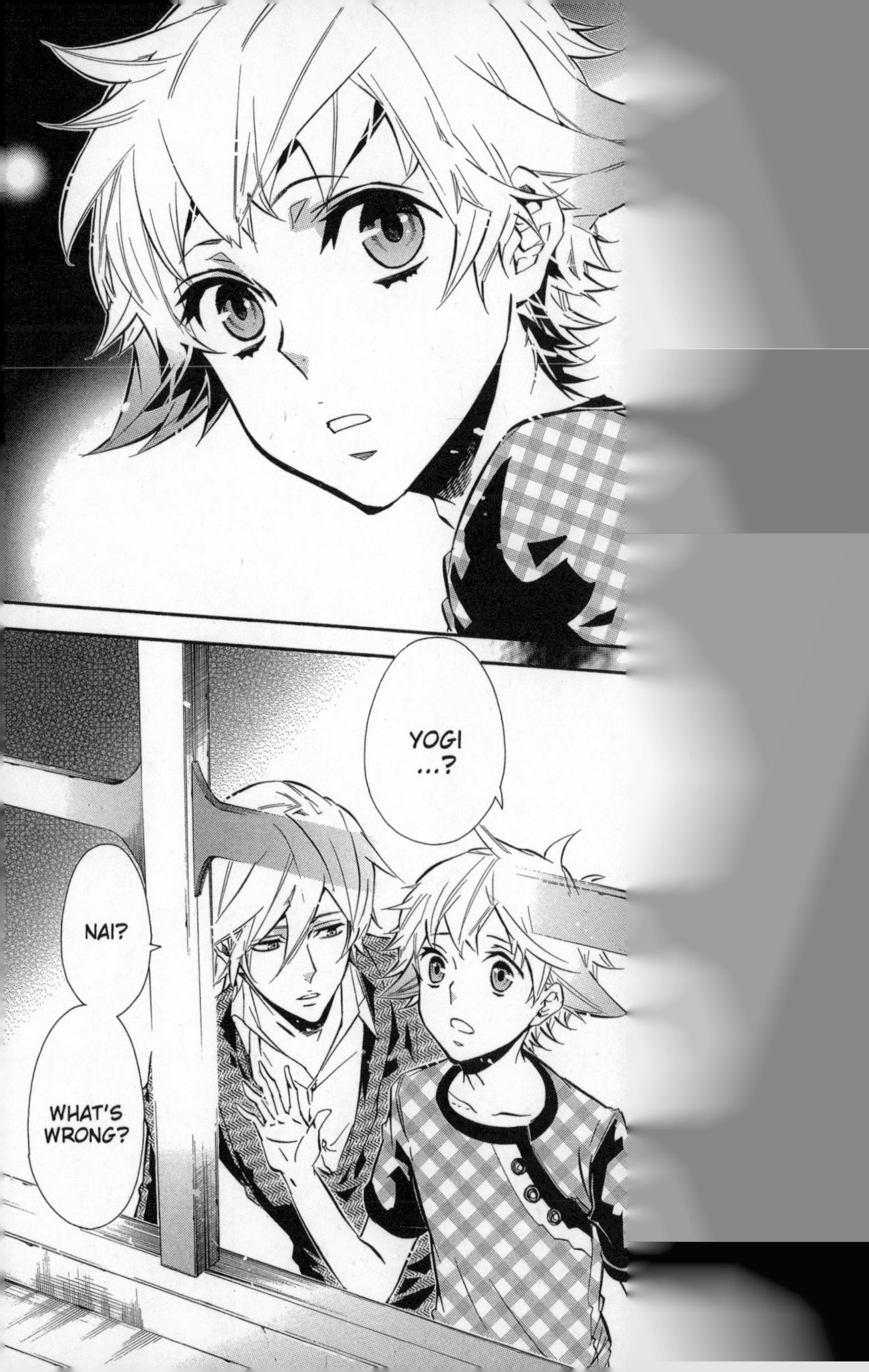
YOGI ...?
NAI?
WHAT'S WRONG?

KARNEVAL

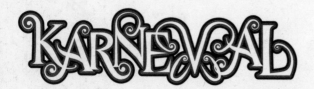

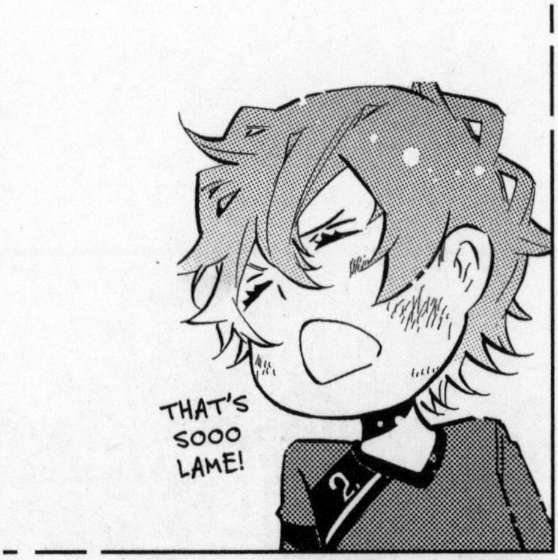

THAT'S
SOOO
LAME!

KARNEVAL

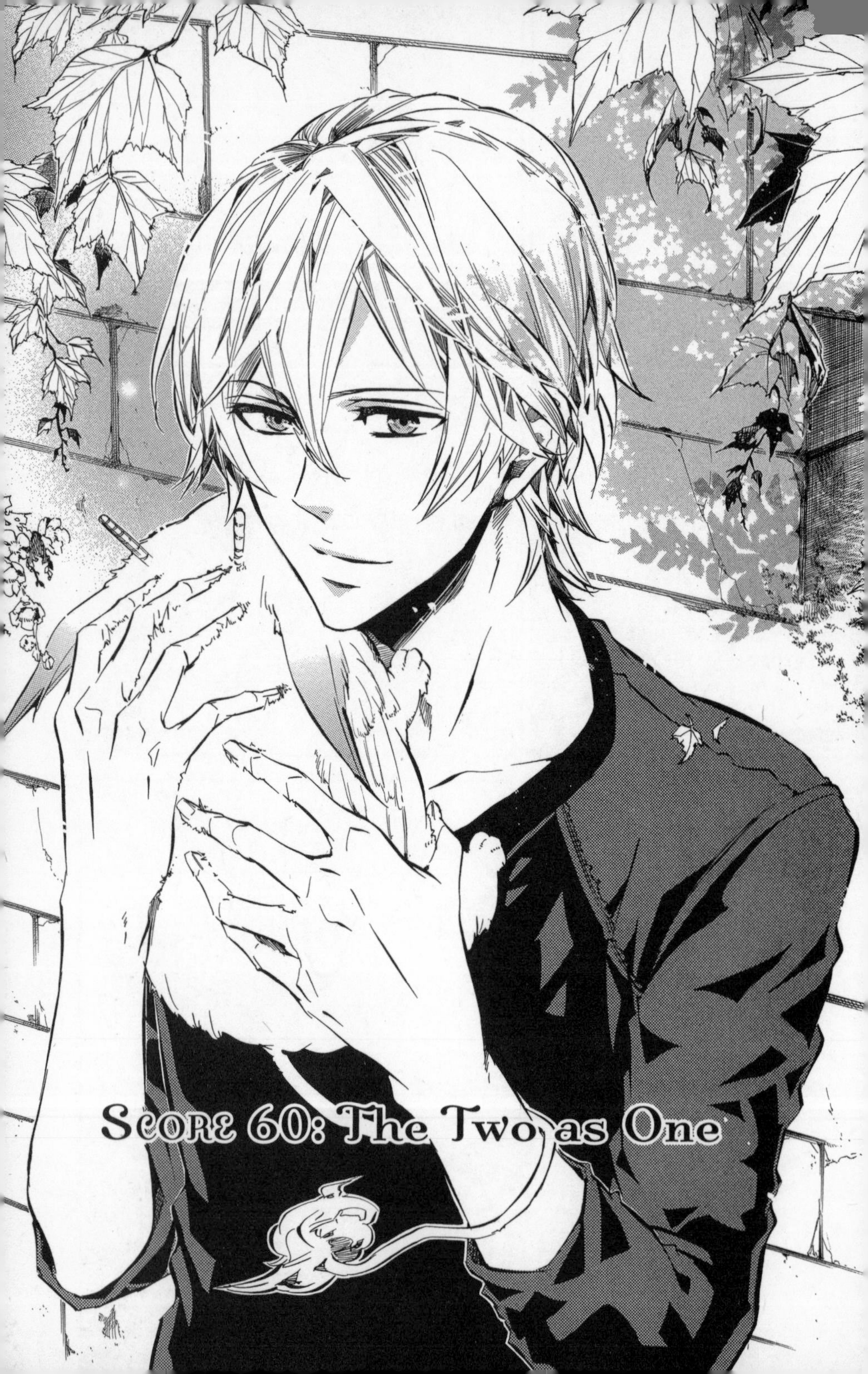
Score 60: The Two as One

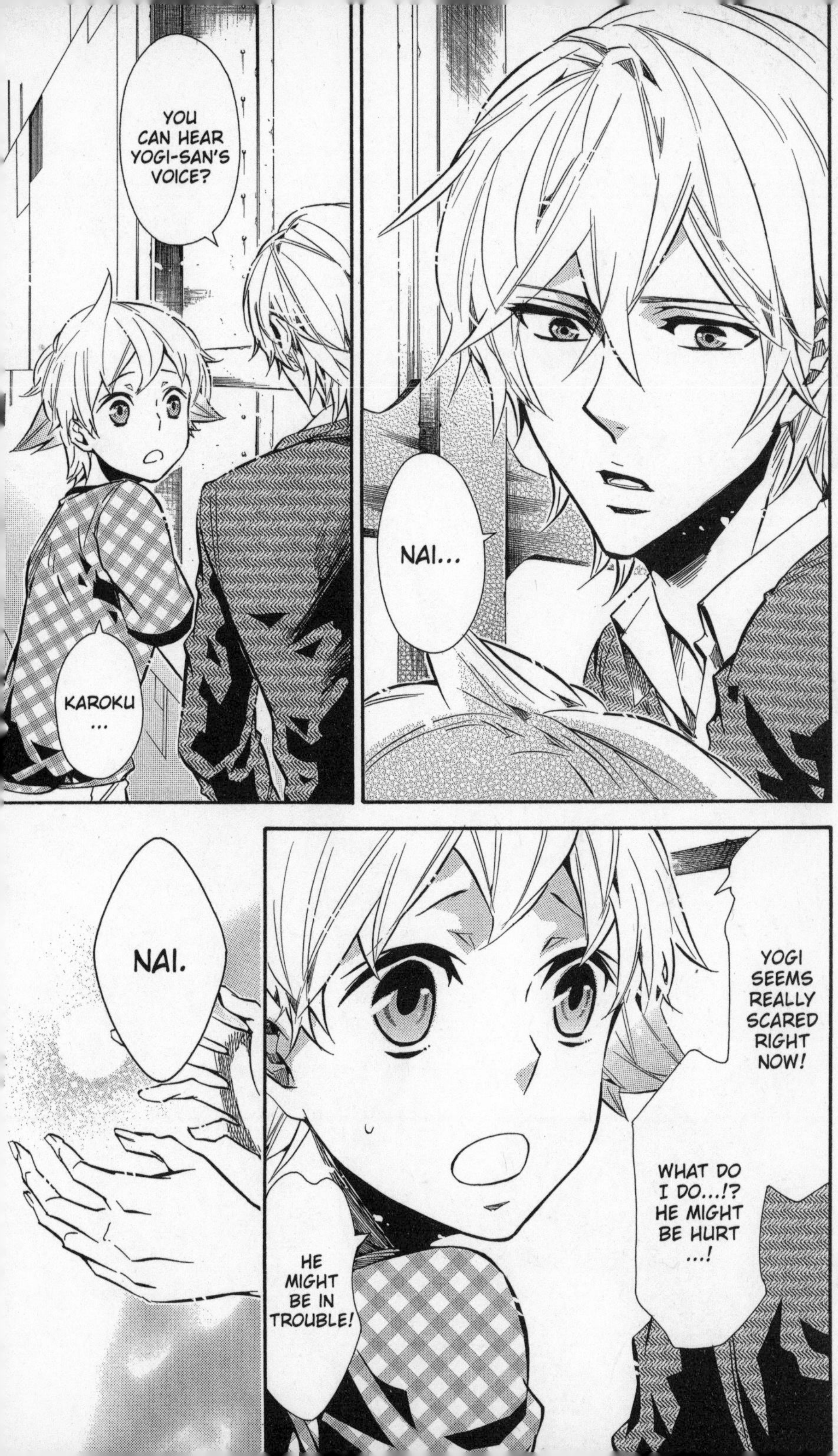
NAI...
YOU CAN HEAR YOGI-SAN'S VOICE?
KAROKU...
YOGI SEEMS REALLY SCARED RIGHT NOW!
WHAT DO I DO...!? HE MIGHT BE HURT...!
HE MIGHT BE IN TROUBLE!
NAI.

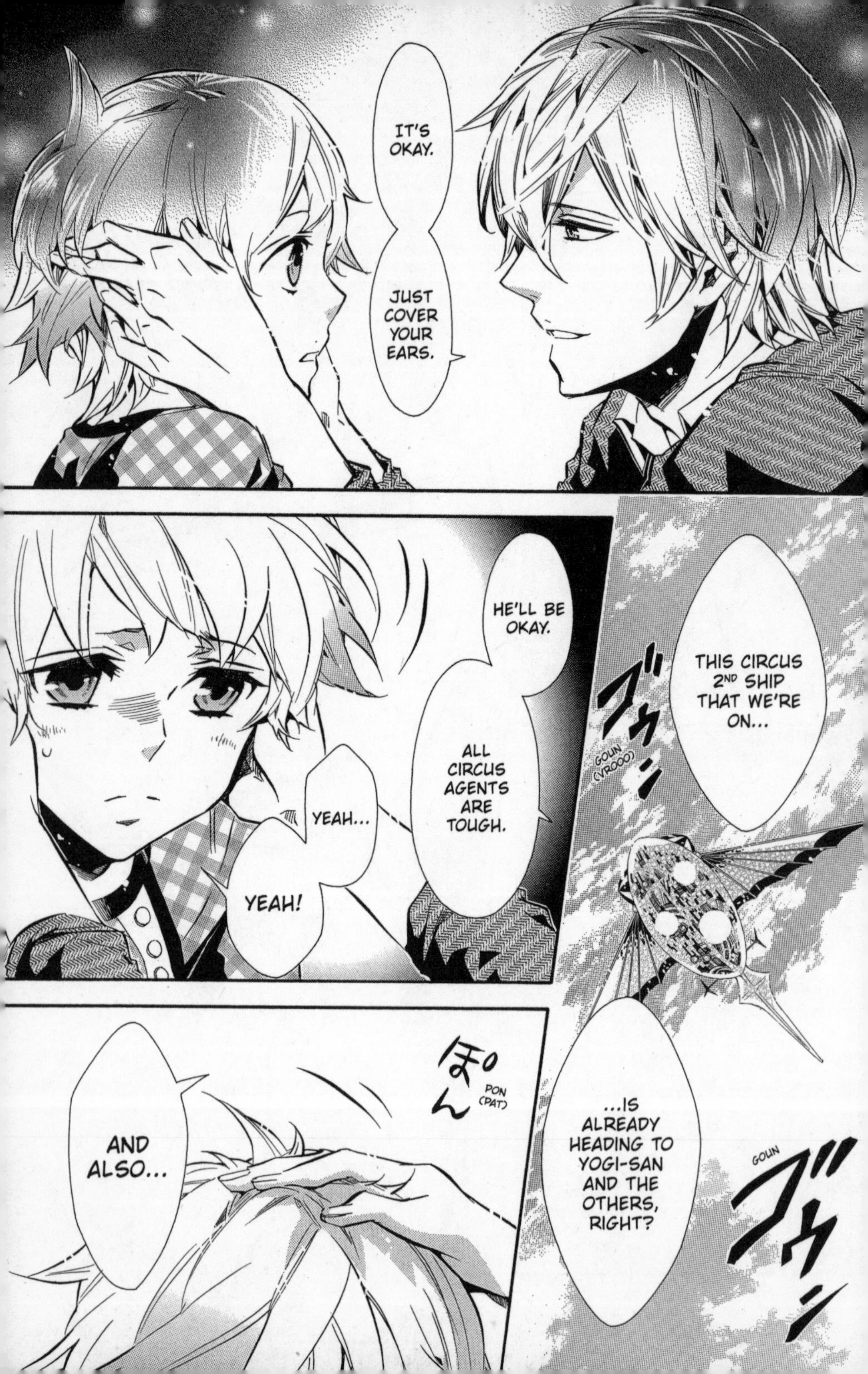
IT'S OKAY.
JUST COVER YOUR EARS.
THIS CIRCUS 2nd SHIP THAT WE'RE ON...
GOUN (VROOO)
...IS ALREADY HEADING TO YOGI-SAN AND THE OTHERS, RIGHT?
GOUN
HE'LL BE OKAY.
ALL CIRCUS AGENTS ARE TOUGH.
YEAH...
YEAH!
PON (PAT)
AND ALSO...

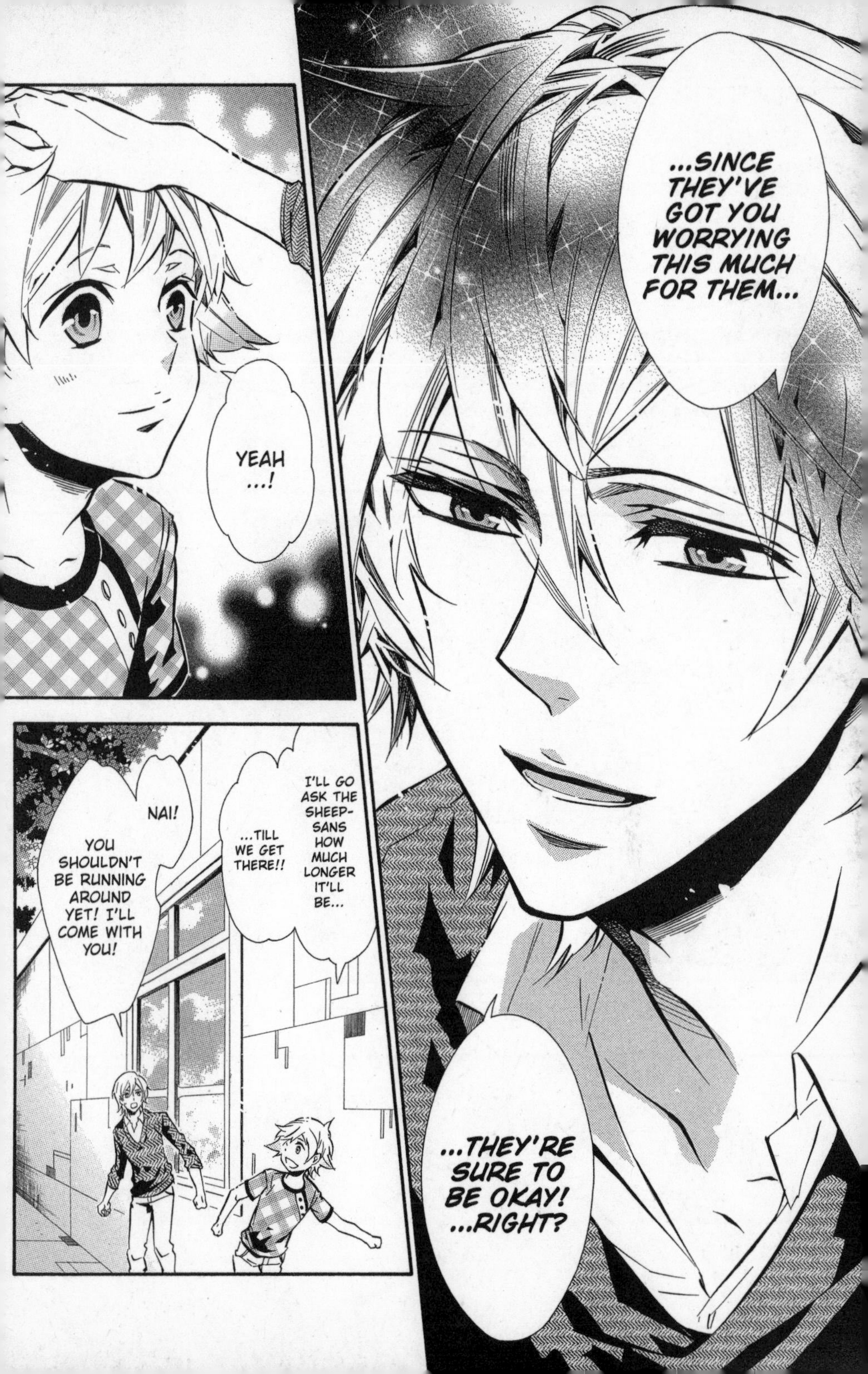
...SINCE THEY'VE GOT YOU WORRYING THIS MUCH FOR THEM...
...THEY'RE SURE TO BE OKAY! ...RIGHT?
YEAH ...!
I'LL GO ASK THE SHEEP-SANS HOW MUCH LONGER IT'LL BE...
...TILL WE GET THERE!!
NAI!
YOU SHOULDN'T BE RUNNING AROUND YET! I'LL COME WITH YOU!

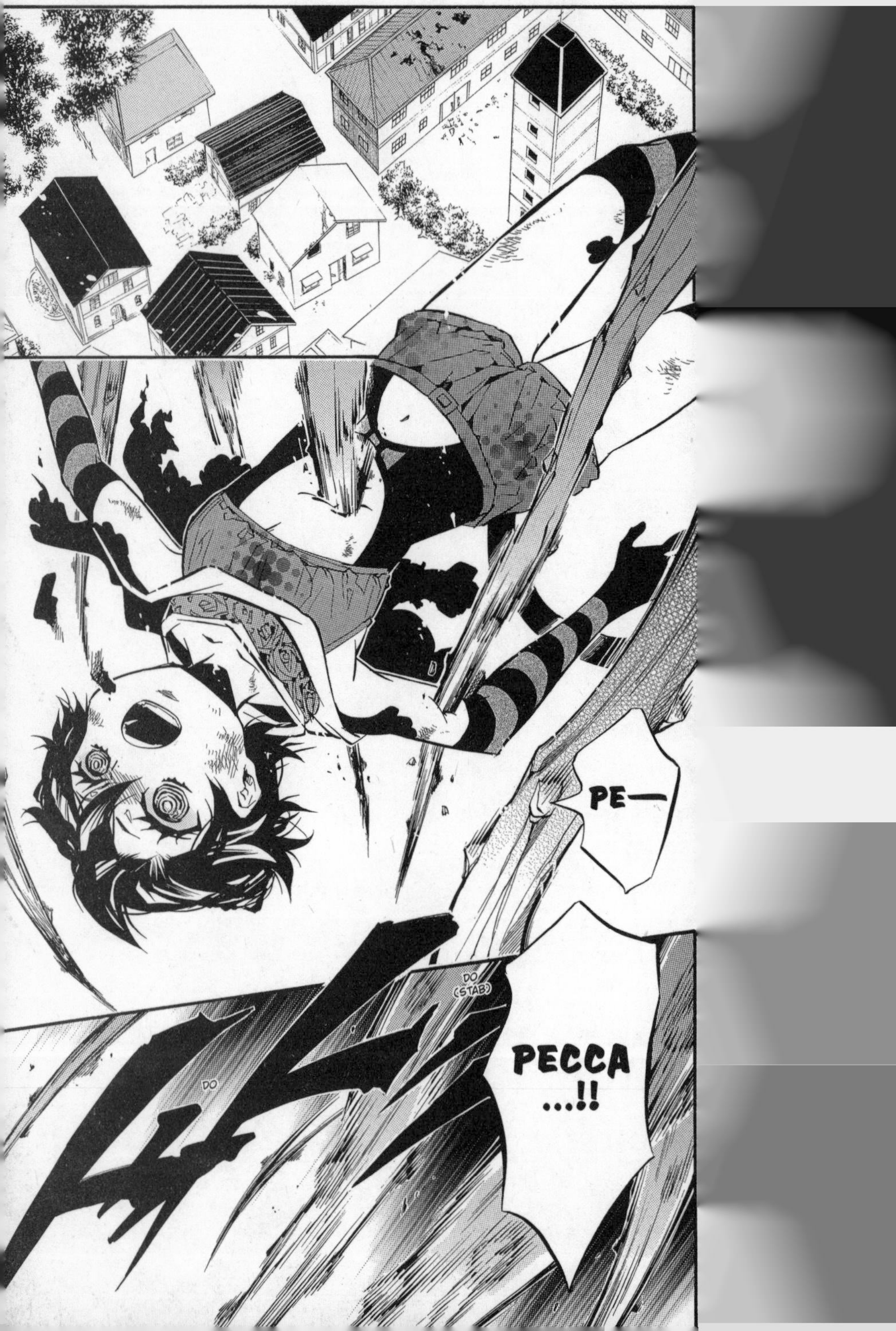
PE—
PECCA ...!!
DO (STAB)
DO

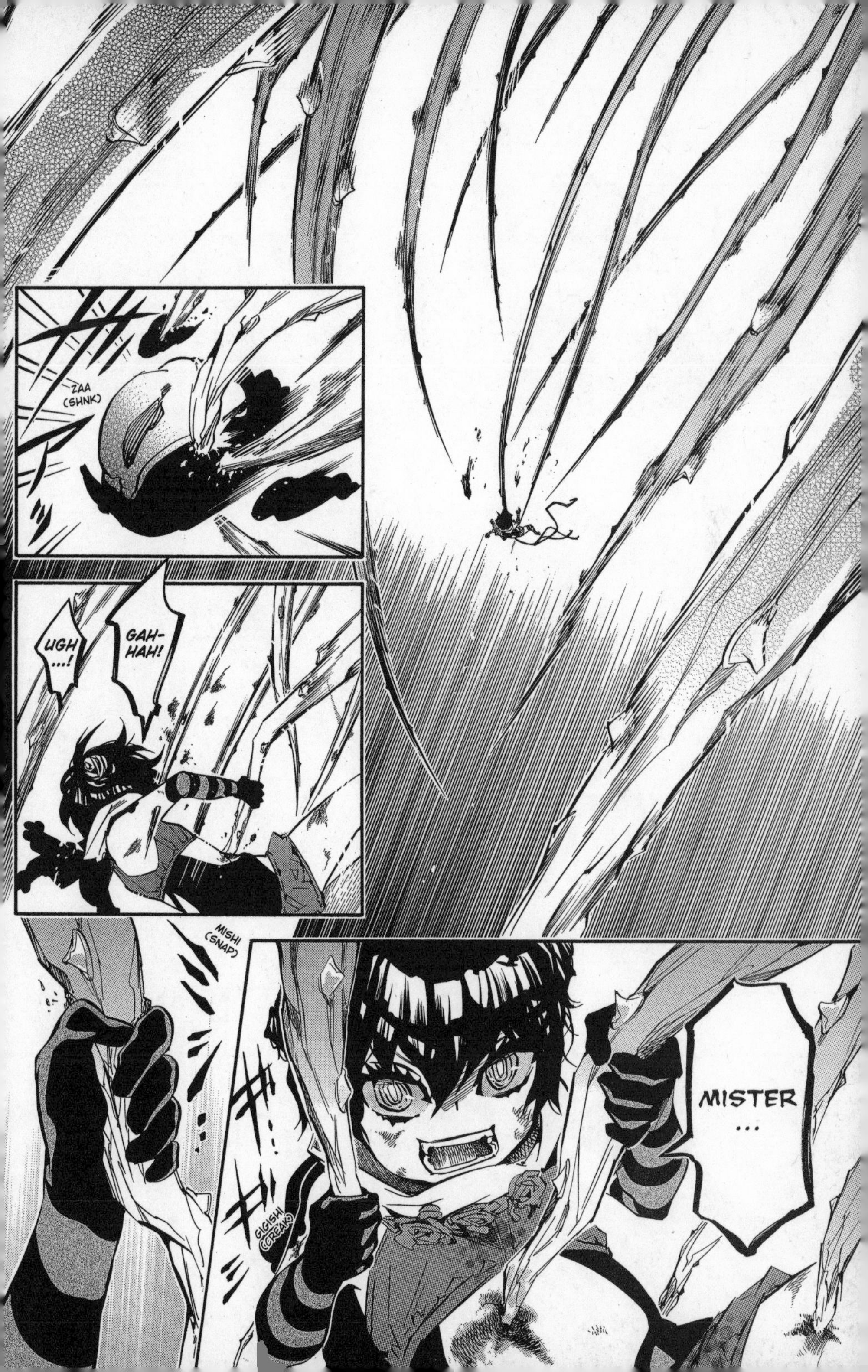
ZAA (SHNK)
GAH-HAH!
UGH ...!
MISTER ...
GIGISHI (CREAK)
MISHI (SNAP)

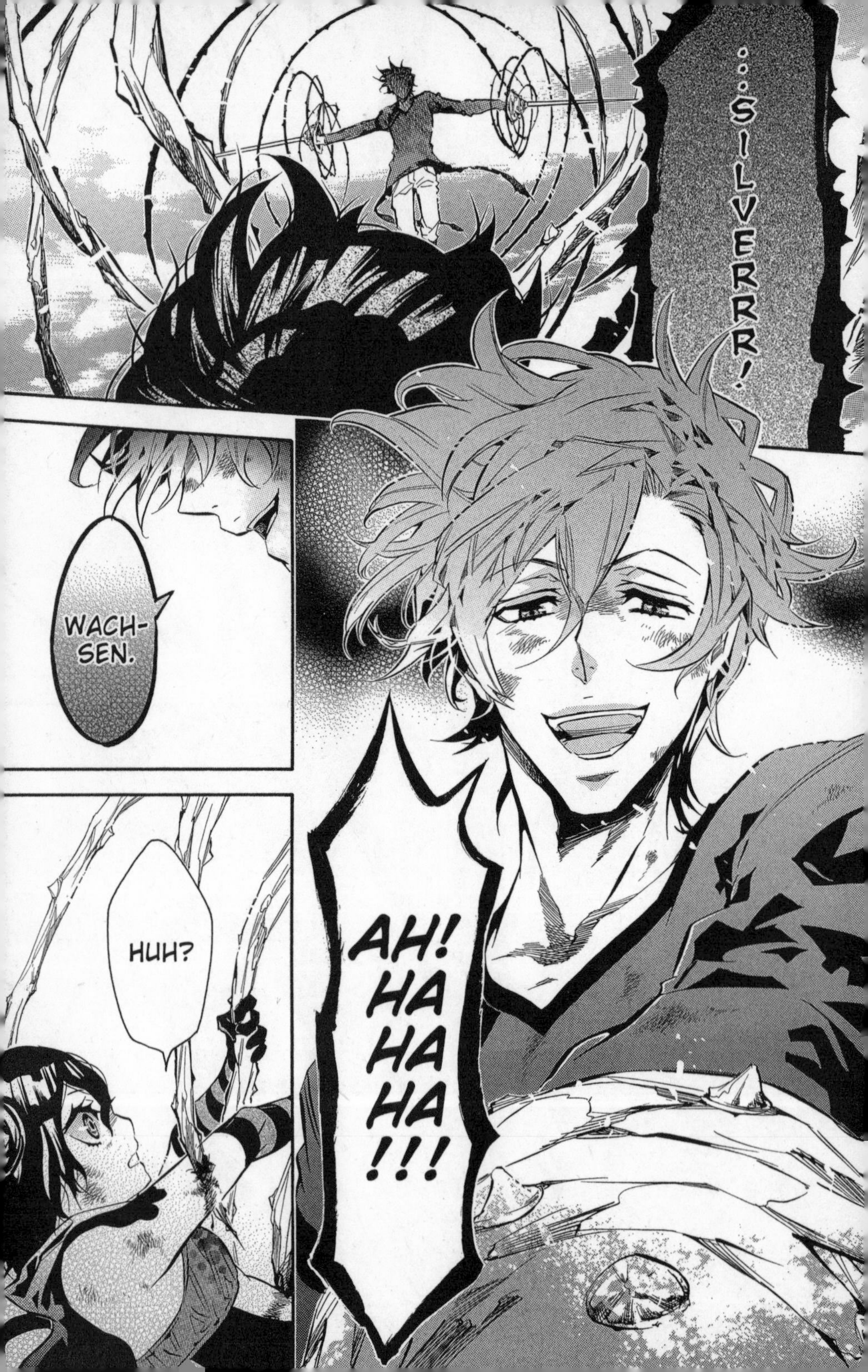
...SILVERRR!
AH! HA HA HA HA!!!
WACH-SEN.
HUH?

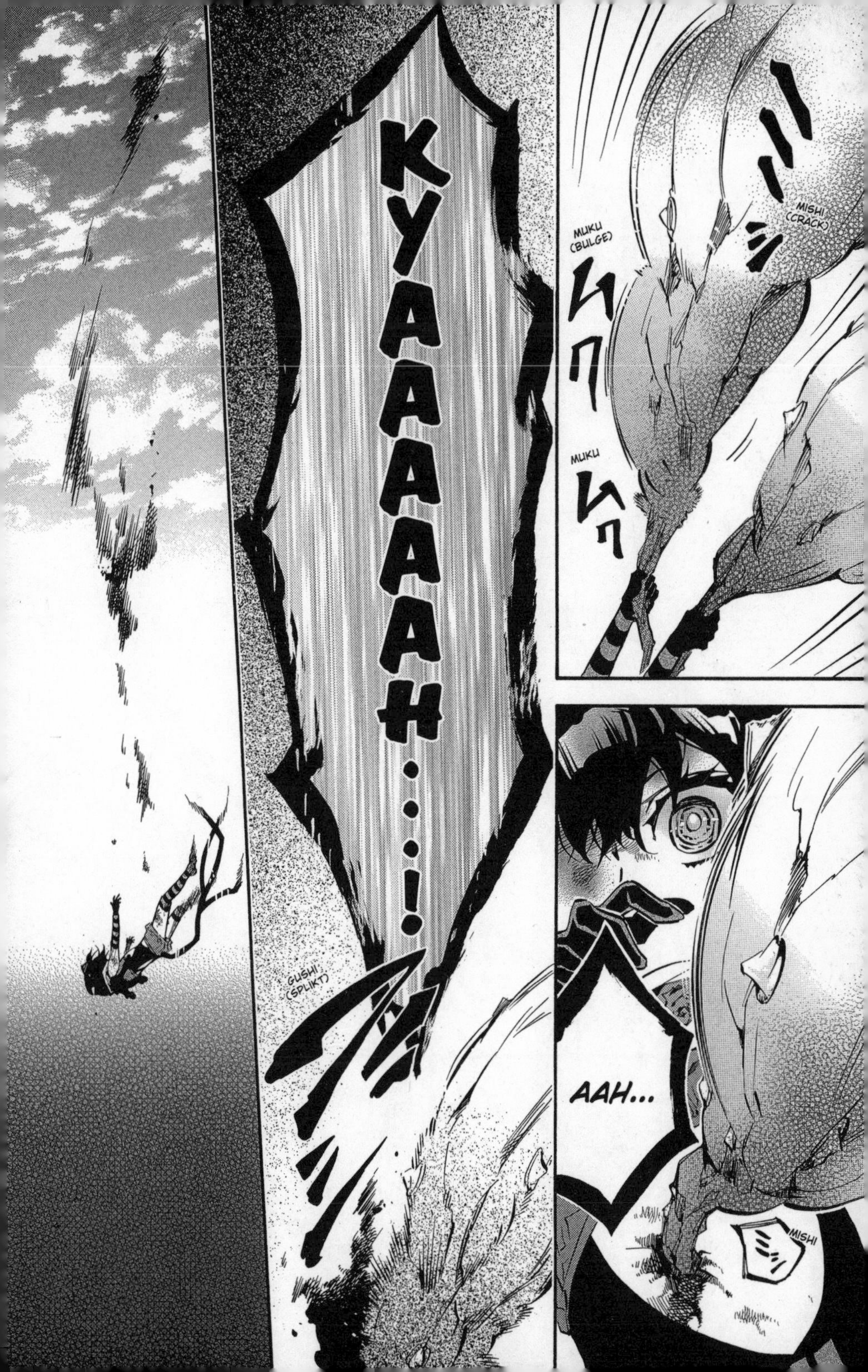
MISHI (CRACK)
MUKU (BULGE)
MUKU
AAH...
MISHI
KYAAAAH...!
GUSHI (SPLIKT)

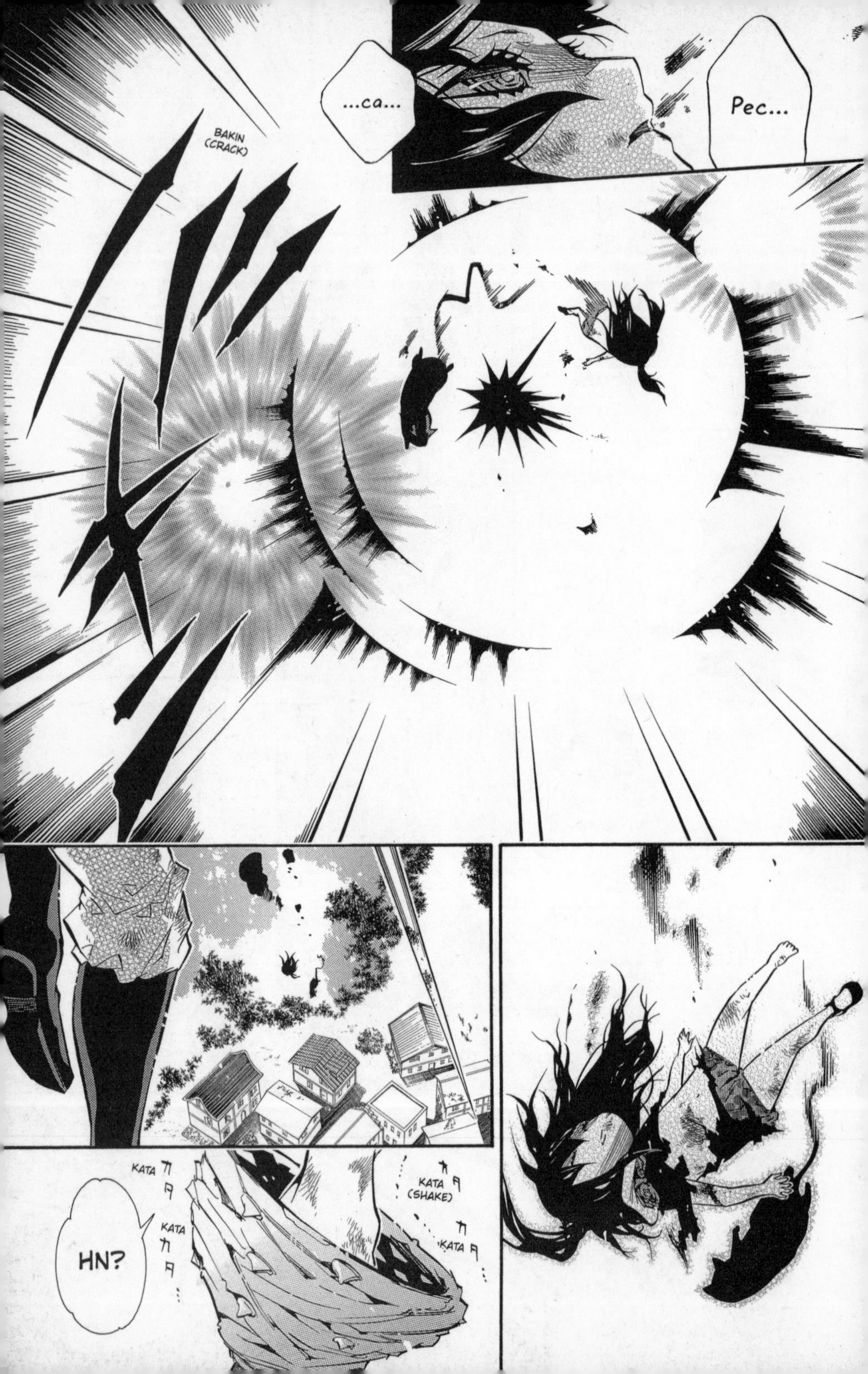
Pec...
...ca...
BAKIN (CRACK)
KATA カタ (SHAKE)
KATA カタ
KATA カタ
KATA カタ
HN?

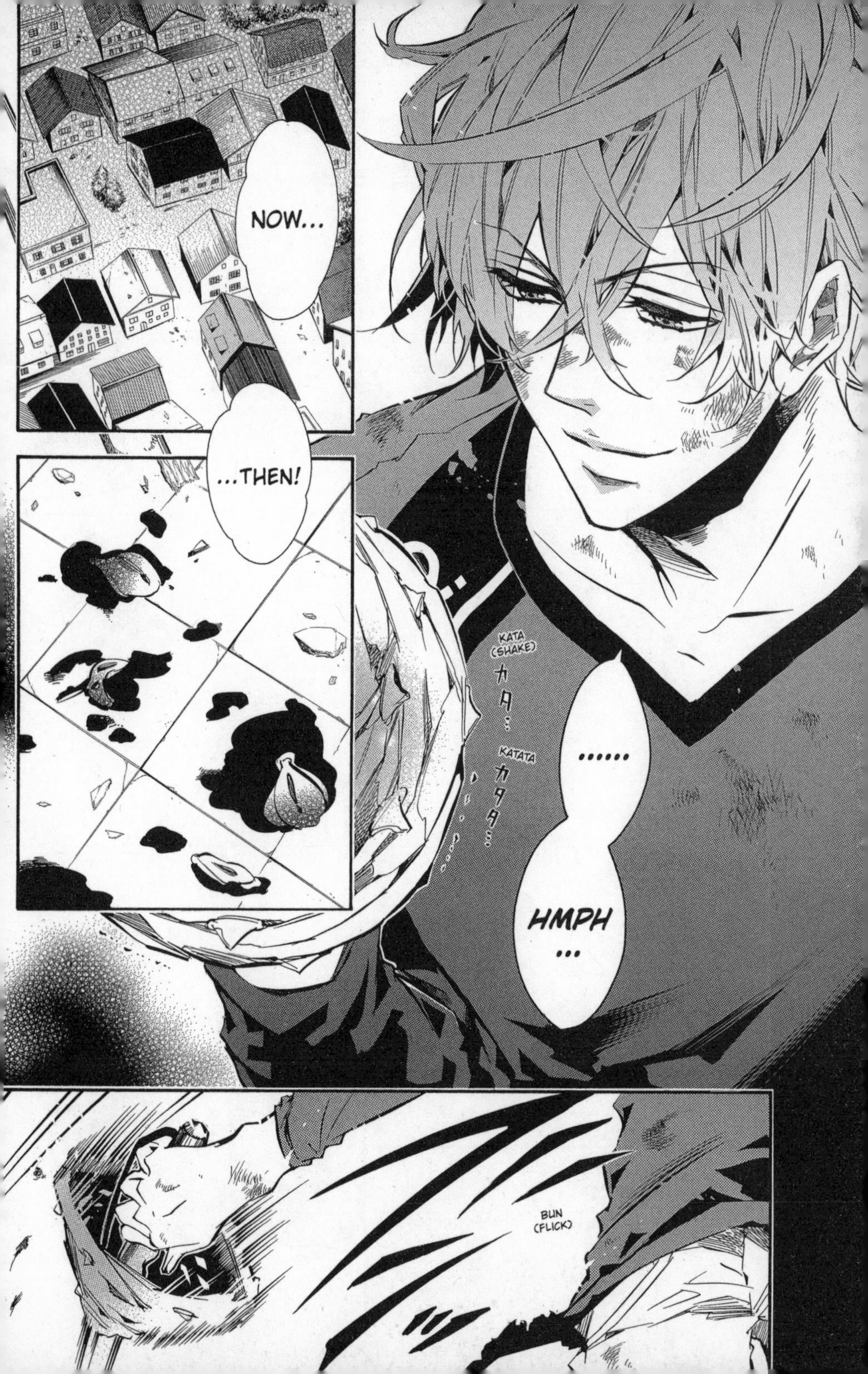
NOW...
...THEN!
KATA (SHAKE)
カタ…
KATATA
カタタ…
......
HMPH...
BUN (FLICK)

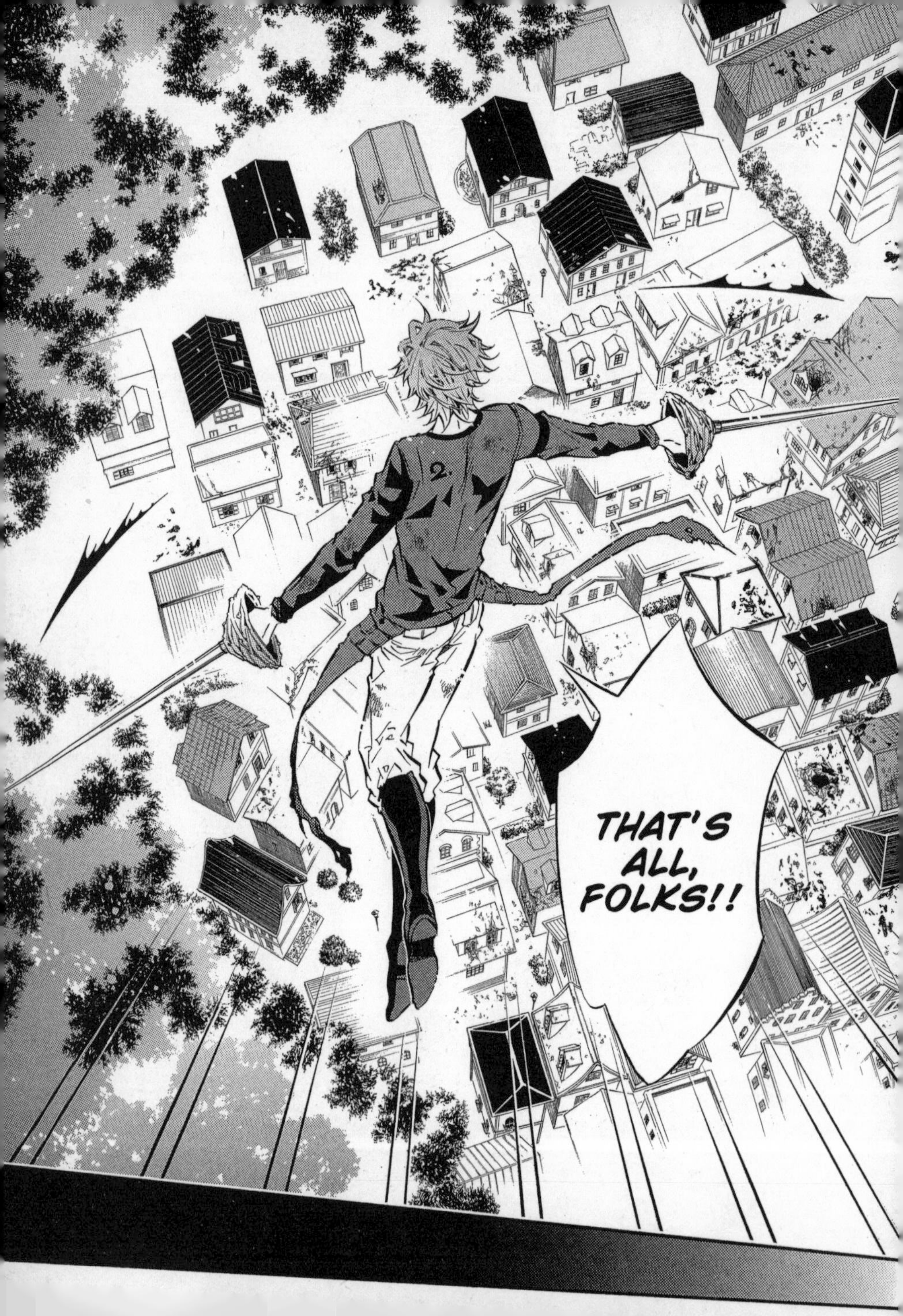
THAT'S ALL, FOLKS!!

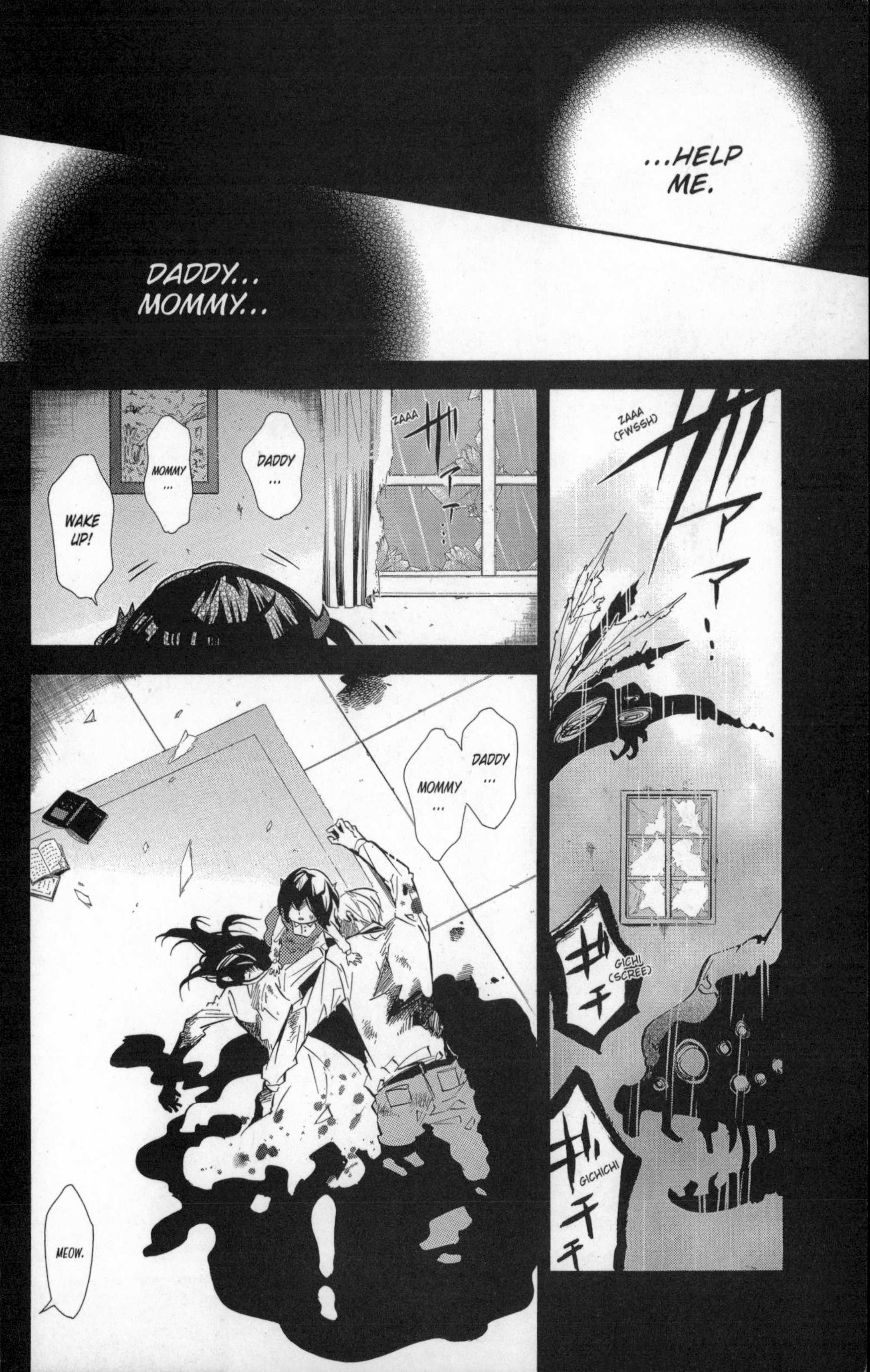
...HELP ME.
DADDY... MOMMY...
ZAAA (FWSSH)
GICHI (SCREE)
GICHICHI
ZAAA
DADDY ...
MOMMY ...
WAKE UP!
DADDY ...
MOMMY ...
MEOW.

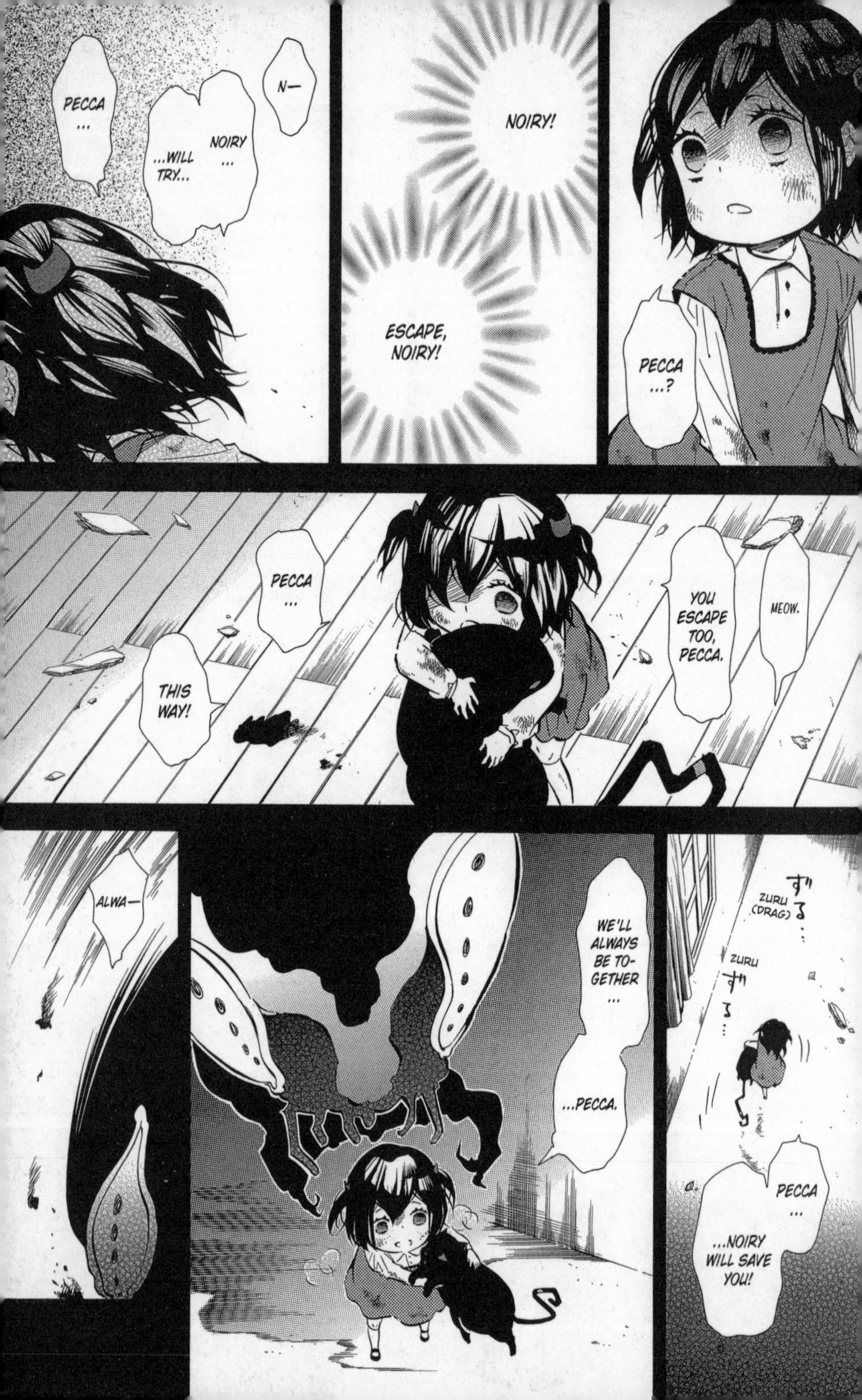
PECCA ...?
NOIRY!
ESCAPE, NOIRY!
N—
NOIRY ... ...WILL TRY...
PECCA ...
MEOW.
YOU ESCAPE TOO, PECCA.
PECCA ...
THIS WAY!
ずる ZURU (DRAG)
ずる ZURU
PECCA ...
...NOIRY WILL SAVE YOU!
WE'LL ALWAYS BE TO-GETHER ...
...PECCA.
ALWA—

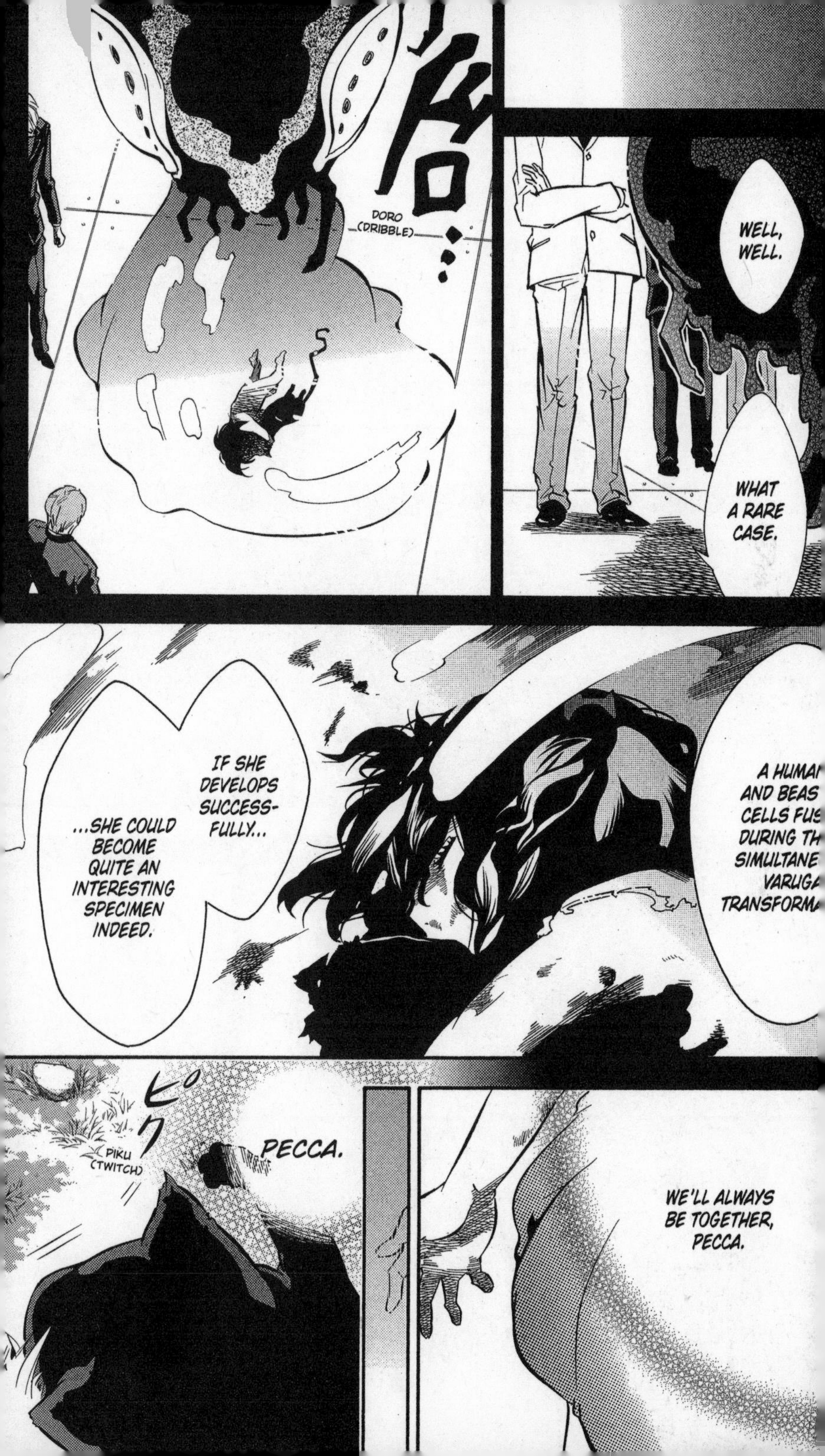
WELL, WELL.
WHAT A RARE CASE.
ドロ
DORO (DRIBBLE)
A HUMAN AND BEAS CELLS FUS DURING TH SIMULTANE VARUGA TRANSFORMA
IF SHE DEVELOPS SUCCESS-FULLY...
...SHE COULD BECOME QUITE AN INTERESTING SPECIMEN INDEED.
WE'LL ALWAYS BE TOGETHER, PECCA.
ピク
PIKU (TWITCH)
PECCA.

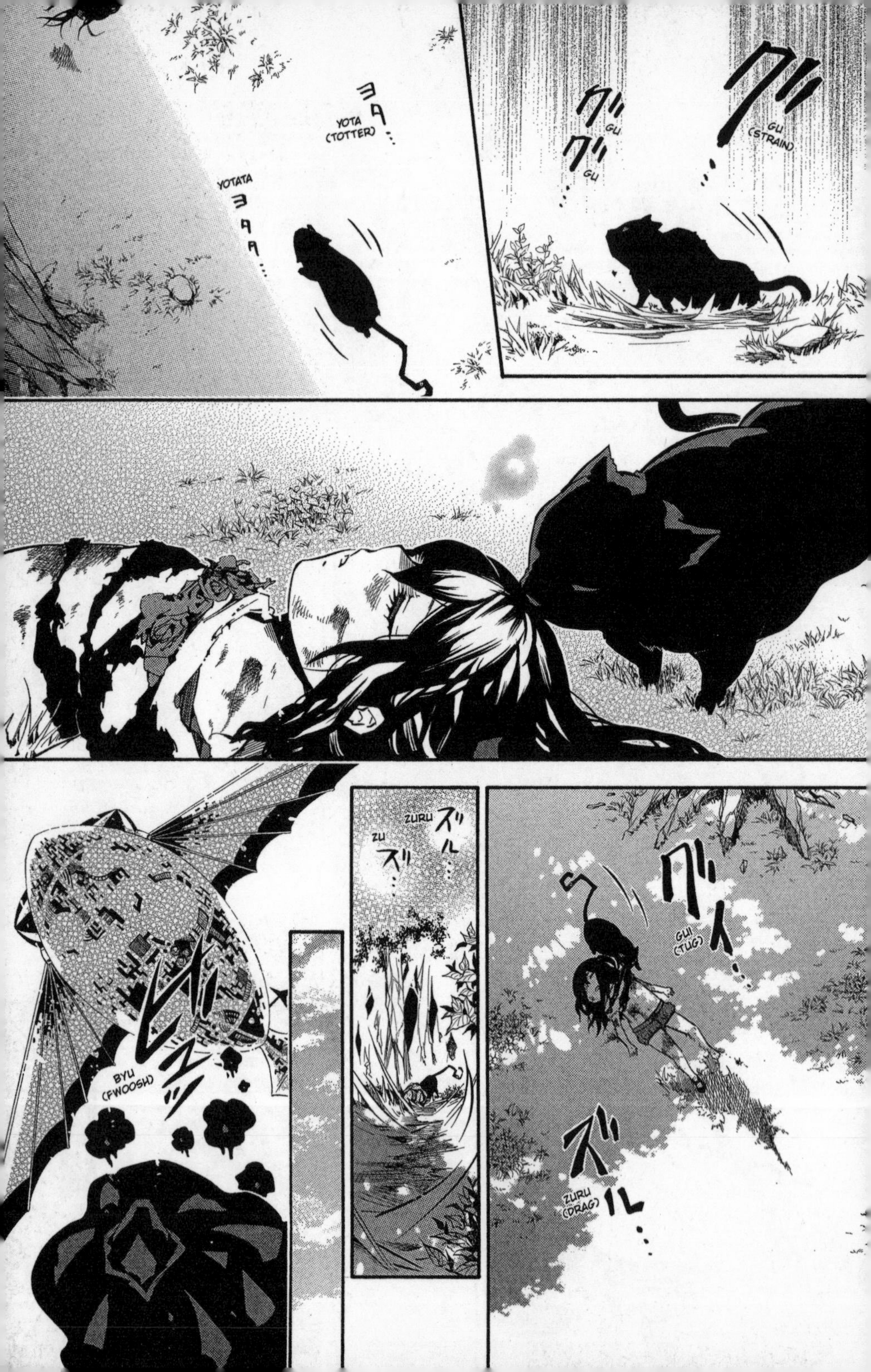

グ…
GU (STRAIN)
グ GU
グ GU
ヨタ…
YOTA (TOTTER)
ヨタタタ…
YOTATA
グイ…
GUI (TUG)
ズル…
ZURU (DRAG)
ズル…
ZURU
ズ…
ZU
BYU (FWOOSH)

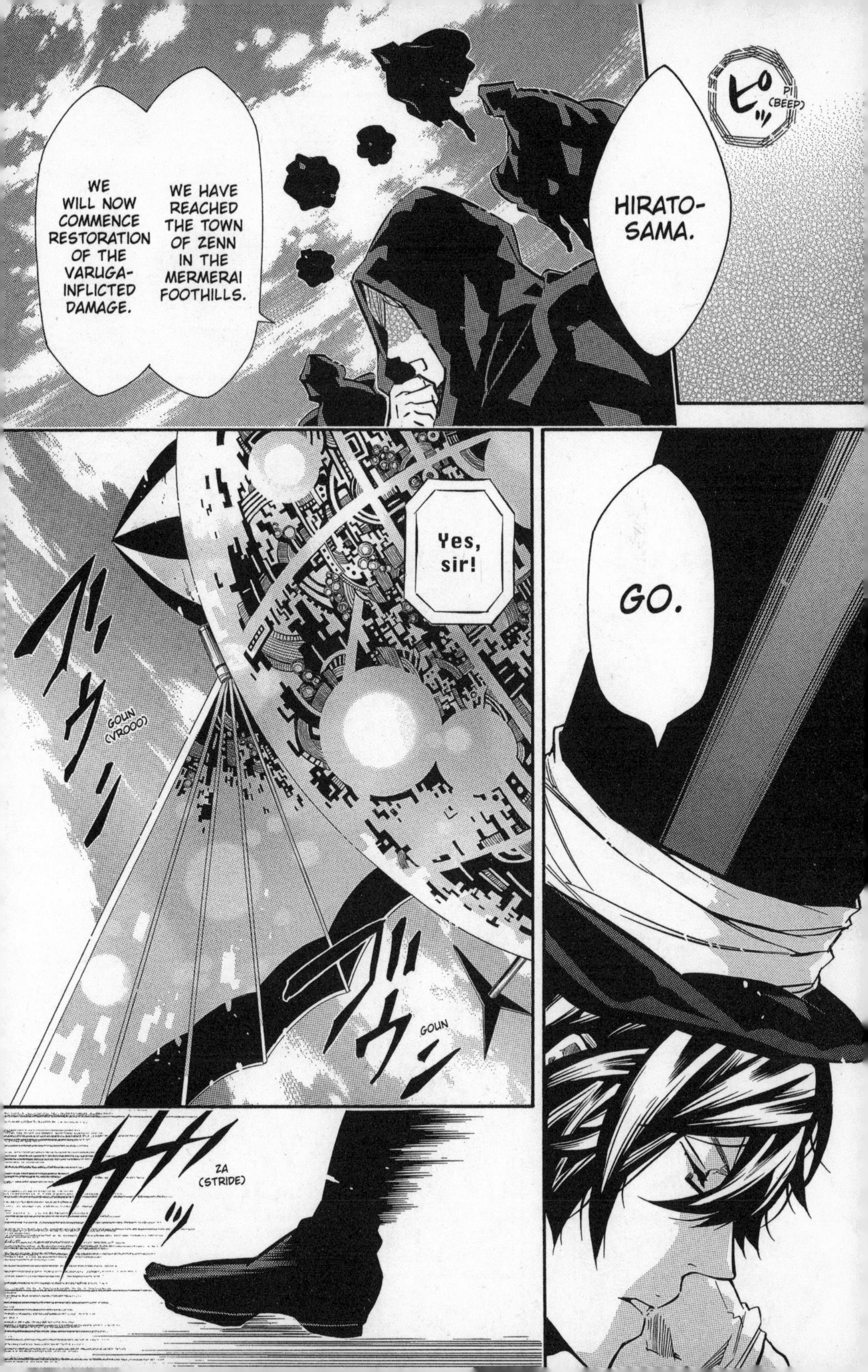
PI (BEEP)
HIRATO-SAMA.
WE HAVE REACHED THE TOWN OF ZENN IN THE MERMERAI FOOTHILLS.
WE WILL NOW COMMENCE RESTORATION OF THE VARUGA-INFLICTED DAMAGE.
GO.
Yes, sir!
GOUN (VROOO)
GOUN
ZA (STRIDE)

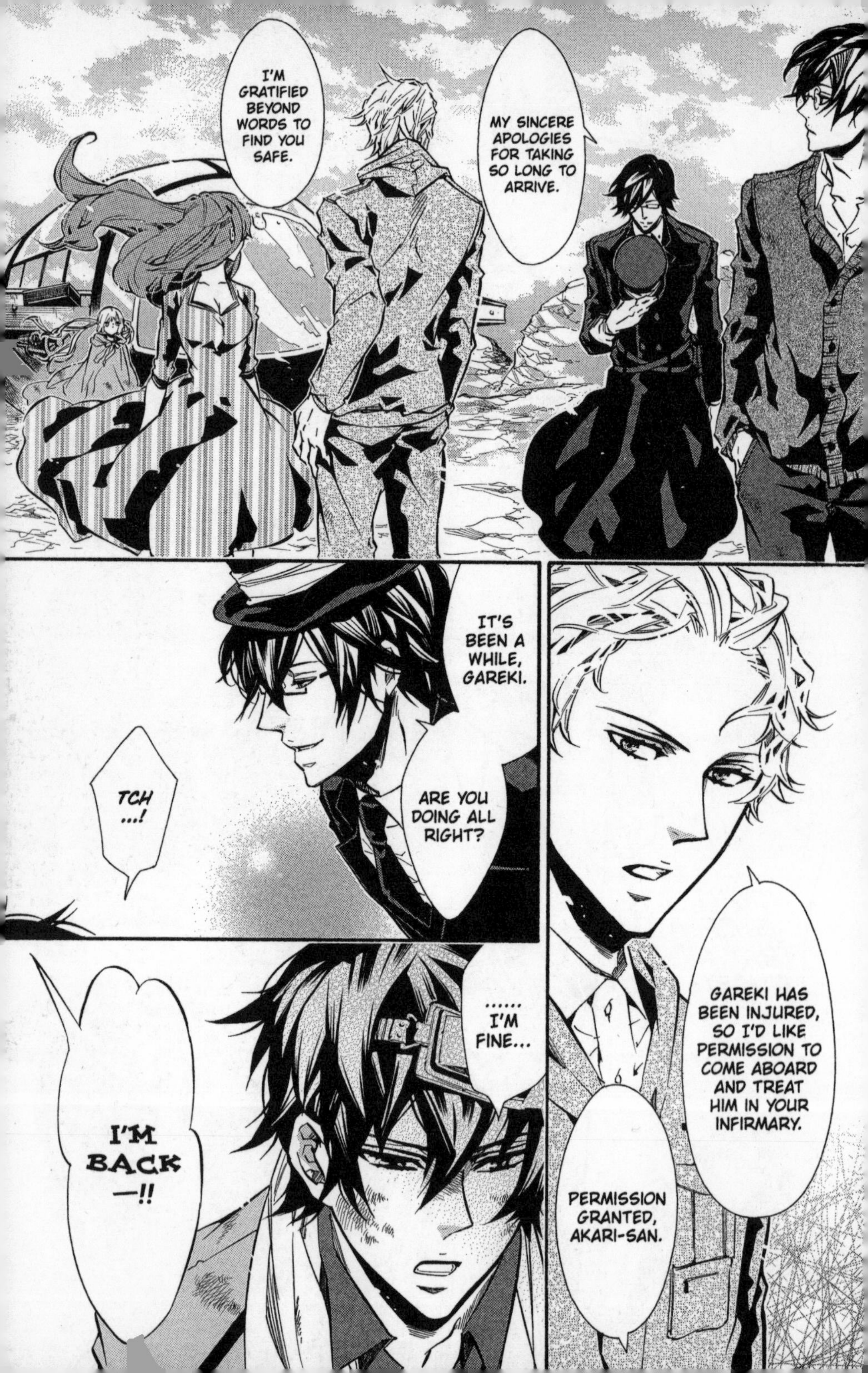
MY SINCERE APOLOGIES FOR TAKING SO LONG TO ARRIVE.
I'M GRATIFIED BEYOND WORDS TO FIND YOU SAFE.
GAREKI HAS BEEN INJURED, SO I'D LIKE PERMISSION TO COME ABOARD AND TREAT HIM IN YOUR INFIRMARY.
PERMISSION GRANTED, AKARI-SAN.
IT'S BEEN A WHILE, GAREKI.
ARE YOU DOING ALL RIGHT?
TCH ...!
...... I'M FINE...
I'M BACK—!!

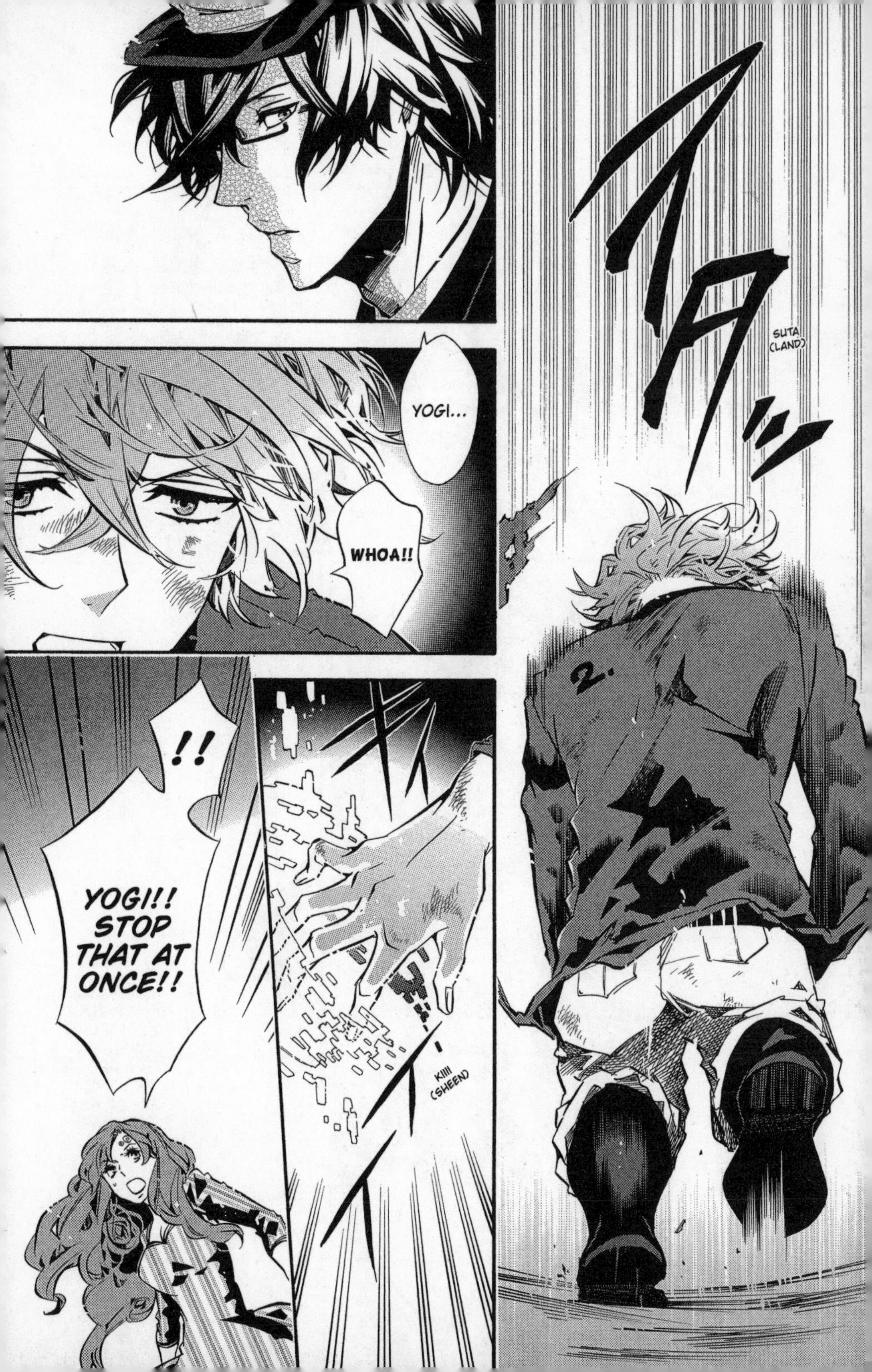
SUTA (LAND)
YOGI...
WHOA!!
KIIII (SHEEN)
!!
YOGI!! STOP THAT AT ONCE!!

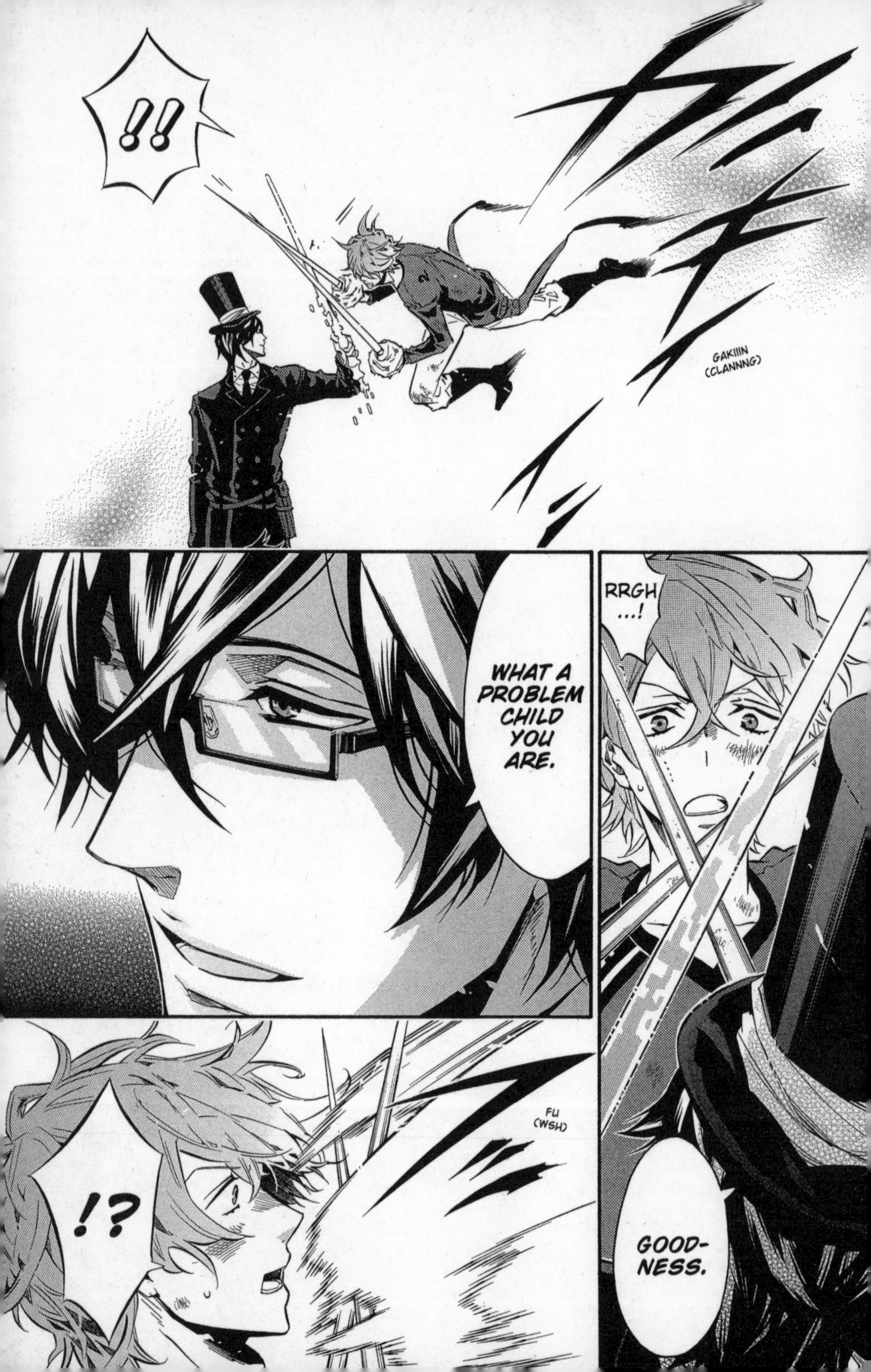
!!
GAKIIIN (CLANNNG)
RRGH ...!
FU (WSH)
GOOD-NESS.
WHAT A PROBLEM CHILD YOU ARE.
!?

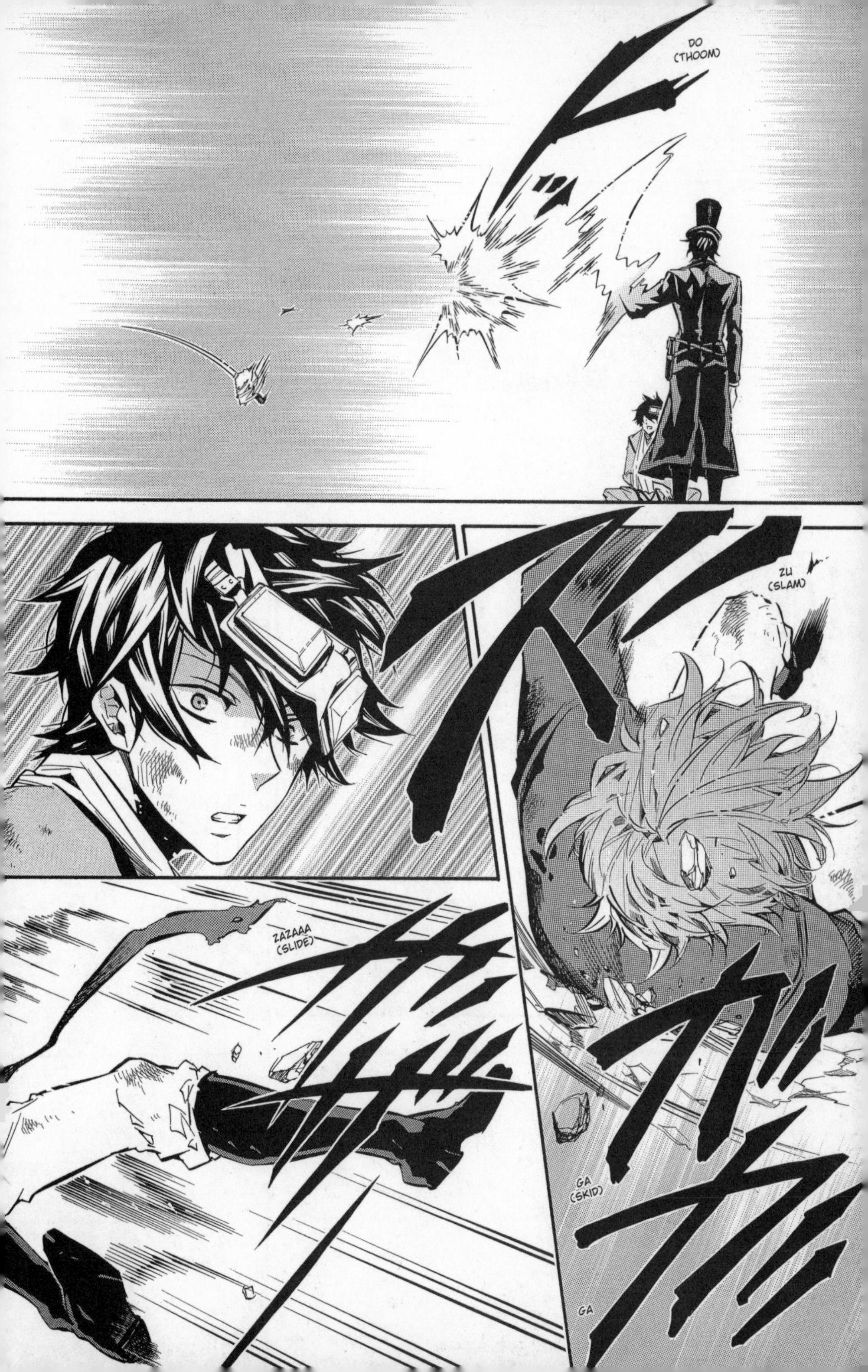
DO
(THOOM)
ZU
(SLAM)
ZAZAAA
(SLIDE)
GA
(SKID)
GA

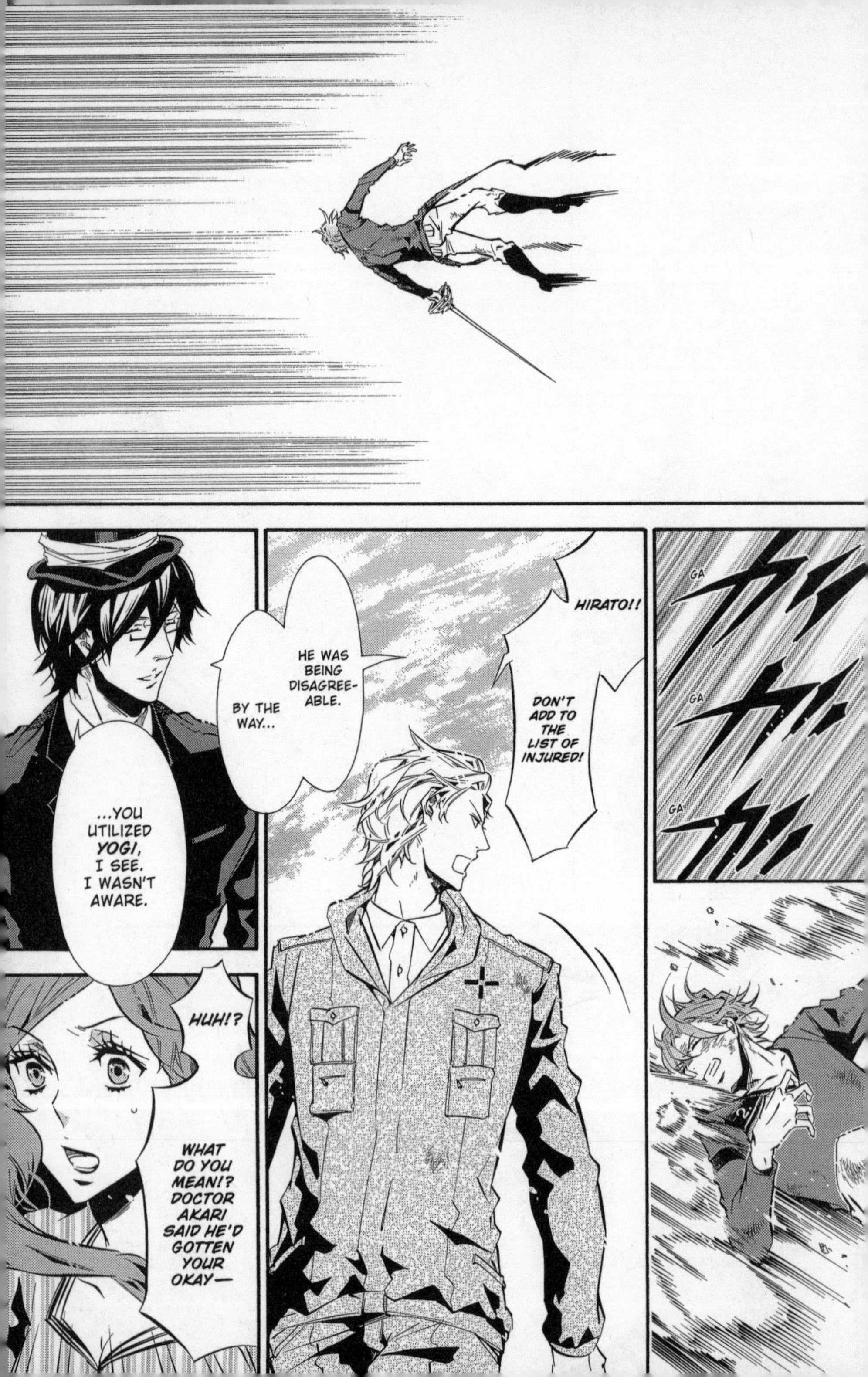
GA
GA
GA
HIRATO!!
DON'T ADD TO THE LIST OF INJURED!
HE WAS BEING DISAGREE-ABLE.
BY THE WAY...
...YOU UTILIZED YOGI, I SEE. I WASN'T AWARE.
HUH!?
WHAT DO YOU MEAN!? DOCTOR AKARI SAID HE'D GOTTEN YOUR OKAY—

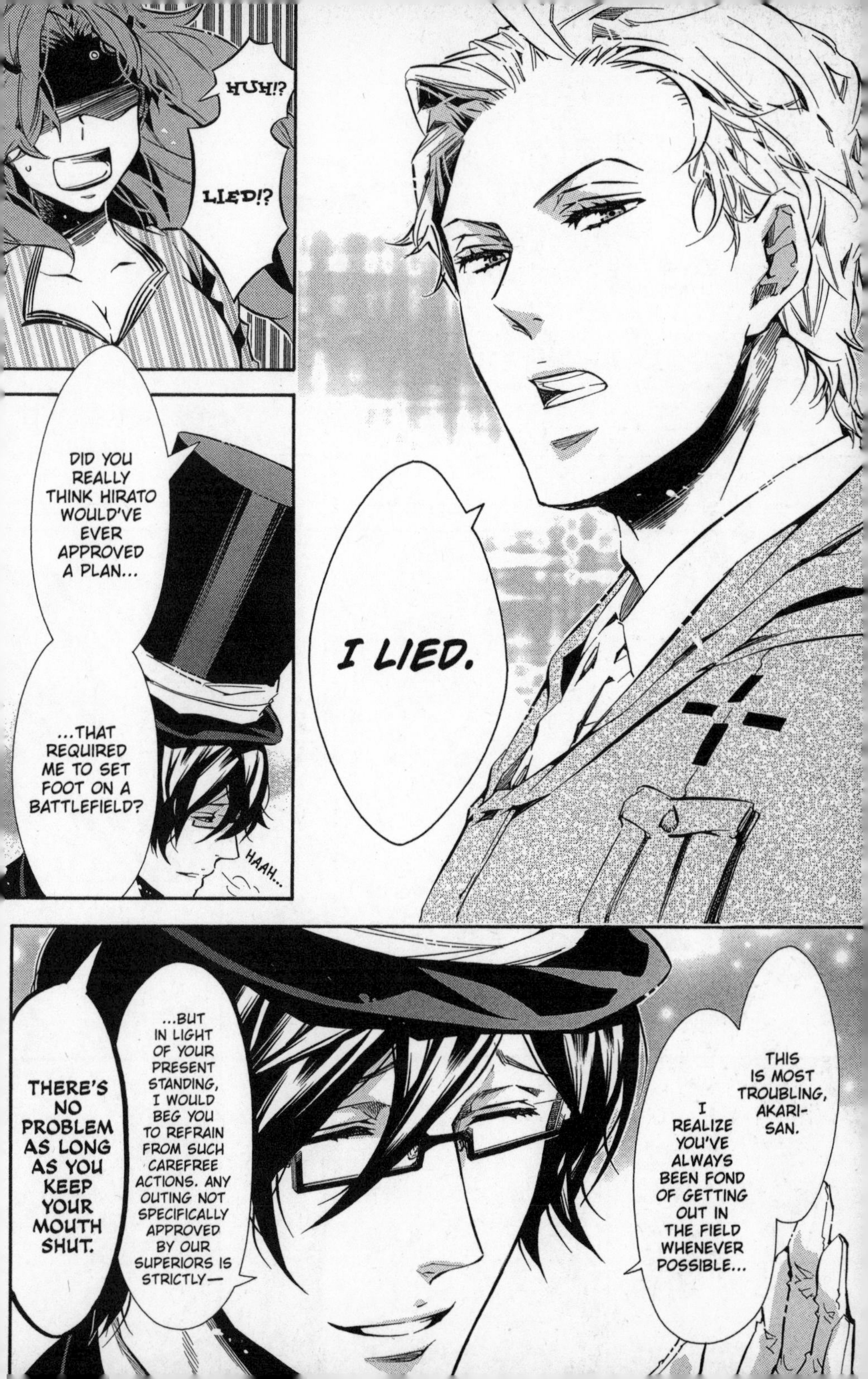
I LIED.
HUH!?
LIED!?
DID YOU REALLY THINK HIRATO WOULD'VE EVER APPROVED A PLAN...
...THAT REQUIRED ME TO SET FOOT ON A BATTLEFIELD?
HAAH...
THIS IS MOST TROUBLING, AKARI-SAN.
I REALIZE YOU'VE ALWAYS BEEN FOND OF GETTING OUT IN THE FIELD WHENEVER POSSIBLE...
...BUT IN LIGHT OF YOUR PRESENT STANDING, I WOULD BEG YOU TO REFRAIN FROM SUCH CAREFREE ACTIONS. ANY OUTING NOT SPECIFICALLY APPROVED BY OUR SUPERIORS IS STRICTLY—
THERE'S NO PROBLEM AS LONG AS YOU KEEP YOUR MOUTH SHUT.

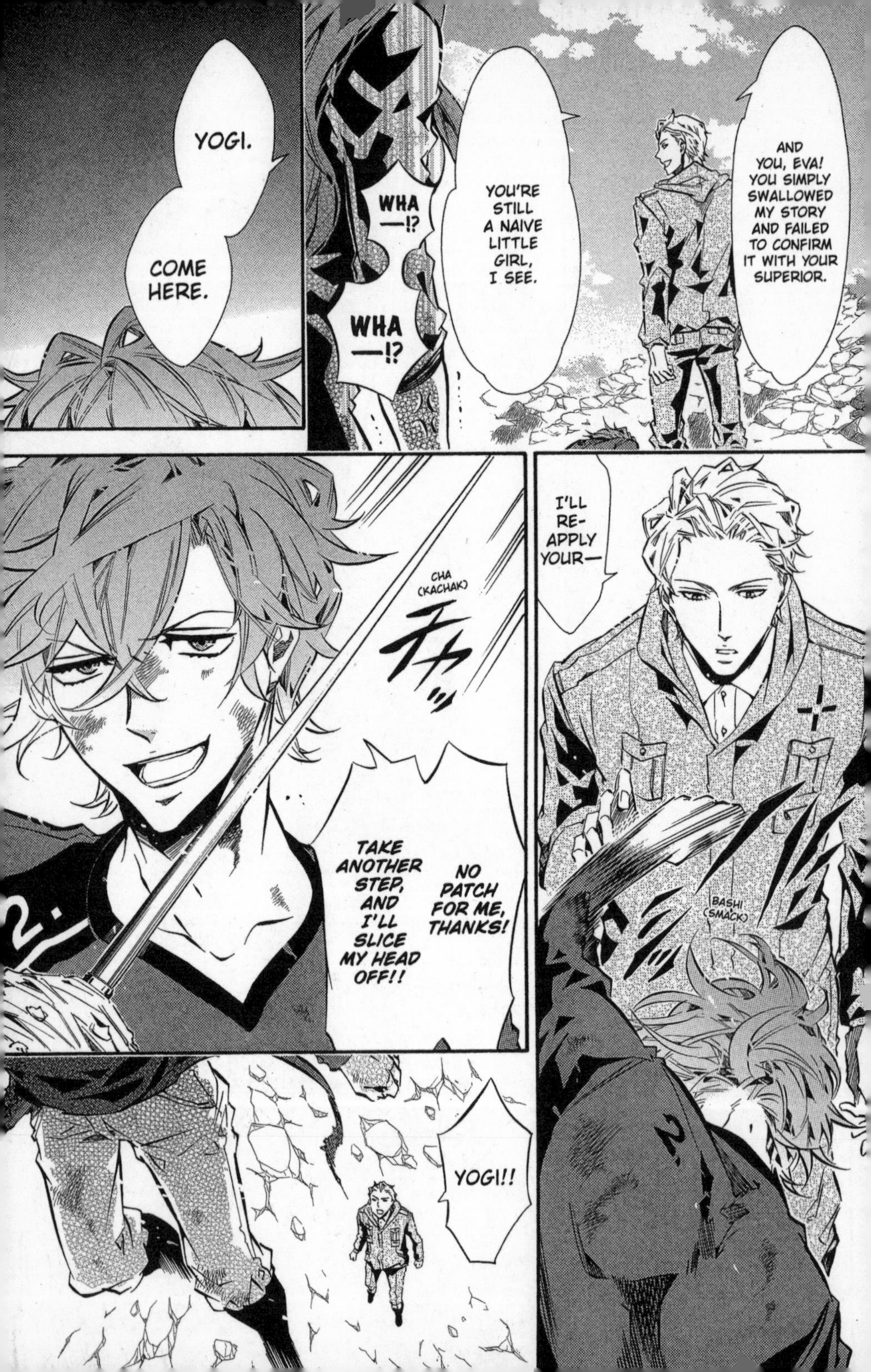
AND YOU, EVA! YOU SIMPLY SWALLOWED MY STORY AND FAILED TO CONFIRM IT WITH YOUR SUPERIOR.
YOU'RE STILL A NAIVE LITTLE GIRL, I SEE.
WHA—!?
WHA—!?
YOGI.
COME HERE.
I'LL RE-APPLY YOUR—
BASHI (SMACK)
CHA (KACHAK)
NO PATCH FOR ME, THANKS!
TAKE ANOTHER STEP, AND I'LL SLICE MY HEAD OFF!!
YOGI!!

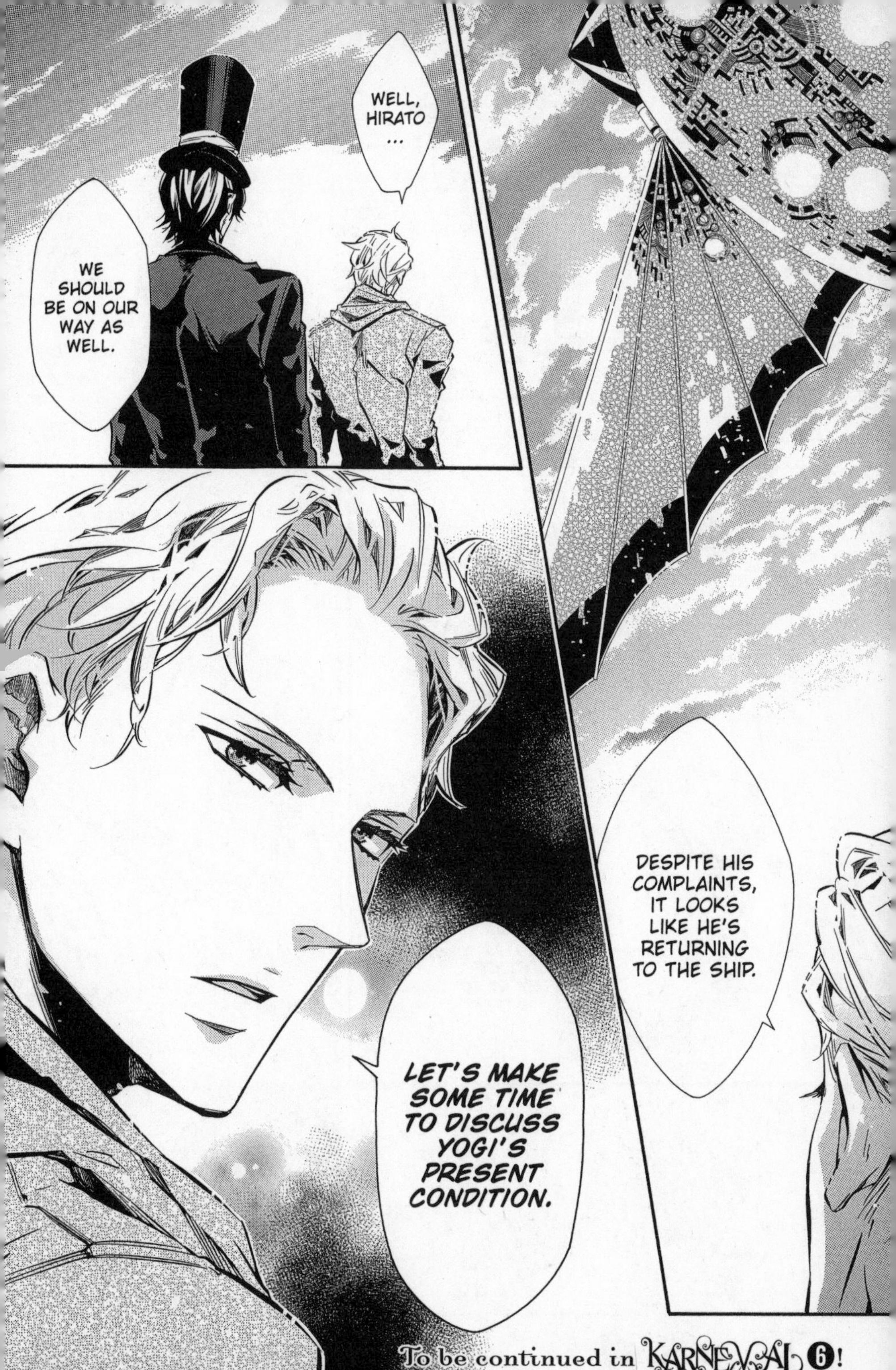
DESPITE HIS COMPLAINTS, IT LOOKS LIKE HE'S RETURNING TO THE SHIP.
WELL, HIRATO ...
WE SHOULD BE ON OUR WAY AS WELL.
LET'S MAKE SOME TIME TO DISCUSS YOGI'S PRESENT CONDITION.

To be continued in KARNEVAL 6!

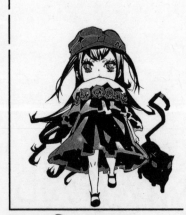

KARNEVAL

KARNEVAL

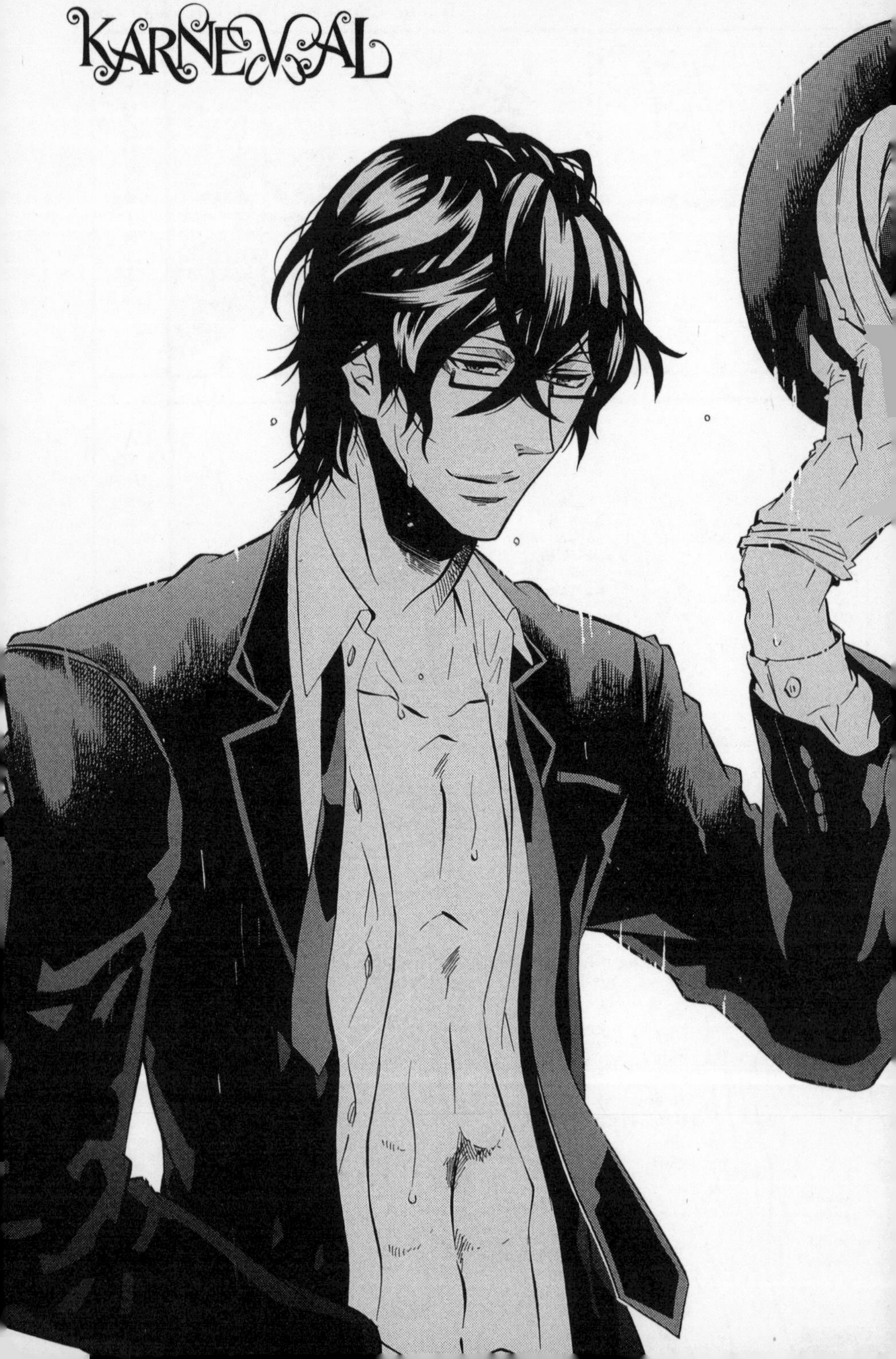
KARNEVAL

Bonus Comic 1 - That Time of Year

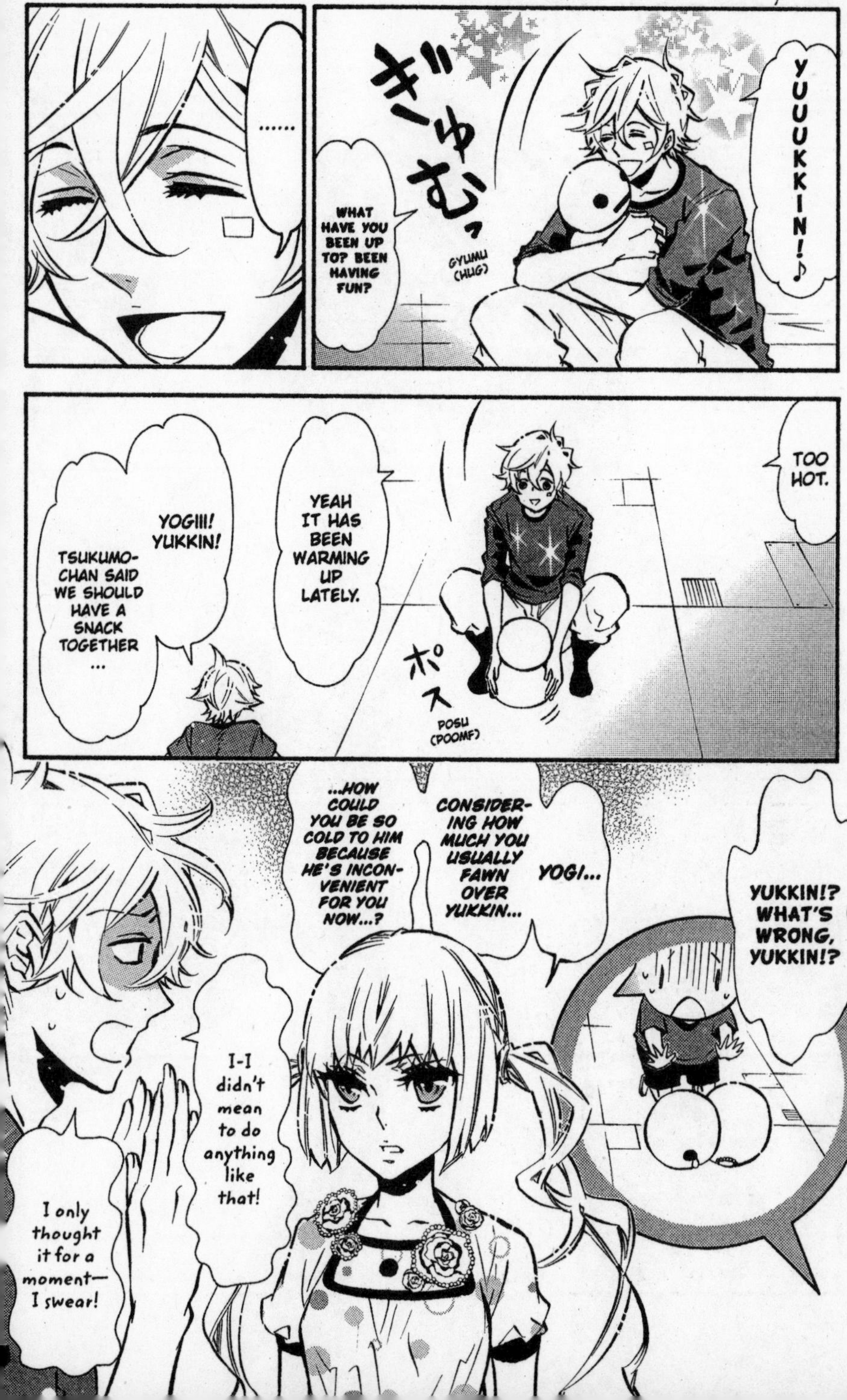

YUUUKKIN!♪
ぎゅむっ
GYUMU (HUG)
WHAT HAVE YOU BEEN UP TO? BEEN HAVING FUN?
......
TOO HOT.
YEAH IT HAS BEEN WARMING UP LATELY.
YOGIII! YUKKIN!
TSUKUMO-CHAN SAID WE SHOULD HAVE A SNACK TOGETHER...
ポス
POSU (POOMF)
YUKKIN!? WHAT'S WRONG, YUKKIN!?
YOGI...
CONSIDERING HOW MUCH YOU USUALLY FAWN OVER YUKKIN...
...HOW COULD YOU BE SO COLD TO HIM BECAUSE HE'S INCONVENIENT FOR YOU NOW...?
I-I didn't mean to do anything like that!
I only thought it for a moment—I swear!

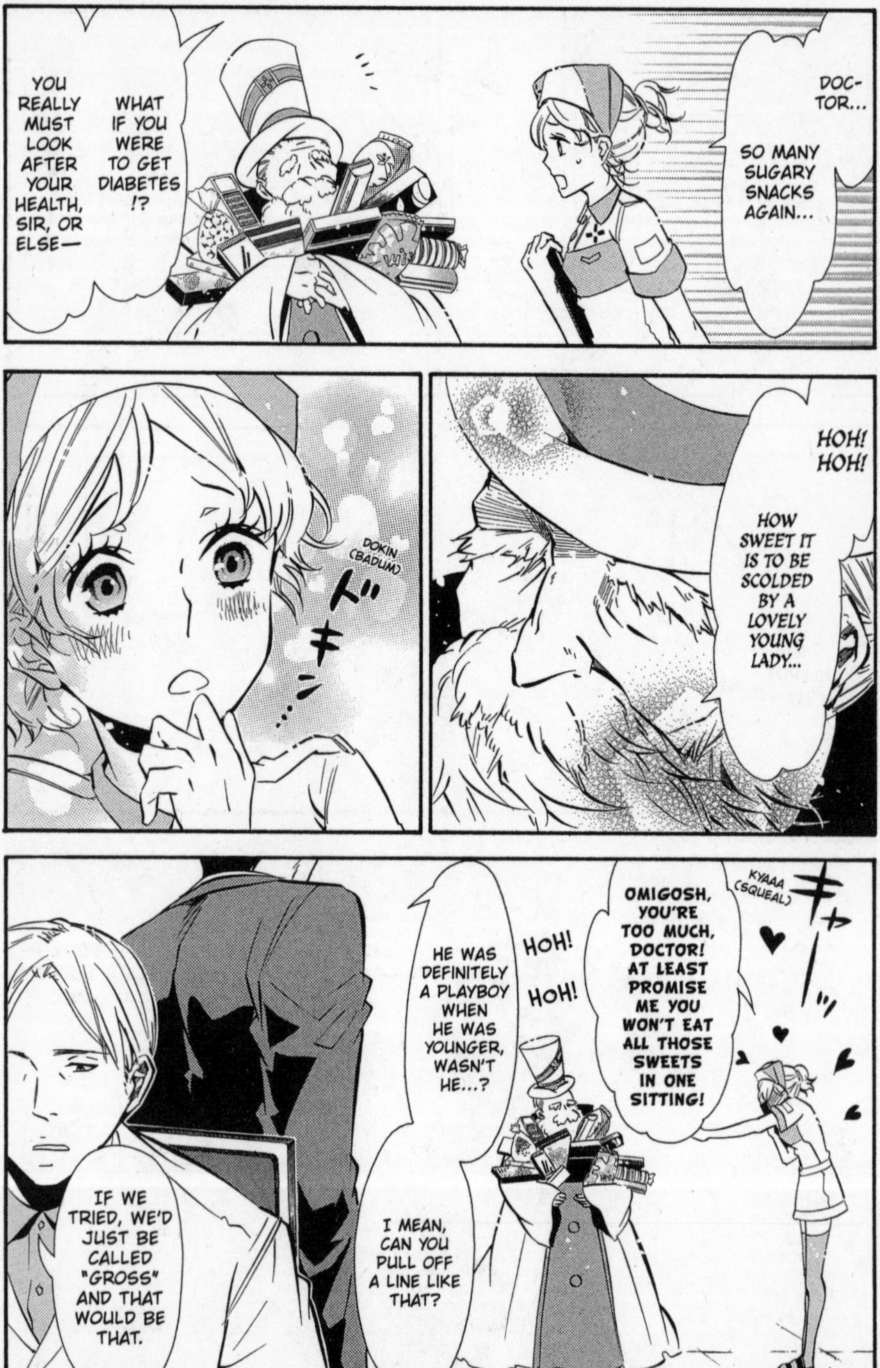
DOCTOR...
SO MANY SUGARY SNACKS AGAIN...
WHAT IF YOU WERE TO GET DIABETES!?
YOU REALLY MUST LOOK AFTER YOUR HEALTH, SIR, OR ELSE—
HOH! HOH!
HOW SWEET IT IS TO BE SCOLDED BY A LOVELY YOUNG LADY...
DOKIN (BADUM)
KYAAA (SQUEAL)
OMIGOSH, YOU'RE TOO MUCH, DOCTOR! AT LEAST PROMISE ME YOU WON'T EAT ALL THOSE SWEETS IN ONE SITTING!
HOH! HOH!
HE WAS DEFINITELY A PLAYBOY WHEN HE WAS YOUNGER, WASN'T HE...?
I MEAN, CAN YOU PULL OFF A LINE LIKE THAT?
IF WE TRIED, WE'D JUST BE CALLED "GROSS" AND THAT WOULD BE THAT.

Bonus Comic 3 - Leaving the Nest

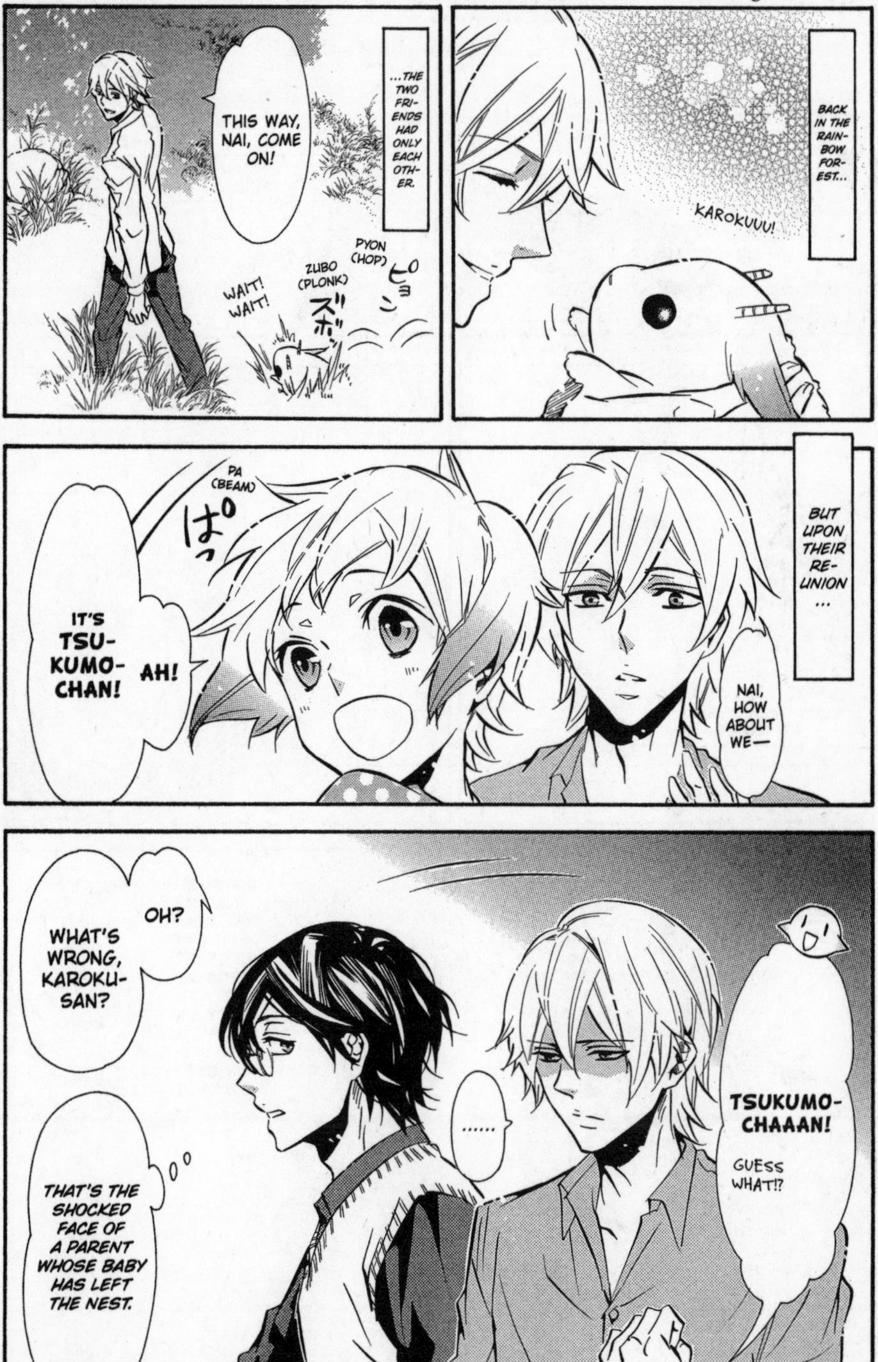
BACK IN THE RAINBOW FOREST...
KAROKUUU!
...THE TWO FRIENDS HAD ONLY EACH OTHER.
THIS WAY, NAI, COME ON!
WAIT! WAIT!
ピョン PYON (HOP)
ズボッ ZUBO (PLONK)
BUT UPON THEIR REUNION...
NAI, HOW ABOUT WE—
AH!
IT'S TSUKUMO-CHAN!
ぱっ PA (BEAM)
TSUKUMO-CHAAAN!
GUESS WHAT!?
......
OH?
WHAT'S WRONG, KAROKU-SAN?
THAT'S THE SHOCKED FACE OF A PARENT WHOSE BABY HAS LEFT THE NEST.

I'D BE GLAD IF YOU WOULD KINDLY WATCH OVER MY GROWN-UP, LITTLE NAI IN THE NEXT VOLUME AS WELL ......
—KAROKU

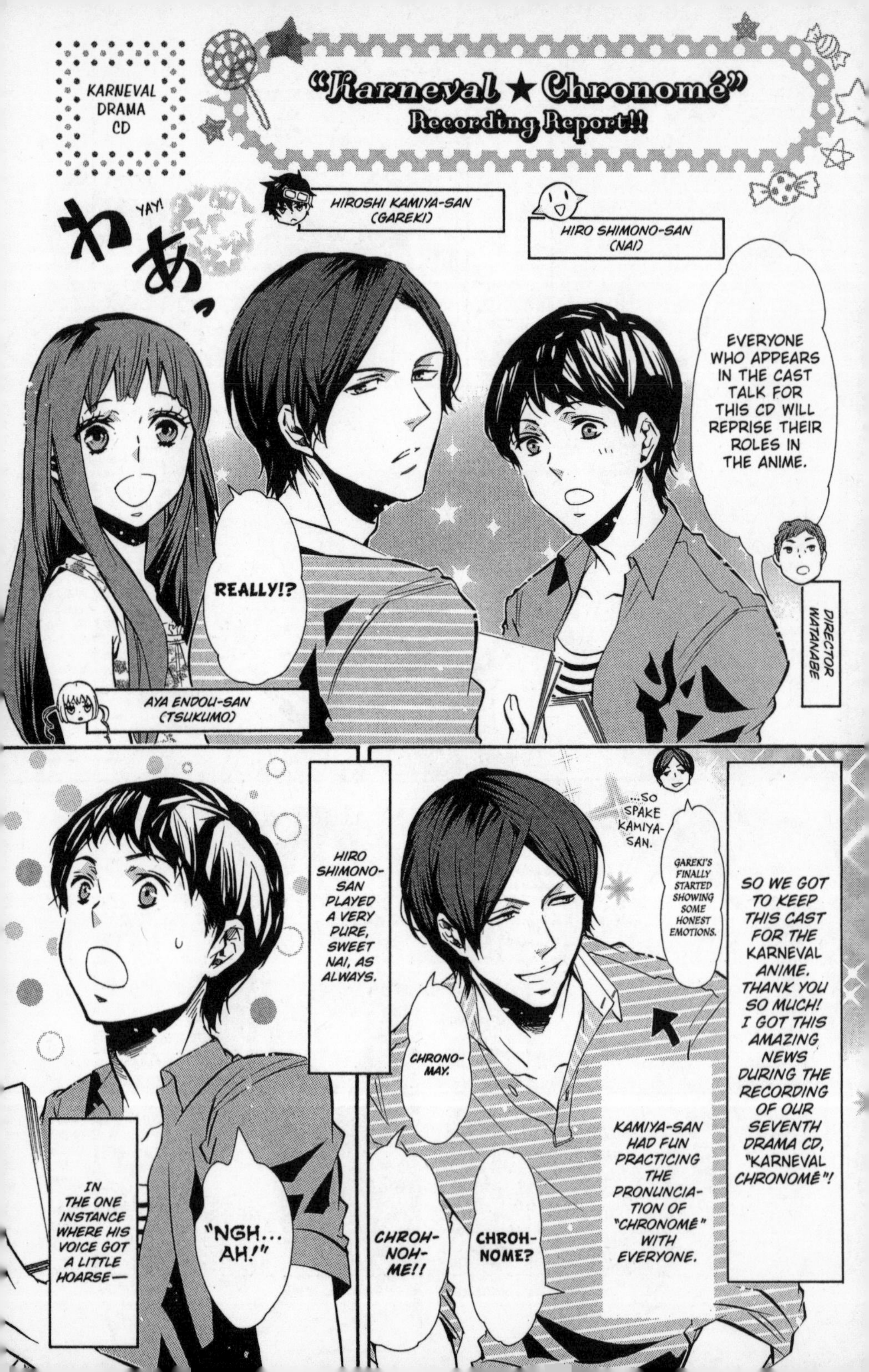
"Karneval ★ Chronomé" Recording Report!!
KARNEVAL DRAMA CD
EVERYONE WHO APPEARS IN THE CAST TALK FOR THIS CD WILL REPRISE THEIR ROLES IN THE ANIME.
DIRECTOR WATANABE
HIRO SHIMONO-SAN (NAI)
HIROSHI KAMIYA-SAN (GAREKI)
わあっ
YAY!
REALLY!?
AYA ENDOU-SAN (TSUKUMO)
SO WE GOT TO KEEP THIS CAST FOR THE KARNEVAL ANIME. THANK YOU SO MUCH! I GOT THIS AMAZING NEWS DURING THE RECORDING OF OUR SEVENTH DRAMA CD, "KARNEVAL CHRONOMÉ"!
...SO SPAKE KAMIYA-SAN.
GAREKI'S FINALLY STARTED SHOWING SOME HONEST EMOTIONS.
CHRONO-MAY.
KAMIYA-SAN HAD FUN PRACTICING THE PRONUNCIATION OF "CHRONOMÉ" WITH EVERYONE.
CHROH-NOME?
CHROH-NOH-ME!!
HIRO SHIMONO-SAN PLAYED A VERY PURE, SWEET NAI, AS ALWAYS.
IN THE ONE INSTANCE WHERE HIS VOICE GOT A LITTLE HOARSE—
"NGH... AH!"

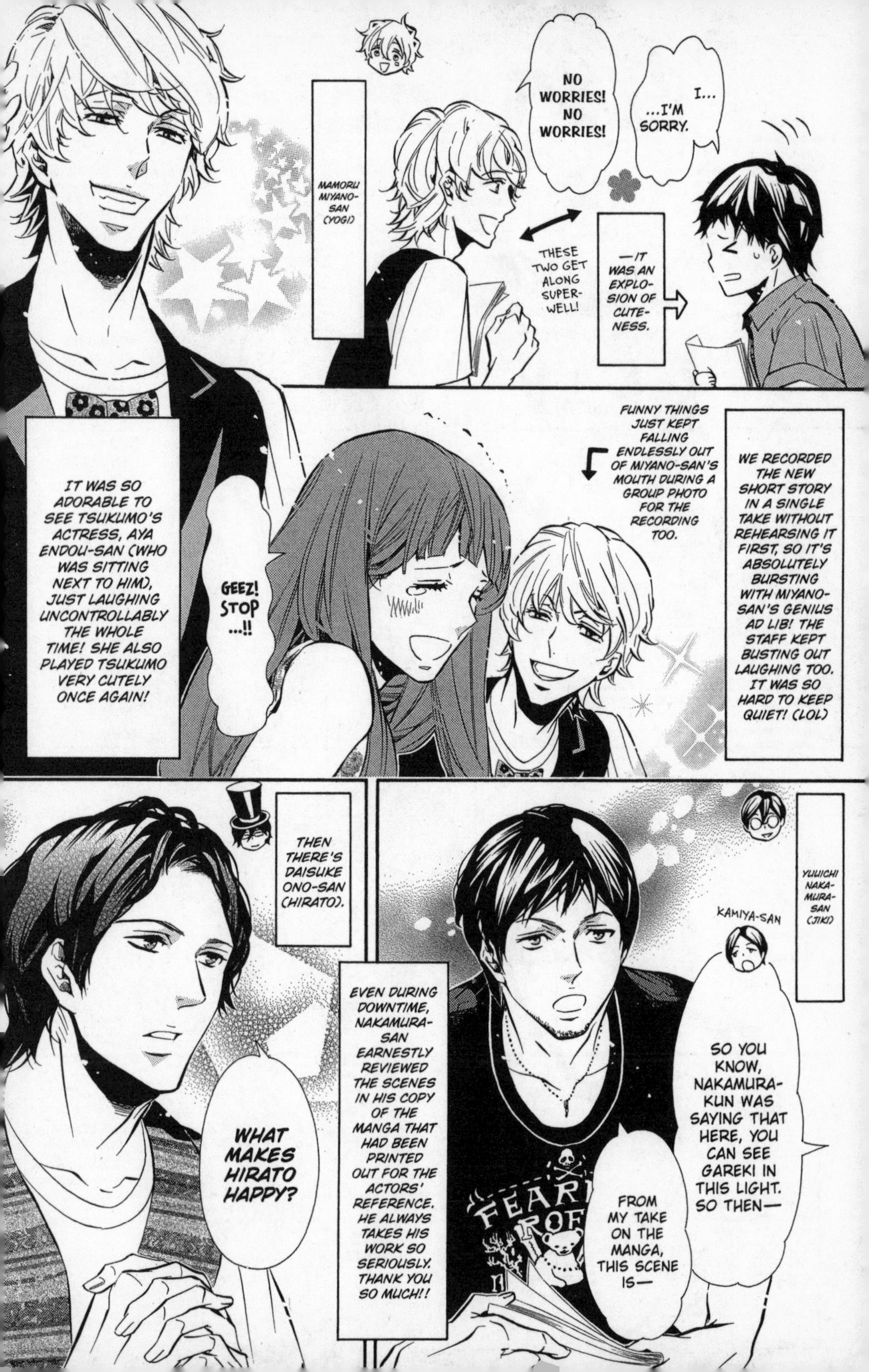
I... ...I'M SORRY.
—IT WAS AN EXPLOSION OF CUTENESS.
THESE TWO GET ALONG SUPER-WELL!
NO WORRIES! NO WORRIES!
MAMORU MIYANO-SAN (YOGI)
WE RECORDED THE NEW SHORT STORY IN A SINGLE TAKE WITHOUT REHEARSING IT FIRST, SO IT'S ABSOLUTELY BURSTING WITH MIYANO-SAN'S GENIUS AD LIB! THE STAFF KEPT BUSTING OUT LAUGHING TOO. IT WAS SO HARD TO KEEP QUIET! (LOL)
FUNNY THINGS JUST KEPT FALLING ENDLESSLY OUT OF MIYANO-SAN'S MOUTH DURING A GROUP PHOTO FOR THE RECORDING TOO.
GEEZ! STOP ...!!
IT WAS SO ADORABLE TO SEE TSUKUMO'S ACTRESS, AYA ENDOU-SAN (WHO WAS SITTING NEXT TO HIM), JUST LAUGHING UNCONTROLLABLY THE WHOLE TIME! SHE ALSO PLAYED TSUKUMO VERY CUTELY ONCE AGAIN!
YUUICHI NAKAMURA-SAN (JIKI)
KAMIYA-SAN
SO YOU KNOW, NAKAMURA-KUN WAS SAYING THAT HERE, YOU CAN SEE GAREKI IN THIS LIGHT. SO THEN—
FROM MY TAKE ON THE MANGA, THIS SCENE IS—
EVEN DURING DOWNTIME, NAKAMURA-SAN EARNESTLY REVIEWED THE SCENES IN HIS COPY OF THE MANGA THAT HAD BEEN PRINTED OUT FOR THE ACTORS' REFERENCE. HE ALWAYS TAKES HIS WORK SO SERIOUSLY. THANK YOU SO MUCH!!
THEN THERE'S DAISUKE ONO-SAN (HIRATO).
WHAT MAKES HIRATO HAPPY?

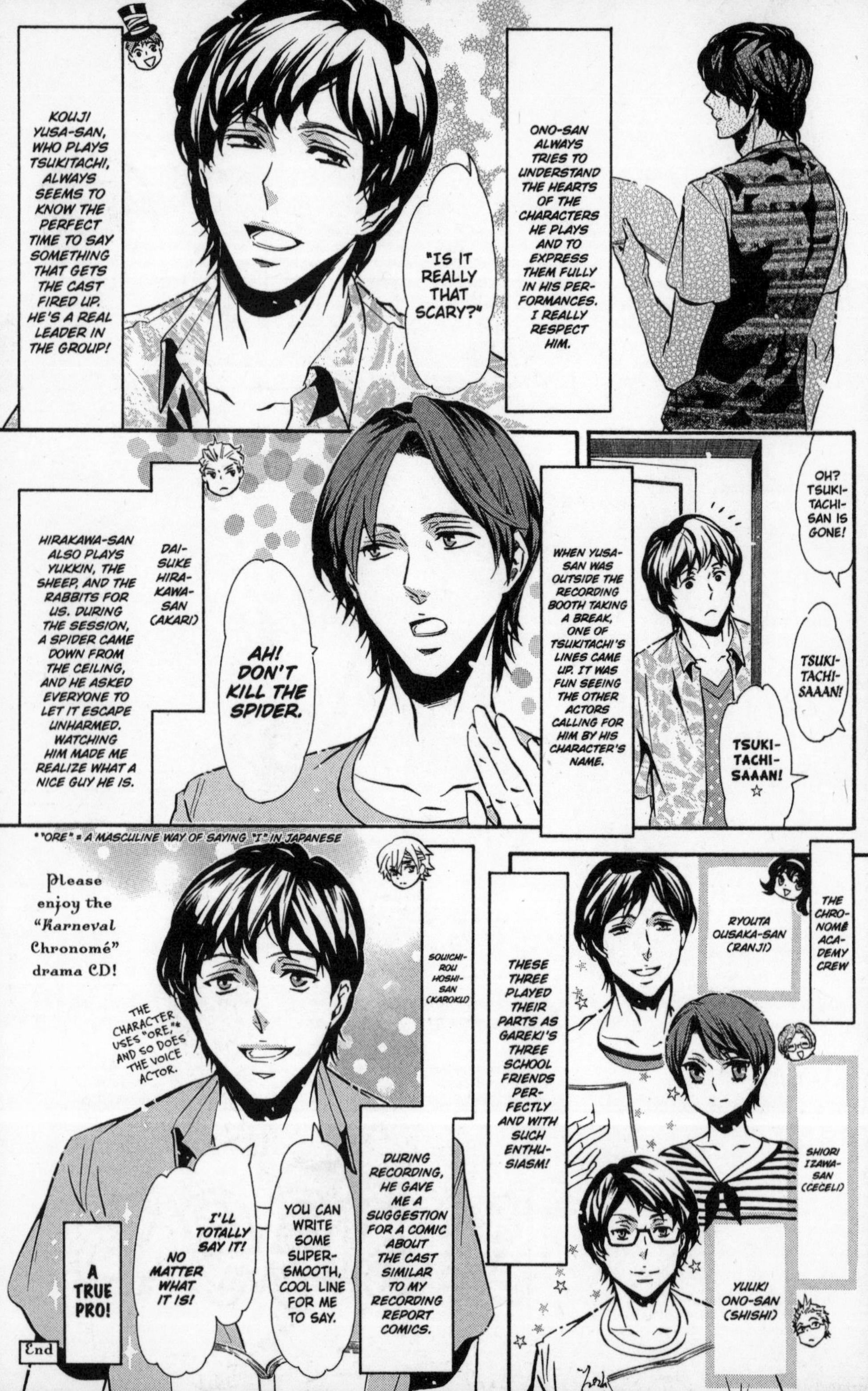
ONO-SAN ALWAYS TRIES TO UNDERSTAND THE HEARTS OF THE CHARACTERS HE PLAYS AND TO EXPRESS THEM FULLY IN HIS PERFORMANCES. I REALLY RESPECT HIM.
"IS IT REALLY THAT SCARY?"
KOUJI YUSA-SAN, WHO PLAYS TSUKITACHI, ALWAYS SEEMS TO KNOW THE PERFECT TIME TO SAY SOMETHING THAT GETS THE CAST FIRED UP. HE'S A REAL LEADER IN THE GROUP!
OH? TSUKITACHI-SAN IS GONE!
TSUKITACHI-SAAAN!
TSUKITACHI-SAAAN! ☆
WHEN YUSA-SAN WAS OUTSIDE THE RECORDING BOOTH TAKING A BREAK, ONE OF TSUKITACHI'S LINES CAME UP. IT WAS FUN SEEING THE OTHER ACTORS CALLING FOR HIM BY HIS CHARACTER'S NAME.
AH! DON'T KILL THE SPIDER.
DAISUKE HIRAKAWA-SAN (AKARI)
HIRAKAWA-SAN ALSO PLAYS YUKKIN, THE SHEEP, AND THE RABBITS FOR US. DURING THE SESSION, A SPIDER CAME DOWN FROM THE CEILING, AND HE ASKED EVERYONE TO LET IT ESCAPE UNHARMED. WATCHING HIM MADE ME REALIZE WHAT A NICE GUY HE IS.
THE CHRONOMÉ ACADEMY CREW
RYOUTA OUSAKA-SAN (RANJI)
THESE THREE PLAYED THEIR PARTS AS GAREKI'S THREE SCHOOL FRIENDS PERFECTLY AND WITH SUCH ENTHUSIASM!
SHIORI IZAWA-SAN (CECELI)
YUUKI ONO-SAN (SHISHI)
DURING RECORDING, HE GAVE ME A SUGGESTION FOR A COMIC ABOUT THE CAST SIMILAR TO MY RECORDING REPORT COMICS.
SOUICHIROU HOSHI-SAN (KAROKU)
YOU CAN WRITE SOME SUPER-SMOOTH, COOL LINE FOR ME TO SAY.
I'LL TOTALLY SAY IT! NO MATTER WHAT IT IS!
THE CHARACTER USES "ORE,"* AND SO DOES THE VOICE ACTOR.
A TRUE PRO!
Please enjoy the "Karneval Chronomé" drama CD!
End
* "ORE" = A MASCULINE WAY OF SAYING "I" IN JAPANESE

KARNEVAL

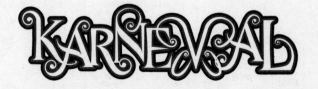

POSTSCRIPT

HI THERE, THIS IS MIKANAGI.
WE'RE ALREADY ON *KARNEVAL* VOLUME 10!
THANK YOU TO EVERYONE WHO CONTINUES TO READ THE STORY LOYALLY!
IT MAKES ME SO HAPPY THAT YOU GUYS ARE ENJOYING IT.

I MENTIONED IT ON MY COVER AUTHOR COMMENTARY AS WELL, BUT AMAZINGLY, IT'S BEEN DECIDED THAT *KARNEVAL* WILL BE MADE INTO AN ANIME! I'M SO HAPPY! THE FACT THAT THE MANGA HAS MADE IT ALL THE WAY TO VOLUME 10 AND THAT WE'RE NOW GETTING THIS INCREDIBLE CHANCE TO HAVE IT ANIMATED IS ENTIRELY THANKS TO ALL THE READERS AND EVERYONE RELATED TO THE PROJECT WHO HAVE SUPPORTED IT ALONG THE WAY. I'M SO VERY GRATEFUL TO YOU ALL.

THROUGH MY WORK, I'VE BEEN ABLE TO MEET ALL SORTS OF PEOPLE IN VARIOUS PROFESSIONS. THOUGH THE AMOUNT OF TIME WE'RE ABLE TO SPEAK DIRECTLY OR MEET FACE-TO-FACE IS VERY LIMITED, I'VE BEEN ABLE TO HEAR THEIR DIVERSE THOUGHTS AND IDEAS AND OBSERVE THEM PERFORMING THEIR CRAFT IN THOSE SHORT MEETINGS, AS WELL AS VIEW THEIR AMAZING FINISHED WORKS. I REALLY LOVE THOSE EXPERIENCES.

I'VE ALSO HAD THE CHANCE TO SEE THE *KARNEVAL* ANIME STORYBOARDS! AS A HUGE FAN OF ANIMATION, THIS WAS UNSPEAKABLY THRILLING FOR ME. AND EVEN MORE AMAZING—SEEING MY WORLD COME TO LIFE IN ANIME STORYBOARDS...I WAS OVERCOME WITH EMOTION THE MOMENT I SAW THEM...! AND ALSO WHEN I GOT THE CHARACTER DESIGNS...! I WAS LIKE—"CHARACTER DESIGNS!!*" AND JUST GOT COMPLETELY PUMPED.

THE JAPANESE LIMITED EDITION OF VOLUME 10 COMES WITH A DVD CONTAINING A TEASER TRAILER FOR THE ANIME AS WELL AS A ROUNDTABLE DISCUSSION WITH THE VOICE CAST. I'M GUESSING SOME OF YOU MAY HAVE ALREADY SEEN THE TEASER ONLINE, BUT IN ANY CASE, I HOPE YOU'LL ENJOY WATCHING IT ON THE DVD TOO.

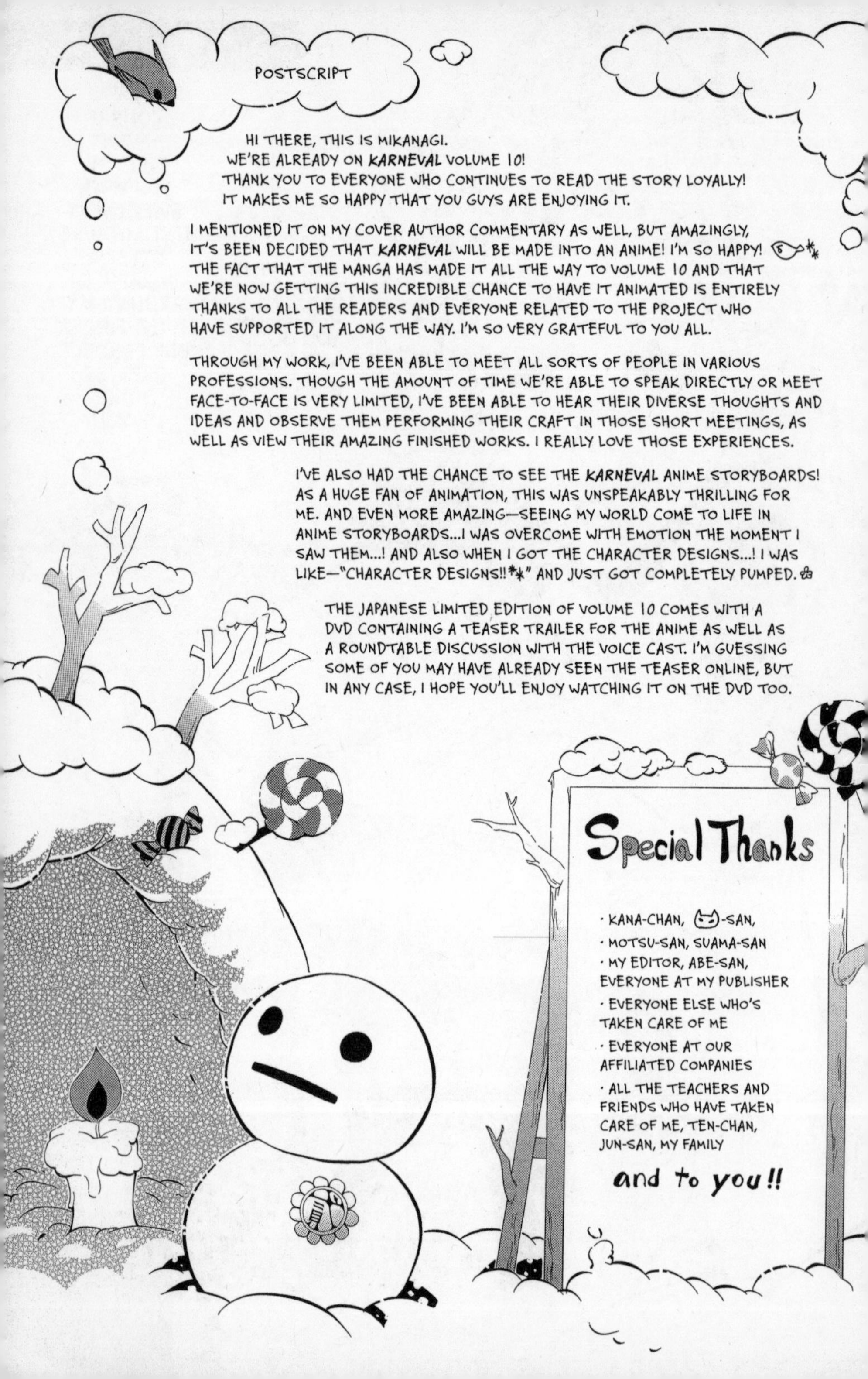
Special Thanks
· KANA-CHAN, -SAN,
· MOTSU-SAN, SUAMA-SAN
· MY EDITOR, ABE-SAN, EVERYONE AT MY PUBLISHER
· EVERYONE ELSE WHO'S TAKEN CARE OF ME
· EVERYONE AT OUR AFFILIATED COMPANIES
· ALL THE TEACHERS AND FRIENDS WHO HAVE TAKEN CARE OF ME, TEN-CHAN, JUN-SAN, MY FAMILY
and to you!!

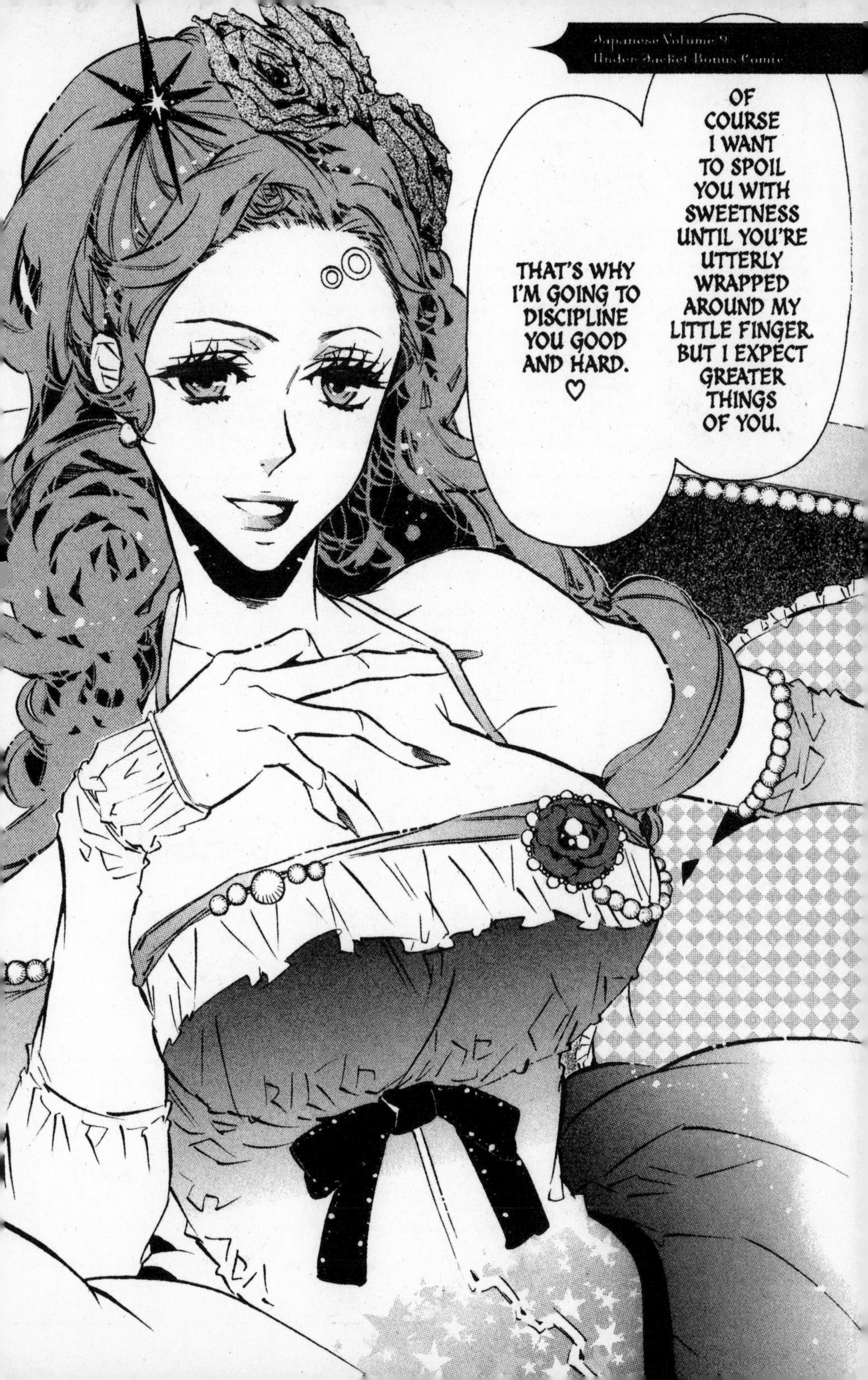
Japanese Volume 9
Under-Jacket Bonus Comic
OF COURSE I WANT TO SPOIL YOU WITH SWEETNESS UNTIL YOU'RE UTTERLY WRAPPED AROUND MY LITTLE FINGER. BUT I EXPECT GREATER THINGS OF YOU.
THAT'S WHY I'M GOING TO DISCIPLINE YOU GOOD AND HARD. ♡

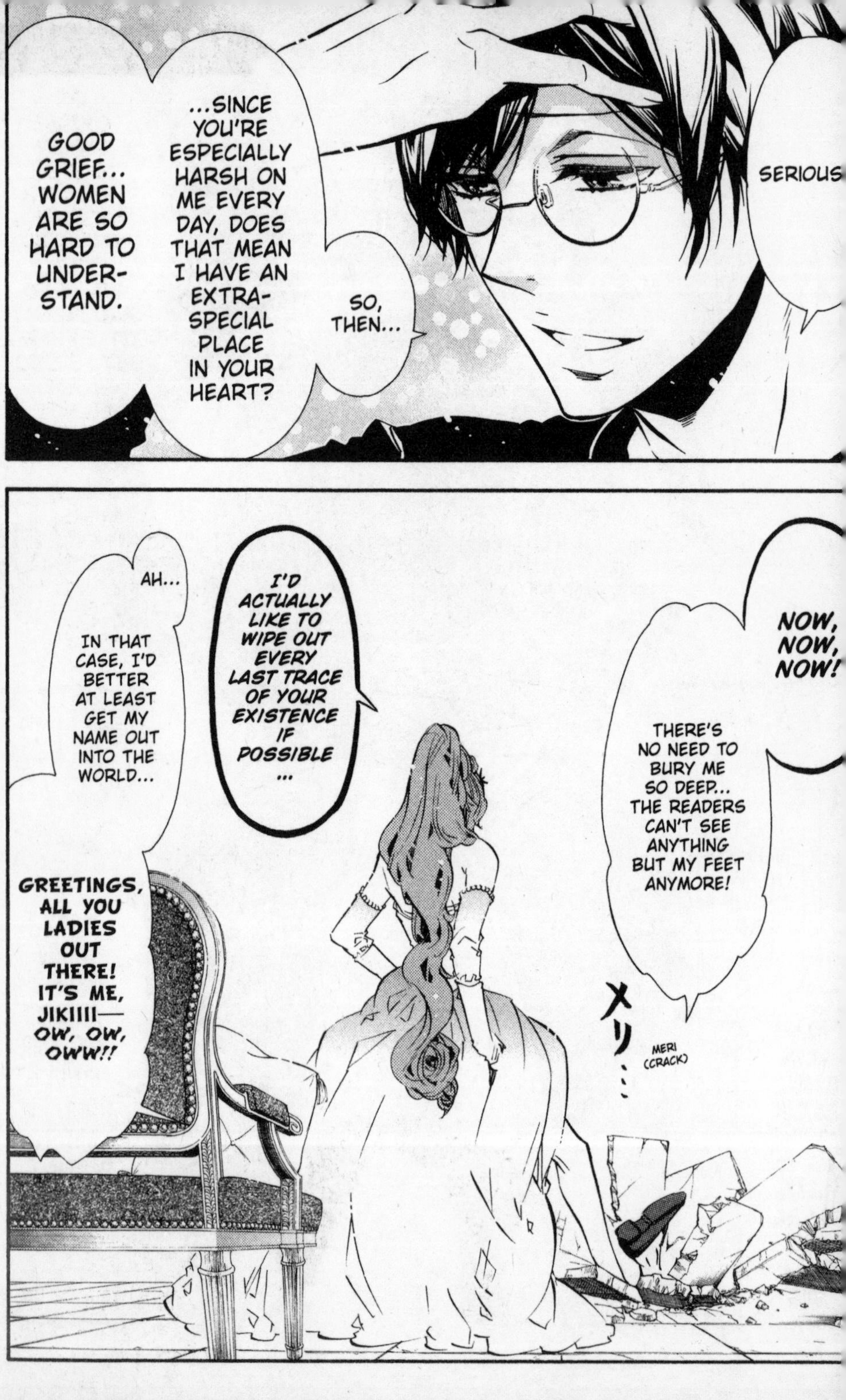
SERIOUS
SO, THEN...
...SINCE YOU'RE ESPECIALLY HARSH ON ME EVERY DAY, DOES THAT MEAN I HAVE AN EXTRA-SPECIAL PLACE IN YOUR HEART?
GOOD GRIEF... WOMEN ARE SO HARD TO UNDER-STAND.
NOW, NOW, NOW!
THERE'S NO NEED TO BURY ME SO DEEP... THE READERS CAN'T SEE ANYTHING BUT MY FEET ANYMORE!
メリ…
MERI (CRACK)
I'D ACTUALLY LIKE TO WIPE OUT EVERY LAST TRACE OF YOUR EXISTENCE IF POSSIBLE...
AH...
IN THAT CASE, I'D BETTER AT LEAST GET MY NAME OUT INTO THE WORLD...
GREETINGS, ALL YOU LADIES OUT THERE! IT'S ME, JIKIIII— OW, OW, OWW!!

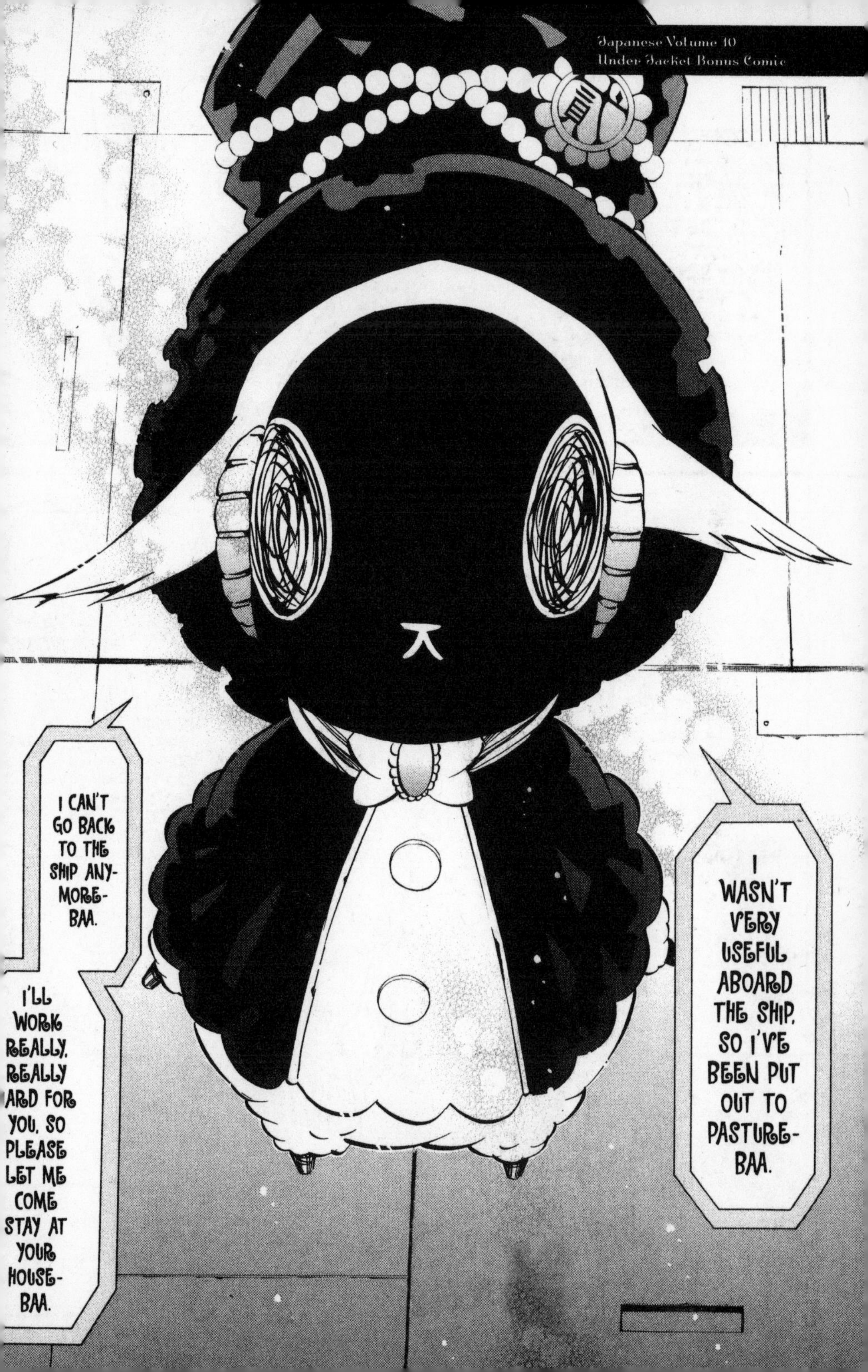
Japanese Volume 10
Under Jacket Bonus Comic
I WASN'T VERY USEFUL ABOARD THE SHIP, SO I'VE BEEN PUT OUT TO PASTURE-BAA.
I CAN'T GO BACK TO THE SHIP ANY-MORE-BAA.
I'LL WORK REALLY, REALLY ARD FOR YOU, SO PLEASE LET ME COME STAY AT YOUR HOUSE-BAA.

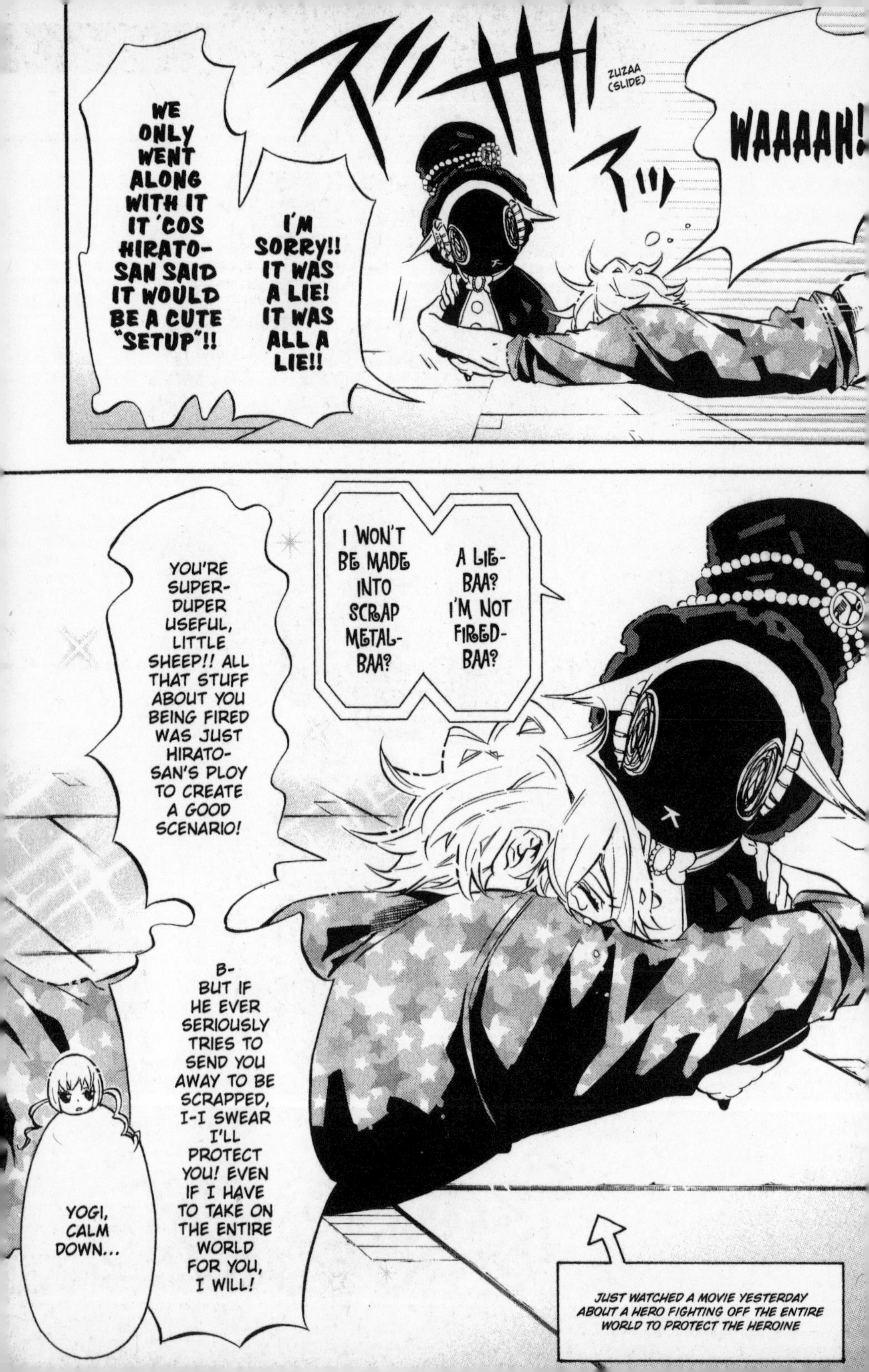
WAAAAH!
ZUZAA (SLIDE)
I'M SORRY!! IT WAS A LIE! IT WAS ALL A LIE!!
WE ONLY WENT ALONG WITH IT IT 'COS HIRATO-SAN SAID IT WOULD BE A CUTE "SETUP"!!
A LIE-BAA? I'M NOT FIRED-BAA?
I WON'T BE MADE INTO SCRAP METAL-BAA?
YOU'RE SUPER-DUPER USEFUL, LITTLE SHEEP!! ALL THAT STUFF ABOUT YOU BEING FIRED WAS JUST HIRATO-SAN'S PLOY TO CREATE A GOOD SCENARIO!
B-BUT IF HE EVER SERIOUSLY TRIES TO SEND YOU AWAY TO BE SCRAPPED, I-I SWEAR I'LL PROTECT YOU! EVEN IF I HAVE TO TAKE ON THE ENTIRE WORLD FOR YOU, I WILL!
JUST WATCHED A MOVIE YESTERDAY ABOUT A HERO FIGHTING OFF THE ENTIRE WORLD TO PROTECT THE HEROINE
YOGI, CALM DOWN...

KARNEVAL

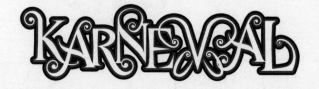

8-16

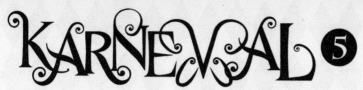

KARNEVAL ⑤

Touya Mikanagi

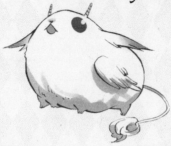

Translation: Su Mon Han   Lettering: Alexis Eckerman

This book is a work of fiction. Names, characters, places, and incidents are the product of the author's imagination or are used fictitiously. Any resemblance to actual events, locales, or persons, living or dead, is coincidental.

Karneval vols. 9-10 © 2012 by Touya Mikanagi. All rights reserved. First published in Japan in 2012 by ICHIJINSHA. English translation rights arranged with ICHIJINSHA through Tuttle-Mori Agency, Inc., Tokyo.

English translation © 2016 by Yen Press, LLC

Yen Press, LLC supports the right to free expression and the value of copyright. The purpose of copyright is to encourage writers and artists to produce the creative works that enrich our culture.

The scanning, uploading, and distribution of this book without permission is a theft of the author's intellectual property. If you would like permission to use material from the book (other than for review purposes), please contact the publisher. Thank you for your support of the author's rights.

Yen Press
1290 Avenue of the Americas
New York, NY 1

Visit us at yenpress.com • facel
twitter.com/yenpress • yen

First Yen Press Editic

Yen Press is an imprint of
The Yen Press name and logo are trad

The publisher is not responsible for websites (or their content) that are not owned by the publisher.

Library of Congress Control Number: 2016936531

ISBNs: 978-0-316-26350-4 (paperback)
978-0-316-26363-4 (ebook)
978-0-316-26364-1 (app)

10 9 8 7 6 5 4 3 2 1

BVG

Printed in the United States of America

D1227462

Tusc. Co. Public Library
121 Fair Ave NW
New Phila., OH 44663